Brian Fleming Library
Ministry of Training, Colleges & Universities
900 Bay St. 13th Floor, Mowat Block
Toronto, ON M7A 1L2

EFFECTIVE EDUCATION FOR LEARNERS WITH EXCEPTIONALITIES

ADVANCES IN SPECIAL EDUCATION

Series Editor: Anthony F. Rotatori

Recently published volumes:

Volume 11: Issues, Practices, and Concerns in Special Education – Edited by Anthony F. Rotatori, John O. Schwenn and Sandra Burkhardt

Volume 12: Multicultural Education for Learners with Exceptionalities – Edited by Festus E. Obiakor, John O. Schwenn and Anthony F. Rotatori

Volume 13: Intervention Techniques for Individuals with Exceptionalities in Inclusive Settings – Edited by Festus E. Obiakor, Sandra Burkhardt, Anthony F. Rotatori and Tim Wahlberg

Volume 14: Autistic Spectrum Disorders: Educational and Clinical Interventions – Edited by Tim Wahlberg, Festus E. Obiakor, Sandra Burkhardt and Anthony F. Rotatori

ADVANCES IN SPECIAL EDUCATION   VOLUME 15

EFFECTIVE EDUCATION FOR LEARNERS WITH EXCEPTIONALITIES

EDITED BY

FESTUS E. OBIAKOR
University of Wisconsin-Milwaukee, USA

CHERYL A. UTLEY
The Juniper Gardens Children's Project, University of Kansas, USA

ANTHONY F. ROTATORI
St. Xavier University, USA

2003

JAI
An Imprint of Elsevier Science

Amsterdam – Boston – London – New York – Oxford – Paris
San Diego – San Francisco – Singapore – Sydney – Tokyo

ELSEVIER SCIENCE Ltd
The Boulevard, Langford Lane
Kidlington, Oxford OX5 1GB, UK

© 2003 Elsevier Science Ltd. All rights reserved.

This work is protected under copyright by Elsevier Science, and the following terms and conditions apply to its use:

Photocopying
Single photocopies of single chapters may be made for personal use as allowed by national copyright laws. Permission of the Publisher and payment of a fee is required for all other photocopying, including multiple or systematic copying, copying for advertising or promotional purposes, resale, and all forms of document delivery. Special rates are available for educational institutions that wish to make photocopies for non-profit educational classroom use.

Permissions may be sought directly from Elsevier Science Global Rights Department, PO Box 800, Oxford OX5 1DX, UK; phone: (+44) 1865 843830, fax: (+44) 1865 853333, e-mail: permissions@elsevier.co.uk. You may also contact Global Rights directly through Elsevier's home page (http://www.elsevier.com), by selecting 'Obtaining Permissions'.

In the USA, users may clear permissions and make payments through the Copyright Clearance Center, Inc., 222 Rosewood Drive, Danvers, MA 01923, USA; phone: (+1) (978) 7508400, fax: (+1) (978) 7504744, and in the UK through the Copyright Licensing Agency Rapid Clearance Service (CLARCS), 90 Tottenham Court Road, London W1P 0LP, UK; phone: (+44) 207 631 5555; fax: (+44) 207 631 5500. Other countries may have a local reprographic rights agency for payments.

Derivative Works
Tables of contents may be reproduced for internal circulation, but permission of Elsevier Science is required for external resale or distribution of such material.
Permission of the Publisher is required for all other derivative works, including compilations and translations.

Electronic Storage or Usage
Permission of the Publisher is required to store or use electronically any material contained in this work, including any chapter or part of a chapter.

Except as outlined above, no part of this work may be reproduced, stored in a retrieval system or transmitted in any form or by any means, electronic, mechanical, photocopying, recording or otherwise, without prior written permission of the Publisher.
Address permissions requests to: Elsevier Science Global Rights Department, at the mail, fax and e-mail addresses noted above.

Notice
No responsibility is assumed by the Publisher for any injury and/or damage to persons or property as a matter of products liability, negligence or otherwise, or from any use or operation of any methods, products, instructions or ideas contained in the material herein. Because of rapid advances in the medical sciences, in particular, independent verification of diagnoses and drug dosages should be made.

First edition 2003

Library of Congress Cataloging in Publication Data
A catalog record from the Library of Congress has been applied for.

British Library Cataloguing in Publication Data
A catalogue record from the British Library has been applied for.

ISBN: 0-7623-0975-X
ISSN: 0270-4013 (Series)

∞ The paper used in this publication meets the requirements of ANSI/NISO Z39.48-1992 (Permanence of Paper).
Printed in The Netherlands.

CONTENTS

LIST OF CONTRIBUTORS	ix
PREFACE *Festus E. Obiakor, Cheryl A. Utley and* *Anthony F. Rotatori*	xiii
FOREWORD *Edward L. Meyen*	xv

1. FOUNDATIONS OF SPECIAL EDUCATION

TRANSFORMING THE TEACHING-LEARNING PROCESS IN GENERAL AND SPECIAL EDUCATION *Festus E. Obiakor*	3
THE FEDERAL ROLE IN TRANSFORMING GENERAL AND SPECIAL EDUCATION *Cheryl A. Utley and Marlene Simon*	17
TRANSFORMING GENERAL AND SPECIAL EDUCATION IN URBAN SCHOOLS *Dianne Ferguson, Elizabeth Kozleski and* *Anne Smith*	43

2. LEARNERS WITH EXCEPTIONALITIES

EDUCATING STUDENTS WITH COGNITIVE DISABILITIES *Cheryl A. Utley and Festus E. Obiakor*	77
STUDENTS WITH LEARNING DISABILITIES *Katherine J. Mitchem and Ann Richards*	99

RESTRUCTURING SERVICE DELIVERY FOR STUDENTS
WITH EMOTIONAL AND BEHAVIORAL DISORDERS
Sujatha S. Hampton and Elisabeth K. Hess-Rice   *119*

STUDENTS WITH ATTENTION
DEFICIT HYPERACTIVITY DISORDER
Marjorie Montague   *139*

GUIDING PRINCIPLES FOR THE EDUCATION
OF CHILDREN AND YOUTH WITH SEVERE
AND MULTIPLE DISABILITIES
*Ernest Rose, Beverly Rainforth and
Daniel Steere*   *155*

STUDENTS WITH SPEECH AND LANGUAGE
DISORDERS
*Jane R. Wegner, Kristin Grosche and
Evette Edmister*   *181*

STUDENTS WITH AUTISM SPECTRUM
DISORDERS
*Tim Wahlberg, Anthony F. Rotatori,
Julie Deisinger and Sandra Burkhardt*   *195*

STUDENTS WITH HEARING LOSS
Deborah S. Stryker and Barbara Luetke-Stahlman   *233*

VISUAL IMPAIRMENT
Wendy Sapp   *259*

EDUCATING CHILDREN AND YOUTH WITH SERIOUS
MEDICAL CONDITIONS: PERILS AND POTENTIAL
Joan Fleitas   *283*

STUDENTS WITH TRAUMATIC BRAIN INJURY
Janet Siantz Tyler and Ronald C. Savage   *299*

STUDENTS WITH GIFTS AND TALENTS
Vera I. Daniels   *325*

3. LIFE SPAN ISSUES AND SPECIAL POPULATIONS

EARLY CHILDHOOD SPECIAL EDUCATION
    Vivian I. Correa and Hazel Jones   *351*

TRANSITIONS TO ADULTHOOD FOR
YOUTH WITH DISABILITIES
    Mary E. Morningstar and Kagendo Mutua   *373*

THE MYTH OF SOCIOECONOMIC DISSONANCE:
WORKING WITH HOMELESS STUDENTS IN
SPECIAL EDUCATION CONTEXTS
    Lynn K. Wilder and Festus E. Obiakor   *401*

FAMILY AND SCHOOL PARTNERSHIPS:
BUILDING BRIDGES IN GENERAL AND
SPECIAL EDUCATION
    Jean Ann Summers, Karen Gavin,
    Tonya Purnell-Hall and Jason Nelson   *417*

MULTICULTURAL LEARNERS WITH
EXCEPTIONALITIES IN GENERAL AND
SPECIAL EDUCATION SETTINGS
    Herbert Grossman, Cheryl A. Utley and
    Festus E. Obiakor   *445*

SUMMARY COMMENTS
    Charles R. Greenwood   *465*

SUBJECT INDEX   *475*

LIST OF CONTRIBUTORS

Sandra Burkhardt	Department of Psychology, St. Xavier University, Chicago, USA
Vivian I. Correa	Department of Special Education, College of Education, University of Florida, USA
Vera I. Daniels	Department of Special Education, Southern University and A & M College-Baton Rouge, USA
Julie Deisinger	Department of Psychology, St. Xavier University, Chicago, USA
Evette Edmister	Intercampus Program in Communicative Disorders, University of Kansas, USA
Dianne Ferguson	Center for Research Synthesis and Product Development, University of Oregon, USA
Joan Fleitas	School of Nursing, Fairfeild University, USA
Karen Gavin	Department of Counseling and School Psychology, Wright School of Education, Indiana University, USA
Charles R. Greenwood	Schiefelbusch Institute for Life Span Studies, Juniper Gardens Children's Project, University of Kansas, USA

LIST OF CONTRIBUTORS

Kristin Grosche	Intercampus Program in Communicative Disorders, University of Kansas, USA
Herbert Grossman	San Jose State University, USA
Sujatha S. Hampton	Department of Special Education, Ruffner Hall, University of Virginia, USA
Elisabeth K. Hess-Rice	Graduate School of Education, Department of Special Education, The George Washington University, USA
Hazel Jones	Department of Special Education, College of Education, University of Florida, USA
Elizabeth Kozleski	National Institute for Urban School Improvement, University of Colorado at Denver, USA
Barbara Luetke-Stahlman	Greene Central High School, North Carolina, USA
Edward L. Meyen	Department of Special Education, University of Kansas, USA
Katherine Mitchem	College of Human Resources and Education, West Virginia University, USA
Marjorie Montague	School of Education, University of Miami, USA
Mary E. Morningstar	Department of Special Education, University of Kansas, USA
Kagendo Mutua	Department of Interdisciplinary Teacher Education, University of Alabama, USA

List of Contributors

Jason Nelson	Department of Counseling and School Psychology, Indiana University, USA
Festus E. Obiakor	Department of Exceptional Education, University of Wisconsin-Milwaukee, USA
Tonya Purnell-Hall	Schiefelbusch Institute for Life Span Studies, Juniper Gardens Children's Project, University of Kansas, USA
Beverly Rainforth	School of Education and Human Development, Binghamton University, State University of New York, USA
Ann Richards	College of Human Resources and Education, West Virginia University, USA
Ernest Rose	School of Education and Human Development, Binghamton University, State University of New York, USA
Anthony F. Rotatori	Department of Psychology, St. Xavier University, Chicago, USA
Wendy Sapp	Department of Special Education, George Peabody College of Vanderbilt University, USA
Ronald C. Savage	Bancroft NeuroHealth, NJ, USA
Marlene Simon	Office of Special Education Programs, U.S. Department of Special Education, Washington, D.C., USA
Anne Smith	Office of Special Education Programs, U.S. Department of Special Education, Washington, D.C., USA

Daniel Steere	Department of Special Education and Rehabilitation, East Stroudsburg University of Pennsylvania, USA
Deborah S. Stryker	Department of Communication Disorders and Deaf Studies, California State University-Fresno, USA
Jean Ann Summers	Schiefelbusch Institute for Life Span Studies, Juniper Gardens Children's Project, University of Kansas, USA
Janet Siantz Tyler	University of Kansas Medical Center, Department of Special Education, USA
Cheryl A. Utley	Schiefelbusch Institute for Life Span Studies, The Juniper Gardens Children's Project, University of Kansas, USA
Tim Wahlberg	Psychology Department, North Illinois University, USA
Jane R. Wegner	Schiefelbusch Speech, Laguage, and Hearing Clinic, University of Kansas, USA
Lynn K. Wilder	Department of Counseling Psychology and Special Education, Brigham Young University, Utah, USA

PREFACE

Effective Education for Learners with Exceptionalities is an innovative survey text that advances the transformation of how general and special education students ought to be educated in inclusive settings. In this book, we argue that effective education must adopt a comprehensive support model (CSM) to facilitate adequate identification, evaluation, placement, and instructional programming for learners with exceptionalities. Based on the CSM, individuals, families, schools, communities, and governments must work together to make programs relevant and inclusive. In addition, we argue that schools must implement intervention techniques that maximize the teaching-learning process of students. In response to the standards-based reform movement, we design this book to examine research from the disciplines of psychology, sociology, organizational theory, curriculum and instruction, and special education.

In more ways than one, this book addresses critical issues related to the effective education for learners with exceptionalities. To achieve our goal, we invited leading scholars and educators in the fields of general and special education to contribute their unique perspectives. These contributors focus on a broad range of topics for restructuring general and special education into a unified system of education. To a large measure, issues pertinent to identification, assessment, labeling, classification, intervention, and service delivery are discussed. To reflect the dimensions of general and special education, the book is divided into three parts: Part 1 focuses on the Foundations of Special Education, Part 2 centers on Learners with Exceptionalities, and Part 3 presents Life Span Issues and Special Populations. Part 1 contains three chapters that focus on transforming the teaching-learning process in general and special education classrooms, the federal role in transforming general and special education, and the unification of general and special education. Part 2 has 12 chapters that center on students with cognitive disabilities, learning disabilities, emotional or behavioral disorders, attention deficit/hyperactivity disorder, severe and multiple disabilities, speech and language disorders, autism, hearing loss, blindness and low vision, chronic illness and other health impairments, traumatic brain injury, and gifts and talents. Part 3 contains five chapters that focus on early childhood special education, working with the homeless in special education contexts, transitions to adulthood, families of learners with exceptionalities, and multicultural learners with exceptionlities.

Effective Education for Learners with Exceptionalities is a survey book of the new millennium. It should be used as a required or supplementary text for preparing undergraduate and graduate students in general and special education. Educators and practitioners interested in transforming the teaching-learning process in special education will find this book informative. We are grateful to the contributors for doing such an excellent job. We especially thank Dr. Edward Meyen and Dr. Charles Greenwood, both of the University of Kansas for writing this book's Foreword and Summary Comments, respectively. In sum, we thank our family members, friends, and well-wishers for their love and support during this book project.

Festus E. Obiakor
Cheryl A. Utley
Anthony F. Rotatori
Editors

FOREWORD

Each year the knowledge base on how to teach children with exceptionalities expands. Research is conducted and reported in the literature. Experiences are shared and validated practices demonstrated. And new products find their way into the market place.

With the emergence of the Internet and the World Wide Web, the expansion of the knowledge base has not only been accelerated and access increased, but the rules have changed. Anyone can now establish a web site and become both a repository of knowledge and the judge of what is added to the knowledge base. Thus, we have more contributors to the knowledge base who set their own standards for what is valid and relevant. While that means more information, it also means that the knowledge base is no longer controlled by professional practices that have stood the test of time. Further, the availability of more avenues to access information that is less controlled than in the past leads to less confidence in such information!

For these reasons, authors of books, such as this one. are now faced with a greater challenge then ever before. Authors must be better informed than at any time in history if they are to create a resource that is useful, timely and helps to position teachers and others to more effectively teach children and youth with disabilities, who represent the most difficult to teach. Thus, the decisions made by Obiakor, Utley, and Rotatori, on what to include or to exclude in this book became more difficult than if the book had been written a mere five years ago. They were committed to using language that enhances the ability of readers in translating new understandings into practice. This is an important feature of this book! Their task was further complicated because of the goal to bring interdisciplinary perspectives into focus in a manner that prepares educators to implement interventions that maximize classroom performance. Had Obiakor and his associates opted merely to inform their readers rather than to improve their effectiveness, the task would have been more easily achieved. It is far less difficult to write about the conditions in schools, the attributes of learners, and the need for advocacy, changing public policy or even how to organize schools to facilitate learning than it is to provide meaningful direction to teachers on how to improve classroom performance of students with exceptionalities.

Obiakor, Utley and Rotatori, in this book, are to be commended for having taken a research-to-practice approach. The context for this approach is couched in a commitment to the unification of general and special education as a comprehensive delivery system. While this decision added to their challenge, the results of their work set the book apart from most other contemporary resources in this area. Unfortunately, it is difficult to write about validated instructional practices in the realm of effective education for learners with exceptionalities without providing the reader a framework of how the educational system has treated this target group of learners throughout history. One cannot simply state that their status in schools has gone from being excluded, to included but segregated to one of presumed equity. If readers are to appreciate the significance of this book, they must be able to place the conditions of the past in perspective with the authors' views on the research and validated practices of today. This is particularly important if readers are to apply this new knowledge in making a difference in the classroom.

The authors have taken this challenge seriously as reflected in each chapter and by the manner in which they integrate the treatment of ideas, concepts and issues across chapters. In addition, they have been able to create a framework that allows readers to apply their personal knowledge to understanding the authors' views on effective education without spending too much time on building that framework. Too often books on effective education presented as offering educational solutions in special education focus mostly on history, identification practices, policy analysis, legislative reviews and case law. While important, this information is not the primary message. In this book, the authors have approached their writing from the perspective of their individual disciplines with the intent of creating a framework for understanding effective education – not an exhaustive discourse on the context. They have achieved this in a way that does not oversimplify the context. In doing so, they serve the needs of both experienced readers and readers who are early in their professional preparation.

Books written for the purpose of contributing to the preparation of a professional work force or as a resource for practicing professionals tend to be judged by how well they match the realities of the contemporary scene. Thus, this book will be judged largely on how it meshes with the issues, emerging practices, and unfolding policies surrounding the education of students with exceptionalities in real time. It is not possible to control how the book will be used or to influence the ever-changing conditions in schools. All the authors can do is to make good judgments about what conditions will prevail during the intended life of the book based on their expertise. This is exactly what this team of authors did! That is, they do not prophesize about what schools should

Foreword

be like over the next decade but acknowledge the power of the standards-based reform movement and the need for schools to adopt principles of school effectiveness while emphasizing the importance of offering classroom instruction that is based upon a clear assessment of instructional needs of learners with exceptionalities. Further, rather than beginning with an advocacy-based essay on inclusion, they begin with a focus on transforming the teaching-learning process in general and special education followed by an emphasis on unification. While this is central to building a framework for the reader, this approach also represents the authors' attempt to set forth the conditions in the schools as they see them.

This book is not designed for the naïve reader. It is written for the person who has a reason for and strong interest in knowing more about effective education for students with exceptionalities, whether as part of preparing for a professional role, ongoing professional development or a need to better understand what is known about effective education and its impact on policy making. It is a substantive treatment of the subject matter with particular attention given to the time and conditions where the reader will apply what he/she has learned. Each reader will bring to the book his/her own perspectives on these conditions. Readers are not asked to hold particular views. But, they are expected to approach the book with motivation to learn more about research-based practices, effective education, the attributes and needs of learners with exceptionalities, and how to improve education for students with exceptionalities within the prevailing conditions of American schools.

The interaction between the readers' backgrounds and the message of the authors is intended to contribute to their learning experiences. To benefit from this book, it is not essential to be an expert on the standards-based reform movement, high-stakes approach to accountability, universal designs for learning, IDEA, or the effective education literature. But it is important to recognize that this book is not written about exceptionalities in isolation from the real world. It requires reflection on the readers' part. The readers are expected to allow their personal experiences and perspectives to challenge the views of the authors and to subject their own observations to the reported research findings. This book will make a difference in the professional growth of general and special educators, and other service providers. No doubt, it can help them make a difference in the education of students with exceptionalities.

Edward L. Meyen

PART 1.
FOUNDATIONS OF SPECIAL EDUCATION

TRANSFORMING THE TEACHING-LEARNING PROCESS IN GENERAL AND SPECIAL EDUCATION

Festus E. Obiakor

"How can I teach these kids? They can't pay attention!" An insistent whine of complaint rises and gathers like a sinister haze over classrooms from preschool through college. Rather than serving as a warning, however, it has become a smoke screen for teachers and parents who belabor the young for failing to learn, and for politicians and professors who take potshots at the schools. While the adult community sanctimoniously bewails erosion of academic rigor and achievement, however, it perpetuates the practices that are shortening children's attention spans and rendering their brains unfit to engage in sustained verbal inquiry. Meanwhile, the schools, inundated with students who can't listen, remember, follow sequences of directions, read anything they consider "boring," or solve even elementary problems, have resorted to classifying increasing numbers of students as educationally sick (Healy, 1990, p. 137).

Healy's notations above reiterate perpetual inconsistencies in efforts to transform the teaching-learning process in general and special education. These inconsistencies are reflected in frequent complaints about how students learn, how teachers teach, how parents respond, how communities support, and how state and federal governments legislate. Despite these rhetorics, education is still the most important tool to uplift citizens, whether they have exceptionalities or not. Dewey (1958) emphasized that education and democracy cannot be divorced from each other. In other words, education has the power to change human beings. As he pointed out:

> Education must have the tendency, if it is education, to form attitudes. The tendency to form attitudes which will express themselves in intelligent social action is something very different from indoctrination.... There is an intermediary between aimless education and the education of inculcation and indoctrination. The alternative is the kind of education that connects the materials and methods by which knowledge is acquainted with a sense of how things are done; not by impregnating the individual with some final philosophy, whether it comes from Karl Marx or from Mussolini or Hitler or anybody else, but by enabling him [her] to so understand existing conditions that an attitude of intelligent action will follow from social understanding (p. 56).

Since education is important in advancing the society, it is imperative that we transform the teaching-learning process to improve achievement of all students, in spite of their exceptionalities. Such a transformation will not be successful unless we redefine what we mean by "good" students, "good" teachers, and "good" schools (Obiakor, 2000a, b). The question then is, How can the teaching-learning process be transformed to accurately reflect an educational program where *all* students achieve academically? In this chapter, I respond to this critical question. Embedded in my response are transformation ideas that are encapsulated in what I call MY DREAM EDUCATIONAL PROGRAM.

TRANSFORMING TEACHING-LEARNING IN GENERAL AND SPECIAL EDUCATION

To transform the teaching-learning process in general and special education, students must be self-motivated, teachers must be dedicated to excellence, parents must be equal partners, communities must be self-directed, and governments must be involved. We cannot be victims of our circumstances, and we must be innovative. From my perspective, a true transformation will come when we stop politicizing special education, and we begin to do whatever it takes to educate *all* students. In their book, *Every Child, Every School: Success for All*, Slavin, Madden, Dolan and Wasik (1996) wrote:

> Every child can learn. Every school can ensure the success of every child. Statements to this effect appear in goals statements, curriculum reports, and school district offices. They are posted in school buildings and appear as mottoes on school stationery. But does our education system behave as if they are true? If we truly believed that every child could learn under proper circumstances, we would be relentless in the search of those circumstances. We would use well-validated instructional methods and materials known to be capable of ensuring the success of nearly all children if used with intelligence, flexibility, and fidelity. We would involve teachers in constant, collaborative professional development activities to continually improve their abilities to reach every child. We would frequently assess children's performance to be sure that all students are on a path that leads to success, and to be able to respond immediately if children are not making adequate progress. If children are falling behind despite excellent instruction, we would try different instructional

approaches and if necessary, we would provide them with tutors or other intensive assistance. We would involve parents in support of their children's school success; we would check to see whether vision, hearing, health, nutrition, or other nonacademic problems were holding children back, and then we would find a solution to those problems. If we truly believed that all children could learn, we would rarely, if ever, assign children to special education or long-term remedial programs that in effect lower expectations for children. If we truly believed that all schools could ensure the success of all children, then the failure of even a single child would be cause for great alarm and immediate, forceful intervention (p. xi).

I believe transforming the teaching-learning process in general and special education is painstaking, but it is not impossible. My ideas about transformation are fully reflected in what I call MY DREAM EDUCATIONAL PROGRAM. For instance, in my dream educational program, all students' potential will be maximized to the fullest. My dream educational program will be located in a school where opportunities and choices for growth are created by well-prepared teachers who understand the true meaning of the teaching profession. Simply put, in my dream educational program, teachers will be truly *good* teachers who have the courage to teach with their real pedagogical power (Dewey, 1958; Henderson & Bibens, 1970; Hilliard, 1992, 1995; Johnson, 1981; Kohl, 1988; Ladson-Billings, 1994, 2000; Orlich, Harder, Callahan & Gibson, 2001; Palmer, 1998). In my dream educational program, "culture" will be a noncontroversial phenomenon that increases the *goodness* and *quality* of school and classroom activities. In fact, my dream educational program will:

(1) Be located in all neighborhoods (i.e. suburb, urban, rural, and inner-city areas).
(2) Have minority and majority students to reflect demographic shifts.
(3) Have minority and majority teachers to reflect demographic shifts.
(4) Have culturally competent teachers.
(5) Produce culturally competent students.
(6) Be dedicated to excellence.
(7) Believe in "quality with a heart."
(8) Have teachers with "soul."
(9) Respond to student stressors and individual differences.
(10) Address issues of student learning styles and multiple intelligences.
(11) Encourage all students to maximize their potential.
(12) Empower parents and community members in all their activities.
(13) Work collaboratively, consultatively, and cooperatively with parents despite their cultural, racial, and socioeconomic backgrounds.
(14) Not get rid of students indiscriminately.
(15) Try its best to educate *all* students.

(16) Prepare students to be responsible and productive citizens through self-knowledge, self-esteem, and self-empowerment.
(17) Prepare students to be nationally and globally aware.
(18) Go beyond traditions to be creative.
(19) Be abreast of the times on how it hires its administrators.
(20) Have administrators who care for students.
(21) Make multiple voices to be heard in classroom activities.
(22) Not support making some students *invisible*.
(23) Create and maintain learning communities.
(24) Not be puritanic (i.e. a perfectionist mentality).
(25) Have truly *good* teachers who will teach *reality*.

Operational Dimensions of My Dream Educational Program

Based on the aforementioned details, it seems clear to me that my dream educational program will have four basic operational dimensions, namely:

(1) It will function with a Comprehensive Support Model (CSM).
(2) It will reflect a learning community.
(3) It will reflect a place to advance the craft of teaching.
(4) It will foster a multidimensional teaching-learning process.

Functioning with a Comprehensive Support Model
Everyone wants a dream educational program that can meet the needs of *all* students! My dream educational program will manifest best practices in all classroom activities for *all* students. In such a program, the COMPREHENSIVE SUPPORT MODEL (CSM) must flourish. Based on the CSM, the "self," family, school, community, and government will be collaboratively and consultatively involved. The "self" will be involved because without the personal powers of all entities involved in learning, self-responsibility may not be maximized. The family will be important because it is the cornerstone of the student and the bridge that connects the student with the school. The school will be a part of the CSM because it will have teachers and professionals who have the power to shift their paradigms regarding demographic changes. The community will be an important part of the CSM because it will provide a variety of opportunities and choices for children and youth, parents, schools, and governmental entities to come together. To make the CSM work, the government will not divorce itself from the happenings in families, schools, and communities. Governmental entities will be involved in generating equitable policies that entice the multiple voices of its citizenry.

Transforming the Teaching-Learning Process 7

In my dream educational program, *all* components of the CSM will listen to each other and communicate as they empower each other. THE BLAME GAME WILL BE OVER as diverse positive forces collaborate, consult, and cooperate for the *common good*. In my dream educational program, the whole village will be at work because "it takes a *responsible* village to raise a *responsible* child" (see Obiakor, 1994). The Milwaukee Catalyst (1998) reiterated these ideas to press for effective educational reforms based on research. This organization highlighted five essential supports for school learning that must be in place to improve school-community relationships. These key forces include:

(1) Effective school leadership.
(2) Family-community partnerships.
(3) A school environment that supports learning.
(4) Effective staff development and collaboration.
(5) A quality instructional program (p. 1).

As the Milwaukee Catalyst concluded, "Making practices like these a reality requires major changes – not only in the classroom but also in the way the entire school is run and in its ties with students, families, and the community. Making these changes allows the schools to focus their resources and attention on improving teaching, learning, and student achievement for all children" (p. 2). In my dream educational program, community forces will be an integral part of its daily functioning. We will not ignore any part of the whole village!

Reflecting a Learning Community
In my dream educational program, the focus will be on maintaining a learning community. According to Peterson (1992), "community in itself is more important to learning than any method or technique. When community exists, learning is strengthened – everyone is smarter, more ambitious, and productive. Well-formed ideas and intentions amount to little without a community to bring them to life" (p. 2). He added:

> Life in a learning community is helped along by the interests, ideas, and support of others. Social life is not snuffed out; it is nurtured and used to advance learning in the best way possible. Learning is social. ... The position taken is that learning awakens a variety of internal processes that operate only when the child is interacting with others in his [her] environment and in cooperation with his [her] peers. Even mainstream educators are beginning to recognize that education fails when it focuses solely on the accumulation of demonstrable facts and skill. An image is taking shape that acknowledges a more complex and irreducible phenomenon, the social person (p. 3).

My dream educational program will reflect a learning community where learning is shared with a *heart*. In such a learning community, life in the classroom will be less intense and there will be fewer restrictions, labels, categories, and illusory generalizations. A well-organized learning community leads to holistic teaching. As Peterson (1992) concluded, holistic teaching entails:

(1) *Teacher orientation* to help students to grow in complicated and critical ways.
(2) *View of knowledge* to help people to construct meaning through experiences.
(3) *Meaning-centered teaching* to help knowledge to be personalized as people search for meaning.
(4) *Skills* to help to negotiate, express, and develop knowledge.
(5) *Curriculum* to help connect students' lives to learning.
(6) *Connectedness* to help students to build upon what makes sense to them.
(7) *Collaboration* to help students and teachers learn together.
(8) *Accountability* to help students to be accountable for their own learning and teachers to be accountable for what they do in the classroom.
(9) *Students* who participate in planning and evaluating their education.
(10) *Competence* to demonstrate how people express meaning, solve problems, work with others, and critique intelligently.

Reflecting a Place to Advance the Craft of Teaching
Good teachers are *good* students. In my dream educational program, general and special education teachers will know what it means to be a teacher, and they will value their profession as change agents. Many years ago, Dewey (1960) explained that:

> Constant and uniform relations in change and a knowledge of them in "laws," are not a hindrance to freedom, but a necessary factor in coming to be effectively that which we have the capacity to grow into. Social conditions interact with the preferences of an individual (that are his or her individuality) in a way favorable to actualizing freedom only when they develop intelligence, not abstract knowledge and abstract thought, but power of vision and reflection. For these take effect in making preference, desire, and purpose more flexible, alert, and resolute. Freedom has too long been thought of as indeterminate power operating in a closed and ended world. In its reality, freedom is a resolute will operating in a world in some respects indeterminate, because open and moving toward a new future (p. 287).

Based on Dewey's statement, in my dream educational program, general and special education teachers will search for answers to problems. In other words, *good* teachers will get liberated when they advance their craft through preservice and inservice trainings. Since my dream educational program will be made up of diverse students and teachers, individuals who refuse to leave their comfort zones and/or shift their paradigms will be unhappy campers. Simply put, in my dream educatio0nal program, learning will be a continuous process of development! Guillaume, Zuniga-Hill and Yee (1995) postulated that teachers of diverse students should:

(1) Develop a knowledge base about diverse ethnic groups and have multiple opportunities to examine personal attitudes toward students of color.
(2) Develop culturally and linguistically supportive strategies and approaches that make learning available and equitable for all students.
(3) Have ample exposure to students of diverse backgrounds and to teachers who can model appropriate instructional approaches.
(4) Commit to professional growth regarding issues of diversity (p. 70).

I believe to understand teaching is to understand communication. In my dream educational program, teachers, principals, and school district personnel will learn to communicate with others. General and special education teachers who are good imparters of knowledge may not necessarily be good communicators. Effective communication will create an environment that fosters success and mutual awareness (Harris-Obiakor, 2000). In my dream educational program, teachers will answer the following questions:

(1) Why is effective communication so necessary?
(2) What is communication all about?
(3) What are the barriers that affect the communication process?
(4) What are the tips for being a good communicator?

Good general and special education teachers must be good communicators. How many of us have ever wondered why some exceptional students do not follow instructions? Maybe, these students do not understand their teachers' directions. As a consequence, in my dream educational program, general and special education teachers will:

(1) Understand that communication is a two-way process between the sender and the receiver.
(2) Be sensitive and aware.
(3) Take great interest in others.
(4) Be specific.
(5) Keep messages clear in terms that will be understood.
(6) Accept the fact that people do things for their personal reasons.
(7) Adjust messages to meet circumstances.
(8) Be sincere.

(9) Know what they do not know.
(10) Not be who they are not.

I am convinced that there are tremendous requirements and demands of being an educator (see Hoyle, 1975; Obiakor, Karr, Utley & Algozzine, 1998). For example, Hoyle described these demands when he noted that:

> The teacher has a much wider public than his [her] pupils and colleagues. Outside the school a number of groups have their own expectations of the teacher's role. These groups include the parents of pupils, local counselors and others who have responsibilities for education, the members of various voluntary organizations which take an interest in education, and members of Parent-Teacher Associations. In addition, members of the public have their conceptions of the teacher. The degree to which these expectations directly impinge upon the teacher and shape his [her] conception of his [her] role varies from society to society (p. 69).

These demands require that *good* general and special education teachers develop techniques to survive in today's changing world. In my dream educational program, all educators will possess "business beatitudes" (Beattie, 1982) that include character, enthusiasm, courage, responsibility, persistence, endurance, self-control, integrity, confidence, knowledge, determination, ambition, teamwork, and wisdom. In such a school, these educators will be frantic as they: (a) build the knowledge base; (b) examine the classroom culture; (c) plan and deliver instruction; (d) negotiate the roles of teaching; (e) build self-concepts through self-efficacy; (f) restructure learning environments; (g) enhance learning with technologies and resources; and (h) work beyond the classroom (see Obiakor et al., 1998). Advancing the craft of teaching is to be aware of positive changes that lead to the *common good*. Surely, general and special education teachers in my dream educational program will be ready to meet the challenges of the new century. They will expand their learning opportunities, value diversity, consult with families and community members, and provide needed support for collaborative systems. "As it appears, educators cannot afford to be divorced from their communities, and their communities cannot afford to be divorced from them. In sum, challenges that face communities will continue to be visible in schools, and the ways educators deal with these challenges will be particularly important in the years ahead" (Obiakor et al., 1998, p. 152).

Fostering a Multidimensional Teaching-Learning Process
As individuals are different so must the teaching-learning process. Ironically, this has not been the precedence in today's general and special education classrooms. Research and practice on effective schools and effective teaching have been somewhat confusing (Bliss, Firestone & Richards, 1991). For

instance, we talk about responding to individual differences as we teach, but very often, inabilities and disabilities are viewed as deficits. In my dream educational program, we will not only talk about differences, we will use them to strengthen and beautify our classrooms. My experiences tell me that people consistently shift their paradigms to respond to society's changes, and that those who refuse to shift their paradigms affect others with their retrogressive behaviors – most frequently, people's futures are negatively affected. Consider Case 1 below:

> *Just a few years ago, on October 6, 1995, I was on one of my trips to present a paper at the Council for Children with Behavior Disorders International Convention in Dallas, Texas. Since I detested driving, I took a Greyhound Bus from Emporia to Wichita, Kansas, where my flight was scheduled to take off around 6.00 a.m. My bus left Emporia around 2.30 a.m. en route to Wichita. Around 3.00 a.m., the bus driver stopped at El Dorado for some rest time. I went briefly to use the restroom, and by the time I came out, the bus had left me at El Dorado. I was stranded and frustrated in the strange hours of the morning. My frustration rose because I did not want to miss my flight in Wichita. I began to talk to anyone who would listen at this rest area. I knew the dangers involved, but I had to take the risk. I asked people (I mean people of all races and cultures) who I saw for a ride to Wichita. Even the African Americans I asked did not respond – they ignored me. I lost hope until I asked a White man (Mr. C. W. Sisemore) who surprised me. He agreed. Remember, it was around 3.40 a.m. in the morning! This White man looked like a construction worker – he wore some mud-ridden "cowboy" clothes. I was dumbfounded that he accepted to give me (a Blackman) a ride this early in the morning. I thought that the well-dressed people, especially the African Americans, would accept to give me a ride, but I was wrong. Anyway, my newfound friend began to speed to catch the bus. We did not catch the bus, but we got there not long after the bus arrived in Wichita. Luckily, my luggage was still in the bus. Mr. C. W. Sisemore waited for me to get my luggage, and he gave me a ride to Wichita airport where I took my flight to Dallas. I tried to give him some money to repay his kindness, but he refused.*

Though this case appears a bit farfetched, many of today's general and special educaiton teachers can learn from Mr. Sisemore. Even though I took a risk to ask for a ride in the early hours of the morning, he took a greater risk to give me a ride. Not only do such risks reduce stereotypes and generalizations, they also make long-term positive impressions on people. How many general and special educators would demonstrate such courage when people are down? Who would have imagined that in these days of racial mistrust that a White man would give a ride to a Black man in the early hours of the morning? I am reminded of the biblical "Parable of the Good Samaritan" where the supposed *good* people left a man stranded and the unsuspected stranger saved him. As it appears, Mr. Sisemore had nothing to gain by giving me a ride, yet he took his time and risk to give me a ride. General and special educators can learn a lot from him! In my dream educational program, teachers will take risks like Mr. Sisemore and be rewarded for taking them.

Consider another example in Case 2, the case of the "Danshiki Man" who frequently wore his African attire to depict his pride as a Black man of African descent.

The "Danshiki Man" was an African American who directed a Black program of a major university. He was known for his pride about Africa. In fact, he was the Faculty Sponsor for the Black Students' Union (BSU) and the Organization of African Students (OAS). For instance, he invited Africans to support his programs and wore African attire to school. As a result, the university administration never wanted to mess with him – they were scared that this man who knew so much about Africa would take them to task. Nobody tried to bother him! He was virtually free to do whatever he wanted to do. The "Danshiki Man" had two daughters who were also students in the same university. These daughters were Beautiful, Black, *and* Brilliant *and commanded great respect on campus. Before long, one handsome Nigerian who was pursuing a graduate degree in chemical engineering got captivated by one of the "Danshiki Man's" daughters. He came from a rich royal family. He made a "pass" at her and she accepted. The two of them began to date and she started strategizing on how to introduce him to her family. The "Danshiki Man" heard through the grapevine that his daughter was dating a Nigerian. He confronted the daughter with the news and she honestly acknowledged that she was falling in love with this Nigerian. The "Danshiki Man" was angry and asked the daughter: "Why are you dating an African? Could you not see other African American men? Do you really know what you're doing? How will your kids look? Do you plan to live with him in the jungle? What will people say when they hear that my daughter is married to an African?" The daughter responded: "I thought you loved Africans, Daddy. I can't believe you are bigoted and closed-minded toward them." The "Danshiki Man" repeated: "I don't care what you say. Do not marry an African! African's are backward." Out of respect for the "Danshiki Man," the daughter stopped dating the Nigerian and their wonderful relationship ended. They were both emotionally devastated.*

Again, this case might be farfetched, but it depicts the fact that people of similar race can be closed-minded. Even though the "Danshiki Man" wore African attire to show his pride for Africa, he was phony. He preached what he never practiced. Some general and special educators play this kind of self-destructive game in schools today. They think that being multicultural means wearing cultural attires, eating at "Taco-Bell," or using chopsticks to eat at Chinese restaurants. I am convinced that *good* general and special education teachers frequently go beyond tradition to challenge their thinking and action. *Goodness* must also go beyond the race, culture, language, and socioeconomic background of students. In my dream educational program, general and special educators like the "Danshiki Man" will be challenged, retrained, and retooled to respond to demographic changes. Paley (2000) recounted her experiences in teaching a multicultural classroom. In doing this, she presented a model for self-examination of teacher prejudices. Such self-examination is necessary to help students in general and special education reach for the *top*. In spite of personal-emotional challenges posed by her students, Paley remained "capable of setting the limits and confronting children with misperceptions, misunderstandings, contradictions, and self-destructive behavior" (Comer & Poussaint, 2000, p. x). As Paley pointed out:

> The challenge in teaching is to find a way of communicating to each child the idea that his or her special quality is understood, is valued, and can be talked about. It is not easy, because we are influenced by the fears and prejudices, apprehensions and expectations, which have become a carefully hidden part of every one of us (p. xx).

In the teaching-learning process, the goal of my dream educational program will be multidimensional and inclusive. Johnson (1981) and Halvorsen and Neary (2001) agreed that multidimensionality should be followed in responding to school order, student interest, school spirit, student discipline, classroom instruction, classroom discussion and mastery, planning class period, study skills, homework, classroom organization, behavior management, selecting and organizing intervals, organizing time, evaluating and testing students, reporting to parents and students, and dealing with written work of students. Even in designing new programs, multidimensionality should be the key! For example, the School District of Shorewood, Wisconsin (1997) continued to offer multiple programs to enrich the minds of *all* its students. These programs included school newspapers, accelerated reader programs, battle of the books, junior great books, writers' club, literary club, young authors' conference, geography hunt, science fair, special projects, and stock market game. This district also offered a variety of educational activities to provide opportunities and choices for their students. These activities included accelerated courses (e.g. foreign language and orchestra); co-curricular activities (e.g. student council and play production); challenge program activities (e.g. international pen pals and quiz bowl); advanced classes (e.g. anthropology and physics); and extracurriculars (e.g. jazz ensemble and multicultural council). In my dream educational program, a variety of enrichment programs will be provided in an inclusive manner to maximize the fullest potential of students in general and special education and to expose them to life's realities. Additionally, general and special educators who lead these activities will be rewarded through merit pay and other forms of professionally enhancing activities.

CONCLUSION

This chapter has addressed how we can transform the teaching-learning process to improve student achievement in general and special education. I believe transformation is painstaking, but it is not impossible. To transform the teaching-learning process, we must be willing to try new experiences; cope with changes; see different points of view; be open-minded; participate in group actions; challenge stereotypes; recognize "self" in relation to larger community; acknowledge quality; and respect other cultures, races, and beliefs. These ideas are encapsulated in what I have called MY DREAM EDUCATIONAL PROGRAM.

Today, we are witnessing tremendous challenges in our society. The critical question continues to be, "Are our schools ready to confront challenges in general and special education?" My answer is "Yes." We have the power to shift our paradigms if we are truly interested in uplifting individual and collective growth in general and special education. This growth will only materialize when we transform the teaching-learning process to improve student achievement. Our goal must be to educate every child – to do this, we must believe every child can learn. As a consequence, in my dream educational program, we will move beyond tradition on the ways we identify, refer, assess, label, categorize, place, include, and instruct students. General and special education teachers will be *good*, but they will not be puritanic. They will be truly *good* teachers who know who they are, learn the facts when they are in doubt, change their thinking, use resource persons, build self-concepts, teach with divergent techniques, make the right choices, and continue to learn. In my dream educational program, a Comprehensive Support Model that values the contributions of students, families, schools, communities, and governments will be in operation. Additionally, this environment will be a learning community where *quality* works with a *heart*. In such an environment, general and special educators will continue to advance the craft of teaching, and the teaching-learning process will be multidimensional.

Finally, my dream educational program will be a *good* school for the 21st century because it will maximize the fullest potential of *all* learners, *all* teachers, *all* parents, and *all* communities. In such an environment, general and special educators will consistently be prepared to learn new ways of looking at all students' experiences in their respective classrooms. Smith (1999) concluded that teachers seem unprepared "to give thought to the way students live through a given classroom learning experience, at least in terms beyond their behavioral manifestations and test scores" (p. xxxiii). Apparently, in my dream educational program, experiences of students in general and special education will matter and the stories they tell will matter. Hopefully, these *new* stories will create *new* directions, *new* hopes, *new* visions, *new* paradigms, and *new* traditions. In the words of Smith:

> Tradition has it that standardized tests, classroom performances on tests, written assignments, special projects, and cumulative grade point averages are the tools used to bracket students off as particular kinds of learners and knowledge seekers and creators . . . such measurements of learning and knowing do not tell the complete story. Without the stories to illuminate the learning journey surrounding such measuring tools, it's not possible to fully understand if what was learned was done to satisfy oneself or someone else. Therefore, in the interest of promoting content mastery beyond a foundational level, assuming of course, that is the goal teachers wish their students to achieve, a curriculum embedded in narratives of its participants, I argue, is an invitation to discover the benefits derived from everyone's unique way of traveling through the classroom maze (p. 153).

REFERENCES

Beattie, W. R. (1982). *A treasury of business beatitudes*. New York: Doubleday.

Bliss, J. R., Firestone, W. A., & Richards, C. E. (1991). *Rethinking effective schools research and practice*. Englewood Cliffs, NJ: Prentice Hall.

Dewey, J. (1958). *Philosophy of education*. Ames, IA: Littlefield, Adams, & Co.

Dewey, J. (1960). *On experience, nature, and freedom*. Indianapolis, IN: The Bobbs-Merrill Company.

Guillaume, A. M., Zuniga-Hill, C., & Yee, I. (1995). Prospective teachers' use of diversity issues in a case study analysis. *Journal of Research and Development in Education, 28*, 69–78.

Halvorsen, A. T., & Neary, T. (2001). *Building inclusive schools: Tools and strategies for success*. Boston: Allyn and Bacon.

Harris-Obiakor, P. (2000). Communicating effectively in the workplace. Paper presented at the Student Technological Conference (June), University of Wisconsin-Milwaukee, Milwaukee, WI.

Healy, J. M. (1990). *Endangered minds: Why children don't think and what we can do about it.* New York: Touchstone Book.

Henderson, G., & Bibens, R. F. (1970). *Teachers should care: Social perspectives of teaching.* New York: Harper & Row.

Hilliard, A. G. (1992). The pitfalls and promises of special education practice. *Exceptional Children, 59,* 168–172.

Hilliard, A. G. (1995). Culture, assessment, and valid teaching for the African American student. In: B. A. Ford, F. E. Obiakor & J. M. Patton (Eds), *Effective Education of African American Exceptional Learners: New Perspectives* (pp. ix–xvi). Austin, TX: Pro-Ed.

Hoyle, E. (1975). *The role of the teacher.* London, England: Routledge & Kegan Paul.

Johnson, E. W. (1981). *Teaching school: Points picked up.* New York: Walker and Company.

Kohl, H. (1988). *Growing minds: On becoming a teacher.* New York: Harper Touchbooks.

Ladson-Billings, G. (1994). *The dreamkeepers: Successful teachers of African American children.* San Francisco: Jossey-Bass.

Ladson-Billings, G. (2000). Teaching in dangerous times. *Rethinking Schools: An Urban Education Journal, 14*(1), 18–19.

Milwaukee Catalyst (1998). *Facts: A resource guide.* Milwaukee, WI: Author.

Obiakor, F. E. (1994). *The eight-step multicultural approach: Learning and teaching with a smile.* Dubuque, IA: Kendall/Hunt.

Obiakor, F. E. (2000a). Redefining "good" schools: Quality and equity in education. Position paper No. 1 presented as Distinguished Visiting Professor (July), West Virginia University, Morgantown, WV.

Obiakor, F. E. (2000b). *Transforming teaching-learning to improve student achievement.* Position paper presented at the Best Practice Conference (October), Institute for the Transformation of Learning. Marquette University, Milwaukee WI.

Obiakor, F. E., Karr, S., Utley, C., & Algozzine, B. (1998). The requirements and demands of being an educator. In: R. J. Anderson, C. E. Keller & J. M. Karp (Eds), *Enhancing Diversity: Educators with Disabilities* (pp. 142–154). Washington, D.C.: Gallaudet University Press.

Orlich, D. C., Harder, R. J., Callahan, R. C., & Gibson, H. W. (2001). *Teaching strategies: A guide to better instruction* (6th ed.). Boston: Houghton Mifflin.

Paley, V. G. (2000). *White teacher.* Cambridge, MA: Harvard University Press.

Palmer, P. J. (1998). *The courage to teach: Exploring the inner landscape of a teacher's life.* San Francisco, CA: Jossey-Bass.

Peterson, R. (1992). *Life in a crowded place: Making a learning community.* Portsmouth, NH: Heinemann.

School District of Shorewood (1997). *Shorewood's gifted and talented education.* Shorewood, WI: Author.

Slavin, R. E., Madden, N. A., Dolan, L. J., & Wasik, B. A. (1996). *Every child, every school: Success for all.* Thousand Oaks, CA: Corwin Press.

Smith, D. J. (1999). *Stepping inside the classroom through personal narratives.* Lanham, MD: University Press of America.

THE FEDERAL ROLE IN TRANSFORMING GENERAL AND SPECIAL EDUCATION*

Cheryl A. Utley and Marlene Simon

> Washington's role in K-12 education needs a major overhaul. The existing programs are ill-suited to today's pressing education problems. Many of them do more harm than good. Washington is funding the forces resisting change rather than those for change. It's time for a fundamental shift to a new mission of raising student achievement and enhancing school effectiveness. Reorienting federal policy so that it is about today's goals rather than yesterday's paradigms will require imagination and courage. Washington should set high academic achievement as the top priority for U.S. schools; parents and states should be trusted with key decisions affecting children; and real accountability for results should replace compliance with rules (Finn, Kanstoroom & Petrilli, 2001, p. 6).

For the American people, improving general and special education has become a national priority. As such, policy makers are faced with articulating the role of the federal government in public education. The U.S. Department of Education's stated mission is to "ensure equal access to education and to promote educational excellence throughout the nation" (U.S. Department of Education: Strategic Plan, 1998–2002). An area that will be facing intense scrutiny will be actions on the part of the federal government to ensure that all students – regardless of race, national origin, color, disability, age, or gender –

---

* The opinions expressed in this chapter are those of the authors and do not necessarily reflect the position or policy of the U.S. Department of Education; official endorsement is neither implied, nor should it be inferred.

Effective Education for Learners with Exceptionalities, Volume 15, pages 17–42.
Copyright © 2003 by Elsevier Science Ltd.
All rights of reproduction in any form reserved.
ISBN: 0-7623-0975-X

have the opportunity to achieve challenging standards of educational excellence. Thus, the primary goal of federal policy, as noted by Ravitch (1999), has been to "ensure equality of opportunity in elementary and secondary education. Title I, Head Start, bilingual education, and other programs enacted in the 1960s and special education for "handicapped" children, enacted in the 1970s, directed resources and established legal rights for children who had previously been poorly served by the education system" (p. 269). However, for the last 35 years, Goertz (2000) noted that while federal programs have funded and promoted expanded educational services for students with special educational needs, and have provided access to a broader range of educational opportunities today, the need for federal support remains. The federal role in elementary and secondary education continues to be viewed by policy makers, researchers, and educators as important, despite the fact that it has been limited in removing legal barriers in educational opportunities based on race, poverty, ethnic origin, and disability. It is, therefore, essential that federal policies continue to improve student achievement for all groups, streamline its own programs to reduce regulatory burdens on schools, and increase incentives for better student performance.

The discussion about the future of the federal role in education is now taking place in a different context. The present context of the U.S., is described by The National Commission on Teaching and America's Future (1996) in its document *What Matters Most: Teaching for America's Future*. It reads as follows:

> Over the last generation, American families and communities have changed profoundly. We lead advanced nations in rates of childhood poverty, homelessness, and mortality rates for those under age 25, and we lag in rates of children enrolled in preschool education. Most children live in a single-parent household at some time while they are growing up. At the same time, our schools are more diverse and rapidly becoming more so. More students, including those with a variety of special needs, enter and stay in school longer than ever before. In addition, by the year 2010, at least a third of all children in this country will be members of groups currently considered "minorities."

Big-city schools are already educating a new generation of immigrants from Eastern Europe, Central America, Asia, and Africa, one that rivals in size the great immigrations of the 19th and early 20th centuries. These statistics impact the direction and dialogue among federal policy makers and the translation of policies into general and special educational programs. This chapter: (a) describes challenges related to the federal role in transforming education; (b) discusses current perspectives about civil rights legislation; (c) outlines federal initiatives in education; and (d) suggests recommendations about the future agenda in federal policy in transforming education.

CHALLENGES RELATED TO FEDERAL ROLES IN TRANSFORMING EDUCATION

Achieving Educational Equity

Children from poor neighborhoods, children with limited proficiency in English, children with hearing impairments, children with preschool language impairments, and children whose parents had difficulty learning to read are particularly at risk of arriving at school with weakness in these areas and hence fall behind from the outset (Snow, Burns & Griffin, 1998, p. 5).

The equality of educational opportunity requires that federal education policies seek to improve student achievement for all groups. This national effort must "improve the education of disadvantaged children that focuses extra funds on poorer schools, that gives principals and teachers the authority to decide how best to help children, and encourages states to raise their academic standards, and to hold accountable low-performing schools" (Jennings, 2000, p. 1).

Evidence exists that important differences do exist between the student background characteristics, school experiences, and outcomes of urban and other students, and that these differences represent more than that which can be attributed to differences in the school concentration of low income students (U.S. Department of Education, 1996). In the document, *Urban Schools: The Challenge of Location and Poverty*, the following findings were reported:

- Urban children were more than twice as likely to be living in poverty than those in suburban locations (30% compared with 13% in 1990).
- Urban students were more likely than suburban or rural students to receive free or reduced price lunch (38% compared with 16 and 18%).
- Urban students were more likely to be attending schools with high concentrations of low income students.
- Urban schools had larger enrollments, on average, than suburban or rural schools at both the elementary and secondary levels.
- Eighth graders in urban poverty schools scored lower on achievement tests.
- Students in urban schools were less likely to complete high school on time.
- Young adults who had attended urban schools had much higher poverty and unemployment rates later in life than those who attended other schools.

The Achievement Gap Between Minority and White Students. One example of the federal role in elementary and secondary education is the federally funded National Assessment of Educational Progress (NAEP). The NAEP reports student performance in relation to standards or achievement levels identified as basic, proficient, or advanced and describes what students in grades four, eight, and twelve should know in subject areas of reading, mathematics, history, and science. In the document titled, *Reaching the Top: A Report of the National Task Force on Minority High Achievement* (1999) the long-term academic achievement trends, as measured by the National Assessment of Educational Progress (NAEP) testing program, reported that in the mid-1990s, the gap in average NAEP math scores between White and Black 17-year olds was about a third less than it had been in the 1970s. In the last half of the 1990s, relatively small percentages of Black, Hispanic (Latino), and Native American high school seniors in NAEP test samples have had scores typical of students who are generally well prepared for college. For example, on the 1998 NAEP reading test, only about one-quarter of the Hispanic and Native American twelfth graders had scores at or above the "Proficient" level (i.e. competency over challenging subject matter) and only two or three percent reached the "Advanced" level (i.e. superior performance). In contrast, nearly half of the Whites reached or exceeded the Proficient level and 7% reached the Advanced level. These scoring patterns for twelfth graders on NAEP tests are also very similar to the NAEP scoring patterns for students in the fourth and eighth grades. These data make it clear that the large achievement gaps that persists among groups emerge very early in students' school careers. In addition, national studies have consistently found that underrepresented minorities are not performing nearly as well as White students early in the first grade and that the very large gaps identified by NAEP develop rapidly during the first three years of school.

Educators are challenged to provide equitable educational outcomes for children living in poverty (Children's Defense Fund, 1997). Shellenberg (1999) noted that the "effects of concentrated poverty both in schools and neighborhoods is a central problem that lowers achievement" (p. i). For example, Gottlieb, Alter, and Gottlieb (1999) reported that "in the New York City school system, there is a 0.90 correlation between the percentage of students in 635 elementary schools who participate in the free or reduced-price lunch program and the percentage of children in those schools where standardized reading test scores fall into the lowest quartile. A -0.94 correlation exists between the percentage of children in the lunch program and the percentage of children whose standardized reading score falls into the fourth quartile" (p. 99).

Promoting Equality of Educational Opportunity. The belief in competitive individualism is at the core of American culture. This can be easily recognized by simply noting the powerful influence such values have had on the functioning of school systems. From its earliest formation, education in the United States was concerned with sorting and selecting students so as to teach only what it considered to be the "best" students. This focus on sorting and selecting students was the impetus for the competitive system of education presently in place to emphasize differences rather than similarities among students. Such a system encourages a "dog-eat-dog" approach to education which, in order to function requires losers. Thus, it focuses on individual success, with little concern for the success of the group as a whole. It rewards and punishes students on the basis of individual merit and achievement. Grading practices, designed to separate students according to inferior or superior achievement, force students to focus on grade averages rather than the process of learning. Such grading practices also tend to limit cooperative student endeavors, as each one is competing with the other for a position on the class rooster of scores. Similarly, schools are routinely ranked as to their "effectiveness" as determined by the outcomes of group achievement tests. Clearly, the philosophy of competitive individualism is one by which no school system (or country for that matter) can ever effect the success of all of its charges. The critical questions are, What happens to students with special needs in the "dog-eat-dog" system of education? Should such a system not be transformed to help every child maximize his/her fullest potential?

Focal Points of Federal Policies: Adults Versus Children

Huston (1991) noted that, for the most part, discussions on federal policies are mostly focused on economics and political perspectives (e.g. the socioeconomic level of adults who are also parents), even though antipoverty policies include children. The logical extension is that policies that reduce parents' poverty will also solve problems of children living in poverty. Policy categories include welfare, education, and family policy – not child policy (Steiner, 1981). Federal policies are aimed at changing parents' income levels, circumstances, and their behavior. As a result, success or failure of federally funded programs depends almost entirely on parents labor force participation and earnings. For example, debates about federal policies on welfare reform are based upon weighting the costs of welfare against the costs of education and training that would lead to employment. Children are left out of the picture!

The perspectives of developmental psychologists, educators, and professionals in the human services are humanitarian, moral, human rights, and social equity principles. Huston (1991) stated that "anti-poverty programs are justified on the grounds that children have a right not to be poor, that is, a right to grow up with reasonable levels of physical and emotional protection and comfort. Children have basic rights to quality of life; they have inherent value as individuals at any point in their lives, not simply as future adults. The welfare of children is taken as a given in a society that values social equity and justice.

Early childhood education, health care, and quality child care are advocated in order to provide for the current developmental needs of children and not simply as adjuncts to parents' labor force participation or as investments as future workers" (p. 6). Important child-focused issues examine a broad range of developmental outcomes for children. It is not assumed that the needs and interests of the parents are identical to the needs and interests of children. In some instances, the specific needs as related to the welfare and schooling of children are dissimilar from their parents and are, unfortunately, absent from political discussions. For example, the economic goal of getting a mother employed or increased family income may not benefit her child if he or she is left unsupervised for long hours after school or if suitable child care supervision is not available. By obscuring the importance of developmental variables and relying solely on parent labor force participation as an index of policy success may be harmful to all children, including those with disabilities.

Current Perspectives on Federal Roles in Education

The United States is one of the few developed countries without a national education system. Barring some limited exceptions (i.e. the Overseas Dependent Schools, Gallaudet University, the armed services academies), the federal government is not responsible for directly providing educational services. States are not required by the U.S. Constitution to provide education. Instead, state constitutions contain clauses explicitly outlining the state's authority with regard to education. The federal government does, however, have some implied authority stemming from the U.S. Constitution's general welfare clause in the First amendment and the due process and equal protection clauses of the Fourteenth Amendment. Federal funding to state and local school systems as well as other mechanisms such as dissemination of research, demonstration projects, and technical assistance enable the federal government to exert influence on the direction of education programs across the country.

Underlying Assumptions. A contrast to the stated value for equity in the United States, is the strong, yet often unstated, endorsement of competitive individualism. Public problems such as drug abuse and unemployment are seen as strongly linked to the individual and less as a product of society's social and economic actions. Such individualism contributes to the conservative argument that structural barriers can be overcome by personal initiative and that present problems represent more a matter of choice than of unequal conditions. Kantor (1996/1997) noted that the liberal consensus that supported the expansion of federal policy-making in education has come under sharp attack from conservative politicians who base their arguments on four assumptions.

First, federal involvement since 1960 constitutes an unprecedented break with past practices. Conservative critics recommend that policy makers reduce the rate of growth in expenditures for federal education programs, eliminate federal programs targeted at poor children and children of color, and, above all, return the control of education to states and local school systems. Second, the federal spending on education for poor and minority children has been excessive. These programs that cost too much, have done little to improve substantially the achievement of low-income and minority children. Third, federal regulations have put schools in a morass of bureaucratic red tape. Teachers and administrators are trapped in a web of bureaucratic regulations that make it impossible for them to perform their essential educational and social functions. And fourth, federal programs have produced little measurable improvement in educational achievement for disadvantaged children. Conservative critics argue that federal involvement in education, particularly federal programs like Title I/Chapter I of the Elementary and Secondary Education Act, bilingual education, and education for exceptional learners has had few beneficial results.

Controversial Issues in Allocation of Title I Funds. Currently, there are three controversial issues focused on the role of the federal government that are currently being debated among policy makers. The first issue is whether or not Title I is a success or failure. There is bipartisan support for maintaining and expanding the presence of the federal government in K-12 education programs. Policy makers have recommended increased federal spending on education and support standards-based reform efforts at the state level. The standards-based reform movement includes high standards for all students, strong accountability systems, and incentives to states that narrow the current achievement gap. Federal initiatives are now focused on reading, teacher preparation, and school improvement. However, there are members of Congress who questioned the effectiveness of Title I and who have criticized this federal program as a failure. This criticism, according to Jennings (2000), has led to the House of Representatives passage of legislation that would allow states to take Title I money away from low performing schools where the majority of children are poor and of minority-status. An important question here is, How can students with exceptionalities maximize their fullest potential based on Congressional negative force?

According to Goertz (2000), the second issue discussed among policy makers is the nature of the federal role and how to balance federal objectives (e.g. student equity objectives) and the state and local governments' need for flexibility and discretion. Today, many federal education programs are designed to be integrated with state and local education reform initiatives. States have been given the responsibility of establishing challenging content and performance standards, implementing assessments that measure students' performance against these standards, therefore, holding schools accountable for the achievement of all students, promoting programmatic flexibility, and fostering instructional and curricular reforms. However, there is no national standard to measure the success or failure of local Title I programs. Critics of Title I have stated that the legislative purpose of Title I has never been to eliminate the achievement gap between minority and White children in affluent schools. If additional dollars are to be focused on expanding Title I funds, then conditions on how states and local school districts allocate funds must be explicitly stated so that excellence and equity can be achieved. As it appears, the third issue revolves around a shift of federal policy makers from procedural accountability to educational accountability (Goertz, 2000). Today, there is considerable controversy among policy makers regarding the federal monitoring of expenditures in relation to performance accountability. Consequently, states and local school districts would be responsible for developing and prioritizing standards, assessing student achievement, and defining levels of student mastery rather focusing on compliance with federal rules and regulations.

LITIGATION, POLICY INITIATIVES, AND GENERAL AND SPECIAL EDUCATION

For the past 25 years, the constitutional equal protection and due process clauses have played a preeminent role in the education of disadvantaged children and children with disabilities. This next section reviews principles of equal protection and due process in case laws and their impact on the provision of equitable educational services for disadvantaged children and children with disabilities.

Case Law and the Courts: Principles of Equal Protection and Due Process

There is no federal constitutional provision establishing a national education system or rights to education. When state rules and regulations provide education, the Fourteenth Amendment comes into play. This means that education must be provided to all citizens on an equal basis, and it cannot be denied without due process of the law. The landmark case of *Brown v. Board of Education* (1954) established a philosophy of integration in America's schools based on constitutional principles established by the Fourteenth Amendment, which provided that people could not be denied "equal protection of the laws" or deprived of "life, liberty, or property, without due process of law (Ysseldyke, Algozzine & Thurlow, 1992). The *Brown* decision extended public school education to African American and other children on equal terms. In the 1960s and 1970s, parents and advocates of children with disabilities questioned the same principles of equal access to education. Heward (1996) stated that "the courts often regarded people with disabilities as belonging to a minority group that has a history of discrimination, political powerlessness, and unequal treatment. Thus, equal protection and certain procedures known as due process of law must be provided to ensure that children with disabilities and their families are fully informed of their rights and are treated fairly and reasonably as citizens" (p. 21). Parents of children with disabilities based their arguments on concepts of equal protection and due process as fundamental rights of their children. Thus, due process is a legal procedure that enables families of children with disabilities to achieve fair treatment and accountability with respect to the quality of their child's education. Turnbull and Turnbull (2000, pp. 9–10) further noted that *Brown v. Board of Education*, 347 U.S. 483 (1954) was a landmark case because it had impact on many issues of educational law and procedure. As they indicated:

- *Brown* illustrates the principle that the federal constitution, as interpreted by the U.S. Supreme Court, is the supreme law of the land binding on all federal, state, and local governments, and is the precedent that must be followed by all federal and state courts in subsequent similar cases.
- *Brown* is a nearly perfect example that all educational issues (such as the educational rights of students with disabilities) are essentially political policy and social issues cast in the guise of constitutional litigation (Should those students be educated and, if so, how, with whom, and by whom?) and, because they are presented in the garments of the law, they ultimately are resolved by the courts.
- *Brown* also demonstrates that the truly difficult educational issues are fought on various civil rights battlefields. Just as *Brown* was the first successful case on the battlefield of racial desegregation of schools, so it was the seed that gave birth to other civil rights battles and to successful challenges to governmental discrimination against certain persons because of their unalterable personal characteristics (such as race, sex, and disability).
- *Brown* gives immense comfort and support to civil rights activists, legitimizing their legal arguments and furnishing them with a powerful tool for persuading legislatures, particularly Congress, to enact entitlements and anti-discrimination laws.
- *Brown* demonstrates that, although the U.S. Constitution never once refers to a public education, the principles of equal protection and due process under the Fifth and Fourth Amendments have a significant effect on public

education. Nowhere is this fact clearer than in the disability right-to-education cases. ... The essential point of *Brown* is that the states were violating the equal-protection clause of the federal Constitution.

Apparently, *Brown* changed the role of the federal government in education. This case shifted the balance of the federal system heavily towards the side of the federal government by diminishing state and local autonomy in education. With the new emphasis on school reforms, standards for student achievement, and standards for educators to provide quality education for *all* students, the federal education agenda will continue to rely on the Constitution as a basis for justifying educational programs with discriminatory intent.

REDEFINING FEDERAL INITIATIVES IN TRANSFORMING EDUCATION

Providing most Americans with an empowering and equitable education has always been a struggle, and it remains one today. Relatively few schools offer all their students a rich, active curriculum that teaches for understanding. Even fewer manage to educate a diverse set of students for constructive social interaction and shared decision making. From the time many Southern states made it a crime to teach an enslaved person to read and Northern states opted to establish differently funded schools for the rich and the poor, through decades of separate and unequal schooling that continue to the present, the right to learn in ways that develop both competence and community has been a myth rather than a reality for many Americans (Darling-Hammond, 1997, p. 7).

Understanding what the best roles are for government, practitioners, and parents is essential for schools. Green (1983) noted that public policy is a crude instrument for securing social ideals, desires, specifying how funds should be spent, how resources should be configured, and how educational interventions should be delivered in schools. Darling-Hammond (1997) advocated the role of government as delegating "decisions about teaching and learning processes and specific curriculum strategies to local schools and professional organizations, which can better determine the needs of individual learners and incorporate advances in knowledge" (p. 221). She reconceptualized the role of the federal government in general and special education from a top-down-bottom-up view that places policy people at the top and school people at the bottom to a set of concentric circles beginning with the student, teacher, and the school and later encompassing the community (see Fig. 1).

The Federal Role in Transforming General and Special Education 27

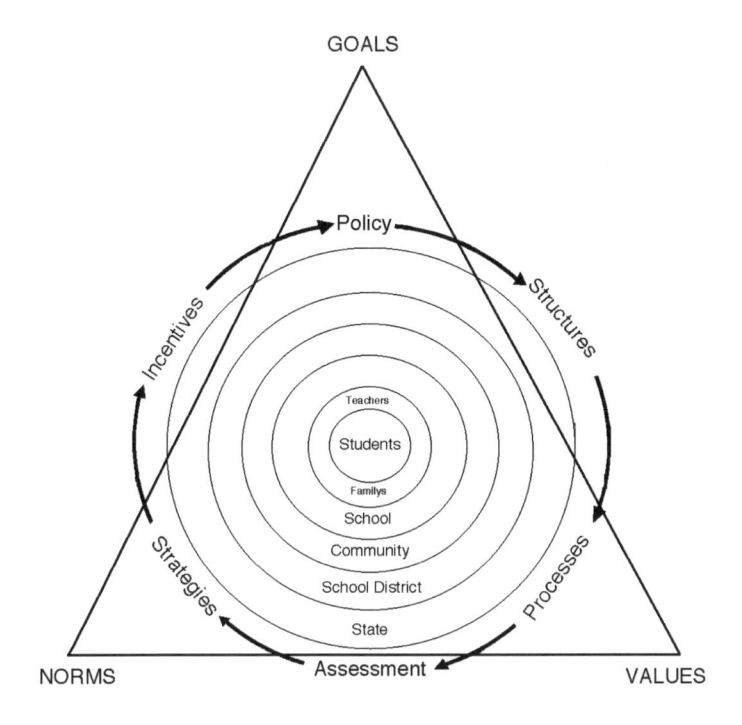

Fig. 1.

Source: Darling-Hammond, L. (1997). *The Right to Learn: A Blueprint for Creating Schools that Work.* San Francisco, CA: Jossey-Bass.

From her perspective, in this model, "each part of the system pursues accountability as shared goals, norms, and values are translated into *policies*, organizational structures, are created to make the policies work, *processes* that guide work are employed within these structures, *feedback and assessment* mechanisms are established to identify needs and progress, *safeguards* are created to ensure that harmful practices do not occur, and *incentives* are designed to promote productive practices" (p. 222).

Policy Initiatives in General and Special Education

This subsection describes in detail an array of federal education polices such as: (a) New Freedom Initiative Act; (b) The No Child Left Behind Act of 2001; (c) GOALS 2000: Educate America Act; (d) Title I of the Elementary and

Secondary Education Act; (e) Special Education Law; (f) School to Work Opportunities Act; (g) Carl D. Perkins Vocational and Technical Education Act of 1998; (h) Workforce Investment of 1998; and (i) Bilingual Education Policies.

New Freedom Initiative. Ten years ago, Congress passed one of the most significant civil rights laws since the Civil Rights Act of 1964 – the Americans with Disabilities Act (ADA). This law enabled Americans with disabilities to improve their access to employment opportunities, public accommodations, commercial facilities, telecommunication services, housing, schools, and polling places. Despite these improvements in the lives of Americans with disabilities, significant challenges remain for them to have full participation in American society. For example, statistics revealed that Americans with disabilities: (a) have a lower level of educational attainment than those without disabilities: and (b) are poorer and more likely to be unemployed than those without disabilities. In order to eliminate discrimination as a barrier to opportunities in America, President George W. Bush proposed the "New Freedom Initiative." The goals of this law are to ensure that Americans with disabilities have the tools to: (a) use their skills in order to make more of their own choices; (b) increase investments in and access to assistive technologies and a quality education; and (c) integrate themselves in the workforce and into community life (Institute on Disabilities, 2001).

The No Child Left Behind Act of 2001. This Act reauthorizes the Elementary and Secondary Education Act (ESEA) of 1965 and is designed to "improve the performance of American's elementary and secondary schools while at the same time ensuring that no child is trapped in a failing school" (U.S. Department of Education, 2002). This comprehensive education reform law passed by Congress and President George W. Bush is to close the achievement gap between disadvantaged and minority students and their peers. Four major principles are incorporated into this Act: (1) increased accountability by requiring states to implement statewide accountability systems covering all public schools and students; (2) increased choices for parents of students attending Title I schools that fail to meet state standards; (3) greater flexibility for states and school districts flexibility in the use of federal education funds in exchange for strong accountability procedures; and (4) increased federal investments in scientifically based reading instruction programs in the early grades in order to reduce the identification of children for special education services due to a lack of appropriate reading instruction in their early years (U.S. Department of Education, 2002). The principles of accountability, choice, and flexibility are also incorporated into the reauthorization of major ESEA programs such as the Eisenhower Professional Development and Class Size Reduction programs and the bilingual and immigrant education grant programs.

GOALS 2000: Educate America Act. The Goals 2000: Educate America was first enacted in 1994 and later amended in 1996. The intent of the act is to "improve student learning through a long-term, broad-based effort to promote coherent and coordinated improvements in the system of education throughout the Nation at the state and local levels" (Goals 2000: Educate America Act, Title III, Sec. 302). Goals 2000 puts into law the National Education Goals agreed to by then President Bush and state governors in 1990 and adds two additional goals on improving the skills of the nation's teaching force and promoting partnerships with parents. Based on the National Education Goals, all children and youth must be involved in the educational system. According to the goals, by the year 2000:

- All children in America should start school ready to learn.
- The high school graduation rate should increase to at least 90%.
- All students should leave grades 4, 8, and 12 having demonstrated competency over challenging subject matter including English, mathematics, science, foreign languages, civics and government, economics, the arts, history, and geography, and every school in America should ensure that all students learn to use their minds well, so they may be prepared for responsible citizenship, further learning, and productive employment in our nation's modern economy. U.S. students should be first in the world in mathematics and science achievement.
- Every adult American should be literate and should possess the knowledge and skills necessary to compete in a global economy and exercise the rights and responsibilities of citizenship.
- Every school in the U.S. should be free of drugs, violence, and the unauthorized presence of firearms and alcohol, and should offer a disciplined environment conducive to learning.
- The nation's teaching force should have access to programs for the continued improvement of their professional skills and the opportunity to acquire the knowledge and skills needed to instruct and prepare all American students for the next century.
- Every school should promote partnerships that should increase parental involvement and participation in promoting the social, emotional, and academic growth of children.

The emphasis in this legislation has been on supporting states, local school districts, and schools as they develop high academic standards and ensure that *all* children meet them. In Fiscal Year 2000, all 50 states and the outlying areas received Goals 2000 funding to support their ongoing school reform efforts (U.S. Department of Education, Goals 2000 Web site, 2001).

The original Goals 2000 legislation tied funding to a state improvement plan outlining strategies for meeting the National Education Goals. These strategies included the development or adoption of three types of standards: *performance standards* that define the results that schools are expected to produce; *content standards* that specify the subject matter that students are expected to engage in; and *opportunity to learn standards* that outline the set of conditions that schools, districts, and states must meet in order to assure that students are being offered an equal opportunity to meet the expectations embodied in performance standards (Elmore & Fuhrman, 1995). Unfortunately, the 1996 amendments to Goals 2000 eliminated all references to opportunity to learn standards or strategies. Holding all students to high content and performance standards without also ensuring that necessary resources are available, puts students from low performing schools in high poverty communities at a disadvantage. The recent annual report of the National Education Goals Panel suggests that overall National progress in reaching the goals may be slow with variation in state performance on particular goals (National Education Goals Panel, 2000).

Title I of the Elementary and Secondary Education Act (ESEA). Since its enactment in 1965, Title I of the Elementary and Secondary Education Act (Title I) has played a critical role in the Nation's efforts to improve achievement for disadvantaged students from low-income families. Funds from Title I are allocated to school districts based on their numbers of children from low-income families. It supplements state and local funding for low-achieving children in high-poverty schools and represents the largest federal education investment with $ 7.9 billion expended in Fiscal Year (FY) 2000. In FY 1996, almost 54,000 schools serving over 7 million students received Title I funding (U.S. Department of Education, 1996). The Improving America's Schools Act (IASA) of 1994 amended the ESEA consistent with the comprehensive reforms described in Goals 2000. Thus, the expressed purpose of Title I is "to enable schools to provide opportunities for children served to acquire the knowledge and skills contained in the challenging state content standards and to meet the challenging state performance standards developed for all children" (IASA of 1994). According to Tirozzi and Uro (1997), five key themes characterized the amendments to ESEA, namely: (1) high standards for all children; (2) a focus on teaching and learning; (3) promoting partnerships among families, communities, and schools to support achievement to high standards; (4) flexibility to stimulate local school-based and district initiative, coupled with responsibility for student performance; and (5) resources targeted to where needs are greatest and in amounts sufficient to make differences.

In the amendments to ESEA, Congress recognized many of the educational inadequacies and inequities faced by students from diverse backgrounds.

Specifically Congress noted that "educational needs are particularly great for low-achieving children in our Nation's highest-poverty schools, children with limited English proficiency, children of migrant workers, children with disabilities, Indian children, children who are neglected or delinquent, and young children and their parents who are in need of family-literacy services." It also recognized that "conditions outside the classroom such as hunger, unsafe living conditions, homelessness, unemployment, violence, inadequate health care, child abuse, and drug and alcohol abuse can adversely affect children's academic achievement and must be addressed through the coordination of services, such as health and social services, in order for the Nation to meet the National Education Goals" (IASA, 1994). Schools and school districts with high concentrations of culturally and linguistically diverse student populations often operate with insufficient resources and inadequate facilities in economically depressed areas (Kozol, 1991). Citing the work of Kozol, Darling-Hammond (1997) described a typical example of differences between public schools serving culturally and linguistically diverse populations and suburban schools serving student populations that are predominantly White. She wrote:

> A typical example contrasts Goudy Elementary School, which serves a predominantly African American student population in Chicago, with the schools in the nearby suburb of nearly all White New Trier. While Goudy uses "15-year-old textbooks in which Richard Nixon is still president," has "no science labs, no art or music teachers . . . [and] two working bathrooms for some 700 children," New Trier provides its students with "superior labs . . . up-to-date technology . . . seven gyms [and] an Olympic pool" (p. 265).

Lawson (2001) further stated that low performing schools "are instrumental in producing and reinforcing social and economic inequalities. Allegations of racism and overall social exclusion run rampant in low-income communities. Some leaders claim that schools are deliberately under funded and unsupported; and that the production of a permanent urban "underclass" is part of an explicit design. Although evidence is lacking in support of an explicit design, evidence is plentiful regarding the short and long term effects of ignoring and neglecting the needs of low performing schools and communities challenged by concentrated disadvantage" (p. 15).

Special Education Law. The right to an *appropriate education* that meets the needs of students with disabilities is undoubtedly one of the most significant provisions outlined in the 1975 Education for All Handicapped Children Act (Public Law 94-142). This legislation, renamed the 1990 Individuals with Disabilities Education Act (IDEA; Public Law 101-476), promotes the provision of individualized educational services designed to meet the unique educational requirements of students with disabilities. The Supreme Court in *Hendrick Hudson District Board of Education v. Rowley* (1982) defined appropriate education as providing a "basic floor of opportunity ... consisting] of access to specialized instruction and related services which are individually designed to provide educational benefit to the ... child [with disabilities]". Under this legislation, eligible students with disabilities have a right to an individualized educational program (IEP); a written statement of the educational program designed to meet the child's needs. In general, to be eligible for services under IDEA, a child must have a disability that fits into one of 13 IDEA categories and the disability must affect the child's educational performance. The IDEA categories of disability are mental retardation, hearing impairments (including deafness), speech or language impairments, visual impairments (including blindness), serious emotional disturbance, orthopedic impairments, autism, traumatic brain injury, other health impairments, specific learning disabilities, mental retardation (including developmental delay). More than $7.4 billion was appropriated for IDEA in FY 2001.

For several years, many in the field have noted with concern the disproportionate representation of some culturally and linguistically diverse students in special education (Chinn & Hughes, 1987; Dunn, 1968; Harry, 1994). Overrepresentation is a particular concern since special education, historically, has involved a student's removal from the typical classroom setting, limited access to the general education curriculum, and low expectations for performance (Oswald & Coutinho, 2001). Underrepresentation is a concern in that students may be denied access to much needed education services in programs for students with gifts and talents (Daniels, 2001). One comprehensive analysis found that "the patterns of disproportionate placement have shifted somewhat, but the main features are that there is now overrepresentation of African American students in most disability categories nationwide, a variety of patterns of over and underrepresentation of Hispanic students in some categories in certain states, and evidence of overrepresentation of Native Americans in some categories in states where their overall population is high" (Harry, 1994, p. 65). The persistent problem of overrepresentation of African-American children in programs for students with learning disabilities, severe emotional disturbance, and mental retardation have been well documented (Patton, 1998).

The recent amendments to IDEA in 1997 (Public Law 105-17), focused on having high expectations for children with disabilities and ensuring their access to the general education curriculum to the maximum extent possible. Congress took steps to coordinate services under IDEA with other federal, state and local school improvement efforts. States are now required to establish goals for the performance of children with disabilities that are consistent, to the maximum extent appropriate, with other goals and standards for children established by the state. Students with disabilities are to be included in general state and district-wide assessments with appropriate accommodations as necessary. The state or school district must develop guidelines for participation in alternate assessments for those students with disabilities who cannot, with accommodations, participate in the state and district-wide assessments.

It is important to note that other legislation that protects the rights of children with disabilities to free appropriate public education include Section 504 of the Rehabilitation Act (Section 504) and the Americans with Disabilities Act (ADA). Section 504 applies to programs or activities that receive federal financial assistance. ADA applies to virtually all other services, programs, or activities of a public entity. Both laws protect individuals with disabilities from discrimination based on their disability (see Table 1).

School to Work Opportunities Act. The School to Work Opportunities Act (STWOA), signed into law in 1994, is jointly administered by the U.S. Departments of Education and Labor. It provides five-year grants to states and local communities to support the development of statewide School-to-Work (STW) systems as a part of comprehensive educational reform and integrated with the systems developed under the Goals 2000 legislation. STW is an educational approach that improves the knowledge and skills of youth by integrating academic and occupational learning, school-based and work-based learning, and building effective linkages between secondary and postsecondary education. Some of the primary purposes of the Act are to: (a) motivate all youths, including low-achieving youths, school dropouts and youths with disabilities, to stay in or return to school or a classroom setting and strive to succeed, by providing enriched learning experiences and assistance in obtaining good jobs and continuing their education in postsecondary institutions; and (b) increase opportunities for minorities, women, and individuals with disabilities, by enabling individuals to prepare for careers that are not traditional for their race, gender, or disability (STWOA, p. 8).

Initial STWOA evaluation findings are showing that more students are making the connection between their academic coursework in school and future career interests. Participation in classes perceived as focused on career goals went from 10% of seniors in 1996 to 20% of seniors in 1998. Growth in this area was significantly greater for African-American students whose participation in academic classes perceived as focused on their career goals went from 13% in the class of 1996 to 28% in the class of 1998. (Mathematica Policy Research, Inc., 1999).

Carl D. Perkins Vocational and Technical Education Act of 1998. The Carl D. Perkins Vocational and Technical Education Act of 1998 (Perkins III) [Public Law 105-332 Section 3(230)] was signed into law in October of 1998. This legislation focuses on services and activities for vocational and technical

Table 1. Federal Legislation Concerning the Education and Rights of Individuals with Disabilities.

Year	Legislation
1958	National Defense Education Act (PL 85-926) Provided funds for training professionals to train teachers for children with mental retardation.
1961	Special Education Act (PL 87-276) Provided funds for training professionals to train teachers of deaf children.
1963	Mental Retardation Facility and Community Center Construction Act (PL 88-164) Extended support given in PL 85-926 to training teachers of children with other disabilities.
1965	Elementary and Secondary Education Act (PL 89-10) Provided money to states and local districts for developing programs for economically disadvantaged and disabled children.
1966	Amendment to Title 1 of the Elementary and Secondary Education Act (PL 89-313) Provided funding for state-supported programs in institutions and other settings for children with disabilities.
1966	Amendments to the Elementary and Secondary Education Act (PL 89-750) Created the Bureau of Education for the Handicapped.
1968	Handicapped Children's Early Assistance Act (PL 91-230) Established the "first chance network" of experimental programs for preschool children with learning disabilities (see Chapter 14).
1969	Elementary, Secondary, and Other Education Amendments (PL 91-230) Defined learning disabilities; provided funds for state-level programs for children with learning disabilities.
1973	Section 504 of the Rehabilitation Act (PL 93-112) Declared that a person cannot be excluded on the basis of disability alone from any program or activity receiving federal funds (adopted 1977).
1974	Education Amendment (PL 93-380) Extended previous legislation; provided money to state and local districts for programs for gifted and talented students for the first time. Also protected rights of children with disabilities and their parents in placement decisions.
1975	Developmental Disabilities Assistance and Bill of Rights Act (PL 94-103) Affirmed rights of citizens with mental retardation and cited areas where services must be provided for people with mental retardation and other developmental disabilities.
1975	Individuals with Disabilities Education Act (PL 94-142) Originally named the Education for All Handicapped Children Act (EHA), PL 94-142 mandates fee, appropriate public education for all children with disabilities regardless of degree of severity of handicap; protects rights of children with disabilities and their parents in educational decision making; requires development of an individualized education program (IEP) for each child with a disability; states that students with disabilities must received educational services in the least restrictive environment.

Table 1. Continued.

Year	Legislation
1983	Amendments to the Education of the Handicapped Act (PL 98-199) Requires states to collect data on the number of youth with disabilities exiting their systems and to address the needs of secondary students making the transition to adulthood (see Chapter 15). Also gave incentives to states to provide services to infants and preschool children with disabilities.
1984	Developmental Disabilities Assistance and Bill of Rights Acts (PL 98-527) Mandated development of employment related training activities for adults with disabilities.
1986	Handicapped Children's Protection Act (PL 99-372) Provided authority for reimbursement of attorney's fees to parents who must go to court to secure an appropriate education for their child. Parents who prevail in a hearing or court case may recover the costs incurred for lawyers to represent them, retroactive to July 4, 1984.
1986	Education of the Handicapped Act Amendments of 1986 (PL 99-457) Encouraged states to develop comprehensive interdisciplinary services for infants and toddlers (birth through age 2) with disabilities and to expand services for preschool children (ages 3 through 5). After the 1990–1991 school year, states must provide free, appropriate education to all three- to five-year-olds with disabilities to be eligible to apply for federal preschool funding (see Chapter 14).
1990	Education of the Handicapped Act Amendments of 1990 (PL 101-476) In addition to renaming the EHA as the Individuals with Disabilities Education Act, this law added autism and traumatic brain injury as two new categories of disability, required all IEPs to include a statement of needed transition services no later than age 16, and expanded the definition of related services to include rehabilitation counseling and social work services.
1994	Goals 2000: Educate America Act (PL 103-227) Provides federal funds to state and local education agencies for the development and implementation of educational reforms to help active eight national goals by the year 2000.

Source: Heward, W. L. (1996). *Exceptional Children: An Introduction to Special Education.* Englewood Cliffs, NJ: Prentice Hall.

education students that integrate academic, vocational, and technical instruction, and that link secondary and postsecondary education. Perkins III restructures and reforms previous provisions governing vocational and technical education and builds on the efforts of state and local communities to develop challenging academic standards. It includes specific provisions for collaboration with other agencies in developing high quality education and workforce systems consistent with the Workforce Investment Act of 1998. Almost $1.2 billion were expended under this legislation in FY 2000.

Perkins III contains specific requirements with regard to special populations. Special populations is defined as including individuals with disabilities, economically disadvantaged individuals (including foster children), individuals preparing for nontraditional employment, single parents (including single pregnant women), displaced homemakers, and individuals with other barriers to educational achievement, including individuals with limited English proficiency. State and local communities receiving Perkins III funding must identify and adopt strategies to overcome barriers to access and success for members of special populations. This includes describing a plan for how members of special populations will not be discriminated against in the provision of services. Perkins also requires state and local communities to provide programs designed to enable members of special populations to meet state performance requirements and prepare them for further learning and for high skill, high wage careers. In addition, Perkins III requires a state assessment to evaluate how the needs of special populations are being met and how programs are designed to enable special populations to meet performance requirements and prepare them for further learning or high skill, high wage careers. States are required to evaluate their progress with regard to meeting the needs of special populations and report annually to the Secretary of the U.S. Department of Education. The report must include a quantifiable description of the progress of special populations in meeting state performance requirements.

Workforce Investment Act of 1998. The Workforce Investment Act (Public Law 105-220), enacted on August 7, 1998, authorizes funds for establishing state workforce investment systems. These workforce investment systems must be designed to meet the needs of job seekers and others wanting to further their careers. These systems call for state Governors to designate local workforce investment areas and oversee the activities of local workforce investment boards. Youth Councils are a subgroup of the local workforce investment board charged with guiding the development and operation of programs for youth ages 14–21. A primary requirement of the legislation is the development of customer-focused, local one-stop delivery systems as the access point for employment-related and training services. Programs funded under this legislation must be designed to prepare youth for postsecondary educational opportunities or employment through appropriate services. These include services such as tutoring, study skills training, instruction leading to completion of secondary school (including dropout prevention); alternative school services; mentoring by appropriate adults; paid and unpaid work experience (such as internships and job shadowing); occupational skills training; leadership development; and appropriate supportive services. The program must provide for guidance and counseling, and follow-up services for at least one year, as appropriate. Statewide and local accountability measures for youth include rates of basic skills and work readiness or occupational skills attainment, attainment of high school diplomas (or equivalent) and placement and retention in postsecondary education, advanced occupational training, apprenticeships, the military or employment.

Eligibility for the Workforce Investment Act is limited to primarily low-income youth ages 14 through 21. Up to 5% of youth who are not low-income may receive services if they face certain barriers to school completion or employment. In addition, for eligibility, youth must face challenges such as: (1) school dropout; (2) basic literacy skills deficiency; (3) homeless, runaway, or foster child; (4) pregnant or a parent; (5) an offender; or (6) need help completing an educational program or securing and holding a job.

Bilingual Education Policies. Not long ago, August and Hakuta (1997) wrote:

> Recent federal policy with regard to educating English-language learners has been based on relatively little research, as a result of both the paucity of research and the predominance of politics. It has endorsed bilingual instruction, both through Title VII of the Elementary and Secondary Education Act of 1968 and the interpretation of the Supreme Court decision in *Lau v. Nichols*. The predominant justification for advocating bilingual education could be characterized as what one observer has called "a leap of faith" (p. 23).

According to Starks, Bransford, and Baca (1998), critical issues facing policy development in the bilingual education and special education are similar to issues in general education. These authors noted that "high unemployment and underemployment figures, concern over interest rates, increasing costs of government services, reduced federal expenditures for education generally, the shift from categorical funding to block grants, and budget balancing are just some of the issues associated with the problem of financing educational programs for the disadvantaged or disabled" (p. 384). Other issues affecting policy development consist of: (a) state and local governments assuming the costs of programs; (b) unwillingness of special interest groups to return to federal spending levels of the past; (c) a lack of support from special interest groups and people supporting public education; (d) increased support for services in private schools at public expense; and (e) reduced support from the federal government for equity in education.

Legislation passed by Congress can be found in Goals 2000 (PL 103-227), Title I (Helping Disadvantaged Children Meet High Standards) and Title VII (Bilingual Education Programs) of the Improving America's Schools Act of 1994 (PL 103-382), and the Reauthorization of the Office of Educational Research and Improvement (Title IX of PL 103-227). Almost one-half billion dollars have been appropriated for the Bilingual Education Act in FY 2001 (specifically $460 million). Inherent within these federal policies are the rationales for developing and implementing bilingual education programs. Gonzalez, Brusca-Vega and Yawkey (1997) highlighted the following points germane to appropriate services for limited English proficient (LEP) students:

- The federal government has a special and continuing obligation to ensure that state education agencies (SEAs) and local education agencies (LEAs) take appropriate action to provide equal educational opportunities to students with LEP.
- Multilingual skills constitute an important national resource that deserves protection and development.
- Quality bilingual programs enable students to learn English and meet high academic standards, including proficiency in more than one language. The use of a student's native language and culture in classroom instruction can: (a) promote self-esteem and contribute to academic achievement; (b) benefit English-proficient students who participate in such programs; and (c) develop our national language resources, thus promoting our competiveness in the global economy.
- Students with LEP face educational challenges, including segregated programs, disproportionate and improper placement in special education and other special programs due to the use of inappropriate evaluation procedures, and a shortage of teachers and other staff qualified to meet their needs.
- Parent and community participation in bilingual education programs contributes to program effectiveness (p. 36).

Several consistent themes regarding student assessment, program evaluation, and standards for English-language learners are presented in the legislative language and content. August and Hakuta (1997) outlined the following themes: (a) standards and assessment are to fully include English-language learners; (b) innovative ways of assessing student performance are encouraged, including modifications to existing instruments for English-language learners; (c) programs are to be evaluated with respect to whether they meet challenging performance standards, rather than on a normative or comparative basis; and (d) evaluations are to be useful for program improvement as well as program accountability.

It is important to note that Title VII of the Elementary and Secondary Education Act (ESEA), also referred to as the Bilingual Education Act (BEA), was reauthorized as part of the Improving America's Schools Act (IASA). The BEA provides discretionary funding for states and local school districts to provide culturally and linguistically appropriate services and programs for LEP students. Instructional programs (i.e. bilingual education or special alternative programs) that are eligible for funding (under Part A, Subpart 1 – Bilingual Education Capacity and Demonstration Grants) must apply in one of four program categories: (1) development and implementation grants; (2) enhancement grants; (3) comprehensive school grants; and (4) system-wide improvement grants. By definition, bilingual education programs are intended to develop the student's native language and/or to enable English proficient students to become proficient in English as a second language. Special alternative instructional programs develop English language curricula, provide services without instruction in the student's native language, address standards identified with the National Education Goals (Goals 2000: Educate America Act of 1994), improve academic mastery of subject area content, and support grade promotion and graduation. In addition to providing funding for instructional programs, the BEA provides funds for activities in the following categories, namely: (a) research, evaluation, and dissemination, including the National Clearinghouse for Bilingual Education, technical assistance centers, and grants to SEAs for data collection and evaluation; (2) professional development, including career ladder programs and training for all teachers; (3) foreign language assistance in elementary and high schools; and (4) emergency immigrant education to assist LEAs with immigrant students (Gonzalez et al., 1997).

FUTURE PERSPECTIVES

Current reform initiatives are beginning to signal a willingness to address the needs of all students, including culturally and linguistically diverse students with and without exceptionalities. Unfortunately, all too frequently, these federal initiatives do not fully achieve their goals. We see a bright future! Conservative politicians are acknowledging the importance of the role of the federal government in maximizing the fullest potential of all learners. As a result, we recommend some perspectives for federal roles in transforming general and special education. Below are our recommendations.

(1) There must be a national commitment to improving the education of poor and minority families and children in low performing schools. Fundamental principles such as excellence, equity, accountability for results, and respect for the roles of state and local governments should be guiding principles of the federal government.
(2) Federal policies must meet the needs of children with and without disabilities, families, and communities so that they may achieve independence, stability, empowerment, and growth.

(3) Federal initiatives must be responsive to individual family- and child-specific service needs in general and special education.
(4) Strategies are needed to engage schools, families, and communities in comprehensive interagency planning to foster school, community, and family partnerships. Strategies are needed to coordinate and integrate family, school, and community initiatives collaboratively and collectively in various federal, state, and local programs.
(5) Federal policies must be designed to maximize current human and fiscal resources at state and local levels.
(6) There must be an emphasis on maintaining a knowledge base for the educational success of federal programs-this knowledge base must be grounded in research and evaluation. Data are needed on the effective implementation and results of planned programs funded at state and local levels.
(7) Federal grants that are realistically inclusive should be funded, and strategies for evaluating whether programs do what they initially indicated must be non-political.
(8) Federal policies must not discriminate on the basis of race, color, national origin, religion, and disability.

REFERENCES

Americans with Disabilities Act of 1990, Pub. L. 101-336.
August, D., & Hakuta, K. (1997). *Improving schooling for language-minority children: A research agenda*. Washington, D.C.: National Academy Press.
Brown v. Board of Education of Topeka, 347 U.S. 483, 74S. Ct.686, 91 L. Ed.873 (1954).
Carl D. Perkins Vocational and Technical Education Act of 1998 Pub. L. 105-332 (1998).
Children's Defense Fund (1997). *Poverty matters: The cost of child poverty in America*. Washington, D.C.: Author.
Chinn, P. C., & Hughes, S. (1987). Representation of minority students in special education classes. *Remedial and Special Education*, 8(4), 41–46.
Daniels, V. I. (2001). Responding to the learning needs of multicultural learners with gifts and talents. In: C. A. Utley & F. E. Obiakor (Eds), *Special Education, Multicultural Education, and School Reform: Components of Quality Education for Learners with Mild Disabilities* (pp. 140–154). Springfield, IL: Charles C. Thomas.
Darling-Hammond, L. (1997). *The right to learn: A blueprint for creating schools that work*. San Francisco, CA: Jossey-Bass.
Dunn, L. M. (1968). Special education for the mildly retarded: Is much of it justifiable? *Exceptional Children*, 35, 5–22.
Education for All Handicapped Children Act, Pub. L. 94-142 (1975).
Elmore, R. F., & Fuhrman, S. H. (1995). Opportunity to learn standards and the state role in education. *Teachers College Record*, 96, 432–457.

Finn, C. E., Kanstoroom, M., & Pintrilli, S. (1999). Overview: Thirty-four years of dashed hopes. In: M. Kanstoroom & C. E. Finn (Eds), *New Directions: Federal Education Policy in the Twenty-First Century* (pp. 10–24) [On-line]. Available at http://www.edexcellence.net/library/ewdrct.htm

Goals 2000: Educate America Act, Pub. L. 103-227 (1994).

Goertz, M. E. (2000). *The Federal Role in an Era of Standards-based Reform. The Future of the Federal Role in Elementary and Secondary Education* [On-line]. Available at: http://www.ctredpol.org

Gonzalez, V., Brusca-Vega, R., & Yawkey, T. (1997). *Assessment and instruction of culturally and linguistically diverse students with or at-risk of learning problems: From research to practice.* Boston, MA: Allyn & Bacon.

Gottlieb, J., Alter, M., & Gottlieb, B. W. (1999). General education placement for special education students in urban schools. In: M. J. Coutinho & A. C. Repp (Eds), *Inclusion: The Integration of Students with Disabilities* (pp. 91–111). Belmont, CA: Wadsworth.

Green, T. F. (1983). Excellence, equity, and equality. In: L. S. Schulman & G. Sykes (Eds), *Handbook of Teaching and Policy* (pp. 318–341). White Plains, NY: Longman.

Harry, B. (1994). *The disproportionate representation of minority students in special education: Theories and recommendations.* Alexandria, VA: National Association of State Directors of Special Education.

Hendrick Hudson Central School District v. Rowley, 102S. Ct. 3034 (1982).

Heward, W. L. (1996). *Exceptional children: An introduction to special education.* Englewood Cliffs, NJ: Prentice-Hall.

Huston, A. C. (1991). *Children in poverty: Child development and public policy.* New York: Cambridge University Press.

Improving America's Schools Act of 1994, Pub. L. 103-382, 108 Stat. 3518 (1994).

Individuals with Disabilities Education Act, Pub. L. 105-17, 111 Stat. 37 (1997).

Institute on Disabilities (2001). New Freedom Intitative [On-line]. Available at: http://www.temple.edu/inst_disabilities

Jennings, J. F. (2000). Title I-A success [On-line]. Available at: http://www.ctredpol.org/articles/Title_IA Success_EdWeekJan26_2000.html

Kantor, H. (1996/1997). Equal opportunity and the federal role in education. *Rethinking Schools, 11*(2), 1–19 [On-line]. Available at: http://www.rethinkingschools.org/Archives/11_02/Kantor.htm

Kozol, J. (1991). *Savage inequalities: Children in American Schools.* New York: Crown.

Lau v. Nichols, 414 U.S. 563 (1974).

Lawson, H. A. (2001). Meeting the needs of low performing urban schools. Unpublished manuscript. The University of Albany, The State University of New York. Albany, NY.

Mathematica Policy Research (1999). *Report to Congress on the National Evaluation of School-to-Work Implementation: Analysis and Highlights.* Washington, D.C.: Author.

National Commission on Teaching and America's Future (1996). *What matters most: Teaching for America's future* [On-line]. Available at: http://www.edweek.org/context/topics/issuespage:cfm?id=16

National Education Goals Panel (2000). *Promising practices: Progress toward the goals 2000* [On-line] Available at: http://www.negp.gov

Oswald, D. P., & Coutinho, M. J. (2001). Trends in disproportionate representation in special education: Implications for multicultural education. In: C. A. Utley & F. E. Obiakor (Eds), *Special Education, Multicultural Education, and School Reform: Components of Quality Education for Learners with Mild Disabilities* (pp. 53–730). Springfield, IL: Charles C. Thomas.

Patton, J. M. (1998). The disproportionate representation of African Americans in special education: Looking behind the curtain for understanding and solutions. *The Journal of Special Education, 32*(1), 25–31.

Ravitch, D. (1999). The national agenda in elementary and secondary education. In: H. J. Aaron & R. D. Reischauer (Eds), *Setting National Priorities: The 2000 Election and Beyond* (pp. 269–302). Washington, D.C.: Brookings.

School to Work Opportunities Act of 1994, Pub. L. 103-239, 108 Stat 568 (1994).

Section 504 of the Rehabilitation Act of 1973, as amended, 29 U.S.C. 794.

Shellenberg, S. J. (1999). Concentration of poverty and the ongoing need for Title I. In: G. Orfield & E. H. Debray (Eds), *Hard Work for Good Schools: Facts Not Fads in Title I Reform* (pp. 130–146). Cambridge, MA: Harvard University.

Snow, C. E., Burns, M. S., & Griffin, P. (1998). *Preventing reading difficulties in young children.* Washington, D.C.: National Research Council.

Starks, J., Bransford, J., & Baca, L. (1998). Issues in policy development and implementation. In: L. M. Baca & H. T. Cervantes (Eds), *The Bilingual Special Education Interface* (p. 372–410). Upper Saddle River, NJ: Merrill.

Steiner, G. (1981). *The futility of family policy.* Washington, D.C.: Brookings Institute.

The College Board (1999). *Reaching the top: A report of the National Task Force on Minority High Achievement.* New York: College Board Publications.

Tirozzi, G. N., & Uro, G. (1997). Education Reform in the United States: National policy in support of local efforts for school improvement. *American Psychologist, 52*(3), 241–249.

Turnbull, H. R., & Turnbull, A. P. (2000). *Free appropriate public education: The law and children with disabilities* (6th ed.). Denver, CO: Love.

U.S. Department of Education (1996). *Justifications of appropriation estimates to the Congress, fiscal year 1997* (Vol. 1). Washington, D.C.: Author.

U.S. Department of Education (1996). *Urban schools: The challenge of location and poverty.* Washington, D.C.: National Center for Education Statistics.

U.S. Department of Education (1997). *U.S. Department of Education: Strategic Plan, 1998–2002* (September). Washington, D.C.: Author.

U.S. Department of Education (2001). *Goals 2000* [On-line]. Available at: http:\\www.ed.gov/pubs/G2KReforming

U.S. Department of Education (2002). *The No Child Left Behind Act of 2001.* Washington, D.C.: Author.

Ysseldyke, J. E., Algozzine, B., & Thurlow, M. L. (1992). *Critical issues in special education* (2nd ed.). Boston, MA: Houghton Mifflin.

TRANSFORMING GENERAL AND SPECIAL EDUCATION IN URBAN SCHOOLS

Dianne Ferguson, Elizabeth Kozleski and Anne Smith

Schools are changing across the United States as educators, politicians, parents, families and communities embark on a new century. An emerging global economy, ongoing demographic shifts, changes in both what "counts" as "knowledge" and who determines what "knowledge" is valued, and advances in technology as well as the skills and abilities demanded by businesses and industries of the future all combine to render much of what schools have been obsolete (Spring, 2000). Further complicating this picture are the political dimensions of school reform that forges debates in what and whom schools are for (Clark, Read & McGree, 1994). For some, the debate remains one of equity in the pursuit of excellence in education for all children (i.e. Darling-Hammond, 1995; Freire, 2000). For others, the debate centers on the preparation of a competitive labor force and service industry as well as the social and economic stratification that implies (Gagnon, 1995). These debates permeate current discussions on teacher preparation, quality, and practice as well as equity in school finance and resource allocation, standards and accountability, school safety, and curricula. The extent to which the professional education community embraces and opens itself to dialogue and partnership with families and communities is another important dimension of the discourse on equity and access to excellence (Haynes & Comer, 1996; Ferguson & Ferguson, 1992). These dimensions of the discussion also hold the promise for the transformation of American schools from a 20th-century educational system dominated by a narrow cultural perspective to one that reflects and values the multicultural nation that the U.S. has become (Banks, 2001; Nieto, 1996). Nowhere is the need for this broadening of cultural perspective more apparent than in the hallways and classrooms of our nations' urban schools (Fine, 1994).

The very nature of our system for funding schools has disadvantaged urban school systems since the Great Depression (Anyon, 2001). Consider that the Government Accounting Office reports that 80% of all urban schools in the U.S. are funded at a lower rate than their suburban counterparts, in spite of the recent influx of state funds to shore up failing urban systems. The lack of equitable funding over an extended period of time has led to increased class sizes, lack of sufficient books and materials, shortages of certified teachers, and to the deterioration of school buildings (Kozol, 1991). The magnitude of these problems should be of grave concern given the fact that urban schools comprise the 4% of American school districts that serve more than 44% of the nation's students (Federal Register, 1997).

Interestingly, it is in urban schools where resources are spread thinly that problems of the overrepresentation of students of color and English language learners in special education is visible (Fusarelli, 1999). For instance, students of African-American descent comprise about 16.3% of the school-age population but are more than 31% of students classified as having mild mental retardation and 23.7% of students classified as severely emotionally disturbed while Latino students are over represented in the categories of learning disabilities and speech and language impairments (Heward & Cavanaugh, 2001). Researchers suggest that patterns of over representation are a result of the narrow cultural preference for particular modes of communication, cognitive schemas, affect, behavior and knowledge (Artiles, Trent, Hoffman-Kipp & Lopez-Torres, 2000; Hilliard, 1992).

Proponents of inclusive education argue that the basic tenets of special education that have led to separate programs and services promote and support the over representation of culturally and linguistically diverse students in special education because they permit the exclusion of those students from general education classrooms (Artiles & Trent, 1994; Ewing, 1995; Patton, 1998; Pugach & Seidl, 1995). Further, the inclusive education movement has focused on poor outcomes that students in special education have achieved as a result of their limited access to the general education curriculum (Berres, Ferguson, Knoblock & Woods, 1996; Ferguson, 1995a; National Association of State Boards of Education, 1990; Sailor & Skirtic, 1995; Skirtic, 1995; Tetler, 1995). To expand this conversation beyond the special education community, practitioners, families and researchers must engage in a conversation that includes multicultural perspectives on inclusion and disproportionality (Artiles, 1998). If these often disconnected conversations can be joined, they will help to create a coherent vision for transforming the current educational system so that the social and educational inequities that currently exist for students of differing abilities, ethnicities, religions, experiences and wealth are no longer present.

All change in urban schools must address differences in culture, gender, language, ability, class and ethnicity (Delpit, 1995). As Banks (2001) recommended, schools need a true multicultural value system that encompasses simultaneously a concept, a process and a reform agenda. Multicultural education is based on the notion that all students must have equal access, and it acknowledges that in current school systems some students are advantaged by their socio-cultural and economic status, ethnicity, and gender (Nieto, 1996). In a true multicultural education system, school practices and climate that convey privilege associated with class, gender, language, ability, ethnicity and culture will not be present (Banks, 2001). Draper (1999) argued that:

> Our nation cannot afford any longer to have disposable children. No longer can systems and policies be built on practices that restrict and restrain; that categorize and seek to find and separate the children and youth who do not "fit" our profiles of successful learners. We must acknowledge that such practices and beliefs have actually done harm to children, disproportionately limiting and constraining the opportunities for children in poverty, children of color, children with disabilities and children with cultural and language differences (p. 2).

The challenge is great, but general and special educators in the United States and other countries are actively engaging the opportunity to transform education and how they can go about teaching and learning in schools. Proposed changes abound, addressing all aspects of schools, students, and teachers. While there are many different ways to address these change agendas, below are six key features that summarize them succinctly:

(1) Family, community and school partnerships (Epstein, 1995; Ferguson & Ferguson, 1992; Haynes & Comer, 1996).
(2) Performance standards for students (McLaughlin, 1995; Darling-Hammond & Falk, 1997).
(3) Performance standards for multicultural teacher preparation and practice (Hollingsworth, 1994).
(4) Aligned curricula and established accountability systems.
(5) Accountable schools for all students (Darling-Hammond & Ancess et al., 1995).
(6) Ongoing professional development system (Smylie, 1995).

Teachers, particularly in urban schools, must understand and value children's differing experiences based on culture, race, ethnicity, disability, economic background, and gender (Briscoe, 1991; Hollins, 1996; Lightfoot, 1983). Urban schools must draw on the strength of student diversity and use that diversity as an asset to foster creativity and leverage new interactions that support learning (Nieto, 1996). The voices of diverse students, parents, and communities can then become integral to the educational process and may suggest changes in policy and practice that better support the education and learning of all students. The opposite of this positive scenario is a bleak one. It has been observed that lack of cultural competence among educators and other service providers can have devastating consequences (Ogbu, 1978; Ogbu, 1993; Ogbu & Matutute-Bianchi, 1986). It can lead to discriminatory identification and diagnosis, improper evaluation and placement, and inadequate or inappropriate services especially to children of color, poverty, and children of limited English proficiency (Patton, 1998; Reynolds & Wang, 1993). Comer (1999) agreed racism affects child development, and in turn, education. He argued that teachers must have an opportunity to learn ways in which their behavior can either facilitate or interfere with child development, and that early childhood educators in particular must be prepared to teach children facing race-based obstacles to success. As he noted, it is important to create a positive school climate to promote children's development and address children's social and emotional needs.

Observing that racism is endemic and deeply ingrained in American life, Ladson-Billings and Tate (1995) called for a "critical race theory" of education that acknowledges that political and social systems are based on property rights rather than human rights. The relationship between ethnicity and poverty in this country present an opportunity for understanding how property rights have contributed to the increasing numbers of persons of color who lack access to high quality educational opportunities that are so closely related to higher paying jobs and economic power. This perspective on the social and political nature of education has led to an examination of social and political issues that are replayed in many urban classrooms. According to Delpit (1988, 1995), many of the academic problems typically associated with children of color are actually the result of miscommunications, inability to deal with imbalances of power in the society, and the complex dynamics of inequality in public school systems. Multicultural education appears to be a response to the context in which learning occurs in the nation's public schools. By adopting a multicultural lens for teaching and learning, students and teachers alike increase their knowledge and appreciation of the rich and fluid nature of different cultures, and of differences and similarities within and among different cultures and individuals (Banks, 2001; Grossman, 1995; Powell, McLaughlin, Savage & Zehm, 2001). Multicultural education is not merely a set of skills and procedures learned at one point in time and applied over and over again. It is a process through which educators and other service providers learn to interpret and adapt to their personal encounters with one another. Through multicultural education, teachers and students become culturally responsive and competent, creating new pathways for communication and knowledge sharing (Liston & Zeichner, 1996). If a key feature of reform focuses on multicultural education as a fundamental social and educational transformation, then we can be assured that opportunities for ALL students to achieve educational equity will be realized in schools.

WHY TRANSFORM SCHOOLS?

Recognizing that there continues to be considerable and legitimate debate surrounding inclusive practices, there is considerable evidence that exclusionary and categorical service delivery models have poorly served students from diverse backgrounds (Artiles, 1998; Artiles & Trent, 1994; Patton, 1998). Traditional strategies for referring, screening, identifying and placing students into specialized services and classrooms have resulted in:

(1) An increase in negative stereotypes based on disability labels.
(2) A lack of learning outcomes for students with disabilities that are comparable to their peers without special education labels (Pugach & Seidl, 1996).
(3) Numbers of minority students in special education that cannot simply be explained by co-varying circumstances of poverty (Artiles & Trent, 1994).
(4) Families and children who walk away from services (Harry, 1992).
(5) A focus of blame for failure on the student while virtually ignoring quality of teaching and learning, both before and after referral and placement in special education (Grossman, 1995).

At the same time, general educators continue to struggle with an increasing diversity of students who challenge the common curriculum and ability-grouping practices long dominant throughout the educational system, whether because of cultural and language differences, differences in ability, or social and family differences (Nieto, 1999). In addition to this increasing diversity, there are ongoing advancements in theories and practices of teaching and learning that focus on students' understanding and use of their learning rather than recall of facts or isolated skills (Brown & Campione, 1998). On a more challenging scale, students must demonstrate their learning via application or performance. Such uses and performances may vary according to students' particular abilities, interests, and life purposes as well as the requirement of state testing (McLaughlin, 1995). How then, do teachers respond to calls for higher standards of achievement and accommodation of the many differences children and youth bring to school? In the face of often-conflicting messages and challenges, urban school professionals are also facing rapid erosion of financial support and public respect. Not only are they being asked to "do more with less," they are also blamed as incompetent for not accomplishing their goals.

Educators are realizing that the efforts of renewal and reform that seemed adequate to resolve the educational problems of the past will simply not suffice. Doing better and more efficient schooling work, or changing existing procedures, rules, and requirements to accommodate new circumstances will not quiet the need, or calls for changes as we begin the new millennium. Instead, educators now argue, schools must begin to engage in the activities that will change the "fundamental assumptions, practices and relationships, both within the organization, and between the organization and the outside world, in ways that lead to improved student learning outcomes" (Elmore, 1996). Since many of these fundamental assumptions helped to create the very separateness between special and general education, it is just such fundamental changes that might realize the vision of inclusive schools.

Changing any school is both a nonlinear and bi-directional task (Fullan, 1993, 1997; Fullan & Miles, 1992). "Top down" policy changes must be met by "bottom up" changes in capacity, commitment and coherence among teachers, students, and families if changes are to become more than superficial accommodations. At the same time, there is no single road map for achieving deeper change (Louis & Miles, 1990). Local events, resources, and personal dynamics combine to create for any particular school or district a unique choreography of change, characterized as much by stepping back as by stepping forward. Students, parents, teachers and parents must become active co-constructors of new school communities, collaborating with one another, with students, and local community members (Berres et al., 1996; Council of Administrators of Special Education, 1993; Cohen, 1995; Darling-Hammond, Ancess & Falk, 1995; Ferguson, 1995). Thus, any school reform effort must focus on assuring that all students are considered as changes are made in instructional delivery, curriculum, student groupings, and school organization (Berres, Ferguson, Knoblock & Woods, 1996). This task is daunting since there are many tensions within education communities including special education (Sarason, 1990). While the ongoing reform discussion deals with many different dimensions, a common ground is emerging. Recent revisions of federal legislation include new language that focuses on access to the general education curriculum (IDEA 1997 U.S. Department of Education, 1996). These revisions suggest that the impetus to ensure that students with disabilities are educated with their non-disabled peers is receiving greater and greater validation both within and outside the special education community (O'Hanlon, 1995).

Inclusive urban schools embody the concepts of community, diversity, and collaboration (Sailor & Skrtic, 1995). The basic premise of inclusive school communities is that schools are about belonging, nurturing, and educating all children regardless of their differences in culture, gender, language, ability, class, and ethnicity (Saldana & Waxman, 1997). The challenge in inclusive school communities is to provide a diverse student body with access to these outcomes and to ensure, to the maximum extent possible, that all students have the opportunities to maximize their quality of life (Spring, 2000). It has become increasingly evident that urban school improvement and renewal activities can help schools to more successfully meet the educational needs of students from diverse backgrounds and their families.

ACHIEVING TRANSFORMED SCHOOLS AND UNIFIED SYSTEMS

A unified educational system is based on the premise that each student represents a unique combination of abilities and educational needs and deserves individual assistance at various times throughout the schooling cycle in order to achieve important outcomes. Key to this approach are schools that are organized around learning supports, not programs and services. Accountability in this approach is based on the use of the same effectiveness indicators for all students – across culture, gender, language, ability, socio-economic background, religion, and ethnicity – and assurance that all students are appropriately and effectively educated as defined by agreed upon standards.

In a successful unified system, educators believe not only that all students can learn but also that they have the skills, knowledge, and dispositions to teach all students. As a result, the lines between general education, special education, Title I, bilingual education, migrant education, vocational education, compensatory education, and other categorical programs become blurred and eventually disappear. Previously separate programs for specific groups of students come together to form a new educational system (Conley, 1991). Such a school system anchors its work in curriculum content, students' performance, and learning assessment strategies, all of which reflect learning outcomes that are valued by local communities and families and informed by national and state standards, curriculum frameworks, and assessment strategies (Fine, 1994).

The task of achieving transformed unified systems *is* complex and it is often made more complex by the sheer number of demands for change that districts, schools, and teachers must address at one time. Change tasks are often different "sizes." Some can be understood and mastered in a relatively short time such as changing to a block scheduling approach in an individual building. Many others require a sustained effort to understand and master, in part because they seek to change more fundamental ways of thinking and working in schools (Evans, 1996). Consider the complexity of redefining the way that practitioners work together to support each other's expertise and meet the needs of diverse learners. To do this requires bringing together all the practitioners within a building and to openly examine how to best organize time and people to deliver services and supports to students (Lambert, 1998). The real challenge of school renewal is changing old assumptions and practices to reinvent schools rather than simply making additions or corrections to existing practice (Abrams & Gibbs, 2000). Task overload and competing demands can turn important and fundamental changes into small, quick fixes that ultimately change little more than what things are called. One way to handle the number and variety of changes required to engage key stakeholders in transforming schools is to have a way to organize efforts in meaningful ways. In response to the complex and sometimes daunting tasks of improving schools, there must be an extraordinary effort to frame and organize the necessary discourse and the complex and interrelated dimensions involved with transforming schools (Bellamy, 1994; Ferguson & Kozleski, 1999).

THE SYSTEMIC CHANGE FRAMEWORK

Systemic reform is the process of identifying the components of a complex system and making strategic choices about levels of change that has a high probability of improving critical outcomes (Banathy, 1996). Using a systemic framework to approach the reform of the educational system helps us to remember that interventions that are seemingly innocuous at one level may produce seismic results at another level (Banathy, 1996). System characteristics are often invisible to the people involved in them, yet they have a life and dynamic of their own (Bateson, 1972).

As a reform is underway there are elements that both reinforce and balance change efforts. Therefore, for every initiative that pushes the system in one direction, another initiative may bubble up to push the system in the opposite direction. This principle helps to explain why large and complex urban systems are so difficult to change. Indeed, systems try to maintain equilibrium in order to sustain what has already been created. These principles from systems theory suggest that change in a complex social and political system like education must be made at multiple levels, from national organizations and government to individual schools, in order to create the intended results.

Achieving an *inclusive, multicultural school system* requires a way to describe the work of districts, schools and people so that change efforts can be organized into meaningful and effective elements. Intuitively, it seems evident that urban schools have many rich and unique contextual features. In order to guide the change effort so that urban schools are inclusive for all learners, it is imperative to provide a framework that encourages educators, community and family members to discuss their beliefs about schools, students and learning, various student outcomes, and multiple family goals but still moves schools toward an inclusive approach for each and every student. If districts and schools were organized around the capacity to change, their systems would look very different than the traditional district and school bureaucracies that have been organized for efficiency and stability (Louis & Miles, 1990). In a change-oriented organization, information is made available "just in time" so practitioners can adjust and improve based on valid information. Built on the premise that practitioners, schools, and districts must be unified, change oriented, and information rich, the *Systemic Change Framework* helps to map the kind of simultaneous change that is necessary at multiple levels of any given urban school system (Bellamy, 1994; Ferguson & Kozleski 1999; National Institute for Urban School Improvement, 1999).

The *Systemic Change Framework* (see Fig. 1) visually represents the varying levels of effort that combine to effect student achievement and learning. The four levels of the framework are interconnected, as represented by the permeable lines that delineate levels and efforts. What occurs at the district level affects the school level, which in turn affects student learning. Of course all these local levels are constantly affected by the agendas, policies, and practices that emerge from state educational organizations and national governmental activities. The district generally mediates these state and national efforts as they are routed to schools and classrooms. Thus, the *Framework* has been designed for use at the local level and emphasize the relationships that most directly affect students' learning and effort. When the efforts at the three outer levels of the *Framework* are maximized or in sync with one another, then the result is a healthy system that can better support student learning.

Student Effort

The Systemic Change Framework begins with student learning since student learning is the heart of all school effort. Learning is defined broadly to include self, social, career, and academic knowledge and competence. Learning is a central, defining function of each human being. How infants, children, youth and adults learn is predicated on the approaches that they use to process,

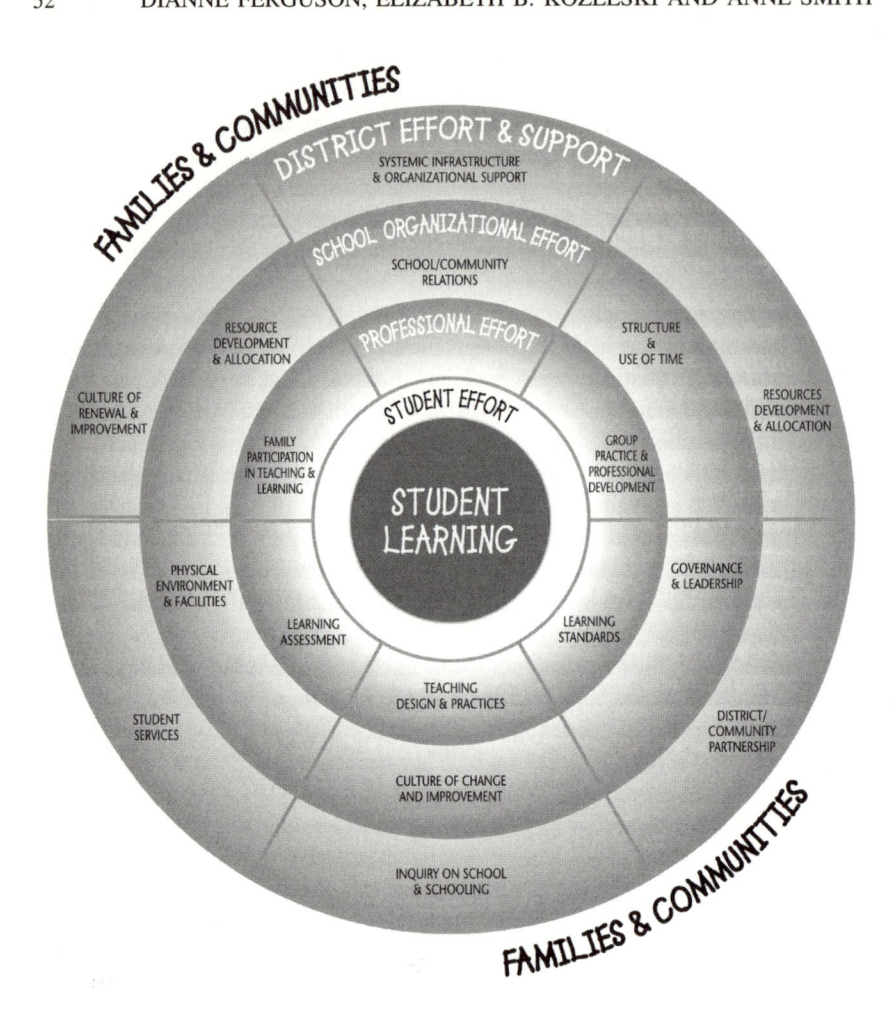

Fig. 1. The Systematic Change Framework.

interpret, and make meaning of the world around them in light of their own cultural perspectives and norms (Ogbu, 1995). The learning process is developmental since information processing, interpreting and meaning making become more sophisticated as children develop tools for learning. Infants use their senses to gather, process, and predict events. Toddlers' language accelerates their access to learning because linguistic symbols can be used to store, retrieve, and share sensory experiences. Social interactions and the collaborative play of preschoolers provide other key ingredients for learning since socially constructed knowledge expands the potential for knowledge acquisition. As children grow into adolescents and adults, their learning tools multiply. Utility, functionality, and context are at the heart of learning rather than a psychological construct of intelligence. While learning is developmental, functional and socially constructed, it also requires effort that focuses and propels learning. Knowledge, skills, and dispositions that are outside of any one person's immediate frame of reference require effort to learn. In order for learning to occur, students must act or expend effort. Therefore, the inner circles of the framework represent both student learning and effort.

While student learning is the school's most important outcome, student learning results from individual and group effort that is only partially accounted for by factors that urban schools and districts can influence (Epstein, 1995; Epstein & Dauber, 1991; Wang, Haertel & Walberg, 1993). As a result, both must focus attention on providing those conditions, opportunities, tasks, role models, relationships, and information that support and nurture student learning. To do this requires thoughtful, caring, and reflective classroom practices supported by building-wide systems for professional development and resource stewardship. The transformation and renewal work of schools becomes more manageable by grouping elements together to focus efforts. The framework provides a shared reference point for diverse members of the school community to support collaborative effort in pursuit of common interests. Further, since these elements describe the work of teaching students with differences in culture, gender, language, ability, class and ethnicity, schools can integrate inclusive, multicultural educational practices with other reform goals to form a coherent approach to renew and transform educational processes.

Professional Effort

While student learning is the urban school's most important outcome, measures of learning are insufficient to guide school improvement efforts since learning results from individual student effort that is only partially accounted for by school controlled factors (Wang et al., 1993). How learning environments get established and maintained rests on the skills and creativity of teachers and other practitioners (Darling-Hammond, 2000; Sanders, 1997). The Systemic Change Framework identifies five core features of this learning environment: (1) Learning standards; (2) assessment for students' academic and social development; (3) teaching design and practice; (4) group practice; and (5) family participation. Where these elements are well designed and implemented, students thrive and their efforts to learn are optimized.

Similarly, practitioners thrive and are better able to innovate and support student effort and outcomes when their organization supports and encourages their creativity and professionalism. Organizational support for teacher learning and innovation must also be supported by initial educator preparation and ongoing professional development opportunities that enable educators to acquire and build accomplished capacity to address the five core features of professional effort. Each of these elements is a critical feature of the learning environment. For instance, learning standards and assessment are essential for identifying what must be taught. Assessment helps teachers understand the knowledge and skills of each student while defining goals for learning, and further represents a complex set of concepts and activities since it is used both to inform instruction and to measure the outcomes of the instructional event. How assessment occurs and the degree of authenticity with which it is conducted is its own field of study. Learning standards are critical to the learning environment because they provide students with the knowledge of "what it is we need to know and be able to do" in the classroom and school. Assessment practices need to be complemented by teaching design and practices that also honor and address each student's particular learning. Thematic, integrated curriculum units that flexibly accommodate students' multiple intelligences, incorporate cooperative learning practices and offer tasks and products provide strategies for planning and teaching in inclusive ways (Gardner, 1999)

As of 1992, 50 of the largest 99 school districts in the U.S. had over a 50% enrollment of "minority" students (Ballou, 1996). By 1995, 35% of all students enrolled in grades 1–12 in public schools were considered to be part of a "minority" group, an increase of 11% from 1976. At the same time that the number of students of color, students who speak languages other than English, and students who live in poverty has increased, the nations' teachers have become more monolithic, monocultural, and monolingual. To illustrate, the percentages of white teachers grew from 88% in 1971 to 90.7% in 1996, while the number of African American teachers decreased from 8.1% to 7.3%. Many of these teachers tend to view diversity of student backgrounds as a problem rather than as a resource that enriches teaching and learning. Such attitudes manifest themselves in low expectations that then get expressed in watered down and fragmented curriculum for students of diverse racial, cultural, and socio-economic backgrounds (Nieto, 1992; Oakes, 1985). Because many teachers understand student diversity from a "cultural deficit" or a "cultural deprivation" (Jensen, 1969) perspective, they attribute urban students' low academic achievement to the students' lack of ability, culture, and motivation to learn (Herrnstein & Murray, 1994). Students who have diverse racial, ethnic, and socio-cultural histories may also put a strain on urban teachers who are often from different backgrounds than their students. The problems that urban students bring to school may also overwhelm urban teachers, therefore, making it more difficult for them to successfully engage with pedagogical issues. Adding to urban students concerns, teachers seldom attribute low scores to teachers' performance in the classroom (Rego & Nieto, 2000), and, therefore, many educators continue to seek the single approach to "good teaching" that will improve all students' achievement (Haberman, 1991). Yet, these teachers must organize pedagogies that will engage and connect the classroom to the urban student's individual experiences.

The literature on effective and inclusive schools – whether urban, suburban, or rural – in addition to identifying specific educator practices, also highlights the need for collaboration among and between general and special educators. Indeed, *group practice* is the hallmark of inclusive schools. Educators must be able to communicate using the same language and collaborate across their traditional role and cultural boundaries. Given the limited preparation for group practice during initial teacher education programs, the limited shared experiences across school professional roles, and the range of new skills that are required to teach an increasingly diverse group of students, school professionals need support, training, and coaching in order to implement high quality inclusionary practices effectively. Yet, school professionals are caught in a double bind. With declining resource allocation for professional development and increasing teacher/student ratios, educators are too often being asked to change without support.

Helping urban schools meet the needs of more and more students and families requires not standardization of procedures but a depth of repertoire that permits adaptations to be made in response to student differences and needs (Lareau & Shumar, 1996). This accommodation requires expertise in assessment, creating opportunities to practice emerging skills, providing assistance, feedback, and organizing classrooms to maximize time spent in learning. Special educators have used these skills for many years in settings with very low pupil-to-teacher ratios. General educators have skills in managing large groups of students, subject matter expertise, group assessment strategies, and the ability to provide multiple levels of instruction. Teaching multiculturally also requires skills and knowledge about language, literacy, and cultural experiences that are so well represented by teachers who come from bilingual, English as a Second Language and multicultural teacher preparation or professional development backgrounds (Nieto, 1996). These teachers have a rich knowledge of how language development and literacy evolve within learning environments that support experiences and abilities that students bring with them. Putting the knowledge base and skills of these varying traditions together will enhance the education for all learners and create a new "hybrid" educator who benefits from the best of all traditions.

One important aspect of group practice is the inclusion of parents and other family members (Epstein, 1995; Epstein & Dauber, 1991, Harry, 1992). Urban schools need families not only to support school efforts outside of school, but more importantly, to contribute to the ongoing mission and operations of the school (Fine, 1994). For example, parents often are the best source of learning data – when their children *use* their learning at home and around the neighborhood teachers can be more assured about the meaningfulness and durability of what their students have learned. Teachers and school administrators are beginning to make their schools accessible to family and community members in new and innovative ways that extend far beyond the cupcake-bearing classroom parents and PTA members of schools of the past. *Family participation* takes on new meaning in restructured inclusive schools. It is obvious that parents and community members now serve on building or instructional leadership teams. They contribute to the school's instruction, public relations, and ongoing operations by offering their talents and resources. Schools are also opening their doors after school so that family and community members can use the school building and resources to continue their own learning through adult courses, access to fitness activities, and another community meeting place. Finally, some comprehensive inclusive schools bring together a variety of other services and resources, and provide "one-stop-shopping" for families that need and use a range of community services (Abrams & Gibbs, 2000).

School Effort

While the core features of the learning environment are most directly linked to student performance, the school organization is most directly linked to professional effort. That is, teachers and other school personnel are able to engage in sustained, thoughtful, continually improving and reflective practice if the school organization creates a milieu or environment that supports professional practice (Beyer, 1996). In recent years, many urban school districts have implemented forms of school-based, shared decision making in their efforts to restructure schools (Bondy, 1995). The traditional bureaucratic, rational, authoritative leadership approach has been challenged and, as a result, many of today's successful schools are based upon shared inquiry and decision-making. Such schools are moving towards a collective-as opposed to an individual-practice of governance, teaching, and learning. These collective practices describe the concept of learning organizations or communities (Joyce, Murphy, Showers & Murphy, 1989). Six essential features of the school organization support professional effort: (1) leadership and governance; (2) culture of improvement and change; (3) physical environment and facilities; (4) structure and use of time; (5) resource development and allocation; and (6) school/community relationships.

Teachers and other staff most directly experience the school organization, staff, policies, structure, and resources. By determining the staff's responsibilities, interactions with each other, and continued development, the organization influences the amount of effort that educators are able to focus on their work. Many urban schools lack the supports that are needed for teachers to make changes in their work. An important focus of school reform efforts has been to help schools organize leadership teams that include school professionals, school board members, family members, students, and administrators. One way to help urban schools manage the complexity of change and improvement is to form and sustain leadership teams that represent the diversity of voices in a building. We find that leadership for change must reside within the collective vision of a learning community rather than within an individual such as a principal (Elmore, 1999–2000). Most of the conventional wisdom in school leadership research places great emphasis on the role of the principal. In our experience, reform and renewal built on individual leadership is difficult to sustain or to scale up because of the mobility of people in such roles. Challenges of changing leadership are even more critical in urban settings where all school personnel seem to move to new schools and districts at a higher rate than is typical in suburban or rural districts. Further, as Miller (1996) pointed out, where vision and drive rests with a leader, only about 25% of the community typically mobilizes to carry out the agenda. The work of urban school reform is too complex and must contend with so much inertia that leadership must be shared.

If one accepts that the most challenging students require the combined expertise of many individuals including administrators, teachers, mental health personnel, community advocates, and students themselves, then it makes sense to create structures that bring this collective resource together. The use of building-level leadership teams for *leadership and governance* creates the opportunity for shared decision making resulting in two important benefits for students with disabilities as well as for many other students in urban schools who require additional learning supports at some time or another in their school careers. First, students benefit from the increased use of diverse instructional procedures in general education classrooms. And, second, special educators and related service providers are involved in general education curriculum decisions and classroom instruction. To a large measure, a Building

Leadership Team (BLT) orchestrates the work of families, school professionals, administrators, and students engaged in the school improvement process (Lambert, 1998). Sometimes these teams have other names, but regardless of the exact title, building leadership teams work together to review practices that work, identify areas that may need improvement, and plan for progress. The synergy of team leadership facilitates rapid and sustained change. Leadership teams provide the needed context for shared decision-making and create a climate of continuous school improvement. The good news is that they may already exist in buildings as site-based management teams, site councils, instructional leadership teams, accountability cadres, or school improvement teams. They are important facilitators of another feature of professional effort: *a culture of improvement and change.*

In a speech at the American Educational Research Association Annual Meeting, Elmore (1996) highlighted the importance of ongoing public conversations in schools and among practitioners about how they intend to improve their practice. A school must provide the intellectual and emotional climate to support sustained improvement of practice. Teachers and other practitioners must use the information that students provide about their learning progress to inform curriculum and teaching decisions. The purposeful improvement of practice must be supported by collective dialogue about practice (Cochran-Smith & Lytle, 1993; Lieberman 1994; Lieberman & Miller, 1991 Lieberman, Saxl & Miles 1988). Sadly, such conversation is absent in many urban schools. But without a collective sense of responsibility for student learning, urban teachers are left to their own resources for making complex decisions about how to support learning for an increasingly diverse student population. There are many urban schools where the staff and faculty understand the urgency to reinvent their roles and redefine their craft. Yet, the way that time is structured and used prevents the planning and collaborative work necessary to achieve sustained change (Louis & Miles, 1990). Without time during the work day to meet, discuss, and challenge one another's ideas and activities, it is difficult to imagine many educators achieving the quality of dialogue and inquiry that Elmore suggested is necessary for sustained, whole school improvement. For instance, some schools have managed to create more time for professional interaction by thoughtful scheduling of physical education, the fine arts, and academic blocks of time. Others reorganize the week in order to release students early one day each week, and others are generating other creative ways to create time for group practice.

As part of the school effort, *Physical facilities* are an essential component of the urban educational experience. In addition to maintaining school buildings that meet contemporary fire and health standards, school buildings need to be architecturally accessible to all students. Further, students' learning preferences can be supported through the way that space and time are used in classrooms. Materials' storage and access should fit instructional goals and independence levels of the students. The noise, temperature and paint color in a room can contribute to or distract from learning just as the sheer numbers of students in a space can enhance or detract from learning. Furniture and seating arrangements can also support or detract from learning. For instance, in kindergarten and first grade, the physical cues provided by carpet squares or chairs help students to monitor and regulate their movement. Furniture can be an important asset in learning. If a child's feet cannot reach the floor, the child is much more likely to squirm, get out of seat often, or be distracted by the discomfort. Students with some kind of physical and mobility impairments also need their chairs and desks to be thoughtfully selected and placed in the room. By using space and equipment thoughtfully, school professionals can also reduce the amount of talking they do to manage the group and so increase the time students spend learning the explicit curriculum. In many urban schools, teachers, building administrators, and staff do not have access to choice in materials, desks, and chairs that their students use so that organizing the physical layout of the class to match the kind of teaching and learning needed is difficult to imagine. Yet, this feature of school effort can make a significant difference in learning outcomes for students.

The reality is that many urban schools are in extremely poor condition. So much so, that in the Fall of 1998, the District of Columbia public schools could not open several of their schools because they were unsafe. Frequently, problems range from dilapidated and poorly maintained physical facilities to the need for careful monitoring of hallways and entrances and exits to prevent intruders and weapons from entering buildings. In some urban systems, the administration has made a concerted attempt to refurbish school buildings, insisting on ensuring that asbestos removal is completed, broken windows are repaired immediately, paint is available to keep the insides and outsides of buildings free of graffiti and that the basic physical plant is kept in good repair. These efforts are critical and visible symbols that the system cares about and is responsive to its children and its teachers. The costs of maintaining older facilities, planning for ongoing renovation, and creating access to the Internet and other forms of digital communication are staggering in many urban school systems. Yet, without significant investment in physical facilities, it will be difficult for schools, faculties, and their local community supporters to provide access to the same quality education that students in more affluent, suburban communities experience.

Embedded in the provision of physical facilities are *resource development and allocation.* They are difficult to reapportion when most schools receive a fixed allocation of teachers with a very limited activities and/or supplies budget. Urban schools face greater challenges than many other districts in this regard perhaps because of their size. Economies of scale simply provide no advantage to urban districts and, thus, size becomes perhaps the biggest challenge. Urban districts also suffer some lack of flexibility in managing fiscal resources both because of the source of some of the funding and unique problems such as the hiring and retention of teachers and substitute teachers. Yet, using these resources well can enhance the motivation and effort that teachers bring to their work. For instance, while the number of faculty and staff assigned to a building may be fixed, there can be fewer constraints imposed on how the staff is organized to teach. Some schools have rethought the traditional class approach where students are assigned to a teacher or set of teachers based on equalizing the number of students across teachers. Instead, some schools have begun to look at flexible class sizes based on team approaches. Thus, a team of teachers responsible for a particular curricular standard or subject can think about how they might increase and decrease class size based on the teaching activity and learning outcome. For instance, a lesson on sentence construction may require only one teacher with 40 students sharing 15 computers, while feedback on a term paper may require more one-on-one or very small group discussions. If two teachers with 50 students between them organize as a team they may be able to accomplish both tasks well and with better outcomes for the students.

Consequently, in a *transformed inclusive urban school*, learning and other educational supports are organized to meet the needs of all students rather than historical conventions or the way the rooms are arranged in the building. Creative reallocation of even limited resources and innovative re-organization of teachers into partnerships and teams offer ways to break old molds and create flexibilities needed to focus on student learning and achievement. Previously separate "programs" like special education, Title I, or bilingual education may come together to form a new educational system that delivers necessary additional supports and instruction in the same spaces to diverse groups of students. The new system anchors both organizational and professional effort in student content, performance, and skill standards that are owned by local communities and families while informed by national and state standards, curriculum frameworks, and effective assessment strategies.

Close *school/community relationships* are at the heart of successful, comprehensive, and inclusive urban schools. To educate all students successfully, accommodate the unique educational needs of each child, and welcome families' participation in their children's education, the school must invite broad participation from families, local religious organizations, advocacy groups, local businesses and government. Education is at the core of all vital communities. Given the challenges and risks faced by both schools and families in most urban communities, there is even greater urgency for forging and sustaining strong school – community linkages (Haynes & Comer, 1996). The sheer size of many urban challenges requires carefully orchestrated initiatives across community agencies, schools, and neighborhood organizations. Any one group working alone may fail to make much progress and some problems may remain unresolved, but working together often generates the shared vision, needed synergy, and practical strategies that can succeed in improving the conditions and outcomes for both students, their families and neighbors. Parents, family, and community members also directly contribute to the work of schools. Parents and families bring an understanding of the broader community and social development needs and strengths of children to the learning environment that can inform school planning and influence curriculum, instruction, and assessment. Strong linkages with families can help school personnel to honor and incorporate different cultural and linguistic perspectives, values, and practices into the life and learning of the school community (Harry, 1992). One of the serious issues facing urban schools is the mismatch between the diversity profile of students, and that of teachers. A disproportionate percentage of urban school personnel are white Americans while the student population reflects a much more diverse cultural and ethnic mix (Hilliard, 1994). Further, teacher preparation programs may not have adequately prepared urban teachers to understand and teach to such multicultural and diverse groups (Cochran-Smith, 1995; Hollins, 1996; Liston & Zeichner, 1996). Without close linkages with families, neighborhood organizations, and other community organizations like churches and grass roots advocacy groups, teachers have little opportunity to acquire this learning.

It is important to acknowledge that urban families benefit directly from being meaningfully involved in their students' education. Both EDC and its ATLAS Communities' partner, the School Development Program (SDP) at Yale University, have documented many cases in which parent volunteers who had dropped out of school were motivated, encouraged, and supported to return to school (Comer, Ben-Avie, Haynes & Joyner, 1999). Some obtained their high school equivalency diploma, and some continued on to college. Drawing upon the work of Epstein, Comer, and others, parents can be involved in many ways (e.g. as teachers, learners, advocates, decision makers, volunteers, outreach workers, and ambassadors to the community-at-large) (Harry, 1992, Haynes & Comer, 1996; Epstein, 1995). While the vast majority of school staff and parents are willing, even eager, to increase parental participation in schools, often they do not know how to do so. It is especially important that parents from every socioeconomic, racial, ethnic, and cultural group be involved and empowered to participate and contribute meaningfully.

All too often, these groups are underrepresented in parent programs for a variety of reasons, including:

(1) Differences in language, culture, and socioeconomic status that serve as both real and perceived barriers to involvement.
(2) Employment constraints, childcare constraints, and/or transportation barriers that make participation particularly challenging.
(3) The use of educational jargon and complex language that distances parents, including those with limited literacy skills.
(4) Frequent moves that impede the development of long-term, trusting relationships.

Research suggests that schools can overcome these barriers by:

(1) Assessing parental interests and needs and engaging families in planning opportunities for participation.
(2) Hiring parent coordinators, using parents to reach other parents, and providing parent centers at the school.
(3) Translating printed materials into the parents' first language and having interpreters available, as needed, to ensure communication and participation at meetings.
(4) Accommodating parents' work schedules as much as possible, providing childcare arrangements and transportation, and/or bringing the school into the community.
(5) Giving parents a valued, equal voice, creating a climate of openness and respect, and providing opportunities for full participation.

As more and more urban schools move to decentralized models of leadership, the focus of decision-making authority shifts to the building and local school community. Unified educational systems ought to employ human and other resources to provide a range of services in a range of settings to students with different educational needs. "Full service" or "community schools" can bring together multiple service agencies, such as health and mental health, social services, and when necessary, juvenile justice, to meet the needs of all students and their families (Fine, 1994). Schools can also become community centers and resources in other ways such as, offering evening English classes for community members who speak other languages, or providing space for health and fitness classes. Additionally, schools can even become the location for community celebrations, and meetings for neighborhood planning and advocacy activities (Anyon, 1997). Developing a core mission, identifying school community needs, determining resource utilization, monitoring progress towards learning standards, and planning for improvement efforts are all variables that require comprehensive input and shared decision-making by the array of individuals who will be affected both directly and indirectly.

District Effort

The last level of effort included in the *systemic change framework* involves the capacities and supports available to schools from central district administration policies and practices. Urban schools need the support and leadership that a district administration can provide. The degree to which district supports and networks meet the needs of schools affects the degree of effort that schools can expend to improve. Of course, central district administrations work within an even broader set of constraints and opportunities that emerges from state education agencies and federal law, policies, and regulations. It becomes the responsibility of a district administration to understand and mediate the requirements and opportunities from states and governments to support local district efforts to accomplish educational outcomes. Managing the state and federal contexts can be challenging for district administrations. Often state and federal policies conflict, especially in times of change. In addition, people may not understand or narrowly interpret policy and, as a result, blame either state or federal policies as a rationale for lack of transformative action. For example, districts and states may be trying to move away from identifying and sorting students by categorical programs while federal regulations continue to require reporting by label. State teacher licensing requirements can conflict with efforts to move schools toward more group practice among teachers and more inclusive grouping and teaching of students. Sometimes, state and federal regulations can limit a district's flexibility in a variety of ways, including using fiscal and other resources creatively to support school and professional effort.

As a consequence, the role of the urban district in supporting the work of schools, teachers, and students is important, and frequently complex. As systems get larger, layers of management and bureaucracy can mask the districts' role in supporting student learning. The task of educating students with disabilities provides an excellent example of the diverse ways that bureaucracies address this responsibility. In New York City, public schools serve over 100,000 students with disabilities. Many of these students are in special schools and classrooms removed from opportunities for social and intellectual discourse with their peers who have no ability labels. In Boston, over 13,950 students receive special education services while the District of Columbia and the Denver Public Schools each serve over 7,000 students in special education. In Chicago, 79% of their 424,454 students are from low-income families and over 20,000 children receive special education services. These numbers are larger than the total number of students in many suburban and rural school systems. In one city district, a system of center-based programs means that students with severe disabilities are clustered in some schools, in disproportionate numbers, while in other schools, only those students with mild to moderate disabilities are served. Other urban districts have more integrated approaches to supporting learning for students with disabilities. Such varied approaches to providing special education services create a set of expectations and skill sets on the part of professionals that are difficult to change. Practitioners and schools cannot meet the needs of all students if many of those students, by district policy, are not in their local schools. Nor can they be expected to accept eagerly students who are challenging to teach if they have not had the opportunity to learn the skills and develop a practice perspective that assumes that all students will be present and involved in the curriculum.

Scarcity of resources, resistance to change, inflexibility of systems, regulatory compliance and broader societal problems all have a serious impact on the ability of school systems to meet the needs of all its students. The district organizational structure has specific roles and tasks that it can, and must, accomplish far more readily than individual schools. Certainly, the school board and central administration have the responsibility for ensuring that students and families receive consistently high quality educational services regardless of the particular school any individual student attends. Further, the school board, as representatives of the local community, has the responsibility for ensuring that each school reflects local values and beliefs. However, local perspectives play out within the parameters imposed by state and federal educational policies, laws and regulations. It is the ongoing implementation of these various agendas that a central administration can carry out while schools and teachers focus on meeting daily needs of their students and families. The *systemic change framework* organizes the work of districts around six tasks: (1) district/community partnerships; (2) a culture of renewal and improvement; (3) systemic infrastructure and organizational support; (4) resource development and allocation; (5) inquiry on schools and schooling; and (6) student services.

District/Community Partnerships. Poverty and its attendant consequences are especially pronounced in urban communities. The Office of Civil Rights indicated that 30% of all inner-city students live in poverty, compared to 18% of students in non-urban areas. Urban areas also have special risk factors such as violence, neglect, child abuse, substance abuse, poor nutrition, sexually transmitted diseases, and high rates of adolescent pregnancy and childbearing. In most urban areas, almost half of the children who are involved in special education (or who have disabilities and remain unidentified) are also involved in the child welfare systems, have case workers because of abuse and/or neglect, are in foster care or residential placement, and/or are involved in the juvenile justice system. Children and youth who live with violence, abuse, and neglect on a daily basis are more likely to adopt patterns of violence themselves as a function of such repeated exposure. All of these children are at high risk for being jailed, placed in juvenile justice programs, out-of-state residential programs, and other restrictive environments because communities and schools lack the capacity and skill to provide an appropriate array of services. For example, in reviewing the cases of three to four children a week, one caseworker commented that many of these same children have lived in 8 to 10 different places a year. The work of schooling and learning is severely compromised in the face of such a lack of basic physical and psychological safety and security.

Urban environmental risks frequently result in high numbers of students identified as needing special education. Many of these urban youth with disabilities are poor as well. Any one of the contributing factors outlined here would place these students at high risk for future educational failure. The frequent combination of several of these factors places an almost impenetrable barrier between many urban children/youth and success. For example, some studies suggest that as many as one-half of students identified as having emotional/behavioral disabilities are victims of physical or sexual abuse. A substantial portion of them has grown up in families involved in alcohol and substance abuse. Nearly 50% are from poor, often single-parent homes. The multiple and cumulative needs of poor children with disabilities in the nation's urban areas present tremendous challenges. The work of school districts is too complex and touches too many of the needs of students and families to make it a solitary enterprise. For many of the same reasons that individual schools need to partner with families and communities, districts need to partner with their local judicial, social, recreational, health and government agencies to ensure that students are able to attend school ready to learn. In addition, they need to reach out to local advocacy agencies and neighborhood organizations to ensure that they are meeting the needs of diverse populations. Often, advocacy organizations can help to surface issues and concerns that a particular faction of the community may have with the school system. Developing and managing local public education campaigns can provide ongoing education for the larger public to learn about and become involved as supporters and participants in public education.

Partnerships for Initial and Continuing Teacher Development. Many governmental, regulatory, and professional educational organizations are currently strong proponents of pre-service and professional development approaches that link the mission and goals of school districts and schools of education in sustainable and productive partnerships. Indeed, works of many scholars (e.g.

Darling-Hammond, 1998) support substantive resourcing of teacher preparation and professional development as the linchpin for better and more durable educational outcomes for all students. Well-educated and supported teachers have always been the backbone of school reform. Yet, all too often previous educational reforms have under invested in teachers (see Darling-Hammond, 1998). Achieving teacher effectiveness, whether in general or special education ultimately requires attention to more than the technical and content mastery so familiar to fields of education. There must also be a broadened definition of teacher roles that includes multi-theoretical fluency, creative problem finding and solving, reflective and inquiry-based teaching, self-management, and ongoing professional growth. The dynamic nature of this process suggests that the traditional division of teacher education into preservice and inservice components is no longer viable, if it ever was. As Goodlad (1994) asked, "What comes first, good schools or good teacher education programs?" His answer was that both must come together.

Partnerships between universities and urban school districts are important strategies for the simultaneous renewal of both organizations (Goodlad, 1994). The arenas of activity within such partnerships address four interrelated and critical goals that: (1) support access to and equity in what all students learn (exemplary education); (2) learning for new educators; (3) learning for experienced educators (teacher preparation and professional development); and (4) new knowledge about teaching and learning (research/inquiry) (Clark, 1994). Some of the activities that can emerge from school/university partnerships include:

(1) *Services to students*, such as mentoring programs, internships, informal education programs, recreational programs, after school programs, tutoring, career education and apprenticeship programs, dropout prevention programs, and medical and social services.
(2) *Services to educators*, such as opportunities for professional development, pre-service programs, school/university partnerships, joint curriculum projects, volunteers, the development of community and school service projects, and participation in the evaluation of student performance.
(3) *Services to schools*, in the form of participation on school improvement teams, support for district and school management, as well as direct resources and grants for special projects.

Culture of Renewal and Improvement. Through professional development schools, the research values of teacher educators are combined with the primary concern of schools to find solutions to practical problems. Anderson, Herr and Nihlen (1994) noted that "practitioner (action) research is done within an action-oriented setting in which reflection on action is the driving force of the research." Action research helps educators work together on problems pertaining to their own practice, a process that Goodlad (1984) found absent in his observations of 1,016 classrooms. Through action research university personnel can collaborate with school and district personnel to address difficult problems of practice in educating K-12 students, including problems related to the learning of students with disabilities, and how teacher preparation and professional development support such learning. Several assumptions undergird the creation of a climate for action research:

(1) The school, district and university play important roles in creating a context that encourages educators to approach teaching as innovation.
(2) All educators – professors, teacher candidates, teachers, and school and district administrators – share responsibility for creating knowledge.
(3) Knowledge produced through action research aims to transform practice.
(4) School and district personnel, as well as university personnel, must commit to explore new roles and responsibilities as they collaborate to engage in action research.

This focus on practitioner-based inquiry is one example of a district-led strategy that signals to the entire organization that renewal and improvement are expected and necessary aspects of a professional organization. To move successfully in this direction, the district needs an overall, explicitly stated, professional development approach that de-emphasizes training and emphasizes research and inquiry. Further, central administration needs to be organized in such a way that data collection and analysis is coordinated and supported so that practitioners and building leadership teams can access information that is "just in time" for their decision-making and school improvement goal setting. Apparently, accountability data are just one type of data schools need. Schools need systems of ongoing data collection about families, the lives of their students, and the learning progress that students make so that they can respond to the changing needs of their constituencies. This is a key component of building a culture across the district that values and rewards inquiry, innovation, and improvement.

Systemic Infrastructure and Organizational Support. The functions of central administration must be organized in such a way that efficiency and individualization are accommodated. In many cases, the systemic infrastructure of districts is rigid and lacks the capacity to personalize and reallocate resources where they are needed. Yet, there are many functions that need to be addressed on daily, weekly, monthly, or yearly cycles that are far better organized and managed at a central level. For instance, teacher recruitment strategies need to be developed and managed at the central administration level. These strategies must involve expanding the number and the diversity of middle and high school students who choose teaching as a career, marketing a teaching career to professionals who are looking to change careers, and working within local district/university partnerships to prepare teachers effectively in the field. It makes little sense for individual schools to create their own processes for doing this work. In this case, since the need for teachers exists throughout a district, centralizing the function is appropriate. On the other hand, professional development strategies must be closely linked to individual needs of schools. Some district schools may need to expand their faculty expertise in teaching math while other schools may need to look at the professional development needs of high school core content teachers around personalized instruction. Individual course offerings may not build the capacity of schools to improve their performance in these particular ways. But, school-based professional development inquiry groups may build capacity. Districts that have more than one school at the preschool, elementary and secondary levels can share expertise across buildings. Hence, a systemic infrastructure for professional development is appropriate – this infrastructure design needs to focus on meeting the needs of the customers, in this case, the buildings.

Technology can play a valuable role in linking teachers in discussion groups, in creating access to units of study, in tracking student performance across grades, and communicating changes in school and district level policies. Technology investment is a systemic infrastructure issue but it cannot be developed apart from the input of individuals who are expected to use it. There are many functions of schools that can make more efficient use of people and financial resources by organizing them at a central level such as curriculum, transportation, food services, building maintenance, and telecommunications. The development and administration of these services must be accomplished by keeping the user (in this case, the schools and their constituencies, students, faculty, and families) at the center of an iterative process of needs assessment, design, implementation, feedback, and redesign.

Student Services. Schools provide a variety of support services to students and families that involve practitioners other than teachers. Many schools use the services of nurses, counselors, school psychologists, reading teachers, special educators, and other specialists. Typically, the budgets that support these functions are managed at the district level. Schools are given a certain number of hours or days per week that they have such specialists available to them. Frequently, the funding that supports these positions comes, not from the general fund, but from the federal or state flow of dollars that are targeted for a particular service. Large bureaucracies are created to manage compliance details that accompany the use of this funding. Hence, a centralized bureaucracy is created to equitably distribute the funding and to ensure that personnel hired to perform these functions are not co-opted at the building level to perform typical instructional functions. Further complicating the picture is the fact that professionals themselves who are hired to perform these specialized student services need ongoing professional development and professional community that value and support their work. Many practitioners are often the only individuals in their specialized roles in their buildings where they work in isolation. One of the roles that student services play is to create this professional community across the district. Unfortunately, student services divisions are often organized by specializations so that special education, nursing, and school psychology may each develop their own bureaucracies in spite of the fact that the professionals fulfilling these roles may be expected to work together in multidisciplinary collaborative teams. More and more, district level administrative structures are moving to multi-disciplinary department structures that focus effort on either articulation areas such as elementary, middle, and senior high school feeder patterns or on preschool, elementary, middle and high school groups that focus on meeting the needs of the buildings. These newer versions of the central administrative bureaucracies are designed to mirror the functions that are performed in the field.

To build the capacity and sustainability of high quality education in urban schools, efforts must be geared toward developing the following:

(1) A deep understanding of the social, political, and learning issues that urban schools face.
(2) Leadership to support strong, building organizations that have the capacity to innovate and flex to meet the needs of students and families.
(3) A vital professional development support structure that builds capacity through action research and professional development schools.
(4) Unified systems of supports to link education, health, and social services.
(5) Efficient, rapid and user-friendly information systems that support genuine school improvement processes.
(6) A focus on culturally responsive ways of knowing and learning.
(7) Active networks that focus work on urban constituencies.
(8) Partnerships among existing urban reform efforts.
(9) Collaborative and cooperative processes that support families and communities in the design and operation of schools.
(10) An ability to influence policy makers in local and state government.

SUMMARY

In spite of the best efforts of educational policy analysts, local, state and federal legislation, researchers, and practitioners, the results of public schooling in the U.S. remains unsatisfactory on a variety of counts. This remains true particularly in our largest and most complex school systems. The limited impact of much school reform has led to a more systemic approach to educational reform. A systems perspective examines the whole organization and the interrelationships between its component parts. The systems approach to change, renewal and innovation is helpful not only as we think about the national picture but as we confront the everyday challenges of our work. The systemic change framework provides an approach to thinking about the work of practitioners, schools, and school districts to help reformers and change agents think about the benefits and counterbalances to innovations and improvements they propose.

REFERENCES

Abrams, L., & Gibbs, J. (2000). Planning for school change: School-community collaboration in a full service elementary school. *Urban Education, 35,* 79–103.

Anyon, J. (1997). *Ghetto schooling. A political economy of urban educational reform.* New York: Teachers College Press.

Anderson, G., Herr, K., & Nihlen, A. S. (1994). *Studying your own school: An educator's guide to qualitative practitioner research.* Thousand Oaks, CA: Corwin Press.

Artiles, A. J. (1998). The dilemma of difference: Enriching the disproportionality discourse with theory and context. *The Journal of Special Education, 32,* 32–36.

Artiles, A. J., & Trent, S. C. (1994). Over-representation of minority students in special education: A continuing debate. *The Journal of Special Education, 27,* 410–437.

Artiles, A. J., Trent, S. C., Hoffman-Kipp, P., & Lopez-Torres, L. (2000). Sociocultural perspectives in special education, Part 2: From individual acquisition to cultural-historical practices in multicultural teacher education. *Remedial and Special Education, 21,* 79–82.

Astuto, T. A., Clark, D., Read. A., & McGree, K. (1994). *Roots of reform: Challenging the assumptions that control change in education.* Bloomington, IN: Phi Delta Kappa Educational Foundation.

Ballou, D. (1996). The condition of urban school finance: Efficient resource allocation in urban schools. In: *National Center for Education Statistics: Selected Papers in School Finance.* Washington, D.C.: National Center for Education Statistics.

Banathy, B. H. (1996). *Designing social systems in a changing world.* New York: Plenum Press.

Banks, J. A. (2001). *Cultural diversity and education foundations: Curriculum and teaching.* Needham Heights, MA: Allyn & Bacon.

Bateson, G. (1972). *Steps to an ecology of mind: Collected essays in anthropology, psychiatry, evolution, and epistemology.* San Francisco, CA: Chandler.

Bellamy, G. T. (1994). The whole-school framework. Unpublished manuscript. Denver, CO: University of Colorado.

Berres, J., Knoblock, D., & Woodes, L. (1996). *Creating tomorrow's schools today, Stories of inclusions, change and renewal.* New York: Teachers College Press.

Berres, M., Ferguson, D. L., Knoblock, D., & Woods, C. (1996). *Creating tomorrow's schools today: Stories of inclusion, change and renewal.* New York: Teachers College Press.

Beyer, L. E. (1996). Introduction: The meanings of critical teacher preparation. In: E. Beyer (Ed.), *Creating Democratic Classrooms: The Struggle to Integrate Theory and Practice* (pp. 1–26). New York: Teachers College Press.

Briscoe, D. B. (1991). Designing for diversity in school success: Capitalizing on culture. *Preventing School Failure, 36,* 13–18.

Bondy, E. (1995). Fredericks middle school and the dynamics of school reform. In: A. Lieberman (Ed.), *The Work of Restructuring Schools: Building From the Ground Up* (pp. 43–63). New York: Teachers College Press.

Brown, A. L., & Campione, J. C. (1998). Designing a community of young learners: Theoretical and practical lessons. In: N. M. Lambert & B. L. McCombs (Eds), *How Students Learn: Reforming Schools Through Learner-Centered Education* (pp. 153–186). Washington, D.C.: American Psychological Association.

Clark, R. W. (1994). *Partner schools and The National Network for Education Renewal: A compact for simultaneous renewal.* Seattle, WA: Center for Educational Renewal, University of Washington.

Cochran-Smith, M. (1995). Color blindness and basket making are not the answers: Confronting the dilemmas of race, culture, and language diversity in teacher education. *American Educational Research Journal, 32,* 493–522.

Cochran-Smith, M., & Lytle, S. (1993). *Inside/outside: Teacher research and teacher knowledge.* New York: Teachers College Press.

Cohen, D. K. (1995). What is the system in systemic reform? *Educational Researcher, 24*(9), 11–17, 31.

Comer, J. P., Ben-Avie, M., Haynes, N. M., & Joyner, E. (Eds) (1999). *Child by child: The Comer process for change in education.* New York: Teachers College Press.

Council of Administrators of Special Education [CASE] (1993). *Future agenda for special education: Creating a unified educational system.* Bloomington, IN: Indiana University.

Darling-Hammond, L. (1998). Teacher learning that supports student learning. *Educational Leadership, 55,* 6–11.

Darling-Hammond, L. (2000). Teacher quality and student achievement: A review of state policy evidence. *Education Policy Analysis Archives, 8*(1).

Darling-Hammond, L., Ancess et al. (1995). *Authentic assessment in action: Studies of schools and students at work.* New York: Teachers College Press.

Darling-Hammond, L., & Falk, B. (1997). Using standards and assessments to support student learning. *Phi Delta Kappan, 79,* 190–199.

Delpit, L. (1988). The silenced dialogue: Power and pedagogy in educating other peoples' children. *Harvard Educational Review, 58,* 280–298.

Delpit, L. (1995). *Other people's children: Cultural conflict in the classroom.* New York: The New Press.

Draper, I. (1999). Preamble. Relationship, Community, and Positive Reframing, Addressing the Needs of Urban Schools. In: *First Annual Urban Schools Symposium Report.* Eugene, OR: National Institute for Urban School Improvement.

Edmonds, R. (1979). Effective schools for the urban poor. *Educational Leadership, 37,* 15–18.

Elmore, R. F. (1996). Getting to scale with good educational practice. *Harvard Educational Review, 66,* 1–26.

Elmore, R. F. (1999–2000). Building a new structure for school leadership. *American Educator,* (Winter), 6–44.

Epstein, J. (1995). School/family/community partnerships. *Phi Delta Kappan, 76*, 701–707.

Epstein, J. L., & Dauber, S. (1991). School programs and teacher practices of parent involvement in inner-city elementary and middle school. *Elementary School Journal, 91*, 289–305.

Evans, R. (1996). *The human side of school change.* San Francisco, CA: Jossey-Bass.

Ewing, N. (1995). Restructured teacher education for inclusiveness: A dream deferred for African American children. In: B. A. Ford, F. E. Obiakor & J. M. Patton (Eds), *Effective Education of African American Exceptional Learners* (pp. 189–208). Austin, TX: Pro-Ed.

Ferguson, D., & Kozleski, E. B. (1999). *The systemic change framework.* Denver, CO: The National Institute for Urban School Improvement.

Ferguson, D., & Ferguson, P. M. (1992). *Building capacity for change: Preparing teachers and families to create inclusive schools and community.* Eugene, OR: Schools Project, Specialized Training Program.

Ferguson, D. L. (1995). The real challenge of inclusion: Confessions of a 'rabid inclusionist'. *Phi Delta Kappan, 77*, 281–287.

Fine, M. (1994). Framing a reform movement. In: M. Fine (Ed.), *Chartering Urban School Reform: Reflections on Public High Schools in the Midst of Change* (pp. 1–30). New York: Teachers College Press.

Freire, P. (2000). *Pedagogy of the oppressed.* New York: Continuum.

Fullan, M. G. (1994). Coordinating top-down and bottom-up strategies for education reform. In: R. F. Elmore & S. H. Fuhrman (Eds), *The Governance of Curriculum: 1994 Yearbook of the Association for Supervision and Curriculum Development* (pp. 186–202). Alexandria, VA: Association for Supervision and Curriculum Development.

Fullan, M. (1996). Turning systemic thinking on its head. *Phi Delta Kapan, 77*(6), 420–423.

Fullan, M. G., & Miles, M. B. (1992). Getting reform right: What works and what doesn't. *Phi Delta Kappan, 73*, 745–752.

Fusarelli, L. D. (1999). Reinventing urban education in Texas: Charter schools, smaller schools, and the new institutionalism. *Education and Urban Society, 31*, 214–224.

Gardner, H. (1999) *The Disciplined Mind: What All Students Should Understand.* New York: Simon & Schuster.

Gagnon, P. (1995). What should children learn? *The Atlantic Monthly, 276*, 65–79.

Goodlad, J. I. (1994). *Educational renewal: Better teachers, better schools.* San Francisco, CA: Jossey-Bass.

Grossman, H. (1995). *Classroom behavior management in a diverse society.* Mountain View, CA: Mayfield.

Grossman, H. (1995). *Special education in a diverse society.* Boston, MA: Allyn & Bacon.

Haberman, M. (1991). The pedagogy of poverty vs. good teaching. *Phi Delta Kappan, 73*(4), 290–294.

Harry, B. (1992). *Cultural diversity, families, and the special education system, Communication for empowerment.* New York: Teachers College Press.

Haynes, N. M., & Comer, J. P. (1996). Integrating schools, families, and communities through successful school reform: The school development program. *School Psychology Review, 25*, 501–506.

Herrnstein, R. J,. & Murray, C. (1994). *The bell curve: Intelligence and class structure in American life.* New York: Free Press.

Heward, W. L., & Cavanaugh, R. A. (2001). Educational equality for students with disabilities. In: J. A. Banks & C. A. M. Banks (Eds), *Multicultural education: Issues and perspectives* (4th ed., pp. 295–326). New York: John Wiley & Sons.

Hillard, A. (1994). Behavioral style, culture, teaching and learning. *Journal of Negro Education, 61*, 370–377.
Hilliard, A. G. (1992). The pitfalls and promises of special education practice. *Exceptional Children, 59*, 168–172.
Hollingsworth, S. (1994). *Teacher research and urban literacy education.* New York: Teachers College Press.
Hollins, E. R. (1996). *Culture in school learning: Revealing the deep meaning.* Mahwah, NJ: Lawrence Erlbaum.
Jensen, A. R. (1969). How much can we boost IQ and scholastic achievement? *Harvard Education Review, 39*(1), 1–123.
Joyce, B., Murphy, C., Showers, B., & Murphy, J. (1989). School renewal as cultural change. *Educational Leadership, 47*, 70–77.
Kozol, J. (1991). *Savage inequalities: Children in America's schools.* New York: Crown.
Ladson-Billings, G., & Tate, W. F. (1995). Toward a critical race theory of education. *Teachers College Record, 97*(1), 47–68.
Lambert, L. (1998). *Building leadership capacity in schools.* Alexandria, VA: Association for Supervision and Curriculum Development.
Lareau, A., & Shumar, W. (1996). The problem of individualism in family-school policies. *Sociology of Education, 12*(12), 24–39.
Lieberman, A., & Miller, L. (1991). Practices that support teacher development: Transforming conceptions of professional learning. In: M. W. McLaughlin & I. Oberman (Eds), *Teacher Learning.* New York: Teachers College Press.
Lieberman, A., Saxl, E., & P. Miles, M. (1988). Teacher leadership: Ideology and practice. In: A. Lieberman (Ed.), *Building a Professional Culture in Schools.* New York: Teachers College Press.
Lightfoot, S. L. (1983). *The good high school.* New York: Basic Books, Inc.
Liston, D. P., & Zeichner, K. M. (1996). *Culture and teaching.* Mahweh, NJ: Lawrence Erlbaum.
Louis, K. S., & Miles, M. B. (1990). *Improving the urban high school: What works and why.* New York: Teachers College Press.
McLaughlin, M. W. (1995). Improving education through standards-based reform. In: *A Report by the National Academy of Education Panel on Standards-Based Education Reform.* Stanford, CA: The National Academy of Education.
Miller, E. (1996). Idealists and cynics: The micropolitics of systemic school reform. *Harvard Education Letter,* (July/August), 3–5.
National Association of State Boards of Education (1990). *Today's children, tomorrow's survival, A call to restructure schools.* Alexandria, VA: National Association of School Boards of Education.
Nieto, S. (1996). *Affirming diversity: The sociopolitical context of multicultural education* (2nd ed.). New York: Longman.
Nieto, S. (1999). *The light in their eyes: Creating multicultural learning communities. Multicultural education series.* New York: Teaching College Press.
Oakes, J. (1985). *Keeping track: How schools structure inequality.* New Haven: Yale University Press.
Ogbu, J. U. (1978). *Minority education and caste: The American system in cross-cultural perspectives.* New York: Academic Press.
Ogbu, J. (1993). Frameworks – Variability in minority school performance: A problem in search of an explanation. In: E. Jacob & C. Jordan (Eds), *Minority Education: Anthropological Perspectives* (pp. 83–111). Norwood, NJ: Ablex.

Ogbu, J. U., & Matute-Bianchi, M. E. (1986). Understanding socio-cultural factors: Knowledge, identity, and school adjustment. In: *Beyond Language, Social and Cultural Factors in Schooling Language Minority Students* (pp. 73–140). Los Angeles, CA: Evaluation, Dissemination and Assessment Center, California State University, Los Angeles.

O'Hanlon, C. (Ed.) (1995). *Inclusive education in Europe*. London, England: David Fulton.

Patton, J. M. (1998). The disproportionate representation of African Americans in special education: Looking behind the curtain for understanding and solutions. *The Journal of Special Education, 32*, 25–31.

Powell, R., McLaughlin, H. J., Savage, T., & Zehm, S. (2001). *Classroom Management: Perspectives on the Social Curriculum*. Columbus, OH: Merrill-Prentice Hall.

Pugach, M., & Seidl, B. (1996). Deconstructing the diversity-disability connection. *Contemporary Education, 68*, 5–8.

Pugach, M., & Seidl, B. (1995). From exclusion to inclusion in urban schools: A new case for teacher education reform. *Teacher Education, 27*, 379–395.

Rego, M., & Nieto, S. (2000). Multicultural/intercultural teacher education in two contexts: lessons from the United States and Spain. *Teaching and Teacher Education, 16*(4), 413–427.

Reynolds, M., Wang, M. et al. (1993). 20/20 Analysis: Taking a close look at the margins. *Exceptional Children, 59*, 294–300.

Sailor, W. T., & Skrtic, T. (1995). Modern and postmodern agendas in special education: Implications for teacher education, research and policy development. In: J. Paul, H. Roselli & D. Evans (Eds), *Integrating School Restructuring and Special Education Reform* (pp. 418–433). New York: Harcourt Brace.

Saldana, D. C., & Waxman, H. C. (1997). An observational study of multicultural education in urban elementary schools. *Equity & Excellence in Education, 30*(1), 40–46.

Sanders, W. L., & Rivers, J. C. (1996). *Cumulative and residual effects of teachers on future student academic achievement*. Knoxville: University of Tennessee Value-Added Research and Assessment Center.

Sarason, S. (1990). *The predictable failure of educational reform*. San Francisco, CA: Jossey-Bass.

Skrtic, T. M. (1995). *Exploring the theory/practice link in special education*. New York, Teachers College Press.

Smylie, M. (1995). Teacher learning in the workplace: Implications for school reform. In: T. Guskey & M. Huberman (Eds), *Professional Development in Education: New Paradigms and Practices* (pp. 69–91). New York: Teachers College Press.

Spring, J. (2000). *The intersection of cultures: Multicultural education in the United States and the global economy*. Boston, MA: McGraw-Hill.

Tetler, S. (1995). The Danish efforts in integration. In: C. O'Hanlon (Ed.), *Inclusive Education in Europe*. London, England: David Fulton.

U.S. Department of Education (1997). *To assure the free appropriate public education of all children with disabilities: 19th annual report to Congress on the implementation of The Individuals with Disabilities Education Act*. Washington, D.C.: Author.

Wang, M. C., Haertel G. D., & Walberg, H. J. (1993). Synthesis of research: What helps students learn? *Educational Leadership*, 74–79.

PART 2.
LEARNERS WITH EXCEPTIONALITIES

EDUCATING STUDENTS WITH COGNITIVE DISABILITIES

Cheryl A. Utley and Festus E. Obiakor

The concept of cognitive disability or mental retardation (MR) as it is traditionally known constantly shifts to reflect changing societal values and attitudes (MacMillan & Hendrick, 1983; Sarason & Doris, 1979; Ysseldyke, Algozzine & Thurlow, 1992, 2000). Not long ago, Trent (1994) described the social construction of the meaning of MR as "construction whose changing meaning is shaped both by individuals who initiate and administer policies, programs, and by the practices, and by the social context to which these individuals are responding" (p. 2). As Smith (2001) pointed out

> ... The social construction of the meaning of retardation is sometimes done in the name of science, sometimes in the name of caring for people, and sometimes in the name of social or economic necessity. Each of these reasons for defining people and their differences, however, has often been used for the purpose of controlling a group of people perceived to be a threat or an inconvenience to society. The construction of the meaning of mental retardation has, from this perspective, been motivated more by a search for social control than by a concern for the best interests of the individuals defined (p. 380).

While the new concept of cognitive disability is used by most states to indicate MR, many fundamental issues continue to haunt the category (Obiakor, 2001; Ysseldyke et al., 2000). For instance, labeling and classifying students as MR are fundamental activities of agencies if they are to receive funds, allocate financial assistance, and provide special services (Lipsky & Gartner, 1997). Earlier, Gallagher (1976) noted that labeling provides:

(1) A means for beginning a classification, diagnosis, and treatment sequence peculiarly designed to counteract certain identifiable negative conditions.
(2) The basis for further research which will give more insight into etiology, prevention, and possible treatment applications of such conditions in the future.
(3) A means of calling attention to a specific problem in order to obtain additional resources through special legislation and funding (p. 3).

The disadvantages of labeling and classifying students as MR have also been highlighted. For example, Gorham, Des Jardins, Page, Pettis and Scherber (1976) decried the use of labels because they "have damaged many children, particularly minority group children whose cultures and lifestyles differ sufficiently from the "norm" to make any measurement of their abilities and aptitudes by norm-based scales a certain disaster for them" (p. 155). Along these same lines, Gallagher (1976) acknowledged that:

(1) By applying labels to children, professionals fail to follow differentiated programs of treatment.
(2) By using labels, professionals preserve a social hierarchy and to keep minority group children at the bottom of the social ladder.
(3) By using labels, professionals focus on "the problem of the individual, rather than on complex social and ecological conditions needing specific change and repair" (p. 3).

In this chapter, we examine divergent professional perspectives that have molded the concept of cognitive disability. We discuss issues of definition, causes, categorical placement, prevalence, and overrepresentation as they have evolved over the last three decades. And finally, we present the learning and social characteristics of persons with cognitive disabilities.

PROFESSIONAL PARADIGMS AND MODELS IN COGNITIVE DISABILITIES

Professionals who work with students with cognitive disabilities use paradigms or models that have become dominant in the field of disability during the decade of the 1990s. Accordingly, these models represent professional thinking and practice. For instance, the *psychometric model* "assumes that "IQ" tests measure "intelligence," a highly heritable trait that is relatively stable throughout an individual lifetime because it is based on the biological substrate" (Mercer, 1992, p. 23). Within the psychometric model, a low score on an IQ test is interpreted as an objective and scientific measure of a symptom of mental subnormality. The *medical model* looks at the physical features of the individual (i.e. inherent features that demonstrate human deficiencies). The *anthropological or social systems model* conceptualizes cognitive disability as a socially constructed category. Society develops a consensus on what they consider to be normal or intelligent behavior. Individuals or groups with the greatest social power have the greatest influence on consensus formation and on establishing standards, values, beliefs, language, and customs by which to judge normal and abnormal/deviant behavior. Thus, an individual's deviant social status is based upon the evaluation of behaviors that are a violation of social norms. Inevitably, persons are perceived, treated, and assigned a label as deviant accorded to the social stigma associated with their status. The *ecological model* is based upon the premise that the: (a) ecology or topographical features of the physical millieu affect a person's behavior; and (b) environment-person relationship is dynamic in which changes or alterations in components of the ecological system affect changes on how individuals interact with their environments (Patterson & Moore, 1979). The ecological dimensions include the "demands and expectations of a given culture for a given cohort and the degree to which the environment affords opportunities for learning and the expression of specific competencies" (Landesman-Ramey, Dossett & Echols, 1996, p. 58). The *sociocultural model* is based upon the assumption that society is heterogeneous and diversified in terms of racial, ethnic, and cultural norms and standards of behavior. Based on this model, the assignment of an individual to the category of cognitive disability does not rely upon IQ test scores. Instead, it measures the individual's social adaptation to his/her own social group in several social settings. The *educational model* focuses on a person's learning problems which are attributed to insufficient use of learning strategies rather than to genetically or biologically based models of disability. Professionals adhering to this model assume that children can learn if they are motivated to apply themselves and are taught learning strategies. The *cognitive psychology model* is focused on the "active processes involved in learning, the development of self-regulation, and on emulating the learning and problem solving of expert learners" (Rueda & Simon, 2001, p. 76). The *legal model* addresses legal definitional changes in statutes and laws that impact the delivery of appropriate services to students with cognitive disability in general and special education classrooms. The *ecobehavioral model* is based upon the hypothesis of intergenerational progression in which "cumulative experiential deficits (defined as hours of engagement with relevant topics/subject matter) is transmitted to low-socioeconomic children over the preadult life span" (Greenwood, Hart, Walker & Risley, 1994, p. 215). This theory represents one approach to knowing where, when, and why environmental variables affect behavior and outcomes, and it represents progress in assessing environmental influences on developmental retardation and in developing the strategic means of preventing it.

DEFINITIONS, CAUSES, AND PREVALENCE OF COGNITIVE DISABILITIES

The American Association on Mental Retardation (AAMR) (formally known as the American Association on Mental Deficiency) is the professional organization that has published earlier definitions on MR. Heber (1961) reiterated the definition of the AAMR classification and terminology committee which reads: "Mental retardation refers to subaverage general intellectual functioning which originates in the developmental period and is associated with impairment in adaptive behavior" (p. 3). Over the next twelve years, the AAMR definition would be hotly debated by professionals. For example, the upper IQ cut off limit for MR was 85 so that no child could be denied educational services (Heber, 1959). Major revisions in the definition of MR were subsequently proposed. These revisions stated that significantly subaverage general intellectual functioning was to be determined by a score of at least two standard deviations below the mean on an intelligence test. This meant that the cut off point for determining MR was moved downward to 85 to 70 (Grossman, 1973). This change lowered the percentage of the population classified as MR from 16% to approximately 2.28%. MacMillan and Reschly (1997) eloquently argued that "slight shifts in the upper limit have rather dramatic consequences in terms of the percentage of the population eligible. For example, a shift from IQ 70 and below to a criterion of IQ 75 and below results in *twice as many people being eligible*. Because of the acceleration of the curve in this portion of the normal curve, there are more cases falling in the interval of 71 to 75 (2.80%) than in the entire range scoring IQ 70 and below (2.68%)" (p. 57). The consequences of this revision meant that fewer people would be labeled as retarded because of minority status, environmental disadvantage, socioeconomic factors, and language difference. In addition, the 1973 definition emphasized the importance of adaptive behavior existing concurrently with subaverage intellectual performance. The definition extended the developmental period from 16 to 18 years of age.

In 1983, the definition of MR was revised and used the intelligent quotient (IQ) scores as the primary diagnostic measure for classifying persons with MR on a continuum as mild, moderate, severe, and profound. As illustrated in Table 1, the 1983 definition of MR used intelligent quotient (IQ) scores as the primary diagnostic measure for classifying persons with MR on a continuum as mild, moderate, severe, and profound.

Table 1. Classification of Mental Retardation by Measured IQ Score.

AAMR 1983 Classification Level	Intelligence Test Score (IQ) Range
Mild or Educable mental retardation	50–55 to approximately 70
Moderate or Trainable mental retardation	35–40 to 50–55
Severe mental retardation	20–25 to 35–40
Profound mental retardation	Below 20–25

To obtain an IQ score, the mental age (MA) is divided by the chronological age (CA) and multiplied by 100 (see formula below):

$$\frac{MA}{CA} \times \frac{100}{1} = IQ$$

The MA reflects a person's mental age capability age and the CA reflects a person's chronological or actual age. If an individual scores within the mild or educable range, the IQ is about 2.0 to 3.0 standard deviations (SD) below the mean (Note: the SD is a score that is positively or negatively deviated from the mean). When an individual scores within the moderate or trainable range, the IQ is 3.0 SD below the mean. Finally, when individuals are within the severe/profound range, the IQ is 4.0 below the mean (see the bell-shaped curve below). It is very important to note that the mean of all IQ tests (e.g. Wechsler Intelligence Scales for Children-Revised [WISC-R] and Stanford-Binet) is 100. The SD for the WISC-R is 15 and that of the Stanford-Binet is 16. While these tests are popular in many areas, the Leiter International Performance scale is popular in some areas because of its emphasis on *performance*.

According to Grossman (1983), impairments in adaptive behavior are defined as "significant limitations in an individual's effectiveness in meeting the standards of maturation, level and cultural group, as determined by clinical assessment and, usually, standardized scales" (p. 11). The debate concerning adaptive behavior has centered upon its inclusion in the definition of MR, its meaning, and assessment. Some researchers have suggested that MR should be determined only by a score of 70 or less on an IQ test, while other researchers have suggested learning, personal independence, and/or social responsibility that are expected for his or her age that the criterion of adaptive behavior must remain in the definition for MR to be socially valid. With regard to adaptive behavior assessment, practices must include in-school behavior (i.e. functional academic skills). As Landesman-Ramey et al. (1996) stated:

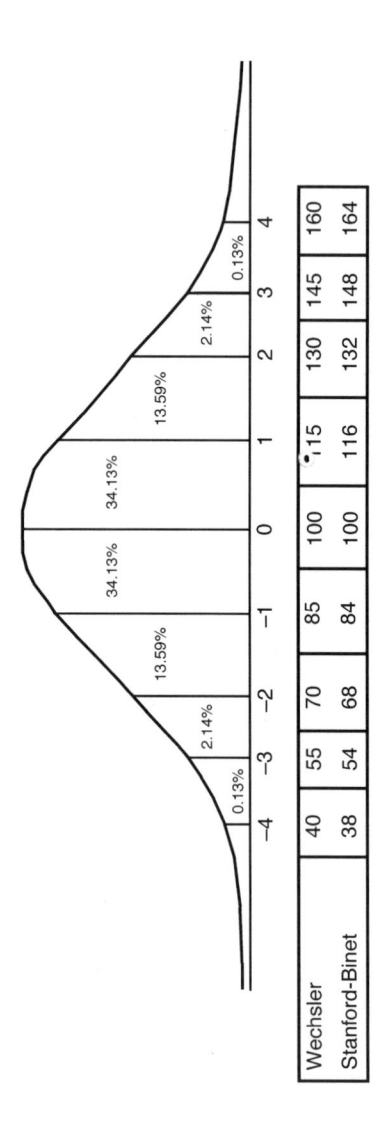

Fig. 1. Bell Shape Curve.

Adaptive behavior encompasses a wide range of functional abilities, from sensorimotor, self-help, communication, and social skills in infancy and early childhood to academic skills, reasoning, community survival skills, social judgment and responsibility, self-direction, and vocational aptitude in later years. Although adaptive behavior and measured intelligence are closely related, their observed correlation is not perfect. Accordingly, assessing intelligence and adaptive behavior independently can minimize the incorrect labeling of a child who scores poorly on an intelligence test for noncognitive reasons such as test anxiety, language differences, poor social compliance, and motivational problems or who lags in adaptive behavior skills because of physical, emotional, or environmental constraints rather than lack of basic intelligence. There are not yet any accurate, useful measures of adaptive behavior that are sensitive to the effects of both age and culture (p. 58).

Definitions of Cognitive Disabilities

Federal Definition. The federal definition of MR (now properly named cognitive disabilities in many states), as described by the U.S. Department of Education, Office of Civil Rights (OCR) (1992), was based on a deficit model. This model defined what a child is not able to do in relation to being served in special education (full-time vs. part-time). Program options do not include access to general educational settings with appropriate supports and services (full-time versus part-time), thus ignoring the potential that children have to function in the general education environment. In addition, this deficit model restricts the educational attainment levels of children with MR. The definition reads as follows:

- Mild retardation: Children capable of becoming self-sufficient and learning academic skills through the upper elementary grades.
- Moderate retardation: Children who are not able to profit from regular instruction or from instruction for the mildly retarded.
- Severe retardation: Children who are significantly subaverage in intellectual functioning and who have concurrent deficits or impairments in adaptive functioning. This is a developmental disorder whose onset occurs before the age of 18 (p. 3).

AAMR Revised Definition. Luckasson, Coulter, Polloway, Reiss, Schalock, Snell, Spitalnik and Stark (1992) revised the definition of MR, one that was supported by the American Association on Mental Retardation (AAMR). As they pointed out, "Mental retardation refers to substantial limitations in present functioning. It is characterized by significantly subaverage intellectual functioning, existing concurrently with related limitations in two or more of the following applicable adaptive skill areas: communication, self-care, home living, social skills, community use, self-direction, health and safety, functional academics, leisure, and work. Mental retardation manifests before age 18" (p. 1). The four assumptions underlying this definition are:

(1) Valid assessment considers cultural and linguistic diversity as well as differences in communication and behavioral factors.
(2) The existence of limitations in adaptive skills occurs within the context of community environments typical of the individual's age peers and is indexed to the person's individualized needs for supports.
(3) Specific adaptive limitations often coexist with strengths in other adaptive skills or other personal capabilities.
(4) With appropriate supports over a sustained period, the life functioning of the person with mental retardation will generally improve.

The 1992 revised definition was based upon a multidimensional approach that requires a comprehensive description of a person with MR along four dimensions: (1) intellectual functioning and adaptive skills; (2) psychological/emotional considerations; (3) physical/health/ etiology considerations; and (4) environmental considerations. A three-step procedure for diagnosing, classifying, and determining the needed supports of persons with MR is outlined in Table 2.

According to the 1992 definition, key elements are capabilities (or competencies), environments, and functioning. Capabilities refer to the notion that functioning in MR is specifically related to limitations in intelligence and adaptive skills. Essential to an understanding of MR is the concept of environments in which individuals live, learn, play, work, socialize and interact. Levels of functioning are influenced by: (a) the intellectual and adaptive skill limitations in MR; (b) the nature, extent, and severity of MR; and (c) the absence or presence of needed supports in the environment. As depicted in Fig. 2, an estimation of the intensity of supports needed to improve functioning in the environments in which the individual lives, goes to school, works, and plays is a procedural recommendation for classifying persons with MR. Weaknesses in four dimensions, as opposed to the IQ score alone.

The changes in the 1992 AAMR supported definition are somewhat controversial. For example, the levels of retardation were reduced to two: mild and severe. With these two levels of disability, the focus is more on a functional orientation and the level of instruction. Dever (1990) explained that:

> It is not an IQ that determines level of retardation but, rather, the amount and intensity of instruction required to move a person out of the category of "retarded." Thus, persons with mild mental retardation are those who know a great deal about living in the community without supervision and who require some instruction that could be provided under relatively nonintensive conditions. On the other hand, persons with severe [or profound] retardation are those who have acquired very few of the skills that are required for living in the

Table 2. Three-Step Procedure for Diagnosing, Classifying, and Describing Systems of Supports.

Dimension I: Intellectual Functioning and Adaptive Skills	Step I. Diagnosis of Mental Retardation Determines Eligibility for Supports Mental Retardation is diagnosed if: (1) The individual's intellectual functioning is approximately 70 to 75 below. (2) There are significant disabilities in two or more adaptive skill areas. (3) The age of onset is below 18.
Dimension II: Psychological/Emotional Considerations Dimension III: Physical/Health Etiology Considerations Dimension IV: Environmental Considerations	Step 2. Classification and Description Identifies Strengths and Weaknesses and the Need for Supports (1) Describe the individual's strengths and weaknesses in reference to psychological/emotional considerations. (2) Describe the individual's overall physical health and indicate the condition's etiology. (3) Describe the individual's current environmental placement and the optimal environment that would facilitate his/her continued growth and development.
	Step 3. Profile and Intensities of Needed Supports Identifies Needed Supports Identify the kind and intensities of supports needed for each of the four dimensions: Dimension I: Intellectual Functioning and Adaptive Skills Dimension II: Psychological/Emotional Considerations Dimension III: Physical Health/Etiology Considerations Dimension IV: Environmental Considerations

Source: American Association on Mental Retardation (1992). *Mental Retardation: Definition, Cclassification, and Systems of Support.* Washington, DC: Author.

community unsupervised and who require an enormous amount of instruction that may have to be provided under very intense conditions (p. 150).

The Board of Directors of the Mental Retardation and Developmental Disabilities Division (MRDD) of the Council for Exceptional Children identified important implications of the revised AAMR definition. Smith (1998)

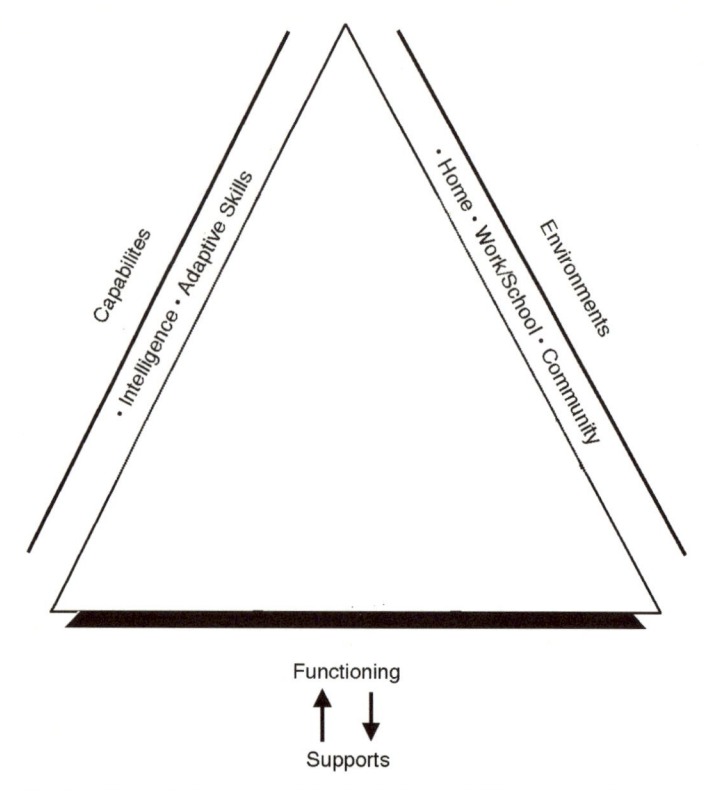

Fig. 2. General Structure of the Definition of Mental Retardation.

identified some questions raised by the Critical Issues Committee of the Board of MRDD, namely:

(1) What are the ramifications of the changes for teacher training?
(2) In what ways will the AAMR definitional changes affect teacher certification requirements?
(3) How will these changes impact special education funding?
(4) Will the four levels of mental retardation no longer recognized in the definition be supplanted by the new equivalents?
(5) How will the movement away from severity levels to levels of needed support affect placement and individual educational programs where classification on the severity of disability still occurs due to child count requirements?

(6) Although the increased specificity of the domains of adaptive behavior in the new definition is a conceptual improvement, what tools are available for measuring these domains?
(7) Among MRDD respondents, a concern was raised about the expanded proportion of the population that is eligible for classification as mentally retarded because of the IQ cutoff of 75 adopted in the definition. What is the impact that this might have on children and adolescents from minority backgrounds?
(8) How will the changes in classification included in the definition jeopardize both the advocacy and the protection that has been afforded those who are touched by the complexities of mild mental retardation? (pp. 18–20).

Causes of Cognitive Disabilities

Mental retardation, now cognitive disability, is caused by a myriad of factors. Coulter (1994) observed that there are more than one thousand causes of MR, and in many cases, it is not clear which causes may apply to particular individuals. In addition, MR results from complex interactions among multiple causes (Batshaw & Shapiro, 1997). A more recent classification system of causes of MR was delineated by Luckasson et al. (1992). As they indicated, these authors, MR is caused by three groups of factors: prenatal (before birth), perinatal (during the birth process), and postnatal (after birth). Prenatal causes include genetic problems, chromosomal abnormalities, maternal drug abuse, maternal illness, sexually transmitted diseases (STD), inborn metabolic disorders, and environmental influences (e.g. living in chemically infested areas). Perinatal causes include accidents, neonatal disorders, and intrauterine disorders. And, postnatal causes include infections, accidents (e.g. head injuries), toxic-metabolic disorders, malnutrition, environmental deprivation, and child abuse and neglect. These causes have been further divided into two broad categories: biomedical or organic (developing within the individual) and psychosocial disadvantage (developing from social and environmental influences). The biomedical category includes prenatal, perinatal, and postnatal factors, genetic factors, biochemical factors, and maturational lag. Environmental causes include poverty, nutrition, toxins, safety, language differences, sensory deprivation, emotional problems, and poor education.

Prevalence and Incidence of Cognitive Disabilities

Prevalence refers to the number of people (or the percent of a population) classified as cognitive disabled at any point in time, while incidence refers to the number of new cases identified in a specific period of time. Incidence is the number of individuals who, at some time in their life, have been identified as having cognitive disabilities (e.g. cases diagnosed at birth). Epidemiologists and researchers estimate the prevalence of cognitive disabilities as ranging between 1% and 3% with 2–3% being the most frequently cited figure (Raymond, 2000). However, there are four major reasons that make it impossible to determine a true prevalence of MR. The first problem preventing the accurate assessment of the prevalence of cognitive disabilities is the definition of the condition (Tarjan, Tizard, Rutter, Begab, Brooke, de la Cruz, Lin, Montenegro, Strotzka & Sartorius, 1972; Tizard, 1972). Earlier, Ramey and Finkelstein (1981) noted that:

> Not only do the criteria for mental retardation [cognitive disability] change over time, but it is likely as well that the criteria for diagnosing mental retardation are not uniformly applied by different groups of professionals at any given time. And, there is more than one classification system extant at any given time. Furthermore, when classification systems that do not permit multiple coding of categories are used, prevalence/incidence may be underestimated by the number of cases where mental retardation [cognitive disability] is the second diagnosis (p. 73).

Second, the instruments used to diagnose cognitive disabilities also present problems for epidemiological studies, particularly those with minority subjects (MacMillan, 1989). The standardization samples of tests do not include members of the cultures groups from whom the epidemiological data are to be collected. Not only is it unethical to use a culture-bound test to assess prevalence of cognitive disabilities among people from a minority culture who are expected to perform only in their own culture, but it is unethical to use this kind of information to plan educational services for minority persons with cognitive disability to function adequately in the majority culture. Third, many persons with IQs in the range of mild cognitive disability (MCD) adjust adequately to the community (e.g. six-hour retarded child). In lower SES urban and rural areas, estimates of MCD are higher than in other areas (e.g. suburban). Using the current definition of cognitive disability, deficits in adaptive behavior must exist concurrently with deficits in IQ test scores. The emphasis on adaptive behavior tends to reduce prevalence. Fourth, the prevalence of MCD will be influenced by epidemiological studies that use different methodologies (e.g. risk registers, or referral lists, versus random or stratified sampling of a particular population). For example, the use of random sampling procedures will give higher prevalence rates than the use of agency referrals. Fifth, children who have MCD are identified during the school years; before and after these years they may not be identified or receive services. Sixth, different states have different criteria and rates of identification. for identifying students with MCD. Seventh, sociopolitical factors and litigation have made it more difficult to test, classify, and place students with the disability label of MCD in special education (Harvard University Civil Rights Project Conference on Minority Issues in Special Education, 2000; Oswald & Coutinho, 2001; Valencia & Suzuki, 2001).

For more than 30 years, the overrepresentation of minority children in special education programs has sparked controversy (Artiles & Trent, 1994; Coutinho, Oswald & Best, 2002; Dunn, 1968; Gottlieb, Alter, Gottlieb & Wishner, 1994; Harry, 1992, 1994; MacDonnell, McLaughlin & Morison, 1997; MacMillan & Speece, 1999; Oswald & Coutinho, 2001; Patton, Polloway & Smith, 2000). The National Institute for Urban School Improvement (2001) recently published a document titled, *On the Nexus of Race, Disability, and Overrepresentation: What Do We Know? Where Do We Go?* Based on the ideas encapsulated in this document (see Meyer & Patton, 2001),

(1) African American students tend to be overrepresented in classrooms for students with mild disabilities and emotional and behavioral disabilities (Oswald, Coutinho, Best & Singh, 1999).
(2) Almost 75% of diagnoses of mild mental retardation [cognitive disabilities] are linked to various socioeconomic-related environmental contingencies. Poor children are more likely than wealthier children to receive special education (U.S. Department of Education, 1998).
(3) Although African Americans represent 16% of elementary and secondary enrollments, they constitute 21% of total enrollments in special education (USDOE, 1998).
(4) Poor African American children are 2.3 times more likely to be identified by their teacher as having mental retardation than their White counterparts (Oswald, Coutinho, Best & Singh, 1999).
(5) The population of Native American children who receive special education services is a one-and-one-half times greater at 16.8% vs. 11% for the general population (Allison & Vining, 1999).
(6) African Americans, especially males, who engage in certain behaviors that represent artifacts of their culture – such as language (ebonics), movement patterns (verve), and a certain "ethnic" appearance – have been found to be over-referred for special education placement (Neal, McCray & Webb-Johnson, 2001).
(7) Although Latino students are often not overrepresented in state and national data, they are likely to be overrepresented in special education when their proportion of a district's diverse student body increases.

A thorough understanding of the phenomenon of overrepresentation involves a very complex combination of theories (Gottlieb et al., 1994; Reschly & Ward, 1991; National Research Council, 2002; Utley & Obiakor, 2001). The National

Academy of Sciences Panel (NASP) (Heller, Messick & Holtzman, 1982), national data from OCR (1997), the National Longitudinal Transition Study (NLTS) (2002), the National Early Intervention Longitudinal Study (NEILS) (2000), and the Committee on Minority Representation in Special Education (National Research Council, 2002) have presented unique perspectives on the issue of overrepresentaion (Hebbeler & Wagner, 2001; Office for Civil Rights, 1997). According to the NASP, the overrepresentation issue implicates the entire special education process as being unfair to students: the quality of instruction prior to referral, the decision to refer, the assessment, placement in special education programs, and the quality of instruction that occurs in that program. Problematic circumstances include the invalid assessment and placement in programs for students with cognitive disabilities where educational progress may be hindered because of teachers' lowered expectations and goals, opportunities for success are restricted, and low-quality instruction exists. OCR investigations have disclosed school discriminatory practices, such as: (1) extensive prereferral interventions in school districts with predominantly Caucasian students than in schools with predominantly African American students; (2) a greater emphasis on students' behavioral problems as opposed to academic reasons; (3) a greater reliance on IQ tests in the evaluation of minority students; and (4) a disproportionate number of minority students labeled as cognitively disabled and placed in restrictive classroom settings. In the words of Meyer and Patton (2001):

> Two elements have emerged as keys to understanding the nexus of race, disability, and overrepresentation. There is a disconnect between the race, culture, and class of teachers in most schools on one hand, and the culture, race, and SES [socio-economic status] of learners they serve on the other. This disconnect is associated with underachievement which contributes significantly to the disproportionate representation of these learners in special education . . . . Increasingly numbers of traditionally trained teachers from the dominant American culture are teaching students who are often nontraditional learners, resulting in cultural, race, and class chasms in our classrooms and schools. Further, too few teachers have been educated to recognize and deal with the cultural, class, and gender "knapsacks" of these learners, or of their own, and may have low expectations shaped by inaccurate assumptions about the innate ability of racial minorities and poor children (p. 6).

LEARNING CHARACTERISTICS OF STUDENTS WITH COGNITIVE DISABILITIES

Students with cognitive disabilities have been found to differ from "normal" achieving peers who exhibit "normal" achievements in several areas related to cognitive functioning. These students are a heterogeneous group of students and some of the characteristics may not apply to all students. Learning characteristics of students with cognitive disabilities manifest themselves in: (a) receptive and expressive language; (b) generalization; (c) attention; (d) memory; and (e) motivation and self-direction.

Receptive and Expressive Language

Receptive and expressive language impairments occur more frequently among students with cognitive disabilities as compared to "normal" achieving peers (Langone, 1996; MacMillan, 1982). Language impairments may consists of an inability to articulate sounds or pronounce words. For these students, speech and language impairments may be diagnosed as a secondary disabling condition. Physiological anomalies (e.g. protruding tongue in individuals with Down Syndrome) and motor development problems affect the individual's ability to produce speech sounds. Impairments may also be due to hearing problems that affect speech production. Additional factors that adversely affect receptive and language developments in students with cognitive disabilities include poor environmental conditions, cultural differences, language barriers, and a lack of exposure to positive role models. Instructional strategies consists of systematically teaching and reinforcing a student's ability to imitate and discriminate gestures or vocalizations, and teaching the generalization of newly learned language skills in different community and school environments.

Generalization of Skills

Generalization refers to the extent to which students with cognitive disabilities have extended what they have learned across settings and over time (Stokes & Baer, 1977; Stokes & Osnes, 1989). Research has shown that these students have impairments in their ability to transfer or generalize information and skills learned in one setting or one way to new situations which involves different people, expectations, and skills (Langone, Clees, Oxford, Malone & Ross, 1995). Instructional strategies consist of behaviorally oriented learning principles such as varying settings, the time of day, materials, and community-based instruction.

Students with cognitive disabilities have difficulty distinguishing and paying attention to relevant cues in learning and social situations and attending to several different cues simultaneously (Zeaman & House, 1963, 1979). In addition, these students tend to exhibit a high level of distractibility when external stimuli are present. Instructional strategies consists of teaching students to pay close attention to the relevant parts of any task by color coding the important components of school tasks.

Memory

The memory capabilities of students with cognitive disabilities differ in the rate at and efficiency with which they can acquire, remember, and use newly learned knowledge as compared to normal-achieving peers. Memory characteristics of students with cognitive disabilities range from problems associated with short-term to long-term memory skills (Ellis, 1970; Scruggs & Laufenberg, 1986). The term "rehearsal" describes the unconscious cognitive strategies students use to remember. The strategy of rehearsal consists of using various verbal strategies, including repetition, rhyme, sub-vocal speech, and verbal self-instruction (Henley, Ramsey & Algozzine, 1993). Research has shown that students with cognitive disabilities are less likely to use spontaneous rehearsal procedures and are unable to benefit from incidental learning cues in their environment as compared to their "normal" achieving peers. However, when these students are taught how to use rehearsal strategies, their short- and long-term memory skills improve (Borkowski & Day, 1987; Mercer & Snell, 1977). Instructional strategies consist of: (a) using mnemonics as mediators to help learners with poor memory to complete a variety of tasks; (b) teaching appropriate problem-solving skills; and (c) computed-based instruction.

Motivation and Self-Direction

Motivation is an important aspect of learning. Because of their past history of negative experiences, students with cognitive disabilities may lack the necessary motivation needed to be successful learners. A frequently mentioned motivational characteristic of students with cognitive disabilities is their low expectancy of success and high expectancy of failure than their "normal" achieving peers (Zigler & Balla, 1981). The cycle of academic failure frequently leads to feelings of learned helplessness in which these students are not motivated to achieve academically (Smith & Luckasson, 1995) or exhibit symptoms of maladaptive motivational orientations on attentional tasks (Obiakor, 1999; Obiakor, Stile & Muller, 1993; Utley, Hoehn, Soraci & Baumeister, 1993).

An important characteristic of students with cognitive disabilities is self-direction. Self-direction is defined as one's ability to control the events that ultimately affect his or her life. Studies of locus of control, an individual's belief concerning the relationship between one's efforts and achievements have shown that students with cognitive disabilities have a history of not being self-directed.. Research suggests that these students demonstrate a tendency toward an external locus of control in which individuals contribute outcomes to forces outside of themselves (e.g. luck and fate) (Levin, 1992). In studies examining locus of control in students with cognitive disabilities. Weisz (1990) found that these students have an external locus of control than their normal-achieving peers and that under conditions of failure feedback showed a significant decline in their use of effective strategies.

MAXIMIZING THE POTENTIAL OF STUDENTS WITH COGNITIVE DISABILITIES

It is clear that the roles and responsibilities of professionals who teach students with cognitive disabilities are in constant flux given the trend to provide services in inclusive classrooms. Special educators must be knowledgeable about how to work collaboratively with professionals to "rethink their habits and culture, their practices, and their beliefs about special education systems, processes, and outcomes" (Smith, Edelen-Smith & Stodden, 1998, p. 333). For example, in working with students with cognitive disabilities, special educators must be required to develop IEPs and implement schoolwide instructional approaches that meet their unique needs. To achieve this transformational change, Shanker (1990) recommended four points. First, people in organizations must change and be given training and assistance to transform new knowledge and practice into existing programs and service delivery systems. Second, transformational opportunities for professionals, family members, agency personnel, and individuals with disabilities must be assured that support will be given when new decisions are made, even though they may be faulty and ineffective. Third, the removal of existing practices, procedures, or programs must be done with caution and reflection about the systemic implications to follow new decisions. Fourth, professionals in state and local educational agencies must have access to information, research data, and technical assistance as roles and responsibilities are redesigned.

To maximize the learning potential of students with cognitive disabilities, culturally competent approaches must be adopted during assessment and intervention (Utley & Obiakor, 2001). Too often, educators mistake cultural differences (e.g. language patterns and diverse behavioral patterns) as deviant. General and special educators must be careful in their use and interpretation of IQ test results. Frequently, culturally different students get labeled as "retarded" even though the tests used to assess them are proven to be unreliable and invalid. It is important, however, to identify students who have cognitive disabilities and who come from different linguistic, cultural, and racial backgrounds (Utley & Obiakor, 2001). To facilitate this process, general and special educators, parents, and communities must work collaboratively and consultatively.

CONCLUSION

This chapter examined pertinent issues (e.g. definition, prevalence) related to the education of students with cognitive disabilities. Given the changing demographics of this student population and the controversial issues related to the classification of these students, their learning characteristics were presented. It is imperative that general and special education practitioners focus their efforts on classroom and school learning environments and move away from perspectives that divert their attention from quality instruction and behavior management issues. These professionals must also examine their collaborative relationships within and across school districts to achieve major changes in how students with cognitive disabilities are provided services.

REFERENCES

Allison, S. R., & Vining, C. B. (1999). Native American culture and language: Considerations in service delivery. In: T. V. Fletcher & C. S. Bos (Eds), *Helping Children with Disabilities and Their Families* (p. 197). Tempe, AZ: Bilingual Press.

American Association on Mental Deficiency, American Association on Mental Retardation (AAMR) (1992). *Mental retardation: Definitions, classification, and systems of support*. Washington, D.C.: Author.

Artiles, A. J., & Trent, S. C. (1994). Overrepresentation of minority students in special education: A continuing debate. *The Journal of Special Education*, 27(4), 410–437.

Batshaw, M. L., & Shapiro, B. K. (1997). Mental retardation. In: M. L. Batshaw (Ed.), *Children with Disabilities* (4th ed., pp. 335–360). Baltimore, MD: Paul H. Brookes.

Banks, J. A., & Banks, C. (1997). *Multicultural education: Issues and perspectives*. Needham Heights, MA: Allyn & Bacon.

Borkowski, J. G., & Day, J. (1987). *Cognition in special children: Comparative approaches to retardation, learning disabilities, and giftedness*. Norwood, NJ: Ablex.

Carr, E. G., Horner, R. H., Turnbull, A., Marquis, J. G., McLaughlin, D. M., McAtee, M. L., Smith, C. E., Ryan, K. A., Ruef, M. B., & Doolabh, A. (1999). *Positive behavior support for people with developmental disabilities: A research synthesis*. Washington, D.C.: American Association on Mental Retardation.

Coulter, D. L. (1994). Biomedical conditions: Types, causes, & results. In: L. Sternberg (Ed.), *Individuals with Profound Disabilities: Instructional and Assistive Strategies* (3rd ed., pp. 41–58). Austin, TX: Pro-Ed.

Coutinho, M. J., Oswald, D. P., & Best, A. M. (2002). The influence of sociodemographics and gender on the disproportionate identification of minority students as having learning disabilities. *Remedial and Special Education*, 23(1), 49–59.

Dever, R. N. (1990). Defining mental retardation from an instructional perspective. *Mental Retardation*, 28, 147–153.

Dunn, L. M. (1968). Special education for the mildly retarded: Is much of it justifiable? *Exceptional Children*, 35, 5–22.

Ellis, N. R. (1970). Memory processes in retardates and normals. In: N. R. Ellis (Ed.), *International Review of Research in Mental Retardation* (Vol. 4, pp. 1–32). New York: Academic Press.

Gallagher, J. J. (1976). The sacred and profane uses of labeling. *Mental Retardation, 14,* 3–7.
Gay, G. (1994). *At the essence of learning: Multicultural education.* West Lafayette, IN: Kappa Delta Pi.
Gorham, K. A., Des Jardins, C., Page, R., Pettis, E., & Scherber, B. (1976). Effect on parents. In: N. Hobbs (Ed.), *Issues in the Classification of Children* (Vol. 2, pp. 154–188). San Francisco, CA: Jossey-Bass.
Gottlieb, J., Alter, M., Gottlieb, B. W., & Wishner, J. (1994). Special education in urban America: It's not justifiable for many. *The Journal of Special Education, 27,* 453–465.
Greenwood, C. R., Hart, B., Walker, D., & Risley, T. (1994). The opportunity to respond and academic performance revisited: A behavioral theory of developmental retardation and its prevention. In: R. Gardner, III, D. M. Sainato, J. O. Cooper, T. E. Heron, W. L. Heward, J. W. Eshleman & T. Grossi (Eds), *Behavior Analysis in Education: Focus on Measurably Superior Instruction* (pp. 214–225). Pacific Grove, CA: Brooks/Cole.
Grossman, H. J. (1973). *Manual on terminology and classification in mental retardation.* Washington, D.C.: American Association on Mental Deficiency.
Grossman, H. J. (1983). *Classification in mental retardation: 1983 revision.* Washington, D.C.: American Association on Mental Deficieny.
Harry, B. (1992). *Cultural diversity, families, and the special education system: Communication for empowerment.* New York: Teachers College Press.
Harry, B. (1994). *The disproportionate representation of minority students in special education: Theories and recommendations.* Washington, D.C.: National Association of State Directors of Special Education.
Harvard University Civil Rights Project Conference on Minority Issues in Special Education (2000). Paper: www.law.harvard.edu/civilrights
Hebbeler, K., & Wagner, M. (2001). *Representation of minorities and children of poverty among those receiving early intervention and special education services: Findings from two national longitudinal studies.* Menlo Park, CA: Stanford Research Institute.
Heber, R. (1959). A manual on terminology and classification in mental retardation. *American Journal on Mental Deficiency, 62*(Monograph Supplement).
Heber, R. (1961). Modifications in the manual on terminology and classification in mental retardation. *American Journal of Mental Deficiency, 65,* 499–500.
Heller, K. A., Holtzman, W., & Messick, S. (1982). *Placing children in special education: A strategy for equity.* Washington, D.C.: National Academy Press.
Henley, M., Ramsey, R. S., & Algozzine, R. (1993). *Characteristics and strategies for teaching students with mild disabilities.* Boston: Allyn & Bacon.
Landesman-Ramey, S., Dossett, E., & Echols, K. (1996). The social ecology of mental retardation. In: J. W. Jacobson & J. A. Mulick (Eds), *Manual of Diagnosis and Professional Practice in Mental Retardation* (pp. 55–65). Washington, D.C.: American Psychological Association.
Langone, J. (1996). Mild mental retardation. In: P. J. McLaughlin & P. Wehman (Eds), *Mental Retardation and Developmental Disabilities* (2nd ed., pp. 113–130). Austin, TX: Pro-Ed.
Langone, J., Clees, T. J., Oxford, J., Malone, M., & Ross, G. (1995). Acquisition and generalization of social skills by high school students with mild mental retardation. *Mental Retardation, 33,* 186–196.
Levin, V. (1992). *Locus of control: Its relationship to gender, ethnicity, and at-risk students.* (ERIC Document Reproduction Service No. ED 360-605.)
Lipsky, D. K., & Gartner, A. (1997). *Inclusion and school reform: Transforming America's classrooms.* Baltimore, MD: Paul H. Brookes.

Luckasson, R., Coulter, D., Polloway, E., Reiss, S., Schalock, R., Snell, M., Spitalnick, D., & Stark, J. (1992). *Mental retardation: Definition, classification, and systems of support.* Washington, D.C.: American Association on Mental Retardation.

MacDonnell, L. M., McLaughlin, M. J., & Morison, P. (1997). *Educating one and all: Students with disabilities and standards-based reform.* Washington, D.C.: National Research Council.

MacMillan, D. L. (1982). *Mental retardation in school and society* (2nd ed.). Boston: Little, Brown.

MacMillan, D. L. (1989). Equality, excellence, and the mentally retarded population: 1970–1989. *Psychology in Mental Retardation and Developmental Disabilities, 15*(2), 1, 3–10.

MacMillan, D. L., & Speece, D. L. (1999). Utility of current diagnostic categories. In: R. Gallimore, L. P. Bernheimer, D. L. MacMillan, D. L. Speece, & S. Vaughn (Eds), *Developmental Perspectives on Children with High-Incidence Risabilities* (pp. 111–134). Mahwah, NJ: Lawrence Erlbaum.

MacMillan, D. L., & Hendrick, I. G. (1993). Evolution and legacies. In: J. I. Goodlad & T. C. Lovitt (Eds), *Integrating General and Special Education* (pp. 23–48). New York: MacMillan.

MacMillan, D. L., & Reschly, D. (1997). Issues of definition and classification. In: W. E. Maclean, Jr. (Ed.), *Ellis' Handbook of Mental Deficiency, Psychological Theory and Research* (3rd ed., pp. 47–74). Mahwah, NJ: Lawrence Erlbaum.

Mercer, J. (1992). The impact of changing paradigms of disability on mental retardation in the year 2000. In: L. Rowitz (Ed.), *Mental Retardation in the Year 2000* (pp. 15–38). New York: Springer-Verlag.

Mercer, C. D., & Snell, M. E. (1977). *Learning theory research in mental retardation. Implications for teaching.* New York: Merrill/MacMillan.

Meyer, G., & Patton, J. M. (2001). *On the Nexus of Race, Disability, and Overrepresentation: What Do We Know? Where Do We Go?* Washington, D.C.: Office of Special education Programs, U.S. Department of Education.

National Institute For Urban School Improvement (2001). *On the nexus of race, disability, and overrepresentation: What do we know? Where do we go?* Washington, D.C.: Office of Special education Programs, U.S. Department of Education.

National Research Council (2002). *Minority students in special and gifted education.* Washington, D.C.: National Academy Press.

Neal, L. I., McCray, A. D., & Webb-Johnson, G. (2001). Something in the way he moves: Teacher's perceptions of African American males' behavior and school achievement. AERA Conference Presentation, April 12, 2001.

Obiakor, F. E. (1999). Teacher expectations: Impact on "accuracy" of self-concepts of multicultural learners. In: F. E. Obiakor, J. O. Schwenn, & A. R. Rotatori (Eds), *Advances in Special Education* (Vol. 12, pp. 205–216). Stamford, CT: JAI Press.

Obiakor, F. E. (2001). *It even happens in "Good" schools: Responding to cultural diversity in today's classrooms.* Thousand Oaks, CA: Corwin Press.

Obiakor, F. E., Stile, S. W., & Muller, D. (1992). Self-concept in school programs: Conceptual and research foundations. In: F. E. Obiakor & S. W. Stile (Eds), *Self-concepts of Exceptional Learners: Current Perspectives for Educators* (pp. 1–17). Dubuque, IA: Kendall Hunt.

Oswald, D. P., & Coutinho, M. J. (2001). Trends in disproportionate representation: Implications for multicultural education. In: C. A. Utley & F. E. Obiakor (Eds), *Special Education, Multicultural Education and School Reform: Components for a Quality Education for Learners with Mild Disabilities* (pp. 53–73). Springfield, IL: Charles C. Thomas.

Oswald, D. P., Coutinho, M. J., Best, A. M., & Singh, N. N. (1999). Ethnic representation in special education: The influence of school-related economic and demographic variables. *The Journal of Special Education, 32,* 194–206.

Patterson, G. R., & Moore, D. (1979). Interactive patterns as units of behavior. In: S. J. Suomi, M. E. Lamb & G. R. Stephenson (Eds), *Social Interaction Analysis: Methodological Issues* (pp. 77–96). Madison, WI: University of Wisconsin Press.

Patton, J., Polloway, E., & Smith, T. E. C. (2000). Educating students with mild mental retardation. In: M. L. Wehmeyer & J. R. Patton (Eds), *Mental Retardation in the 21st Century* (pp. 71–89). Austin, TX: Pro-Ed.

Ramey, C., & Finkelstein, N. W. (1981). Psychosocial mental retardation: A biological and social coalescence. In: M. J. Begab, H. C. Haywood & H. L. Garber (Eds), *Psychosocial Influences in Retarded Performance: Issues and Theories in Development* (Vol. 1, pp. 65–92). Baltimore, MD: University Park Press.

Raymond, B. E. (2000). *Learners with mild disabilities: A characteristics approach.* Needham Heights, MA: Allyn & Bacon.

Reschly, D. J., & Ward, S. M. (1991). Uses of adaptive behavior measures and overrepresentation of Black students in programs for students with mild mental retardation. *American Journal on Mental Retardation, 96,* 257–268.

Rueda, R., & Simon, K. (2001). Cultural and linguistic diversity as a theoretical framework for understanding multicultural learners with mild disabilities. In: C. A. Utley & F. E. Obiakor (Eds), *Special Education, Multicultural Education, and School Reform: Components of Quality Education for Learners with Mild Disabilities* (pp. 74–89). Springfield, IL: Charles C. Thomas.

Sarason, S. B., & Doris, J. (1979). *Educational handicap, public policy, and social history.* New York: Free Press.

Scruggs, T. E., & Laufenberg, R. (1986). Transformational mneumonic strategies for retarded learners. *Education and Training of the Mentally Retarded, 21*(3), 165–173.

Shanker, A. (1990). Staff development and the restructured school. In: B. Joyce (Ed.), *Changing School Culture Through Staff Development* (pp. 101–115). Alexander, VA: Association for Supervision and Curriculum Development.

Smith, G. J., Edelen-Smith, P. J., & Strodden, R. A. (1998). Effective practice for generating outcomes of significance: The complexities of transformational change. In: A. Hilton & R. Ringlaben (Eds), *Best and Promising Practices in Developmental Disabilities* (pp. 331–342). Austin, TX: Pro-Ed.

Smith, J. D. (1998). Defining mental retardation: The natural history of a concept. In: A. Hilton & R. Ringlaben (Eds), *Best and Promising Practices in Developmental Disabilities* (pp. 15–21). Austin, TX: Pro-Ed.

Smith, J. D. (2001). Social construction of mental retardation: Impersonal histories and the hope for personal futures. In: M. L. Wehmeyer & J. R. Patton (Eds), *Mental Retardation in the 21st Century* (pp. 379–394). Austin, TX: Pro-Ed.

Stokes, T. F., & Baer, D. M. (1977). An implicit technology of generalization. *Journal of Applied Behavior Analysis, 10,* 349–367.

Stokes, T. F., & Osnes, P. G. (1989). An operant pursuit of generalization. *Journal of Learning Disabilities, 23,* 32–37.

Tarjan, G., Tizard, J., Rutter, M., Begab, M., Brooke, E. M., de al Cruz, F., Lin, T. Y., Montenegro, H., Strotzka, H., & Sartorius, N. (1972). Classification and mental retardation: Issues arising in the fifth WHO seminar on psychiatric diagnosis, classification, and statistics. *American Journal of Psychiatry, 128,* 34–35.

Tizard, J. (1972). A note on the international statistical classification of mental retardation. *American Journal of Psychiatry, 128,* 25–29.

Trent, J. W. (1994). *Inventing the feeble mind: A history of mental retardation in the United States.* Berkeley: University of California Press.

U.S. Department of Education (1998). *Twentieth annual report to Congress on the implementation of the Individuals with Disabilities Education Act.* Washington, D.C.: Author. (ERIC Document Reproduction Service No. ED 424-722.)

U.S. Department of Education, Office of Civil Rights (1992). *Elementary and secondary school civil rights compliance report.* Washington, D.C.: Author.

Utley, C. A., Hoehn, T. P., Soraci, S. A., & Baumeister, A. A. (1993). Motivational orientation and span of apprehension in children with mental retardation. *The Journal of Genetic Psychology, 154*(3), 289–295.

Utley, C. A., & Obiakor, F. E. (2001). *Special education, multicultural education and school reform: Components for a quality education for learners with mild disabilities.* Springfield, IL: Charles C. Thomas.

Valencia, R. R., & Suzuki, L. A. (2001). *Intelligence testing and minority students: Foundations, performance factors, and assessment issues.* Thousand Oaks, CA: Sage.

Weisz, J. R. (1990). Cultural-familial mental retardation: A developmental perspective on cognitive perspective and "helpless" behavior. In: R. M. Hodapp, J. A. Burack & E. Zigler (Eds), *Issues in the Developmental Approach to Mental Retardation* (pp. 137–159). New York: Cambridge University.

Ysseldyke, J. E., Algozzine, B., & Thurlow, M. L. (1992). *Critical Issues in Special Education* (2nd ed.). Boston: Houghton Mifflin.

Ysseldyke, J. E., Algozzine, B., & Thurlow, M. L. (2000). *Critical Issues in Special Education* (3rd ed.). Boston: Houghton Mifflin.

Zeaman, D., & House, B. J. (1963). The role of attention in retardate discrimination learning. In: N. R. Ellis (Ed.), *Handbook of Mental Deficiency* (pp. 159–223). New York: McGraw Hill.

Zeaman, D., & House, B. J. (1979). A review of attention theory. In: N. R. Ellis (Ed.), *Handbook of Mental Deficiency: Psychological Theory and Research* (2nd ed., pp. 31–51). Hillsdale, NJ: Erlbaum.

Zigler, E., & Balla, D. (1981). Issues in the personality and motivation in mentally retarded persons. In: M. Begab, H. C. Haywood & H. L. Garber (Eds), *Psychosocial Influences in Retarded Performance* (pp. 197–218). Baltimore, MD: University Park Press.

STUDENTS WITH LEARNING DISABILITIES

Katherine J. Mitchem and Ann Richards

Prior to the 1975 enactment of PL 94-142, later reauthorized as the Individuals with Disabilities Education Act (IDEA) (1997), many children with learning disabilities (LD) were unidentified, unrecognized, and included in the general education classroom. As both professionals and parents realized that the specific needs of this group of students were not being met in the general education classroom, various options, including resource rooms and self-contained rooms (Deno, 1970) were developed to meet these needs. Since this time, the number of students identified as LD has grown more rapidly than any other disability category. The most recent data available (1996–1997) indicate that 2,756,046 students are now identified as having a learning disability, an increase of 10% since 1994–1995 (U.S. Department of Education, 2000). Due to this trend, current educational reform efforts identify the need to include all students when setting educational standards.

The standards-based reform movement, currently being discussed throughout the nation, is a frame of thought based on improving education by first setting standards (Boundy, 2000). Standards delineate the essential knowledge that students should gain within their educational careers thereby shifting attention to actual results (Vohs, Landau & Romano, 2000). Strategies, services, and supports that assist students in reaching these standards are addressed while developing curriculum. Assessment is then based on both content, knowledge of a specific subject area, and performance, which describes how a student must perform to demonstrate achievement (Vohs, Landau & Romano, 2000). Linking students with LD to this standards-based reform movement, Congress amended

IDEA (1997) to emphasize that effective educational systems now and in the future must:

(a) maintain high academic standards and clear performance goals for children with disabilities, consistent with the standards and expectations for all students in the educational system, and provide for appropriate and effective strategies and methods to ensure that students who are children with disabilities have maximum opportunities to achieve those standards and goals;
(b) create a system that fully addresses the needs of all students, including children with disabilities by addressing the needs of children with disabilities in carrying out educational reform activities (Pub. L. No. 115-17, Section 671, p. 101).

With the increase in students being serviced by special education under the definition of LD and the public interest in the standards-based reform movement comes increased questioning concerning their education. Some of these questions include: (1) How are students classified as having LD under the current federal definition and is the current process the best one?; (2) Where do these students receive special education services and how has this changed over the past two decades?; (3) How does the assessment of a student's learning impact instructional objectives?; and (4) What does the research on effective education indicate is the most appropriate setting for service delivery for students with LD? In this section, we first provide the IDEA's definition of LD, describe the classification process for students with LD, and how assessment is related to this. We then address the continuum of placements typically available to students with LD and trends in the placement of these students over the past two decades. Next we review the research on effective instruction and effective practices for students with LD. Finally, we discuss the implications of this review for research and practice.

CLASSIFICATION

IDEA (1997) defines a learning disability as:

> a disorder in one or more of the basic psychological processes involved in understanding or using language, spoken or written, which disorder may manifest itself in imperfect ability to listen, speak, read, write, spell, or do mathematical calculations. Such term includes conditions such as perceptual disabilities, brain injury, minimal brain dysfunction, dyslexia, and developmental aphasia. Such term does not include a learning problem that is primarily the result of visual, hearing, or motor disabilities, of mental retardation, of emotional disturbance, or of environmental, cultural, or economic disadvantage (Pub. L. No. 105-17, Section 26, p. 13).

This definition is based on Kirk and Bateman's (1962–1963) work in which they identified a need to focus on describing students' learning behaviors rather than etiological concerns when diagnosing a student with LD. Today, for students to receive services under an LD classification they need to have obtained a discrepancy between their aptitude and achievement scores on standardized tests (Bocian, Beebe, MacMillan & Greshman, 1999; Fletcher, Francis, Shaywitz, Lyon, Foorman, Stuebing & Shaywitz, 1998; Johnson, 1988; MacMillan, Greshman & Bocian, 1998; Mercer, Jordan, Allsopp & Mercer, 1996). The use of a discrepancy formula in the diagnosing of students with LD is also based on the work of Kirk and Bateman. This was operationalized when the United States Office of Education (1977) published the procedures for evaluating LD in the Federal Register as:

> A severe discrepancy between achievement and intellectual ability in one or more of the areas: (1) oral expression; (2) listening comprehension; (3) written expression; (4) basic reading skill; (5) reading comprehension; (6) mathematics calculation; or (7) mathematic reasoning. The child may not be identified as having a learning disability if the discrepancy between ability and achievement is primarily the result of: (1) a visual, hearing, or motor handicap; (2) mental retardation; (3) emotional disturbance; or (4) environmental, cultural, or economic disadvantage (p. G1083).

Twenty-four years later, 98% of the states still incorporate discrepancy in either their definition of LD or in criteria outlined in identifying students with LD (Bocian et al., 1999; Fletcher et al., 1998; Mercer et al., 1996).

Traditionally, the procedure for classifying a student as LD begins when teachers identify that a student is not achieving the same academic progress as others in the classroom. Once it is established that the student is still not making progress after educational interventions, school personnel administer psychological and academic standardized tests. The scores obtained from these tests, as well as information gathered from school personnel, are then used against state guidelines for classification of students with an LD label. MacMillan et al. (1998) found that 50% of students referred for learning disabilities were classified; however, had State guidelines concerning discrepancy been followed, only 30% of students would have been. This finding is supported by other researchers (Lyon, 1996; MacMillan et al., 1998; Shaywitz, Shaywitz, Fletcher & Escobar, 1990; Shepard, Smith & Vojir, 1983) who have found that a large proportion of students identified as LD fail to meet eligibility criteria. This is further impacted by the growing body of research that questions the use of discrepancy formulas when classifying students with LD.

Researchers do not discount that a discrepancy model can identify and be a valid means of determining students with LD but are suspect of the model's ability to differentiate between students with LD and students who are low achievers rendering many students ineligible for educational support (Bocian et al., 1999; Fletcher et al., 1998; Fletcher, Shaywitz, Shankweiler, Katz, Lieberman, Fowler, Francis, Stuebing & Shaywitz, 1994; Foorman, Francis, Fletcher & Lynn, 1996; Francis, Fletcher, Shaywitz, Shaywitz & Rourke, 1996; Fuchs & Fuchs, 1998; MacMillan et al., 1998; Stanovich & Siegel, 1994). Kirk (1993) contended that the earlier an intervention begins, the greater the likelihood of effectiveness. By solely using a discrepancy formula, schools are forced to identify students in their later elementary years, thus preventing their access to educational interventions at an early age (Fletcher et al., 1998). To combat this dilemma, MacMillan et al. found that school districts disregarded psychometric profiles when classifying students as LD and instead looked at a student's achievement in academic areas. This finding implies that assessments based on general education objectives would eliminate the fundamental and ethical gaps now evident within classification processes.

In response to the debate over discrepancy formulas, several researchers have advocated for treatment validity approaches such as curriculum-based measurement (CBM) or performance-based assessment to be used in the classification process of students with LD (Bocian et al., 1999; Elloit, 1998; Fletcher et al., 1998; Fuchs & Fuchs, 1998; Johnson, 2000; MacMillan et al., 1998; Morgan, Singer-Harris, Berstein & Waber, 2000; Reschly & Grimes, 1995; Shinn, 1995). This is supported by Fletcher and his colleagues in their finding that scores or performance on academic achievement measures were a better predictor of students with LD than IQ tests. The proponents of treatment validity approaches also recognize that when assessment is tied to classroom curriculum the word classification becomes obsolete and assessment is the basis for decisions regarding placement, instructional goals, and service delivery.

ASSESSMENT

Elliot (1998) stated, "that the central purposes of most educational assessments are to guide instruction and to facilitate communication among primary educational stakeholders-teachers, students, parents-about valued education accomplishments" (p. 235). States have been using large-scale assessments as the basis for this transformation of curriculum in conjunction with the standards-based reform movement (Johnson, 2000). In the past, students with LD have been left out of these large-scale assessments which resulted in "students with disabilities being excluded from the curriculum or from reform initiatives designed to improve student performance" (Yssedyke, Thurlow, Kozleski & Reschly, 1998, p. 7). With new requirements under IDEA 1997, students with disabilities now must be included in general state and district-wide assessments, with appropriate accommodations where necessary (Yssedyke et al., 1998).

Johnson (2000) conducted a study in which she looked at the effects of reading mathematics questions on a state-wide assessment to students with and without LD. She found that there was no significant difference in test scores between students with and without LD when the test was read. Her findings are consistent with a similar study conducted by Tindal, Heath, Hollenbeck, Almond & Harniss (1998) in which they also found no significant effects for reading math items to students with and without LD. In addition, Johnson noted that even when students with LD received the accommodation of a reader, their average mathematics scores were still below the state standard. This implies that even when students with LD are afforded accommodations on standardized tests, their progress may not be accurately assessed. Current stakeholders within the standards-based reform movement recognize the weaknesses of standardized testing and are investigating assessment instruments that will connect instructional curriculum to real-world tasks (Elliott, 1998).

With the cost of per pupil expenditures for students with special education being 2.3 times that of general education students (Parrish, 1995), constituencies are looking for systematic assessment processes that yield information on how to enhance the overall quality of an instructional program for students with LD (Fuchs & Fuchs, 1998). Fuchs and Fuchs viewed a treatment validity approach as being able to accomplish this goal because it is based on: (a) assessing whether a student is making progress within the general classroom environment; (b) comparing students' performance progress in relation to each other; (c) assessing whether individual students achieve better academic growth if adaptations are made within the general education setting; and (d) assessing if special education services are effective for individual students. CBM accomplishes these goals by delineating the academic competence and progress of individual students. It is important to note that CBM was developed by Deno (1985) to establish an assessment system to be used efficiently within a classroom setting so that data could be gathered that had the capacity to drive educational practices for both individual and group instruction. Fuchs and Fuchs (1998), Fuchs, Fuchs and Hamlett (1994), Fuchs, Fuchs, Hamlett and Allinder (1989), Fuchs, Fuchs, Hamlett, Thompson, Roberts, Kubec and Stecker (1994) found that CBM produced reliable and valid data used in describing student performance. These researchers also found that by embedding assessment into local curriculum, teachers were able to transform the curriculum to individual students needs more readily. In the 1998 study conducted by Fuchses and associates, three of the 10 teachers studied positively influenced the educational growth of students identified as LD. By using CBM to assess students' performances, teachers had the data to adapt or provide adaptations within general classroom instruction to address individual needs of the student.

Performance assessment provides another method to assist educational constituents in defining educational standards for all students while also allowing for the individual assessment of learning (Elliot, 1998). Performance assessment is defined as "testing methods that require students to create an answer or product that demonstrates their knowledge or skill" (U.S. Office of Technology Assessment, 1992). It has been described as an extension of CBM because it observes students' inquiries and responses to the general education curriculum through their permanent products (See Elliot, 1998). To develop curriculum that gives students opportunities to link instruction to producing permanent products, teachers must strive to link classroom objectives to authentic tasks. Many researchers (Choate & Evans, 1992; Coutinho & Malouf, 1992, Taylor, Tindal, Fuchs & Bryant, 1993) have supported the use of performance assessment because of its responsiveness to local settings and norms although there are no published reports on its use for classification or placement purposes (see Elliot, 1998). By combining the component of performance assessment with CBM, educators are able to track students' skill and knowledge development.

Although both CBM and performance assessment, unlike standard psychometric measures; (a) require students to construct knowledge rather than just respond to a question; (b) include the ability to observe the child's behaviors while constructing knowledge; and (c) illustrate the student's thought processes (Elliot, 1998), they are still not all encompassing. For a group of students the transformation of general education as a result of these assessments is not enough to achieve academic gains. The lack of student responsiveness to adapted general education supports the need for various placement options for students with learning disabilities. To classify a student as LD using performance assessment or CBM, school personnel must first assess how a student is performing in comparison to his/her peers. Once this is done, teachers must then assess and develop an approach that maximizes the student's performance in a general education setting or provide evidence that a special education placement is more appropriate.

PLACEMENT

One of the most controversial and hotly debated issues currently facing special educators is the extent to which students with LD should be included in general education classrooms (Baker & Zigmond, 1995; Fuchs & Fuchs, 1994; McCleskey & Waldron, 1995; Roberts & Mather, 1995; Stainback & Stainback, 1992). Inclusion refers to the placement of children with disabilities into regular or general education classes for instruction, with appropriate supports (Lerner, 2000). Proponents of full inclusion (e.g. Lipsky & Gartner, 1991) aimed to develop a restructured and unified system of general and special education (Skrtic, 1991) in which the inclusive school is viewed as a setting devoid of special education with all students included in age-appropriate classrooms. Although research on the effectiveness of inclusive practices for students with learning disabilities is mixed, the debate on inclusion essentially reflects two perspectives (see Lerner, 2000). Some advocates contend that children with disabilities have a right to participate in environments as close to normal as possible and to benefit socially and academically from being in the mainstream of society and school (McCleskey & Waldron, 1995; Stainback & Stainback, 1992). Others argue that the nature of problems encountered by students with learning disabilities requires individual, intensive, and explicit instruction that cannot be easily provided in the general education classroom (Fuchs & Fuchs, 1994; Kauffman & Hallahan, 1995; Zigmond & Baker, 1997).

Schools are to ensure that a continuum of alternative placements is available to meet the varied needs of students with disabilities. Placement settings for students with disabilities as defined in Reports to Congress (U.S. Department of Education, 2000) include *Regular Education Class* – students who receive special education and related services outside of the general education classroom for less than 21% of the school day; *Resource Room* – students who receive special education and related services outside the general education classroom from 21% to 60% of the school day; *Separate Class* – students who receive special education and related services outside of the general education classroom for more than 60% of the school day; *Separate School* – students who receive special education and related services in separate day schools (more than 50% of the school day), residential facilities (more than 50% of the school day), or homebound/hospital environments. The Reports to Congress do not include a placement setting for students with disabilities who are included in general education classroom for 100% of the school day; therefore, even students who are classified as being educated in general education may spend up to 20% of the day in separate, special education classrooms. This cascade of services model became part of the regulations governing the IDEA and for 20 years has guided the educational placement of students with disabilities across the country (Fuchs, Roberts, Fuchs & Bowers, 1996). Somewhat troubling to both advocates and critics of this model is this fact that "once a student is placed in separate special education program, that program too often becomes a terminal assignment" (Fuchs et al., 1996, p. 214). Clearly, this does not speak well for services these students are provided, nor does it bode well for the notion of students with disabilities accessing services, to the extent appropriate, in the least restrictive environment (LRE).

Placement trends for students with learning disabilities have changed over the past two decades. McCleskey and Pacchiano (1994) found that between 1979 and 1989, the trend was to educate students with learning disabilities in more rather than less restrictive settings. More specifically, they found that the proportion of students with learning disabilities who were being educated in restrictive, separate class settings almost doubled between 1979 and 1989, while much of the increase that occurred during this time in placements in less restrictive settings was probably due to increasing identification rates for students with learning disabilities. McCleskey, Henry and Axelrod (1999) sought to update the previous study by examining data from Reports to Congress to identify placement practices for students with LD from 1989 to 1995. Findings suggest a reversal of previous trends noted by McCleskey and Pacchiano (1994) such that the number of students with LD who were educated in general education classrooms for 80% or more of the school day increased by 151% from 1988–1989 to 1994–1995, reflecting a gain of almost 614,000 students. McCleskey and colleagues (1999) pointed out that this increase was no doubt influenced by the considerable increase in the number of students identified with LD over the past 6 years (approximately 509,000 students) as well as the movement of students from resource rooms into general education classrooms. During the same time frame, students educated in resource rooms and separated school settings decreased 18% and 31% respectively, while the percentage of students with LD placed in separate classes increased slightly (McCleskey et al., 1999).

Although there are variations across states in the restrictiveness of placement for students with disabilities, overall data on placement trends for general education classrooms and separate school settings illustrate that students with LD are being educated in less restrictive settings across the U.S. The most recent data available (U.S. Department of Education, 2000) suggest that this trend toward general education placement continues with over 43% of students (1,146,168) identified as learning disabled now served in regular education settings at least part of the school day. That large numbers of students with learning disabilities are now being served in general education settings clearly has implications for inservice and preservice preparation of general and special education teachers. Attempts to address this restructuring of services are further complicated by the recent emphasis on accountability influenced by education reform. State boards of education and local school districts are setting high academic standards for all students, including students with learning disabilities. The 1997 reauthorization of Individuals with Disabilities Education Act ensures the involvement of both general and special education teachers in the development of individualized education programs (IEPs) to address the skills needed by students with learning disabilities so that they can access the general education curriculum and participate in state wide and district-wide assessments.

In light of what is known about effective education for students with learning disabilities, some interesting questions seem to surface. What are the likely implications of this for restructuring general and special education? What challenges will a unified system of education present for students with learning disabilities, general education teachers, special education teachers, teacher educators, and staff developers? How might these challenges be constructively addressed? The next section of this chapter reviews the research on effective instruction and effective practices for students with learning disabilities, especially with regard to those practices that can be and are implemented in the general education classroom. We discuss these findings in the context of what we know about why teachers choose and continue to use interventions and explore the implications for research, practice, and professional development.

EFFECTIVE INSTRUCTION

Recent reviews of the literature and meta-analyses of intervention research indicate great strides have been made in developing powerful, effective interventions for students with learning disabilities (Gersten, 1998; Swanson, 1999; Swanson, in press). Vaughn, Gersten and Chard (2000) distilled from the large number of recent intervention research syntheses of LD some common principles of best practices for this population. They concluded that effective instructional approaches consist of both visible and explicit components. Those instructional practices that are effective for students with LD include procedural facilitators and strategies to help students develop a plan of action. In addition, interactive groups/partners, and interactive dialogue between students and teachers or between students and proficient peers is critical for effective interventions in reading and writing. Variables that appear to influence learning outcomes include motivation to learn, task difficulty, and task persistence. Vaughn et al. also identified practices that are beneficial for all learners such as reciprocal teaching and its offspring, classwide peer tutoring, peer assisted learning strategies, and content enhancement. Of most significance are findings supporting the use of these effective instructional approaches with all students.

There clearly exists a data base of empirically validated interventions effective at improving performance outcomes of students with and without LD. For example, in order to address increasing diversity within the classroom, researchers have developed and investigated a variety of practices using peers to mediate instruction that capitalize and depend on diversity within the classroom. Such strategies include research by the Juniper Gardens Children's Project on ClassWide Peer Tutoring (CWPT) (e.g. Greenwood, Delquadri & Hall, 1989), works on Peer Assisted Learning Strategies (PALS) (e.g. Fuchs, Fuchs, Mathes & Simmons, 1997), classwide peer assisted self-management strategies (e.g. Mitchem & Wells, 2002; Mitchem, Young, West & Benyo, 2001; Mitchem & Young, 2001); and small grouping practices including cooperative learning strategies (e.g. Stevens, Madden, Slavin & Farnish, 1987). Unfortunately, there is also sobering evidence that general education teachers consider themselves neither prepared nor responsible for implementing instructional adaptations to meet the needs of students with LD (Baker & Zigmond, 1990; McIntosh, Vaughn, Schumm, Haager & Lee, 1993; Schumm, Vaughn, Gordon & Rothlein, 1994; Semmel, Abernathy, Butera & Lesar, 1991; Vaughn & Schumm, 1995; Vaughn, Schumm, Jallad, Slusher & Saumell, 1996). For instance, Baker and Zigmond found that routine adaptations by teachers, such as variations in goals, materials, and grouping practices, were seldom seen. McIntosh et al. found that students with disabilities had lower rates of interaction with teachers and peers and that their instruction was undifferentiated and few adaptations were provided. Even those teachers who endorse such efforts in principle have been shown to make only the most minimal instructional accommodations. For example, in a series of studies, Vaughn and Schumm (1996) found that the most feasible accommodations were those that required limited instructional or curricular alterations. In general, teachers were reluctant to alter content and felt that a student with LD should be expected to cover the same content and complete the same assignments as other students in the class (Schumm & Vaughn, 1992).

EDUCATIONAL AND SERVICE DELIVERY ALTERNATIVES

Baker and Zigmond (1995) provided an integrative review of five case studies in which co-teaching was the primary model of service delivery. They noted that there was little assessment of individual students with which to monitor their progress through the curriculum and that the instruction provided in the co-taught classroom most often reflected the instruction provided to other students with the addition of an extra teacher, smaller groups, or peer tutoring. They also commented that "concern for the individual was replaced by concern for the group... No one seemed concerned about individual achievement, individual progress, individual learning" (p. 171). Weiss and Brigham (2000), in their review of the literature on co-teaching, identified three studies that examined the actual behavior of teachers in co-taught classrooms and found that this varied widely. One study (Boudah, Schumaker & Deshler, 1997) examined the effects of training in collaboration on the behavior of teachers in co-teaching. Although the results suggested that with proper support, teachers could dramatically increase the amount of instructional time and support provided to students with disabilities, the impact on student outcomes was disappointing. Students with disabilities obtained lower scores on classroom tests and quizzes under enhanced instructional conditions in co-taught classes (as cited in Weiss & Brigham, 2000).

The above issue is highlighted in Deshler's (1998) tribute to Samuel Kirk, where he noted that some of the current trends in service delivery for students with LD bring forth two areas of possible concern: (a) failure to differentiate between inclusion and inclusive teaching; and (b) collaborative and coteaching efforts that focus more on process than student outcomes. The first concern refers to Baker and Zigmond's (1995) findings that merely placing students with LD

> in the general education classroom (inclusion) is no guarantee that the unique needs of these children will be understood and incorporated into the instructional plan. To the contrary, their (Baker & Zigmond, 1995) data clearly indicate that children with LD who are placed in the general education classroom often fail to receive intensive, individualized instruction that enables them to benefit from the curriculum content being covered as well as to master the skills and strategies that they are lacking (inclusive teaching) (Deshler, 1998, p. 33).

Deshler's point is well made and important to consider in the assessment of what constitutes effective education for students with learning disabilities. Even in the first grade, academic abilities in typical classrooms range across several grade levels (Mathes, 1998, as cited in Mathes, Grek, Howard, Babyak & Allen, 1999). This diversity creates challenges for teachers to meet the unique needs of individual students and makes it difficult for teachers to provide adequate instructional intensity for all learners (Vaughn & Schumm, 1995).

In communicating advances made toward educating students with learning disabilities by general education teachers, there is the need to remember that LRE is not a particular setting. Although LRE for some students with disabilities may be the general education classroom, it is not required or desirable in all cases (Abeson, Burgdorf, Casey, Kunz & McNeil, 1975 as cited in Kavale & Forness, 2000). Evidence suggests that there are limitations to the effectiveness of inclusive service delivery for all students with learning disabilities. Fuchs and Fuchs (1998) reported that their interventions were less effective for students with learning disabilities than for other students in the classroom (Fuchs, Fuchs

& Burish, 2000). Klingner, Vaughn, Hughes, Schumm and Elbaum (1998) reported that the lowest readers benefited the least from the relatively intensive inclusive model that they investigated. Mastropieri and Scruggs (1998) reported that the magnitude of learning effects for mnemonic instruction was smaller for classroom implementation than for earlier experimental interventions.

In grappling with questions related to how students with learning disabilities should be served in a unified system of education, it is important to remember that the setting is just one part of placement. Kavale and Forness (2000) described an earlier meta-analysis that synthesized findings from 50 of the best efficacy studies that had been used to demonstrate the lack of effectiveness of a separate special education. They found that placement per se had only a modest influence on outcomes and that there were differential positive effects in favor of special class placement for those students with learning and behavior problems vs. a slight negative effect for those with mild mental retardation. They noted that the place where students with disabilities resided was not a critical factor, suggesting the need for an examination of what goes on instructionally and socially in those placements. The most recent research syntheses on intervention research for students with learning disabilities (Elbaum, Vaughn, Hughes, Moody & Schumm, 2000; Gersten, 1998; Mastropieri & Scruggs, 1997; Swanson, 1999; Swanson, in press; Swanson & Hoskyn, 1998; Swanson, Hoskyn & Lee, 1999) indicate that what occurs within the setting or placement is of far more significance to the outcomes of students with LD than the placement itself.

IMPLICATIONS AND CONCLUSIONS

In chapter one of this book, Obiakor describes the possibilities of his dream educational program (i.e. a program that can help student to maximize their fullest potential). Attention now turns to how we might make these possibilities a reality. The issue of how this might be accomplished has become even more urgent given the current emphases on accountability and high stakes assessment in which all students, with and without disabilities, must demonstrate evidence of serious engagement with the general curriculum (Gersten, 1998). These considerations highlight the pressing need to find effective means for translating research into practice and incorporating validated special education practices into general education instructional activities (Mitchem & Wells, 2000; Mitchem & Young, 2001; Stone, 1998). Gersten (1998) attested to this crucial need to share advances made with those in general education (e.g. teachers, counselors, and administrators) so that they develop a sense of the logic behind special education services and adaptations.

Effective education for students with LD appears to involve the strategic integration of research-based practices in assessment, instructional design, and instruction tailored to the unique needs of the student and situated in the context of the school. Throughout this chapter, three related themes have emerged: first, the continuing challenge facing the field regarding teachers' adoption and sustained use of research-validated practices; second, the ongoing perception of teachers concerning preparation for and ability to meet the needs of students with LD in the general education classroom; and third, the small, but significant, percentage of students that continues to make inadequate progress even when research-validated practices are implemented. If we are to provide effective education for students with LD within a unified system of education, we must address these and other issues.

Teachers' infrequent use of validated instructional practices is a clear example of the research-to-practice gap. Interestingly, Fuchs and Fuchs (1998) contended that the main reason why this occurs "is because of an inadequate *demand* (italics in original). To create demand, the following must be in place: reasonably high standards for student performance; a valid means for measuring student progress; and appropriate consequences for schools, teachers, and students meeting and failing to meet them" (p. 136). If this is so, then the focus on standards based reform, assessment, and accountability means that many of these contingencies must now be in place. Fuchs and Fuchs also indicated that there must be meaningful professional development and site-based decision making to facilitate and support widespread use of validated practices. Effective education for students with learning disabilities requires that students receive individualized and intensive, needs-based instruction. In a similar fashion, teachers must receive the administrative, technical, and financial support necessary to implement this type of intensive instruction. In fact, we hypothesize that identifying and providing the supports that teachers need to be willing and able to implement research-validated practices may provide the mechanism through which one outcome may be students' improved performance (see Mitchem & Wells, 2000).

Related to the above point is the perception of many teachers that they are unprepared and unable to meet the needs of students with disabilities in the general education classroom. It has become evident that inservice and preservice preparation of teachers for inclusive practices is sporadic at best. Sindelar, Brownell and Rennells (1997) reviewed current efforts in teacher education reform to support the development of inclusive programs for students with learning and behavioral disorders. They found that innovation at the preservice level was not widespread and the need to assist practicing teachers in the development of inclusive practices was largely unmet. Further, they indicated that institutional change would be necessary to support teachers as they adopt new practices and to provide beginning teachers an environment in which they might establish themselves professionally. In describing teachers' reluctance to embrace educational innovations, Stone (1998) drew an analogy with research on strategy training with students and noted that those who received strategy training did not use those strategies "in new situations, or in the same situations in the future, unless the instructor helped them to attribute their greater success to the strategy and helped them predict when the strategy would and would not be useful" (p. 124). The same may be true when educators begin using instructional innovations. We agree with Gersten, Chard and Baker's (2000) recommendations for training to ensure sustainability, realistic expectations, opportunities for teachers to understand and think through an approach, systems to enhance teacher efficacy such as peer networks and support, sufficient administrative support, and explicit links between change and student data.

Teaching cannot be separated from the context in which it takes place (Kame'enui, Simmons & Coyne, 2000). Although many students with LD benefit from research-based instruction, not all special instructional activities can be successfully adapted for the general education classroom. Carroll (1963, 1989) and Mosenthal (1984) contended that there are multiple considerations and influences that need to be investigated when analyzing teaching and learning practices. Often educators only consider the learner with disregard for the learning, teaching, and schooling process. Repeated findings indicate the need to continue providing a continuum of services (Baker & Zigmond, 1995; Fuchs et al., 2000; Klingner et al., 1998; Mathes et al., 1999). Future research needs to investigate systematically which types of students can have their needs met successfully with appropriately modified mainstream instruction and which students will need more specialized support in separate settings.

REFERENCES

Abeson, A., Burgdorf, R. L., Casey, P. J., Kunz, J. W., & McNeil, W. (1975). Access to opportunity. In: J. N. Hobbs (Ed.), *Issues in the Classification of Children* (Vol. 2, pp. 270–292). San Francisco: Jossey-Bass.

Baker, J. M., & Zigmond, N. (1990). Are regular education classes equipped to accommodate students with learning disabilities? *Exceptional Children, 56*, 515–526.

Baker, J. M., & Zigmond, N. (1995). The meaning and practice of inclusion for students with learning disabilities: Themes and implications from five cases. *Journal of Special Education, 29*(2), 163–180.

Bocian, K. M., Beebe, M. E., MacMillan, D. L., & Greshman, F. M. (1999). Competing paradigms in learning disabilities classification by schools and the variations in meaning of discrepant achievement. *Learning Disabilities Research & Practice, 14*(1), 1–14.

Boudah, D. J., Schumaker, J. B., & Deshler, D. D. (1997). Collaborative instruction: Is it an effective option for inclusion in secondary classrooms? *Learning Disability Quarterly, 20*, 293–316.
Boundy, K. B. (2000). *Opportunity to learn and education reform: Ensuring access to effective education for all students.* Boston: Center for Law and Education. www.fcsn.org/peer/ess/opportunityfs.html
Carroll, J. B. (1963). A model of school learning. *Teachers College Record, 64*, 723–733.
Carroll, J. B. (1989). The Carroll model: A 25-year retrospective and prospective view. *Educational Researcher, 18*, 26–31.
Choate, J. S., & Evans, S. S. (1992). Authentic assessment of special learners: Problem or promise? *Preventing School Failure, 37*, 6–9.
Coutinho, M., & Malouf, D. (1992). *Performance assessment and children with disabilities: Issues and possibilities* (November). Washington, D.C.: Division of Innovation and Development, U.S. Department of Education.
Deno, E. (1970). Special education as developmental capital. *Exceptional Children, 37*, 229–237.
Deno, S. L. (1985). Curriculum-based measurement: The emerging alternative. *Exceptional Children, 19*, 219–232.
Deshler, D. D. (1998). Grounding interventions for students with learning disabilities in "powerful ideas." *Learning Disabilities Research & Practice, 13*(1), 29–34.
Elbaum, B., Vaughn, S., Hughes, M., Moody, S. W., & Schumm, J. S. (2000). How reading outcomes of students with disabilities are related to instructional grouping formats: A meta-analytic review. In: R. Gersten, E. Schiller & S. Vaughn (Eds), *Contemporary Special Education Research* (pp. 105–135). Mahwah, NJ: Lawrence Erlbaum Associates.
Elliot, S. N. (1998). Performance assessment of student's achievement: Research and practice. *Learning Disabilities Research & Practice, 13*, 233–241.
Fletcher, J. M., Francis, D. J., Shaywitz, S. E., Lyon, G. R., Foorman, B. R., Stuebing, K. K., & Shaywitz, B. A. (1998). Intelligent testing and the discrepancy model for children with learning disabilities. *Learning Disabilities Research & Practice, 13*, 186–203.
Fletcher, J. M., Shaywitz, S. E., Shankweiler, D. P., Katz, L., Liberman, I. Y., Fowler, A., Francis, D. J., Stuebing, K. K., & Shaywitz, B. A. (1994). Cognitive profiles of reading disability: Comparisons of discrepancy and low achievement definitions. *Journal of Educational Psychology, 86*, 1–18.
Foorman, B. R., Francis, D. J., Fletcher, J. M., & Lynn, A. (1996). Relation of phonological and orthographic processing to early reading: Comparing two approaches to regression-based, reading-level-match designs. *Journal of Educational Psychology, 88*, 639–652.
Francis, D. J., Fletcher, J. M., Shaywitz, B. A., Shaywitz, S. E., & Rourke, B. (1996). Defining learning and language disabilities: Conceptual and psychometric issues with the use of IQ tests. *Language, Speech, and Hearing Services in Schools, 27*, 132–143.
Fuchs, D., & Fuchs, L. S. (1994). Sometimes separate is better. *Educational Leadership, 52*(4), 22–26.
Fuchs, D., & Fuchs, L. S. (1998). Researchers and teachers working together to adapt instruction for diverse learners. *Learning Disabilities Research & Practice, 13*, 126–137.
Fuchs, D., Fuchs, L. S., & Burish, P. (2000). Peer-assisted learning strategies: An evidence-based practice to promote reading achievement. *Learning Disabilities Research & Practice, 15*, 85–91.
Fuchs, L. S., Fuchs, D., & Hamlett, C. L. (1994). Strengthening the connection between assessment and instructional planning with expert systems. *Exceptional Children, 61*, 138–146.
Fuchs, L. S., Fuchs, D., Hamlett, C. L., & Allinder, R. M. (1989). The reliability and validity of skill analysis within curriculum-based measurement. *Diagnostique, 14*, 203–221.

Fuchs, L. S., Fuchs, D., & Hamlett, C. L., Thompson, A., Roberts, P. H., Kubec, P., & Stecker, P. M. (1994). Technical features of a mathematics concepts and applications curriculum-based measurement system. *Diagnostique, 19*(4), 23–49.

Fuchs, D., Fuchs, L. S., Mathes, P. G., & Simmons, D. C. (1997). Peer-assisted learning strategies: Making classrooms more responsive to diversity. *American Educational Research Journal, 34,* 174–206.

Fuchs, D., Roberts, P. H., Fuchs, L. S., & Bowers, J. (1996). Reintegrating students with learning disabilities into the mainstream: A two-year study. *Learning Disabilities Research & Practice, 11,* 214–229.

Gersten, R. (1998). Recent advances in instructional research for students with learning disabilities: An overview. *Learning Disabilities Research & Practice, 13,* 162–170.

Gersten, R., Chard, D., & Baker, S. (2000). Factors enhancing sustained use of research-based instructional practices. *Journal of Learning Disabilities, 33,* 445–457.

Greenwood, C. R., Delquadri, J. C., & Hall, R. V. (1989). Longitudinal effects of classwide peer tutoring. *Journal of Educational Psychology, 81,* 371–383.

Individual with Disabilities Education Act, Pub. L. No. 105-17, 111 Stat (1997).

Johnson, D. J. (1988). Review of the research in specific reading, writing, and mathematics disorders. In: J. F. Kaveanagh & T. J. Truss, Jr. (Eds), *Learning Disabilities: Proceedings of the National Conference* (pp. 79–103). Parkton, MD: York Press.

Johnson, E. S. (2000). The effects of accommodations on performance assessment. *Remedial and Special Education, 21,* 261–267.

Kame'enui, E. J., Simmons, D. C., & Coyne, M. D. (2000). Schools as host environments: Toward a schoolwide reading improvement model. *Annals of Dyslexia, 50,* 33–51.

Kauffman, J. M., & Hallahan, D. P. (Eds) (1995). *The illusion of full inclusion: A comprehensive critique of a current special education bandwagon.* Austin, TX : Pro-ED.

Kavale, K. A., & Forness, S. R. (2000). The great divide in special education: Inclusion, ideology, and research. In: T. E. Scruggs & M. Mastropieri (Eds), *Advances in Learning and Behavioral Disabilities* (pp. 179–215). Greenwich, CT: JAI Press.

Kirk, S. A. (1993). Autobiographical remarks. In: G. A. Harris & W. D. Kirk (Eds), *The Foundations of Special Education: Selected Papers and Speeches of Samuel A. Kirk* (pp. 9–41). Reston, VA: Council for Exceptional Children.

Kirk, S. A., & Bateman, B. (1962–1963). Diagnosis and remediation of learning disabilities. *Exceptional Children, 29,* 73–87.

Klingner, J. K., Vaughn, S., Hughes, M. T., Schumm, J. S., & Elbaum, B. (1998). Outcomes for students with and without learning disabilities in inclusive classrooms. *Learning Disabilities Research & Practice, 13,* 153–161.

Lerner, J. W. (2000). *Learning Disabilities: Theories, Diagnosis, and Teaching Strategies* (8th ed.). Boston: Houghton-Mifflin.

Lipsky, D. K., & Gartner, A. (1991). Restructuring for quality. In: J. W. Lloyd, A. C. Repp & N. N. Singh (Eds), *The Regular Education Initiative: Alternative Perspectives on Concepts, Issues, and Models* (pp. 43–56). Sycamore, IL: Sycamore.

Lyon, G. R. (1996). Learning disabilities. *The Future of Children, 6*(Spring), 54–76.

MacMillan, D. L., Gresham, F. M., & Bocian, K. M. (1998). Discrepancy between definitions of learning disabilities and school practices: An empirical investigation. *Journal of Learning Disabilities, 31,* 314–327.

Mastropieri, M., & Scruggs, T. E. (1997). Best practices in promoting reading comprehension in students with learning disabilities. *Remedial and Special Education, 18,* 197–215.

Mastropieri, M., & Scruggs, T. E. (1998). Constructing more meaningful relationships in the classroom. Mnemonic research into practice. *Learning Disabilities Research & Practice, 13*, 138–148.

Mathes, P. G. (1998). Preventing Early Reading Failure by Enhancing Classroom Technologies – Project PERFECT (Unpublished raw data).

Mathes, P. G., Grek, M. L., Howard, J. K., Babyak, A. E., & Allen, S. H. (1999). Peer-assisted learning strategies for first-grade readers: A tool for preventing early reading failure. *Learning Disabilities Research & Practice, 14*, 50–60.

McCleskey, J., Henry, D., & Axelrod, M. I. (1999). Inclusion of students with learning disabilities: An examination of data from Reports to Congress. *Exceptional Children, 66*, 55–66.

McCleskey, J., & Waldron, N. (1995). Inclusive elementary programs: Must they cure students with learning disabilities to be effective? *Phi Delta Kappan, 77*, 300–303.

McCleskey, J., & Pacchiano, D. (1994). Mainstreaming students with learning disabilities: Are we making progress? *Exceptional Children, 60*, 508–517.

McIntosh, R., Vaughn, S., Schumm, S., Haager, D., & Lee, O. (1993). Observations of students with learning disabilities in general education classrooms. *Exceptional Children, 60*, 249–261.

Mercer, C. D., Jordan, L., Allsopp, D. H., & Mercer, A. R. (1996). Learning disabilities definitions and criteria used by state education departments. *Learning Disabilities Quarterly, 19*, 217–232.

Mitchem, K. J., & Wells, D. L. (2000). When does training in functional behavioral assessment lead to implementation? A prescription for institutionalizing best practice. Paper presented at the Annual National Conference of the Teacher Educators for Children with Behavioral Disorders (TECBD) (November), Scottsdale, AZ.

Mitchem, K. J., & Wells, D. L. (2002). A classwide peer assisted self-management program: Adaptations, implications, and a step-by-step guide for rural educators. *Rural Special Education Quarterly, 21*(2), 3–15.

Mitchem, K. J., & Young, K. R. (2001). Adapting self-management for classwide use: Acceptability, feasibility, and effectiveness. *Remedial and Special Education, 22*(2), 75–88.

Mitchem, K. J., Young, K. R., West, R. P., & Benyo, J. (2001). CWPASM: A classwide peer-assisted self-management program for general education classrooms. *Education and Treatment of Children, 24*(2), 111–140.

Morgan, A. E., Singer-Harris, N., Berstein, J. H., & Waber, D. P. (2000). Characteristics of children referred for evaluation of school difficulties who have adequate academic achievement scores. *Journal of Learning Disabilities, 33*, 489–500.

Mosenthal, P. (1984). The problem of partial specification in translating reading research into practice. *The Elementary School Journal, 85*, 199–227.

Office of Technology Assessment, U.S. Congress (1992). *Testing in American schools: Asking the right questions* (OTA-SET-519) (February). Washington, D.C.: U.S. Government Printing Office.

Parrish, T. B. (1995). *What is fair? Special education and finance equity*. Palo Alto, CA: American Institute for Research.

Reschly, D. J., & Grimes, J. P. (1995). Best practices in intellectual assessment. In: A. Thomas & J. Grimes (Eds), *Best Practices in School Psychology* (Vol. III, pp. 763–773). Washington, D.C.: National Association of School Psychologist.

Roberts, R., & Mather, N. (1995). The return of students with learning disabilities to regular classrooms: A sellout? *Learning Disabilities Research & Practice, 10*, 46–58.

Schumm, J. S., & Vaughn, S. (1992). Planning for mainstreamed special education students: Perceptions of general classroom teachers. *Exceptionality, 3*, 81–98.

Schumm, J. S., Vaughn, S., Gordon, J., & Rothlein, L. (1994). General education teachers' beliefs, skills, and practices in planning for mainstreamed students with learning disabilities. *Teacher Education and Special Education, 17*, 22–37.

Semmel, M. I., Abernathy, T. V., Butera, G., & Lesar, S. (1991). Teacher perceptions of the regular education initiative. *Exceptional Children, 58*, 9–25.

Shaywitz, S. E., Shaywitz, B. A., Fletcher, J. M., & Escobar, M. D. (1990). Irrelevance of reading disability in boys and girls: Results of the Connecticut longitudinal study. *Journal of the American Medical Association, 264*, 998–1002.

Shepard, L. A., Smith, M. L., & Vojir, C. P. (1983). Characteristics of pupils identified as learning disabled. *American Educational Research Journal, 20*, 309–331.

Shinn, M. R. (1995). Best practices in curriculum-based measurement and its use in a problem-solving model. In: A. Thomas & J. Grimes (Eds), *Best Practices in School Psychology* (Vol. III, pp. 547–567). Washington, D.C.: National Association of School Psychologist.

Skrtic, T. M. (1991). The special education paradox: Equity as the way to excellence. *Harvard Educational Review, 61*, 148–162.

Stainback, S., & Stainback, W. (1992). *Curriculum considerations in inclusive classrooms: Facilitating learning for all students*. Baltimore, MD: Brookes.

Stanovich, K. E., & Siegel, L. S. (1994). Phenotypic performance profiles of children with reading disabilities: A regression-based test of the phonological-core variable difference model. *Journal of Educational Psychology, 86*, 24–53.

Stevens, R. J., Madden, N. A., Slavin, R. E., & Farnish, A. M. (1987). Cooperative integrated reading and composition: Two field experiments. *Reading Research Quarterly, 22*, 433–454.

Stone, C. A. (1998). Moving validated instructional practices into the classroom: Learning from examples about the rough road to success. *Learning Disabilities Research & Practice, 13*(3), 121–125.

Swanson, H. L. (1999). *Interventions for students with learning disabilities: A meta-analysis of treatment outcomes*. New York: Guilford.

Swanson, H. L. (in press). Intervention research for adolescents with learning disabilities: A meta-analysis of outcomes related to high-order processing. *Elementary School Journal*.

Swanson, H. L., & Hoskyn, M. (1998). Experimental intervention research on students with learning disabilities: A meta-analysis of treatment outcomes. *Review of Educational Research, 68*, 277–321.

Swanson, H. L., Hoskyn, M., & Lee, C. (1999). *Interventions for students with learning disabilities: A meta-analysis of treatment outcomes*. New York: Guilford.

Taylor, R. L., Tindal, G. Fuchs, L., & Bryant, B. R. (1993). Assessment in the nineties: A possible glance into the future. *Diagnostique, 18*, 113–122.

Tindal, G., Heath, B., Hollenbeck, K., Almond, P., & Harniss, M. (1998). Accommodating students with disabilities on large-scale tests: An experimental study. *Exceptional Children, 64*, 439–450.

U.S. Department of Education, Office of Special Education Programs (2000). *To assure the free an appropriate public education of all children with disabilities: Twenty-second annual report to Congress on the implementation of the Individuals with Disabilities Education Act*. Washington, D.C.: Author.

U.S. Office of Education (1977). Assistance to states for education for handicapped children: Procedures for evaluating specific learning disabilities. *Federal Register, 42*, G1028–G1085.

Vaughn, S., Gersten, R., & Chard, D. (2000). The underlying message in LD intervention research: Findings from research syntheses. *Exceptional Children, 67*, 99–114.

Vaughn, S., & Schumm, J. S. (1995). Responsible inclusion for students with learning disabilities. *Journal of Learning Disabilities, 28*, 264–270, 290.

Vaughn, S., & Schumm, J. S. (1996). Classroom ecologies: Classroom interactions and implications for inclusion of students with learning disabilities. In: D. L. Speece & B. K. Keogh (Eds), *Research on Classroom Ecologies: Implications for Inclusion of Children with Learning Disabilities* (pp. 107–124). Mahwah, NJ: Lawrence Erlbaum Associates.

Vaughn, S., Schumm, J. S., Jallad, B., Slusher, J., & Saumell, L. (1996). Teachers' views of inclusion. *Learning Disabilities Research & Practice, 11*, 96–106.

Vohs, J. R., Landau, J. K., & Romano, C. A. (2000). *Raising standards of learning students with disabilities and standards based reform* [On-line]. Available: www.fcsn.org/peer/ess/standardsib.html

Weiss, M. P., & Brigham, F. J. (2000). Co-teaching and the model of shared responsibility: What does the research support? In: T. E. Scruggs & M. Mastropieri (Eds), *Advances in Learning and Behavioral Disabilities* (pp. 217–245). Greenwich, CT: JAI Press.

Yssledyke, J. E., Thurlow, M. L., Kozleski, E., & Reschly, D. (1998). *Accountability for the results of educating students with disabilities: Assessment Conference report on the new assessment provisions of the 1997 amendments to the individuals with disabilities education act* (April). Minneapolis, MN: National Center on Educational Outcomes [On-line]. Available: http://www.coled.umn.edu/nceo/OnlinePubs/awgfinal.html

Zigmond, N., & Baker, J. M. (1997). A comprehensive examination of an experiment in full inclusion. In: T. E. Scruggs & M. A. Mastropieri (Eds), *Advances in Learning and Behavioral Disabilities* (pp. 101–134). Greenwich, CT: JAI Press.

RESTRUCTURING SERVICE DELIVERY FOR STUDENTS WITH EMOTIONAL AND BEHAVIORAL DISORDERS

Sujatha S. Hampton and Elisabeth K. Hess-Rice

At the dawn of our new millennium, the field of emotional and behavioral disorders (EBD) faces a furious imperative. In the last decade the number of students with EBD served under the IDEA increased from 381,639 in 1989–1990 to 463,262 in 1998–1999 (U.S. Department of Education, 2001). This amounts to a 2% increase in students served, but what does this number or this increase mean? A modest estimate acknowledges that at any given time 2% of the school population has emotional or behavioral disorders that could benefit from special education services, however the U.S. Department of Education admits that only half that number ever receive those services. And the outlook for those students who receive services is so bleak it begs the question: what exactly are general and special educators offering students with EBD when we provide them with special education? The following statistics highlight the problem: the 22nd Annual Report to Congress finds that 53.46% of students with EBD dropped out of school (U.S. Department of Education, 2000). The challenge to keep these children in school is enormous, but the necessity of doing so is startlingly clear: 58% of students with EBD are arrested within five years of leaving school, but among dropouts the arrest rate is a staggering 73% (Wagner, D'Amico, Marder, Newman & Blackorby, 1992).

Effective Education for Learners with Exceptionalities, Volume 15, pages 119–138.
© 2003 Published by Elsevier Science Ltd.
ISBN: 0-7623-0975-X

The difficulty of successfully graduating students with EBD is echoed in the difficulty in recruiting and retaining qualified teachers. In the Seventh Annual Report to Congress, 43 states reported shortages of teachers trained to work with children with EBD (U.S. Department of Education, 1985). In 1987, a survey of 126 school districts found that 32% reported that the EBD teachers in their schools held emergency certification, and 6.6% were less than fully certified (Knitzer, Steinberg & Fleisch, 1990). More than a decade later, the 20th Annual Report (U.S. Department of Education, 1998) gives the certification information for 32 states and Puerto Rico which shows 43% of EBD teachers to be less than fully certified, and reports that in the 32 states surveyed, there were 231 vacant EBD positions during the 1995–1996 school year. It has been further estimated that EBD loses 1/3 of its teaching force every three years to attrition (Meadows, 1996; Schmid, 1990). These data show that there is not only a shortage in the number of EBD teachers, but that there is also a question as to the quality, or at least the qualifications, of teachers being prepared. The data suggest that the nation is moving in a dangerous direction of more needy students, and fewer prepared teachers.

The situation becomes even more grave when it is put in the context of our current political climate where high-stakes assessment is more likely to dictate funding for new teachers and new programs and where research into innovative practice may be limited by a federal commitment to rhetoric over sound empirical data.

Our fundamental belief in this chapter is that as much as we know now and as much progress as has been made in terms or educational availability for students with EBD, there is still so much that needs to be done. Our students, too often, are not offered an education that affords them access to the health, happiness, and fulfillment of normal adulthood. This basic bias stated, our purpose in this chapter is to consider a new way of thinking about the educational policies and practices that affect students with EBD, from the way we fund our programs to the way we train our teaching force.

SPECIAL EDUCATION FUNDING

From its inception, special education has been tied inextricably to funding, regardless of the social and moral obligation of a nation to provide education for all its children. The history of the United States shows us that before the 1960s, public education for children with disabilities was entirely dependent on "the generosity of private charity and the largess of state and local governments" (Tweedie, 1983, p. 49). Some states authorized discretionary special education programs, but many were largely babysitting services with little attention paid to teaching or learning. As a result, taking their lead from the civil rights movement, parents and advocates for people with disabilities began to demand their own right to a free and appropriate public education, and based on the legal precedent set by Brown v. Board of Education in 1954, they prevailed. Through the late 1960s and into the 1970s, right-to-education litigation proliferated throughout the country, but these lawsuits focused on state, not federal, constitutions. Threatened not only by these expensive lawsuits, but also by the economic difficulty of implementing programs to accommodate students with disabilities while not cutting into existing programs, the states sought financial assistance from Congress (Verstegen, 1999).

In 1966, Congressional hearings revealed that only about one third of the 5.5 million children with disabilities were receiving appropriate special education services. The remaining children were either completely excluded from education or were languishing in regular education classrooms waiting to drop out (Verstegen, 1999). This finding led to the addition of a new Title VI to the Elementary and Secondary Education Act (PL 89-750). With this initiative, a program of grants to states was established to assist with the education of students with disabilities, including the training of new teachers and the establishment of new programs. But the succeeding decade showed little progress in access to and adequacy of educational services for children with disabilities. Frustrated with a system that was unable to address their needs, advocates for these students brought landmark cases including *PARC v. the Commonwealth of Pennsylvania* and *Mills v. Board of Education of the District of Columbia*, which essentially ensured the right to a public education, despite any financial hardship to the states. The court used strong language stating:

> The defendants are required by the constitution of the United States, the District of Columbia Code, and their own regulations to provide a publicly-supported education for these "exceptional" children. Their failure to fulfill this clear duty to include and retain these children in the public school system, or otherwise provide them with publicly-supported education, and their failure to afford them due process hearings and periodical review cannot be excused by the claim that there are insufficient funds (Mills, 1972, p. 876).

The above landmark litigation and the strong stance of the courts brought about a near crisis situation with states struggling, with little federal assistance, to comply with legally mandated rulings regarding provision of services. New hearings held by the House Subcommittee on Select Education and the Senate Subcommittee in the Handicapped in 1975 revealed the abysmal state of service provision. Statistics provided by the Bureau of Education for the Handicapped estimated that of the more than 8 million children with disabilities requiring special services, only half were receiving an appropriate education; 1.75 were receiving no education at all and 2.5 were receiving an inappropriate education.

The Committee presciently acknowledged the economic reality of such numbers of uneducated citizens:

> The long-range implications of these statistics are that public agencies and taxpayers will spend billions of dollars over the lifetimes of these individuals to maintain such persons as dependents and in a minimally acceptable lifestyle. With proper education services, many would be able to become productive citizens, contributing to society instead of being forced to remain burdens. Others, through such services, would increase their independence, thus reducing their dependence on society (U.S. Senate, Committee on Labor and Public Welfare [Report No. 92–168] The Education of the Handicapped Act, p. 199).

The Committee found that financial constraints were often hindering states from providing appropriate educational services for students with disabilities and recommended that Congress take a more active role under its responsibility for equal protection under the law to support states financially in accomplishing the goal of a free and appropriate education for all children. The subsequent passage of Public Law 94-142 The Education for All Handicapped Children Act in 1975 expanded Part B of the Education of the Handicapped Act into a multi-billion-dollar federal assistance commitment to assisting state and local education agencies in providing special education services.

Public Law 94-142 included several new provisions: a state funding formula based on need rather than on census; a new intrastate funding formula that required 75% of funds to go directly to localities according to need; and a limit of 12% of the population that could be supported by federal aid. The Senate Committee stipulated that federal monies were to be used to assist states in carrying out their responsibilities under state laws, not to provide full funding of special education (Verstegen, 1999). The funding system for special education was not substantially changed until the 1997 Reauthorization of the Individuals with Disabilities Education Act of 1990. A key feature of the IDEA reauthorization was a new state and substate funding formula where enactment of appropriations over $4.9 billion triggers a new state formula which distributes a base amount to states equal to their allocations in the year before the trigger was reached. Any additional money is allocated based on the total school-age population (weighted 85%) and the total school-age population in poverty (weighted 15%), with minimum and maximum grant provisions. Within-state allocations are distributed similarly (Aleman & Jones, 1997b).

Funding Programs for Students with EBD

For students with EBD, funding very often means identifying fewer students than those who really require services. From the mid 1950s until 1980, the U.S. Department of Education conservatively estimated that 2% of students would qualify for special education services for behavior disorders. During the early 1980s, they revised their estimate to 1.2–2%. Since then, they have not published a prevalence estimate (Kauffman, 2000). A truer representation based on population surveys puts the estimate between 3–6% of the student population (Costello et al., 1998). Some more liberal estimates based on teacher and parent reports cite the prevalence of disordered behavior in children as high as 14% (Mash & Dozois, 1996). Research indicates that although less than 2% of students are offered services to address their behavior disorders, closer to 7% are found to have persistent behavior problems that negatively impact their academic and social development and which are unlikely to be remediated without intervention (Colvin, Greenberg & Sherman, 1993, see Kauffman, 2000).

Thus, every empirical indication demonstrates that the number of students provided with special education services to address serious behavioral disorders is much less than half the number of students who require services. For a government that has mandated that all students with disabilities be given an appropriate education, it is far more manageable to allow a confusing and easily circumvented definition of emotional and behavioral disorders (or emotional disturbance) to remain the diagnostic cornerstone than to find the money to serve this difficult population of children (Hallahan, Keller & Ball, 1986). For example, 25 years ago it was estimated that nearly 1 billion dollars more per year of federal funds would be necessary plus almost 1.4 billion dollars from state and local funds to serve 2% of students in public schools (Grosenick & Huntze, 1979). These funds did not include funds for personnel preparation nor did they allow for inflation. Today, serving 2% of the school population would cost substantially more in extra federal, state, and local funds and these funds are unlikely ever to become available. As Kauffman (2000) so eloquently puts it:

> The tragedy is that social policy (IDEA) mandates the impossible and that the public – and a growing number of professionals-are likely to change their perceptions to match economic realities. The social policy mandate changes the question, at least for those who manage budgets, from "How many students with emotional or behavioral disorders are there in our schools?" to "How many can we afford to serve?" And to save face and try to abide by the law, it is tempting to conclude that there are, indeed, precisely as many students with emotional or behavioral disorders as one is able to serve (p. 50).

The Cost of Funding

More than half the states in the U.S. are considering or have already made major changes to their funding mechanisms for special education, moving toward a census-based approach to funding. Census-based approaches fund on the basis of the total number of students enrolled in the district, assuming that all districts have approximately the same percentages of special education students and then providing a fixed amount of additional resources for these students (Chambers, 1999). The critical issue with regard to a census-based funding strategy is that not all special education students cost the same to educate. The more important question is, what are the needs of students in special education and what are the costs of each of these variables? These are the data that must inform the budgetary decisions of states and local school districts.

Chambers, Hikido and Dueñas (1995) conducted a comprehensive study for the Commonwealth of Massachusetts for the Center for Special Education Finance after the Education Reform Act of 1993 that called for a new funding formula to provide more equitable funding for education. With this act, Massachusetts shifted from a system of pupil weights to one that was more census based. Part of the argument for the change was that the new formula did not provide any fiscal incentive for identification and labeling of students for special education. Chambers and colleagues conducted the analysis such that it would reflect educational, behavioral and medical-physical needs of students. These needs were translated into criteria under five categories, namely: (1) type of environment, referring to departmentalized vs. nondepartmentalized settings; (2) grade levels according to preschool, kindergarten, primary grades 1–3, intermediate grades 4–8, traditional high school grades 9–12, and ungraded; (3) service prototype: such as a combination of the type of placement (regular classroom, outside the regular classroom, separate school) and the percentage of time spent in that placement; (4) primary disability, under the IDEA; and (5) student need, based on the subjective response of the special educator who rated each student according to their level of need for curricular, behavioral, and medical-physical adaptations in the learning environment necessary to provide instructional services. The results of this study have serious implications for the future of funding for students with EBD. Specifically this study highlights important information that will almost certainly impact the way services are provided, and where we services are provided for students with EBD. These issues must be rectified before services for students with EBD can be improved.

In the study identified above, Chambers et al. (1995) provides the per pupil expenditures for regular education and then for special education. At the elementary school level, a student in regular education costs $2,168. A student with EBD costs $6,299, or almost three times as much. This figure comes as no great surprise, it is widely estimated that on the average, a student in special education costs about twice as much, and this is because most students in special education fall into the category of learning disabilities which costs $4,499 per pupil, or roughly twice that of a student in general education. The additional cost of educating students with EBD results from the extraordinary numbers who are educated outside the general education classroom. The 22nd Annual Report to Congress states that 39.86% of elementary aged students with EBD spend over 60% of their time outside the general education classroom (U.S. Departament of Education, 2001). Chambers et al. found that for this age group it costs 32% more to educate a student who spends between 25–60% of his or her time outside the general education classroom and 84% more to educate him or her in a separate classroom within a regular school. With this information, the cost of educating a 40% of elementary school students with EBD jumps from $6,299 to about $7,151. This would amount to a national expenditure of approximately $450 million for the 40% of elementary school children with EBD who are educated outside the classroom for over 60% of the day. At the high school level, the numbers are only slightly better (Chambers et al., 1999; U.S. Department of Education, 2001).

Innovations in Funding

MacMillan (1999) reported the results of a longitudinal study in California on the costs of educating students in public vs. private settings. In response to the astronomical costs of providing restrictive, nonpublic placements for students with EBD, the California legislature encouraged school districts to develop cost-effective programs for students who would otherwise be placed in nonpublic schools. The Contra Costa County school district designed a program in concert with their existing continuum of services to provide intensive services with low teacher-student ratios for students whose behaviors would otherwise have warranted transfer to a more restrictive, nonpublic placement to receive the appropriate education and related services. The program, called the 1261 Project was housed within an existing special education center and the state grant allowed the district to hire additional teachers and a wraparound staff including representatives from social services and mental health disciplines. The 1261 Project established a multidisciplinary advisory committee and a school-based intake committee that serve as project evaluators. A social-cognitive approach is used in the program, and children are given regular on-site therapy 1–2 times per week, and have medical monitoring of medication. They have weekly counseling with the school social worker, and crisis intervention support as needed. Also, the 1261 Project encourages the active support of family and/or caregivers in the therapeutic education of the students, and the students have contact with their parents or guardians approximately every day. Adult-student ratios in the 1261 Project are four adults to 8–10 students, at a cost of $23,000 per student per year. The Marchus School Day Classroom, from which many of the students come, has ratios of 2 adults to 8–10 students and the cost is $18,000 per student per year.

Interestingly, it may appear that the 1261 Project is moving in the wrong direction, supporting more expensive more exclusive educational settings, but just the opposite is true. Development of the 1261 Project is a pilot program to see if it would be possible to provide services comparable to those available in a nonpublic residential facility at a savings. The students placed in the 1261 Project would have been placed in a nonpublic facility at a cost of $44,000 per student per year if such public program had not been available. Services provided in a nonpublic residential placement were similar except that there was much less parental contact, approximately twice a month. To underscore their claim that with innovative programs it is possible to save thousands of dollars and still provide appropriate services for children with EBD, MacMillan (1999) provided three case studies that showed the savings, not only with the program itself, but in the students' behavioral improvements that allowed them to be moved out of expensive group homes, off of expensive state financed medications, and into gainful employment.

In several individual cases, the meaningful and appropriately conceived wraparound services offered to students in the 1261 Project resulted in their movement out of restrictive placements back into general education classrooms with supports. Not only did this reduce per pupil expenditures, but also it qualitatively improved the lives of children. Clearly, great strides towards improving service delivery for students with EBD can be achieved through innovative programs that strive to maintain students as close to the general education environment as possible while still meeting their diverse social and learning needs.

RESTRUCTURING TEACHER EDUCATION IN THE FIELD OF EBD

Society faces the *serious challenge* of providing an enriched and valuable education to children with EBD because of the lack of a sufficient quantity and quality of teaching professionals (American Association for Employment in Education, 1998). Without an increase in the quantity and quality of teachers for students with EBD, true restructuring in the education of students with EBD will never occur. Simpson (1999) warned that: "One need not be capricious or an alarmist to conclude that the field (of special education) is perilously close to losing significant ground in its struggle to educate and support students who are behaviorally troubled" (p. 284). The disheartening result of this crisis in personnel is that the adults are failing and thus making it difficult for students to succeed. Students with EBD who are struggling to cope with emotional or behavioral issues are now also lacking the appropriate personnel to guide them through potential academic and social successes. There is no factor that contributes more to improving student success than the guarantee of a qualified teacher in every classroom (Seidel & Ross, 2000). Thus, personnel preparation and retention are paramount.

Students with EBD need teachers who understand and care about them, who can work collaboratively with other professionals, and who have a myriad of research-based techniques to help change behavior. The strength of good, dedicated teachers is of particular concern for students with EBD who are at high risk for failure in school and after leaving school. Examining the facts about children with EBD, one realizes how critical educators' efforts are to improve their services and results. Children with ED:

- Frequently fail to obtain a high school diploma despite intellectual ability and potential (U.S. Department of Education, 1999).
- Are likely to be involved in interpersonal difficulties and dysfunctional family situations (Kauffman, 2000; Stephens & Repa, 1992; Walker, Colvin & Ramsey, 1995).
- Comprise 44% of all the special education suspensions even though they comprised only 8.7% of all students with disabilities (Whelan & Kauffman, 1999).
- Are more frequently educated outside of their local schools and outside general education classrooms (U.S. Department of Education, 1999).
- Miss more days of school per year than do students in any other disability category (Chesapeake Institute, 1994).
- Are more likely to grow up to become adults who are underemployed, involved in criminal behavior and abuse substances (Landrum & Tankersley, 1999).

Teaching students with EBD is *not* a skill that naturally develops in teachers or that can be addressed through generic teacher education coursework. The natural response of unqualified or under qualified teachers to students with EBD is to *avoid* students with disruptive and challenging behaviors. This reduces the amount of time these students spend academically engaged (Carr, Taylor & Robinson, 1991). In addition, the unconscious response of many untrained professionals to students with EBD is to mirror the deviant behaviors that they are facing (Long & Fescer, 2000). For example, when students are aggressive, the untrained teacher can become counter aggressive; and when students are depressed, the untrained teacher begins to feel hopeless (Long & Fescer, 2000). These negative attitudes affect the quality of services students receive as well as the feeling of self-efficacy that helps teachers remain in the field. Specific training is needed to combat these reactions to students with EBD and to provide a structured, strength-based school environment. This point is further substantiated when examining some of the literature about inclusion and students with EBD. Attitudinal research reveals that students with EBD experience the highest rejection rates of any other disability group (Downing, Simpson & Miles, 1990; Landrum & Kauffman, 1992). A body of professional literature shows that teacher attitudes and expectations toward children with EBD are often stereotypic and negative and that negative expectations breed futility in both students and teachers (Brendtro, Brokenleg & Van Bockern, 1990).

One of the primary objectives of the inclusion movement is to place all children with disabilities in the general education setting to increase social competence and foster positive peer relationships. By definition, however, these are the areas that are most difficult for students with EBD (Cheney & Muscott, 1996). Students with EBD need teachers who understand their needs and can assist general educators with developing learning activities and social interactions that benefit all children. When qualified teachers assist others to have positive experiences with students with EBD, additional positive experiences and attitudes will occur and thus benefit the student and teacher (Shapiro, Miller, Sawka, Gardill & Handler, 1999).

As it appears, these students with EBD have become a predominant concern in special education, with administrators and teachers scrambling to provide interventions that foster positive school experiences. As schools deal more with serious behavioral challenges, they often respond inappropriately with policies such as zero tolerance, suspension, and isolation (Kauffman, 2000). These punitive measures are not effective and merely exacerbate the strain in relationships between adults and students. Research suggests that such practices are at best ineffective and at worst counterproductive (Mayer & Leone, 1998; Shores, Gunter & Jack, 1993). Providing successful school experiences for these students is urgent and qualified professionals must lead the way. Therefore, a key aspect of the restructuring solution should be intensive pre-service training that provides research-based strategies to work effectively with students with EBD, thus empowering professionals to provide quality services and to remain in the field.

Preparing sufficient numbers of qualified professionals to educate children with EBD is arguably the most immediate and long-term challenge facing the field of special education. Allowing unqualified or under qualified individuals to work in the profession detracts from students' potential for positive outcomes and thereby has the potential to exacerbate their problems (Simpson, 1999). Intensive preservice training in teacher education is "needed to guarantee better prepared and more effective classroom teachers and higher achieving students," (Ross & Thompson, 2000, p. 7). Preservice training, "when done well, becomes the *essential* link that translates reforms into a different way of practice" (Meyers, Kaufman & Goldman, 1998, p. 26). A successful training experience should develop the skills, rules, concepts, or attitudes that result in improved performance in another environment. The combination of an increasing number of students in special education and teacher shortages can only mean that the number of well-trained professionals available to provide quality education to students with emotional and behavioral disorders is distressingly insufficient. In relation, evidence suggests the number of graduates in special education teacher preparation programs is much too low to satisfy the need for teachers (U.S. Department of Education, 1999). However, such training is imperative, considering the dismal outcomes often seen in the literature regarding students with EBD (Maag & Katsiyannis, 1999). In a recent study, teacher education programs that focus specifically on the needs of students have received feedback that their graduates believed they were prepared to teach and "that they possessed extensive knowledge that enabled them to manage the day-to-day activities of the classroom with professionalism and success" (Ross & Thompson, 2000, p. 49). As a result, students within classroom walls must be geared toward greater academic and social success.

A New Way of Training

In order to prepare teachers to work effectively with students with EBD, teacher education must be reformed. Instead of merely talking about these students, pre-service teachers must experience working with them under the tutelage of qualified special educators and university researchers. Traditional teacher preparation in general and special education has been criticized for inadequately preparing teachers for the realities of the classroom because it does not tie the theory of education to the practice of education (Darling-Hammond, 1996). One response to this criticism has been the creation of the professional development school (PDS) movement. Universities and schools across the nation have begun to collaborate in partnerships called professional development schools (PDSs)(the Holmes Group), or clinical schools (the Carnegie Foundation), or partner schools (National Educational Renewal Network) in order to improve teacher preparation and school practice. PDSs are collaborative mergers between universities and school sites. According to the Holmes Partnership, PDSs are schools that serve teacher education as the teaching hospital serves medical education, and as agricultural extension services serve the agricultural community (Holmes Group, 1990). PDSs train teachers in the theory and the practice of the profession of teaching. They value diversity, the growth of students, educative communities, inquiry, and continual learning (Goodlad, 1990; Holmes Group, 1990). Across the nation, PDS reform efforts are projected to resolve two significant problems in the work of schools and universities. First, schools become revitalized and transform out-of-date practices through the partnership. Second, new teachers become better teachers because of a sustained interaction between schools and universities (Zimpher, 1990). PDSs have become a major initiative in the reform and restructuring movement in public education and are intended to reform teacher education and student education through the development of simultaneous renewal between partner schools and universities (Goodlad, 1990; Holmes, 1990).

Partnerships are the most recent response to training effective teachers and transforming teacher education throughout the country (Darling-Hammond, 1994; Goodlad, 1990; Holmes Group, 1995; 1990; Slick, 1995). The PDS idea was strongly influenced by the teaching hospital (Levine, 1992). Many years ago Flexner (1910) wrote a report on scathing conditions of medicine that influenced the conceptualization and development of the teaching hospital. The teaching hospital was designed to prepare doctors to be 'thinking practitioners' just as PDSs were designed to help prepare thinking teaching practitioners (Levine, 1997; Ludmerer, 1985). The aims of PDSs are to provide exemplary education for preservice teachers, support continuing professional development of experienced teachers, and involve schools and universities in collaborative research (Bullough, Hobbs, Kauchak, Crow & Stokes, 1997). Apparently, the PDS movement is gaining popularity and momentum such that it is estimated that "... PDSs are much more than a fashionable new idea. They are an imperative of professional responsibility in education," (Robinson & Darling-Hammond, 1994, p. 217). Universities and schools are responding to the calls to reform teacher education as evidenced by the growing number of PDSs. In 1994, Darling-Hammond approximated that there were 100 PDSs across the country. Two years later, in 1996, there were more than 650 PDSs documented nationwide (Abdal-Haqq, 1996). More recently, it is estimated that there are over 1,000 PDSs in 47 states (Abdal-Haqq, 1998). Most of these PDSs have come into existence since 1991 and are found in urban, suburban, and rural settings in this country and in several foreign countries (Abdal-Haqq, 1995).

The PDS structure is perceived to improve the preparation of preservice teachers because it enhances the experience levels of preservice teachers and provides more authentic preparation for the realities of today's classrooms (Kochan, 1999). In addition, learning communities are formed that help bind education professionals together. Authentic preparation is especially needed for teachers of students with EBD who cannot afford to react with natural counter aggressive responses to aggressive or disturbing behavior (Long & Morse, 1996). The PDS movement cannot be a reform that occurs solely in general education. Meaningful partnerships between schools serving students with EBD and university training programs preparing teachers to teach these students must join together to reap the benefits of simultaneous renewal. Without school laboratories, preservice teachers cannot grapple with instructional strategies and behavior management tools in a supervised setting. Without consistent, long-term exposure to students with EBD, preservice teachers can never grasp the full import of their interventions. Without university research and support, programs serving these students will not utilize or publicize effective approaches with this needy population. PDSs provide hands on training for preservice teachers while also providing research opportunities for university faculty and professional development for inservice teachers.

Landrum and Tankersley (1999) believed "the future can be brighter for children and youths with emotional disturbance... but we must act sooner rather than later. For children who may be already on a course toward behavioral problems, it is indeed clear that the future is now" (pp. 327–328). Students with EBD need qualified teachers to help them learn and meet their complex needs. An innovative training model is needed to produce the most rich, realistic and supportive training environment. One such environment that has been successful in teacher preparation is the PDS movement.

A Model Program that Works for Students with EBD

One program utilizing the PDS structure is the Marshall Road Center Professional Development School, an elementary placement for students with EBD in Fairfax County, Virginia. Fairfax County and the George Washington University established a partnership in 1995 and each year about eight graduate students complete a 39 credit hour Master's degree in EBD while working in place of assistants in the school. The program is one year in length and provides the opportunity for the bridging of theory and practice. The program is funded through an arrangement with Fairfax County were money for assistants is used to pay for some of the tuition for the graduate interns. While both the university and the school have struggled through issues in the collaboration process, both acknowledge positive change in both the school and the university over the course of five years (Belknap, Mosca & Marston, 2000). The goals of this PDS have been to: (a) involve graduate student interns with professionals from the discipline of education, social work, psychology, and related fields; (b) to build reflective practice by tying theory directly to practice during the full-time, one year internship; and (c) to prepare highly qualified and skilled special education professional who provide psychoeducational services for students with emotional and behavioral problems.

The outcomes of this new way of training are still being studied. Preliminary results suggest that teachers trained in the full time PDS are socialized to the field of EBD more quickly and therefore can 'hit the ground running' when they begin their careers working with students with EBD (Marston, Hess, Mosca & Belknap, 2001). Employer follow-up reported that employers particularly valued the skills of graduates to work effectively in interdisciplinary teams, to problem solve, and to behave more like experienced teachers than other graduates from a different training program (Marston, 1999). In addition, training teachers involved at the PDS site report that through the partnership they have grown more reflective about their practice and have been able to further refine their skills in teaching students with EBD (O'Brien, 2001). This professional development is needed by teachers in the field in order to avoid high attrition rates and providing the structure to nurture professionals working with students with EBD begins to fill the needs of this troubled and troubling population.

Implementing and facilitating a PDS is not without its concerns. Preliminary study results indicate that the time and labor needed to facilitate change on the part of the school and the university is not rewarded within current structures as has been identified in other PDS studies (Hess, 2000). For example, training teachers are generally not compensated for their time coaching graduate students, and university faculty members are not granted tenure or promotion based upon fruitful work in school-university partnerships. In addition, the nature and needs of students with EBD seem to heighten the stress levels and the delicacies of the collaboration process with adults. Nevertheless, the preliminary results provide an impetus for forming school-university partnerships specifically for training teachers to effectively work with students with EBD. Preservice teachers become stronger teachers because of the intensive experiences and amount of qualified professionals surrounding them, school faculty become connected to a community of professionals and are able to share their expertise while becoming more reflective, and university faculty are forced to reconcile the gaps between theory and practice in their teacher education programs.

As schools across the nation cope with increasingly troubling behavior, they are experiencing shortages in teacher availability and retention, particularly in special education. Miller, Brownell and Smith (1999) noted that, "The provision of a free and appropriate public education (FAPE) to students with disabilities is dependent on the retention of qualified special education teachers in the classroom" (p. 201). Teacher education for preservice special education teachers is a contributing factor to job satisfaction and willingness of teachers to remain in the classroom (Billingsley & Cross, 1991). One model that is providing quality teacher education that is specific to the needs of students with EBD is the professional development school model. This model blends theory and practice of teaching and helps teachers grapple with the complexities of teaching students with EBD in supervised, supportive settings. Developing models similar to this model helps alleviate the shortage of qualified professionals in the field of EBD and therefore improves services to students with EBD – the first step in restructuring services.

CONCLUSION: A TIME FOR BOLD ACTION

Restructuring of service delivery for students with EBD in the new millennium will require a commitment to innovative programming, both for student achievement and for teacher preparation, and also an understanding of the fiscal issues associated with implementation of any plan of action. Our federal budgetary surplus does not extend far enough to serve all the students identified as requiring services for EBD, let alone to serve all the students who remain unlabeled despite clear indications that their needs could be better met with access to special education. The current service delivery models available for students with EBD are staggeringly expensive, as much as three times as expensive as general education. They are, furthermore, notoriously ineffective with over half of students with EBD dropping out of school. These numbers beg several questions. What are we paying for? Where is all this money going, and is it worth it? Is there a better way of doing things, a new way of thinking?

Successes in various pilot programs and PDS programs across the nation have encouraging data that support the premise that excellent outcomes for teachers and for students can be achieved in a cost effective manner. Pilot programs aimed at reducing long term costs while improving service delivery and educational and behavioral outcomes for students have included innovative strategies including the following:

- Integration of wraparound services that include individual and group therapy on a regular and frequent basis, as well as a strong commitment to improving family communication and interaction
- Reduction in teacher-student ratios, and recruitment of experienced and well prepared teachers

- Emphasis on improving academic and social achievement thereby increasing students' success in moving back up the continuum of services to less expensive and more inclusive environments

Programs implementing these measures have resulted in substantial cost savings, both initially and in the long term. Students selected for these pilot programs were those who would otherwise have been sent to high priced residential treatment centers. The improvements they made as a direct result of the schools' educational and therapeutic programs allowed many students to move out of the more restrictive settings and receive educational services in less expensive environments.

Innovative programs for students with EBD, such as the 1261 Project described above, must be led by qualified, competent, and confident teachers. Thus, non-traditional thinking must also extend to teacher preparation, which is woefully suboptimal for the students with EBD. The PDS offers an authentic environment in which preservice teachers can develop their skills. This model blends theory and practice in a supervised and supportive setting, which though controlled to some extent by the presence of master teachers, is intensive and real. Preliminary research in the use of the PDS model to prepare teachers to teach students with EBD has yielded positive results. Teachers graduated from such a program consider themselves highly confident and thoroughly aware of the difficulties that this population presents for the teacher. They were also highly confident in their ability to navigate the real school culture, having taught full time in a real school for an entire year. This confidence could translate to longer tenure in the field of EBD, which would alleviate the shortage of teachers for this population, and in turn then, improve services for students with EBD through a more experienced and better prepared teaching force.

The future of service delivery for students with EBD need not be bound by the failures of the past. Promising new thinking in educational programming and teacher preparation give hope that these students can have the full complexity of their educational, social, psychological, and behavioral needs addressed in school. The current state of education for students with EBD suggests that the time has come for a radical restructuring of service delivery for this population.

REFERENCES

Abdal-Haqq, I. (1995). *Professional development schools: A directory of projects in the United States* (2nd ed.). Washington, D.C.: American Association of Colleges for Teacher Education.

Abdal-Haqq, I. (1996). An information provider's perspective on the professional development school movement. *Contemporary Education, 67*(4), 237–240.

Abdal-Haqq, I. (1998). *Professional development schools: Weighing the evidence*. Thousand Oaks, CA: Corwin Press.

Aleman, S. R. & Jones, N. L. (1997b). *Individuals With Disabilities Education Act Reauthorization Legislation: An Overview*. Washington, D.C.: Library of Congress, Congressional Research Services.

American Association for Employment in Education (1998). *Job search handbook for educators*. Evanston, IL: Author.

Belknap, N., Mosca. F., & Marston, J. (2001). Preparing teachers for students with emotional disturbance: A professional development school approach. *The Capital educators: Leadership through collaboration*. The Capital Educators Monograph Series. Washington, D.C.: The George Washington University.

Billingsley, B., & Cross, L. (1991). General education teachers' interest in special education teaching. *Teacher Education and Special Education, 14*(2), 162–168.

Brendtro, L. K., Brokenleg, M., & Van Bockern, S. (1990). *Reclaiming youth at risk*. Bloomington, IN: National Educational Service.

Bullough, R. V., Hobbs, S. F., Kauchack, D. P., Crow, N. A., Stokes, D. (1997). Long-Term PDS development in research universities and the clinicalization of teacher education. *Journal of Teacher Education, 48*(2), 85–95.

Chesapeake Institute for the U.S. Department of Education (1994). *National agenda for achieving better results for children and youth with serious emotional disturbance* (ERIC Document Reproduction Service No. ED 376-690). Washington, D.C.: Office of Special Education Programs.

Carr, E. G., Taylor, J. C. & Robinson, S. (1991). The effects of severe behavior problems in children on the teaching behavior of adults. *Journal of Applied Behavior Analysis, 24*, 523–535.

Chambers, J. G. (1999). The patterns of expenditures on students with disabilities: A methodological and empirical analysis. In: T. B. Parrish, J. G. Chambers & C. M. Guarino (Eds), *Funding Special Education* (pp. 89–123). Thousand Oaks, CA: Corwin Press, Inc.

Chambers, J. G., Parrish, T. B., Hikido, C. & Dueñas, I. (1995). A comprehensive study of education for the Commonwealth of Massachusetts: Final report. Palo Alto, CA: American Institutes for Research, Center for Special Education Finance.

Cheney, D., & Muscott, H. (1996). Preventing school failure for students with emotional and behavioral disabilities through responsible inclusion. *Preventing School Failure, 40*(3), 109–116.

Colvin, G., Greenberg, S., & Sherman, R. (1993). The forgotten variable: Improving academic skills for students with serious emotional disturbance. *Effective School Practices, 12*(1), 20–25.

Costello, E. J., Messer, S. C., Bird, H. R., Cohen, P., & Reinherz, H., Z. (1998). The prevalence of serious emotional disturbance: A re-analysis of community studies. *Journal of Child and Community Studies, 7*, 411–432.

Darling-Hammond, L. (Ed.) (1994). *Professional development schools: Schools for developing a profession*. New York: Teachers College Press.

Darling-Hammond, L. (1996). What matters most: A competent teacher for every child. *Phi Delta Kappan, 78*(3), 193–202.

Downing, J., Simpson, R., & Miles, B. (1990). Regular and special educators' perception of non-academic skills needed by mainstreamed students with behavioral disorders and learning disabilities. *Behavioral Disorders, 15*, 217–226.

Flexner, A. (1910). *Medical education in the United States and Canada: A report to the Carneige Foundation for the Advancement of Teaching*. New York City.

Fruchter, N., Parrish, T. B., Berne, R. (1999). Financing special education: Proposed reforms in New York City. In: T. B. Parrish, J. G. Chambers & C. M. Guarino (Eds), *Funding Special Education* (pp. 176–200). Thousand Oaks, CA: Corwin Press, Inc.

Goodlad, J. (1990). *Teachers for our nation's schools*. San Francisco: Jossey-Bass.

Grosenick, J. K., & Huntze, S. L. (1979). *National needs analysis in behavior disorders: A model for a comprehensive needs analysis in behavior disorders*. Columbia: University of Missouri, Department of Special Education.

Hallahan, D. P., Keller, C. E., & Ball, D. W. (1986). A comparison of prevalence rate variability from state to state for each of the categories of special education. *Remedial and Special Education, 7*(2), 8–14.

Hess, E. K. (2000). An investigation of the facilitators of and the barriers to the collaboration process in professional development schools (PDSs): A meta-ethnography 1990–1998. Unpublished dissertation, The George Washington University, Washington, D.C.

Holmes Group (1990). *Tomorrow's School: Principles for the design of professional development schools*. East Lansing, MI: Holmes Group, Inc.

Holmes Group (1995). *Tomorrow's schools of education*. East Lansing, MI: Author.

Maag, J., & Katsiyannis, A. (1999). Teacher preparation in E/BD: A national survey. *Behavioral Disorders, 24*(3), 189–96.

Kaufman, J. (2000). Future Directions with Troubled Children. *Reclaiming Children and Youth, 9*(2), 119–124.

Kochan, F. (1999). *Professional development schools: A comprehensive view*. ATE 1999 Annual Yearbook.

Landrum, T., & Kauffman, J. (1992). Reflections on characteristics of general education teachers perceived as effective by their peers: Implications for the inclusion of children with learning and behavioral disorders. *Exceptionality: A Research Journal, 3*, 185–188.

Landrum, T., & Tankersley, M. (1999). Emotional and behavioral disorders in the new millennium: The future is now. *Behavioral Disorders, 24*, 319–330.

Levine, M. (Ed.) (1992). *Professional practice schools; Linking teacher education and school reform*. New York: Teachers College Press.

Levine, M. (1997). Can professional development schools help us achieve what matters most? *Action in Teacher Education, 14*(2), 63–73.

Long, N., & Fecser, F. (2000). *LSCI Senior Training Manual*. (Available from Life Space Crisis Intervention Institute, 226 Landis Road, Hagerstown, MD 21740.)

Long, N. J., & Morse, W. (1996). *Conflict in the classroom: The education of at-risk and troubled students*. Austin, TX: Pro-Ed.

Ludmerer, K. (1985). *Learning to heal: The development of American medical education*. New York: Basic Books.

MacMillan, R. C. (1999). A longitudinal study of the cost effectiveness of educating students with emotional or behavioral disorders in a public school setting. *Behavioral Disorders, 25*(1), 65–75.

Marston, J. R. (1999). Professional development school employer evaluation data. Unpublished raw data.

Mash, E. J., & Dozois, D. J. A. (1996). Child psychopathology: A developmental systems perspective. In: E. J. Mash & R. A. Barkley (Eds), *Child Pychopathology* (pp. 3–60). New York: The Guilford Press.

Mayer, M., & Leone, P. (1998). A structural analysis of school violence and disruption: Implications for creating safer schools. Paper presented at the annual meeting of the Teacher Educators for Children with Emotional and Behavioral Disorders (November), Scottsdale, AZ.

McLaughlin, M. J. (1996). Consolidating categorical resources to support local school improvement: Issues and perspectives. *Journal of Educational Finance, 21*, 506–526.

McLaughlin, M. J. (1999). Consolidating categorical educational programs at the local level. In: T. B. Parrish, J. G. Chambers & C. M. Guarino (Eds), *Funding Special Education* (pp. 22–40). Thousand Oaks, CA: Corwin Press, Inc.

Mills v. Board of Education of the District of Columbia, 348 F. Supp. 866 (D.D.C.1972).

O'Brien, K. (2001). Lessons learned from being a training teacher. Paper presented at the Holmes Partnership Annual Meeting (January), Albuquerque, NM.

Parrish, T. B., & Wolman, J. (1999). Trends and new developments in special education funding: What the states report. In: T. B. Parrish, J. G. Chambers & C. M. Guarino (Eds), *Funding Special Education* (pp. 203–229). Thousand Oaks, CA: Corwin Press, Inc.

Robinson, S., & Darling-Hammond, L. (1994). Change for collaboration and collaboration for change: Transforming teaching through school-university partnerships. In: L. Darling-Hammond (Ed.), *Professional Development Schools: Schools for Developing a Profession* (pp. 203–219). New York: Teachers College Press.

Ross, F., & Thompson, S. (2000). Becoming a teacher in a professional development school. *Teaching and Change, 8*(1), 31–50.

Schmid R. (1990). Teaching emotionally disturbed adolescents: A study of selected teachers and teacher characteristics. *Behavioral Disorders, 9*, 105–112.

Seidel, S., & Ross, S. (2000). Introduction to the NEA Teacher Education Initiative. *Teaching and Change, 8*(1), 5–9.

Shapiro, E., Miller, D., Sawka, K, Gardill, M., & Handler, M. (1999). Facilitating the inclusion of students with EBD into general education classrooms. *Journal of Emotional & Behavioral Disorders, 7*(2), 83–93.

Shores, R. E., Gunter, P. L., & Jack, S. L. (1993). Classroom management strategies: Are they setting events for coercion? *Behavioral Disorders, 18*, 92–102.

Slick, G. A. (1995). *Emerging trends in teacher preparation*. Thousand Oaks, CA: Corwin Press.

Stephens, R. T., & Repa, J. T. (1992). Dropping out and its ultimate consequence: A study of dropouts in prison. *Urban Education, 26*, 401–422.

Simpson, R. (1999). Children and youth with emotional and behavioral disorders: A concerned look at the present and a hopeful eye for the future. *Behavioral Disorders, 24*(4), 284–292.

Tweedie, J. (1983). The politics of legalization in special education reform. In: J. G. Chambers & W. T. Hartman (Eds), *Special Education Policies: Their History, Implementation and Finance* (pp. 48–73). Philadelphia, PA: Temple University Press.

U.S. Department of Education. (1999). *Twenty-first annual report to Congress on implementation of the Individuals with Disabilities Education Act*. Washington, D.C.: Author.

U.S. Senate, *The Education of the Handicapped Act* (pp. 131, 198, 199).

Verstegen, D. A., & Whitney, T. (1997). From courthouses to schoolhouses: Emerging judicial theories of adequacy and equity. *Educational Policy, 11*(3), 330–352.

Verstegen, D. A. (1995). *Consolidating special education funding and services: A federal perspective*. Palo Alto, CA: Center for Special Education Finance (CSEF).

Verstegen, D. A. (1998). *Landmark court decisions challenge state special education funding*. Palo Alto, CA: Center for Special Education Finance (CSEF).

Walker, H. M., Colvin, G., & Ramsey, E. (1995). *Antisocial behavior in school: Strategies and best practices*. Pacific Grove, CA: Brookes/Cole.

Whelan, R., & Kauffman, J. (1999). Educating students with emotional and behavioral disorders: Historical perspective and future directions. In: L. M. Bullock & R. A. Gable's (Eds), *Third CCBD Mini-Library Series: What Works for Children and Youth with E/BD: Linking Yesterday and Today with Tomorrow*. Reston; VA: Council for Children with Behavioral Disorders.

Zimpher, N. (1990). Creating professional development school sites. *Theory into Practice, 29*(1), 42–49.

STUDENTS WITH ATTENTION DEFICIT HYPERACTIVITY DISORDER

Marjorie Montague

How often have you heard the following comments about children and adolescents from parents, teachers, or other adults? Sara doesn't pay attention. Derrick never seems to listen. Amy won't follow instructions. James never finishes his schoolwork. Ellen is so disorganized. Homework time is a nightmare. She does her homework but usually doesn't turn it in. Even though I remind him, he forgets to take out the garbage and do his other chores. Allison sits still only when she's playing video games; then I can't get her attention. Jaime is always out of his seat. Eliette never stops talking. She's constantly moving. Jennifer blurts out without thinking.

Most individuals display one or more of these idiosyncratic behaviors to some degree at some time in their lives. Individuals with attention deficit hyperactivity disorder (ADHD), however, have serious and ongoing problems with attention, impulsivity, and hyperactivity that cause considerable difficulty functioning in school, at home, and in the community. The purpose of this chapter is to: (a) provide a brief historical view of ADHD focusing on why and how, in just the past ten years, ADHD has become a major concern for teachers, school administrators, and other school personnel; and (b) describe what ADHD is, how children are assessed and diagnosed with ADHD, and "best practice" for helping students with ADHD succeed in school.

ADHD: CONCERNS FOR EDUCATORS

ADHD as a disorder had been virtually ignored by educators until the past decade. In 1990 when Congress was reauthorizing P.L. 94-142 as the Individuals with Disabilities Act (IDEA), parent and advocacy groups requested that ADHD be recognized as a disability category like learning disabilities and emotional disturbance. They argued that students with ADHD have attention and behavioral problems that adversely affect their educational performance and success in school and, thus, should qualify for special education and related services under IDEA. Educational organizations such as the National Association of State Directors of Special Education and the National Education Association, however, had strong objections to ADHD as a separate disability category. They rebutted that many children with ADHD already qualify for special education programs because they have co-occurring learning, emotional, or behavior disorders and, as a result, receive special education services under one of these categories. They were also concerned that resources would limit services that students with more serious disabilities need. Finally, they argued that defining ADHD and identifying children who have the disorder would be difficult from an educational perspective because historically ADHD had been viewed as a medical problem.

Following much debate, Congress authorized the Department of Education to collect comments from consumers about ADHD and report those findings. The *Federal Register* (November 29, 1990) contained a "Notice of Inquiry" soliciting responses to questions about characteristics and educational needs of children and youth with ADHD. A summary of the responses was submitted to Congress in May 1991 and in September of that year the Office of Special Education and Rehabilitative Services, the Office of Civil Rights, and the Office of Elementary and Secondary Education of the Department of Education issued a policy statement based on the comments (Davila, Williams & MacDonald, 1991). In sum, the statement indicated that children with ADHD may qualify for special assistance, adaptations, or accommodations in general education under Section 504 of the Rehabilitation Act of 1973 or, if they meet the criteria for another disability or it can be established that they are not achieving due to ADHD, may qualify for services under IDEA. That is, these children and youth may have a co-occurring learning disability or emotional/behavioral disorder (IDEA disability categories) or, if the ADHD is severe to the extent that it interferes substantially with school performance, then the student with ADHD may qualify for special education services under the category of "other health impaired." This policy statement was extremely important because it emphasized the responsibility of both general and special education to appropriately educate all students who have been identified as having ADHD. All state departments of education and local education agencies were now required to assess, identify, and serve students with ADHD in either general education classrooms under Section 504 or in special education under both IDEA and Section 504. Students with ADHD in general education required a written Accommodation Plan and students with ADHD in special education required a written Individual Educational Plan.

At the same time, Congress authorized the Department of Education to fund five centers to synthesize research in ADHD and disseminate their findings with regard to the ADHD knowledge base (Aleman, 1991). Interestingly, the Centers found a voluminous research base, but very few studies had been conducted by educators with school-based samples of children. The vast majority of the studies were reported in the psychology and psychiatry journals. The Miami Center, for example, reviewed over 1,300 studies on ADHD assessment and identification published between 1980 and 1992 and found only 11% of these in educational journals (Hocutt, McKinney & Montague, 1993). Only 38 of these 152 articles pertained to assessment and identification and were conducted, for the most part, by psychologists. Only one of the 38 articles was published in a general education journal; the others were published in special education journals. A report summarizing the findings of the centers was submitted to Congress in 1992. Despite the acknowledgement of ADHD as a disorder that affects millions of individuals and the tremendous knowledge base on ADHD, the disorder still generates considerable controversy about diagnosis and treatment and even its very existence as indicated in a consensus statement by the National Institutes of Health (NIH, 2000). Despite the controversy, based on the sheer amount of research focusing on the behavioral, neurophysiological, psychological, and genetic aspects of the disorder, NIH concluded that it has validity as a disorder. Despite this acknowledgement, it is unlikely that Congress will approve ADHD as a category of disability in the near future.

ADHD: WHAT IS IT?

The American Psychiatric Association (APA, 1994) estimated the prevalence of ADHD to be between 3% and 5% of the school-age population, and research supports this estimated rate although prevalence studies vary substantially in the percentages reported. Longitudinal studies have found that approximately 75% of children continue to display symptoms of ADHD into adulthood (e.g. Biederman, Faraone, Milberger, Curtis, Chen, Marrs, Quellette, Moore & Spencer, 1996). ADHD has undergone several reconceptualizations since its symptoms were first noted in the second edition of the *Diagnostic and Statistical*

Manual of Mental Disorders (DSM II) (APA, 1968) as hyperactive-impulsive behavior. The term *attention deficit disorder* (ADD) was first used in DSM-III (APA, 1980), which actually specified two distinct subtypes based on the presence (ADDH) or absence (ADDnoH) of hyperactivity. DSM-III-R (APA, 1987) eliminated the distinction between ADD with and without hyperactivity but maintained the three primary behavioral indicators: inattention, impulsivity, and hyperactivity. This revision also adopted the inclusive term *attention deficit hyperactivity disorder*. In the fourth and latest edition of the manual, DSM-IV (APA, 1994), extensive national field trials and consensus meetings delineated three subtypes of ADHD: (a) ADHD – predominately inattentive type; (b) ADHD – predominately hyperactive-impulsive type; and (c) ADHD – combined type.

Because there is no established educational definition of ADHD, general and special educators must rely on the DSM-IV criteria for identifying individuals with ADHD. Primary characteristics of ADHD are inattention, hyperactivity, and impulsivity (see Fig. 1 below for a list of the DSM-IV behavioral indicators). For diagnosis of ADHD, not only must students display the

---

INATTENTION
- Does not give close attention to details or makes careless mistakes.
- Has difficulty attending to tasks.
- Does not seem to listen when spoken to.
- Fails to finish schoolwork, chores, or other tasks.
- Is disorganized.
- Avoids or dislikes tasks that require sustained attention.
- Loses things necessary for tasks or activities.
- Is easily distracted by extraneous stimuli.
- Is forgetful in daily activities.

HYPERACTIVITY
- Fidgets with hands and feet and squirms in seat.
- Leaves seat without permission where remaining in seat is expected.
- Runs about or climbs excessively in situations where it is inappropriate.
- Has difficulty playing or engaging in quiet leisure activities.
- Is "on the go" or acts as if "driven by a motor."
- Talks excessively.

IMPULSIVITY
- Blurts out answers before question is completed.
- Has difficulty waiting in lines or taking turns in group situations.
- Interrupts or intrudes on others.

Fig. 1. Primary Behavioral Indicators of ADHD Based on DSM-IV Symptoms.

symptoms associated with the primary characteristics, but they must also meet the following criteria regarding persistence, time of onset, pervasiveness, and severity. Persistence relates to the length of sustained time an individual has exhibited symptoms of inattention and/or hyperactivity-impulsivity. DSM-IV requires that symptoms be present for at least six months. Age of onset refers to the age of the individual at which the behaviors were first evident. DSM-IV states that an individual must have displayed symptoms prior to seven years of age. Pervasiveness refers to the number of settings and situations in which the symptoms are evident. DSM-IV requires that symptoms be severe enough to cause clinically significant problems for individuals in at least two settings (e.g. school, home, and/or work situations).

Inattention means that an individual has difficulty sustaining attention when effort is required. Attentional problems may be less or more noticeable depending on contextual factors. Children with ADHD usually have difficulty staying on task and are easily distracted, appear not to listen, and seldom finish their work without close supervision. They seem to have an attentional bias toward novelty because they generally respond favorably to novel and stimulating activities and frequently are able to sustain attention in these situations. Hyperactivity implies an inordinate activity level. Individuals with hyperactivity frequently fidget constantly, cannot sit for long periods of time, display agitation, and act as if "driven by a motor." Impulsive individuals seem unable to control their behaviors and appear to act without thinking. Impulsivity implies a problem with self-regulation (see Fig. 1).

For diagnosis of ADHD, students must display at least six of the symptoms of inattention and/or display at least six of the symptoms of hyperactivity/impulsivity for at least six months in a developmentally inappropriate manner. Three subtypes are possible. For the ADHD: Predominately Inattentive Type, students will display symptoms of inattention but display less than six of the hyperactivity/impulsivity symptoms. For the ADHD: Predominately Hyperactive-Impulsive Type, students will display symptoms of hyperactivity/impulsivity but display less than six of the inattention symptoms. For the ADHD: Combined Type, students will display at least six symptoms of inattention and six of the hyperactivity/impulsivity symptoms. Students with the Combined Type or Predominately Hyperactive-Impulsive Type have more behavioral and acting out problems, whereas students with the Predominately Inattentive Type have more learning problems. Diagnosis depends also on meeting the criteria of persistence, pervasiveness, severity, and time of onset. That is, behaviors associated with inattention or impulsivity/hyperactivity must be persistent, frequent, severe and developmentally inappropriate. Additionally, the child must have displayed these behaviors before seven years of age. This pattern of behavior must be evident in at least two settings (e.g. home and school) and must seriously impede functioning in a developmentally appropriate manner academically, socially, personally, or occupationally and must not be due to other developmental or personality disorders.

School performance problems seem to characterize all students with ADHD because the behaviors associated with ADHD interfere with a student's productivity in school. In other words, students with ADHD may fail not because they cannot do their schoolwork, but because they do not finish their work and perform poorly on tests. In addition to production problems, students with ADHD may have learning and/or serious behavioral and emotional problems (McKinney, Montague & Hocutt, 1993). ADHD co-occurs with learning disabilities in at least 10% to 20% of the students when stringent identification criteria are applied for both conditions. Students with ADHD and learning disabilities are often described as inattentive and distractible, but not necessarily hyperactive. ADHD can also co-occur with behavioral disorders. Approximately 30% to 50% of these students are seriously aggressive, oppositionally defiant, or conduct disordered. Students with ADHD who have serious emotional problems may be withdrawn, depressed, moody, or anxious. Regardless of the type of ADHD diagnosis, research has consistently reported that students with ADHD are at significantly greater risk than other children for poor academic, social, personal, and vocational outcomes (Barkley, 1990). In sum, ADHD is a life-long condition that is manifested differently over the different developmental stages.

ADHD: ASSESSMENT AND IDENTIFICATION

Educational assessment for ADHD relies on the DSM-IV criteria as described in the last section. To measure severity of behavior, assessment typically involves teacher and parent checklists and rating scales, observational techniques, and interviews. Checklists and rating scales usually reflect the current DSM criteria. One of the primary limitations of keying these measures to the DSM criteria is that the same threshold and operational behaviors are used with all age levels and both boys and girls, which may lead to overidentification of young children and underidentification of girls who may not present with as many of the acting out behaviors as boys but, nonetheless, have serious attentional problems.

Many of the checklists and rating scales have been revised to reflect the DSM-IV criteria (APA, 1994) and to facilitate diagnosis of the DSM-IV ADHD subtypes. For example, the Attention Problems Scale (Achenbach, 1996) is a norm-referenced teacher report form consisting of 20 items that reflect the behavioral indicators listed in DSM-IV for diagnosis of ADHD (e.g, fails to finish things he or she starts, is apathetic or unmotivated, can't sit still/is restless or hyperactive, fidgets, and does messy work). There are several multifactor rating scales that have been used to clinically assess ADHD or for research purposes but these scales are used as well to identify other problem behaviors such as aggression, passivity, anxiety, and immaturity. The Conners teacher and parent rating scales are examples of these multifactor instruments (e.g, Conners, 1969; Goyett, Conners & Ulrich, 1978).

Measuring time of onset and persistence if the child is over seven years of age is critical to diagnosis of ADHD. Persistence is the notion that symptoms as listed in DSM-IV must have been observed and evident for a period of at least six months to a degree that is developmentally inappropriate. Generally, interviews with parents are used to ascertain early age of onset and persistence. Parents are asked a series of structured questions to determine the nature and severity of the ADHD symptoms and to ensure that the behaviors were present in early childhood and have persisted over time. Parent interviews also provide information about current life and family circumstances, the child's developmental history, previous treatment, educational and social experiences, and current behavioral and educational concerns. One example of a structured parent interview intended to gather a comprehensive history and current concerns is Barkley's (1990) ADHD Parent Interview.

To measure situational and temporal variation in behavior and to meet the criterion of pervasiveness (i.e. the behavior occurs across situations and settings), rating scales are usually used. DuPaul and Barkley (1992) developed the Home Situations Questionnaire (HSQ) and the School Situations Questionnaire (SSQ) specifically for the purpose of assessing pervasiveness of symptoms across situations and contexts. The HSQ-Revised has parents rate the severity of problem behaviors in 14 different situations at home such as mealtime, TV time, and playing with friends. The SSQ-Revised has teachers rate the severity of problem behaviors in eight school contexts (e.g. seatwork and small-group work). Observations are usually conducted to confirm or support a diagnosis of ADHD and may be used as well to assess situational and temporal variation in symptoms during different types of lessons and school activities and at different times during the school day. One such standardized procedure is Barkley's (1990) ADHD Behavior Coding System, which has been used to observe ADHD symptoms in clinic playrooms and classroom settings in schools.

Educational Assessment

Assessing students for ADHD from an educational perspective takes into account their academic achievement, productivity, social behavior with teachers and peers, emotional well being, and co-occurring disabilities. A comprehensive assessment for educational purposes is a multistage, multimodal process that considers information and data from a variety of sources to make informed decisions about: (a) the nature and extent of their educational problems; (b) their ability to self-regulate performance and use compensatory strategies appropriately in the context of school activities; (c) their need for specialized programs and related services; and (d) the effectiveness of the educational program and services they receive (Montague & Warger, 1998). Assessment and identification of youngsters with ADHD is a three-stage process.

The first stage of educational assessment is screening, referral if appropriate, and individual evaluation for symptoms or characteristics that may be indicative of ADHD and/or other disabilities. At this stage, the concern is to determine the presence or absence of ADHD and other disabilities. The second stage entails additional assessment to further identify the educational needs of students who have been identified as ADHD in the academic, behavioral, and social-emotional domains. The results of assessment at stage two are used to design either an Individualized Educational Program (IEP) if the student with ADHD qualifies for special education or an Accommodation Plan as required by Section 504 of the Vocational Rehabilitation Act of 1973 for students with ADHD who do not qualify for special education and remain in general education classes. The third stage of assessment has to do with evaluating the efficacy of educational programs. At this stage, based on student progress, modifications to the program may be made in terms of instructional methods, classroom management strategies, and organization of the learning environment.

At the foundation of effective implementation of this multistage process of assessment is the multidisciplinary team composed of general and special education teachers, school administrators, and related service personnel such as school psychologists, nurses, and speech and language clinicians, as well as parents and students. Consultants might be the student's medical doctor or therapist. All of the team members should be involved in making decisions about assessment and identification from the outset for students who have been screened and referred for problems associated with ADHD.

Educational assessment necessitates going beyond the ADHD clinical assessment methods and applying current methods for assessing educational/instructional needs to determine individual needs of students. These methods are much more informal but more useful in designing instructional programs for students. Techniques such as criterion-referenced tests, functional analyses of behavior, systematic observations of classroom performance, student interviews, and work sample analysis provide insight into how students approach school tasks and activities and interact in the school environment.

Planning and modifying educational programs for students with ADHD is vital to their success. Follow-up studies of students with ADHD have indicated that they are retained and suspended from school and also drop out of school more frequently than average students (Barkley, Fischer, Edelbrock & Smallish, 1990). Continued school failure can have a negative impact on a variety of educational, vocational, social, and personal outcomes. As a consequence, it is important that school personnel recognize these students' ADHD problem behaviors but also provide appropriate programming to help them experience success (see Fig. 2).

All school districts must have an evaluation process in place to assess and identify students with ADHD. Figure 2 below presents a typical assessment, identification, and placement process used by school districts to identify students with ADHD. First, a teacher or parent referral is made to the child study team if the youngster is experiencing serious attentional or behavioral problems. The child study team is multidisciplinary in composition very much like the assessment team usually consisting of administrators, special education teachers, classroom teachers, social workers, counselors, school psychologists, and service providers depending on the needs of the child or youth. An assessment plan is

	Teacher or Parent Referral	
Problems Resolved Stop	Child Study Team Recommendations	
No ADHD Diagnosis Stop	Problems Persist Psychoeducational Evaluation	
General Education Class Accommodation Plan	ADHD Diagnosis Placement Recommendation	Special Education Program Individualized Education Program
	Ongoing Evaluation	

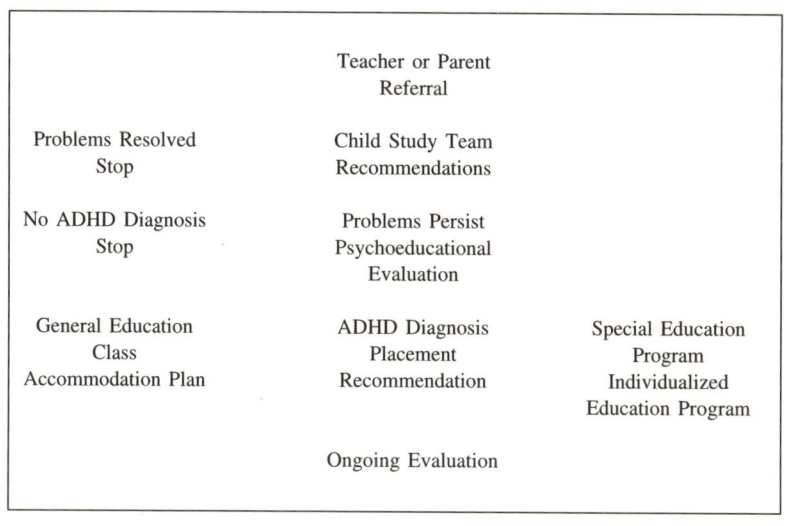

Fig. 2. ADHD Assessment and Identification Process.

Source: Montague & Warger, 1998).

developed to collect additional information about the student's school functioning before a formal referral is made to the district-level special education evaluation team. The team usually asks for additional information about the child's performance and recommends instructional strategies that can be implemented in the general education classroom by the student's teacher. About a month later, they review the case and may stop the process because students' problems have been resolved, continue performance monitoring for a designated period of time, or decide to make a referral to the psychoeducational evaluation team for formal assessment. Following formal assessment, a multidisciplinary committee decides whether or not the student meets the criteria for ADHD and, if so, whether he or she qualifies for special education or remains in the general education program. Evaluation, however, does not stop here for a student with ADHD. The student's behavior must be monitored on an ongoing basis and the IEP or Accommodation Plan must be reviewed periodically to ascertain whether the student is making appropriate progress. If not, the program or plan must be revised.

ADHD: TREATMENT AND INTERVENTIONS

"Best practice" for students with ADHD requires that classroom instruction, management, and curriculum are matched with the individual student's characteristics. Along with the school-based intervention programs, more frequently than not, medication is part of the treatment. Present estimates suggest that approximately 60% to 90% of all students who have been diagnosed with ADHD will be on some form of medication and between 85% and 90% of students with ADHD will be served in the general education classroom for part or all of the school day (Montague & Warger, 1997). Consequently, teachers not only need to have a basic understanding of the behaviors of students with ADHD and how these behaviors interfere with school performance, but also an understanding of the medications that students take as part of their treatment program. Teachers play a major role in monitoring medication and implementing the comprehensive treatment plan. This section describes medical treatments, classroom management approaches, self-monitoring strategies, and parent involvement that, together, may comprise a comprehensive accommodation plan for students with ADHD. Figure 3 provides a list of effective instructional practices that may be useful for teachers in promoting success for students with ADHD in their classrooms.

Medication Programs

Stimulant medication refers to a class of drugs that includes Ritalin, Dexedrine, Cylert, and Adderall (Wilens, 1999) that can help students with ADHD to focus

- *Strength model:* Identify students' strengths and capitalize on them.
- *Brief tasks:* Provide frequent, brief drills or lessons covering chunks of information.
- *Variety:* Present a variety of activities and use a variety of instructional formats.
- *Structure:* Use consistent routines and highly organized formats for activities. Develop and post the daily schedule. Plan smooth transitions between activities and lessons. Clearly state and post rules, expectations, and consequences. Keept to at most three or four rules.
- *Cues and prompts:* Use visual and auditory cues to facilitate learning and transitions (e.g., charts, graphs, color coding, numbering system).
- *Key phrases:* Develop a repertoire of key phrases to keep students focused (e.g., "pencils down," "one, two, three," "eyes on me").
- *Directions:* Keep directions simple, ordered, and clear. Check students' understanding.
- *Modeling:* Use teacher and peer modeling to demonstrate for students the correct way to complete a task or assignment. Use photographs to sequence a set of behaviors to complete a task.
- *Fidgeting:* Allow the student to hold an object (e.g., small rubber ball or sandpaper square).
- *Redirection:* Redirect the child who is having difficulty maintaining attention.
- *Tapping:* Model "quiet tapping" by tapping an arm or leg instead of the desk or table.
- *Physical tasks:* Pair auditory presentations with physical cues (e.g., thumbs up or down for question/answer times). Allow students to doodle on a pad while listening. Have students underline or highlight important information or take notes using diagrams or schematic maps.
- *Positive and corrective feedback:* Give immediate and positive feedback to students when they respond appropriately. Use a token system.
- *Peer tutoring:* Allow students to work with peers but pre-select the pairs or small groups.
- *Mnemonic strategies:* To help students remember, teach the student simple mnemonic strategies. Teach students to use verbalization and visualization as memory aids. Allow students to audiotape material and then play back for review.
- *Self-regulation:* Teach students to use self-monitoring strategies to control their behavior.
- *Social skills instruction:* Explicitly teach students classroom behavior and peer interaction social skills and provide plenty of practice opportunities. Reward appropriate behavior.
- *Computer-based instruction:* Use computers to develop and build skills and for written assignments.

Fig. 3. "Best Practice" for Classroom Teaching.

their attention and control their behavior. Medication may alleviate distractibility, concentration difficulties, attention problems, and disruptive behaviors. Although medication does not in itself improve academic performance, it may improve behaviors that interfere with task completion and thus increase a youngster's productivity. Stimulant medication does not necessarily result in improvement in long-term adjustment in either social behavior or academic achievement (Swanson et al., 1993).

Teachers do not recommend or prescribe medication; that is the responsibility of the child's medical doctor and the ultimate decision of the parent. However, teachers are generally responsible for making sure that students receive their medication on schedule. The school nurse or some designated person is responsible for administering the medication, but the teacher often must remind the youngster to go to the office or clinic at the appropriate time. The student's confidentiality should be respected at all times. Some students do not like to be singled out and often resist leaving the classroom to take their medication. Special arrangements may need to be made for certain children. Teachers are also responsible for monitoring the effects of the medication by observing the student's behavior and noting any anomalies. Side effects can include decreased appetite, insomnia, motor tics, or mood swings. Periodic reports to the school nurse or to the child's parent and/or doctor are necessary. Also, documenting improvement in a student's behavior that supports the use of medication is important. Interfering behaviors need to be noted as to when they occur and under what conditions. As a student's behavior improves, the Accommodation Plan may be modified. As with most treatment or intervention plans, medication is only one part of the overall program to help students achieve success in school. For all practical purposes, medication does not cure ADHD or affect academic achievement; rather, it improves the conditions for learning so that students with ADHD can be more successful academically, socially, and personally.

Classroom Management

Some students can work quite well in a disorganized environment, but most students respond better to an organized classroom environment. Students with ADHD, however, require organization, structure, and routine. Teachers should establish three, or, at most four, rules that are clear and concrete and then communicate the expectations and consequences for infractions of rules. They should also keep in mind that, contrary to popular belief, students with ADHD need variety, novelty, and stimulation in their educational programs. Therefore, although the classroom environment should be predictable, orderly, and free of unnecessary distracters, most students with ADHD need short assignments that are interesting and challenging. They may need to take short breaks during longer lessons and be actively involved. Visual and auditory cues and signals often help students follow directions and stay with the class.

Procedures for performing tasks, completing activities, and making transitions between lessons or between classrooms need to be well defined and communicated to students. Practicing procedures until students can perform them without prompting helps students to internalize routines. Ongoing positive and corrective feedback is a must when students are first acquiring skills and routines. Understanding consequences is difficult for students with ADHD because their underlying problem is an inability to think ahead and monitor themselves. They often do not understand what they did wrong and do not equate the "punishment with the crime," so to speak. The transgression needs to be made clear to these students and an alternative, acceptable behavior must be provided and practiced so students learn appropriate behaviors. Positive reinforcement is a powerful procedure if used correctly. Although most teachers have a basic understanding of principles underlying reinforcement and punishment, they frequently do not apply them appropriately. A solid understanding of why, how, and when these procedures are used effectively as well as consistency in application are critical to their success. Many students with ADHD receive a great deal of negative feedback, which may inadvertently become reinforcing for inappropriate and unacceptable behavior. Therefore, it is essential that teachers carefully plan reinforcement programs and apply them consistently and directly.

Self-Monitoring Strategies

Typically, students develop self-monitoring strategies throughout elementary school. By middle school, these students have a repertoire of effective strategies that help them listen to their teachers and parents, understand directions, complete tasks, and follow rules. Students with ADHD, however, have significant problems managing and monitoring their behavior. They may not tell themselves what to do, ask themselves questions, or reinforce themselves, which are strategies for successfully negotiating daily life. They have a limited self-control system that seems to develop naturally in other students. Because they have difficulty monitoring themselves, they often become dependent on repeated directions and explanations, which wastes valuable learning time and effort (Walker, Shinn, O'Neill & Ramsey, 1987). These students have difficulty getting and staying on task.

As an example, the following simple self-monitoring strategy teaches students self-control and helps them stay on task and complete assignments. This strategy involves being cued to perform necessary steps and then immediately reinforced for completing them. Students who have necessary academic skills can be directly taught to use self-monitoring. This strategy consists of teacher cues, a student checklist, and a systematic reinforcement chart. To focus students' attention on the task, the teacher uses both verbal and nonverbal cues to trigger specific behaviors. The cues can be as simple as:

- Am I listening to my teacher?
- Do I know what to do?
- Did I finish my work?

Students who have difficulty sustaining attention and staying on task may need cues from the teacher (visual icons and/or verbalizations of statements) that correspond with the three important questions above until they have internalized the strategy. Students can be taught to monitor their progress and then are rewarded with privileges and activities when they complete their work.

Parent Involvement

Behaviors associated with ADHD occur across settings and situations. Thus, the treatment plan for individual children must involve parents and others (e.g. after-school care workers, Little League coaches, and therapists) who deal directly with the child in different situations throughout the day. The level of involvement may vary considerably from family to family due to time constraints, interest, and commitment. At the very least, parents need to be encouraged and supported as they learn to responsibly monitor their child's medication program if that is part of the comprehensive treatment plan. With further encouragement, parents can learn to communicate and collaborate with their child's teachers and therapists, use effective strategies for improving their child's behavior and learning, and coordinate their efforts with the school program. Parent support groups and parent education programs are very important and should be part of the total intervention program (Barkley, 1990). Parents of children with ADHD often need outside assistance to help them deal with the recalcitrance of their children. Family counseling may be necessary to help parents understand the nature and extent of their child's problems and deal with their guilt and blame. Although research on the effects of parent education and support systems is limited, it makes sense that parent involvement is critical if we expect behavior improvement to generalize across settings.

CONCLUSION

Students with ADHD are required by law to have a written Individualized Educational Program or Accommodation Plan to help them succeed in school. It is thus incumbent on general and special educators to be well informed about policies governing service provision for these students. Educators and other related professionals also need to be knowledgeable about the characteristic behaviors of these students, procedures for identifying and diagnosing ADHD, and instructional approaches and strategies that are considered "best practice" for these students. A cooperative, multidisciplinary approach to identification, assessment, and service delivery that involves professionals, parents, and students themselves is critical to success for these students. There is ample evidence that with well designed treatment/intervention plans that consider the needs of students and capitalize on their strengths will provide them the opportunity to achieve and be successful in school, at home, and in the community.

REFERENCES

Achenbach, T. M. (1996). Subtyping ADHD: A request for suggestions about relating empirically based assessment to DSM-IV. *The ADHD Report, 4,* 5–9.

Aleman, S. R. (1991). *CRS report for Congress: Special education for children with attention deficit disorder: Current issues.* Washington, D.C.: Congressional Research Service.

American Psychiatric Association (1968). *Diagnostic and statistical manual of mental disorders* (2nd ed., DSM-II). Washington, D.C.: Author.

American Psychiatric Association (1980). *Diagnostic and statistical manual of mental disorders* (3rd ed., DSM-III). Washington, D.C.: Author.

American Psychiatric Association (1987). *Diagnostic and statistical manual of mental disorders* (3rd ed., rev., DSM-III-R). Washington, D.C.: Author.

American Psychiatric Association (1994). *Diagnostic and statistical manual of mental disorders* (4th ed., DSM-IV). Washington, D.C.: Author.

Barkley, R. A. (1990). *Attention-deficit/hyperactivity disorder: A handbook for diagnosis and treatment.* New York: Guilford Press.

Barkley, R. A., Fischer, M., Edelbrock, C. S., & Smallish, L. (1990). The adolescent outcome of hyperactive children diagnosed by research criteria: An 8-year prospective follow-up study. *Journal of the American Academy of Child & Adolescent Psychiatry, 29,* 546–557.

Biederman, J., Faraone, S., Milberger, S., Curtis, S., Chen, L., Marrs, A., Quellette, C., Moore, P., & Spencer, T. (1996). Predictors of persistence and remission of ADHD into adolescence: Results from a four-year prospective follow-up study. *Journal of the American Academy of Child and Adolescent Psychiatry, 35,* 343–351.

Conners, C. K. (1969). A teacher rating scale for use in drug studies with children. *American Journal of Psychiatry, 126,* 884–888.

Davila, R. R., Williams, M. L., & MacDonald, J. T. (1991). *Memorandum to chief state school officers re: Clarification of policy to address the needs of children with attention deficit disorders with general and/or special education.* Washington, D.C.: U.S. Department of Education.

DuPaul, G. J., & Barkley, R. B. (1992). Situational variation of attention problems: Psychometric properties of the revised Home and School Situations Questionnaires. *Journal of Clinical Child Psychology, 21*, 178–188.

Goyett, C. H., Conner, C. K., & Ulrich, R. F. (1978). Normative data on Revised Conners Parent and Teacher Rating Scales. *Journal of Abnormal Child Psychology, 6*, 221–236.

Hocutt, A. M., McKinney, J. D., & Montague, M. (1993). Issues in the education of students with attention deficit disorder: Introduction to the special issue. *Exceptional Children, 60*, 103–106.

McKinney, J. D., Montague, M., & Hocutt, A. M. (1993). Educational assessment of students with attention deficit disorder. *Exceptional Children, 60*, 125–131.

Montague, M., & Warger, C. (1997). Helping students with Attention Deficit Hyperactivity Disorder succeed in the classroom. *Focus on Exceptional Children, 30*, 1–16.

Montague, M., & Warger, C. L. (1998). *Attention Deficit Hyperactivity Disorder Knowledge and skills: A training program for educators.* Reston, VA: Exceptional Innovations, Inc.

National Institutes of Health (2000). Consensus and development conference statement: Diagnosis and treatment of attention-deficit/hyperactivity disorder. *Journal of the American Academy of Child and Adolescent Psychiatry, 39*, 182–193.

Swanson, J. M., McBurnett, K., Wigal, T., Pfiffner, L. J., Lerner, M. A., Williams, L., Christian, D. L., Tamm, L., Willcutt, E., Crowley, K., Clevenger, W., Khouzam, N., Woo, C., Crinella, F. M., & Fisher, T. D. (1993). Effect of stimulant mediation on children with attention deficit disorder; A "review of reviews." *Exceptional Children, 60*, 154–162.

Walker, H. M., Shinn, M. R., O'Neill, R. E., & Ramsey, E. (1987). A longitudinal assessment of the development of antisocial behavior in boys: Rationale, methodology, and first year results. *Remedial and Special Education, 8*, 7–16.

Wilens, T. E. (1999). *Straight talk about psychiatric medications for kids.* New York: Guilford Press.

GUIDING PRINCIPLES FOR THE EDUCATION OF CHILDREN AND YOUTH WITH SEVERE AND MULTIPLE DISABILITIES

Ernest Rose, Beverly Rainforth and Daniel Steere

INTRODUCTION

The design of appropriate education for children and youth with severe and multiple disabilities is based upon a foundation of philosophical values. For the past three decades, values such as the principle of normalization (Nirje, 1970), age appropriateness (Brown, Branston-McClean, Baumgart, Vincent, Falvey & Schroeder, 1978; Brown, Branston, Hamre-Nietupski, Pumpian, Certo & Gruenewald, 1979), and functionality of curriculum (Brown, Nietupski & Hamre-Nietupski, 1976; Wehman, 1997) have fundamentally shaped the way curriculum is designed and implemented for learners with severe and multiple disabilities. Each of these values emerged as individuals with severe disabilities sought to be part of everyday life in American society. Although the aforementioned values also influence and shape the conceptualization of an appropriate education for learners with severe disabilities, the chapter offers additional guiding principles that form the foundation for current educational discourse. These principles are discussed in the following subsections.

Emphasis on Abilities, Not Deficits

Historically, educators have focused efforts on trying to remediate deficits in students with disabilities. By remediating deficit areas, it was thought that the child would become more "normal" and therefore able to engage in typical activities to a greater degree. There are, however, two major fallacies with this logic. First, because individuals with severe and multiple disabilities may require support in a number of areas, an inordinate amount of time may be spent trying to "fix" areas in which difficulty is experienced. This, in turn, can reduce the time during which such children could be participating in other activities with age peers. Secondly, the deficit-remediation orientation fails to identify and build upon the strengths, gifts, and unique characteristics of individuals that may be valued by others. These positive attributes become points of commonality among people within inclusive schools and communities. Consequently, our orientation is that the design and implementation of education for learners with severe and multiple disabilities must be based largely on identifying and strengthening their abilities, talents, and gifts.

Readiness of Supports versus Readiness of People

A corollary of deficit remediation is the assessment of readiness of people. That is, despite efforts to remediate identified deficits, too often it was determined that students with severe and multiple disabilities were not yet ready for: (a) participation in a particular activity; (b) interaction with nondisabled individuals; or (c) participation in everyday community environments. These decisions, made typically by professionals, held individuals with severe disabilities back from full participation in and benefit from school and other social institutions. Instead, they were held in a perpetual limbo, "caught in the continuum" (Taylor, 1988), residing in a permanent state of getting ready for something that typically never came. As Taylor (1988) pointed out, the existence of a continuum of placement options, whether in educational, residential, or adult day services, has three obvious problems:

- The need for support and where one spends time are confused;
- People need to move from one option to another as their needs change;
- People with severe disabilities are often denied the opportunity for movement to less restrictive placements.

Our orientation is that individuals with severe disabilities are ready to fully participate in school and community life once proper and necessary support systems have been established. This orientation is also a hallmark of current legislation that supports individuals with disabilities. For example, the Least Restrictive Environment (LRE) mandate of the Individuals with Disabilities Education Act (IDEA; PL 105-17) clearly specifies that students with disabilities should be educated in the typical classroom with their nondisabled peers, unless it is clearly demonstrated that an appropriate education cannot be provided, even with supplementary aids and services. Likewise, the Rehabilitation Act Amendments of 1998 (part of the Workforce Investment Act of 1998) contains language clarifying that individuals with disabilities are capable of obtaining competitive employment in the community. Finally, the Americans with Disabilities Act (ADA; PL 101-336) provides protections for the participation of individuals with disabilities in the areas of employment, telecommunications, and access to community services. The onus of responsibility is not upon the individual with severe and multiple disabilities to "earn" the right to participate in school in society; rather, it is upon those who support the individual to design creative and flexible support systems that allow participation to occur.

Inclusive Schools and Communities

The pieces of legislation mentioned above share a common focus on inclusion in school and community life. In particular, the LRE mandate is clear in its statement in favor of placement in regular education with supplementary aids and services. However, IDEA recognizes a continuum of placement options to meet the unique needs of individual students. This continuum, based upon the work of Reynolds (1962), was incorporated into the Education of All Handicapped Children Act of 1975 (PL 94-142), which was subsequently renamed IDEA (1990, 1997). It should be noted, however, that Reynolds and Birch (1977) later amended Reynolds' original recommendations to focus instead on a continuum of supports as needed to assist students to be successful in regular education.

In recent years, the attitude of supporting students with severe and multiple disabilities in inclusive regular education settings has gained strength. Advocates, families, and professionals have refocused their efforts on the original intent of the LRE provision of PL 94-142, particularly the need for creative and unique supplementary aids and services. A similar refocusing on supporting inclusion has occurred within the employment arena, as individuals with severe disabilities enter the workforce through supported employment programs. In each of these movements, the underlying philosophy is the presumption that the individual is ready for participation once the necessary supports are in place. Across the country, this is affirmed by countless examples of participation in schools and communities by people who were at one time deemed not ready for those environments (Brown et al., 1976; Brown et al., 1978; Brown et al., 1979; Wilcox & Bellamy, 1982).

Importance of Parents, Family, and Friends in Education and Supporting Services

Parents, family, and friends have important roles as advocates, informants, planners, and problem solvers for children and youth with severe and multiple disabilities (Fishbaugh, 1997; Rainforth & York-Barr, 1997; Steere, Rose & Fishbaugh, 1999). Parent groups established the first educational programs for this population, and litigation by parents on behalf of their children with severe and multiple disabilities led to the Education of All Handicapped Children Act of 1975 (Osborne, 1996; Rose & Hueffner, 1984). As a result, parent involvement in planning their child's special education program is a central tenet of the current IDEA. While school personnel may be deeply involved with a student for one or two years, parents and other family members are involved for a lifetime, so they have commitments to and vested interests in the outcomes of the educational program. Families and friends also bring perspectives on the history, gifts, talents, needs, and personality of their child or friend with severe and multiple disabilities that are rarely captured in school records. Friends without disabilities often look past the deficits on which professionals focus and recommend attention to qualities that would improve acceptance of their friend, like haircuts and clothing. These perspectives are essential to planning programs that are worthwhile.

School personnel often struggle with the concept and practice of family participation. Ongoing research has demonstrated that the type, amount, and quality of family involvement will vary, depending upon: (a) family resources and demands; (b) match between culture of school and home; and (c) school attitude toward parents (Salisbury & Dunst, 1997; Soodak & Erwin, 2000; Welch & Sheridan, 1995). Extra efforts are needed to find ways of involving family members whose own education was unpleasant, whose employment status and support networks limit the times and ways they can participate, or whose lives are occupied with other issues (Welch & Sheridan, 1995). In contrast, parents with greater educational, financial, and interpersonal resources often desire a greater role in their child's education than school personnel have offered. Parents feel more welcome and enjoy greater collaboration when schools have an "open-door policy" and ongoing exchange of information about the content and effectiveness of the educational program (see Soodak & Erwin, 2000).

Collaboration Among Teachers, Related Service Providers, Students, and Their Families

Developing effective program plans for students with severe and multiple disabilities usually require input from many specialists, including special education, communication, occupational and physical therapy, and nursing. Coordinating all these services is challenging and, unfortunately, parents have reported that failure of school personnel to work together presents a significant barrier to inclusive education (Soodak & Erwin, 2000). Two strategies to achieve the collaboration required for an appropriate education are a transdisciplinary approach and integrated therapy (Rainforth & York-Barr, 1997). A transdisciplinary approach is one in which educational team members cross discipline boundaries to exchange knowledge and skills (known as "role release") so they can incorporate methods from all relevant disciplines into a comprehensive plan of instruction. Integrated therapy means that, rather than therapists contriving tasks to practice isolated skills, they embed their instruction on communication and sensory-motor skills into natural routines and everyday activities in home, school, and community. Students with severe and multiple disabilities and their families provide important input about which activities are priorities for participation, and can also provide a "reality check" as to whether instructional strategies are effective and manageable in daily routines (Friend, 2000). Real collaboration is also promoted by scheduling meetings around others' commitments, soliciting input from all, working toward consensus, and finding the communication modes that work best for a particular team, for example, phone calls, email, fax, or form notes, in addition to face-to-face meetings (Fishbaugh, 1997, 2000; Friend & Cook, 2000; Rainforth & York-Barr, 1997).

The Concept of an Extended Classroom

In keeping with the principle of *Inclusive Schools and Communities*, the educational needs of children and youth with severe and multiple disabilities would be an almost insurmountable challenge if those needs were thought to be met only in a school classroom (Steere et al., 1999). The school, home, and community are integral domains in the relevant curricula and have long been shown to be productive environments for teaching and learning (Brown et al., 1979; Cross & Villa, 1992; Steere, 1997; Wilcox & Bellamy, 1987). Likewise, the role of the teacher is more expansive in the extended classroom model so that she or he has responsibilities as a service coordinator organizing the activities of parents, family, friends, school administrators, related services specialists, community agency providers, and employers. And, by extending the classroom into the community, individuals with severe and multiple disabilities are able to develop and maintain a larger and more stable network of friends and advocates than with school peers alone (see Steere et al., 1999).

From Advocacy to Self Determination

For persons with severe and multiple disabilities to gain the greatest benefit from their education, individual support plans, and learning experiences, a process of planning that includes family, friends, and advocates should be enacted throughout the school years. An important characteristic of this planning process should be the preparation of individuals with disabilities to assume as much personal advocacy or self-determination as possible (Wehmeyer, 1996). The 1992 and 1998 amendments to the Rehabilitation Act specified policy related to self-determination (West, Kregel & Revell, 1994). These amendments required that Individualized Plans for Employment (IPE) be developed by the consumer and the vocational rehabilitation counselor in consideration of the individual's employment goals and job preferences (West et al., 1994). Thus, the importance of individuals learning to participate as advocates on their own from the school years through the adult years is now a well-recognized practice (Steere et al., 1999; Wehmeyer, 1996).

An example of planning and advocacy through the process of positive futures planning (Mount & Zwernik, 1988; O'Brien, 1987) is the McGill Action Planning System (MAPS) (Forest & Pierpoint, 1992). This system is a departure from traditionally formal meetings between professional staff, parents, and "clients." MAPS promotes a conversation about choosing desirable outcomes in a comfortable setting (Forest & Pierpoint, 1992). Participants include the individual with a disability, parents, and professional staff, but also included are siblings, extended family, friends, and others as invited by the individual or parents. This non-clinical approach to planning focuses on the hopes and fears of the individual, and depending upon the individual's age, those of the parents. This process focuses on what it will take for the hopes to be realized and the fears to be diminished. From this activity, priorities of goals and activities can be set and responsibilities to accomplish them assigned (Rainforth & York-Barr, 1997). As mentioned previously, a significant benefit of the process is the encouragement of the individual to participate as fully as possible in setting priorities and responsibilities. For individuals with severe and multiple disabilities, there may be significant challenges to communicating desires and responsibilities, but any such participation is progress and can lead to greater self-advocacy and self-determination for making life's choices (Wehmeyer, 1996).

Transition as a Function of the Extended Classroom

IDEA requires annual transition planning for children with disabilities beginning at age 14; gaining greater specificity by age 16 and beyond (Friend & Bursuck, 1999). While this is accepted as good policy for students with mild or moderate disabilities, children with severe and multiple disabilities need greater longitude in planning transitions from home to school, from school level to school level (e.g. elementary school to middle school), from school to community, and from school to employment (Hunter, 1999). The environments individuals and communities construct as living, learning, and working spaces may work for those of us who do not have disabilities and for those who have mild to moderate disabilities, but they often create significant barriers or "handicaps" for persons with severe and multiple disabilities. Thus, as a society, we must be ever mindful of how children with such disabilities might interact in the various environments of their lives. Every change in environmental space and personal interaction constitutes a transition for children with severe and multiple disabilities. It becomes particularly important then, that transition planning includes micro-level activities (e.g. moving from the bus into the school building) with the same attitude of importance as macro-level activities (e.g. using the city transportation system to go to work and to shop).

UNDERSTANDING CHARACTERISTICS OF CHILDREN AND YOUTH WITH SEVERE AND MULTIPLE DISABILITIES

The Individuals with Disabilities Education Act of 1997 (PL 105-17) defines many categories of disabilities and requires states to report the number of students assigned each label. However, IDEA does not define the term "severe and multiple disabilities" so there is a lack of agreement about this population. Another federal law, the Developmental Disabilities Assistance and Bill of Rights Act Amendments of 1994 (PL 103-230) provides a definition that helps explain some of the characteristics of students with severe and multiple disabilities. This act defines "developmental disability" as:

> a severe, chronic disability, . . . that is attributable to a mental or physical impairment or combination of mental and physical impairments; results in substantial functional limitations in three or more of the following areas of major life activity:

(i) self-care;
  (ii) receptive and expressive language;
  (iii) learning;
  (iv) mobility;
  (v) self-direction;
  (vi) capacity for independent living; and
  (vii) economic self-sufficiency; and

reflects the individual's need for a combination and sequence of special, interdisciplinary, or generic services, supports, or other assistance that is of lifelong or extended duration and is individually planned and coordinated... (42 U.S.C. 6000 Sec. 102 (8)).

Brown, Nisbet, Ford, Sweet, Shiraga, York and Loomis (1983) suggested a professional definition that looks at the one percent of the school-age population with the most significant disabilities as "severely handicapped." Directly, this definition refers to a very small portion of the population who need extensive supports to participate in education, community living, and work due to their disabilities. Children with severe and multiple disabilities might also have medical diagnoses such as cerebral palsy, autism, Down syndrome, Rett syndrome, or hydrocephaly, to name just a few, but these labels do not necessarily indicate severe and multiple disabilities. Students with severe and multiple disabilities have "functional limitations" in their ability to learn and frequently are considered to have mental retardation. Nevertheless, when a student has multiple disabilities it is extremely difficult to conduct valid measures of cognitive ability. Due to the nature of their disabilities, children with severe and multiple disabilities are usually identified at birth or in early childhood. Rarely is diagnostic testing required to determine that disabilities are present. However, such testing may be useful in determining the intensity of the disabilities.

To understand the population better, we introduce Tamara. We are using her experiences as an individual with severe and multiple disabilities to illustrate points of discussion. She lives with her mother and older brother and has attended regular classes at the same schools her brother attended. She has a long and complex medical history and many medical labels, including brain damage, cerebral palsy, and legal blindness. She requires support to sit, but with support she is able to drive her power wheelchair and use her electronic communication system. Tamara's speech is quite limited, but she can signal "yes" and "no" with head movements, press keys on her electronic "talker" and sometimes when she is quite excited, she says a few words. Because of her other limitations, assessing her understanding of academic content has been an ongoing challenge. She has some use of one hand, and needs careful positioning of materials to handle them. She needs assistance with all self-care. At home and throughout her school day, she needs a high level of support to participate and have her needs met, and her requirements for support services are expected to continue indefinitely. Tamara's IEP calls for her to use her electronic communication system more spontaneously and for more activities; to improve reading skills (e.g. listening comprehension, sight vocabulary); to write using a computer and keyboard adaptation; to improve understanding and application of number concepts (e.g. object sets, and coins and values); to learn main ideas from science and social studies; to improve oral motor skills for speech and eating; and to increase use of her power wheelchair. To achieve her IEP objectives, Tamara has received services from a special education teacher, physical therapist, occupational therapist, speech-language pathologist, and teacher for persons with visual impairments.

It is important to understand Tamara's abilities and needs, but the information above doesn't tell much about who Tamara is as a person. It does not convey that she loves her mom and brother, likes some school personnel much more than others, has a crush on a boy in her class, and likes to cook. She does not like being different from other students, being left out of activities, or missing school. Tamara's team, including Tamara, her mother, her brother, and two friends, have created a vision of a positive future for her, and have determined what her ideal day should look like. Her team agreed that, during the next few years, they would like to see her keep living at home, going to the same schools and classes that her brother did, and start using more of the community for recreation. For example, Tamara could go to the library for reading club, shop at the mall, and use local parks and the community pool in the summer. More immediately, they would like to see Tamara become a more active member of her class, and receive instruction that is both geared to her abilities and closely aligned with class activities. Her team would like to function more like a multidisciplinary team, with special education and related services providing more support for her within regular classroom activities and routines. In the end, the team would like to see greater communication and collaboration between home and school.

EDUCATION AND SUPPORTING SERVICES

Based on the aforementioned details, we make the case for continuous curricula that longitudinally focus on adult outcomes in inclusive settings. Such curricula must concentrate on immediate needs of children with severe and multiple disabilities, but do so in ways that build foundations and skill sets, and establish support systems that will progressively serve these children as they become adolescents and eventually adults. Therefore, it is important to teach Tamara greater independence in getting to the school bus stop using her power wheelchair, not solely because it makes mornings easier for her mother and brother, but because in years to come it should give her more independence in getting to a metro bus stop to get to work or to shop. Likewise, it is important for her to improve her communication skills not only to communicate better with her peers and her teachers, but also to enable her to communicate with other members of society (e.g. inquiring of a clerk the location of a department in a store or ordering food from a waiter in a restaurant).

Most children with severe and multiple disabilities will be identified as disabled very early in their lives, and over the next 21 years will receive instruction in a variety of educational environments. Although these children continue to have severe and multiple disabilities throughout their lives, the characteristics of effective instructional settings will change as they grow up. The supports that are provided will shift and change over their lifespan. Thus, the balance of settings and responsibilities shifts as individuals grow and move through early childhood programs, to elementary school, to middle school, to high school, and then, fully into the community.

Early Childhood Education

A physician is usually the one who determines that an infant or toddler has severe and multiple disabilities, and soon after refers the family to an agency that provides early intervention or early childhood special education services. Although it is convenient for service providers to centralize their programs, home and possibly day care are the natural "centers" for infants and toddlers. Effective early intervention services will keep the home and family in their focus, integrating "education" and "therapy" into family daily routines rather than creating additional tasks for parents to perform (Rainforth & York-Barr, 1997). For infants and toddlers up through the age of two, IDEA (PL 105-17) requires an Individualized Family Service Plan (IFSP), which addresses the needs of the child, like an IEP, as well as the needs of the family as a whole. For example, when Tamara was an infant, her IFSP team identified needs for family counseling, parent education, and infant development.

Depending on needs identified by the team, services might also include home programs, parent-child groups at a center, preschool classes, or some combination of these services. For infants and toddlers, IDEA also requires assignment of a service coordinator to ensure that all required services are provided and well aligned. One strategy for selecting the service coordinator is to determine who could best address one of the family's primary needs. This person has a central role in working with the family and, when using a transdisciplinary approach (Rainforth & York-Barr, 1997), the service coordinator works closely with other service providers to synthesize strategies from all assigned disciplines. This approach eliminates duplication and contradictions among service providers while reducing the number of professionals with whom the family must interact. Tamara's IFSP team selected an occupational therapist (OT) as the service coordinator. When Tamara and her mother attended the *Mothers and Babies* group at the Community Preschool Center, the OT worked with all the professionals to determine the intervention strategies most important to address her needs. Then, rather than impose "teaching" or "exercises" on top of demanding daily care tasks, the OT and Tamara's mother looked at bathing, dressing, play, mealtime, naptime, and outings to see where it made sense to incorporate positioning, language stimulation, movement, hand use, and other areas of development. Addressing Tamara's special needs in the course of the daily routine also provided the OT with many opportunities to help her mother improve her parenting skills without being judgmental.

When children with disabilities reach their third birthday, IDEA requires either an IEP or an IFSP. Although the lives of three, four, and five-year-olds are still centered at home and, perhaps, daycare, many start to attend preschool programs, and these educational settings become relevant to young children with severe and multiple disabilities. Special education and related services are often provided in cooperation with Head Start programs, preschool programs at public day care facilities, and private preschools. The play and self-care activities that are developmentally appropriate practice for typical preschoolers (Bredekamp, 1997) offer excellent opportunities for instruction in sensory-motor, communication, cognitive, and social skills (Rainforth & York-Barr, 1997). Although children with severe and multiple disabilities may need adaptations to participate, their learning objectives remain similar to preschool students without disabilities. During preschool years, Tamara's team discovered that she was very motivated by activities with other children. She learned to make choices between friends to sit next to, toys she wanted to play with, and songs she wanted to sing during circle time by touching the picture of her choice. She started shaking her head "yes" or "no" to answer questions about the weather, stories that were read, and what she wanted to eat. She was learning to sit on the floor with support and crawl short distances in play areas. Using a transdisciplinary and integrated therapy approach, teachers and therapists provide their services within the context of the preschool's daily routine (McWilliam, 1996). In Tamara's class, an OT and a speech-language pathologist worked closely with the teachers to plan activities that would address student needs, to co-teach these lessons, and to share information that would allow teachers and paraprofessionals to use "therapy methods" when related service providers were away.

Because parents' perspectives are valued, professional personnel must continue to communicate regularly with them through journals and phone calls, home visits that fit the family's schedule, and an open door policy at school. In Tamara's case, ongoing communication prepares and encourages parents to have a leadership role in shaping the IEP. School personnel also explore roles that parents want to play in their child's education, while also recognizing the family system dynamics that may limit parent participation (Lambie, 2000).

Elementary School

During the elementary years, curricular demands rise and transitions increase rapidly. It is often assumed that children with severe and multiple disabilities cannot "keep up" and would be better served in special classes or special schools. As discussed in our *Guiding Principles*, however, educating students with severe and multiple disabilities in regular classes is an important and effective practice, when appropriate supports are provided. The classroom team for a student with severe and multiple disabilities will usually include the regular education teacher, special education teacher, paraprofessional, and related service providers as determined by needs of the individual student (Ryndak, 1996).

Designing appropriate instruction starts with the special education teacher and regular education teacher carefully examining the regular education curriculum, activities, and routines, and identifying the opportunities that already exist to address the student's IEP objectives (Rainforth & York-Barr, 1997). Even when academic tasks need significant adaptation, class activities and routines usually offer numerous opportunities for a student with severe and multiple disabilities to develop important sensory-motor, communication, cognitive, social, and self-care skills. As indicated earlier, when Tamara's fourth grade class worked on oral reading, she worked on listening comprehension and answering factual questions, using her electronic communication system. During journal writing, Tamara was learning to type a short sentence on the computer, using an adapted keyboard, word prediction program, and voice output system that would allow her to "read" her journal entries to others. During spelling and math, Tamara used many of the same materials as her classmates, but was learning to point to the correct word or number, from a choice of two. For science and social studies, main concepts were identified for her to learn. She often led the Pledge of Allegiance and announced correct answers for homework or quizzes by pressing a micro-switch attached to a tape recorder. These tasks allowed Tamara to work alongside her classmates and play valued roles in the class routine, while she worked on fine motor (pointing and pressing), cognitive (symbol recognition), and communication skills.

The special education teacher and related service providers take responsibility for: (a) designing instructional strategies; (b) providing or developing adapted equipment and materials; and (c) teaching other members of the team to use new strategies, equipment, and materials through "role release" (Rainforth & England, 1997). Tamara's team worked closely with their OT and vision specialist to make sure materials were sized, colored, and positioned appropriately for her to see and touch. She also wore splints on her hands for part of the day, to prevent deformity, and the OT helped figure out how she could both wear the splints and use her hands to participate. The physical therapist (PT) worked with the classroom team to determine appropriate times to teach her to drive her power wheelchair in the classroom, and to position her on a standing board, to strengthen her legs, improve her circulation and digestion, and prevent deformities (Rainforth & York-Barr, 1997).

While classroom team members are teaching specific skills, they also keep in mind that they are facilitating inclusion. As a result, supports are provided in ways that do not inadvertently prevent interactions with other students (Giangreco, Edelman, Luiselli & McFarland, 1997). Because friendships take on increasing importance during the elementary years, both at school and at home after school and on weekends, school has an important role in promoting social networks for children with severe and multiple disabilities (Sapon-Shevin, Dobbelaere, Corrigan, Goodman & Mastin, 1998). Tamara had a circle of friends who enjoyed helping her with her work in class (when their own work permits), helping her make transitions to other areas of the classroom, opening doors for her when she drove her wheelchair to other areas of the school, sitting with her in the cafeteria, and playing during free time and recess. The team taught all the students how to communicate with Tamara and how to help her reach for and hold materials when they were playing. Her mother was pleased to report that children in the neighborhood knew her and included her in some after school and weekend activities.

For instruction to be effective, in any setting, it must be intentional (i.e. goal directed) and systematic (Snell & Brown, 2000). For students with severe and multiple disabilities, systematic instruction usually involves a specific set of two or three prompts (e.g. verbal, visual, and physical), separated by a short pause (e.g. 5 seconds) to give the student time to respond. This "prompting sequence" is individualized to reflect best learning modes for the student and task. For example, Tamara's team determined that, for most tasks, they could use a prompt sequence involving the following three steps:

(1) Ask a question or give an instruction (e.g. "Point to an *ocean* on the map" or "Press the button to tell everyone the answers"), and wait five seconds for Tamara to start to respond.
(2) If she doesn't respond, or responds incorrectly, rephrase the question/instruction while pointing to direct her gaze toward the desired response (e.g. "which one is an ocean?" or "press the button"), and wait five seconds for Tamara to start to respond.
(3) If she doesn't respond, or responds incorrectly, gently guide Tamara's hand to the correct position and give a brief explanation if needed (e.g. "this is an ocean").

After the student learns a new skill, systematic instruction continues to ensure routine use, improve proficiency (speed and quality), and apply the skill in a variety of situations (Snell & Brown, 2000).

It is a time-consuming process for professionals from different disciplines to organize themselves into a classroom team, learn the unique needs of students with severe and multiple disabilities, design systematic instruction plans, and engage in role release needed to provide effective instruction. Elementary schools that include students with severe and multiple disabilities in regular education classes often find that creating a new team each year is neither efficient for staff nor effective for students. One strategy to improve continuity is for a special education team to link with a multi-grade team (e.g. K-1-2 team, or 3-4-5 team). This regular education-special education team would commit to educating students with severe and multiple disabilities together for a series of years, enabling them collectively to develop the expertise needed to provide effective education. No more than two students with severe and multiple disabilities are assigned to each of the three classrooms, to maintain appropriate diversity in the classroom (Rainforth & England, 1997). Although these students present new challenges for many regular education teachers, practitioners who already use learner-centered, activity-based, and multi-level instruction recognize that the needs of students with severe and multiple disabilities can be accommodated in the same ways as other types of diversity in the classroom.

At the elementary level, the special education teacher usually serves as team leader and service coordinator for students with severe and multiple disabilities. In this capacity, the teacher maintains home-school communication, supervises paraprofessionals, and assists related service providers in defining their roles and responsibilities to provide their services in the context of classroom activities (Rainforth & York-Barr, 1997). As noted, Tamara's school had an open-door policy and encouraged her mother to visit school whenever possible. The special education teacher did not have time to write daily journal entries about Tamara, so the team developed one-page forms that addressed the topics most important to her mother and the classroom team, including changes in health, new abilities, special activities, and services provided. Just prior to her annual review, representatives of the classroom team met with her mother to discuss progress, goals for the next year, and any concerns. Because of the ongoing home-school communication, the team had already agreed on most matters before they arrived at the IEP meeting. Additionally, the special education teacher takes the lead in developing a portfolio for each student with severe and multiple disabilities, to document student achievements with videotape, photographic, and paper evidence. This portfolio supports smooth transitions through elementary grades, and from elementary to middle school while also fulfilling state mandates for student evaluation (Kleinert & Kearns, 1999).

Middle School

By the sixth or seventh grade, students typically begin to have more than one major teacher for core academic subjects. Consequently, the ability to stay organized and to handle increased academic demands becomes important. Different teachers also provide special subjects, such as music, art, health, physical education. Thus, students at the intermediate or middle school level need to generalize their academic, communication, and social behaviors to multiple classrooms and instructors. Special educators and related services personnel continue to work as part of the educational team with a representative group of subject area teachers. The role and scope of peers increase as important supporters and advocates in the learning process (Wilcox & Bellamy, 1984; Wilcox & Bellamy, 1987).

This can be an especially confusing time for students with severe and multiple disabilities and educators who work directly with them. As more students with severe disabilities are remaining in general education classrooms for a good portion of the school day, some fundamental questions on how instruction should be directed in the inclusive classroom arise for both general and special educators. McDonnell (1998) suggested a two-fold model to answer such questions. The first part of the model addresses strategies for improving the instructional foundation of inclusive classrooms. These strategies, which are supported by the instructional behavior of teachers, are the use of heterogeneous groupings, cooperative learning, and peer tutoring (McDonnell, 1998).

Heterogeneous grouping has been advocated for some time, but homogenous groupings have been the historical practice in both general and special education. Some recent studies (Slavin, 1996; Veeman, 1995) have questioned the efficacy of homogenous grouping, finding no apparent advantage to this traditional practice. For instance, Slavin suggested that heterogeneous grouping focuses teacher attention on the individual needs of all students in a group rather than attending primarily to elements of the lesson, which are presumed to be appropriate for all students in a homogeneous group.

Cooperative learning has emerged as a popular strategy for minimizing competition and maximizing collective efforts among students to facilitate learning. Working in heterogeneous groups, students are directed to work together to get the most out of their own potential and those of other group members (Johnson, Johnson & Holubec, 1993). Cooperative learning enables teachers to establish clear outcomes for learning just as companies set up objectives for project teams. In both cases, group members may be changed and outcomes may be adjusted depending upon the progress of the group (Thousand, Villa & Nevin, 1994). In addition, peer tutoring has been found to be an effective strategy that benefits students with severe disabilities and those with average to above average abilities (McDonnell, 1998). With very specific planning by the teacher, students without disabilities can help and benefit from the opportunity to tutor their peers with significant disabilities. The process of tutoring can reinforce learning in the tutor and provide encouragement and incentive in the tutee who is working with a peer (McDonald, Mathot-Buckner & Ferguson, 1996; Salisbury, Gallucci, Palombaro & Peck, 1995).

The second part of the model emphasizes student specific strategies. These strategies include parallel instruction, naturalistic teaching procedures, and embedded instruction (McDonnell, 1998). Parallel instruction is typically within a common curriculum domain, but is directed toward the ability level of the student. Thus, while students without disabilities are studying a Shakespearian play, students with severe disabilities can be learning to speak phrases based upon specific cues. McDonnell cautioned overusing parallel instruction because it could lead to "zoning" within inclusion, which would defeat the purpose. However, used in conjunction with heterogeneous grouping, parallel instruction can be planned and used to provide the appropriate instruction for all students in an inclusion classroom.

Another promising strategy appears to be naturalistic teaching procedures. Here, the teacher plans for opportunities to create learning situations within the context of another activity or lesson. For example, when transitioning to any writing activity, Tamara needs to use special hand tools that make it possible for her to press the keys on the computer keyboard. She calls these tools, "keyboard helpers." Tamara's teacher has been trying to get her to ask for her keyboard helpers when she is told the class is going to be engaged in a writing task. The teacher sets the situation by announcing to the class that they will be doing a writing assignment. At that point she points to Tamara's keyboard helpers and asks her, "What do you need?" The plan is for Tamara to ask for the keyboard helpers when so prompted. As time goes on, the teacher will gradually fade the prompt so that she will learn to automatically ask for her keyboard helpers whenever a writing task is announced.

Embedded instruction is another student specific strategy that has been found to be effective in a number of environments and is beginning to be used in inclusive classrooms. As the name implies, embedded instruction refers to teaching discrete skills from a particular domain during regularly scheduled routines and activities in a student's day (McDonnell, 1998). This distributed model of instruction has been demonstrated to be as effective as massed trial instruction for students with severe disabilities and facilitates generalization of learning due to the diversity of teaching environments (Helmstetter & Guess, 1987). Evidently, the elements of the model proposed by McDonnell have been empirically proven in specific situations and environments. They look promising as instructional strategies for inclusive classrooms, but are in need of further investigation in that venue.

High School

In high schools, education in the community outside of the school assumes increasing importance. This is the concept of the extended classroom. Because it is typically difficult to simulate the complex constellation of cues to which one must attend in community environments, experience in community work sites and other community environments are essential. Preparation for employment becomes a focus for students who will enter the workforce after graduation (Wehman, 1996). This includes work exploration, situational assessments, and work training, all of which assist students and their families in planning for the transition to adult working life. A key support role at the secondary level is that of the transition coordinator, who serves as the service coordinator for a student at the transition age (starting at age 14). Course selection decisions and a design for community-based instruction must be chosen from an individual student's desired post-school outcomes in the areas of employment, post-secondary education and training, and community participation. Because the student will spend increasing time away from the school for community-based instruction, the need for such coordination increases throughout high school years. In Tamara's case, she will spend most of her afternoons away from school in the community. She will learn work skills three days a week and independence skills two days a week. These experiences are designed to help Tamara achieve her post-school outcomes of working, living, and recreating in the local community. The members of her service planning team do not want her to end up in a segregated adult program. Community experiences are therefore an essential part of her high school curriculum. Her work preparation takes place at a local catalog distribution center. Tamara's job coach uses systematic instructional strategies, including the system of least prompts as she improves her use of a hand held scanner and performs the job with greater independence. Her success provides a natural motivator for her to continue to develop additional work skills.

Community-based Instruction. The community becomes an important instructional environment during the secondary educational years. As mentioned previously, it is extremely difficult to recreate or simulate the range of complex stimuli or cues that one must attend to for success in community environments. These cues often vary in subtle ways from situation to situation (e.g. the differences across automatic teller machines or ATMs), and direct experience with such variations is essential. For Tamara, such community training involves finding her way from one place to another in the community. This requires the ability to cross multiple streets using her wheelchair and to determine the correct buses to take to work and to other community locations. She is also learning to select items in stores and to use her check/debit card to purchase products.

A particular challenge with the provision of community-based instruction is the provision of sufficient opportunities for students to master needed skills. Although scheduling and transportation constitute formidable logistical challenges, teams must provide students with frequent enough opportunities to perform skills within community environments. Students with severe and multiple disabilities typically need more practice than their nondisabled peers, so the provision of sufficient opportunities for instruction becomes critical (Wehman, 1996). For instance, during Tamara's high school years, she began to receive instruction in the community. One of her initial work experiences was an unpaid intern at a catalog distribution center. Her transition team was aware they had to ensure that Department of Labor regulations were met to allow non-paid work experiences take place in a legal manner. Guidelines for adherence to the Fair Labor Standards Act (PL 99-150) are available in school district offices and clarify how schools can provide their students with needed experience while ensuring that employers meet their legal obligations (Wehman, 1996).

Family Support and Involvement. As we have previously stated, the secondary level curriculum should be driven by the desired post-graduation outcomes for adult living. IDEA (PL 105-17) describes transition as an outcome-oriented process that promotes the movement of students from school to post-school life. Desired outcomes in the areas of employment, post-secondary education or training, community living, and recreation and leisure are clarified on an individual student basis. These outcomes then provide the rationale for the selection of annual goals and short-term objectives within the rest of the IEP. Table 1 shows an example of the relationship between desired transition (post-school) outcomes and annual goals and short-term objectives.

Naturally, this selection of desired outcomes necessitates the involvement of family members who will provide longitudinal support for students. Because family members are typically one of the most enduring sources of support, their involvement in secondary education is essential. Not only do family members coordinate with school personnel to support instruction throughout the school day, they also provide needed instruction at home and within their home community. This is important for any secondary level student, as the school cannot provide all needed instruction across all skill areas necessary for success in adulthood.

Systematic Instruction. Students with severe and multiple disabilities in secondary schools continue to require systematic instruction. Teachers and job coaches must be skilled in using a number of teaching strategies that have been shown to assist students with disabilities (Steere et al., 1999). Table 2 lists essential instructional strategies that are used to teach students with severe disabilities in school and community environments. These are organized into antecedent strategies that occur before responding takes place and help the learner to respond correctly; task modification strategies that shape or change the quality of the learner's response; and consequent strategies, that either reinforce or correct the learner's responding. For additional information regarding these instructional strategies, the reader is referred to Alberto and Troutman (1999).

Functional Assessment. Students whose behaviors put them at odds with others can impede efforts to include them in school and community environments. Because it is presumed that inappropriate behaviors serve a function or purpose for the student (e.g. to communicate the need for attention

Table 1. Example Transition Outcome and Associated Annual Goal and Short-Term Objective.

Student: Tamara	
Transition Outcome:	Tamara will live in her own apartment with a roommate of her choice, with necessary supports.
Annual Goal:	Tamara will learn to cook simple meals.
Short-Term Objective:	Given pictorial prompting sequence, Tamara will heat up a prepared macaroni and cheese casserole in a microwave oven. Without teacher assistance, on three consecutive trials.

Table 2. Systematic Instructional Strategies.

Antecedent Strategies (strategies that precede the learner's response and that help the learner to respond correctly to relevant stimuli):
- prompts (verbal statements, gestures, physical assistance, diagrams, etc.);
- prompting sequences or hierarchies:
  – least to most prompting;
  – most to least prompting;
  – graduated guidance;
  – progressive time delay.

Response modification strategies (strategies that modify the quality of the learner's responding):
- shaping (reinforcing successive approximations of the desired response);
- forward chaining;
- backward chaining.

Consequent Strategies (strategies that follow the learner's responding):
- positive reinforcement (verbal praise, desired activities, etc.);
- error correction.

---

or the wish to avoid a specific task), instructors must become skilled in determining the function that is being met through the inappropriate behavior. The set of strategies for determining the purpose(s) of such inappropriate behaviors are referred to collectively as functional assessments (Steere et al., 1999). These include structured observations and data recording strategies, such as scatterplots and A-B-C (Antecedent-Behavior-Consequence) recording forms (Alberto & Troutman, 1999), and interviews with significant others who know the individual well (O'Neil, Horner, Albin, Sprague, Storey & Newton, 1997).

An essential outcome of the functional assessment process is that the team be able to predict when, with whom, where, and in which activities the disruptive behavior is most and least likely to occur (see Table 3). These predictions help the team to correctly identify the function(s) of the challenging behavior. Once the function(s) of a behavior are known, then the focus of effort is on: (a) restructuring activities or the environment to reduce the need for the inappropriate behavior; and (b) teaching the individual a more socially acceptable manner for communicating his or her wishes.

Generalization and Maintenance. A key approach to promoting generalization of skills is referred to as general case instruction (Horner, Sprague & Wilcox, 1982; Steere, 1997). In using this approach, the instructor surveys all examples of an activity (e.g. crossing a street, using an ATM machine, or asking for help) within the environments that the student is likely to spend time. This survey

Table 3. Functional Assessment Prediction Chart.

Student: Tamara

Behavior: Crying

Predictions:

	Most Likely to Occur	*Least Likely to Occur*
With whom	With Maria	With her brother
Activity	During gym/PE	During lunch
Time of Day	Mid-morning	Not during lunch or in the afternoon
Environment	Multipurpose room at school	School Cafeteria; Wendy's Restaurant
Other Considerations	Transition times are extremely difficult, particularly if she is not prepared	Enjoys eating and watching food preparation

yields a description of the range of situations to which the individual might need to generalize his or her abilities. Then, examples of the activity that represent the range of stimulus and response variations are selected for use in instruction. It is critical that these teaching examples represent variations in activities that the student is likely to encounter. This approach has been used to teach a range of complex activities within the community such as crossing streets and selecting items at a grocery store. It has recently been extended to the instruction of social interaction skills, such as asking for assistance (Chadsey-Rusch & Halle, 1992; Chadsey-Rusch, Drasgow, Reinoehl, Halle & Collet-Klingenberg, 1993).

A promising avenue for enhancing maintenance of skills is to teach self-management skills to students with severe disabilities (Alberto & Troutman, 1999). These skills include self-monitoring skills (e.g. recording how many items were completed), self-prompting (e.g. talking oneself through the steps of an activity), and the self-provision of consequences (e.g. self-reinforcement or self-correction). These strategies have been used to teach a variety of skills including academic and vocational skills, and are considered to be an important aspect of self-determined behaviors (Wehmeyer, Agran & Hughes, 1999).

A GOOD ENDING

Imagine if Tamara had been born just 35 years ago. At her birth, the obstetrician and the family doctor would have recommended that she be placed in the State Hospital and Training Center for the Mentally Retarded. Her life would have been one of being maintained rather than one of being educated. Depending upon the distance of the State Hospital and Training Center from the family home, her mother and brother would have visited monthly or infrequently. Her brother would have never really known her as a sister, only as someone he was obligated to visit. Tamara and the other residents may have exacted his pity, fear, or scorn. He may have come to consider the sister he never knew as an embarrassment to the family.

Tamara's life would have been set by a rigid schedule of when to rise, eat, engage in some form of activity, bathe, and retire. There would have been no effort to prepare her for transitions. She would have been moved from one unit to another, without her consent, as she aged. There would have been no effort to prepare her for competitive employment or other outcomes related to life in the general community. The State Hospital and Training Center would have been her only community for her entire life. Although the State Hospital would employ a competent medical staff, it is likely Tamara's life expectancy would be somewhat less than current expectations.

Today, because of advances in law, policy, education, social services, medical and health services, technology, and a basic understanding of disabilities, Tamara lives in her family home and attends her neighborhood school. The comprehensive model of services and education she has received since birth have enabled her to learn and do far more than anyone might have anticipated. She is loved by her mother and brother; she has neighborhood friends and school friends. Although she faces multiple challenges everyday of her life, Tamara is a visible and contributing member of society. We all, including Tamara, can be thankful that strong advocacy over the last half of the 20th century helped to produce a change in attitudes, laws, and policies that created the foundation for new and effective methods for teaching and learning for individuals with disabilities. Many positive comprehensive activities have set the stage for amazing progress in technologies that make it possible for Tamara to learn, work, and communicate better than any generation of persons with disabilities that have come before. We believe advances in medicine and biotechnology will continue to improve the overall health of individuals with severe and multiple disabilities and likely make vast improvements in strengthening vision, hearing, the use of arms and legs, hands and feet, and muscular-skeletal integrity. Current laws, policies, practices, and *guiding principles* along with ongoing research and development will also continue to improve conditions for Tamara and other individuals with severe and multiple disabilities. Thus, we can say with more certainty than ever before, a disability does not have to be a handicap.

REFERENCES

Alberto, P., & Troutman, A. (1999). *Applied behavior analysis for teachers* (5th ed.). Upper Saddle River, NJ: Merrill Publishing Company.
Education of All Handicapped Children Act of 1975, PL 94-142, U.S.C. Section 1401 *et seq.*
Americans with Disabilities Act of 1990, PL 101-336, 42 U.S.C. Section 12101 *et seq.*
Bredekamp, S. (1997). *Developmentally appropriate practice in early childhood programs.* Washington, D.C.: National Association for Education of Young Children.
Brown, L., Branston-McLean, M., Baumgart, D., Vincent, L., Falvey, M., & Schroeder, J. (1978). Using the characteristics of current and subsequent least restrictive environments in the development of curricular content for severely handicapped students. *AAESPH Review, 4*, 407–424.
Brown, L., Branston, M., Hamre-Nietupski, S., Pumpian, I., Certo, N., & Gruenewald, L. (1979). A strategy for developing chronological age-appropriate and functional curricular content for severely handicapped adolescents and young adults. *Journal of Special Education, 13,* 81–90.
Brown, L., Nietupski, J., & Hamre-Nietupski, S. (1976). Criterion of ultimate functioning. In: M. Thomas (Ed.), *Hey! Don't forget about me!* (pp. 212–242). Reston, VA: Council for Exceptional Children.
Brown, L., Nisbet, J., Ford, A., Sweet, M., Shiraga, B., York, J., & Loomis, R. (1983). The critical need for non-school instruction in educational programs for severely handicapped students. *Journal of the Association for the Severely Handicapped, 8*(3), 71–77.
Chadsey-Rusch, J., & Halle, J. (1992). The application of general-case instruction to the repertoires of learners with severe disabilities. *Journal of the Association for Persons with Severe Handicaps, 17,* 121–132.
Chadsey-Rusch, J., Drasgow, E., Reinoehl, B. Halle, J., & Collet-Klingenberg, L. (1993). Using general-case instruction to teach spontaneous and generalized requests for assistance to learners with severe disabilities. *Journal of the Association for Persons with Severe Handicaps, 18,* 177–187.
Cross, G., & Villa, R. (1992). The Winooski school system: An evolutionary perspective of a school restructuring for diversity. In: R. Villa, J. Thousand, W. Stainback & S. Stainback (Eds), *Restructuring for Caring and Effective Education: An Administrative Guide to Creating Heterogeneous Schools* (pp. 219–237). Baltimore, MD: Paul H. Brookes.
Developmental Disabilities Assistance and Bill of Rights Act Amendments of 1994, PL 103-230, 42 U.S.C. Section 6000 *et seq.*
Education of All Handicapped Children Act of 1975, PL 94-142. U.S.C. Section 1401 *et seq.*
Fair Labor Standards Act of 1985, PL 99-150, 29 U.S.C. Section 201 *et seq.*
Fishbaugh, M. S. (1997). *Models of collaboration.* Needham Heights, MA: Allyn & Bacon.
Fishbaugh, M. S. (2000). *The collaboration guide for early career educators.* Baltimore, MD: Paul H. Brookes.
Forrest, M., & Pierpoint, J. C. (1992). Putting all kids on the MAP. *Educational Leadership, 50,* 26–31.

Friend, M. (2000). Myths and misunderstandings about professional collaboration. *Remedial and Special Education, 21,* 130–132.

Friend, M., & Bursuck, W. (1999). *Including students with special needs: A practical guide for classroom teachers* (2nd ed.). Needham Heights, MA: Allyn & Bacon.

Friend, M., & Cook, L. (2000). *Interactions: Collaboration skills for school professionals* (3rd ed.). Reading, MA: Addison-Wesley Longman.

Giangreco, M. F., Edelman, S. W., Luiselli, T. E., & McFarland, S. Z. (1997). Helping or hovering? Effects of instructional assistant proximity on students with disabilities. *Exceptional Children, 64,* 7–18.

Helmstetter, E., & Guess, D. (1987). Application of the Individualized Curriculum Sequencing Model to learners with severe sensory impairments. In: L. Goetz, D. Guess & K. Stremel-Campbell (Eds), *Innovative Program Design for Individuals with Dual Sensory Impairments* (pp. 255–282). Baltimore, MD: Paul H. Brookes.

Horner, R., Sprague, J., & Wilcox, B. (1982). General-case programming for community activities. In: B. Wilcox & G. T. Bellamy (Eds), *Design of High School Programs for Severely Handicapped Persons* (pp. 61–98). Baltimore, MD: Paul H. Brookes.

Hunter, D. (1999). Systems change and the transition to inclusive systems. In: M. J. Coutinho & A. C. Repp (Eds), *Inclusion: The Integration of Students with Disabilities* (pp. 135–151). Belmont, CA: Wadsworth.

Inclusive education: Needs of Minnesota parents (1994). *What's Working: Topics in Inclusive Education, 15,* 2–3.

Individuals with Disabilities Education Act (IDEA) Amendments of 1997, PL 105-17, 20 U.S.C. Section 1400 *et seq.*

Johnson, D. W., Johnson, R. T., & Holubec, E. J. (1993). *Circles of learning: Cooperation in the classroom* (4th ed.). Edina, MI: Interaction.

Kleinert, H., & Kearns, J. F. (1999). A validation study of the performance indicators and learner outcomes of Kentucky's alternate assessment for students with severe disabilities. *Journal of the Association for Persons with Severe Handicaps, 24*(2), 100–110.

Lambie, R. (2000). *Family systems within educational contexts: Understanding at-risk and special needs students* (2nd ed.). Denver, CO: Love.

McDonnell, J. (1998). Instruction for students with severe disabilities in general education settings. *Education and Training in Mental Retardation and Developmental Disabilities, 33,* 199–215.

McDonnell, J., Mathot-Buckner, C., & Ferguson, B. (1996). *Transition programs for students with moderate/severe disabilities.* Pacific Grove, CA: Brooks/Cole.

McWilliam, R. A. (1996). *Rethinking pull-out services in early intervention: A professional resource.* Baltimore, MD: Paul H. Brookes.

Mount, B., & Zwernik, K. (1988). *It's never too early, it's never too late: A booklet about personal futures planning.* Mears Park Center, MN: Metropolitan Council.

Nirje, B. (1970). The normalization principle and its human management implications. *Journal of Mental Subnormality, 16,* 62–70.

O'Brien, J. (1987). A guide to lifestyle planning: Using the Activities Catalog to integrate services and natural support systems. In: B. Wilcox & G. T. Bellamy (Eds), *The Activities Catalog: An Alternative Curriculum Design for Youth and Adults with Severe Disabilities* (pp. 175–189). Baltimore, MD: Paul H. Brookes.

Osborne, A. (1996). *Legal issues in special education.* Needham Heights, MA: Allyn & Bacon.

O'Neil, R., Horner, R., Albin, R., Sprague, J., Storey, K., & Newton, J. (1997). *Functional assessment and program development for problem behavior* (2nd ed.). Pacific Grove, CA: Brooks/Cole.

Rainforth, B., & England, J. (1997). Collaborations for inclusion. *Education and Treatment of Children*, 20(1), 85–104.

Rainforth, B., & York-Barr, J. (1997). *Collaborative teams for students with severe disabilities: Integrating therapy and educational services* (2nd ed). Baltimore, MD: Paul H. Brookes.

Reynolds, M. C. (1962). A framework for considering some issues in special education. *Exceptional Children*, 28, 367–370.

Reynolds, M. C., & Birch, J. W. (1977). *Teaching exceptional children in all America's schools: A first course for teachers and principals*. Reston, VA: Council for Exceptional Children.

Rose, E., & Hueffner, D. (1984). Cultural bias in special education assessment and placement. In: T. Jones & D. Semler (Eds), *School Law Update . . . Preventive School Law* (pp. 179–188). Topeka, KS: National Organization on Legal Problems of Education.

Ryndak, D. (1996). Education teams and collaborative teamwork in inclusive settings. In: D. Ryndak & S. Alper (Eds), *Curriculum Content for Students with Moderate and Severe Disabilities in Inclusive Settings* (pp. 77–96). Needham Heights, MA: Allyn & Bacon.

Salisbury, C. L., & Dunst, C. J. (1997). Home, school, and community partnerships: Building inclusive teams. In: B. Rainforth & J. York-Barr (Eds), *Collaborative Teams for Students with Severe Disabilities: Integrating Therapy and Educational Services* (2nd ed., pp. 57–87). Baltimore, MD: Paul H. Brookes.

Salisbury, C. L., Gallucci, C., Palombaro, M. M., & Peck, C. A. (1995). Strategies that promote social relations among elementary students with and without severe disabilities in inclusive schools. *Exceptional Children*, 62, 125–137.

Sapon-Shevin, M., Dobbelaere, A., Corrigan, C. R., Goodman, K., & Mastin, M. C. (1998). Promoting inclusive behavior in inclusive classrooms: "You can't say you can't play." In: L. H. Meyer, H. S. Park, M. Grenot-Scheyer, I. S. Schwartz & B. Harry (Eds), *Making Friends: The Influences of Culture and Development* (pp. 127–148). Baltimore, MD: Paul H. Brookes.

Slavin, R. E. (1996). *Education for all: Contexts of learning*. Lisse, France: Swets & Keitlinger.

Snell, M. E., & Brown, F. (Eds) (2000). *Instruction of students with severe disabilities* (5th ed.). Upper Saddle River, NJ: Prentice Hall.

Soodak, L. C., & Erwin, E. J. (2000). Valued member or tolerated participant: Parents experiences in inclusive early childhood settings. *Journal of the Association for Persons with Severe Handicaps*, 25(1), 29–41.

Steere, D. (1997). *Increasing variety in adult life: A general-case approach* (Innovations, No. 10). Washington, D.C.: American Association on Mental Retardation.

Steere, D., Rose, E., & Fishbaugh, M. S. (1999). Integration in the secondary school for students with severe disabilities. In: M. J. Coutinho & A. C. Repp (Eds), *Inclusion: The Integration of Students with Disabilities* (pp. 333–365). Belmont, CA: Wadsworth.

Taylor, S. (1988). Caught in the continuum: A critical analysis of the principle of the least restrictive environment. *Journal of the Association of Persons with Severe Handicaps*, 13, 41–53.

Thousand, J. S., Villa, R. A., & Nevin, A. I. (1994). *Creativity and collaborative learning: A practical guide to empower students and teachers*. Baltimore, MD: Paul H. Brookes.

Veeman, S. (1995). Cognitive and noncognitive effects of multigrade and multi-age classes: A best evidence synthesis. *Review of Educational Research*, 65, 319–382.

Wehman, P. (1996). *Life beyond the classroom: Transition strategies for young people with disabilities* (2nd ed.). Baltimore, MD: Paul H. Brookes.

Wehman, P. (1997). Curriculum design. In: P. Wehman & J. Kregel (Eds), *Functional Curriculum for Elementary, Middle, and Secondary Age Students with Special Needs* (pp. 1–17). Austin, TX: Pro-Ed.

Wehmeyer, M. (1996). Self-determination as an educational outcome: Why is it important to children, youth, and adults with disabilities? In: D. Sands & M. Wehmeyer (Eds), *Self-Determination Across the Lifespan: Independence and Choice for People with Disabilities* (pp. 17–36). Baltimore, MD: Paul H. Brookes.

Wehmeyer, M., Agran, M., & Hughes, C. (1999). *Teaching self-determination to students with disabilities: Basic skills for successful transition.* Baltimore, MD: Paul H. Brookes.

Welch, M., & Sheridan, S. (1995). *Educational partnerships: Serving students at risk.* Fort Worth, TX: Harcourt Brace.

West, M., Kregel, J., & Revell, W. (1993–1994). A new era of self-determination. *Impact*, 6(Winter).

Wilcox, B., & Bellamy, G. T. (1982). *Design of high school programs for severely handicapped students.* Baltimore, MD: Paul H. Brookes.

Wilcox, B., & Bellamy, G. T. (Eds) (1987). *A comprehensive guide to the Activities Catalog: An alternative curriculum for youth and adults with severe disabilities.* Baltimore, MD: Paul H. Brookes.

Workforce Investment Act of 1998, PL 105-220, HR 1385 (1998).

STUDENTS WITH SPEECH AND LANGUAGE DISORDERS

Jane R. Wegner, Kristin Grosche and
Evette Edmister

INTRODUCTION

Communication is the cornerstone of the teaching and learning process. A successful school is one in which communication is good. Such a school focuses on communication between teachers and students, students with each other, faculty and staff with each other, and faculty and staff with families and community members.

Because instruction is typically delivered via spoken and written language, students who have adequate speech and language skills participate in the school experience more easily than those with speech and/or language disorders. More than a million students ages six through 21 who have speech or language disorders have more difficulty (U.S. Department of Education, 2000). In addition, 50% of students who have some other primary disability such as mental retardation, autism or hearing impairment also have speech and/or language disabilities that affect their participation in school (Hall, Oyer & Haas, 2001). Approximately 8–12% of preschoolers have speech and/or language disorders (National Institute on Deafness and Other Communication Disorders, 1995).

Speech and/or language disorders have both social and learning effects on students. Some students with speech and/or language disorders are reluctant to participate in activities in and out of the classroom, some have difficulty understanding the "instructional conversation", and some students have difficulty reading and writing. Because of the fundamental, reciprocal relationship between spoken and written language, students with speech and/or language problems are at greater risk for reading and writing difficulties (ASHA, 2000a).

Speech-language pathologists provide support to students with speech-language disorders in the schools. According to the American Speech-Language-Hearing Association's (ASHA) 2000 Schools Surveys, almost one-half of these students receiving speech-language services in the schools are between the ages of six and 11. Approximately half of the students served have moderate impairments. Most students on the speech-language pathologists' caseloads had articulation/phonological disorders with learning disabilities and specific language impairment being the next most frequently served.

A traditional approach to service provision in the schools includes assessment to determine need and then intervention to address the "areas of weakness". This has, in the past, meant an intervention program that generally included the speech-language pathologist and the student engaged in activities designed to focus on the area of concern. The activities may or may not have related to the curriculum. Recent changes in the Individuals with Disabilities Education Act (IDEA) of 1997 have focused the services of the speech-language pathologist toward students' progress within the general education curriculum. Speech-language pathologists are being guided toward educationally relevant services that impact students' participation in the educational process (ASHA Ad Hoc Committee on the Roles and Responsibilities of the School-Based Speech-Language Pathologist, 1999). The focus is directed toward making the curriculum comprehensible and participation possible for all students. This new direction expands the roles of the speech-language pathologists and offers opportunities to modify their delivery of services. Speech-language pathologists will need to understand the curriculum and the classroom teaching/learning process, use more contextually based assessments, provide a variety of service delivery options, and expand services beyond the school to homes and communities to support all forms and types of communication including classroom and social. The speech-pathologist's primary role in our dream education program would be to support communication for learning for everyone including students with and without speech-language disorders, teachers, staff, administrators, and families in a flexible collaborative manner.

ASSESSMENT

The more traditional role of assessment has included predominately formal and informal, norm-referenced and criterion-referenced assessments along with language samples and category inventories (Losardo & Notari-Syverson, 2001).

These assessments have been traditionally used to establish eligibility and have had little to do with the student's classroom learning experiences. These assessments, completed in an environment away from the classroom, may give only a thumbnail sketch of an individual's abilities. A more meaningful assessment with respect to access to the curriculum, would include a combination of naturalistic, dynamic and performance assessments utilizing a team approach.

Naturalistic Assessment

Naturalistic assessments involve observing the student within a natural context with a familiar communication partner and documenting the student's participation through checklists, descriptions, and/or narration (Losardo & Notari-Syverson, 2001). The student is assessed in natural contexts of importance to the student's participation in school and/or considered to be problematic to his/her participation. A naturalistic assessment could also include a peer comparison. A naturalistic assessment initiates a collaborative relationship with families and other professionals within the school setting.

For instance, the speech language pathologist would interview the family and the teachers to identify specific areas of concern for the student and environments that may be difficult as well as environments or activities that the student performs well. From this information the speech language pathologist may choose an environment or environments (i.e. snack time, class participation during large group lecture, small group interactions such as science experiments) to observe and document the communication interactions observed. The components of such communication interactions could include such things as conversation initiation, topic maintenance, conversational turn taking, social awareness, syntax, word finding ability, and language comprehension. A checklist, including a list of all of the target communication interactions could be developed. Other members of the team, which includes the parents, could also make observations of the child's communication in various settings. The team would then meet to review observations and determine communication patterns, communication strengths, and communication weaknesses.

Dynamic Assessment

If differences are found in the naturalistic assessment, a dynamic assessment could be used to determine what modifications might be helpful for the student to be successful. Dynamic assessment is based on the assumption that all children can learn (Pena, 1996). It is also considered to be a culturally non-biased assessment because of the test-teach-retest structure (Lidz & Pena, 1996; Pena, 1996;

Losardo & Notari-Syverson, 2001). The dynamic assessment focuses on the student's learning rather than his/her weaknesses or ability to complete an item. The assessment also seeks intervention strategies and contexts where change can be seen (Lidz & Pena, 1996; Pena, 1996; Losardo & Notari-Syverson, 2001).

Without dynamic assessment, particular needs of a student could be missed. For example, a fifth grader with autism and a language disorder could follow and attend during the teacher "read aloud" time if she had the book to follow along and if she had the story verbally "recapped" for her with a friend prior to the teacher's reading.

Performance Assessment

Progress is best monitored using performance assessments such as portfolios. With this type of assessment, progress can be monitored over a specific period of time and referenced to the student's progress through the curriculum. A performance assessment requires a team approach which includes the student and his/her family (Losardo & Notari-Syverson, 2001). One example of a portfolio would be a daily journal kept by the student. For many classrooms this is a class requirement. The child's independent writing skills could then be assessed daily and progress monitored over the school year. Another example may include the use of videos to record various communication interactions and presentations through out the year. The expressive communication could be captured on tape at various times of the year. The goal of this documentation would be to record a student's progress through the curriculum.

SERVICE DELIVERY

Service Delivery Models

When choosing a service delivery model, the individual needs of the student should be considered as well as the advantages and limitations of potential models. No one model is right for every student. In fact, it is recommended that a combination of service delivery models be used (ASHA, 1993; Cirrin & Penner, 1995). Despite which model(s) are used, they should be selected based on individual needs, they should be dynamic in nature and involve collaboration among speech-language pathologist, teachers and family (ASHA, 1993).

Service delivery models vary among the location, context, role of the professionals and communication partners, and outcomes or goals. Models include pullout, classroom based and consultative.

Pullout. According to ASHA's National Outcomes Measurement System school report (2000), most intervention in the schools is provided in a pullout model in small groups of two to four students. This model is used regardless of the type of speech-language disorder (i.e. receptive and expressive language, articulation, fluency). The frequency and intensity of intervention sessions is also consistent across types of disorders, with 30 minute sessions being most common (75.6%) and sessions occurring two times a week (63.4%).

In the traditional pullout model, the speech-language pathologist plays a direct role in providing services, which occur individually or in groups outside of the classroom. Speech and language skills are taught outside of the setting they are used in. Students' goals are separate from the classroom curriculum. The communication partners are typically adults. Peers can also serve as partners when they are brought into the artificial setting of the therapy room. Coordination and collaboration can occur but less often than in other models (ASHA, 1993; McWilliam, 1995; Paul-Brown & Caperton, 2001)

The pullout model is used to teach a specific skill or new behavior in a controlled environment. (Paul-Brown & Caperton, 2001). In this model, the speech-language pathologist has control over variables such as the arrangement of the room and materials, the conversation and the activity. In a national survey of early interventionists, advantages to this model included perception of increased intensity and minimized distractions (McWilliam, 1996b).

Problems with pullout include the lack of generalization of skills to the settings or environments in which they are needed. By learning a skill in isolation, it is more difficult to carry it over into the classroom or community (McWilliam, 1996b; Paul-Brown & Caperton, 2001). Why not teach a skill where it will be used right from the beginning? A meaningful context for teaching and learning should be used rather than stripping away the context (Nelson, 1998).

Classroom Based. In a classroom-based model, direct services are provided but in the context of the classroom. Goals are integrated into the classroom and the curriculum is used as both content and context for intervention. Collaboration needs to occur between the speech-language pathologist, teachers and students (ASHA, 1993; Cirrin & Penner, 1995; Paul-Brown & Caperton, 2001). Some classroom-based services may include groups of children within a classroom working on similar goals or skills. The teacher and speech-language pathologist may also team teach. By working in the classroom, the speech-language pathologist can reach larger numbers of children and enhance generalization (ASHA, 1993).

Other advantages include working on goals relevant to classroom functioning, leading to better generalization. Students are taught in the environment they are expected to use the behaviors they are being taught, thereby alleviating any problems with generalization (McWilliam, 1996c). In addition, the skills targeted are functional in that they support classroom learning. Skills can also be taught through a variety of activities throughout the day (McWilliam, 1996). The student receives more intervention than the two 30 minute sessions a week in the traditional model since teachers and other staff become knowledgeable and skilled in supporting the student while the speech-language pathologist is not in the classroom. In addition, all students in the classroom benefit from the speech-language pathologist's expertise. By using the natural context of the classroom, interactions between students and students and teachers are facilitated. Peers and teachers learn how to facilitate speech and language skills even if they are not directly taught (Cirrin & Penner, 1995).

Ehren (2000) presents ways speech-language pathologists can maintain a therapeutic focus in the classroom while at the same time share responsibility for students success. She suggests planning in advance for classroom activities rather than "going with the flow", planning with the teacher face to face at least once per marking period to understand the curriculum, selecting time for classroom work carefully, knowing what will take place during that time, establishing a collaborative relationship so that mutual decision making takes place, and analyzing the curriculum at specific grade levels for the speech/language components that are integral to the curriculum.

Collaborative consultation. In a consultative model, the speech-language pathologist, teachers and parents "work together to facilitate a student's communication and learning in educational environments" (ASHA, 1993 p. 108). Shared decision making, planning and problem solving are critical. Together goals are developed, implemented and evaluated (ASHA, 1993; Paul-Brown & Caperton, 2001; McWilliam, 1996c). The speech-language pathologist plays an indirect role supporting the teachers in implementing communication goals in the classroom. Intervention occurs in the natural setting of the classroom with adults and peers as communication partners. Goals are integrated and consistent with and relevant to the general education curriculum. These goals are achieved through naturally occurring opportunities for speech and language learning (Cirrin & Penner, 1995). A high amount of collaboration is needed in setting goals, implementing and evaluating them. The speech-language pathologist's role is to collaborate with the teachers to insure that they teachers have the information and support they need (Paul-Brown & Caperton, 2001).

A collaborative consultation model is the most compatible with ASHA's (1996) recommendations for inclusive practices. These practices include the use of typical language models, provision of support in the natural educational environment, integration within the classroom curriculum and activities, bringing services to the child, and collaboration among professionals. A collaborative, consultative model has the same advantages described for a classroom based model. In addition, it allows the speech-language pathologist to spend his/her time brainstorming and sharing expertise with the professionals who spend the most time educating the students directly. The primary role of the speech-language pathologist in this model is to work with the classroom teachers to support all children in their participation in the education process.

A consultative model for speech and language service provision is the most consistent with inclusive practices, but remains as the least used model. An average of 23 hours in a speech-language pathologist's week is spent providing traditional pullout services, while two hours are spent using collaborative consultation and one hour in classroom/curriculum based (ASHA, 2000b).

Support Beyond the Classroom

The goals for students receiving speech-language intervention must be relevant to the school curriculum. Students should be supported in their learning and development of communication skills, such as listening, reading, writing, thinking and speaking, throughout the school day and across all subject areas (ASHA, 1993).

In thinking of how services are provided to students in schools, aspects other than the location of services are important. The involvement of communication partners, the context, and the goals of students should also be considered in choosing a service delivery approach (McWilliam, 1996b). Communication occurs during all times of day and during all activities. Students have conversations in the hallways and on the play yards. They need to follow directions in the cafeteria line and on the bus. Both understanding and use of speech and language happens throughout the day. It is therefore, critical that the activities a student participates in be the "location" and "activity" in which support is provided. In addition, the communication partners who interact with children in these settings should play an important role in the services as well.

Blosser and Kratcoski (1997) propose an alternative framework for service delivery in which the providers, activities and contexts (PACs) serve as the foundation. The providers include all communication partners whether they be speech-language pathologists, teachers, family and community members. Interventionists should include any partners who communicate with the student. In addition, these individuals may serve different roles in different activities. The contexts for intervention include all potential opportunities for enhancement of communication. It is the role of the providers to identify and facilitate communication during these opportunities.

The speech-language pathologist's role in schools should be to support the school staff, families, community members and students to enhance communication for everyone. The speech-language pathologist's role should be flexible. Speech-language pathologists need to share their expertise with classroom teachers, special educators, cafeteria staff, bus drivers, etc. as well as provide intervention focused services to students. These individuals are the ones who spend the most time with students with speech and language difficulties and are part of the child's daily activities. They have the knowledge of the classroom, school and hidden curriculum that the speech-language pathologist may not have. The speech-language pathologist should use their expertise in communication to educate others on how to observe communication, how to identify problems and how to facilitate communication during any activity. Through methods such as in services, informal conversations, modeling, joint problem solving sessions, etc., speech-language pathologists and other school personnel can collaboratively enhance the communication skills of children throughout the day.

Speech-language pathologists should spend their time in the classroom and in other school environments, supporting school personnel and students. They should work with teachers and others to observe, identify communication difficulties, design, implement, monitor and adapt interventions. This can be accomplished by establishing a systematic way to share information between all parties. Resources, both materials and information, should be provided to teachers and others.

Important to the collaboration among speech-language pathologists, teachers, and families are both interpersonal and organizational factors. Interpersonal skills such as shared responsibility and releasing and expanding of roles are critical to successful collaboration. In addition, organizational factors such as administrative support in the form of collaboration time, space, funding, resources to educate one another, are equally as important.

Initially, a shift to a collaborative, consultative model will require time and effort on the part of all participants. Time is needed to develop relationships, share information and begin implementation. However, the long-term outcomes should far outweigh the initial expense. Long-term outcomes include the prevention rather than remediation of speech and language difficulties. School staff will be more able to recognize potential problems and facilitate communication before difficulties arise. In addition, more students will be supported. Not only will speech-language support be provided to students who qualify for these services throughout the day, but all students could conceivably benefit in the form of enhanced communication skills.

IMPLEMENTING A COLLABORATIVE INTERVENTION MODEL

To implement a collaborative service delivery model that is consistent with inclusive practices, there are several factors to consider. A common shared vision, collaborative relationships and administrative support are essential.

To begin with, school personnel and families need to have a common philosophy or shared vision of individualized, dynamic speech-language support. Programmatic decisions should be made as a team, considering the student's individual needs. These decisions should change as needed over time as the student's needs change. Having a shared philosophy affects how services are delivered, what resources or options are available and how teams work together (Dinnebeil, Hale & Rule, 1999).

In order to implement a flexible, collaborative model, partnerships need to be built between all team members. Partnerships should include speech-language pathologists, teachers, other school personnel, families and community members. Good relationships are built on trust, mutual respect, equality, and good communication. Team members must communicate effectively by sharing information. They must also share their knowledge and expertise along with power. Flexibility and sensitivity to individual differences and needs of all team members is important. These characteristics facilitate joint problem solving and decision making and can only be developed over time (Tuchman, 1996; Winton, 1996).

It is important to establish a relationship built on respect and equality where the teacher and the speech-language pathologist are learning from each other and engaging in shared decision making. Collaboration would require the speech-language pathologist to work with teachers, students and families to create IEP goals, select a service delivery option and implement intervention programs.

Collaboration can be a difficult thing to accomplish given personal and structural constraints. Collaboration, to some speech-language pathologists, may cause concern that they will lose their independence or professional identity and create more work for them (McWilliam, 1996a). Some speech-language pathologists, though they agree philosophically, have concerns that they will become classroom teachers or aides and water down their therapy (Ehren, 2000). Teachers and other partners have similar concerns. A collaborative model requires all individuals to take on new or different roles and share expertise or release roles (Bruder & Bologna, 1993). Individuals may not know how or be comfortable trying new things. They may be hesitant due to more time that may be involved and added responsibilities. They may also be reluctant to share control with others (McWilliam, 1996c).

Speech-language pathologists face many challenges in serving students in schools, including lack of time. In a recent survey of school speech-language pathologists lack of planning or collaboration time (81%) and high caseloads (60%) were reported as the greatest challenges in schools (ASHA, 2000b). Speech-language pathologists are often serving high numbers of children with varying degrees of need. The average monthly caseload for speech-language pathologist is 53 children (median, range 15–110) (ASHA, 2000a).

Given these challenges, it would seem that a shift to a more consultative model would require more time. When in fact, a consultative model offers speech-language pathologists the opportunity to serve more students and to expand the services provided to students throughout the curriculum. Although more time is needed to come to these shared decisions and in taking shared responsibility, the intervention is enhanced for the child, occurs more often and is more meaningful.

Since lack of planning or collaboration time is a significant challenge for school speech-language pathologists (ASHA, 2000b), it is critical that this time is provided by the administration. Despite the service delivery model used, collaboration time is important for the success of intervention. It is important to provide opportunities to share and exchange information among staff members and families (Paul-Brown & Caperton, 2001) whether it is an informal exchange such as conversations at recess or in the lunchroom, time set aside periodically or more formal inservice or presentations. Frequent visits and conversations to trouble shoot and problem solve initially are necessary (McWilliam, 1996c).

Education and training are necessary to support the provision of collaborative services. As a consultant the speech-language pathologist will need to have the knowledge and skills necessary to plan and implement and make adaptations within the classroom context. They also need the skills and training in service delivery models and collaboration (Paul-Brown & Capeton, 2001).

More inservice and preservice training is needed and should be expanded beyond the discipline specific content. It should include information across disciplines, in team and collaborative behaviors, service delivery models and consultative roles (McWilliam, 1996c). Our university training programs need to reflect these changes in the way they prepare speech-language pathologists to provide services in the schools.

Programmatic changes are needed. School administrations must provide support in terms of collaboration and planning time (ASHA, 1993), funding, supportive policies, education (Winton, 1996). With administrative support, a shared vision and collaborative partnerships, speech-language pathologists, teachers and families can provide the communication support needed for all children to successfully participate in their education.

CONCLUSION

Ehren (2001, p. 225) state that "in actuality, speech-language pathologists and classroom teachers need to assume shared responsibility for the functional outcomes related to school success for students with speech and language disorders." She suggests that speech-language pathologists can assist the teacher in making modifications in curriculum, instruction and assessment. She also suggests that teams write IEP goals that they can collaboratively achieve as opposed to discipline specific ones. Ehren recommends that speech-language pathologists make suggestions as to how to modify lessons, tests, and assignments based on student speech and language skills.

These are new roles for speech-language pathologists that will take adjustments from their perspective as well as the expectations of others. In our dream education program, students with speech and/or language disorders would be supported by a speech-language pathologist who collaborates with teachers, school staff, students and families. The speech-language pathologist would be involved in the literacy program at the school. She would understand the curriculum and teaching/learning process in classrooms and use these in her service delivery, responding to student, family and teacher needs. She would feel a shared responsibility with teachers and families for the successful learning of students in the classroom. The speech-language pathologist would be viewed as the "communication specialist" in the school rather than the person who corrects speech and language problems.

REFERENCES

American Speech-Language-Hearing Association (1996). Inclusive practices for children and youths with communication disorders: Position statement and technical report. *ASHA, 38*(Suppl. 16), 35–44.

American Speech-Language-Hearing Association, Ad Hoc Committee on the Roles and Responsibilities of the School-Based Speech-Language Pathologist (1999). *The guidelines for the roles and responsibilities of the school-based speech-language pathologist.* Rockville, MD: Author.

American Speech-Language-Hearing Association (2000a). *2000 omnibus survey.* Rockville, MD: Author.

American Speech-Language-Hearing Association (2000b). *2000 schools survey: Executive summary.* Rockville, MD: Author.

American Speech-Language-Hearing Association (1993). Guidelines for caseload size and speech-language service delivery in the schools. *ASHA, 35*(Suppl. 10), 33–39.

Blosser, J. L., & Kratcoski, A. (1997). PACs: A framework for determining appropriate service delivery options. *Language, Speech and Hearing Services in the Schools, 28*, 99–107.

Bruder, M. B., & Bologna, T. (1993). Collaboration and service coordination for effective early intervention. In: W. Brown, S. K. Thurman & L. F. Pearl (Eds), *Family-Centered Early Intervention Services with Infants and Toddlers: Innovative Cross-Disciplinary Approaches* (pp. 103–127). Baltimore, MD: Paul H. Brookes.

Cirrin, F. M., & Penner, S. G. (1995). Classroom-based and consultative service delivery models for language intervention. In: S. F. Warren & J. Reichle (Series Eds) & M. Fey, J. Windsor & S. F. Warren (Vol. Eds), *Communication and Language Intervention Series: Vol. 5. Language Intervention: Preschool Through the Elementary Years* (pp. 333–362). Baltimore, MD: Paul Brookes.

Dinnebeil, L. A., Hale, L., & Rule, S. (1999). Early intervention program practices that support collaboration. *Topics in Early Childhood Special Education, 19*, 225–235.

Ehren, B. (2000). Maintaining a therapeutic focus and sharing responsibility for student success: Keys to in-classroom speech-language services. *Language, Speech, and Hearing services in schools, 31*(3) 219–229.

Hall, B. J., Oyer, H., & Haas, W. (2001). *Speech, language, and hearing disorders: A guide for teachers*. Boston, MA: Allyn and Bacon.

Lidz, C. S. & Pena, E. D. (1996). Dynamic assessment: The model, its relevance as a nonbiased approach, and its application to Latino American preschool children. *Language, Speech, and Hearing Services in Schools, 27*, 367–372.

Losardo, A., & Notari-Syverson, A. (2001). *Alternative approaches to assessing young children*. Baltimore, MD: Paul H. Brookes.

McWilliam, P. J. (1996). Collaborative consultation across seven disciplines: Challenges and solutions. In: R. A. McWilliam (Ed.), *Rethinking Pull-Out Services in Early Intervention: A Professional Resource* (pp. 315–340). Baltimore, MD: Paul Brookes.

McWilliam, R. A. (1995). Integration of therapy and consultative special education: A continuum of early intervention. *Infants and Young Children, 7*, 29–38.

McWilliam, R. A. (1996a). Service delivery issues in center-based early intervention. In: R. A. McWilliam (Ed.), *Rethinking Pull-Out Services in Early Intervention: A Professional Resource* (pp. 3–25). Baltimore, MD: Paul Brookes.

McWilliam, R. A. (1996b). A program of research on integrated vs. isolated treatment in early intervention. In: R. A. McWilliam (Ed.), *Rethinking Pull-Out Services in Early Intervention: A Professional Resource* (pp. 71–102). Baltimore, MD: Paul Brookes.

McWilliam, R. A. (1996c). Implications for the future of integrating specialized services. In: R. A. McWilliam (Ed.), *Rethinking Pull-Out Services in Early Intervention: A Professional Resource* (pp. 343–371). Baltimore, MD: Paul H. Brookes.

National Institute on Deafness and Other Communication Disorders. (1995). *National strategic research plan for language and language impairments, balance and balance disorders, and voice and voice disorders* (NIH Publication No. 97-3217). Bethesda, MD: Author

Nelson, N. (1998). *Childhood language disorders in context: Infancy through adolescence*. Boston: Ally and Bacon.

Paul-Brown, D., & Caperton, C. J. (2001). Inclusive practices for preschool-age children with specific language impairment. In: M. J. Guralnick (Ed.), *Early Childhood Inclusion: Focus on Change* (pp. 433–464). Baltimore, MD: Paul H. Brookes.

Pena, E. (1996). Dynamic assessment the model and its language applications. In: K. N. Cole, P. S. Dale & D. J. Thal (Eds), *Assessment of Communication and Language* (Vol. 6, pp. 281–308). Baltimore, MD: Paul H. Brookes.

Tuchman, L. I. (1996). The team and models of teaming. In: P. Rosin, A. D. Whitehead, L. I. Tuchman, G. S. Jesien, A. L. Begun & L. Irwin (Eds), *Partnerships in Family-Centered Care: A Guide to Collaborative Early Intervention* (pp. 119–144). Baltimore, MD: Paul H. Brookes.

U.S. Department of Education (2000). *Twenty-second annual report to Congress on the implementation of the Individuals with Disabilities Education Act.* Washington, D.C.: Author.

Winton, P. J. (1996). Family professional partnerships and integrated services. In: R. A. McWilliam (Ed.), *Rethinking Pull-Out Services in Early Intervention: A Professional Resource* (pp. 49–70). Baltimore, MD: Paul H. Brookes.

STUDENTS WITH AUTISM SPECTRUM DISORDERS

Tim Wahlberg, Anthony F. Rotatori,
Julie Deisinger and Sandra Burkhardt

HISTORICAL ASPECTS AND DEFINITION

Kanner (1943) provided the first record of autism. His record occurred after examining a group of 11 children who, from infancy, exhibited impairment in social and communication interactions, and repetitive and stereotyped patterns of behavior, interests and activities. Kanner was the first to give a name to the pattern of behaviors, namely, "early infantile autism". He defined autistic children as "children who exhibit: (a) serious failure to develop relationships with other people before 30 months of age; (b) problems in development of normal language; (c) ritualistic and obsessive behaviors (insistence in sameness); and (d) potential for normal intelligence" (p. 3). Autism has a poor prognosis and is "a condition marked by severe impairment in intellectual, social, and emotional functioning. Its onset occurs in infancy, and the prognosis appears to be extremely poor" (Lotter, 1978, p. 359). It was not until 1990 that autism was defined educationally by the Individuals with Disabilities Education Act (IDEA) (1990) as a:

> developmental disability significantly affecting verbal and nonverbal communication and social interaction, generally evident before age three, that adversely affects a child's performance. Other characteristics often associated with autism are engagement in repetitive activities and stereotyped movements, resistance to environmental change or change in daily routines, and unusual responses to sensory experiences.

The term does not apply if a child's educational performance is adversely affected primarily because the child has serious emotional disturbance (34 C.F.R. Section 300.7-[b] [1] [1992]).

A more comprehensive definition of autism is provided in the DSM-IV (see Table 1).

The DSM-IV definition stresses that persons with autism have severe deficits in a number of areas: language development, attachment to their parents, self

Table 1. Diagnostic Criteria for 299.00 Autistic Disorder.

A. A total of six (or more) items from (1), (2), and (3), with at least two from (1), and one each from (2) and (3):
  (1) qualitative impairment in social interaction, as manifested by at least two of the following:
    (a) marked impairment in the use of multiple nonverbal behaviors such as eye-to-eye gaze, facial expression, body postures, and gestures to regulate social interaction;
    (b) failure to develop peer relationships appropriate to developmental level;
    (c) a lack of spontaneous seeking to share enjoyment, interests, or achievements with other people (e.g. by a lack of showing, bringing, or pointing out objects of interest);
    (d) lack of social or emotional reciprocity.
  (2) qualitative impairments in communication as manifested by at least one of the following:
    (a) delay in, or total lack of, the development of spoken language (not accompanied by an attempt to compensate through alternative modes of communication such as gestures or mime);
    (b) in individuals with adequate speech, marked impairments in the ability to initiate or sustain speech with others;
    (c) stereotyped and repetitive use of language or idiosyncratic language;
    (d) lack of varied, spontaneous make-believe play or social imitative play appropriate to developmental level.
  (3) restricted repetitive and stereotyped patterns of behavior, interests, and activities, as manifested by at least one of the following:
    (a) encompassing preoccupation with one or more stereotyped and restricted patterns of interest that is abnormal either in intensity or focus;
    (b) apparently inflexible adherence to specific, nonfunctional routines or rituals;
    (c) stereotyped and repetitive motor mannerisms (e.g. hand or finger flapping or twisting, or complex whole body movements).
B. Delays or abnormal functioning in at least one of the following areas, with the onset prior to age three years: (1) social interaction, (2) language as used in social communication, or (3) symbolic or imaginative play.
C. The disturbance is not better accounted for by Rett's Disorder or Childhood Disintegrative Disorder.

care skills, toy play, interactions with peers, and attentiveness to their surroundings. Also, persons with autism have high rates of aggression directed against themselves or others and self-stimulatory behaviors such as repeatedly rocking their bodies and flapping their hands.

Prior to the early 1970s, no cure for autism existed and most persons ended up institutionalized at some point in their lives. In fact Rutter (1970) reported that only one of 64 subjects with autism (fewer than 2%) could be considered free of clinically significant problems by adulthood, as evidenced by holding a job, living independently, and maintaining an active and age-appropriate social life.

Early theorists believed that an "autistic child's failure to learn was the result of inadequate parenting, which prevented social stimuli such as praise and attention from acquiring reinforcing properties for the children" (Rutter & Schopler, 1987, pp. 17–18). Today, this hypothesis is no longer acceptable and researchers indicate that autism is considered "a disease caused by as-yet unspecified neurological disorder" (Fester, 1961, p. 18). A number of researchers (Ciaranello & Ciaranello, 1995: Kanner, 1943: Mundy, 1995), indicated that the neurological implications of autism are attributed to severe deficits in early social-emotional approach behaviors (e.g. joint attention bids) and subsequent social cognitive disturbances. These researchers reported there is a possible connection between affect, social behavior, and neurological disturbances in persons with autism. For example, persons with autism can exhibit excesses in their behavior such as: self-stimulatory behavior: this consists of repetitive ritualistic behavior which gives the child internal pleasure (e.g. rocking, stacking, balancing, lining up objects, or spinning); negativistic behavior, which consists of noncompliance and tantrums; aggression, which includes aggression towards self, others, and property; rigidity/insistence on sameness, the child does not like anything to change; and sensitivity to external stimuli. Additionally, persons with autism exhibit behavioral deficits such as: receptive language, child does not understand instruction (come here, sit down, or get your shoes); expressive language, child does not understand how to give verbal gestures (what is your name); social-emotional attachment, they have no fear of strangers, no separation anxiety; play behavior: they do not play like normal children and do not have any friends, they just sit passively by, and they do not want to share; attention (eye contact is almost nonexistent); failure to develop proper self help skills (they can not drink from a cup or use the bathroom); and apparent sensory deficit (they are thought to be deaf at first, and do not react to pain). In contrast, persons with autism do show some "normal" behaviors in the following: motor development (they function at an age appropriate stage in motor skills); memory: (they show a normal to above average memory both auditory and visually); interests: (they have interests in music, dance, and motorized things such as VCRs or train cars); special fears: (they show fear towards distinct items like the vacuum cleaner, or loud sirens).

GENERAL CHARACTERISTICS OF INDIVIDUALS WITH AUTISTIC SPECTRUM DISORDER

According to the American Psychiatric Association (2000), Autistic Spectrum Disorders (ASD) include the following categories Autistic Disorder, Rett's Disorder, Childhood Disintegrative Disorder, Asperger's and Pervasive Developmental Disorder Not Otherwise Specified. The common characteristics that these disorders share are serious impairment in social interactions and communication skills. Additionally, persons with ASD have noted restricted interests or repetitive behaviors.

The American Psychiatric Association has guidelines (see DSM-IV-TR, 2000) that specify the characteristics for each of the ASD. For example, an individual with Autistic Disorder would exhibit the following characteristics before the age of three years: (1) has at least two deficit social interaction parameters (e.g. eye contact, inappropriate use of facial expression or body language, difficulty in maintaining friendships, or failure to exhibit social reciprocity); (2) significant impairment in communication skills (e.g. documented lack of or delay in spoken language, inability to initiate or sustain conversation, a tendency to repeat certain words or phrases, or a lack of imaginative or imitative play; (3) presence of an usual pattern of interests (e.g. abnormal preoccupation with a particular topic, persistent fascination with parts of objects), a rigid adherence to unusual routines or repetitive patterns of unusual bodily movements (e.g. hand or finger flipping).

Individuals with Rett's Disorder exhibit normal development up until the age of five months. Sometime between the ages of five to 48 months, the individual's rate of head growth declines and they display a loss of purposeful hand movements, a decline in social interaction, the appearance of repetitive hand-wringing gestures, uncoordinated gait, and slowed movements. Also, these individuals have serious deficits in receptive and expressive language. This disorder is only found in females.

Individuals with Childhood Disintegrative Disorder develop normally up to the age of 24 months. After this age, these individuals exhibit significant losses in the following areas: language, motor, adaptive, and play accompanied by difficulties with bladder and bowel control. Lastly, prior to the age of ten years, these individuals will exhibit noted problems in social and communication behavior along with the appearance of restricted interests or repetitive mannerisms. This disorder is more typically found in males.

Individuals with Asperger's Disorder exhibit marked deficits in social interaction and restricted interests or stereotyped movements, which significantly interfere in social, occupational or other types of functioning. These individuals do not exhibit cognitive or expressive or receptive language delays but they have pragmatic language deficits. This disorder is more typically found in males.

Individuals with Pervasive Developmental Disorder Not Otherwise Specified exhibit some characteristics of ASD but they do not meet all the necessary criteria for any single diagnostic category. For instance the individual may have very mild symptoms of the disorder or the age of onset is later.

Prevalence

The prevalence rate of autism has been estimated to be about one out of every 2,000 live births and it is four times more common in males than females (Ciaranello & Ciaranello, 1995). However, the American Psychiatric Association states that the prevalence may be five cases per 10,000 live births (APA, 2000). Recently, Nash (2002) reported that "the latest studies suggest that as many as one in 150 kids age 10 and younger may be affected by autism or a related disorder-a total of nearly 300,00 children in the U.S. alone" (p. 48). Hardman, Drew, and Egan (2002) indicate, "the wide variation in prevalence is likely due to differences in definition and diagnostic criteria employed but may diminish over time as greater consensus about what constitutes autism is achieved" (p. 379).

Etiology

The presence of cold distant parents and dysfunctional parenting practices as a factor in the etiology of autism has not been supported (Tsai & Ghaziuddin, 1992; Wenar, 1994). In fact, "This idea is a most destructive one, not only because it is incorrect, but because all successful treatment programs require active parental participation" (Kaplan, 1996, p. 577). Current research on the causes of autism focuses on neurobiological underpinnings and neurochemistry factors (see Baker, Piven, Schwartz & Patil, 1994; Bauman & Kemper, 1994; Lee & Gotlib, 1994). Neuroimaging studies which attempt to identify abnormalities in persons with autism are becoming more frequent (see Nash, 2002). Most researchers generally accept that autism is present at birth. The research seems to support that idea that the underlying cause of autism may vary with different children (Koegel, Koegel, Frea & Smith, 1995). For example, Ciaranello and Ciaranello (1995) reported that autism is a severe neurological disorder with neuronal maturation defects, particularly in the cerebellum and the limbic structures. These authors stressed that the underlying etiology of autism can be attributed to nongenetic and genetic causes. The nongenetic causes can be associated with disruption, usually prenatal, to the normal pattern of development. Ciaranello and Ciaranello hypothesized that "the genetic forms of autism arise from mutations in genes controlling brain development and that both genetic and nongenetic etiologies cause damage to the same brain centers and regions" (p. 108). The main nongenetic cause of autism is prenatal viral infection. Autism may be triggered by infections such as rubella, toxoplasmosis, syphilis, varicella and rubeola. These infectious agents constitute evidence that prenatal infection can disrupt brain development in a way that causes autism. It should be pointed out that every time one of these infections occur autism does not automatically develop, but the research does show increased incidence of autism when the infections are present (Ciaranello & Ciaranello). Other non-genetic factors that may lead to autism include hypothyroidism and maternal cocaine and alcohol abuse during pregnancy (Ciarenello & Ciaranello, 1995). Epidemiological studies (Rutter & Bartak 1971), twin studies (Folstein & Rutter 1977, 1978), family studies (Folstein & Rutter 1977), and linkage and association studies all support the theory that genetic factors have an influence on autism (Ciaranello & Ciaranello, 1995). These studies which have looked at the frequency with which siblings of autistic probands are affected with autism, report estimates ranging between two and six percent, or 50 to 150 times the frequency in the general population (Rutter & Bartak 1971). Nash (2002) reported that "if one identical twin has autism, there is a 60% chance that the other will too and a better than 75% chance that the twin without autism will exhibit one or more autistic traits" (p. 50).

UNDERSTANDING HOW INDIVIDUALS WITH ASD THINK

A number of cognitive oriented theories exist today that attempt to shed some light on this unique psychological disorder (see Wahlberg 2001; Wahlberg & Rotatori, 1996). Many of these theories postulate that various cognitive mechanisms appear to be malfunctioning, giving rise to the symptomology of autism (Happe & Frith, 1996; Mundy, 1995; Smith & Bryson, 1994). Five of these theoretical positions, namely: (1) theory of mind (Happe, 1993; Happe, 1994; Happe, 1995; Happe & Frith, 1996; Hughes & Russell, 1993; Karmiloff-Smith, Klima, Bellugi, Grant & Baron-Cohen, 1995; Phillips, Baron-Cohen & Rutter, 1998;); (2) weak central coherence (Frith, 1989; Frith & Happe, 1994; Happe, 1997; Happe & Frith, 1996; Jarrold & Russell, 1997; Shah & Frith, 1993); (3) impaired executive function (Happe & Frith, 1996; Ozonoff,

Pennington & Rogers, 1994; Pennington & Ozonoff, 1996); (4) social impairment (Happe & Frith 1996; Hobson, 1993; Mundy, 1995); and (5) control theory (Wahlberg 2001) are discussed below.

Theory of Mind

One potential explanation of many of the symptoms of autism is that these individuals suffer from a weak theory of mind. Theory of mind can be best described as a person's ability to attribute mental states such as knowing and believing to other people while understanding that other people have their own thoughts and beliefs about the world around them (Flavell & Miller, 1998; Happe, 1995; Happe & Frith, 1996; Smith & Bryson, 1994). It also involves ones understanding that individuals other than themselves are able to appreciate and evaluate the actions taken by other people and use this understanding to form mental concepts or ideas based on these actions (Happe, 1993; Hobson, 1994; Hughes & Russell, 1993; Phillips et al., 1998). Normal individuals (with a sound theory of mind) are able to understand that others may form different perspectives than theirs about other people or objects that exist within the environment. Individuals with autism have been hypothesized to suffer from a specific impairment in the ability to represent the mental states of themselves and others and to understand and predict behavior in terms of these states (Happe, 1993). They are unable to attribute mental states, such as knowing and believing, to other people. The mental states individuals with autism have are constrained by what is observable within the concrete, physical, environment. According to Nash (2002), "Children on the autistic spectrum, however, are 'mind blind': they appear to think that what is in their mind is identical to what is in everyone else's mind and that how they feel is how everyone else feels. The notion that other people-parents, playmates, teachers – may take a different view of things, that they may harbor concealed motives or duplicitous thoughts, does not readily occur" (p. 51).

One of the primary ways in which a child can demonstrate a theory of mind is through the administration of a false belief task (Flavell & Miller, 1998; Hughes & Russell, 1993; Phillips et al., 1998). The following is an example of a highly used false belief task:

> If three people are sitting in a room and a pen is placed into a box with a cover, all involved realize that a pen is in the box. One of the persons in the room is asked to leave and while out of the room, the pen is replaced with a pencil. Upon the person's return to the room, the question is posed, "What does the person who exited the room think is in the box?"

The correct answer is the pen. In order to pass a false belief task, such as the one above, one has to understand that the individual that left the room has no idea about the switch. In order to pass this task, individuals have to understand a belief that is different from their own. Normal children are typically able to pass first order false belief tasks consistently by four to five years of age (e.g. see Flavell & Miller, 1998; Phillips et al., 1998).

In order to assess the extent to which autistic individuals possess a theory of mind, Happe (1994) presented 18 high functioning individuals with autism, who ranged in age between nine and 45 years old, and a false belief task. Happe found that six of the participants were unable to pass first order false belief tasks. These subjects averaged 17.6 years of age with a lower than average Verbal IQ ranging between 52 and 76.

Baron-Cohen, Leslie and Frith (1985) conducted a study and found that children with autism were unable to predict where a protagonist would look for an object moved in his absence. In contrast, normal four-year-olds and children with Down's syndrome that were matched with the autistic participants were able to make the distinction. These results provided evidence of deficits in theory of mind for autistic children because the children with Down's syndrome passed the first order false belief tasks, while children with autism failed.

A weak theory of mind can explain the following autistic symptoms; inability to share joint attention and perspectives (see Happe & Frith, 1996; Mundy, 1995); weak interpersonal relatedness (see Hobson, 1993); dysfunction in the appreciation of the significance of incoming stimuli; attaching motivational value to stimuli (see Fotheringham, 1991); and imagination, communication, and socialization deficiencies (see Happe & Frith, 1996). For example, individuals with autism have a hard time coordinating objects and perspectives with others in the environment. Additionally, individuals with autism seem to lack the ability to share joint attention and perspectives (Happe & Frith, 1996; Mundy, 1995) and suffer from the ability to initiate joint shared attention relative to an object or event (see Mundy, 1995). Presumably, one needs an intact theory of mind in order to share the perspectives of others (i.e. joint attention). Theory of mind accounts for joint attention because individuals need to understand that others have perspectives in order to share that perspective.

A weak theory of mind deficit in individuals with autism may be due to joint attention problems as infants. They lack social reciprocity as infants, which can lead to a lack of understanding of the mental state of another individual which eventually leads to a theory of mind deficit later on in development. Another example which is closely related to joint attention, is that individuals with autism suffer from weak interpersonal relatedness (Hobson, 1993). Weak interpersonal relatedness is the inability to effectively coordinate perspectives of others to a shared object. Individuals need an intact theory of mind in order to be able to coordinate another person's perspective onto an object of interest. Furthermore, they would need to understand that others have perspectives different from their own in order to coordinate and share a perspective with another individual.

It has also been hypothesized that individuals with autism suffer from a dysfunction in the appreciation of the significance of incoming stimuli and attaching motivational value to the stimuli (Fotheringham, 1991). Within this hypothesis, Fotheringham believes that individuals with autism cannot understand the significance of incoming stimuli and suffer difficulties in making meta-representations. Making meta-representations involves the process of forming beliefs about another person's mental state. Fotheringham believes this is accomplished by being able to put oneself in another's shoes and take his/her point of view. Again, it becomes apparent that one would need a sound theory of mind to understand the significance of incoming stimuli so as to attach motivational value to take another's point of view.

Happe and Frith (1996) argue that the theory of mind deficit can explain various symptoms associated with autism. These researchers state that a deficit in theory of mind would explain the impairment's which individuals with autism have with imagination, communication, and socialization. Happe and Frith state that the key element which individuals with autism seem to suffer from is "mentalizing". A deficit in mentalizing is supported by the inability of individuals with autism to correctly complete a false belief task. Happe and Frith described this deficit as the "failure to attribute mental states independent of reality and of the child's own belief" (p. 1386). These researchers stress that this mentalizing deficit accounts well for the above three impairments.

Within all the aforementioned symptoms associated with autism, it becomes apparent that a causal relationship exists. It seems that individuals with autism suffer from a weak theory of mind as well as the deficits that were mentioned above. As was pointed out, theory of mind can account for all of the previously mentioned deficits associated with autism.

Executive Function Deficits

Individuals with autism exhibit rigid repetitive behaviors, deficits in pretend play, as well as socially inappropriate behaviors (see Wahlberg & Rotatori, 1996). In order to explain these symptoms, the executive function theory has been proposed that describes the behaviors individuals with autism exhibit in terms of an impairment in executive processing (see Normal & Shallice, 1986). Executive function is described as the control of continuous planned behavior while engaging in future goal directed activities (Normal & Shallice, 1986). This process allows one to retrieve and use knowledge and prior experience as part of the planning and inhibiting of responses, while at the same time monitoring progress. Individuals with autism seem to exhibit certain skill deficits related to impairments in executive functioning. For example, they are unable to inhibit inappropriate responses while interacting with other individuals or to monitor responses while providing feedback to others. Also, they are deficit in the ability to disengage from context which prevents them from using previously learned knowledge to interpret and understand a certain context of events, without the knowledge necessarily appearing within the context under interpretation (Ozonoff, Pennington & Rogers, 1994). This process can be described as learning from your mistakes or learning from past experience and changing your perceived notion of a certain context. Finally, individuals with autism lack another key element of executive function, namely, flexibility. To succeed and function in life people need to be flexible, to a certain degree, due to the fact that nothing in life is ever a "sure thing".

Ozonoff et al. (1994) tested the hypothesis that individuals with autism do indeed suffer from executive function deficits. In their study, individuals with autism and matched control participants were given a number of tasks to perform. Two information processing paradigms were used to examine three cognitive operations required in many traditional executive function measures. The first was a Go-No-Go task consisting of three conditions with a hierarchy of processing demands. The first neutral inhibition condition required subjects to respond to a neutral stimulus, while simultaneously inhibiting responses to another neutral stimulus; this condition required no shifting of cognitive set. The second proponent inhibition (i.e. dominant) condition required inhibition of a previously reinforced well-learned response. The final flexibility condition necessitated frequent shifting from one response pattern to another, which placed high demands on cognitive flexibility (Ozonoff et al., 1994). The second task was the H&S task. This task examined local-global processing (which is described as detail orientation as opposed to seeing the big picture). Participants were presented with large letters on a computer screen. Each of the large letters was, in turn composed of small letters. The small letters were either the same letter as the large pattern or different than the larger pattern. The ability to process small letters (local processing) was compared to the ability to attend to large letters (global processing). Three groups participated in the study: the experimental group consisting of those diagnosed with autism and two control groups, one diagnosed with Tourette's syndrome and the other that was developmentally normal.

Ozonoff et al. (1994) found that the performance of the autistic and the Tourette's syndrome groups were similar on tasks requiring inhibition of neutral stimuli and global-local processing, but differed on a measure of cognitive flexibility and on a task that appeared to require inhibition of inappropriate responses. Overall, the autistic participants were less flexible than the Tourette's syndrome group on the tasks performed. The ability to shift attention from various informational sets was also found to be lacking in the autistic group in comparison with the Tourette's syndrome group.

Central Coherence

Central coherence is another theory that explains various symptoms associated with autism (Happe, 1997). This theory purposes that individuals with autism have a weak drive for central coherence, which is needed for general information processing. This perspective is based on a body of research that centers around the relative failure of individuals with autism to extract and use global meaning from a situation or written context (see Happe, 1997). Frith (1989) states that the underlying cognitive deficit associated with autism is displayed by a failure to process information for meaning in context. Frith argues that individuals with autism are processing the information in a very different way than normal individuals. Due to their weak drive for central coherence individuals with autism are unable to derive overall meaning from a situation or written text. This weakness results in individuals with autism making less use of content while paying more attention to parts rather than wholes. For example, research has shown that individuals with autism are just as good at recalling meaningless information as they are at recalling meaningful information (Happe & Frith, 1996). In comparison, normal and mentally handicapped individuals showed a superior ability in processing meaningful and patterned information over random and meaningless stimuli (Hermelin & O'Connor, 1967). Within the same context, normal subjects typically extract the gist of a passage or story while forgetting the surface form (Bartlett, 1932), while children and adults with autism may retain the actual words used but fail to extract the meaning (Happe & Frith, 1996).

Frith and Happe (1994) proposed that the weak drive for central coherence theory can account for symptomology that does not quite fit under the theory of mind account for autism. Specifically, these researchers argue that high functioning adults with autism, who can pass theory of mind tasks, continue to show patterns of performance characteristic of weak central coherence. An example of this would be their above average block design performance (Happe, 1994) and poor sentence-specified pronunciations of homographs (Happe, 1997). Other examples are their: savant skills (Grandin, 1995; Wahlberg & Rotatori, 1996); inherent insistence on sameness (DSM-IV, 1994; Happe & Frith, 1996; Wahlberg & Rotatori, 1996); specific odd interests (DSM-IV, 1994; Grandin,

1995; Powers, 1989); and poor comprehension of text (Frith & Snowling, 1983; O'Connor & Hermelin, 1994; Prior & Hall, 1979; Snowling & Frith, 1986; Tager-Flusberg, 1981b; Yuill et al., 1989).

Theorists have hypothesized those individuals with autism process information differently than normal individuals. Jarrold and Russell (1997) describe individuals with autism as processing information at an analytic rather than a global level. They assessed whether individuals with autism would rapidly and automatically enumerate a number of dots presented in a canonical form, or count each dot individually to obtain the total. Jarrold and Russell found that individuals with autism counted each dot individually, which suggests that they counted the dots at an analytic level rather than a global level. The researchers stated that this analytic performance by children with autism supports a weak drive for central coherence theory.

Processing information in such a manner causes impairments in making sense of stimuli and deriving meaning, consistency, and structure when processing information (Frith, 1989). Frith and Happe (1994) explain that individuals with autism may not show the normal bias towards processing certain types of information at a global level. The tendency to draw together diverse information and use this information to construct higher-level meaning in context is not present. Frith and Happe argue that instead of integrating low-level features into a coherent whole, individuals with autism may process information in a more piecemeal and bottom-up fashion. In other words, individuals with autism struggle to incorporate learned information when formulating higher level meaning.

There has been some speculation as to the mechanisms that support the weak drive for central coherence perspective. Experimental subjects' performance on the block design test has been used frequently to demonstrate a weak drive for central coherence. For example, researchers (Bolles & Goldstein, 1938; Nadel, 1938; Reissenweber, 1953; Shapiro, 1952) have reported that psychiatric patients and patients suffering from certain cerebral lesions perform poorly on the block design test (cited in Shah & Frith, 1993). Also, children with Williams's syndrome are substantially impaired on this task (Bihrle, Bellugi, Delis & Marks, 1989). Kaplan (1983) found that different types of errors on the block design test can be distinguished in adult patients with left-hemisphere and right-hemisphere lesions (cited in Shah & Frith, 1993). In contrast, individuals with autism excel on the block design test (Shah & Frith, 1993).

Happe and Frith (1996) assessed evidence for the weak drive for central coherence theory when they presented individuals with autism and normal individuals various forms of text. The participants read sentences as well as paragraphs that were either meaningful or not meaningful. The researchers assessed comprehension by requiring participants to recall information the participants had previously read in various forms of text. Participants were asked to recall either the text itself or the underlying meaning of what they had read. Happe and Frith found that individuals with autism were able to recall the written text verbatim, but were unable to recall meaning of text they had read. Recall for both forms of sentences were equal (those that had underlying meaning and those that did not) for individuals with autism. Normal participants were found to recall sentences with underlying meaning better than meaningless sentences. This was also found to hold true for reading paragraphs. Individuals with autism were able to recall the text they read, but struggled to describe any underlying meaning or connotations made within the paragraph. Happe and Frith hypothesized that individuals with autism perform well on the recall of written text and block design tests because they are able to resist the overall pattern (the global picture) and perceive it instead in terms of individual cubes (the analytic level).

A weak drive for central coherence may lead to the development of certain brain anomalies in individuals with autism such as making interpretations at an analytic rather than global level. This way of processing information may lead to the various symptoms associated with autism such as: savant skills (Grandin, 1995; Wahlberg & Rotatori, 1996), inherent insistence on sameness (DSV-IV, 1994; Happe & Frith, 1996; Wahlberg & Rotatori, 1996), and specific odd interests (DSM-IV, 1994; Grandin, 1995; Powers, 1989). Processing information at an analytic rather than a global level could also have an impact on the poor text comprehension of individuals with autism (see Frith & Snowling, 1983; O'Connor & Hermelin, 1994; Prior & Hall, 1979; Snowling & Frith, 1986; Tager-Flusberg, 1981b; Yuill et al., 1989).

Social Impairment

Theorists purposing a social impairment position hypothesize that autism is a direct manifestation of a deficit in social insight (Happe & Frith, 1996). In fact, Mundy (1995) postulates that the developmental anomalies in the neurological systems associated with autism may result in disturbances associated with cognitive or affective processes related to social development. One such disturbance is a lack of interpersonal relatedness (Hobson, 1993). This can be best described as an individual's failure to effectively coordinate perspective of others to share perspectives on objects in a similar way. Typically, normal children mirror others and learn to interact with them in a variety of tasks. However, individuals with autism are unable to perform such tasks and their social development suffers significantly. According to Hobson (1993), this process takes place in the earliest months of life when children with autism are unable to perform these tasks.

Hobson (1994) examined interpersonal relatedness in older children with autism. They found that these children demonstrated an inability (relative to matched controls) at identifying emotions. According to these researchers individuals with autism are unable to recognize the emotional states of others because of their inability as children to understand that other individuals share thoughts and feelings relative to external stimuli.

Another disturbance of social impairment, which children with autism exhibit is a deficit in joint attention. Typically, this involves sharing the focus of attention, through eye contact or pointing, between an object and another person. Mundy (1995) reported that joint attention disturbances in children with autism "reflects a failure of the adequate development, or operation of social-emotional executive function" (p. 65). Such a failure results in an inadequate allocation of resource to social problem solving procedures, which in turn yields the developmental anomalies that exist within the social-cognitive systems of individuals with autism (Mundy, 1995).

Another social development deficit associated with autism is a dysfunction of the appreciation of the emotional significance of incoming stimuli and attaching motivational value to the stimuli (see Fotheringham, 1991). This deficit prevents children with autism from perceiving and interpreting social-emotional type stimuli, which leads to difficulties in making meta-representations. According to Fotheringham, this deficit interfers with an individual with autism being able to put oneself in another's shoes and take on his or her point of view.

The final disturbance of social impairments in children with autism is imitation. This involves the ability of infants to imitate facial expressions of caregivers. This early form of imitation (it is hypothesized) leads to later social understanding. Happe and Frith (1996) stress that infants learn to share the emotional state felt by the other person by imitating various facial expressions, however, an early imitation problem may result in significant problems or delays in later social development. Smith and Bryson (1994) contend that the social deficit(s) of children with autism is diagnostic of a basic information processing problem rather than a social function deficiency.

Due to these disturbances of social impairment, children with autism are unable to form a strong social understanding of others. This lack of social understanding creates a barrier, which force children with autism to withdrawal from society and in turn to develop very odd stereotypical behaviors and poor communication skills. The development of these latter behaviors further alienates children with autism from society.

Control Theory

Very few theories exist that attempt to describe the neurological development of autism. Neurological deficits in individuals with autism are generally taken as a given, and research and theories tend to focus on the behavioral manifestations of the neurological anomalies inherent in individuals with autism. Wahlberg (2001) has used clinical findings, previous knowledge, and current research to develop a theory that attempts to explain the development of autism at the neuronal level starting at birth. This researcher has postulated a theory that attempts to explain how autism manifests itself in certain individuals. His theory is an attempt to "bridge the gap" between theories that exist to date.

Wahlberg (2001) postulates that individuals with autism suffer from environmental over-stimulation (O'Neill & Jones, 1997) which leads to many, if not all, of the symptoms associated with autism. Wahlberg indicates that this over-stimulation forces individuals with autism to process incoming stimuli in a very different manner, than normal individuals. This researcher argues that the brain of an individual with autism learns to think and handle information in a very different manner due to environmental over-stimulation. His theory is referred to as the Control Theory of autism.

O'Neill and Jones (1997) state that abnormalities in sensory or perceptual experiences can occur in the following areas, perception of sound, vision, touch, taste, smell, as well as kinesthetic and proprioceptive sensation. This stimulation may include hyper- and/or hyposensitivity to stimulation. According to O'Neill and Jones these stimulation distortions may lead individuals with autism to have problems in the processing of incoming sensory information.

Wahlberg (2001) describes over-stimulation as the effect environmental stimuli have on the neuronal activity within the human body. An example of over-stimulation would be wearing a wooly sweater without a tee shirt underneath. To most individuals this would be very over-stimulating to the tactile senses in the human body. This feeling is produced by the activation of neurons in the body that describe the "feel" of the sweater to the brain. The brain then suppresses this activation of the senses through chemical exchanges. This suppression is what allows us to wear clothing and not feel it unless we consciously think about it. This term is referred to as habituation (Willott, 1999). In the above example, the body may not be able to suppress the high level of over-stimulation produced by the sweater (i.e. it is to stimulating for suppression to take hold). Wahlberg hypothesizes that this over-stimulation of the senses is what causes individuals to develop autism and the various symptoms associated with it. In essence individuals with autism are unable to suppress the incoming stimuli and as information enters their respective "field", it does so much in the same way the sweater does for normal individuals, as over-stimulating, but to a much greater effect. Normal individuals have control over the sweater example as they can take it off or put on a tee shirt. In contrast individuals with autism cannot take off clothing that is over-stimulating to them as many may be walking around with no clothes on. This example can be applied to all forms of incoming stimuli entering the body's sensation field such as sight, sound, touch, and smell.

Wahlberg (2001) hypothesizes that individuals with autism learn to take in information in such a way as to screen out anything in the environment that is over stimulating. Within this information processing paradigm, individuals with autism learn to perceive information in a manner that is recognizable and understandable to them without the information over-stimulating them. Individuals with autism learn to control their surrounding environment in such a way as to make it understandable and less painful. They in turn learn very effective strategies that suppress over-stimulating events that surround them. These strategies, it is argued, are manifested in many of the odd behaviors classic to individuals with autism, such as stereotypic behaviors. For example, individuals with autism often will begin to stimulate themselves, when over-stimulated, by flapping their hands in front of their faces. In essence, they are removing themselves from whatever is over-stimulating them in the environment.

Individuals with autism learn to control over-stimulating environmental stimuli very early on in life. For example, infants with autism avoid eye contact and tense up when held (Van Hasselt & Hersen, 1994; Wahlberg & Rotatori, 1996). This is evident in almost 25% of cases of autism. Additionally, children with autism are often found sitting in a corner, almost as if they are attempting to tune out the external environment that they deem to be over-stimulating. Similarly, the way children with autism play with toys is suggestive of a form of control over the environment as they will take a toy car, turn it over, and spin the tires for extended periods of time. In doing so they are controlling the action of the toy, as well as tuning out external stimuli that they perceive as over-stimulating. All these interactions effect the way children with autism interact and draw information from their environment.

Wahlberg (2001) argues that individuals with autism can be over-stimulated by the external environment in a number of ways via tactile, auditory, or visual stimuli. Their reaction to controlling this over stimulation leads to brain development that is different than typical normal brain development. During normal brain development in childhood, individuals are attempting to acquire information dealing with every aspect of the world around them. In contrast individuals with autism expend the same amount of energy learning to remove the over-stimulating environment around them. They attempt to find ways to "tune out" the external, at times painful, environmental stimulation. Whereas in normal brain development, children take in information, the brains of individuals with autism tune out over stimulating external stimulus. The brain of an individual with autism continues to develop and learn to harness the energy it's provided, but it learns to screen out information deemed over-stimulating or painful by developing very concrete ways of processing information to make it meaningful without being painful or over-stimulating. This process results in the individual with autism appearing rigid and inflexible, socially inept, and lacking proper communication skills. The focus for individuals with autism becomes "sameness". They crave information that is consistent and concrete. Individuals with autism focus on environmental stimuli that are concrete, such as numbers, or calendars because they never change.

Recently, Wahlberg and Jordan (2001) tested a child with autism's ability to control a short-term memory task. The researcher used the Sternberg short-term memory task to assess both normal children and a child with autism's reaction times and delay times in completing the task. All subjects were asked to complete a task that required them to respond to a probe that either appeared in a previously presented word or did not. This response was referred to as a reaction time response. Subjects in the study had to press a button to initiate the next trial. This was referred to as the delay time. Upon analysis of the subject's reaction and delay times, Wahlberg and Jordan found that the child with autism had a longer overall delay time, while at the same time having a very structured set of data. In other words, the child with autism was controlling the task. The researchers reported that the length of the delay time represents the child's apprehension in initiating the next trial as it represented an unknown set of new variables. Wahlberg and Jordan concluded that the subject's control of the unknown next trial placed him in an awkward and uncomfortable position due to his craving for sameness.

Wahlberg (2001) hypothesizes that the over-stimulation felt by individuals with autism causes them to attempt to create order within the chaos of the world. They do this by filtering the information they take in. In essence individuals with autism take "flexible" information and filter it to make it more "concrete". The over-stimulation they experience forces them to control the influx of information, while at the same time feeding their desire for "sameness". This insistence on sameness is paramount in the diagnosis of autism and it is referred to as rigid stereotypic behavior. This pattern of behaviors is what Wahlberg and Jordan (2001) found in their study. In essence the child controlled the task and at the same time controlled how he was processing information (Wahlberg & Jordan, 2001). For a more detailed description of the Control Theory, see Wahlberg (2001).

DIAGNOSIS AND ASSESSMENT

A major problem with ASD is the fact that it is extremely hard to diagnose a child with this disorder at an early age. In fact correct identification may not occur for several years (Bax, 1999; Howlin & Asgharian, 1999; Lord & Risi, 2000). The diagnosis is complicated according to Rutter (1978) because all behaviors shown by ASD children are shown by other children, including normal children. Similarly, Kravitz and Boehm (1971) found that self-stimulatory behaviors such as rocking and hand flapping, which autistic children exhibit at high rates, are quite common in infants. Along these lines, Perlman (2000), Ryan. (1992), and Wolf (1991) indicated that misdiagnosis can occur due to the similarities in ASD symptoms and those associated with psychiatric disorders such as schizophrenia, mania, anxiety, obsessive-compulsion, or schizoid personality. Further, Howlin and Asgharian (1999) reported that some individuals with ASD might not get diagnosed until adulthood. Because of this DeMyer, Hingsten and Jackson (1981) and Rutter (1978) have suggested, "the diagnosis of autism may represent a multiplicity of behavior problems with a multiplicity of etiologies" (p. 19). In the following section, specific screening instruments, interview procedures, checklists and rating scales and observational assessment methods for diagnosing ASD are discussed.

Specific Screening Instruments

A popular instrument for screening symptoms of children with ASD is the Checklist for Autism in Toddlers (CHAT; Baron-Cohen, Allen & Gillberg, 1992). The CHAT is a simple 14-question test to detect symptoms of ASD as early as 18 months. The "CHAT" test "asks questions pertaining to social play, social interest, pretend play, joint-attention skills, communicative pointing, and imitation. Parents answer nine questions (e.g. "Does your child take and interest in other children?") and physicians answer five (e.g. "During the appointment, has the child made eye contact with you?)" (p. 839). Baron-Cohen, Allen, and Gillberg (1992) had the test administered to 50 randomly selected and 41 "high risk" 18-month-old toddlers who had autistic siblings. They found that no children in the normal functioning group failed more than one item pertaining to pretend play, social pointing, joint attention, social interest, or social play. The researchers did find that four children in the "high risk" group failed two or more of these items and these children received a diagnosis of autism by 30 months. Convincingly, "the CHAT detected all four cases of autism in a total sample of 91, 18-month-olds" (p. 839). This test is a great breakthrough in the search for an easier way to diagnose autism in early childhood. It is both

Table 2. Specific Screening Instruments for ASD.

Name Age Range Areas.		
Pervasive Developmental Screening Test-Stage – 1 (PDDST; Siegel, 1998 cited in Filipek et al., 1999)	Children up to three years	Presence of negative and positive symptoms
Autism Screening Questionnaire (ASQ; Berument, Rutter, Lord & Bailey, 1999) years	Version 1: under six years Version 2: over six communications, and	40 questions on reciprocal social interactions, repetitive behaviors
Autism Spectrum Screening Questionnaire (ASSQ; Ehlers & Gillberg, 1993)	Elementary school aged students	27 items-restricted interests, literal interpretation of clumsiness, social naivety, and peer relationships
Australian Scale for Asperger's Syndrome (ASAS; Garnett & Attwood, 1995 as cited in Attwood, 1998)	Elementary school aged children behaviors	Social, emotional, cognitive, and motor
Screening Tool for Autism Two-Year-Olds (STAT; Stone, 1998 cited in Filipek et al., 1999)	Two-year-old children	Pretend and reciprocal play, imitation of movements and nonverbal communications

economical and an early detector of autism. Additionally CHAT includes many items that children with autism pass but most children with mental retardation fail, which makes the CHAT more specific for autism. Positively, this test would allow parents to start a treatment program as soon as possible in their autistic child's life. While there is support for the CHAT, there some instances when it failed to detect children with ASD (see Baird et al., 2000; Cox et al., 1999; Filipek et al., 1999; & Tanguay, 2000). Other screening instruments appear in Table 2.

Interview Procedures

When information from a screening instrument suggests that more detailed knowledge is attained, a comprehensive interview should be carried out.

Wicks-Nelson and Israel (2001) recommend that the interview cover information on the individual's birth, developmental, medical and family histories. Two structured interview devices that may be helpful in gathering the above information are The Parent Interview for Autism (PIA; Stone & Hogan, 1993) and the Autism Diagnostic Interview-Revised (ADI-R; Lord et al., 1994). The PIA is a 118-item interview that assesses social behavior, communication abilities and repetitive movements. This device is psychometrically adequate and takes about 30 to 45 minutes to administer (Filipek et al., 1999).

The ADI-R is composed of the following areas: communication abilities, social development. Play behaviors, repetitive movement and behavioral problems. It can be used with individuals from 18 months through adulthood. The ADI-R is very helpful for mental health clinicians as it was designed in accordance with DSM-IV diagnostic criteria for autism (Lord et al., 1994). Volkmar and Marans (1999) reported that the ADI-R has good psychometric properties and can be administered in an hour or more.

Checklists and Rating Scales

Table 3 provides the reader with information on seven scales that have been developed to identify ASD symptoms. One of these, namely, the Gilliam Autism Rating Scale (GARS; Gilliam, 1991, cited in Carr, 1999) is a broad ranged scale that can be used with individuals aged three through 22 years. This scale is very useful for clinicians because the items correspond to the DSM-IV criteria for autism. Parents, teachers, and mental health professionals can complete the scale. It takes about ten minutes to administer and its reliability and validity scores are reported to be psychometrically strong (see Pro-Ed, 2001). Another useful scale is the Asperger Syndrome Diagnostic Scale (ASDS; Myles, Bock & Simpson, 2001, cited in Pro-Ed, 2001). This comprehensive scale covers the following areas: language, cognitive abilities, social interactions, maladaptive behaviors and sensorimotor functioning. Individuals aged five through ten years can be assessed with the ASDS. Parents, teachers, speech-language pathologists and mental health professionals who know the behaviors of the individual being assessed, can complete the scale. In addition to providing an "AS Quotient", which indicates the likelihood of Asperger's Disorder, ASDS can be used to identify behaviors for intervention and assess treatment success.

Observational Procedures

Deisinger (2001) recommends that naturalistic observations be carried out to evaluate individuals for the diagnosis of an ASD. According to Deisinger, such

Table 3. Checklists and Rating Scales to Identify ASD Symptoms.

Name	Age Range	Areas
Autism Rating Scale (CARS; Schopler, Reichler, DeVelles & Daly, 1980)	Children over two years	15 items – impairment in relationships, stereotypic movements, resistance to change, eye contact, ecolalia, pronoun reversal
Autism Behavior Checklists (ABC; Krug, Arick & Almond, 1980, cited in Volker & Marans, 1999)	Elementary school aged children	57 items – sensory and relational symptoms, use of body and objects, language use and self help abilities
Gilliam Autism Rating Scale (GARS; Gilliam, 1991, cited in Carr, 1999)	3 to 22 years	Stereotyped behaviors, communication, social interactions, and developmental disturbances
Revised Behavior Summarized Evaluation Scale (BSE-R, Barthelemy et al., 1997)	Elementary school aged children	29 items – social interactions, eye contact, communication odd utterances and movements, resistance to change, sleep disturbances, and mood difficulties
Gilliam Asperger's Disorder Scale (GADS, Gilliam, 2001, cited in Pro-Ed, 2001)	Elementary school aged children	40 items – developmental history, cognitive patterns, restricted behaviors and pragmatic abilities
Asperger Syndrome Diagnostic Scale (ASDS; Myles, Bock & Simpson, 2001, cited in Pro-Ed, 2001)	5 to 18 years	50 items – language, cognitive abilities, social interactions, maladaptive behaviors and sensorimotor
Chidren's Social Behavior Questionnaire (CSBQ; Luterijn Jackson, Volkmar & Minderaa, 1998)	Elementary school aged children	96 items – disruptive behaviors, social interaction problems, social cues, resistance to Change and stereotypic behaviors

observations should include interactions between the person and the evaluator as well as the examinee and family members and peers. Inaddition to naturalistic observational procedures, standardized observational devices can be used. For example, the Autism Diagnostic Observation Schedule (ADOS; Lord, Rutter, DiLavore & Risi, 2001, cited in Western Psychological Services, 2001), is an excellent schedule to observe and record the behavior of individuals with ASD. It is composed of four modules, which contain set activities to be observed during a 35 to 40-minute period. Module One can be used with nonverbal children, whereas, Module Two is appropriate for children who communicate in phrases but are not considered verbally fluent. Modulae Three is used with children that have fluent language, whereas, Module Four is used with verbally fluent adolescents and adults. According to Lord et al. information gathered from the ADOS can assist the clinician in classifying the examinee for DSM-IV diagnosis. The ADOS has excellent reliability and good discriminant validity (Lord et al., 2000).

TREATMENT

Language Intervention

Bakken and Bock (2001) indicated that individuals with ASD display language disorders that range from no verbalizations " to recitation of monologue in an area of obsessional interests" (p. 111). At times these individuals exhibit echolalia, delayed language, topic preseveration and lack of initiation or maintenance. Due to these deficits, Koegel and Koegel (1995) stressed that spontaneous language training is of vital importance in a child with autism's life so that the child can function in the community with others. In the following section, promising language practices and strategies are discussed.

Facilitated communication is a relatively recent instructional strategy for individuals with autism. It allows the individual to communicate using a keyboard and the "help" of a facilitator (Taylor, Sternberg & Richards, 1995). Initially the individual with autism is taught to use the keyboard with a hand-over-hand method, where the facilitator actually takes the child's hand and touches a key. Eventually the child learns to touch the keys and respond on his/her own. The major problem that skeptics have about the use of facilitated communication is whether or not the child with autism is coming up with the output or if the facilitator is. Biklen, Morton, Gold, Berrigan, and Swaminathan (1992) offered:

> the following six factors in support of facilitated communication: (1) the style, speed, and accuracy of a student's fine motor movement to the communication device were generally

consistent across facilitators; (2) typographical errors made appear to be unique to the communicator; (3) photonetic or invented spellings appear to be unique to the communicator; (4) some of the typed phrases and sentences were so unusual as to be unexpected from a facilitator; (5) content produced is sometimes not known to the facilitator; and (6) personality appears to be revealed through the various communications.

It should be pointed out that while their are success stories for the use of facilitated communication (see Biklen & Duchan, 1994; Biklen et al., 1992; Biklen & Schubert, 1991; Crossley & Remington-Gurney, 1992; Spake, 1992), it is important to note that not all professionals believe that the communication exhibited in these studies are being communicated by individuals with autism (see Prior & Cummins, 1992). Also controlled research has not supported this independent communication from nonverbal subjects when the facilitator cannot be appraised of the response asked of the subjects (see Cabay, 1994; Green & Shane, 1994; Wheeler, Jacobson, Paglieri & Schwartz, 1993).

Language Experience Approach: Shepherd and Arther (1986) modified the language experience approach (LEA) into what they called experience language (EL). Experience language is best served for children who are high functioning but have difficulty in communicating. Shepherd and Arther place emphasis on working on many different language areas at all times, as well as in all areas of communication by providing modeling, demonstrations and by giving examples (Bakken & Bock 2001). The incorporation of the EL involves many different components to stimulate language. It is important to establish a routine that allows for modifications, have children tested for vision, hearing, and vocal abilities, to use instant pictures to provide a concrete visualization for language development, to use colors, and the use specific life experiences of each child to promote language development.

Milieu Teaching: Cavallaro (1983) uses the naturally occurring change and developments in the milieu to teach children to generalize language. Milieu teaching involves teaching children that language can be used to obtain various objects, to gain the attention of others, and to teach children language that is appropriate in differing social contexts (Bakken & Bock, 2001).

Behavior Chain Interruption Strategy: Sigafoos and Littlewood (1999) assessed the effectiveness of the behavior chain interruption strategy (BCIS). The BCIS involves the interruption of an activity and the correct evoked response of the student in order to continue with the activity. In their study they interrupted playground activity and had the participants with autism respond by saying the word "play" in order to continue playing. They found that a high level of correct responses was obtained over the course of approximately 100 instructional trails. The BCIS can be an effective strategy for the promotion of communicative language in naturalistic settings (Bakken & Bock, 2001).

Sign Language: Studies have shown that the use of sign language for children with autism can be beneficial to the development of communicative language (Bonvillian & Nelson, 1976; Carr, 1979). Sign language allows children with autism a means to communicate wants and needs when the spoken form of language does not. Research studies on the acquisition of sign language in children with autism has found a decrease in many negative behaviors associated with autism such as self-stimulation and tantrums as well as an increase in spontaneous communication and social skills (Bonvillian & Nelson, 1976; Carr, 1979).

Language Shaping Technique: Another techniques used to teach language to children with autism is the structured methods in language education (SMILE) (Bakken & Bock, 2001; Wolf-Schein, 1995). SMILE incorporates a hierarchy of skill progression from phonology to morphology to syntax. This technique is used in a small group setting at the beginning of the school day with short lessons. The duration of the lessons is increased with time to a maximum of 30 minutes.

Semantic/Pragmatic Language Instruction: Beisler and Tsai (1983) developed a program for increasing communication that involved the establishment of reciprocal communication exchanges. Intensive modeling of verbal responses with joint activity routines were used in conjunction with a reinforcement system that provided the child with the fulfillment of the intent of the communication (Beisler & Tsai, 1983; Bakken & Bock, 2001). Research has also found benefits from role-playing video segments (Ogletree, Fischer & Sprouse, 1995). Videotaped vignettes were viewed, discussed and eventually role-played by a clinician and a child with autism depicting positive interactions. This was shown to be beneficial to increasing appropriate gazing behaviors, response time and topic maintenance (Bakken & Bock, 2001; Ogletree, Fischer & Sprouse, 1995). Similarily, social stories can be developed specifically for each child to help teach them appropriate strategies to use in social situations while at the same time decreasing maladaptive behaviors (Hagiwara & Myles, 1999; Kuttler, Myles & Carlson 1998; Swaggart et al., 1995).

Modifying Maladaptive Behaviors

"Today the most promising treatment for autistic persons is behavior modification as derived from modern learning theory" (DeMyer, Hingtgen & Jackson, 1981, p. 3). Empirical results from behavioral intervention have shown positive and negative results (see Lovaas, Koegel, Simmons & Long, 1973). The positive side of behavioral treatment allows the child to build complex behaviors, such as language, and can help to suppress pathological behaviors, such as aggression and self-stimulatory behavior. On the negative side, the client's gains have been specific to the particular environment in which the client was treated. Also substantial relapse has been noted and no client fully recovered (Lovaas et al., 1973).

Over the years many researchers have looked at trying to teach children with autism (Lovaas et al., 1973). O. Ivar Lovaas has done a large amount of research (see Lovaas, 1987; Lovaas & Smith, 1989) on autistic children over the years and has developed a behavioral program for the autistic child. Lovaas stated that, "the problem is that the existence of an entity called "autism" is a hypothesis (Rutter, 1978), an attempt to organize data and direct research, rather than a proven fact. Moreover, autism remains a poorly supported hypothesis despite the extensive research that has been conducted in an effort to conform it" (p. 19).

Lovaas and Smith (1989) indicated that the emphasis should be on, "separate behaviors rather than "autism" as a whole, on discovering causes in the immediate environment rather than on etiology, and on inductive rather than hypothetico-deductive research together provide the basis for the behavioral theory" (p. 21). They propose:

> Four tenets for behavioral therapy: First, the laws of learning adequately account for autistic children's behaviors and provide the basis for treatment. Second, autistic children have many separate behavioral deficits best described as developmental delays, rather than a central deficit which, if corrected, would lead to broad-based improvement. Third, autistic children give evidence of being able to learn like other human beings if they are placed in special environments. Fourth, autistic children's failure in normal environments and success in special environments indicate that their problems can be viewed as a mismatch between their nervous system and the environment, solved by manipulating the environment, rather than as the result of a diseased nervous system, curable only by identifying and eliminating the disease (p. 21-22).

Lovaas and Smith (1989) go on to say that:

> behavioral treatment centers on reinforcement control, effecting behavior change by manipulating the consequences of behavior. In contrast, traditional behavior centers on stimulus variables, which precede behavior. Behavioral treatments aim to build behavior and traditional treatments aim to cue behavior (p. 25).

In 1970, Lovaas started research on a behavioral program aimed at treatment for autistic children at the UCLA clinic for the Behavioral Treatment for Children. In Lovaas' first major study on autistic children (1987), he hypothesized that "construction of a special, intense, and comprehensive learning environment for very young autistic children would allow some of them to catch up with their normal peers by first grade" (p. 4). The subjects in the study were diagnosed by a medical doctor or a licensed Ph.D. psychologist, and had chronological ages of less than 40 months. Subjects were assigned to one of two groups: an intensive-treatment experimental group or the minimal-treatment Control Group one ($N = 19$). The experimental group received more than 40 hours of one-to-one treatment per week and the Control Group one received 10 hours or less of one-to-one treatment per week. Both treatment groups received treatment for two or more years.

Each subject in the experimental group was assigned several well-trained student therapists who worked (part-time) with the subjects in the subject's home, school, and community for an average of 40 hours per week for two or more years. During the first year, treatment goals consisted of reducing self-stimulatory and aggressive behaviors, building compliance to elementary verbal requests, teaching imitation, establishing the beginnings of appropriate toy play, and promoting the extension of the treatment into the family. During the second year, treatment emphasized teaching expressive and early abstract language and interactive play with peers. The third year emphasized the teaching of appropriate and varied expression of emotions: such as reading, writing, arithmetic, and observational learning.

Lovaas (1987) found that nine out of the 19 subjects in the experimental group (47%) did show improvement. They showed normal intellectual and educational functioning. In contrast, only two percent of the subjects in the Control Group one showed these same results. These results demonstrated that Lovaas' behavioral treatment method does offer relief of the problems associated with autism to almost 50% of those treated to the extent that children with autism can lead normal lives.

Use of Psychotropic Medication for Aberrant Behaviors

Hoover (2001) provides an extensive description of the medication management for target symptoms that individuals with ASD may exhibit. These symptoms include agitation, aggressiveness, stereotyped behaviors, social fears, dysphoric mood and depression, obsessions and compulsions, anxiety, hyperactivity, attention deficits and impulsivity. Hoover states that these symptoms "are not the unique features of either an individual ASD or the family of ASDs" (p. 259) but for individuals with ASD who have severe symptoms, they need to be treated to improve their: social coping capacity, acceptance of educational and vocational training and the management of own affairs. Hoover stresses that medications for altering the psychological and biological functioning of individuals with ASD work more efficiently in conjunction with a psychological, medical, social and educational treatment plan which focuses on the improvement of the individual's life functioning. Lastly, Hoover cautions mental health professionals that no medication is without side effects as such "an analysis of the potential benefits and risks of the use of a medication must be undertaken when medication to enhance an individual's' functioning is considered" (p. 266).

SPECIAL ISSUES

Therapeutic Interventions

Individuals with ASD engage in maladaptive behaviors (eg. rigidness, insistence on sameness, stereotyped or restricted play or interests. aggression, and self-injurious behavior) which interfere with their educational, social-emotional, and vocational learning. Parents, teachers, vocational trainers, mental health professionals, and self-care staff are frequently challenged by these maladaptive behaviors as they attempt to educate, counsel and train individuals with ASD. Positively, successful educational and environmental interventions are now available for individuals with ASD. These include peer-mediated instruction (Odom & Watts, 1991), pivotal response training (Stahmer, 1995), play based therapy (Baker, Koegel & Koegel, 1998; Jahr, Eldevik & Eikeseth, 2000), music therapy (Wimpory, Chadwick & Nash, 1995) and social stories (Swaggart et al., 1995). A growing therapeutic service that can assist higher functioning individuals with ASD and their families in the management of these maladaptive behaviors is counseling (see Arthur, Rotatori & Wahlberg, 2001; Burkhardt, 2001).

Arthur, Rotatori and Wahlberg (2001) provide mental health professionals, whom counsel high functioning individuals with ASD, extensive information on successful counseling interventions that were developed from clinical practice. The information addresses the following topics: setting goals for counseling; procedures to enhance and unlock communications; ways to understand how clients with ASD think; strategies to deal with misperceived social interactions; ways to understand fragmented social skills; techniques to improve social skills dealing with faulty emotional responses; and interventions to improve decision making and practices to support parents. Similarly, Burkhardt (2001) provides mental health professionals comprehensive understanding and guidelines to counsel parents of clients with ASD. This understanding stresses that parents can offer social and emotional assistance to their child with ASD in the management of problematic behavior. The basis for parental assistance stems from research in the area of "expressed emotion" (see Mueser et al., 1993) which is concerned with " how people display their feelings with others, offers potential insight into the role that families, particularly parents, may play in triggering and managing behavioral excesses and deficits" (p. 218). Burkhardt uses hypothetical cases to illustrate for mental health professionals how parental assistance can alter their child's maladaptive behavior. This assistance is based on the following guidelines: "make criticism of persons with ASD as benign and constructive as possible; avoid negatively expressed emotions when possible; offer family members constructive outlets for their frustrations, hostility and disappointments to reduce negatively expressed emotions; have a safety plan in place to respond to tantrums following exposure to high levels of expressed emotions; introduce new behavior goals in the family environment to increase the likelihood that the child with ASD will make progress in social and emotional functioning; preserve parental resources through respite, planning, support and encouragement; create option for success for families of persons with ASD by defining a hierarchy of goals to be worked on; and help family members to understand the difference between the inability of persons with ASD to identify and respond to social expectations and an insensitive refusal to be considerate of others" (p. 230).

WORKING WITH FAMILIES AND LIVING ARRANGEMENTS

Children with ASD impact family dynamics in a very profound and often times debilitating way. Families that have a child with ASD are forced to deal with a number of extremely difficult tasks while raising their child. Past research suggesting that the parents themselves were responsible for their child's autistic condition, did not help matters either (Bettelheim, 1967; Kanner, 1943). This research described parents as being cold and refrigerator like and therefore leading their children into the condition known as autism. Obviously that is not the contention today, as this chapter previously made mention to within the etiology section.

Some of the difficulty for parents with a child with ASD stems from the fact that no specific guidelines for treatment exists and therefore parents are left to try and navigate the large number of standard and alternative treatments that exist (American Academy of Pediatrics, 2001). Making the task of treatment choice even more difficult is the "Internet" where web sites exist that talk about various treatments that work. At times, these web sites offer misleading results due to the fact that the sites are usually not refereed by anyone and are not supported by scientific research.

Teaching parents how a child with ASD perceives the world may help alleviate problematic interactions with the family system. Understanding sameness and a child with ASD's craving for consistency will help the family learn ways to interact and make an environment that is conducive to a child with ASD. "Natural" reactions and the normal treatment of children in the family without ASD may not provide the same results for the child of children in the family with ASD. Educating the parents to this is important. They may need to learn other ways to interact, discipline and communicate with their child with ASD. It can be hard for family members without ASD to "think outside the box" and develop strategies to enhance the familial system.

It is also important to teach family members that the ways in which a child with ASD functions as a whole may seem rather distant and cold. Even the things they say (if communicative) may come across as painfully honest or rude. Educating family members about autism as a whole may help all those involved understand the actions of the child with ASD. As family members become more educated to the condition, they are more apt to change not only their perceptions and expectations but also the way they interact with a family member with ASD. The family may be "doing the best it can" before they learn about the disorder. When their resources become exhausted, problematic interaction and frustration can emerge resulting in negatively spiraling consequences for the individual with ASD and family members.

COLLEGE AND/OR CAREER PLANNING FOR STUDENTS WITH AUTISM

Some individuals with high functioning autism and Asperger Disorder have the ability to attend a Junior College, Community College, or a University of their choice after high school. While these individuals are the minority, they need to be provided with strategies to help them transition into what they perceive as a chaotic and overwhelming setting. Individuals with ASD that plan to enroll in post-secondary education can benefit from information concerning what happens in this new environment. A discussion about information in a college catalog or student handbook helps ease their tension and presents a more favorable picture of what the college experience is. Also, students with ASD can benefit from a first hand rendition of college life provided by a friend, relative, or counselor which describes some of the experiences they had entering and completing college.

Another post secondary possibility for high functioning individuals with autism and Asperger Disorder is enrollment in a trade or professional school. For example, some individuals may be very capable and enjoy working with computers. They can be encouraged to attend a technical school that trains them to be proficient data processors. By learning such technical skills, they position themselves for high demand job opportunities in the economy.

State agencies can also help an individual with ASD learn vocational skills and find employment after school. Such an agency exists in Illinois and is called the Department of Rehabilitation Services (DORS). This agency provides training and job placement opportunities for many individuals with exceptionalities in the state of Illinois. A high school graduate with ASD can choose from a number of career options and receive free training at state funded facilities. In addition to specific job training skills, these programs provide opportunities in job interviewing, resume writing, and assistance in job placement.

FUTURE RESEARCH

The fact that autism is characterized as a neurological disorder creates a very difficult paradigm for researchers. Technology limits our understanding of the human brain and its development. Further complicating the issue is the fact that individuals with ASD are very different with respect to their abilities and prognosis. The aforementioned research does not provide a very clear, pronounced understanding of the neurological implications of ASD. Research is underway which provides new information on the neurology of autism. For example, Carlucci (1999) reports that Minshew and her colleagues have recently received a grant from the National Institutes of Health (NIH) to conduct research in the area of autism. There are a number of researchers working with Minshew on neurology and autism. Minshew (as cited in Carlucci, 1999) states that, "contemporary theories hypothesize deficits in complex or higher order cognitive abilities and disturbances in the development of neural networks that link brain regions to subserve complex cognitive functions" (p. 8). Minshew feels that the deficits seen in individuals with autism are due to the 'wiring' or connections between brain regions, as opposed to the deficits being caused by one region alone (which is in agreement with the control theory of autism previously mentioned).

Minshew (as cited in Carlucci, 1999) has used the fMRI to study the amygdala, which is involved in emotion, and the hippocampus, which is involved in memory. This researcher has found that these two brain regions are smaller in individuals with ASD. Minshew hypothesized that this finding may explain why individuals with ASD have problems experiencing and/or understanding subtle emotions and remembering complex information.

Researchers (see Carlucci, 1999) at the University of Pittsburgh (also part of the research team) approach autism, "as a disorder of complex information processing resulting from the abnormal development and dysfunction of neocortical systems" (p. 8). Their research has suggested that abnormalities do exist in the circuitry of the neocortical systems, but not in the brainstem or cerebellum. These findings have led them to the hypothesis that abnormalities associated with autism involve the neocortical systems.

Carpenter and Just (as cited in Carlucci, 1999) are using functional magnetic resonance imaging (fMRI) to focus on language comprehension, visuospatial processing and executive processing in individuals with ASD. These researchers are interested in studying the prefrontal cortex. Preliminary research findings suggest that when high functioning individuals with ASD are given complex sentences to comprehend, their left prefrontal cortex, which provides executive support, is activated. Such activation did not occur with matched control subjects. The researchers concluded that a complex sentence is much harder for individuals with ASD to solve in comparison to control subjects who perform the task more automatically.

Sweeney (as cited in Carlucci, 1999) is looking at the reflexive and voluntary eye movements in people with high functioning autism. This researcher is investigating the basic motor control of eye movements in terms of velocity and latency and the executive and attentional factors regulating these movements. Sweeney's preliminary results suggest that individuals with ASD do not have difficulties with eye movements controlled by the cerebellar vermis as previous research has suggested. In contrast Sweeney found that individuals with ASD experience problems on the eye movement tasks due to aspects of the prefrontal cortex. In fact, Sweeney found that individuals with ASD had great difficulty if they were told to look toward a remembered location or if they were asked to stop themselves from looking at suddenly appearing lights.

Nash (2002) reported that recently researchers (Courchesne – University of California) noted that "At birth ... the brain of autistic child is normal in size. But by two to three years of age, their brains are much larger than normal. This abnormal growth is not uniformly distributed. Using MRI-imaging technology, Courchesne and his colleagues were able to identify two types of tissue where this mushrooming in size is most pronounced" (p. 53). Courchesne raises the question "What's driving this abnormal growth?" (p. 54). Nash stresses that Courchesne is "looking at specific genes that might be involved" (p. 54).

SUMMARY

The number of individuals with ASD is growing tremendously since autism was recognized as a category for special education services in IDEA. While the disorder was first described by Kanner in 1943 and again by Asperger in 1944, it did not receive substantial attention until 1981, when Dr. Lorna Wing wrote an influential article which revived the early work of Kanner and Asperger

(Nash, 2002). Since then there has been an increase in research related to etiology, prevalence, educational and social-emotional intervention, and assessment and diagnosis. This research has highlighted that: ASD appears to run in families; their may be as many as 20 genes involved in autism; individuals with ASD think, socialize and emote differently; there appears to be some neurological misconnection present in the brains of individuals with ASD (Nash, 2002). Positively, there have been advances in educational, therapeutic and medication management that has allowed individuals with ASD to be more inclusively involved in our society.

REFERENCES

American Academy of Pediatrics Committee on Children with Disabilities (2001). Policy Statement: The pediatrician's role in the diagnosis and management of autistic spectrum disorder in children (RE060018). *Pediatrics, 107*(5), 1221–1226.

American Psychiatric Association (2000). *Diagnostic and statistical manual of mental disorders* (4th ed., Text Revision). Washington, D.C.: Author.

Arthur, M. R., Rotatori, A. F., & Wahlberg, T. (2001). Counseling techniques for individuals with autistic spectrum disorders. In: T. Wahlberg, F. Obiakor, S. Burkhardt & A. Rotatori (Eds), *Autistic Spectrum Disorders: Educational and Clinical Interventions* (pp. 234–254). New York: JAI Press.

Attwood, T. (1998). *Asperger's syndrome: A guide for parents and professionals*. Philadelphia, PA: Jessica Kingsley Publishers.

Baird, G., Charman, T., Baron-Cohen, S., Cox, A., Swettenham, J., Wheelwright, S., & Drew, A. (2000). A screening instrument for autism at 18 months: A 6-year follow-up study. *Journal of the American Academy of Child and Adolescent Psychiatry, 39*(6), 694–702.

Baker, M. J., Koegel, R. L., & Koegel L. K. (1998). Increasing the social behavior of young children with autism using their obsessive behavior. *The Journal of the Association for Persons with Severe Handicaps, 23*, 300–308.

Baker, P., Piven, J., Schwartz, S., & Patil, S. (1994). Brief report: Duplication of chromosome 15 Q 11–13 in two individuals with autistic disorder. *Journal of Autism and Developmental Disorders, 24*, 529–535.

Bakken, J. P., & Bock, S. T. (2001). Developing appropriate curriculum for students with autism spectrum disorders. In: T. Wahlberg, F. Obiakor, S. Burkhardt & A. Rotatori (Eds), *Autistic Spectrum Disorders: Educational and Clinical Interventions* (pp. 109–132). New York: JAI Press.

Baron-Cohen, S., Allen, J., & Gillberg, C. (1992). Can autism be detected at 18 months? The needle, the haystack, and the CHAT. *British Journal of Psychiatry, 161*, 839–843.

Baron-Cohen, S., Leslie, A. M., & Frith, U. (1985). Does the autistic child have a 'theory of mind'? *Cognition, 21*, 37–46.

Barthelemy, C., Roux, S., Adrien, J. L., Hameury, L., Guerin, P, Garreau, B., Fermanian, J., & Lelord, G. (1997). Validation of the Revised behavior Summarized Evaluation Scale. *Journal of Autism and Developmental Disorders, 27*(2), 139–153.

Bartlett, F. C. (1932). *Remembering: A study in experimental and social psychology*. Cambridge: Cambridge University Press.

Bauman, M., & Kemper, T. L. (1994). Neuroanatomic observations of the brain in autism. In: M. L. Bauman & T. L. Kemper (Eds), *The Neurobiology of Autism*. Baltimore: Johns Hopkins University Press.

Bax, M. (1999). Diagnoses made too late. *Developmental Medicine and Child Neurology, 41*(12), 795.

Beisler, J. M., Tsai, L. Y. (1983). A pragmatic approach to increase expressive language skills in young autistic children. *Journal of Autism and Developmental Disorders, 13*, 287–303.

Berument, S. K., Rutter, M., Lord, C., Pickles, A., & Bailey, A. (1999). Autism Screening Questionnaire: Diagnostic Validity. *British Journal of Psychiatry, 175*, 444–451.

Bettelheim, B. (1967). *The empty fortress*. New York: Free Press.

Bihrle, A. M., Bellugi, U., Delis, D., & Marks, S. (1989). Seeing either the forest or the trees: Dissociation in visuospatial processing. *Brain and Cognition, 11*, 37–49.

Bilken, D., & Duchan, J. E. (1994). I am intelligent: The social construction of mental retardation. *The Journal of the Association for Persons with Severe Handicaps, 19*, 173–185.

Bilken, D., Morton, M. W., Gold, D., Berrigan, C., & Swaminathan, S. (1992). Facilitated communication: Implications for individuals with autism. *Topics in Language Disorders, 12*, 1–28.

Bilken, D., & Schubert, A. (1991). New words: The communication of students with autism. *Remedial and Special Education, 12*, 46–57.

Bolles, M., & Goldstein, K. (1938). A study of impairment of abstract behaviour in schizophrenic patients. *Psychiatric Quarterly, 12*, 42–65.

Bonvillian, J. D., & Nelson, K. E. (1976). Sign language acquisition in a mute autistic boy. *Journal of Speech and Hearing Disorders, 41*, 339–347.

Burkhardt, S. (2001). Counseling issues for parents of children with autistic spectrum disorders. In: T. Wahlberg, F. Obiakor, S. Burkhardt & A. Rotatori (Eds), *Autistic Spectrum Disorders: Educational and Clinical Interventions* (pp. 211–234). New York: JAI Press.

Cabay, M. (1994). Brief Report: A controlled evaluation of facilitated communication using open-ended and fill-in questions. *Journal of Autism and Developmental Disorders, 24*, 517–527.

Carlucci, D. (1999). Brain wiring in autism. Research probes cognitive processing in people with high-functioning autism and Asperger's syndrome. *Advance for Speech-Language Pathologists and Audiologists, 9*(1), 6–9.

Carr, A. (1999). *The handbook of child and adolescent clinical psychology: A contextual approach*. New York: Routledge.

Carr, E. G. (1979). Teaching autistic children to use sign language: Some research issues. *Journal of Autism and Developmental Disorders, 30*, 553–567.

Cavallaro, C. C. (1983). Language intervention in natural settings. *Teaching Exceptional Children, 15*(3), 65–70.

Ciaranello, A. L., & Ciaranello, R. D. (1995). The neurobiology of infantile autism. *Annual Review of Neuroscience, 18*, 101–128.

Cox, A., Klein, K., Charman, T., Baird, G., Baron-Cohen, S., Swettenham, J., Drew, A., & Wheelwright, S. (1999). Autism spectrum disorders at 20 and 42 months of age: Stability of clinical and ADI-R diagnosis. *Journal of Child Psychology and Psychiatry, 40*(5), 719–732.

Crossely, R., & Remington-Gurney, J. (1992). Getting the words out: Facilitated communication training. *Topics in Language Disorders, 12*, 29–45.

Deisinger, J. (2001). Diagnosis and assessment of autistic spectrum disorders. In: T. Wahlberg, F. Obiakor, S. Burkhardt & A. Rotatori (Eds), *Autistic Spectrum Disorders: Educational and Clinical Interventions* (pp. 181–210). New York: JAI Press.

DeMyer, M. K., Hingtgen, J. N., & Jackson, R. K. (1981). Infantile autism reviewed: A decade of research. *Schizophrenic Bulletin, 7,* 388–451.

Education for All Handicapped Children Act of 1975, P.L. 94-142, United States Code, 20, Sections 1401 *et seq.*

Ehlers, S., & Gillberg, C. (1993). The epidemiology of Asperger syndrome: A total population study. *Journal of Child Psychology and Psychiatry, 34*(8), 1327–1350.

Fester, C. B. (1961). Positive reinforcement and behavioral deficits in autistic children. *Child Development, 32,* 437–456.

Filipek, P. A., Accardo, P. J., Baranek, G. T., Cook, E. H. Jr., Dawson, G., Gordon, B., Gravel, J. S., Johnson, C. P., Kallen, R. J., Levy, S. E., Minshew, N. J., Priznat, B. M., Rapin, I., Rogers, S., Stone, W. L., Teplin, S., Tuchman, R. F., & Volkmar, F. R. (1999). The screening and diagnosis of autism spectrum disroders. *Journal of Autism and Developmental Disorders, 29*(6), 439–484.

Flavell, J. H., & Miller, P. H. (1998). Social cognition. In: W. Damon, D. Kuhn & R. S. Siegler (Eds), *Handbook of Child Psychology: Cognition, Perception, and Language* (Vol. 2, pp. 851–898). New York: John Wiley & Sons, Inc.

Folstein, S., & Rutter, M. (1978). A twin study of individuals with infantile autism. In: M. Rutter, & E. Schopler (Eds), *Autism a Reappraisal of Concepts and Treatment* (pp. 219–242). New York: Plenum.

Fotheringham, J. B. (1991). Autism: Its primary psychological and neurological deficit. *Canadian Journal Of Psychiatry, 36,* 686–692.

Frith, U. (1989). *Autism: Explaining the enigma.* Oxford: Basil Blackwell.

Frith, U., & Happe, F. (1994). Autism: Beyond "theory of mind." *Cognition, 50,* 115–132.

Frith, U., & Snowling, M. (1983). Reading for meaning and reading for sound in autistic and dyslexic children. *Journal of Developmental Psychology, 1,* 329–342.

Grandin, T. (1995). *Thinking in pictures and other reports from my life with autism.* New York: Doubleday.

Green, G., & Shane, H. C. (1994). Science, reason, and facilitated communication. The *Journal of the Association for Persons with Severe Handicaps, 19,* 151–172.

Hagiwara, T., & Myles, B. S. (1999). A multimedia social story intervention: Teaching skills to children with autism. *Focus on Autism and Other Developmental Disabilities, 14,* 82–95.

Happe, F. G. (1993). Communicative competence and theory of mind in autism: A test of relevance theory. *Cognition, 48,* 101–119.

Happe, F. G. (1994). An advanced test of theory of mind: Understanding of story characters' thoughts and feelings by able autistic, mentally handicapped, and normal children and adults. *Journal of Autism and Developmental Disorders, 24,* 129–154.

Happe, F. G. (1995). The role of age and verbal ability in the theory of mind tasks performance of subjects with autism. *Childhood Development, 66,* 843–855.

Happe, F. G. (1997). Central coherence and theory of mind in autism: Reading homographs in context. *British Journal of Developmental Psychology, 15,* 1–12.

Happe, F. G., & Frith, U. (1996). The neuropsychology of autism. *Brain, 119,* 1377–1400.

Hardman, L. M., Drew, C. J., & Egan, M. W. (2002). *Human exceptionality: Society, school, and family* (7th ed.). Boston: Allyn and Bacon.

Hermelin, B., & O'Connor, N. (1967). Remembering of words by psychotic and subnormal children. *British Journal of Psychology, 58,* 213–218.

Hobson, R. P. (1993). Understanding persons: The role of affect. In S. Baron-Cohen, H. Tager-Flusberg & D. Cohen (Eds), *Understanding Other Minds: Perspectives from Autism.* New York: Oxford University Press.

Hobson, R. P. (1994). On developing mind. *British Journal of Psychiatry, 165*, 577–581.
Hoover. M. (2001). The role of medication in the management of autistic spectrum disorders. In: T. Wahlberg, F. Obiakor, S. Burkhardt & A. Rotatori (Eds), *Autistic Spectrum Disorders: Educational and Clinical Interventions* (pp. 254–268). New York: JAI Press.
Howlin, P., & Asgharian, A. (1999). The diagnosis of autism and Asperger syndrome: Findings from a survey of 770 families. *Developmental Medicine and Child Neurology, 41*(12), 834–839.
Hughes, C., & Russell, J. (1993). Autistic children's difficulty with mental disengagement from an object: Its implications for theories of autism. *Developmental Psychology, 29*(4), 498–510.
Jahr, E., Eldevik, S., & Eikeseth, S. (2000). Teaching children with autism to initiate and sustain cooperative play. *Research in Developmental Disabilities, 21*, 151–169.
Jarrold, C., & Russell, J. (1997). Counting abilities in autism: Possible implications for central coherence theory. *Journal of Autism and Developmental Disorders, 27*(1), 25–37.
Kanner, L. (1943). Autistic disturbances of affective contact. *Nervous Child, 2*, 217–250.
Kaplan, E. (1983). A process approach to neuropsychological assessment. In: T. K. Boll & B. K. Bryant (Eds), *Clinical Neuropsychological Brain Function: Research Measurement and Practice* (pp. 129–167). Washington, D.C.: APA.
Kaplan, P. S. (1996). *Pathways for exceptional children: School, home and culture*. St, Paul, MN: West Publishing Company.
Karmiloff-Smith, A., Klima, E., Bellugi, U., Grant, J., & Baron-Cohen, S. (1995). Is there a social module? Language, face processing, and theory of mind in individuals with Williams syndrome. *Journal of Cognitive Neuroscience, 7*(2), 196–208.
Koegel, R. L., & Koegel, L. K. (1995). *Teaching children with autism*. York, PA: Maple Press Co.
Koegel, R. L., Keogel, L. K., Frea, W. D., & Smith, A. E. (1995). Emerging interventions for children with autism. In: R. L. Koegel & L. K. Koegel (Eds), *Teaching Children with Autism* (pp. 1–16). York, PA: Maple Press Co.
Kravitz, H., & Boehm, J. J. (1971). Rhythmic habit patterns in infancy: Their sequence, age of onset, and frequency. *Child Development, 42*, 399–413.
Kuttler, S., Myles, B. S., & Carlson, J. K. (1998). The use of social stories to reduce precursors to tantrum behavior in a student with autism. *Focus on Autism and Other Developmental Disabilities, 13*(3), 176–182.
Lee, C. M., & Gotlib, I. H. (1994). Mental illness and the family. In: L. L'Abate (Ed.), *Handbook of developmental family psychology and psychopathology* (pp. 243–264). New York: Wiley.
Lord, C., & Risi, S. (2000). Diagnosis of autism spectrum disorders in young children. In: A. M. Wetherby & B. M. Prizant (Eds), *Autism Spectrum Disorders: A Transactional Developmental Perspective* (Vol. 9, pp. 11–30). Baltimore, MD: Paul H. Brookes Publishing Company.
Lord, C., Risi, S., Lambrecht, L., Cook, E. H. Jr., Leventhal, B. L., DiLavore, P. C., Pickles, A., & Rutter, M. (2000). The Autism Diagnostic Observation Schedule-Generic: A standard measure of social and communication deficits associated with the spectrum of autism. *Journal of Autism and Developmental Disorders, 30*(3), 205–223.
Lord, C., Rutter, M., & LeCouteur, A. (1994). Autism Diagnostic Interview-Revised: A revised version of a diagnostic interview for caregivers of individuals with possible pervasive developmental disorders. *Journal of Autism and Developmental Disorders, 24*(5), 659–685.
Lotter, V. (1978). Follow-up studies. In: M. Rutter & E. Schopler (Eds), *Autism: A reappraisal of concepts and treatment*. London: Plenum Press.

Lovaas, O. I. (1987). Behavioral treatment and normal educational and intellectual functioning in young autistic children. *Journal of Consulting and Clinical Psychology, 55*, 3–9.

Lovaas, O. I., Koegel, R. L., Simmons, J. W., & Long, J. S. (1973). Some generalization and follow-up measures on autistic children in behavioral therapy. *Journal of Applied Behavioral Analysis, 6*, 131–161.

Lovaas, O. I., & Smith, T. (1989). A comprehensive behavioral theory of autistic children: Paradigm for research and treatment. *Journal of Behavioral Therapy and Experimental Psychiatry, 20*, 17–29.

Luteijn, E., Jackson, S., Volkmar, F. R., & Mindera, R. B. (1998). The development of the Children's Social Behavior Questionnaire: Preliminary data. *Journal of Autism and developmental Disorders, 28*(6), 559–565.

Mueser, J. J., Bellack, A., Wade, J., Sayers, S., Tierney, A., & Haas, G. (1993). Expressed emotions, social skills, and response to negative affect in schizophrenia. *Journal of Abnormal Psychology, 102*(3), 339–351.

Mundy, P. (1995). Joint attention and social-emotional approach behavior in children with autism. *Developmental and Psychopathology, 7*, 63–82.

Nadel, A. B. (1938). A qualitative analysis of behaviour following cerebral lesions diagnosed as primarily affecting the frontal lobes. *Archives of Psychology*, (Whole No. 224).

Nash, J. M. (2002). The secrets of autism. *Time*, (May), 47–56.

Norman, D. A., & Shallice, T. (1986). Attention to action: Willed and automatic control of behavior. In: R. J. Davidson, G. E. Schwartz & D. Shapiro (Eds), *Consciousness and Self-Regulation* (Vol. 4, pp. 1–18). New York: Plenum.

O'Connor, N., & Hermelin, B. (1994). Two autistic savant readers. *Journal of Autism and Developmental Disorders, 24*(4), 501–515.

Odom, S. I., & Watts, E. (1991). Reducing teacher prompts in peer-mediated interventions for young children with autism. *The Journal of Special Education, 25*(1), 26–43.

Ogletree, B. T., Fischer, M. A., & Sprouse, J. (1995). An innovative language treatment for a child with high-functioning autism. *Focus on Autistic Behavior, 10*(3), 1–10.

O'Neill, M., & Jones, R. S. P. (1997). Sensory-perceptual abnormalities in autism: A case for more research? *Journal of Autism and Developmental Disorders, 27*(3), 283–292.

Ozonoff, S., Pennington, B. F., & Rogers, S. J. (1994). Executive function deficits in high functioning autistic children: Relationship to theory of mind. *Journal of Child Psychiatry, 32*, 1081–1105.

Pennington, B. F., & Ozonoff, S. (1996). Executive functions and developmental psychology. *Journal of Child Psychology and Psychiatry, 37*(1), 51–87.

Perlman, L. (2000). Adults with Asperger disorder misdiagnosed as schizophrenic. *Professional Psychology: Research and Practice, 31*(2), 221–225.

Phillips, W., Baron-Cohen, S., & Rutter, M. (1998). Understanding intention in normal development and autism. *British Journal of Developmental Psychology, 16*, 337–348.

Powers, M. D. (1989). *Children with autism.* Rockville, MD: Woodbine House Inc.

Prior, M., & Cummins, R. (1992). Questions about facilitated communication and autism. *Journal of Autism and Developmental Disorders, 22*, 331–338.

Prior, M. R., & Hall, L. C. (1979). Comprehension of transitive and intransitive phrases by autistic, retarded and normal children. *Journal of Communication Disorders, 12*, 103–111.

Pro-Ed. (2001). *2001 spring catalog.* Austin, TX: Author.

Reissenweber, M. (1953). The use of modified block designs in the evaluation and training of the brain injured. *Psychological Monographs: General and Applied, 67*(Whole No. 371), 1–28.

Rutter, M. (1970). Autistic children: Infancy to adulthood. *Seminars in Psychiatry, 2*, 435–450.

Rutter, M. (1978). Diagnosis and definition. In: M. Rutter, & E. Schopler (Eds), *Autism: A Reappraisal of Concepts and Treatment*. New York: Plenum Press.

Rutter, M., & Bartak, L. (1971). Causes of infantile autism: Some considerations from recent research. *Journal of Autism in Children Schizophrenia, 1*(1), 20–32.

Rutter, M., & Schopler, E. (1987). Autism and pervasive developmental disorders: Concepts and diagnostic issues. *Journal of Autism and Developmental Disorders, 17,* 159–186.

Ryan, R. M. (1992). Treatment-resistant chronic mental illness: Is it Asperger's syndrome? *Hospital and Community Psychiatry, 43*(8), 807–811.

Schopler, E., Reichler, R. J., DeVellis, R. F., & Daly, K. (1980). Toward an objective classification of childhood autism: Childhood Autism Rating Scale (CARS). *Journal of Autism and Developmental Disorders, 10*(1), 91–103.

Shah, A., & Frith, U. (1993). Why do individuals show superior performance on the block design task? *Journal of Child Psychiatry, 34*(8), 1352–1364.

Shapiro, M. B. (1952). Experimental studies of perceptual anomaly: Two confirmatory and explanatory experiments. *Journal of Mental Science, 98,* 605–617.

Shepherd, T. R., & Arther, B. (1986). Experience language: An autistic case example. *Academic Therapy, 21,* 605–613.

Sigafoos, J., & Lettlewood, R. (1999). Communication intervention on the playground: A case study on teaching requesting to a young child with autism. *International Journal of Disability, Development, and Education, 46,* 421–429.

Smith, I. M., & Bryson, S. E. (1994). Imitation and action in autism: a critical review. *Psychological Bulletin, 116,* 259–273.

Snowling, M., & Frith, U. (1986). Comprehension in 'hyperlexic' readers. *Journal of Experimental Psychology, 42,* 392–415.

Spake, A. (1992). Autistic children and breaking through. *Education Digest,* (November), 41–45.

Stahmer, A. C. (1995). Teaching symbolic play skills to children with autism using pivotal response training. *Journal of Autism and Developmental Disorders, 25*(2), 123–141.

Stone, W. L. & Hogan, K. L. (1993). A structured parent interview for identifying young children with autism. *Journal of Autism and Developmental Disorders, 23,* 639–652.

Swaggart, B. L., Gagnon, E., Bock, S. J., Earles, T. L., Quinn, C., Myles, B., & Simpson, R. L. (1995). Using social stories to teach social and behavioral skills to children with autism. *Focus on Autistic Behavior, 10*(1), 1–16.

Tager-Flusberg, H. (1981). Sentence comprehension in autistic children. *Applied Psycholinguistics, 2,* 5–24.

Tanguay, P. E. (2000). Pervasive developmental disorders: A 10-year review. *Journal of the American Academy of Child and Adolescent Psychiatry, 39*(9), 1079+. Retrieved November 6, 2000 from Infotrac database on-line (Article A65329815) on the World Wide Web: http://infotrac.galegroup.com

Taylor, R. L., Sternberg, L., & Richards, S. B. (1995). *Exceptional children integrating research and teaching.* San Diego: Singular Publishing Group.

Tsai, L. Y., & Ghaziuddin, M. (1992). Biological medical research in autism. In: D. E. Berkell (Ed.), *Autism: Identification, Education and Treatment* (pp. 53–77). Hillsdale, NJ: Erlbaum.

Van Hassalt, V. B., & Hersen, M. (1994). *Advanced abnormal psychology.* New York: Plenum Press.

Volkmar, F. R., & Marans, W. D. (1999). Measures for assessing pervasive developmental and communication disorders. In: D. Shaffer, C. P. Lucas & J. E. Richters (Eds), *Diagnostic Assessment in Child and Adolescent Psychopathology* (pp. 167–205). New York, NY: Guilford Press.

Wahlberg, T. (2001). The control theory of autism. In: T. Wahlberg, F. Obiakor, S. Burkhardt & A. Rotatori (Eds), *Autistic Spectrum Disorders: Educational and Clinical Interventions* (pp. 254–268). New York: JAI Press.

Wahlberg, T., & Jordan, S. (2001). A case study in the dynamics of autism. In: T. Wahlberg, F. Obiakor, S. Burkhardt & A. Rotatori (Eds), *Autistic Spectrum Disorders: Educational and Clinical Interventions* (pp. 254–268). New York: JAI Press.

Wahlberg, T. J., & Rotatori, A. (1996). Various treatment modalities for autistic individuals. In: A. F. Rotatori, J. O. Schwenn & S. Burkhardt (Eds), *Advances in Special Education* (pp. 109–131). Greenwich, CT: JAI Press.

Wenar, C. (1994). *Developmental psychopathology* (3rd ed.) New York: McGraw Hill.

Western Psychological Services (2001). *Catalog 2001*. Los Angeles, CA: Author.

Wheeler, D. L., Jacobson, J. W., Paglieri, R. A., & Schwartz, A. A. (1993). An experimental assessment of facilitated communication. *Mental Retardation, 31*, 49–61.

Wicks-Nelson, R., Israel, A. C. (2000). *Behavior disorders of childhood* (4th ed.). Upper Saddle River, NJ: Prentice Hall.

Willott, J. F. (1999). *Neurogerontology: Aging and the nervous system*. DeKalb, IL: Northen Illinois University: VCB Custome Packets.

Wimpory, D., Chadwick, P., Nash, S. (1995). Brief report: Musical interaction therapy for children with autism: An evaluative case study with two-year follow-up. *Journal of Autism and Developmental Disorders, 25*, 541–552.

Wolf-Schein, E. G. (1995). Structured methods in language education: SMILE. Paper presented at the 18th International Congress on Education of the Deaf (July), Tel-Aviv, Israel. (ERIC Reproductive Service No. ED 391-282).

Wolff, S. (1991). 'Schizoid' personality in childhood and adult life: I. The vagaries of diagnostic labeling. *British Journal of Psychiatry, 159*, 615–620.

Yuill, N., Oakhill, J., & Parkin, A. (1989). Working memory, comprehension ability and the resolution of text anomaly. *British Journal of Psychology, 80*, 351–361.

STUDENTS WITH HEARING LOSS

Deborah S. Stryker and Barbara Luetke-Stahlman

INTRODUCTION

Most hearing people have little concept of what it is like to be unable to hear. Sound is so much a part of their lives that they cannot imagine a world without waking to the radio in the morning or startling to the ring of the telephone in the middle of the night. So, it is easy to understand why most people have a difficult time relating to a world in which the spoken sound is never heard or not heard well enough to understand. Nobody feels this gap in understanding more acutely than hearing parents who have a child with a hearing loss or school personnel who have never experienced a student who is deaf or hard of hearing in their classroom.

Although deafness is categorized as a special need, it involves many unique characteristics when compared with some of the other areas of exceptionality such as learning disability, blindness, mental retardation, and so forth. Just as an example, consider that Gallaudet University, in Washington, D.C. is the only liberal arts university in the world for students who are deaf or hard of hearing. Hearing students can not enroll there as undergraduates. Yet, there is no college or university only for students with learning disabilities, autism, blindness, or behavioral challenges. In addition, there are more national organizations serving as advocates for individuals who are deaf and hard of hearing, with resources to meet their needs, than there are for any other exceptionality. This chapter addresses the need for general and special educators who work with children and youth who are deaf or hard of hearing to critically examine traditional views of teaching methods and expectations for these students. As teachers of deaf and hard of hearing students we know firsthand how difficult our task is in educating and nurturing this population of students. We also know how rewarding the experience can be when we realize that the changes we are making can make a difference in the lives of these students.

Definition of Terms

Students with a hearing loss are an incredibly diverse group of individuals. To better understand this varied group of children, it is necessary to understand something about audition; how it is measured and by whom. In addition, it is important to realize how a hearing loss might impact the education of students at various periods in their lives.

A hearing loss is categorized into three types according to site of lesion; conductive, sensorineural, and mixed. A conductive hearing loss involves the external or middle ear, a sensorineural loss involves the inner ear or auditory nerve, and a mixed loss has components of both conductive and sensorineural hearing loss. The term peripheral applies to sites of lesions in the outer, middle, and inner ear; the term central applies to hearing loss related to brainstem or cortex disorders.

Various terms, such as mild, moderate, severe, or profound, are used to indicate the degree of severity of the hearing loss. Hearing loss can also be described as either being unilateral, involving only one ear, or bilateral, involving both ears. A hearing loss that is present at birth is called congenital; a hearing loss that is sustained after birth is called acquired or adventitious. If a hearing loss is present prior to the development of language, it is described as prelingual; a hearing loss that occurs after the development of language is described as postlingual. Terminology that categorizes a student's hearing loss is often confusing because two students with identical audiograms may function very differently. An audiogram is only a rough estimation of what a person hears and does not usually take into consideration a child's cognitive level of functioning or language level. A student with a severe or profound hearing loss, who benefits from high powered hearing aids and who has received training since a young age, may be able to understand enough of what is heard to function "auditory/oral" and not use cues or signs. Another child with a similar audiogram may need to rely much more on vision and communicate primarily by signing.

Terms associated with the degree of hearing loss, as outlined on a child's audiogram, include mild through profound. Hearing loss is often measured in decibel (dB) loss. A student with a mild hearing loss (27–40 dB) will experience difficulty hearing faint sounds or speech from a distance, while a student with a moderate loss (41–55 dB) will begin to experience difficulty communicating outside a distance of five feet. Both of these students can benefit from hearing aids or an assistive listening device. Students with a moderate severe hearing loss (56–70 dB) will experience difficulty hearing conversational speech and especially group discussions at any distance and will benefit from the same services provided a student with a mild or moderate hearing loss. A severe hearing loss (71–90 dB) in a student typically means that he or she may only hear a loud voice within one foot of his/her ear and may be able to distinguish vowels from consonants. Students with a profound hearing loss (90 dB and above) will not be able to rely on their hearing for their primary means of communication, although he/she may hear some loud sounds. Students experiencing any level of hearing loss should be given preferential seating in any academic setting. These classifications are based on a child's ability to detect or hear sound (not necessarily understand it!). Again, although these classifications have been established to aid parents and professionals working with these students, one must be careful not to "pigeonhole" or label someone based on this information.

The various labels associated with a student who has a hearing loss include: deaf, Deaf, hard of hearing, and hearing impaired. These are all related terms and sometimes used synonymously. It was reported in 1995 that of the 47,616 students in the United States receiving services because of their hearing loss, 36% of these students were classified as deaf (Schildroth & Hotto, 1996). The term "deaf" means any loss of hearing that is so severe or profound that the individual is substantially limited in processing linguistic information through auditory channels, with or with out amplification. Therefore, a child might be deaf when not wearing hearing aids, but not measure within this classification of deafness when using them. Deaf children are the most adversely affected educationally. As a result, communication, learning, and socialization must be conducted through visual methods. These might include the use of manual signs or visual cues. Another label for a student with a hearing loss is Deaf, emphasizing the use of capital *D*, which refers to culturally Deaf individuals as well as a particular set of beliefs and practices shared by other Deaf people. Students considered part of the Deaf community share a common language, American Sign Language (ASL), and a common culture. Sharing deaf culture means the student shares beliefs, values, behaviors, arts, customs, schools, social forms, and knowledge that are characteristic of people in their Deaf community.

The term "hard of hearing" means that students have a permanent or fluctuating hearing loss in their ability to hear, ranging from mild to severe as defined by audiological measurement. Such a loss can affect students' processing of auditory signals and, therefore, also affect their academic performance, even when hearing aids or other assistive listening devices are utilized. Students who are hard of hearing usually benefit from such equipment and can understand speech depending on the noise level in the environment. Because linguistic development is primarily auditorily based, with vision serving as a secondary or supplemental channel, most students who are hard of hearing usually benefit from amplification and other assistive listening devices. If they cannot obtain such equipment or refuse to wear it, educational development will most likely be adversely affected. Children with a 20 to 90 dB hearing loss are considered hard of hearing and account for 64% of the students receiving deaf education services in schools (Schildroth & Hotto, 1996). Historically, these students were not given due consideration regarding individual communication needs and the varying differences their hearing loss presented. This unique population has been called the most misunderstood group of students because they appear to hear at times, but at other times, they are negatively affected by colds, noise, and distractions (Henwood & Pope-Davis, 1994). Children who are deaf or hard of hearing are educated in either general education classrooms with hearing peers, in segregated public school classes with other deaf children, or in separate residential schools.

Medical professionals often use the term "hearing impaired" to refer to students with any amount of hearing loss; however, it carries a negative connotation, particularly for members of the Deaf community and more recently with professionals in educational settings. They avoid the term because it implies an inability when audiologic definitions are used and prefer that students with a hearing loss be viewed in terms of what they can do instead of what they cannot. The term "hearing impairment" is also used differently in various programs. It is recommended that the terms "deaf" or "hard of hearing" be used when recognizing a student's hearing loss. How students perform in the educational setting can be influenced by these differences, as well as by the age that the student looses his/her hearing, the reason that the hearing loss occurred, the availability of services, and the family's response to services.

DEAFNESS AND HARD OF HEARING

Approximately 28 million Americans, or about one in every ten people in this country, have a hearing loss. Projections indicate that this number and percentage will grow larger as "baby boomers" age and as increasing noise pollution continues to take its toll. It is interesting to note that hearing loss affects more people than blindness, cancer, kidney disease, multiple sclerosis, and tuberculosis combined. Deafness is considered a low incidence disability, affecting approximately one percent of all schoolchildren. Although there are fewer children classified as deaf or hard of hearing than those classified with a learning disability, mental retardation or behavioral disorder, the impact of their hearing loss educationally, communicatively, and socially constitutes a significant concern. Regarding the deaf and hard of hearing student population, within the last two decades an increase has occurred in the number of minority students in the United States, although there has been a drop in the overall number of students who are deaf and hard of hearing. The greatest swell has occurred among Hispanic children (up 19%) and Asian/Pacific Islander children (up 50%) (Schildroth & Hotto, 1994).

Causes

Knowledge of the cause of hearing loss in children is important for several reasons. In the case of conductive loss, the cause dictates the treatment, which is usually medical or surgical. In the case of sensorineural loss, which is permanent, knowledge helps families gather information about the probability of hearing loss in any subsequent children and may help them master the feeling of stress and guilt related to having a child with this disability. The following are the most common causes of conductive hearing loss in school-age children:

(a) Ear infection or otitis media, affects 70% of all infants and young children.
(b) Blockage of the outer ear by an excessive amount of wax.
(c) An occluded auditory canal or atresia.
(d) An anomaly in the middle ear evidenced by missing or malfunctioning ossicles or tympanic membrane.

Children with a conductive hearing loss experience damage to their middle or outer ear. The problem lies with the child not being able to conduct sound to the remainder of the hearing mechanism. Although conductive hearing loss usually can be successfully treated in young children, and it is not usually a basis for placement of school-age children in special education programs, this type of loss can have a serious effect on speech production and language-dependent skills (Webster, Saunders & Bamford, 1984). One particularly challenging group to teach are those children with a fluctuating conductive hearing loss.

Children with sensorineural hearing loss experience damage to the structure of the inner ear and/or the nerves that carry sound to the brain. It can be characterized by a student's inability to perceive sounds at varying frequencies with the same level of intensity. This loss is usually permanent and can not be medically treated, but is usually responsive to an assistive listening device. Still, special education services are usually necessary. Following is an overview of four etiologies most commonly associated with a sensorineural hearing loss in school-age children.

(a) Heredity is the passing of traits transferred in genes from parent to child. When a child is born with a hereditary hearing loss, he or she typically demonstrates better academic achievement and psychological adjustment than if the hearing loss were caused by other etiologies.
(b) Maternal Rubella is a common viral disease that attacks a developing fetus. The virus can remain active from 6–18 months following birth, thereby continuing to negatively affect the infant. Rubella is also associated with blindness and high rates of aphasia (the inability to speak), which is commonly associated with learning disabilities (Mauk & Mauk, 1992). Possible effects of rubella include cognitive delays, rigidity, hyperactivity, impulsivity and autistic-like behaviors.
(c) Meningitis is a disease of the central nervous system brought about by either bacterial infections or viruses that cause the covering of the brain to become inflamed. The disease is associated with high fever that destroys the hair cells that conduct sound to the brain. In many cases, meningitis extends to other organs, including the ear, and causes severe damage. Although incidence of the condition has declined in recent years as a result of medical advances (Moores, 1996), cases of meningitis continue to occur. Mauk and Mauk (1992) reported that almost 13% of children with a hearing loss caused by meningitis also had one or more cognitive disabilities. This type of sensorineural hearing loss is considered an acquired hearing loss, meaning it developed after the child was born.
(d) Consequences of prematurity also account for the highest rate of pregnancy related causes of hearing loss.

CHALLENGES AND CHOICES IN DEAF EDUCATION

In the history of "Western civilization, attitudes toward children with a hearing loss have varied. Some societies protected them, others ridiculed them, persecuted them, and even put them to death" (Smith, 2001, p. 421). The first school for the deaf in the U.S. was the Connecticut Asylum for the Education and Instruction of Deaf and Dumb Persons. The American School for the Deaf, as it is known now, is located in Hartford, Connecticut. Since the founding of this school until after the Civil War in 1817, students who were deaf or hard of hearing almost exclusively received their education in residential institutions. However, during the past 25 years, landmark federal and state legislation and regulations have been designed in order to provide children appropriate and necessary education for children with disabilities. These have included the Rehabilitation Act of 1973 (PL 93-112); Education for All Handicapped Act of 1975 (PL 94-142); Education of the Handicapped Act Amendments of 1986 (PL 99-457); Individuals with Disabilities Education Act of 1990 (IDEA, PL 101-476); IDEA Amendment of 1997 (PL 105-17); and the Children's Health Insurance Program of August 1997. These laws have reversed the trend of educating children and youth who are deaf or hard of hearing in residential schools.

Today over 80% of students who are deaf or hard of hearing are enrolled in public schools. These statutes and their accompanying regulations greatly contributed to establishing programs and provision of services for children who are deaf and hard of hearing in the public schools. The biggest challenge facing professionals in the field of deaf education is helping students develop the communication skills they will need to interact with others and obtain literacy skills required for personal, educational, and professional successes. Unfortunately national achievement test scores for deaf high school graduates indicate little success in attaining this goal. These scores reported the reading abilities of deaf and hard of hearing youth at the end of high school averaged at the third grade level (Paul, 1998), and math scores averaged around the sixth grade level (Stewart & Kluwin, 2001). Certainly there are exceptions, but in general, students with hearing loss do not graduate with the English language abilities and literacy skills that their hearing peers acquire.

The art of teaching students who are deaf or hard of hearing has been and continues to be mired in philosophical, methodological and instructional differences of opinion. Controversy and disagreement has made it difficult to move forward in the field and find solutions to even the most basic challenges. Educators have accepted low rates of learning, argued over modality of instruction, and offered students who are deaf or hard of hearing a vastly different curriculum than hearing students are offered. "Although there are differences, to be sure, they have been taken to far outweigh the similarities that exist between Deaf and hearing learners and have been magnified to create a system of education that smacks of remediation and repair. For far too long, the fact that we teach Deaf students has precluded the more important fact that we teach, first and foremost, human learners who just happen to be deaf" (Livingston, 1997, p. xi). To consider how best to meet this challenge of changing professionals' attitudes regarding differences in expectations, philosophical approaches, curriculum, and modality of instruction, parents and professionals must first understand what choices are currently available in deaf education. It is important to review these, before introducing and discussing new and innovative ways of approaching the education of this unique population of students in the new millennium. Thus, within deaf education there traditionally have been three teaching philosophies; auditory/oral, total or simultaneous communication, and bilingual/bicultural education. The next section will discuss these approaches.

Philosophical Instructional Choices

Oral approach. Until the early 1970s, oral methods were used to teach nearly all children who were deaf or hard of hearing in public schools and residential schools for the deaf. At present about one-third of these students continue to be instructed in an auditory/oral environment. There are whole schools, large programs, and tracks within districts in which only an oral approach is utilized. Some of these programs allow students to both listen and speech read. Other oral programs use an auditory only approach in which children are not allowed to speech read or use other visual cues to augment what they are able to hear (i.e. Auditory-Verbal). Generally, teachers employ methods that maximize the use of hearing and speech reading, and, that do not use cues or signs. The underlying philosophy is that most students have some amount of residual hearing that can be made usable with amplification or a cochlear implant device (Flexler, 1997). Since they are members of hearing families and the hearing society, simply, the underlying premise of this philosophy is that they need to adapt to the majority, the hearing community. Much emphasis is given to the appropriate selection of hearing aids, cochlear implants, and other assistive listening devices, and the use of systematic auditory training in the development of oral language skills, including both speech and speech reading. Because the first few years of life are critical for the development of oral language and speech pronunciation (Whitehead & Barefoot, 1992), early identification, auditory training, and speech reading are viewed as essential for success.

Upon reaching adulthood, many students who are deaf or hard of hearing who were educated orally, find they begin to incorporate sign into their lives. Many of these adults resent that no form of manual communication was ever formally introduced to them during their years of schooling. They feel that had sign been introduced to them at an earlier age (i.e. before graduating high school when many deaf and hard of hearing young adults then learn or "pick up" signs), adjustment to school and acquiring social friendships would have been easier. This might be one consideration that personnel working in oral programs take into consideration when developing programs for children and youth. For instance, a manual hand cue system invented to augment speech reading, Cued Speech, used in oral programs, helps a student who is deaf or hard of hearing to differentiate sounds that appear similar on a speaker's face (i.e. bop, mop, top, cop). Consonants are represented by eight hand configurations, vowels by placing those hand cues in four different locations around the face and neck, and diphthongs by gliding from beginning to ending vowel locations. These hand cues, together with speech reading, assist in the visual identification of sounds and are meant to create a full visible representation of spoken English (Stewart & Kluwin, 2001).

It is important to note that cued speech is not a language, but rather a teaching tool that transmits a visual form of spoken sound patterns. It is considered an oral approach to educating children and youth who are deaf or hard of hearing, because manual signs are not used. Accuracy rates in reception of greater than 95% can be achieved by adding cued speech to speech reading (Shea & Bauer, 1997).

Total communication approach. This is the most prevalent teaching approach in deaf education. This approach utilizes simultaneous communication; signing and voicing at the same time. It was developed in the late 1960s by educators who were dissatisfied with the results traditional oral instruction was providing and today is used by about two thirds of the school age deaf and hard of hearing population. Total communication methods combine voice and signed communication in one or several sign systems along with speech reading, audition, gestures, and written English in order to develop students' English skills to the fullest extent possible. The philosophy of total communication involves creating an environment totally accessible to a child who is deaf or hard of hearing. The two most commonly used manual codes of English (MCE) sign systems used in the U.S. to enhance total communication are Signed English and Signing Exact English (SEE). These were developed in the early 1970s and are used with a wide range of accuracy in today's classrooms. The reference book for Signed English is *The Comprehensive Signed English Dictionary* (Bornstein, Saulnier & Hamilton, 1983), also known as "the blue book" and for SEE it is *Signing Exact English* (Gustason & Zawklaw, 1994; Gustason, 1990), referred to as "the yellow book." The authors of these texts encourage people using their systems to incorporate as many ASL features in to their signing as possible. Another form of sign used in classrooms today is called Pidgin Sign English (PSE). Teachers utilizing PSE in their academic instruction should realize that they are not providing their students a complete language model, neither ASL nor English (Woodward, 1990). Although PSE appears to be an acceptable alternative in the Deaf community because of its non-reliance on English syntax, users of PSE should realize that what they communicate to their students is not a language. PSE is a combination of

English and ASL that is considered a contact language and has no reference text. It provides signs in English word order although often omits words, prefixes, and suffixes in no systematic method.

Bilingual bicultural approach. This approach to educating children who are deaf or hard of hearing, also known as "BiBi," incorporates immersion in an environment where the dominant language is ASL. English is read and written only. ASL is a visual-gestural language. It has its own syntax, grammar, rules, and structure and is able to convey the same meanings, information, and complexities as English. It is used by almost 5% of students who are deaf. Supporters of the BiBi approach contend that even children who are deaf who have hearing parents are members of the deaf community; again, a strong subculture in the United States supported by its own social mores and language. The foundation of this culture is ASL. Proponents of bilingual bicultural education recognize the importance of learning English; however, they believe that ASL should be the first language of all children who are deaf and receive instruction in written English. Additional contentions of this philosophy include educational placement in residential schools for the deaf in order to foster the development of ASL, Deaf culture, and self-identity. Research is needed to determine the efficacy of the method (Paul, 1998).

A New Twist to Philosophical Approaches

No research study can predict what philosophical approach will be most successful for each individual child who is deaf or hard of hearing (and there are wonderful success stories as well as devastating failures associated with each). Methodological decisions can be *mind boggling* for parents and teachers alike. Regardless of what method is chosen, it can only be as strong as the model communicating and teaching within the constraints of that approach. These language models, or teachers of the deaf, *must* provide instruction in a complete and comprehensible language for the students to learn. Input equals output in the education of children and youth who are deaf or hard of hearing and thus it bears repeating that caution should be advised if considering the use of PSE in reading or other literacy building subjects. It may be that a combination of instructional methods incorporating complete and comprehensible forms of MCE or ASL is warranted. For instance, daily instruction in English (manual, spoken or cued) for reading, with language instruction in the child's dominant language, ASL or English. The alternate language could be introduced as supplemental, attempting to better secure comprehension. Again, regardless of the philosophical approach used to instruct students, all have the potential to be effective if best practices are employed. In other words, research-based teaching methods can benefit all students if used correctly.

BEST PRACTICES IN DEAF EDUCATION

Most children who are deaf or hard of hearing are educated today in public schools. Federal laws and regulations guide the placement of these students. An important clause in the legislation is the Least Restrictive Environment (LRE) clause within the IDEA. LRE supports that all children with disabilities be placed in general education classrooms with their non-disabled peers for as much of the school day as possible. Opinions in deaf education vary concerning LRE. For example, members of the deaf community view deafness as a cultural difference and believe that the residential schools are the "regular classroom" for students who are deaf (Innes, 1994; Pitman & Huefner, 2001). The experience of others is that these students learn better speech articulation, English language, and academic skills when they are enrolled in settings with hearing peers. Because there are several placement options available for these students under the continuum of services, appropriate placement decisions should be based upon issues related to communication and socialization, deaf culture, and the availability of qualified teachers and support services. It is paramount that such decisions not be driven by financial concerns, but by discussion of what conditions will enable an individual student to develop to the fullest extent possible.

In larger cities, many school districts now centralize their programs for students who are deaf or hard of hearing in order to consolidate resources and support services and create the needed critical mass of students with a hearing loss in one school. Services the educational system provides to these students are varied and include the following.

(1) Students in itinerant programs typically attend their neighborhood public schools and are enrolled in general education full time. They receive support services from an itinerant teacher of the deaf. This teacher often travels to several different schools to work individually with these students. These services may vary from daily, weekly, monthly or possibly service only once a semester, depending on a student's individual needs.

(2) Students who are deaf or hard of hearing and receive services from a teacher in a resource room are typically assigned to a general education classroom teacher for the majority of their school day. These students come and go from the resource room depending upon the special or additional attention they may need in certain subject areas, as outlined in their Individualized

Education Plan (IEP). Generally, a teacher of the deaf in a resource room is expected to provide individualized instruction to a very heterogeneous group of students who are deaf and hard of hearing. Often, a teacher of the deaf in this setting teaches or organizes other personnel or staff to teach the hearing students and staff sign language.

(3) Day class programs (also referred to as special day classes or self-contained classrooms) are classes for students who are deaf and hard of hearing located in a public school building. Students may receive their academic instruction completely in this classroom, or they may spend some of their academic time in general education classrooms. For students receiving the majority of their instruction in the day class program, a part of their day should be spent integrating and socializing with hearing peers. Integrated times should include physical education, lunch, recess and when appropriate, music.

(4) In larger metropolitan areas, programs may be established in separate day schools for the deaf. Children commute to these schools daily, and hearing children are not enrolled (Moores, 1996).

(5) Residential school programs, available in each state (with the exception of Alaska, Nebraska, Nevada, New Hampshire, and Wyoming), provide facilities to house and educate students. In areas of large populations 40% of the children who are deaf or hard of hearing live at home and commute daily (Moores, 1996). Those living farther away stay at the school on a residential basis, commuting to their homes on a weekend or bimonthly weekend basis.

At present, guidelines have not been established to guide a determination of the circumstances under which these students choosing the public school option should be included in the general education classroom. This is especially important since the degree of hearing loss, as previously mentioned, is no predictor of a pupil's success in an integrated educational program.

Innovative Placement Options in Deaf Education

Any number of options could be conceivable when coordinating a student's time in school and possible division of services for the student between a residential and public school program. Luetke-Stahlman (1998) suggested placement choices that multidisciplinary IEP teams should take into consideration when making a placement decision for students who are deaf or hard of hearing. If a public school placement was determined as the most appropriate for a student, the variety of instructional opportunities, or any combination of them, might be placement possibilities. The variety of instructional opportunities might include: (a) a contained classroom with, at a minimum, integration for lunch, art, PE, and so forth; (b) a resource room with integration and possible collaboration between the general educator and the teacher of the deaf (with any variety of time split between these two arrangements); (c) an inclusive general education program with monitoring from a teacher of the deaf; or (d) a fully inclusive placement within the general education classroom in the student's neighborhood school. An interpreter should be provided as determined necessary. Dependent upon an individual's long-term goals and short-term objectives, placement options should always be reviewed at least annually, but can be discussed whenever there is concern.

One interesting arrangement to educating students who are deaf or hard of hearing in an inclusive environment is called "clustered inclusion." This model provides the structure for collaboration among professionals who have a shared responsibility for supporting students with a hearing loss in the general education classroom. Collaboration describes the activities to achieve shared goals (Friend & Bursuck, 1999). These activities must be shared by parents, general and special education teachers and support personnel who work together to build a team for a shared purpose. Willingness to share expertise and responsibility to organize, plan, or co-teach students with special needs is a cornerstone to building teams for successful collaboration. In the clustered inclusion model, students who are deaf or hard of hearing are placed together in a classroom at each grade level. Included is a common planning time for general and special education teachers, reduced class size, availability of appropriate consultants and paraprofessionals, a supportive attitude, and a positive school climate (Simpson, Myles & Simpson, 1997). One type of clustered inclusion model effective for students who are deaf or hard of hearing is the Class Within A Class Model (CWC) (Hudson, 1989; Luetke-Stahlman, 1999). In this model, two professionals co-plan and co-present lessons with strategic interventions that focus on modifications that illustrate concepts presented and organizational techniques that ensure all students understand the content. Additionally, these strategies should focus on developing routines to encourage students to learn subsequent lessons independently. Another component of CWC is the role definition between the two professionals, a general education teacher and a teacher of the deaf. Roles are negotiated as professionals co-plan for collaborative co-teaching. Friend and Bursuck explained co-teaching as the instructional arrangement where two professionals share responsibility for one or more special needs students (i.e. deaf or hard of hearing). Various levels of co-teaching may be implemented within the model. According to Friend and Bursuck these are five common approaches to co-teaching:

(1) *One teach, one support* – One teacher assumes primary instructional responsibility while the other teacher assists students with work and monitors behavior, or corrects assignments. (This approach can be successful if used only occasionally with the other approaches described here; its main disadvantage is that students who are deaf or hard of hearing may receive group rather than small group or individualized instruction).
(2) *Station teaching* – Curriculum content is divided into two parts. One teacher teaches one part while the other presents the other part. The two groups switch for the other part to be presented by the second teacher.
(3) *Parallel teaching* – Students are divided into heterogeneous groups where each student has twice the opportunity to participate in discussions. Different presentations accommodate various student learning styles.
(4) *Alternative teaching* – One teacher instructs students in one group while the other pre-teaches for the lesson to follow or re-teaches material using alternative methods.
(5) *Team teaching* – Both teachers share leadership and are equally engaged in instructional activities. Two teachers may role-play, stage debates or model note-taking strategies (pp. 82–85).

These levels of co-teaching, as well as the need for an interpreter in any of these arrangements, are decided when the IEP is discussed and documented. Roles are determined by individual student needs and will differ for each student.

As just described, one collaborative approach to educating students who are deaf or hard of hearing is the teaming of general educators and teachers of the deaf. Luetke-Stahlman and Stryker (1996a, b) provided the following suggestions for both professionals, relative to 12 different areas involved in the education of these students.

1. Pre/Post Assessment of Knowledge and Skills of Content

| *General Educators* (a) give frequent quizzes or project assignments to assess if all students have obtained competencies; (b) grade all work done in the general classroom; and (c) raise concerns with the team when students who are deaf or hard of hearing are not acquiring competencies. | *Deaf Educators* (a) conduct academic and linguistic assessment using formal, criterion-referenced curriculum-based, and process-based tools; (b) help write tests and design projects that allow students to demonstrate their obtainment of competencies; (c) monitor and record weekly progress and problem-solve when it doesn't occur; and (d) task analyze to discover abilities and needs. |

2. Learning Experiences

General Educators (a) promote unit-based, thematic instruction within individual or small groups, using games, simulations, role plays, and other activity-based learning formats; (b) use cooperative learning groups and peer tutoring; (c) teach to students' learning style; and (d) teach learning strategies.

Deaf Educators (a) provide individual or small group planning and instruction in specific skills or content; (b) prepare graphic organizers; (c) teach study skills; and (d) monitor the use of learning strategies.

3. Instruction

General Educators (a) slow the pace; (b) provide directions as to what's expected, homework assignments, and roles; (c) utilize effective instruction principles; and (d) observe activities the teacher for the deaf implements and begin to incorporate them into the teaching routine.

Deaf Educators (a) add examples to make content meaningful and linked to student's life; (b) provide advanced organizers, outlines, sample discussion and quiz probes to structure learning activities for these students; (c) highlight or underline essential directions or content in written materials; (d) paraphrase or sequence directions out loud for students who may need them repeated or restated; (e) read or sign to students if reading is not the lesson's target objective; (f) demonstrate effective teaching; (g) provide question prompts; and (h) use a wide range of questioning levels.

4. Monitor Student Participation

General Educators (a) be aware of students' abilities and linguistic levels; (b) ask frequent comprehension questions; (c) discuss needs for additional support with the team; and (d) account for student participation and progress.

Deaf Educators (a) ask frequent comprehension questions at different cognitive levels; and (b) reverse interpret a student's response and contribution to questions/discussion if there is not an interpreter in the room when teaming occurs.

5. Behavior

General Educators (a) establish rules collaboratively with the students and reinforce them for adherence to the behavioral plan; and (b) observe the activities the teacher of the deaf incorporates and begin to incorporate them into the teaching routine.

Deaf Educators (a) provide leadership in the implementation of behavioral plans; (b) reinforce contingencies for behavior management during instruction, guided practice, and independent activities; (c) collect data; and (d) fade prompts as needed.

6. Placement

General Educators (a) participate with the team in determining if the resource room, an alternative school, or a community setting is more appropriate than the general classroom; and (b) work cooperatively with team members to make placement a collaborative decision.

Deaf Educators (a) discuss alternative placement within the public school (e.g. CWC, contained classroom, etc.) or at a residential school; and (b) suggest a functional activity or a community-based experience for student with cognitive challenges.

7. Emotional Observation

General Educators (a) observe and note medical and emotional needs of students and physical or psychological abuse, or neglect.

Deaf Educators (a) observe and note medical and emotional needs, and discuss special needs; and (b) assist the team in determining an action plan.

8. Deaf Culture

General Educators (a) advocate for the use of deaf or hard of hearing adult role models, deaf paraprofessionals, volunteers, peer-coaches, and so forth.

Deaf Educators (a) locate and train adult deaf or hard of hearing role models, deaf paraprofessionals, and volunteers for a variety of roles in public schools.

9. Inservice

General Educators (a) express needs for desired inservice training; and (b) support the need for those working with deaf and hard of hearing students to attend workshops and conferences about deafness.

Deaf Educators (a) provide/distribute information about inservice opportunities for administrators, general teachers, paraprofessionals, volunteers, and hearing, hard of hearing, and deaf peers; and (b) advocate for funding and credit obtainment.

10. Team Meetings

General Educators (a) meet whenever there is cause; (b) participate in these meetings and be prepared with daily, weekly, and semester progress information; and (c) don't wait until concerns become problems to seek assistance and support.	*Deaf Educators* (a) participate in team meetings, and assist with the writing of goals and objectives that correspond to the school curriculum; and (b) don't wait until concerns become problems.

11. Peers

General Educators (a) teach students about special equipment (e.g. hearing aids, Assistive Listening Devices (ALDs), cochlear implants, TTY's, etc.), communication strategies, and social skills; and (b) consult the school social gworker if eneral social skills training is needed.	*Deaf Educators* (a) provide information and demonstration about equipment, communication strategies, and social skills to meet the needs of deaf and hard of hearing students.

12. Families

General Educators (a) keep the parent/guardian informed of the student's weekly/monthly progress.	*Deaf Educators* (a) use forms to monitor information going to parent/guardians; (b) regularly provide a checklist on progress with input from the general education teacher and interpreter to those who would be interested; and (c) advocate for consultation time during appropriate times (e.g. not always during lunch).

Continuing our discussion of innovative placement options, another alternative could be dual options between a residential school for the deaf and a public school (traveling time between the two schools must be taken into consideration for coordinated placements to be considered). These dual placement options should be considered, with either school determined to be the student's primary program, depending upon a student's individual needs. A multidisciplinary team should have the choice whether a child attends either program for part or all of the morning and then is transported to another program for the remainder of the day to attend classes or activities. If the residential school was the later placement, dinner and overnight activities could be considered, supporting the potential cultural and social challenges a student might encounter when educated mainly with hearing peers. Full-time placement in a residential school for the deaf, naturally, is an option. These schools offer not only a quality education but also a culturally and linguistically rich environment for many children and youth who are deaf or hard of hearing to learn and grow. Placement within state schools for the deaf must be considered an option, especially for children in need of opportunities to socialize with a critical mass of peers and adults who are also deaf, and should never be considered a more restrictive placement for this unique group of individuals.

It is unfortunate that public schools often do not consider residential schools as options when determining placements of these students. Public school districts often shy away from considering this placement for a variety of reasons, but often for financial ones. School districts state that they are able to provide a similar learning environment, but consider that the deaf role models a state school employs for the deaf includes administrators, teachers, office and residential personnel and custodial staff attuned to deaf community needs. The LRE, for many deaf students, is in a residential school because of the environment and role models it can provide the students.

Regardless of where a student who is deaf or hard of hearing receives his or her education, professionals in the schools should reassess their curriculum choices. Traditionally, children in deaf education classrooms receiving full instruction in one or more school subject areas, use different textbooks than their hearing peers. Not only should curriculum available to teachers in general education classrooms be made available to teachers of the deaf, for each grade level of student they teach, but these same teachers must follow through and take advantage of such curriculum. Teachers of the deaf may adapt or modify the text or level of textbook offered to their students, depending on each student's individual needs as outlined in their IEP. The level of expectation for children and youth who are deaf or hard of hearing must be raised for these students to better compete once they exit high school.

PROFESSIONALS IN DEAF EDUCATION CLASSROOMS

As stated earlier, much federal and state legislation has been designed to better meet the needs of individuals with disabilities. These regulations and legislation, however, do not specify various roles assumed by professionals serving these children. As a result, misunderstandings related to specific professionals' roles continue to affect developmental, academic, and social/emotional outcomes for children who are deaf or hard of hearing (Seal, Rossi & Henderson, 1998). The following section provides descriptions of different professionals who might be involved in the education of such students. These professionals include teachers of the deaf, interpreters, speech language pathologists, and educational paraprofessionals.

Teachers of the deaf have the specialized preparation, experiences, and opportunities to integrate the development of communicative competence within the student's whole educational program, including a variety of social, linguistic, and cognitive/academic contexts. Such teachers have majored in deaf education programs and typically are certified to teach in general education classrooms. These teachers are prepared to deliver educational programming to children and youth who are deaf or hard of hearing in a variety of settings and are able to advocate for a wide range of instructional methods. Each state has established certification standards for teachers of the deaf. These standards vary from state to state, but always require that a trained professional monitor the IEP of a student with a hearing loss.

Interpreters in today's schools have job titles such as educational interpreter, oral interpreter, or cued speech transliterator. These professionals are hearing individuals who change or clarify spoken language into either ASL or English. These interpreters may communicate what has been said in some form of sign or finger spelling. When an interpreter or transliterator is being used, it is important to remember that there could be processing delays, called "lag time". Pausing to allow for lag time ensures that all students can participate in responding to questions and in discussions. The interpreter or transliterator should be free to ask a teacher for clarification and is usually expected to voice any message communicated by a student who is deaf or hard of hearing. The role of an educational interpreter is relatively new and very valuable. Educational interpreters communicate using an MCE system or ASL while oral interpreters facilitate communication by inaudibly repeating the message more slowly and with clearer enunciation so that speechreading is facilitated. They might include natural gestures but not formal signs. For more information about educational interpreters see *Best Practices in Educational Interpreting* (Seal, 1998).

Speech-language pathologists (SLP) in educational settings have become vital contributors to the language development and academic achievement of students who are deaf or hard of hearing. SLPs should be trained to recognize the complex interplay of the areas of listening, speaking, signing, reading, writing, and thinking. Furthermore, they should understand how skill expansion in one of these components enhances performance in another area, ultimately contributing to the overall development of literacy. In other words, it is behind the times to facilitate speech articulation without materials from students' actual curriculum and without the promotion of listening skills as well. With increasing responsibility for establishing environments and activities that foster the development of literacy skills, increased literacy will be one of the primary functional outcomes of successful skill facilitation for students who are deaf or hard of hearing (Moore-Brown, 1998; Montgomery, 1998). It seems unfair for a student who would benefit from articulation, audition, or English language facilitation to be denied any or the appropriate amount of services from an SLP. Unfortunately, this does occur. IEP teams must remember to focus on individual students and offer them all the services necessary, and in sufficient amounts, in order to provide them the opportunity to improve in these areas.

Educational paraprofessionals are individuals who support teachers in providing educational experiences to students in different classrooms. Although the use of a special education paraprofessional was intended to assist the teacher in providing a cost-effective alternative to improve deaf and hard of hearing children's quality of education, finding a qualified person who can meet the unique communicative needs of these students is difficult. Just adding an additional staff member to a deaf education classroom does not create a better learning environment. Because there are no certification requirements for an educational paraprofessional, careful selection and ongoing training must occur. When this happens a student's learning environment is maximized.

TECHNOLOGICAL ADVANCES

Technology for students who are deaf or hard of hearing has been improving rapidly. During the past three decades, technological developments, such as closed captioning on television (TV) e-mail and the Internet, two-way pagers, text telephones, telecommunications relay services, video interpreting services, visual alerting devices, vibro-tactile devices, hearing aids, amplification devices, audio loop, and listening systems have had an important role in leveling the playing field for this population of students. Cochlear implants have also played a part in improving the lives of many students. The increase in the prevalence of cochlear implants is reflected in the recent position statement issued by the National Association for the Deaf (NAD): The NAD recognizes that cochlear implantation is a technology that represents a tool to be used in some forms of communication, and not a cure for deafness. Cochlear implants provide sensitive hearing, but do not, by themselves, impart the ability to understand spoken language through listening alone. The position statement has been met with approval from consumers, parents, educators, the media, and health professionals. "Balanced" has been the most commonly used description of their revised and updated position, although this procedure continues to be controversial. Cochlear implants do not eliminate deafness. An implant is not a "cure," and an implanted student is still deaf when his/her equipment is off. Many children, though, have demonstrated impressive speech and literacy progress. It is important for parents and teachers to stay current regarding this and other technological advancements.

Hearing aids and other equipment that help children and youth who are deaf or hard of hearing make better use of their residual hearing are called ALDs. Hearing aids are the most commonly used ALD. It is, however, important to recognize that hearing aids do not solve problems associated with hearing loss for many students. One ALD available in schools for students with a hearing loss is the FM (frequency-modulated) transmission device. This equipment is used in many classes for students with hearing loss. It allows direct oral transmission from the teacher, who wears a microphone, to each individual student wearing this type of an ALD. Another FM transmission device available in today's classroom is the audio loop. This system directs sound from its source directly to a child's ear through a specially equipped hearing aid or earphone. Sound may travel through a wire connection or through radio waves. Audio loops are inexpensive and easy to install. Since 1972, the captioning technology available has improved tremendously. Captioning, or the printed words that appear on a TV screen, like subtitles that translate foreign films, is an important tool in schools today. It allows students who are deaf or hard of hearing equal access when material is presented on the TV.

DEAF AWARENESS

Throughout the developmental years, children and youth who are deaf or hard of hearing – implanted or not, signing or not, mainstreamed or not – should receive education in deaf studies. This curriculum should include deaf heritage, history of deafness and people who are deaf, and particularly stories and accounts of individuals who are deaf who have succeeded in many areas of life. Obviously, if students are educated at residential schools they will see Deaf role models and have ample opportunities to discuss how these adults interact with and adapt to the hearing society. Historically, such education has been absent in many public school programs. The challenge is how to integrate it into existing curriculum.

If a student who is deaf or hard of hearing attends a public school, suggestions for incorporating curriculum related to deaf studies may be met by teachers and related professionals in a variety of ways. They include:

(a) Providing the media specialist in the school(s) they teach a recommendation list of a variety of material related to Deaf Studies for all students to check out.

(b) Making parents aware of Deaf cultural events and then encouraging them to attend.
(c) Providing the general education teachers at various grade levels specific information on successful Deaf people from history, as they appropriately fit into the subject areas being taught.
(d) Inviting Deaf people to the classroom or school.
(e) Acknowledging and organizing National Deaf Awareness Week, which occurs every September.
(f) Visiting Deaf adults working out in the community.
(g) Presenting information about hearing loss to general education students in other grade levels.
(h) Starting a sign language club.

In sum, schools should purposefully provide all students, regardless of hearing status, information on deafness, the people, customs and culture. By providing this curriculum in schools, especially schools where students are deaf or hard of hearing attend, it will aid in better developing their self-image and self-awareness, in addition to community building.

WHERE DO WE GO FROM HERE?

An effective teacher of the deaf does more than just present curricular activities to students. This teacher plans instruction based on comprehensive and on-going evaluation of each student, chooses instructional materials, arranges the environment and teaching sequence to promote student learning, instructs, and evaluates student learning, and plans future instruction accordingly. Obviously decision-making plays a key role in being a good teacher. It is the teacher of the deaf's responsibility to advocate for his/her students and educate and assist building principals and school psychologists in learning new and improved methods to complete their jobs. Effective practices are learned in texts, modeled by effective teachers and borrowed from those teachers, and modified to fit unique needs and styles. That is why keeping up to date with what is new and researched is so important. School districts must recognize this need and provide staff development specific to the needs of students with a hearing loss enrolled in their programs. In addition, teachers working in both general and special education must raise their level of expectations for students with a hearing loss, introduce alternate or supplemental instructional philosophies and methodologies to support student learning, and consider alternate ways of teaching and/or communicating. This requires attendance at regional and national meetings and attention to published articles in the field of deaf education. General and special education professionals must put personal philosophies and opinions aside and be guided by a sound theory of practice and research. They must be flexible, because just as there are multiple intelligences, no two children with deafness learn the same.

Certainly, an appropriate education is one that involves access to information in a language or communication mode that reduces communication barriers for students who are deaf or hard of hearing. It is time to honestly evaluate needs of these students and not make decisions based on historically available options and methods. As Pittman and Huefner (2001) stated, "Instruction in a child's first language and communication mode should be seen as more of an issue of equal access than an issue of educational methodology" (p. 197). Children and youth who are deaf or hard of hearing can learn to read on grade level and achieve, as do their hearing peers. It is the responsibility of general and deaf education professionals to use assessment results to create a successful learning environment where progress is documented. If teachers of the deaf do not utilize effective teaching methodology to create a successful environment, then all of the assessment results and up-to-date materials in the world cannot produce literate students that our complex society demands. It is that simple. However, unlike their hearing peers who have had the advantage of hearing the linguistic structures of English from birth, students with hearing loss have not been provided with access to phonological awareness and cognitive academic language proficiency (Cummins, 1984). Studies have shown that most of these students leave high school to become illiterate adults in regards to English language functioning (Paul, 1998). It follows that there are many adults who are deaf or hard of hearing who never reach their productivity potential and who, as a result, are often under or unemployed. It seems more important than ever to examine effective teaching practices, past opinions and modes of communication, and differences in curriculum used with students with a hearing loss, as well as try to reverse this trend of poor readers among this student population.

REFERENCES

Bornstein, H., Saulnier, K. L., & Hamilton, L. B. (1983). *The Comprehensive Signed English Dictionary*. Washington, D.C.: Gallaudet University Press.

Cummins, J. (1984). *Bilingualism and special education: Issues in assessment and pedagogy*. Clevedon, Avon, England: Multilingual Matters.

Education for All Handicapped Children Act of 1975 (1975). Public Law 94-142, 20, U.S.C. 1401-1461: *U.S. Statutes at Large*, 89, 773–779.

Education of the Handicapped Act Amendments of 1974 (1974). Public Law 93-980.

Education of the Handicapped Act Amendments of 1986 (1986). Public Law 99-457, 20, U.S.C. *et seq*: *U.S. Statutes at Large, 100,* 1145–1177.

Flexer, C. (1997). Individualized sound field FM systems: Rationale, description, and use. *Volta Review, 99*(3), 133–162.

Friend, M., & Bursuck, W. D. (1999). *Including students with special needs: A practical guide for classroom teachers* (2nd ed.). Needham Heights, MA: Allyn & Bacon.

Gustason, G., & Zawklaw, E. (1994). Signing exact English. Los Alimitos, CA: Modern Signs Press.

Henwood, P. G., & Pope-Davis, D. B. (1994). Disability as cultural diversity: Counseling the hearing impaired. *The Counseling Psychologist, 22*(3), 489–503.

Hudson, F. G. (1989). *Class within a class staff development workshop: Module III and Module IV.* Jefferson City, MO: Missouri Department of Elementary and Secondary Education.

Individuals with Disabilities Education Act of 1990 (IDEA) (1990). Public Law 101-476, 20, U.S.C. 1400 *et seq*: *U.S. Statutes at Large, 104,* 1103–1151.

Individuals with Disabilities Education Act Amendments of 1997 (IDEA) (March 12, 1999). Public Law 105-17, III, Stat. 38 (1997). Codified as amended at 20 U.S.C. Section 1400-1485. *Federal Register, 34,* CFR Parts 300 and 303.

Innes, J. (1994). Full inclusion and the deaf student: A deaf consumer's review of the issue. *American Annals of the Deaf, 139*(2), 152–156.

Livingston, S. (1997). *Rethinking the education of Deaf students: Theory and practice from a teacher's perspective.* Portsmouth, NH: Heinemann.

Luetke-Stahlman, B. (1995). Some thoughts on models of inclusion. *Association of Canadian Educators of the Hearing Impaired, 20*(3), 119–121.

Luetke-Stahlman, B. (1998). *Language issues in Deaf education.* Hillsboro, OR: Butte.

Luetke-Stahlman, B. (1999). *Language across the curriculum: When students are deaf or hard of hearing.* Hillsboro, OR: Butte.

Luetke-Stahlman, B., & Stryker, D. (1996a). The teaming of general educators and teachers of the Deaf: Part I. *Perspectives in Education and Deafness, 17*(3), 10–13.

Luetke-Stahlman, B., & Stryker, D. (1996b). The teaming of general educators and teachers of the Deaf: Part II. *Perspectives in Education and Deafness, 17*(4), 6–7, 20.

Mauk, G., & Mauk, P. (1992). Somewhere out there: Preschooler children with hearing impairment and learning disabilities. *Topics in Early Childhood Special Education, 12*(2), 174–195.

Moore-Brown, B. (1998). Membership message (from the President). *CASHA Magazine, 27*(3), 3, 7.

Moores, D. (1996). *Educating the Deaf: Psychology, principles, and practices.* Boston: Houghton Mifflin.

Montgomery, J. K. (1998). Reading and the SLP: Using discourse, narratives, and expository text. *CASHA Magazine, 27*(3), 8–9.

Paul, P. V. (1998). *Literacy and deafness: The development of reading, writing, and literate thought.* Needham Heights, MA: Allyn & Bacon.

Pittman, P., & Huefner, D. S. (2001). Will the courts go bi-bi? IDEA 1997, the courts, and deaf education. *Exceptional Children, 67*(2), 187–198.

Rehabilitation Act of 1973 (1973). Section 504, 29, U.S.C. 794 *U.S. Statutes at Large, 87,* 335–394.

Schildroth, A. N., & Hotto, S. E. (1996). Changes in student and program characteristics, 1984–1985 and 1994–1995. *American Annals of the Deaf, 141*(2), 68–81.

Seal, B. C. (1998). *Best practices in educational interpreting.* Needham Heights, MA: Allyn & Bacon.

Seal, B. C., Rossi, A., & Henderson, C. (1998). Speech-language pathologists in schools for the Deaf: A survey of scope of practice, service delivery, caseload, and program features. *American Annals of the Deaf, 143*(3), 277–283.

Shea, T. M., & Bauer, A. M. (1997). *An introduction to special education: A social systems perspective* (2nd ed.). Madison, WI: Brown & Benchmark.
Simpson, R. L., Myles, B. S., & Simpson, J. D. (1997). Inclusion of students with disabilities in general education settings; Structuring for successful management. In: P. Zionts (Ed.), *Inclusion Strategies for Students with Learning and Behavior Problems: Perspectives, Experience, and Best Practices* (pp. 171–196). Austin, TX: Pro-Ed.
Smith, D. D. (2001). *Introduction to special education: Teaching in an age of opportunity* (4th ed.). Boston: Allyn & Bacon.
Stewart, D. A., & Kluwin, T. N. (2001). *Teaching Deaf and hard of hearing students: Content, strategies, and curriculum.* Needham Heights, MA: Allyn & Bacon.
Webster, A., Saunders, E., & Bamford, J. M. (1984). Fluctuating conductive hearing impairment. *AEP: Association of Educational Psychologists Journal*, 6(5), 6–9.
Whitehead, B. H., & Barefoot, S. M. (1992). Improving speech production in hearing impaired children and youth: Theory and practice. *The Volta Review*, 94(5), 119–134.
Woodward, J. (1990). Sign English in the education of deaf students. In: H. Bornstein (Ed.), *Manual Communication: Implications for Education* (pp. 67–80). Washington, D.C.: Gallaudet.

VISUAL IMPAIRMENT

Wendy Sapp

INTRODUCTION

Many children in public schools today have visual impairments, but what exactly does visual impairment mean? Can children with visual impairments see? Why do they seem to see differently on different days, in different settings, or at different times of day? Can children with visual impairments have other disabilities? Can they be taught in their neighborhood school or do they need a special school setting? Why do two children with visual impairments act and learn very differently from each other? These are only some of the questions that arise when people first encounter children with visual impairments. This chapter is written to respond to the questions of what is a visual impairment and how can learners with visual impairments receive an appropriate education.

DEFINITIONS AND ELIGIBILITY

A visual impairment is "any degree of vision loss that affects an individual's ability to perform the tasks of daily life, caused by a visual system that is not working properly or not formed correctly" (Corn & Koenig, 1995, p. 452). The Individuals with Disabilities Act (1990) uses a similar definition but states that the visual impairment affects the child's educational performance. Across the U.S., approximately 93,600 school-aged children have a visual impairment requiring specialized educational services (Kirchner & Diamonte, 1999). Some children with visual impairments are totally blind, meaning that they see nothing or see only light and dark; however, approximately 90% of children with visual impairments have low vision meaning they use vision for some activities (Kahn & Moorhead, 1973). People with low vision have a visual impairment that with correction still interferes with their ability to complete daily tasks, though vision remains their primary method of learning (CEC, 2000).

Legal blindness is another term that is frequently mentioned in relation to visual impairments. Legal blindness refers to an acuity, or sharpness of image, of 20/200 or worse in the better eye after correction or a visual field of less than 20 degrees. Figure 1 provides an image of what a person with typical acuity (20/20) might see, and Fig. 2 simulates the same image seen by a person with an acuity of 20/200. To provide a rough idea of a visual field of 20 degrees, make a fist with a very small opening and look through the opening. Legal blindness is a definition used to determine eligibility for certain federal, state, and private services, but it is not a useful term for identifying children requiring specialized educational services (Koestler, 1976).

Some children with visual impairments have additional disabilities. In a recent study of children from birth to five years of age with visual impairments, Ferrell (1998) reported that 40% of these children were identified with only a visual impairment. 22% of the children had mild additional disabilities, and 38% had severe additional disabilities. All children with visual impairments, regardless of the presence or severity of additional

Fig. 1. Image as Seen by Person with 20/20 Acuity.

Fig. 2. Simulation of Image as Seen by Person with 20/200 Acuity.

disabilities, have the right to specialized services to meet their needs as children with visual impairments.

Despite the variety of terms and definitions related to visual impairments, identifying children who will require specialized educational services due to a visual impairment is a relatively straightforward process. Most children are referred for educational services for visual impairments by doctors who have diagnosed a visual impairment, by parents who are aware that their child has a visual impairment, or by teachers who notice behaviors common to children with visual impairments. Once a child is referred, medical records documenting the visual impairment are acquired, and a teacher of students with visual impairments (TVI) conducts a series of formal and informal tests. These tests determine how well the child uses his or her vision and the ways the visual impairment affects the child's functioning in school and community environments. Though the specific eligibility criteria to receive services varies from state to state, most states require that: (1) the visual impairment reduces the child's acuity or visual field; and (2) the visual impairment impacts the child's educational performance.

THE VISUAL SYSTEM

The visual system is made up of many different components, all of which play important roles in a person's ability to see. This section briefly describes the structures and roles of major components of the visual system: the eye, the optic nerve, and the visual cortex. Though this section cannot cover all aspects of the visual system in great detail, it provides a brief conceptual understanding of how the visual system works. There are many components to the visual system (i.e. sclera, cornea, iris, pupil, lens, retina, optic disc, optic nerve, and visual cortex).

The eyeball is the sense organ that provides visual information to the brain. The sclera is the white outer layer of the eyeball that provides protection to the eye. The cornea, found in the center of the front of the eye, is the clear portion of the eye's outer covering that allows light to enter the eye. Behind the cornea is the iris, the colored disk that expands and contracts through muscle movement to adjust the amount of light that enters the eye. In the center of the iris is an opening known as the pupil. The iris adjusts its size to allow more or less light through the pupil and into the eye. The lens is located behind the iris and is a transparent structure that changes shape to focus the light rays to create the clearest image based on the distance from the object to the eye. The light rays pass through the eye to the retina, the inner sensory layer of the back of the eyeball consisting of photo receptor cells. The photoreceptor cells activate a chain of related cells that transfer impulses to the optic disc at the back of the eyeball. The optic disc is the ocular end of the optic nerve, which is made up of one million nerve fibers that transmit the image received by the retina to the visual cortex in the posterior of the brain. The visual cortex is then primarily responsible for interpreting the image.

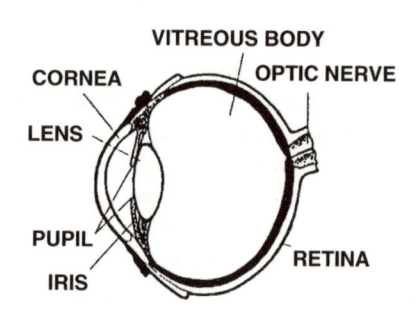

Fig. 3. Simplified Diagram of the Human Eye.

Graphic courtesy of Prevent Blindness America®.

MANIFESTATIONS OF VISUAL IMPAIRMENTS

As you can see from the above description of the eye's anatomy, many different structures are involved in the process of seeing and each serves an important function. When there is an anomaly, trauma, or disease in any part of the visual system, a visual impairment can result. While there are many ways a visual impairment can affect a person's ability to see (e.g. an inability to see color, or an inability to tolerate normal levels of light), there are three primary manifestations of visual impairments: reduced acuity, restricted visual fields, and cortical damage.

Acuity refers to how clearly a person is able to see. For distance vision, most people see 20/20 though many require glasses or contacts to see that clearly. The top number of an acuity refers to the distance at which the person can distinguish an image and the bottom number denotes at what distance a typically sighted person can see the same image. For example, an acuity of 20/100 means that the person can see at 20 feet what a typically sighted person could see at 100 feet. Reduced acuities can affect the clarity with which a person sees at near distances, far distances, or both near and far distances.

The second manifestation of a visual impairment is a restriction to a person's visual field, the area in which a person can see without moving his or her eyes. People with typical vision have approximately 160 to 180 degrees of vision from left to right and approximately 120 degrees of vision from top to bottom. The visual field of both eyes overlap in the center so images directly in front of a person are seen by both eyes, known as binocular vision. Visual fields may be damaged in many ways. A person may lose the outer edges of the visual field but still be able to see clearly items that are directly in front of them. Alternatively, a person may be able to see in the periphery but not have any vision in the center of the visual field. A third possibility is that a person has scotomas often referred to as "blind spots." Scotomas are one or more areas scattered through the visual field in which the person is unable to see.

Contrary to popular belief, field loss does not produce blacked out areas; the areas without vision are simply not there. Try to imagine what you can see out of the back of your head. You don't see blackness; you simply don't see anything. This is similar to how a person experiences a peripheral field loss. When a person experiences a scotoma, there are many ways visual images can be perceived. For images in the central field, the other eye may fill in the missing information. For images in the peripheral field, the brain may fill in the missing area with images similar to those around it.

The third possible manifestation of a visual impairment occurs when the optic nerve or the visual cortex is damaged or was not formed properly. When this happens, the visual image is distorted or lost as it passes through the nerves or as it is received by the visual cortex. When cortical damage exists, the child may have no damage to the eye itself, so the person is able to perceive normal acuities and visual fields; however, the cortical damage may prevent or reduce the child from understanding what he or she sees. This is not the same as visual perceptual difficulties that are associated with learning disabilities.

Reduced acuities, restricted visual field, and cortical damage may occur singly or in combination. One child may experience only a reduced acuity, another only a field loss, and a third only cortical damage. Alternatively, children may demonstrate any combination of these manifestations. For example, a child may have a reduced acuity and a small visual field, or have a reduced acuity, several blind spots, and a cortical visual impairment. It is also important to remember that not all visual impairments are stable. Some may improve over time, but others may deteriorate, and still others remain constant throughout the individual's lifetime. Additionally, some children may experience better vision on one day than another or at certain times of day.

People often ask why a child has a visual impairment or what caused the visual impairment. Though there are many cases in which the cause of the visual impairment is unknown, there are etiologies that can be traced to specific internal or external causes. Many visual impairments are associated with syndromes. For example a child with CHARGE syndrome will most likely have retinal damage along with several other physical, sensory, and/or cognitive impairments. Other visual impairments are hereditary and are passed through families though often parents are unaware that they are carriers of the genes. For example, retinitis pigmentosa and ocular albinism are both the result of hereditary factors. External factors also can produce visual impairments; prematurity, prenatal exposure to toxins such as drugs, and trauma to the head or eyes may result in visual impairments.

CHARACTERISTICS OF CHILDREN WITH VISUAL IMPAIRMENTS

Children with visual impairments are more like typically developing children than they are different. They laugh and cry, learn and make mistakes, make friends and occasionally lose friends. It is important to keep the image of the child at the forefront and to focus on the similarities they share with other children. Despite the similarities among children with and without visual impairments, children with visual impairments may demonstrate some unique characteristics.

Children with visual impairments are extremely diverse in their characteristics and cannot easily be described as a group. Some children with visual impairments may give no outward indication that they have difficulty seeing. Other children may obviously have trouble seeing and openly employ alternative techniques for gaining access to visual information. Still other children may engage in behaviors that seem odd or unusual but do not appear to be directly related to vision. Being aware of these characteristics may help teachers and service providers to understand children who are identified as having visual impairments or may help to identify a child who should be evaluated for possible visual problems. Remember, each child will be different and no two children are likely to exhibit the same characteristics.

Visual impairments are often the result of damage to the visible portions of the eye or to portions of the visual system that affect the appearance of the eyes. In these cases, you may notice that the child's eyes do not look normal. Additionally, children may position their heads or bodies in unusual ways to improve their ability to see. Table 1 outlines several ways the eyes of children with visual impairments may appear unusual. Table 2 lists visual behaviors in which children with visual impairments may engage.

Children with extremely low vision or blindness may demonstrate other unusual behaviors. Some behaviors that are frequently observed include head swaying, body rocking, hand flapping, and eye poking. The causes of these behaviors are not well understood, but it is believed that they provide stimulation to the vestibular system that is normally stimulated through visual input. Teachers and parents should work together to reduce the frequency and severity

Table 1. Appearance of Eyes of Children with Visual Impairments.

Description	Medical term
Eye turns in	Esotropia or esophoria
Eye turns out	Exotropia or exophoria
Eyes "shake"	Nystagmus
Eye is small	Microphthalmos
Eye is large	Macrophthalmos
Iris is missing	Aniridia
Red eyes	None
Puffy eyes	None
Watery eyes	None
Dry eyes	None

Note: This is only a partial list. Not all children with visual impairments will display these characteristics and not all children who display these characteristics will have a visual impairment.

Table 2. Possible Visual Behaviors of Children with Visual Impairments.

Blinking
Squinting
Holding material close
Holding material far away
Tilting head to side
Looking beside, above, or below object rather than at object
Moving body or hands to block light
Moving body to allow in more light
Complaining of headaches when engaged in extensive visual tasks

---

Note: This is only a partial list. Not all children with visual impairments will display these behaviors and not all children who display these behaviors will have a visual impairment.

of these behaviors to prevent children from harming themselves and to assist them in fitting in better in social, school, and work settings.

PROFESSIONALS IN THE FIELD OF VISUAL IMPAIRMENTS

Many professionals are involved in providing medical and educational services for children with visual impairments. While not all children will be served by all of the specialists discussed below, each professional plays an important and unique role in the lives of children with visual impairments. Children are best served when these professionals work together in interdisciplinary teams with some educational services being provided in a transdisciplinary approach.

Medical Personnel

Medical professionals are responsible for diagnosing visual impairments. Occasionally, a pediatrician will diagnose a visual impairment, but more often the diagnosis is made by an ophthalmologist or optometrist (Corn & Koenig, 1996). Ophthalmologists are medical doctors who have specialized training in the diseases and treatment of the eye. They can diagnose visual impairments, prescribe glasses and optical medicines, and perform eye surgeries. Optometrists are health care providers who specialize in identifying refractive errors (e.g. nearsightedness or farsightedness), prescribing glasses or contact lenses and managing other aspects of vision care as allowed by state law.

Some optometrists and ophthalmologists have specialized training in treating patients with low vision and may refer to themselves as clinical low vision specialists (Corn & Koenig, 1996). They can use specialized testing to accurately pinpoint the visual abilities of children and adults with low vision. They are experienced in prescribing optical and non-optical devices to increase a person's visual independence. They also provide helpful clinical low vision evaluations of children with visual impairments and additional disabilities.

Educational Personnel Specializing in Visual Impairments

The primary professional in the education of a child with a visual impairment is the teacher of students with visual impairments (TVI). Spungin and Ferrell (2000) identified six major roles of TVIs, namely:

(1) TVIs are responsible for ensuring complete and accurate assessment and evaluation of students with visual impairments so their educational needs are met.
(2) TVIs are required to provide an appropriate learning environment including, but not limited to, providing materials in the appropriate media, recommending appropriate seating and classroom arrangements, and collaborating with other professionals to ensure an appropriate environment.
(3) TVIs adapt curriculum to meet the needs of students with visual impairments as well as provide instruction in areas that are unique to children with visual impairments.
(4) TVIs provide guidance and counseling to students and their families on issues related to the child's visual impairment.
(5) TVIs carry out many administrative duties, which include communicating with local, state, and national administrators, maintaining records, and participating in screenings and child find activities.
(6) TVIs are responsible for educating schools and communities about the needs and abilities of children and adults with visual impairments.

TVIs must be prepared to work with all students with visual impairments including those who have additional disabilities (Silberman & Sacks, 2000). Children with visual and additional disabilities may have a combination of impairments that affect their physical, sensory, and/or cognitive abilities. To adequately work with students with visual and additional disabilities, their families, and other educational staff, TVIs must be knowledgeable about the needs of children with multiple disabilities. TVIs encourage vision use through instructional activities and environmental modifications as well as recommend visual, tactile, and auditory modifications to assist the child in meeting his or her educational goals.

Orientation and mobility (O&M) refers to the skills and knowledge a person with a visual impairment requires in order to move safely, efficiently, and independently in familiar and unfamiliar environments (Hill, Rosen, Correa & Langley, 1984). Certified orientation and mobility specialists are education or rehabilitation personnel who are specially trained to teach knowledge, concepts, and skills related to O&M. In addition to improving a student's ability to travel independently, O&M skills provide psychological benefits from an improved self concept, physical benefits from the increased walking exercise, and social benefits from being able to participate in more activities (Hill, 1986). Certified orientation and mobility specialists work closely with TVIs and other school personnel to ensure that skills are generalized to a variety of settings and practiced on a daily basis. Some basic O&M skills may occasionally be taught by regular educators or parents (e.g. body parts) or by the TVI (e.g. sighted guide technique). Other skills are extremely specialized and may involve some danger to the child if not taught properly. These skills are *only* taught by the O&M specialist (e.g. cane travel or street crossing). In addition to working with students who are totally blind, the O&M specialist works with students who have low vision on skills such as using distance vision for travel.

The vocational rehabilitation counselor will become part of the educational team as the student prepares to transition into post-secondary schooling and/or the work force depending on the student's interests and abilities. Most states employ vocational rehabilitation counselors who specialize in visual impairments, though some states hire generic rehabilitation counselors. When the student graduates from high school, the vocational rehabilitation counselor becomes his or her link to specialized services. These services include college services (e.g. finding readers), job placement, and specialized training. Specialized training might be needed due to a change in visual functioning, a new career, a change in job responsibilities, or new disability specific technology.

Other Educational Personnel

In addition to personnel trained specifically in visual impairments, many other school personnel are part of a child's educational team. Because most students with visual impairments are served in their neighborhood schools, general education teachers are frequently responsible for providing most of the child's basic education. General education teachers are essential for ensuring that these children receive an appropriate education. Close communication between the general education teacher and the TVI ensures that appropriate modifications are made for the child to participate in classroom activities and problems are addressed quickly before they adversely affect the student's education. In addition, special education teachers may also be part of the team for a child with a visual impairment. As indicated earlier in this chapter, many children with visual impairments have additional disabilities. Those with mild additional disabilities may receive part of their instruction from a special education teacher who specializes in learning disabilities or mild intellectual disabilities. Just like a general education teacher, the special education teacher stays in contact with the TVI to ensure that the child's needs are being met. For children with additional severe disabilities, a special education teacher who works with children with multiple impairments will most likely be involved. This special education teacher should also work closely with the TVI so that the child is encouraged to learn as much as possible and is not penalized for his or her low vision or blindness.

Paraprofessionals are frequently employed to assist in providing services for children with visual impairments, especially if the impairment is severe. Paraprofessionals can provide important services such as transcribing materials into Braille. The paraprofessional may also support instruction of the TVI or general education teacher but should not provide instruction that sighted children would receive from a certified teacher (e.g. reading instruction). It is important that the student is not allowed to become dependent on the paraprofessional, because this limits the child's independence rather than increases it. For this reason, it is usually best if paraprofessionals are assigned to assist in a classroom and not assigned one-on-one to a child. Other school personnel play a role in the education of children with visual impairments. Cafeteria staff, janitors, secretaries, librarians, administrators, and school bus drivers have daily contact with children with visual impairments. It is important that all staff be trained to treat the child respectfully. They should understand what modifications the child may need to use (e.g. a cane to travel to and from the school bus), as well as the need for the child to act independently.

EDUCATIONAL IMPLICATIONS OF VISUAL IMPAIRMENTS

People with typical sight gain 60–80% of their information about the world through their eyes (MacCuspie, 1996). People, including those with visual impairments, need to be able to access information that is near to them as well as information at a distance. This access is necessary to participate fully in general education activities (e.g. reading a textbook, viewing a science demonstration), in extracurricular activities (e.g. reading a script for a school play, watching a football game), in social activities (e.g. looking up a friend's telephone number, attending a concert), and other age appropriate activities. Modifications can allow a child with low vision or total blindness to access this information and participate more fully in their school and community activities.

Learning Media Options and Issues

One of the first issues to be decided when a child has a visual impairment is what type of learning mode will be most beneficial for the child: visual, tactile, or auditory (Koenig & Holbrook, 1995). Many children will find that a combination of learning media for different types of activities will help them learn most efficiently. This section will describe the four most common learning media, how these may be combined and how they may be modified for children with additional disabilities.

Braille. Children with little or no sight, frequently use Braille to access written material. Braille is a code consisting of six raised dots arranged in two vertical rows of three dots each. The code includes 64 possible combinations of dots that represent letters, combinations of letters, or words. Additionally, certain combinations of symbols produce words without writing out all letters, similar to the way shorthand works. Children require special instruction to learn to read and write Braille due to the unique characteristics of tactual reading and the Braille code. Additionally, children who use Braille will also need to learn to read graphs and diagrams in tactile format, another specialized skill.

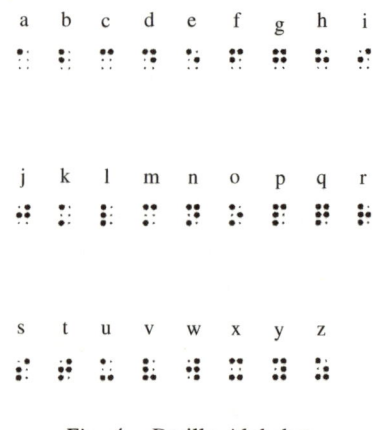

Fig. 4. Braille Alphabet.

Visual Impairment 271

Optical Devices. Children with low vision often find that their vision, while not typical, is still their strongest learning mode. A clinical low vision specialist should examine these children to determine if optical devices can enhance their ability to see. Optical devices are specialized lenses that enhance a child's ability to see near, intermediate, and distance. A common near vision device is a magnifier that enlarges the image on a page and may be handheld, spectacle mounted, or stand mounted. A common distance vision device is a monocular, a hand held telescope that allows the person to enlarge images seen at a distance. Other optical devices can be used to reduce the size of an image (e.g. for a child with 20/20 acuity but a small visual field), move the location of an image on the retina (e.g. for a child with damage to part of the retina), or to reduce light (e.g. for a child who is sensitive to light).

Large type. At times, children with low vision may benefit from large type, providing printed material in a larger font than the standard material. Large type can be provided either by ordering large type books, enlarging pages on a copy machine, or reprinting material in a larger font size. Large type can be beneficial in some circumstances, such as for a child with cerebral palsy who

Fig. 5. Student with a Visual Impairment Reading Off a Chalkboard with an Optical Device.

has difficulty holding a magnifier, or to label items that may be more difficult to view with a magnifier such as files in a file drawer or information on a computer screen. However, large type has many disadvantages. Large type books are heavy and bulky and usually provide pictures and graphs in shades of black and white making images difficult to interpret. Because large type also must be ordered or produced well in advance of its use in the classroom, children who only use large type are rarely able to access materials such as newspapers, magazines, and library books. Additionally, large type primarily provides access to textbooks. Most leisure reading materials are not available in large type, and distant information (e.g. information on a chalkboard) is not available using large type. For these and other reasons, large type is rarely sufficient for meeting all of a student's needs unless it is used in combination with other media.

Auditory. Providing material in an auditory format can be a supplemental learning media for many children with visual impairments. Information can be provided on tapes, through synthesized speech, or by a live reader. While children with visual impairments should learn to read using print or Braille, they often have slower reading speeds and experience visual fatigue when reading for extended periods of time. For these reasons, students with visual impairments may benefit from using taped materials in the evening when their eyes are tired after reading during the day. Additionally, children who are blind may need to have a peer or adult narrate events that are happening at a distance such as material the teacher writes on the board or events on a video. On rare occasions, a child may need to use auditory methods as his or her primary learning media. For example, when a child is blind and has a physical impairment that reduces fingertip sensitivity to the point that Braille cannot be distinguished, auditory methods may be the only practical way for the child to access material.

When the TVI conducts an assessment to select a primary learning media, other methods are not completely eliminated. Often children with low vision will use a variety of media to meet their needs. For example, a high school student with extremely low vision might use all of the above media throughout a day. The student could read and write with Braille in most classes, use a telescope to read material on a chalkboard, access a computer with large print on the screen to look up information for a report, and listen to a science chapter on tape in the evening for homework. Each student is unique and his or her teachers will have to work closely with the student to determine what medium or combination of media will help the student be as academically successful as possible. It is important to note that for children with visual impairments who also have additional severe disabilities, finding appropriate learning media can be challenging but is essential to ensuring they receive an appropriate education. Children with usable vision often use optical devices or enlarged materials. Children who are blind can learn Braille or alternative tactile codes, such as a texture to represent a particular item. Many children with visual and additional disabilities benefit from auditory instruction as a primary method of learning.

Accessing the Regular Curricula

Lowenfeld (1973) proposed three instructional methods to reduce the limitations on learning imposed by visual impairments, namely: (1) providing frequent and varied concrete experiences; (2) arranging instruction so that children learn by doing; and (3) using unifying experiences to help children understand how what they learn is connected to the rest of the world. These three instructional methods are appropriate for all children and can easily be incorporated into general education classrooms. In addition to the aforementioned tactile and auditory adaptations, five basic visual elements can be modified to enhance the ability of students with low vision to see material. These five elements are space, color, contrast, illumination, and time (Corn, 1989). Some students with visual impairments will require very few modifications in order to succeed in a general education environment, but others may need extensive modifications. Due to the infinite variety of modifications that can be made, a TVI should always take the lead in designing these modifications so that the child's needs are met.

Space. The space surrounding a visual item contains several elements that can be adjusted. The size of an object can be changed to help a student with a visual impairment. By enlarging an image, a child with a reduced acuity may be better able to see the image. Reducing the size of the image might be appropriate for a child with typical acuities but with a severe field restriction. The exact size needed to adequately see print or pictures without excessive fatigue will vary from child to child. TVIs and clinical low vision specialists work together to ensure children have the proper optical devices and/or size of large type to use their vision most efficiently. By moving closer to an object in space, the size of the image on the retina is increased, and the child may be able to see more clearly. Providing clear uncluttered space around an object can also increase a child's ability to see the item. Other spatial characteristics, such as font style and spacing between letters, words, and lines, can also affect a child's ability to see material.

Color. Color plays an important role in helping a child to see. Some children with visual impairments also experience color deficiency making it difficult to distinguish between certain colors. Red-green color deficiency is the most common form and occurs more frequently in males than females, but blue-green color deficiency also occurs. For children with color deficiency, it is important to know what colors the child cannot distinguish. Additionally, darker colors are usually more easily seen than lighter colors. For example, a black or blue marker on a white dry erase board will be more easily seen than using a red or yellow marker, or elementary school students may use black ink pens rather than pencils to improve their ability to read their own work.

Contrast. The contrast between the background and the item being viewed is also important. When the background and the print are similar in color, brightness, or shading, a child with a visual impairment may have difficulty seeing the print even if the size is appropriate. As a general rule, clear simple displays with high contrast tend to be most easily seen by children with visual impairments. Black on white has traditionally been considered the best contrast for reading and viewing, though other color combinations are also effective if there is a large difference in the amount of light reflected by the background and the letters (Eperjesi, Fowler & Kempster, 1995). Children may vary in which contrasts are most effective, and most prefer to occasionally receive materials using color even if the contrast is lower than it would be with black and white.

Illumination. Illumination is another important factor to consider when adjusting visual items. Many children with visual impairments function well in situations with typical lighting, however, some do not. Some children will require brighter light to enable them to see print or to use their vision to move through the environment. Other children may require less light in order to see either because they primarily use their peripheral vision, which works best in low light situations, or because their eyes are sensitive to light. Regardless of whether a child needs typical, high, or low lighting, he or she will benefit from avoiding glare from windows or artificial lighting. Additionally, children who are blind may still be able to perceive light and dark and may benefit from certain lighting situations.

Time. The fifth modification, time, is not directly related to the visual environment but can be essential for a child to function in a general education environment. Children with visual impairments may take longer to interpret visual information, including print, so that it takes them longer to complete assignments. By allowing extended time, children are not penalized for their visual impairment. At the same time, it is important to encourage children to increase their reading speeds, because they will be expected to work as quickly as sighted peers when they enter the work force. The TVI plays an important role in determining when extended time should be allowed and how much extra time should be given.

Most of the examples provided above apply to students with visual impairments who are participating in general education curricula, however, the same modifications can help students with visual impairments who are following alternative curricula. For example, if a child uses a picture communication board, the pictures should be clear and uncluttered with high contrast between the background and the picture. The pictures should be in colors the child can see and large enough for the child to see comfortably from his or her normal position when using the device. Lighting should be adjusted as needed and the child and communication board should be positioned to avoid glare on the device or in the child's face. The child should be given adequate time to visually identify the communication board and the pictures before being prompted for a response. The TVI should work closely with the special education teacher and other specialists to ensure that the child's visual needs are being met in all instruction and materials.

Expanded Core Curriculum for Students with Visual Impairments

In addition to needing modifications to access the general education curricula, children with visual impairments require instruction in disability specific skills (Corn, Hatlen, Huebner, Ryan & Siller, 1995; Hatlen, 1996). Hatlen discussed eight areas of disability specific instruction needed to expand the core curriculum for students with visual impairments. The areas of the expanded core curriculum, presented below, are important for all children with visual impairments regardless of their age, the severity of their visual impairment, or the presence of additional disabilities. Not all children with visual impairments will experience deficits in all the areas of the expanded core curriculum, but all areas should be assessed and instruction provided as needed.

Academic and compensatory skills. Children with visual impairments are expected to achieve in all of the basic academic areas, such as reading, writing, math, science, social studies, physical education, foreign language, home economics, to mention a few. Compensatory skills are the adaptive skills children with visual impairments use to complete academic tasks, such as Braille for reading and writing and abacus for computation. While academic instruction is usually the responsibility of the general education teacher, the TVI will consult on appropriate modifications and provide direct instruction when the visual impairment prevents the child from learning the skill in the general education setting. Obviously, the TVIs and orientation and mobility specialists are responsible for providing instruction in compensatory skills so that the child will be successful in the classroom.

Career education. Though career education is part of the general curriculum, this is not always sufficient for children with visual impairments. These children usually lack opportunities to visually learn about jobs, often face discrimination from employers, and may require specialized adaptations to complete jobs. Unfortunately, approximate 74% of adults with severe visual impairments are unemployed or underemployed (McNeil, 1993). Intensive career education is needed for students with visual impairments throughout their education so that future generations of people with visual impairments are able to participate more fully in society. TVIs can incorporate career education opportunities into regular classroom routines as well as providing direct instruction to small groups or individual students (Wolffe, 1996).

Independent living skills. Children with visual impairments often have difficulty learning independent living skills without direct instruction. Typically sighted children learn to manage routine activities such as eating, grooming, hygiene, and dressing primarily by watching others around them. Other tasks, such as housekeeping and money management, are generally learned with minimal instruction and extensive observations of others. Children with severe visual impairments are unable to observe these activities occurring around them or are unable to pick up on all details of what they observe. Additionally, the methods for completing some tasks need to be adapted due to the visual impairment, and children and parents may need instruction on making these adaptations. Independent living skills, from basic eating and toileting skills for preschoolers to household management for high school students, require direct instruction.

Orientation and mobility. Orientation and mobility (O&M) instruction provides students with the knowledge and skills necessary to travel as independently as possible. Probably the most well known symbol of O&M is the long white cane used by many people with visual impairments to aid in their independent travel. As discussed above, some aspects of O&M can be taught by TVIs or other educators, but other specialized skills should only be taught by a certified O&M specialist. The eight components of O&M which are addressed from preschool to adulthood are concept development, sensory training, mobility skills, orientation systems, solicitation of aid, use of community resources and public transportation, safety issues, and assistive technology (Griffin-Shirley, Trusty & Rickard, 2000). The recent reauthorization of IDEA specifically lists O&M as a related service, which encourages school systems to provide this much needed instruction.

Recreation and leisure. Children and adults with visual impairments often engage in few if any recreation and leisure activities resulting in feelings of

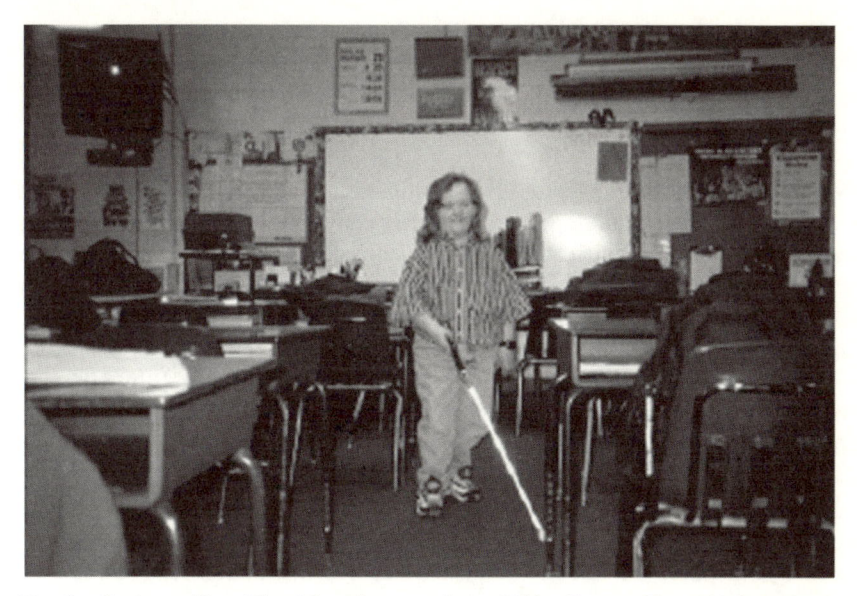

Fig. 6. Student with a Visual Impairment using a White Cane to Travel Independently.

isolation and poor physical health (Leiberman & Cowan, 1996). Typically sighted people usually become aware of recreation opportunities and learn how to engage in recreational activities through observing others. Children with visual impairments often cannot make these observations. Additionally, children with visual impairments may feel insecure about their ability to engage in a recreation activity or be unaware of appropriate adaptations they could use. Given appropriate instruction and modifications, virtually any recreation activity can be safely experienced by a person with a visual impairment. By providing instruction in active and sedentary recreation activities and in activities that involve groups as well as individual activities, TVIs can help students increase their recreation and leisure skills.

Social skills. Children with visual impairments often need intervention to develop social skills that typically sighted peers exhibit. Social interactions contain many visual cues that a person with a visual impairment may not be able to observe, such as body posture and eye contact. Children with visual impairments will also have to deal with questions and teasing about their eyes that will require high levels of social skills. TVIs provide direct instruction on social skills through a variety of models, as well as honest feedback to the student on how he or she interacts with peers and adults. Opportunities to interact with other children with visual impairments can assist children in feeling less isolated due to their visual impairment. When appropriately structured, interactions with non-disabled peers provide good opportunities to improve social skills in natural contexts (Sacks, Kekelis & Gaylord-Ross, 1992).

Technology. Technology provides multiple advantages for children with visual impairments that were not available even a few years ago. Technology can provide visual modifications such as enlarging the image on a computer screen or changing its color or contrast. It can also provide auditory modifications such as a screen reader that reports the information on a computer screen or a talking book machine that reads taped books at various speeds. Additionally, it can provide tactile modifications as well by allowing Braille code to be used to input information and by outputting Braille to an embosser (i.e. a Braille printer) or to a refreshable Braille display (i.e. a device using rounded metal pins that raise and lower to form Braille symbols). These are only a few examples of the many technological devices that are available for students with visual impairments. In order to benefit from this technology, students require extensive instruction from TVIs who are proficient in the use of the technology.

Visual efficiency skills. Visual efficiency skills are important for children with low vision so that they can make the best use of the vision they have. Hall and Bailey (1989) identified three types of visual behaviors in which children engage: visual attending behaviors (e.g. fixates on an object), visual examining behaviors (e.g. identifies pictures), and visually guided motor behaviors (e.g. reaches for face or toy). Some young children will require direct instruction to learn these skills; others may only need structured opportunities to practice the skills in appropriate environments; and others may develop these skills with little assistance. Older children may also require instruction in order to use optical devices effectively and efficiently. Because of the importance of visual efficiency as well as differences from etiologies, two children with similar acuities or visual fields may use their vision very differently. For example, one student with an acuity of 20/200 may read with optical devices and use a bioptic device to drive a car, but another student with the same acuity may use Braille to read and not meet state requirements to receive a drivers license.

SERVICE DELIVERY MODELS

The above review of the effects of visual impairments, the modifications made in the general curricula, and the specialized instruction needed, leaves one to wonder how and where children with visual impairments can receive an appropriate education. Several documents (e.g. Heumann & Hehir, 2000; Erin & Pugh, 1999) provide direction and guidance on service delivery for children with visual impairments. As with all children with disabilities, children with visual impairments must be provided with a free and appropriate public education (FAPE) in the least restrictive environment. There are many ways these services can be provided and each is appropriate under certain circumstances. This section discusses these service delivery models.

Historically, residential schools provided almost all education services for children with visual impairments; however, by the mid-20th century many children with visual impairment were served in their local schools (Hatlen, 2000). Despite the shift towards providing instruction in children's local schools, residential schools still serve important functions. Some residential schools continue to offer long term general education options, especially when students do not have access to certified TVI in their home schools. More frequently, residential schools are providing short-term instruction on skills that may be difficult for children to learn in their regular school. They also offer intensive skills instruction for students who lose their vision and need to learn many new skills quickly. Residential schools provide a place where children with visual impairments can meet and develop relationships with other children and adults with visual impairments. The concentration of skilled personnel and materials at residential schools, allows these facilities to act as resources for families, students, and professionals.

Self-contained classrooms in local schools are occasionally used to provide services for children with visual impairments. These classrooms are in general education schools but the majority of the student's education is provided in a classroom specifically designed for children with visual impairments. In this setting, as in the residential school, the TVI is responsible for the child's entire education program with only limited support from other professionals. Unlike residential schools, self-contained classrooms provide more opportunities for interaction with typically sighted peers.

Resource rooms taught by a TVI are frequently set up to meet the needs of children with visual impairments. Resource room settings allow the TVI to provide primary and supplemental instruction in academic areas when vision is a factor in the child's ability to complete academic tasks. Resource rooms also provide time for instruction in other areas of the expanded core curriculum described above. Additionally, TVIs may leave the resource room to provide inclusive services for children with visual impairments in their general education classrooms. In this setting, the general education teacher is responsible for the majority of the child's curricula instruction, and the

TVI provides supplemental support and instruction in areas of the expanded core curriculum.

The final service delivery model is the itinerant model which is used most frequently to provide educational services to children with visual impairments (Corn & Huebner, 1998). In this model, children attend their local schools and are served by TVIs who travel to different schools providing a variety of educational services to their students and the general education teachers. In this setting, general education teachers are responsible for the child's curricula and the TVI provides instruction in areas of the expanded core curriculum, as well as consultation to teachers on modifications for use in their classrooms. Students served by itinerant TVIs may be seen daily, weekly, or monthly depending on their needs. Itinerant models allow the child to be most fully included in his or her local school with only minimal time spent in special education instruction.

CONCLUSION

Children with visual impairments offer exciting challenges to teachers responsible for providing their education. Unfortunately, there is a severe shortage of teachers of students with visual impairments and certified orientation and mobility specialists (Council for Exceptional Children, 2000) making it difficult for children to receive the services they need. Because most children with visual impairments are educated in their neighborhood schools, it is essential that all teachers have at least a basic understanding of visual impairments and their effects on a child's learning. Children with visual impairments deserve the same quality of education as their typically sighted peers, thus requiring that schools provide certified teachers of students with visual impairments, appropriate modifications, and specialized instruction as needed.

RESOURCES

American Foundation for the Blind (AFB)
11 Penn Plaza
Suite 300
New York, NY 10001
800-232-5463
TDD: 212-502-7662
www.afb.org

The Lighthouse, Inc.
111 East 59th St
New York, NY 10022
800-334-5497
TDD: 212-821-9713

Library of Congress National Library Service for the Blind and Physically Handicapped
1291 Taylor St., N.W.
Washington, D.C. 20542
800-424-8567

American Printing House for the Blind
1839 Franfort Ave
PO Box 6085
Louisville, KY 40206-0085
800-223-1839
www.aph.org

REFERENCES

Corn, A. L. (1989). Instruction in the use of vision for children and adults with low vision. *RE:view*, *21*, 26–38.

Corn, A. L., Hatlen, P., Huebner, K. M., Ryan, F., & Siller, M. A. (1995). *The national agenda for the education of children and youths with visual impairments, including those with multiple impairments*. New York: AFB Press.

Corn, A. L., & Huebner, K. M. (1998). *A report to the nation: The national agenda for the education of children and youths with visual impairments, including those with multiple disabilities*. New York: AFB Press.

Corn, A. L., & Koenig, A. J. (1996). *Foundations of low vision: Clinical and functional perspectives*. New York: American Foundation for the Blind.

Council for Exceptional Children (2000). *National plan for training personnel to serve children with blindness and low vision*. Reston, VA: Author.

Eperjesi, F., Fowler, C. W., & Kempster, A. J. (1995). Luminance and chromatic contrast effects on reading and object recognition in low vision: A review of the literature. *Ophthalmic and Physiological Optics*, *15*, 545–551.

Erin, J., & Pugh, G. S. (Eds) (1999). *Blind and visually impaired students: Educational service guidelines*. Watertown, MA: Perkins School for the Blind.

Ferrell, K. A. (1998). *Project PRISM: A longitudinal study of developmental patterns of children who are visually impaired. Executive summary*. Greeley: University of Northern Colorado.

Griffin-Shirley, N., Trusty, S., & Rickard, R. (2000). Orientation and mobility. In: M. C. Holbrooks & A. J. Koenig (Eds), *Foundations of Education (Volume 2): Instructional Strategies for Teaching Children and Youth with Visual Impairments* (2nd ed., pp. 529–568). New York: American Foundation for the Blind.

Hall, A., & Bailey, I. L. (1989). A model for training visual functioning. *Journal of Visual Impairment and Blindness*, *83*, 390–396.

Hatlen, P. (1996). The core curriculum for blind and visually impaired students, including those with additional disabilities. *RE:view*, *28*, 25–32.

Hatlen, P. (2000). Historical perspectives. In: M. C. Holbrook & A. J. Koenig (Eds), *Foundations of Education* (Vol. 1, 2nd ed., pp. 1–54). New York: AFB Press.

Heumann, J. E., & Hehir, T. (2000). *Policy guidance on educating blind and visually impaired students*. United States Department of Education, Office of Special Education and Rehabilitative Services.

Hill, E. W. (1986). Orientation and mobility. In: G. T. Scholl (Ed.), *Foundations of Education for Blind and Visually Handicapped Children and Youth* (pp. 315–340). New York: American Foundation for the Blind.

Hill, E. W., Rosen, S., Correa, V. I., & Langley, M. B. (1984). Preschool orientation and mobility: An expanded definition. *Education of the Visually Handicapped*, *16*(2), 58–72.

Kahn, H. A., & Moorhead, H. B. (1973). *Statistics on blindness in the model reporting area 1969–1970* (Publication No. (NIH) 73-427). Washington, D.C.: U.S. Government Printing Office.

Kirchner, C., & Diamonte, S. (1999). Estimates of the number of visually impaired students, their teachers, and orientation and mobility specialists: Part one. *Journal of Visual Impairment and Blindness*, *93*, 600–606.

Koenig, A. J., & Holbrook, M. C. (1995). *Learning media assessment of students with visual impairments: A resource guide for teachers* (2nd ed.). Austin, TX: Texas School for the Blind.

Koestler, F. A. (1976). *The unseen minority: A social history of blindness in the United States*. New York: David McKay.

Lieberman, L. J., & Cowart, J. F. (1996). *Games for people with sensory impairments: Strategies for including individuals of all ages*. Champaign, IL: Human Kinetics.

MacCuspie, P. A. (1996). *Promoting acceptance of children with disabilities: From tolerance to inclusion*. Halifax, NS: Atlantic Provinces Special Education Authority.

McNeil, J. (1993). *Americans with disabilities 1991–1992*. Washington, D.C.: U.S. Department of Commerce, Bureau of the Census.

Sacks, S. Z., Kekelis, L. S., & Gaylord-Ross, R. J. (1992). *The development of social skills by blind and visually impaired students*. New York: AFB Press.

Silberman, R. K., & Sacks, S. (2000). *Expansion of the role of the teacher of students with visual impairments: Providing for students who also have severe/multiple disabilities*. Washington, D.C.: Council for Exceptional Children.

Spungin, S. J., & Ferrell, K. A. (2000). *The role and function of the teacher of student with visual handicaps*. Washington, D.C.: Council for Exceptional Children.

Wolffe, K. E. (1996). Career education for students with visual impairments. *RE:view*, *28*, 89–93.

EDUCATING CHILDREN AND YOUTH WITH SERIOUS MEDICAL CONDITIONS: PERILS AND POTENTIAL

Joan Fleitas

INTRODUCTION

This chapter examines issues central to the education of students with serious medical conditions in classroom settings. It defines the parameters of the population and focuses on the challenges to education from the point of view of children, parents, teachers, and health care providers. Additionally, it reviews relevant legislation and suggests non-categorical intervention strategies to prevent this vulnerable population from falling through the cracks of the system.

WHO ARE CHILDREN WITH SERIOUS MEDICAL CONDITIONS?

Children with serious medical conditions (SMCs) encounter myriad problems in schools and communities. Consider the following case:

> Anthony reflects on his second grade experience following treatment for leukemia, "... some of the kids called me "fat cheeks" and "blow up boy." It especially hurt me, but I tried to ignore it." Brian complains, "I can never be just me ... it's all about the wheelchair. A chair that I have because of muscular dystrophy, but I am not the wheelchair. And I am definitely not the muscular dystrophy. You'd never believe it, though, because even my friends treat me like I'm perishable. They want to push my wheelchair and carry my books.

Some kids I definitely do not like talk to me like I'm four years old instead of ten." And Jessica counsels teachers to be sensitive to issues surrounding chronic illness, explaining that, "when my teacher asked if there was anything she needed to know about her students for gym, I told her I was diabetic. When she responded 'oh well, I don't mean eating disorders', that hurt. I do not have anorexia or bulemia, yet I was put into that category" (Fleitas, 2000).

Youngsters with SMCs speak for legions more who live bifurcated existences, with one of their feet in the health care system and the other in school. It is a precarious footing, and many of them fall through the cracks in the ground that separates their roles of patient and student. Almost 31% of U.S. children and adolescents have a chronic physical condition, with 18% (representing 12.6 million children) having special health care needs. Add to this an uncalculated number of children and youth "at risk" for such needs, and it becomes apparent that the situation demands focused attention (Newacheck & Halfon, 1998). This emerging population reflects the success of medical advances. While the incidence rates of childhood chronic conditions remains relatively stable, the prevalence of these disorders has shown a substantial increase.

Today, most children survive conditions that would have in the past resulted in their deaths. A child with cystic fibrosis (CF), for example, had a life expectancy of 11 years in 1966, yet today, children born with this genetic disease have a median life expectancy of more than 30 years (National Patient Registry data, Cystic Fibrosis Foundation, 1997). New categories of childhood chronic conditions add to the prevalence picture. For instance, infants are surviving very low birth weights, children with acquired immunodeficiency syndrome (AIDS) are living longer due to advances in drug treatment, and babies born with prenatal drug exposure are presenting new challenges to both the health and educational systems. Yet another category of children and youth bear the iatrogenic marks of U.S. health care successes. Children coping with bronchopulmonary dysplasia as a sequela of surviving prematurity, children requiring immune suppression following organ transplantation, and childhood cancer survivors with residual effects of toxic treatments – all present with special health care needs (Jackson, 2000). The success of the health care system in saving lives of large numbers of children and the introduction of new medical problems mandate educational reform to better ensure a parallel success in schools. Because diagnoses alone fail to predict the need for educational adaptations, policy makers in pediatric public health have endorsed a non-categorical approach to better define medical conditions and their consequences. Such an approach looks at chronic conditions that have a biological base that lasts or is expected to last from 3–12 months and is accompanied by either: (a) limitations in day-to-day functioning; (b) reliance on compensatory medications, diets and/or assistive devices; or (c) the need for services beyond routine medical care (Stein, Coupey, Bauman, Westbrook & Ireys, 1993).

THE LAWS THAT PROTECT CHILDREN AND YOUTH WITH SMCS

In a perfect society, children with SMCs would be furnished every health care and educational service they need, with school districts having sufficient personnel and financial resources to enthusiastically meet those needs. The reality, however, is different. Even when educators want to provide what they or parents perceive to be necessary services, they often are challenged by a lack of expertise among existing (and often insufficient) staff, and funding priorities that do not include this burgeoning group of students. Unfortunately, no legal mandate exists specifically to address needs of students with chronic illness, and children with diseases like cancer, asthma, and diabetes may be ineligible for programs created by the Individuals with Disability Education Act (IDEA), and do not qualify for special education services. And even more problematic is the eligibility criteria for IDEA that limits services to children with health problems adversely affecting their educational performance. Many of the children who might fit the definition have not been identified, guidelines for determining the adverse effects on academic performance remain vague, and no system exists for assessing the relationship between academic performance and chronic medical conditions (Thies, 1999).

Even recognizing such dilemmas, children and youth with SMCs deserve protection and education. Legislative and judicial programs and rulings over the past 25 years have dramatically changed the role of public schools in providing services to children with any type of disabling condition. Beginning with the landmark decision of *Brown v. the Board of Education* (1954) that banned segregated schools, the civil rights movement affirmed the right of all Americans to an education. Later, the Supreme Court ruled that a free, public education must be provided to all school-age children regardless of disability or degree of impairment (*Mills v. Board of Education of the District of Columbia*, 1972). This decision paved the way for an educational bill of rights for children articulated by Public Law 94-142, the Education of All Handicapped Children Act of 1975. Later renamed the Individuals with Disabilities Education Act, or IDEA (Public Law 101-476), it was enacted by Congress with the soundest of motivations: to provide every child with a disability a free and appropriate education in the least restrictive environment. However, the failure to adequately fund its mandates has placed a heavy financial burden on both states and school districts (i.e. instead of funding at 40% of the national average expenditure – the amount specified in statute – federal funding more typically has been in the 7% to 9% range) (McCarthy & Cambron-McCabe, 1992).

Although most children falling under IDEA guidelines have developmental disabilities, there are provisions in the legislation to provide necessary assistance to those whose needs fall under the category, "other health problems." In 1995, the Federal Maternal and Child Health Bureau's Division of Services for Children with Special Health Care Needs (DSCSHCN) noted that "children with special health care needs are those who have or are at elevated risk for chronic physical, developmental, behavioral, or emotional conditions and who also require health and related services of a type or amount not usually required by children" (p. 1). This definition focuses on the need for additional services rather than on identified medical conditions or functional impairment because of the variability in severity and need among children with the same or differing diagnoses. Conditions identified as disabilities in children under IDEA were divided into 13 categories. The category, "other health impairments", however, defines those students who have "limited strength, vitality or alertness due to chronic or acute health problems that affect their educational performance" (Shenkman, 2000, p. 2).

From the 1989–1990 to the 1998–1999 school years, there was a 318.7% increase in students served under the category "other health impairments," representing a shift from 52,733 to 220,831 students. Although the marked increase in this category reflects better identification of children in need of services and the growing number of children diagnosed with attention deficit hyperactivity disorder, it also includes children with chronic illnesses like cancer, asthma, heart conditions, sickle cell anemia, hemophilia, epilepsy, HIV/AIDS or medical fragility in need of adaptations in their educational programs (U.S. Department of Education, Office of Special Education Programs, Data Analysis System, 2000).

Children with SMCs are living longer, and medical technology is permitting them access to educational experiences in neighborhood schools, yet school personnel are often inadequately equipped to meet their complex needs. PL 94–142 defined the appropriate personnel to provide school health services as the "school nurse or other qualified person" (PL 94-142, 1975). Interestingly, while the complexity of SMCs increases, the number of school nurses has not shown a parallel rise, with over 90,000 public schools and only 40,000 school nurses (Igoe & Duncan, 1999). Section 504 of the Americans with Disability Act of 1973 is another piece of protective legislation, ensuring that students with "other health impairments" are not discriminated against because of the need for accommodations in their education. Like many of governmental acts intended to ensure a free and appropriate education for all children, regardless of their degree of disability, it is hampered by a lack of adequate funding. To date, Federal programs have mandated services, but have failed to provide financial resources necessary to supply those services (Vessey & Jackson, 2000).

Children and youth with SMCs are challenged by another barrier to the acquisition of appropriate supports. Many of them are not identified by the school system because of parental fear that once earmarked; they would be classified as "special ed children" and would be relegated to a dark self-contained classroom in the basement of the school. Myths abound, despite significant changes in the prognosis and services for students with developmental and mental health disabilities, the group usually thought of as "special." Special education services for students with SMCs may well be inappropriate for many of them for more cogent reasons, though. Such services generally focus on the individual in need and fail to address the concerns of teachers and other students. When classmates encounter students with overt SMCs, they have questions and fears; fears about causation, contagion, prognosis, and death. Without education and support, all students fail to learn important lessons about diversity and respect. Parents are concerned that special education services might further stigmatize their children who already feel different. Many parents, and most children and youth with SMCs, do not want to be singled out or treated differently as a result of their condition. Because of these factors, students with hidden disorders are vulnerable in school systems that fail to identify the SMCs. Children with heart disease, lupus, sickle cell disease, AIDS and cancer, and a myriad of other SMCs may be present in the classroom, without the awareness of teachers, support staff, the school nurse, or mental health professionals. They attempt to 'fit in' while their parents cross their fingers and pray that nothing bad will happen during the school day.

CHILDREN AND YOUTH WITH SMCS AS STUDENTS

In addition to such illness-related stressors as complying with complicated medical regimes and coping with physical ailments, limitations, discomfort, and fatigue, children and youth with SMCs have additional challenges as they attempt to don the role of student:

- If they have spent a great deal of time in hospitals, they must learn to relate to classmates in a non-clinical environment. As one student, Sophie, explains, "when I first started school, I had a difficult time because I didn't know how to relate to my classmates. Since I had spent so much time in the hospital with doctors, nurses, and older family members, when it was time for me to start kindergarten, I literally clutched onto my teachers' skirts." And another student, Donald, aches to be considered just one of the gang as he navigates between the role of patient and that of student, "I just started school after a summer spent in and out of the hospital, and kids look at me as if No. 1, I just dropped in from another planet, or No. 2, was about to drop dead on the floor. I especially hate the pity!" (Fleitas, 2000).

- They must prepare for and get to school. As one student, Martin, recalls, "I had to climb up and down those big school bus steps both to get on and off the bus, twice a day. And I had to walk farther to get to my room. One of the scariest things was if the bus was late, everybody else would already be inside the school. I would have to try to open those giant heavy school-building doors all by myself. I worried that I might be trapped on the wrong side, and would miss school because of it."
- They must adjust to being students while coping with the teasing and exclusion that is often part and parcel of being different in appearance or behavior, or of being treated preferentially by teachers. As one student indicated, "I get picked on, pick, pick, pick, and I get called the horriblest names, and when I go off crying, people go and tell (the teacher), but she doesn't do anything at all" (Lightfoot, Wright & Sloper, 1999, p. 277). Another eleven-year-old student, Liz, asserts that ". . . had I known I'd be alone (on a field trip), I probably would've stayed at home. I thought that segregation was illegal in this nation" (Fleitas, 2000).
- They must attempt to keep up with their school work, despite the need for extended or frequent absences. The more school absences, the greater the likelihood of poor academic achievement and impaired social relationships. Studies report significantly higher absences among children with SMCs (Newacheck & Halfon, 1998).
- They must deal with exclusion from school life when their SMCs limit their participation in activities, and when their recesses are relegated to treatment or personal care tasks. As an adolescent with SMC, ankylosing spondylitis, commented:

    Once I even had the humiliation of being put into study hall where I was watched by a security guard who growled at everyone . . . it was really a place for detention, fighting, or truancies. Kids thought I was a "criminal" because I was in a closed classroom in the back of the school for an hour each day (Fleitas, 1999).

- They must cope with their teachers' reactions to the SMCs. Teachers are often ill-equipped to provide appropriate support, as this child illustrates in a web page offering tips for teachers, "I wish you would treat me like a student instead of like a patient. I'm not sick, so when you ask me if I

feel OK all the time, this heart problem that I have feels like a heavy weight" (Fleitas, 2000).
- They must bear the brunt of poor communication between health professionals and school staff. One adolescent student was forced to take part in physical activities she felt unable to manage:

  > He had me running around the field... I said, "Sir, I can't do this, I'm going to be sick," I was in such a state, I was blue... and I felt really poorly after. I was upset because I thought, well, all the teachers know, but they don't seem to care (Lightfoot et al., 1998).

- They must attempt to engage with teachers who question the validity of their symptoms. As one student with SMC noted, "Some of my teachers were not very understanding about my "lavatory needs", and even the school nurse thought it strange at times that I needed to go to the bathroom so much" (Fleitas, 2000).
- They must cope with feelings of being "damaged goods" and alienated from their normal peer networks during prolonged absences.

Because SMCs result in lifestyle interruptions that often impede continued social interaction with peers, either the severity of the condition or the extent of disruption in the lives of these students may affect social adjustment. For example, Graetz and Shute (1995) reported that among children with moderate to severe asthma, those with more hospitalizations were less preferred as playmates, were perceived by their peers as more sensitive and isolated, and admitted loneliness. Epidemiological studies demonstrate that children with SMCs are at higher risk for school problem as well, particularly those with physical disabilities or chronic illnesses affecting the brain. Factors contributing to this risk are the primary effects of either the sequelae of the SMCs or the iatrogenic effects of treatment protocols, and the secondary effects of the illness in terms of absenteeism and psychological stressors and distress (Thompson & Gustafson, 1996).

Students with SMCs assert that teachers' responses are crucial to how they feel about school. In one qualitative study focusing on the views of youngsters with illness and disability, students reported that even within the same school, teachers reacted very differently to their medical needs. A strong theme in the report was the value students felt for teachers who "understood." They defined an understanding teacher as one who was aware of the health condition and understood the impact it had on school work and behavior, and who made appropriate arrangements based on this knowledge without making the child "stand out in the crowd" (Lightfoot et al., 1999).

TEACHERS' ROLES IN WORKING WITH STUDENTS WITH SMCS

While children with SMCs are challenged by their dual roles of patient and student, teachers are challenged by the presence of these youngsters in the classroom. Teachers for the most part have been educated to educate, not to attend to health problems of their students, which had been the purview of nurses in school settings. Yet the growing number of students with SMCs in classrooms has necessitated a change; that teachers be aware of the educational ramifications of a number of childhood diseases and disabilities, and that they be responsive to individualized needs that these health conditions activate. Children no longer remain in hospitals for weeks and months, and following discharge after a few days, they may return to school with medical needs that create tension in the classroom. Such tension are visible with teachers who are often poorly informed of the nature of the health problems and of their roles should problems occur. Similar tensions occur in students with SMCs who must cope with an imbalanced focus on the illness. "I hate it", complained one youngster, using the anonymity of a web page to share his concern, "when you keep asking if I can eat this or do that. I know what my limitations are and I can look after myself." There is a fine line that must be drawn between paying too little attention to students with SMCs and patronizing them, thus increasing both physical risks and frustration (Weist, Finney, Barnard, Davis & Ollendick, 1993).

Teachers are challenged by:

- Inadequate orientation to the needs presented by students with SMCs.
- Concern that they will be unable to respond to medical crises in the classroom.
- Fear that the education of other students will be negatively affected by attention given to children and youth with SMCs.
- The need to maintain the balance necessary to ensure the safety of students with SMCs while normalizing them into the classroom.
- The need to remember that most SMCs, whether they are visible or invisible, have an impact on students' ability to learn.
- Communication breakdowns with parents, health professionals, and school administrators.
- Lack of up-to-date knowledge of Federal laws that mandate educational accommodations for students with SMCs.
- Lack of knowledge of technical skills they are often asked to perform.

Parental Roles in Maximizing the Potential of Students with SMCs

In the best of circumstances, parents are a major source of information for the schools. They frequently suggest educational implications of the SMCs in their children, and provide guidelines for dealing with emergencies, assist in demonstrating necessary procedures to relevant staff members, and act as mediators between their children and the teachers, helping to resolve problems secondary to a lack of understanding or insensitivity to individual needs. Prior to the Education of All Handicapped Children Act (later named IDEA), parents were denied a role in the special education process. This law considered parental involvement essential, however, and afforded parents a primary role in decision making. For example, school officials were required to notify parents whenever there was a proposed change to their children's program, and obtain parental consent, as parents were involved in the development and review of their child's individualized educational plan (IEP).

With IDEA, these processes have become solidified and stabilized. The Office of Special Education Programs (OSEP) funded three primary initiatives beginning in 1999 for students with disabilities, their parents and families, and advocates: the National Information Center for Children and Youth with Disabilities (NICHCY); The Families and Advocates Partnership for Education (FAPE) project; and the establishment of Parent Training and Information (PTI) centers (http://www.ncd.gov/newsroom/publications/backtoschool_3.html#10). The goals of the Parent Program are to provide information, training, and support to the families of children with disabilities, including those with SMCs, in advocating for supports and services their children need to receive the benefits of a free appropriate public education under IDEA. The Parent Program recognizes the critical role of parents in their children's education and aims at preparing them to be active participants in the IEP process.

Parents are challenged, however, by:

- Expending resources in confronting obstacles to their child's most basic right to an appropriate education, often at the expense of their personal lives.
- Poor communication with classroom teachers. Most "regular" classrooms do not have telephones, and when students with SMCs present with crises secondary to their conditions, the teacher must wait for the nurse to intervene and contact the parents. One parent argues against such delays, "when Bobby was irritable, he was told to stand in the back of the room, and all the while he was having a reaction to low blood sugar" (Fleitas, 2000).

- Complex time demands. Another parent writes for many when she expresses frustration over inordinate time demands and a lack of sensitivity of the school to her son's SMC:

  > Craig has cystic fibrosis and has a very hard time in school. Many of his teachers just don't understand that children can be so cruel. I spend the good portion of my days speaking with principals and teachers. One time he was approached by a student asking him when he was going to die. It turns out that the science teacher had told the class what he had when he was absent one time and that he wasn't going to live very long (Fleitas, 2001).

- Concerns that school staff have inadequate knowledge and resources to monitor the SMCs of their children, to support the children in the management of their conditions, to sensitize other students to the nature of any visible conditions, and to understand the issues central to specific diseases and disabilities.

It is important that teachers and administrators understand the learning potential of students with SMCs. Thies (1999) discussed the educational implications of having this group of students in school, and concluded with recommendations that warrant attention:

(1) Schools should recognize the growth in this population of students, and understand the need to work closely with health care providers and parents in the shift away from inpatient acute care to community-based management of chronic illness.
(2) Schools should identify students with chronic illness, remembering that health records reflect only self-disclosed medical diagnoses.
(3) School nurses, teachers, administrators, and mental health professionals should develop a systematic approach for identifying and working with students with chronic illness.
(4) Schools should differentiate between accommodations of health problems and provision of educational services; accommodations meaning, for example, that children with asthma be allowed to carry inhalers to class, while provision of appropriate educational services is seen as broader intervention for that same child (e.g. accommodating chronic absenteeism by providing extra time to make up missed homework).
(5) Schools should nurture personnel who think creatively about this group of students, rather than routinely moving them into existing programs not developed to meet their educational and heath needs.

Meeting the educational needs of students with SMCs requires the coordinated efforts of health care providers, schools, parents and their children. Successful integration of this group of youngsters into the classroom involves enhancing their academic and social skills, modifying the school environment as necessary, and encouraging parents to be effective advocates for their children. (Thompson & Gustafson, 1996). It also involves enhancing the knowledge and sensitivity of their healthy classmates when students with SMCs present with obvious physical or behavioral differences. Eliciting and maintaining peer support have been identified as key objectives in integration and re-integration (after hospitalization) programs for students with SMCs, since maintaining positive relationships with peers serves as a protective factor in their adaptation to their illnesses/disabilities. Varni, Katz, Colegrove & Dolgin (1993) found that children with cancer who received explicit training in social skills reported higher perceived classmate and teacher social support. Coupled with parental reports of a decrease in behavior problems and an increase in school competence for these children, the findings suggest the value of identifying situation-specific deficits in social skills and planning individualized programs to address them.

School-based health centers (SBHCs) are coordinated resources most appropriate to manage the chronic care needs of students with SMCs. They offer a means of providing primary care and physical/mental health services to all children and youth as well. Originally designed to address problems of adolescents, their success prompted diffusion of the concept and practice into the elementary schools. The number of SBHCs in the United States climbed to 1,380 in school year 1999/2000, representing a 20% increase over two years and nearly a seven-fold increase over the past decade. Currently, 33 states provide grant support to SBHCs and 43 states permit them to bill Medicaid for patient care (Lear, 2001). These centers are usually organized by health care institutions and focus on both primary and tertiary care. Nurses, physicians and mental health professionals work together to provide physicals, offer education and treatment of chronic conditions, provide family counseling, and work with school staff to address student problems.

Since the early 1990s, funding and political support for SBHCs has increased dramatically. Paul Jellinek, Vice-President with The Robert Wood Johnson Foundation, explains that "like shopping malls, frozen dinners and online banking, part of the beauty of school-based health centers is their convenience. They make life easier for parents, for their employers and for the students they serve. As the pace of society becomes more hectic, I think their appeal will become more universal" (Lear, 2001). What he failed to note was the tremendous potential that SBHCs hold for students with SMCs, who are under such systems and able to receive both primary and disease specific support in an effective and coordinated fashion.

Teachers are powerful people in the lives of students, and as such, they have tremendous influence in the quality of the educational and social climate in the classroom. There are several strategies they should employ to ensure that students with SMCs are integrated into the life of the classroom in a safe and socially integrative manner. They should:

- Participate in a multi-disciplinary planning process to ensure success in school re-entry after hospitalization or extended absences.
- Fully understand the diseases of any students who will be spending a year of their lives in the classroom. As a result of such information, teachers will feel more in control, less afraid of the situations that may be present, and better able to distinguish the onset of real emergencies.
- Learn CPR and determine how to handle health emergencies.
- Advocate for a classroom phone to communicate with parents and health care providers, summon help, call 911, and get assistance during a fire drill if any of their students with SMCs are not ambulatory.
- Encourage physical activities for students with SMCs to their ability, recognizing that the level of activity may change daily.
- Ensure that students with SMCs are not pushed to go beyond their limits as defined by them.
- Be sensitive to the need for parental involvement in decision-making
  Plan alternative activities for the class or for students with SMCs if the original activity poses a significant health risk, and ensure that this group of students is not simply excluded from any activity.
- Encourage class discussion about SMCs in general and, with the permission and involvement of the students who have particular ones, about them as well.

In order that students with SMCs have a successful school experience, school nurses need to be active members of the interdisciplinary school and community team. When re-entering school after home absences and hospitalizations, these children and youth should enjoy a sense of safety, accomplishment and social acceptance. Strategies of nursing support that best achieve those goals are to:

- Develop an individual health care plan for these students.
- Concentrate on abilities, not disabilities, because focusing on what students with SMCs are able to do promotes self-esteem and positive self-image.
- Communicate with these students in a manner appropriate to their abilities. The presence of a SMC does not ordinarily carry with it a cognitive impairment.

- Meet with parents and obtain careful histories. Their assistance in interpreting behaviors and responses can provide a better understanding of student needs.
- Become familiar with respiratory emergency interventions since they are the most common emergencies encountered with this population of students.
- Develop a plan identifying appropriate follow-up after emergency incidents.
- Educate parents and staff members in prevention and early intervention techniques.
- Work collaboratively with administrators, staff, health care advisors and providers, the local EMS and parents to establish a comprehensive emergency care plan.

Service providers (e.g. nurses and mental health professionals) can facilitate psychosocial outcomes by ensuring that students with SMCs are physically and emotionally ready to return to school. One successful program involves role-playing, wherein the health professionals play the role of classmates, and the students with SMCs play themselves. The goal is to act out a number of common re-entry scenarios so that the children and youth can develop a repertoire of responses to potentially embarrassing questions and comments. (Rabin, 1994). Coupled with this preparation is the need to facilitate the adjustment of teachers and classmates. Different strategies have proven to be effective. For instance, hospitalized youngsters keeping in touch with their class through letters, e-mails, and videotapes or photos of their experiences can facilitate smooth transitions. When the tapes and photos are shared with classmates and teachers several days prior to the anticipated return to school, they have an opportunity to adjust to any changes in appearance like alopecia or scarring. This "sanctioned staring" and opportunity to ask questions and express concerns without fear of recrimination improves the likelihood of a successful school experience. (Vessey & Jackson, 2000). In Australia, a model program was provided in schools for nurses and mental health professionals who work with a number of children and youth with SMCs. A "Chronic Illness Peer Support" program had as its goal the assistance of young people in their adjustment to life with a chronic illness by developing positive connections with other young people facing similar circumstances. As a result, coping skills were enhanced, school absences were handled effectively, peer networks were maintained, and family relations were improved. Given the move in the United States towards comprehensive school health services, such a program might go a long way to protecting students from the negative psychosocial sequela of their SMCs (Olsson, C. A., 1997).

Perspectives

Because children with SMCs must cope not only with significant absences from the classroom but with the emotional and sometimes sensory responses to their conditions and treatment protocols, their return to regular school environments can be overwhelming. Goals of such programs should include: (a) educating students, parents and school personnel about the unique needs of children with SMCs; (b) informing parents and schools about specialized education and support resources in the community when necessary; (c) addressing specific emotional and educational challenges through coordinated community services; and (d) advocating for students with special needs at school and collaborating in the development of an action plan to best meet their goals. The Liaison for Effective Academic Resource and Networking (LEARN) is one such program that might serve as a model for others. For example, it provides educational guidance to children with cancer and blood disorders. Its goal is to share information and provide practical assistance to families and school personnel regarding the impact of the disease on educational success. The program has been effective in providing counsel and support to families facing school challenges. School with its homework assignments and peer relationships provides reassurance to children with cancer that there is still some stability and normalcy in their lives, and this program serves as a liaison between families and school personnel to ensure that stability. It involves such activities as obtaining school records, securing tutoring while children are unable to attend school, and working directly with their teachers to design necessary classroom modifications to address both medical and academic needs. From the time of diagnosis, special considerations need to be made to address individual educational needs. The LEARN coordinator serves as an advocate in assisting parents and school staff to determine the educational needs of affected children, and then in working with them to implement necessary modifications (Tomorrow Children's Institute for Cancer and Blood Disorders, 2000).

Although advances in treatments and therapies have greatly enhanced long-term survival and rates of cure, the LEARN program acknowledges that certain cancer therapies may affect academic performance, with effects on learning subtle and appearing slowly over time. The LEARN coordinator assists in the early detection of treatment-related learning problems through regular screenings and interviews with parents and teachers. If more thorough psycho-educational testing is thought necessary, the coordinator facilitates it to assist in the development of an appropriate educational plan. Services of the program that might serve as a model for the coordination of programs for all students with SMCs include: (a) advocacy on behalf of families; (b) consultation on school placement and use of resources; (c) school staff education about disease, treatments, and related effects; (d) educational/developmental screenings; (e) coordination of diagnostic educational evaluation; and (f) coordination of tutoring services for children in both the inpatient service and the outpatient clinic.

This chapter has focused on the challenges inherent in successfully educating students with SMCs in the regular classroom setting, and on guidelines and initiatives to address those challenges in a creative manner. Comments from students with SMCs have been integrated throughout to focus attention on the issues they must deal with and the solutions that only a coordinated team will be able to achieve. As one youngster reminds, "look beyond my illness... look into my world, see the many pieces, not just one". In order to see her, and educate her, and help her achieve her goals, it is imperative to have a comprehensive plan that allows educators, parents, health professionals, and other service providers to work together in a collaborative manner.

REFERENCES

Back to School on Civil Rights (2001) [on line]. Available: http://www.ncd.gov/newsroom/publications/backtoschool_3.html#10

Brown vs. Board of Education, 347 U.S. 483 (1954) (USSC+), 1954 [on line]. Available: http://www.nationalcenter.org/brown.html

Cystic Fibrosis Foundation (1999). Patient Registry 1997 Annual Data Report (September). Bethesda, Maryland.

Fleitas, J. (2000) Band-Aides and Blackboards [on line]. Available: http://www.faculty.fairfield.edu/fleitas/contents.html

Graetz, B., & Shute, R. (1995). Assessment of peer relationships in children with asthma. *Journal of Pediatric Psychology, 20*, 205–216.

IDEA and special education for children and youth (1995). *National information center for children and youth with disabilities* (p. 2) [on line]. Available: http://www.ldonline.org/ld_in-depth/general_info/gen-4.html

Igoe, J. B., & Duncan, P. (1998). School health services. In: E. Marx & S. Wooley (Eds), *Health is Academic: A Guide to Coordinated School Health Programs*. New York: Teachers College Press.

Jackson, P. L. (2000). *The Primary care of the child with a chronic condition* (pp. 3–19). St. Louis, MO: C. V. Mosby.

Lear, J. (2001). Center for Health and Health Care in Schools [on line]. Available: http://www.healthinschools.org/press/PR00002.asp

Lightfoot, J., Wright, S., & Sloper, P. (1999). Supporting pupils in mainstream school with an illness or disability: Young people's views. *Child: Care, Health and Development, 25*(4), 267–283.

McCarthy, M., & Cambron-McCabe, N. (1992). *Public school law* (3rd ed.). Needham Heights, MA: Allyn and Bacon.

Mills v. Board of Education of the District of Columbia United States District Court (D.D.C.) (1972) [on line]. Available: http://wind.uwyo.edu/edec5250/assignments/Mills.pdf

Newacheck, P. W., & Halfon, N. (1998). Prevalence and impact of disabling chronic conditions in childhood. *American Journal of Public Health, 88*, 610–617.

Newacheck, P. W., Strickland, B., Shonkoff, J. P., Perrin, J. M., McPherson, M., McManus, M., Lauver, C., Fox, H., & Arango, P. (1998). An epidemiologic profile of children with special health care needs. *Pediatrics, 102*, 117–123.

Olsson C. A., Walsh B. W., Toumbourou J. W., & Bowes G. (1997). Chronic illness peer support (ChIPS). *Aust Fam Physician, 26*, 500–501.

Rabin, N. B. (1994). School reentry and the child with a chronic illness: The role of the pediatric nurse practitioner. *Journal of Pediatric Health Care, 8*, 227–232.

Shenkman, E. A. (2000). Strategies for identifying children with special health care needs. *Institute for Child Health Policy*, 1 [on line]. Available: http://www.ichp.edu/rtitlexxi/materials/StrategiesforID.pdf

Stein, R., Coupey, S., Bauman, L., Westbrook, L., & Ireys, H. (1993). Framework for identifying children who have chronic conditions: The case for a new definition. *Journal of Pediatrics, 122*, 342–347.

Thies, K. M. (1999). Identifying the educational implications of chronic illness in school children. *Journal of School Health, 69*, 392–396.

Thompson, R., & Gustafson, K. (1996). Social adjustment, peer relationships and school performance. *Adaptation to chronic childhood illness* (pp. 115–130). Washington, D.C.: American Psychological Association.

Tomorrow Children's Institute for Cancer and Blood Disorders (2000) [on line]. Available: http://www.tcikids.com/psychosocialservices.htm#L.E.A.R.N.

U.S. Department of Education, Office of Special Education Programs, Data Analysis System (2000) [on line]. Available: http://www.ed.gov/offices/OSERS/OSEP/Products/OSEP2000AnlRpt/PDF/Chapter-2.pdf

Varni, J. W., Katz, E. R., Colegrove, R., & Dolgin, M. (1993). The impact of social skills training on the adjustment of children with newly diagnosed cancer. *Journal of Pediatric Psychology, 18*, 751–767.

Vessey, J. A., & Jackson, P. L. (2000). The school and children with chronic conditions. In: P. L. Jackson, & J. A. Vessey (Eds), *Primary Care of the Child with a Chronic Condition* (3rd ed., pp. 83–100). St. Louis: Mosby-Yearbook.

Weist, M. D., Finney, J. W., Barnard, M. U., Davis, C. D., & Ollendick, T. H. (1993). Empirical selection of psychosocial treatment targets for children and adolescents with diabetes. *Journal of Pediatric Psychology, 18*, 11–28.

STUDENTS WITH TRAUMATIC BRAIN INJURY

Janet Siantz Tyler and Ronald C. Savage

INTRODUCTION

In terms of acquired injuries (i.e. taking place after birth), traumatic brain injury (TBI) remains the greatest cause of death and disability for children, according to various medical registries. Yet, according to the United States Department of Education statistics gathered from individual states, students with TBI make up a miniscule population when compared to students with learning disabilities, developmental disabilities, or autism (U.S. Department of Education, 1999). Misunderstanding that there is only a small population of children/youth who have TBI, may stem from the fact that many of these children are frequently misclassified under other diagnostic categories (e.g. learning disabilities, other health impairment). Apparently such misunderstandings and inconsistencies have affected the development of effective instructional practices to serve children with TBI.

Despite enormous variability, the population known as TBI, also shares a number of commonalities and issues that make this group unique and sets it apart from other disabilities. An understanding of typical patterns of functioning following TBI, as well as issues specifically related to this population, will help to increase educators' awareness of the special needs of these students. This chapter begins with a general orientation to TBI, including incidence and prevalence of TBI in children and adolescents, classification issues, and common sequelae from TBI. The centerpiece of the chapter is a discussion of effective educational practices for students with TBI, including a proposed model of integrating special education, rehabilitation services, and recommended practices to foster innovative programming for these students.

TRAUMATIC BRAIN INJURY

Incidence and Prevalence

Each year approximately one million youngsters are admitted to hospital emergency departments with traumatic brain injuries resulting from motor vehicle collisions, falls, sports, assault, and abuse (Brain Injury Association, 1997). It is estimated that traumatic brain injuries to children between birth and 19 years of age annually result in:

- 7,000 deaths of children;
- 150,000 hospitalizations;
- hospital care costing over one billion dollars;
- 30,000 children becoming permanently disabled (see Brain Injury Association).

According to data from the National Pediatric Trauma Registry (NPTR), in an analysis of 15,024 children with TBI from birth through 19 years of age, males outnumber females approximately 2:1, and in terms of age more children were injured under the age of 9 years than between 10–19 years (Savage, 2000). See Table 1 below.

NPTR data collected from 85 pediatric trauma centers/hospitals indicate that for all children (0–19 years of age) who are admitted to the hospital for an acute

Table 1. Prevalence of Traumatic Brain Injury by Sex and Age.

Sex	Number	Percentage
Male	9,447	62.9
Female	5,432	36.2
NA	145	1.0
Age (years)	Number	Percentage
Under 1	1,198	12.3
1–4	4,205	27.0
5–9	4,008	25.6
10–14	3,596	22.7
15+	2,017	12.4

Source: National Pediatric Trauma Registry (NPTR) as cited in Savage (2000).

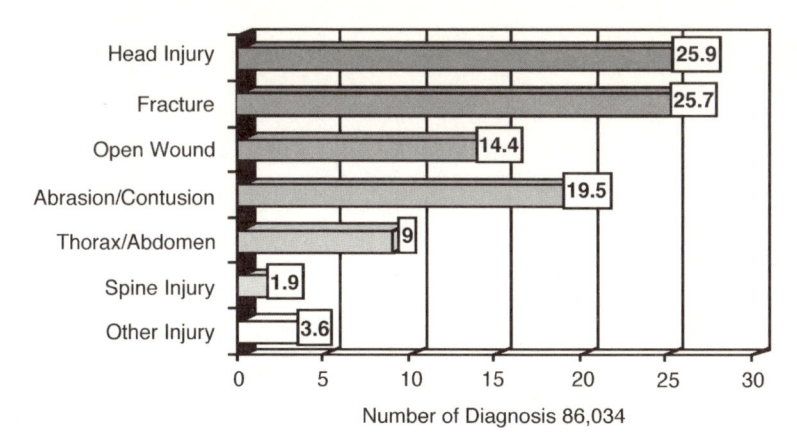

```
Head Injury        25.9
Fracture           25.7
Open Wound         14.4
Abrasion/Contusion 19.5
Thorax/Abdomen     9
Spine Injury       1.9
Other Injury       3.6
```
Number of Diagnosis 86,034

Fig. 1. Incidence of Traumatic Head Injury Compared to Other Categories of Acute Injury.

Source: Savage, R. C. (2000 August). An analysis of 15,024 children with TBI. Paper presented at the Brain Injury Association 20th Symposium, Chicago, IL.

injury, TBI is the most common diagnosis (see Fig. 1). For example, the incidence of TBI is twelve times greater than spinal cord injury in children and adolescents.

As illustrated in Fig. 2, motor vehicle crashes and falls exceeded all other mechanisms for injury, with pedestrian and bicycle accidents also involving significant numbers. Many children included in the NPTR database were not using restraints (seatbelts) or helmets (bicycle, motor cycle, and all-terrain vehicle recreational vehicle) at the time of their injuries. Percentages range from a high of 43.4% using motorcycle restraints, to a low of 8.3% for bicycles.

CLASSIFICATION OF TRAUMATIC BRAIN INJURY

There are both medical and educational classifications of TBI, and educators and families must fully grasp the nature and severity of the child's injury (Kraemer & Blacher, 1997). While there is not an exact correlation between medical classification of TBI and outcome, in general students with the most severe injuries do the poorest in terms of overall physical, cognitive, and emotional functioning.

Medical Classification of TBI.

Using the medical model, brain injuries are classified according to level of injury severity (i.e. mild, moderate, and severe). In practice, medical personnel may use different methods for arriving at these classifications, but one method commonly

[Bar chart showing mechanism of injury percentages:
MV Crash 27.1%, Motorcycle 1.2%, Bicycle 9.7%, ATV/RV 1.8%, Pedestrian 13.7%, Gunshot 0.8%, Cutting/Piercing 0.2%, Beating 4.4%, Sport 5.0%, Struck 4.4%, Animal 1.5%, Machine 0.1%, Caught 0.1%, Fall 26.5%, Other 3.6%]

Motor Vehicle Restraint:	37.4%
Motorcycle Restraint:	43.4%
Bicycle Helmet:	8.3%
All-Terrain/Recreational Vehicle Restraint:	21.6%

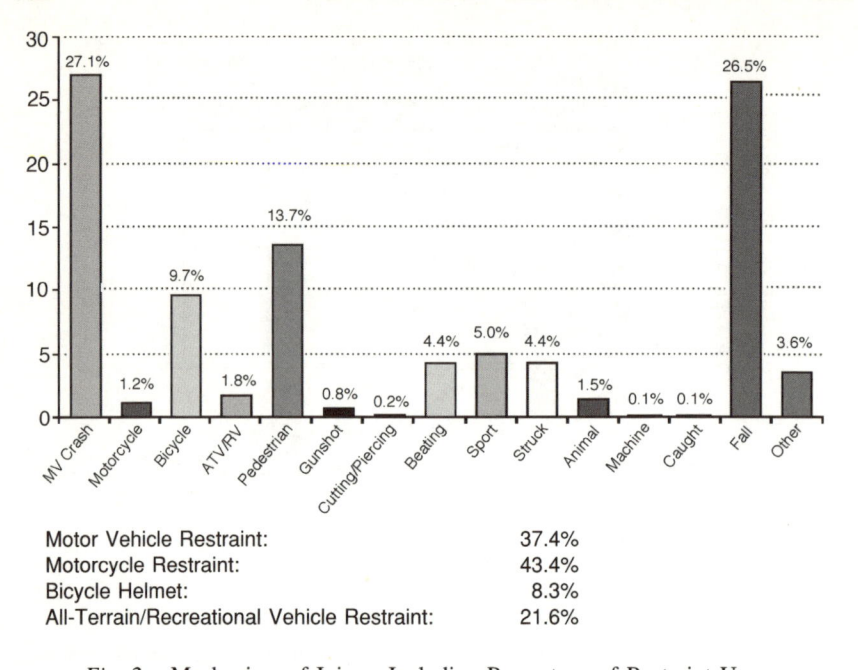

Fig. 2. Mechanism of Injury, Including Percentage of Restraint Usage.

Source: Savage, R. C. (2000 August). An analysis of 15,024 children with TBI. Paper presented at the Brain Injury Association 20th Symposium, Chicago, IL.

employed is the *Glasgow Coma Scale* (GCS) (Teasdale & Jennett, 1974). Since the traditional benchmark classification of TBI is an alteration in the level of consciousness, the GCS is used to quantify the depth of coma based on the patient's response to commands and stimuli upon admission to the hospital. Using the GCS, mild brain injury is defined as a score of 13–15, moderate brain injury is a score of 9–12, and severe brain injury is a GCS of 3–8. While the GCS does not necessarily predict level of outcome, studies have shown a relationship between lower GCS scores and poor outcomes (Weiner & Weinberg, 2000). It should be pointed out that the accepted severity classifications for TBI using the GCS are based primarily upon adult cases, thus the relationship between GCS and outcome in children is more tentative (Savage, 1991). While separate scales for rating severity of injury have been developed for children (e.g. *Children's Coma Scale*, *Children's Rancho Los Amigos Recovery Scale*), they are not routinely employed. In addition to using level of consciousness as an indicator of severity of brain injury, medical personnel may also factor in symptoms of brain injury, neuroimaging results, and predicted outcome. Using this method, the severity of a TBI is commonly defined as follows.

Mild brain injury:
- brief or no loss of consciousness.
- signs of concussion (e.g. headache, drowsiness, and confusion).
- evidence of post-concussion syndrome (e.g. memory and attention problems, irritability, fatigue, and sleep difficulties)
- good recovery within 6–8 weeks, often within hours or days.

Moderate brain injury:
- coma lasting more than 20–30 minutes, but less than 24 hours.
- possible skull fractures with bruising and bleeding.
- focal findings on electroencephalogram (EEG), computed axial tomography (CAT) scan, or magnetic resonance imaging (MRI).
- some long-term problems in one or more areas.

Severe brain injury:
- coma lasting more than 24 hours, often lasting days or weeks.
- evidence of contusion (brain tissue damage) or intracranial hematoma (bleeding within the brain).
- focal findings on EEG, CAT scan, or MRI.
- long-term impairments.

Classification systems such as the aforementioned ones can be used as general indicators for severity, but they should not be regarded as exact science. Differences in diagnostic procedures and practice patterns can affect severity classification (Torner, Choi & Barnes, 1999), and the medical definition of the terms is not consistent throughout the medical literature. Furthermore, as mentioned in relation to the GCS, accepted classifications are based primarily on adult cases, so their application to children may be less predictive. Several major studies of children with TBI (Ewing-Cobbs et al., 1997; Klonoff, Clark & Klonoff, 1993; Yeates et al., 1999) have shown that even a so-called mild brain injury can create significant learning and behavior problems for some children. Thus, present medical definitions of mild, moderate, and severe brain injuries may not be the best indicators of outcome or potential for school-related problems. For example, children with mild TBI may experience problems months or even years after the injury that are just as disabling as problems experienced by students with more severe injuries (Savage & Wolcott, 1995).

Educational Classification of TBI

In 1990, traumatic brain injury was added to the list of disabilities that qualify students for special education services under the Individuals with Disabilities

Education Act (IDEA). The purpose of creating a distinct category was to enable educators to better identify and classify a distinct group of school-age children, and consequently more efficiently plan educational programs for these students. The following definition of TBI is given in IDEA:

> "Traumatic brain injury" means an acquired injury to the brain caused by an external physical force, resulting in total or partial functional disability or psychosocial impairment, or both, that adversely affects a child's educational performance. The term applies to open or closed head injuries resulting in impairments in one or more areas, such as cognition; language; memory; attention; reasoning; abstract thinking; problem-solving; sensory, perceptual and motor abilities; psychosocial behavior; physical functions; information processing; and speech. The term does not apply to brain injuries that are congenital or degenerative, or brain injuries induced by birth trauma (Section 300.7b[12] 1999).

A recent survey of state education agencies (Markowitz & Linehan, 2001) revealed that the majority of states adhere to the federal definition of TBI for qualifying students for special education services. Although a few states have adopted a broader definition, in most states the TBI category is limited to students who have received open or closed head injuries caused by an external physical force. Therefore, students with brain injuries from "internal" occurrences such as brain infections, strokes, anoxia, brain tumors, neurotoxic poisonings, or metabolic disorders do not qualify for special services under the educational definition of TBI. Nevertheless the learning needs of students with brain injuries from external physical force and those with brain injuries from internal occurrences are often very similar, although their course of recoveries may differ. Perhaps the most profound similarity between the two groups is the sudden onset of disability. Prior to the injury, the majority of these students had a history of normal development that is drastically altered following the injury. Additionally, both populations of students face similar issues with school re-entry, ongoing medical needs, and coordination of medical and educational therapies.

AGE EFFECTS ON TRAUMATIC BRAIN INJURY

It was once believed that children were resilient little beings who could "bounce back" after even severe brain trauma. However, the theory that younger children recover more successfully from brain injury than older children or adults because of greater plasticity of the brain has been challenged with new evidence showing that young children are particularly vulnerable to the effects of TBI (Taylor & Alden, 1997). To appreciate the profound effects of TBI in a child, one must keep in mind that the injury occurs to a developing brain. That is, the course of recovery from the injury is superimposed on the child's ongoing process of development, in contrast to the recovery process of an injured adult, whose brain is mature. Since young children's brains are still developing during the first years of life, the effects of an early trauma may not be evident for some time. For example, preschoolers with injuries to their frontal lobes often look fine within a few weeks or months after an injury. However, later in life, when these children are challenged by more complex integrated activities or demonstrate difficulties in acquiring new learning skills, subtle psychological deficits or more serious cognitive and behavioral problems often become apparent (Valko, 1999). Therefore, it is important to assess and monitor the effects of early brain injury (Ewing-Cobbs et al., 1997; Fletcher, Ewing-Cobbs, Francis & Levin, 1995).

New research utilizing advanced scanning technology is identifying how a child's brain grows and matures from birth through adolescence. In particular, five peak maturation periods have been identified in normally developing children. Thus in addition to the type of brain injury sustained and the region of the brain affected, the child's age at the time of injury is of critical importance. The five peak maturation mileposts are:

- ages 1–6
- ages 7–10
- ages 11–13
- ages 14–17
- ages 18–21

As illustrated in Fig. 3, the greatest percentage of brain maturation occurs in the early years, birth through age five. Thus, injury to a child's brain before age five may be the most devastating. This may be why infants and toddlers

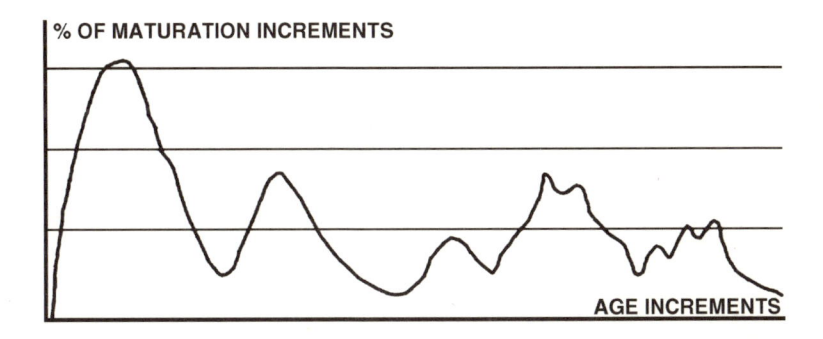

Fig. 3. Percentage of Brain Maturation Increments Compared with Years of Age.

Source: Savage, R. C. (2000 August). An analysis of 15,024 children with TBI. Paper presented at the Brain Injury Association 20th Symposium, Chicago, IL.

who have suffered severe head trauma from being "shaken and impacted" have such poor outcomes (Duhaime, Christian, Rorke & Zimmerman, 1998) and why children who sustain frontal lobe injuries early in life tend to develop long-term psychosocial and behavioral problems (Eslinger, Grattan, Damasio & Damasio, 1992). For many developmental psychologists and neuropsychologists, this is not ground-breaking news, as cognitive and social development theorized by Piaget, Luria, and others has been understood for years. However, whereas previously scholars studied child development by observing the "outside" world of the child, they are now able to look "inside" the child to see if the psychology and neurology support each other. Obviously, they do. Unfortunately, it may well mean that for a child whose brain is injured early in his/her life, or at a critical developmental milestone, the real problems for the child are "yet to be seen."

PERSISTING EFFECTS OF BRAIN INJURY ON A CHILD

Children who have sustained a TBI may experience a number of challenges – physically, cognitively, and behaviorally. The pattern of deficits resulting from a TBI depends on a number of factors, including age, mechanism of injury, pathophysiology of injury, preinjury personality and ability, family support and the availability of appropriate services (Valko, 1999). The effects of injury are most pronounced in the period immediately following the injury, with the first 6 months following an injury being characterized by early rapid recovery. During this period, many of the initial effects resolve, so the child may appear to be free of major aftereffects of the injury. However, six months to a year (or longer) after a moderate to severe TBI (and sometimes even mild brain injury), the child may continue to exhibit a variety of physical, sensory, cognitive, and behavioral sequelae. Long-term follow-up studies indicate that despite improvements in functional adaptation, cognitive and behavioral disorders may persist (Klonoff et al., 1993). These deficits will affect daily functioning and have a major impact on educational achievement. Educators must be familiar with these problems so they can evaluate their implications and modify the student's educational program accordingly.

Physical Effects

Following brain injury, a student may experience reduced stamina and fatigue due to prolonged hospitalization and inactivity, seizures, or medications. Motor impairments may occur as a result of damage to the brain and can include spasticity, ataxia (loss of ability to coordinate smooth movements), or apraxia (inability to plan and carry out movements purposefully on command), tremors, and disturbances of balance and gate. Approximately 5% of children have seizures following a TBI, with the incidence increasing to over 50% depending on medical variables (Hahn, Fuchs, Flannery, Barthel & McLone, 1988).

Sensory Effects

A significant incidence of hearing loss and visual impairment follows TBI in children (Michaud, Duhaime & Jaffe, 1999). Post-traumatic hearing loss is most commonly the result of a fracture of the temporal bone. Depending on the type of fracture, conductive hearing loss or sensorineural deficits can occur, with prognosis for recovery being better for conductive than for sensorineural hearing impairments. Visual deficits following TBI include diplopia (double vision), problems of visual tracking, or visual field defects.

Cognitive Effects

Memory impairments and disorders of attention have been identified as the most common cognitive effects of TBI (Ewing-Cobbs & Fletcher, 1987; Ewing-Cobbs et al., 1997; Kaufmann, Fletcher, Levin & Miner, 1993; Levin & Eisenberg, 1979). Impairments in executive functions such as organization, planning, problem solving, and judgment have also been noted (Garth, Anderson & Wrennal, 1997; Levin et al., 1993). Additionally, TBI has been found to be associated with decreased speed of information processing (Beers, 1992). Since TBI has the most profound effect on learning of new information, even mild TBI can lead to academic impairment (Ewing-Cobbs et al 1991; Faye et al., 1994; Kinsella et al., 1997).

Language Effects

Following TBI, both expressive and receptive language problems may occur. Dysarthria (oral motor dysfunction) and dysphasia (difficulty with naming and word retrieval) are the most common expressive language problems in children with TBI (Michaud, Duhaime & Lazar, 1997). Receptive language impairments result from auditory-perceptual problems and are most affected in complex listening situations.

Behavioral/Emotional Effects

Research has shown that students with TBI tend to experience more behavior problems than their typically developing peers (Asarnow, Satz, Light, Lewis & Neumann, 1991; Brown, Chadwick, Shaffer, Rutter & Traub, 1981; Greenspan & MacKenzie, 1994; Parker, 1994). Behavior problems following TBI may include overactivity, impulsivity, low frustration tolerance, irritability, apathy, poor anger control, aggression, and social disinhibition. Injury to the frontal lobe is associated with impairments in attention, executive functioning, reasoning, and problem solving.

Table 2 provides examples of how possible long-term effects of brain injury manifest themselves in the classroom setting and affect a child's educational functioning. Because of the severe nature of deficits many children experience following a brain injury, the child may not be able to succeed in school without some form of specialized programming and services. The provision of appropriate services for such students requires coordinated, interdisciplinary planning involving all parties, including the health care providers, the educators, the family and child, and the community.

DEVELOPING EDUCATIONAL PROGRAMS

Integrating Special Education and Rehabilitation Services

It is critical for educators to understand that brain injury is a medical condition that is treated by both medical and education professionals. Many students with moderate and severe brain injuries re-enter schools after being treated in hospitals and/or rehabilitation centers. These students will have received medical services from a variety of physicians (trauma specialists, neurologists, and physiatrists) and allied health professionals (e.g. nurses, physical therapists, occupational therapists, speech/language therapists, neuropsychologists, and behavioral psychologists) (Savage, 1997). Most students with brain injuries return to their schools still requiring ongoing medical management and rehabilitation services. The "medical" impact of the brain injury on students affects their learning. Therefore, students requiring special education services need individualized education plans that incorporate their ongoing medical needs (e.g. medication management for seizures or spasticity; physical, occupational, and/or speech/language therapies; cognitive rehabilitation). For example, a comparison study of 50 children with autism and 50 children with brain injuries found that the students with autism only required 1–4 hours of consultative physical, occupational, and speech/language therapies per month, whereas the

Table 2. Possible Long-Term Effects of Brain Injury on Classroom Functioning.

Cognitive Effects

Memory

The student
- is unable to recall previously learned information that serves as the foundation for new learning;
- cannot remember a series of two- to three-step directions;
- is unable to grasp new concepts without repeated exposure;
- has difficulty recalling the day's schedule, what was assigned for homework, or what materials to bring to class.

Attention and Concentration

The student
- is distracted by normal classroom activity;
- has difficulty staying on topic during a class discussion;
- is unable to complete a task without prompting;
- blurts out answers in the middle of a class session;
- becomes fatigued by mid-afternoon and appears to be uninterested in activities.

Higher-Level Problem Solving

The student
- has difficulty organizing and completing long-term projects;
- lacks the ability to sequence the steps necessary to plan and complete an activity;
- is unable to come up with solutions to problem situations (e.g., lost lunch money);
- has difficulty drawing conclusions from facts presented.

Language Skills

The student
- has difficulty taking turns in a conversation;
- is unable to summarize and articulate thoughts;
- talks around subject or use indefinite words;
- does not understand the meaning of a conversation when figures of speech or metaphors are used.

Sensorimotor Effects

The student
- takes an inordinate amount of time to produce written material;
- is unable to take notes while listening to the class lecture;
- has difficulty copying information from the board or overhead projector;
- has difficulty completing simple math problems when presented with a worksheet full of problems;
- completes only problems on one half of the paper because of difficulty seeing objects in part of the visual field;
- becomes disoriented in the hallway and has difficulty finding classroom.

Behavioral/Emotional Effects

The student
- says or does socially inappropriate things;
- is unable to start or stop an activity without assistance;
- impulsively leaves seat or classroom;
- becomes easily frustrated;
- is unaware of and denies any impairments resulting from the injury.

students with brain injuries required 1–4 hours of direct therapy each week. Also, the students with autism were prescribed a total of 12 medications averaging one dose per day, whereas the students with brain injuries were prescribed 108 different medications with 312 doses per day (Savage, 1998).

The demands upon the school system require a different model that stretches beyond more traditional special education programs. Such a model proposes an integrated approach that combines rehabilitation therapies with special education therapies to avoid gaps in service delivery (Kaufman & Blanchon, 1996). Conceptually, the answer to the questions "What is 'rehabilitation' and what is 'special education'?" becomes blurred when providing services for these students. While hospitals treat these students in their initial course of recovery, it is ultimately the schools that become the long-term providers of services for this population. Thus, full integration of rehabilitation and special education therapies into a more cohesive model will potentially better serve the multiple needs of students with TBI.

For example, students with brain injuries commonly have problems with new learning. As a result, they need to be taught not only what to learn (i.e. academic content) but how to learn it (i.e. information processing). The use of neuropsychological reports that specify how students best learn and what kinds of compensatory strategies they need in order to learn will help educators create the appropriate instructional strategies (Lazar & Mendalino, 1995). Teachers who study cognitive rehabilitation, a common therapy in brain injury rehabilitation, will find it offers many strategies to help students strengthen attention/concentration skills, improve memory skills, and utilize problem-solving skills. For students with behavioral challenges, methodologies from applied behavioral psychology, especially the use of antecedent management techniques, will help teachers understand the reasons for particular behaviors and subsequently develop appropriate behavioral management plans. Since many students will need various medications, special educators also need to understand how these medications work, the side effects of the medications (e.g. fatigue and irritability), and how these medications impact the student's learning (Singer & Savage, 2000).

Preparing for School Re-Entry

The process of integrating educational and rehabilitation services begins with preparing for the child's return to school following the injury. This transition from hospital to school requires a well-coordinated plan that involves the hospital/rehabilitation staff, school, parents, and the student (Mira & Tyler, 1991; Savage, 1991; Ylvisaker, Hartwick & Stevens, 1991). The school reintegration process begins as soon as a student is admitted to a health care facility. Ideally, hospital staff immediately inform school personnel that they are caring for one of their students and the family and/or attending physician formally requests that the school begin the evaluation process. However, hospital staff are not always efficient at recognizing the need for specialized educational services or planning for school re-entry, so school personnel must take an active role in this process by gaining parental permission to contact the hospital staff as soon as they are aware that an injury has occurred. School personnel can then begin communicating with the child's doctors, therapists, hospital social worker, hospital teacher, psychologist, and neuropsychologist to gather relevant information and to start planning for the child's return to school. Such information includes mechanism and date of injury; child's current medical condition; anticipated discharge date; child's present cognitive and behavioral functioning; anticipated long-term medical needs (including medications, need for special equipment, environmental accommodations); and anticipated therapy needs (DePompei, Blosser, Savage & Lash, 1999).

To gain additional information on the child's functioning, it is recommended that school personnel observe the student during therapy sessions or in the hospital classroom and attend the hospital predischarge meeting. Information gathered from these meetings, coupled with results of hospital-based evaluations (e.g. neuropsychological, speech/language, physical/occupational therapy) helps school personnel decide if the child is in need of special education services and determine how to best coordinate such services with the hospital or rehabilitation facility (Blosser & DePompei, 1994; Savage, 1991; Savage & Wolcott, 1995; Ylvisaker et al., 1991). This evaluation is the important first step in initiating the special education process for identification and classification purposes (i.e. does this student need special education services and how is he/she best classified?). Unfortunately, many students are not referred to the school system for evaluation but are merely discharged back to school with little if any support services in place (DiScala, Osberg & Savage, 1997).

Developing the Individual Education Plan (IEP)

After the student has been determined to be eligible for special education and has appropriately been identified as having a TBI, the school can begin to develop the IEP. Because of the underlying medical cause of the disability, the resulting cognitive and behavioral deficits, and the evolving needs of the students, IEPs written for students with TBI require procedures that vary from traditional IEP development. For example, information from a variety of sources and disciplines outside the school system needs to be translated to determine present levels of functioning; goals need to address cognitive processes rather than strictly academic impairments; and IEP reviews need to be conducted more frequently (e.g. every 2–4 months initially) to address dramatically changing needs. In addition, the initial IEP should be a joint venture among the health care facility, the school, and the family.

The IEP should reflect the cognitive, psychosocial, and neuromotor needs of the student using a functionally based and holistic approach that enables the student to become increasingly more involved in school, family, and community as the recovery process continues. In addition, a student's IEP should designate the involvement of vocational rehabilitation and community transition services by outside state and local agencies to ensure continuity of services prior to graduating from the public school system, if applicable. In the case of students whose brain injuries are mild and who are not showing evidence of cognitive or behavioral deficits, special education programming may not be necessary immediately. Such students may only need to be monitored or to have their schedules modified for a period of time to ensure that any neurologic sequela has been resolved. However, it is important to remember that the currently used medical definitions of mild, moderate, and severe brain injury may not be the best indicators of outcome or potential for school-related problems. Therefore, it is crucial that the school nurse, classroom teachers, and family closely monitor the child's performance and reevaluate the need for services if problems emerge. The use of a protocol for school re-entry following mild brain injury, such as the one developed by Ylvisaker, Feeney and Mullins (1995), will help to ensure that these students are appropriately monitored by school personnel.

The possibility of delayed developmental consequence of TBI, as well as rapidly changing neurologic functioning in children, necessitates ongoing assessment of students with TBI (Ylvisaker, Chorazy, Feeney & Russell, 1999). Initial evaluation information may only provide an accurate description of the student for a short period of time. Ongoing functional assessment of the student in the school environment is required to accurately determine the student's current functioning and needs.

Instructional Interventions

In conjunction with developing the IEP, educators must identify teaching strategies that meet the specialized needs of the student. Although long-term deficits following TBI are well documented, noticeably lacking is empirical research on the effectiveness of particular instructional practices for dealing with subsequent learning problems. This means that teachers should examine effective teaching practices and proven instructional strategies for varied populations of students with and without disabilities to find what works best with a particular student (Ylvisaker et al., 2001). Ylvisaker and colleagues recommended identifying students by functional need and connecting identified needs with research-based strategies. For example, organizational impairments following TBI will necessitate proven instructional strategies for organization, such as task analysis and advance organizational support; decreased speed of processing will necessitate using appropriate pacing strategies; and the possibility of gaps in the student's knowledge base will require teaching to mastery.

Other empirically supported techniques such as strategy instruction (Deshler, Ellis & Lenz, 1996) often prove useful for TBI-related impairments, including impaired acquisition of new learning and organizational functioning deficits. Additionally, components of techniques such as Direct Instruction and Circle of Friends, which have been validated in students with developmental disabilities, have also been proven effective for addressing specific deficits areas for students with TBI (Cooley, Glang & Voss, 1997; Glang, Singer, Cooley & Tish, 1992). By identifying the student's strengths and deficits and matching them with validated instructional strategies, educators will have a wide range of effective teaching practices with which to begin programming. Evaluation of the effects of instructional methods is important for all students, but Ylvisaker and Feeney (1998) emphasized that this type of active experimentation is particularly important to identify best educational programs for students with TBI. In conjunction with matching specific strategies to identified needs, a number of accommodations should be considered to address problem areas. Tyler, Blosser and DePompei (1999) provided the following examples of common deficit areas and suggested techniques for dealing with them.

Attention/Concentration

To improve attention/concentration, educators should:

- Reduce distractions in student's work area (remove extra materials).
- Divide work into smaller sections and have student complete one section at a time.
- Provide timelines for task completion.
- Ask student to orally summarize information that has just been presented.
- Establish nonverbal cueing system (e.g. eye contact, touch, etc.) to remind student to pay attention.

Memory

To improve memory, educators should:

- Frequently repeat and summarize information.
- Teach student to use devices such as sticky notes, calendars, and assignment books as self-reminders to compensate for memory problems.
- Teach student to categorize or chunk information to aid retention.
- Demonstrate techniques such as mental rehearsal and use of special words or examples as reminders.
- Link new information to student's relevant prior knowledge.

Organization

To improve organization, educators should:

- Provide student with: (a) additional time for review; (b) written checklists of steps for complex tasks; (c) written or oral cues for organizing an activity (e.g. step one, step two . . .); (d) practice sequencing material; (e) color-coded materials for each class (book, notebook, supplies); (f) assigned person to review schedule at start of school day and organize materials for each class; and (g) outlines coordinated to class lectures (require student to take notes within each section).

Following Directions

To help improve student's ability to follow directions, educators should:

- Provide oral as well as written instructions.
- Ask student to repeat instructions back to teacher or a peer.
- Underline or highlight significant part of directions on written assignments.
- Rewrite complex directions into simple steps.
- Ask students to perform task, check for accuracy, then give immediate feedback.

Behavioral Interventions

Behavioral problems are common following TBI. Consequently, school personnel must have a well-established plan for managing behavior when the child returns and be ready to modify and revise the plan as the student's needs change. In developing an intervention plan, educators must be aware that a number of factors may influence behavioral functioning following TBI. These factors can include: (a) preinjury behaviors; (b) damage to behavior-regulating areas of the brain (i.e. frontal lobes); (c) cognitive impairments; and (d) emotional reaction to a life-altering injury. Because a student's behavior problems may be the result of a variety of factors, an important first step in developing and intervention plan is to conduct a functional analysis of the student's behavior (Feeney & Ylvisaker, 1997). Accurate assessment of the rate, cause, and function of a particular behavior provides important information for choosing intervention strategies (Deaton, 1997).

Since many challenging behaviors following TBI are the result of frontal lobe dysfunction and cognitive impairments, traditional behavioral management approaches that focus on consequential management of behavior may be inappropriate (Ylvisaker & Feeney, 1998). Instead, Ylvisaker, Feeney, and Szekers (1998) advocated a positive, antecedent-focused, communication-based approach to problem behavior following TBI. This type of approach seeks to prevent behavior problems by providing the student with positive cognitive and behavioral supports. While the use of positive, antecedent-focused behavior supports has been validated with a subpopulation of students with TBI (e.g. Feeney & Ylvisaker, 1995), there is limited research to support the use of other specific behavioral interventions for students with TBI. However, as in the case with identifying instructional strategies, if students are identified by functional need, a number of strategies that have been empirically supported with children who have similar behavior problems becomes available (Ylvisaker et al., 2001). Critical to identification of strategies to address specific behavioral problems is the need to adapt such strategies in accordance with the student's current level of cognitive functioning (Kehle, Clark & Jenson, 1996).

PLANNING FOR TRANSITIONS

The need for transition planning for students with disabilities is well documented in the literature (Halpern, 1985; Patton & Blalock, 1996; Wehman, 1996). Transition planning for students with TBI differs from traditional transition planning because it involves school re-entry planning following the injury, within-school transition planning, as well as the transition from school to adulthood. Thus, planning and programming for students with brain injury is an ongoing process, that begins with the school reintegration process and continues through transition from high school to postsecondary education, employment, and community living. Ongoing monitoring and planning for transitions is critical because the impact of the injury to an individual's brain is most likely to continue to show up even years after the injury itself (Eslinger et al., 1992; Klonoff et al., 1993; Price, Doffner, Stowe & Mesulam, 1990). Additionally, new problems may arise, as the demands of school and life in general become greater and more challenging for the student.

The ongoing involvement of hospital and rehabilitation staff is of paramount importance in the transition planning process because of the child's ongoing medical, rehabilitation, psychological, and cognitive needs. Information gained from follow up medical, rehabilitation, and neuropsychological evaluations provide valuable information to assist the school in determining current functioning and assessing progress. Ongoing communication between school staff and the child's physicians, psychologist, and therapists allows room for discussing any concerns that arise (e.g. late-onset seizures), and provides important data to evaluate a current course of treatment (e.g. behavior charting of the effects of medication on behavioral performance).

Within School Transitions

Following the child's return to school, a series of transitions will take place over the years before the child finishes high school. Such transitions include passage from grade level to grade level, the change from elementary to middle and then high school, and finally, graduation. While these transitions can be difficult at times for any student, for students with brain injury, they can be particularly troublesome. The difficulties students encounter may be partially due to cognitive and behavioral impairments that often occur following a brain injury, including problems of adjusting to changes in environments, routines, and expectations. Additionally, as the child progresses through the educational system, the increasing complexity of content, coupled with requirements for higher-level thinking skills and more independent learning, may cause new difficulties to surface (Tyler & Wilkerson, 1999).

Tyler, Wilkerson and DePompei (2002) offered the following suggestions for helping to ensure smooth in-school transitions, namely:

- Recognize the need for transition planning.
- Begin transition planning early.
- Assess the new environment and determine student's needs.
- Prepare receiving teachers (e.g. brain injury inservice).
- Provide teachers with specific information about the student.
- Involve ancillary personnel (medical, psychological, rehabilitation).
- Continually monitor the student's progress.

Transition to Postsecondary Education

For students choosing to pursue postsecondary education (e.g. vocational school, community college, junior college, and four-year university), school personnel must devote a considerable amount of time to: (a) examining the available options; (b) determining the most suitable placement; and (c) preparing the student to make the transition. Students who require special education services in high school are likely to need special assistance or accommodations at the postsecondary level. Individuals with brain injury can access such services under Section 504 of the Rehabilitation Act in postsecondary settings. Section 504 requires all postsecondary institutions that receive federal education funds to provide accommodations to enable students with disabilities to participate. Accommodations are made on a case-by-case basis and may include untimed exams, extended time on assignments, tape-recorded textbooks, and preferential seating. The types of accommodations provided are determined by individual institutions and, therefore, vary widely among schools. Therefore, evaluating a particular institution's capacity to provide services needed by a particular student is critical (Goodwin & Larson, 1999). In addition to providing required accommodations, some colleges offer special services such as study skills classes, tutoring in subject areas, support groups and special counselors. These services are offered voluntarily and may involve a fee. Finally, a limited number of colleges offer special programs designed specifically for students with brain injury. Information about such programs is available from the national office of the Brain Injury Association (BIA) and local state Brain Injury Association chapters. [Note: The BIA's web address is www.biausa.org].

Transition to Work and Community

In planning for transition to employment, coordinating with community vocational resources is essential (Bergland, 1996). The transition planning team must be aware of and informed about the range of available vocational services. For example, students with brain injury may be eligible for services from their state vocational rehabilitation agency, including aptitude assessment, post-high school training opportunities, and supervised trial job placement. Transition to employment planning should include vocational assessment and counseling to help identify occupations that would be most suitable for an individual. A strict commitment to using the assessment information coupled with student's preferences and goals is essential in establishing vocational objectives (Tyler & Mira, 1999).

In planning for the transition from school to community living, linkages with adult service providers must be established during the high school years. Such linkages include social security programs, independent living centers, and residential service providers. Coordination with programs that provide assistance to adults with disabilities (e.g. state head injury waiver programs) is essential. Transition planners need to be aware of the type and kind of services available, qualification requirements, availability of services at the local level, and procedures for completing applications. Because some programs have waiting lists for services, it is important to begin planning well in advance of the need for such services. The process of determining eligibility for services should be facilitated by the student's transition planning team.

TEACHER TRAINING FOR STUDENTS WITH TRAUMATIC BRAIN INJURY

As the field of special education continues to move toward progressive inclusion, all teachers must be prepared to help accommodate students with special needs in general education classrooms. Because students with TBI receive educational services in a variety of settings, both general and special education teachers need to be knowledgeable about TBI. Moreover, special education teachers need an in-depth understanding of all aspects of TBI to be prepared to provide consultation to general education teachers, related services personnel, and parents (Tyler, 1997). While it is generally agreed that specialized training is essential for meeting the needs of individuals with TBI (Becker, Harrell & Keller, 1993), in the past very few educators receive training specifically addressing these students (Ylvisaker et al., 1991). In addition, information about TBI has only been minimally addressed in most teacher training programs. Indeed, the absence of teacher preparation in the area of TBI has been identified by state educational agencies as one of the major educational issues in the provision of services to such students (Janus, 1996).

The educational success of students with TBI is dependent on the availability of appropriately trained educators. Teacher preparation programs must meet this need by incorporating TBI training into their curriculum for all educators and offering in-depth training for special educators who will be serving as consultants to general education teachers. School systems must supplement this preparation by providing ongoing in-service training to upgrade teacher skills (Tyler, 1997). In addition, school systems must ensure that teachers have access to a TBI specialist for ongoing consultation, as well as access to literature and other instructional materials related to TBI (Ylvisaker et al., 2001). Increasingly, state departments of education are realizing the need for specialized training in TBI, and a number of states have implemented specialized training models (e.g. Kansas, Iowa & Oregon), and many have developed specific training materials for teachers (Savage 1997). Such training programs are necessary in all states to ensure that educators have the knowledge and skills to provide effective educational programs for students with TBI.

SUMMARY

Educators are faced with a number of unique challenges when programming for students with TBI. Issues of widespread lack of recognition of TBI among educators and differing medical and educational classification systems complicate identification of this population of students. Once students are properly identified, the challenge of developing appropriate programs for individual students with TBI is compounded by the lack of research based instructional and behavioral intervention strategies designed specifically for this student population. However, despite these challenges, effective educational programs can be developed for students with TBI if educators recognize the features that distinguish this population of students from other disability groups, address the functional needs of individual students, and adhere to specialized planning procedures. An understanding of the influence of age at time of injury and typical patterns of functioning following TBI provides educators with requisite information with which to begin planning. Identification of specific needs of individual students coupled with the selection of effective teaching strategies to meet such needs enables educators to design effective intervention plans. Additionally, observance of specialized procedures, such as early and ongoing collaborative planning between health care and school systems, frequent IEP reviews, and extensive transition planning, as well as adequate teacher training further ensures the educational success of students with TBI.

REFERENCES

Asarnow, R. F., Satz, P., Light, R., Lewis, R., & Neumann, E. (1991). Behavior problems and adaptive functioning in children with mild and severe closed head injury. *Journal of Pediatric Psychology, 16*, 543–555.

Becker, H., Harrell, W. T., & Keller, L. (1993). A survey of professional and paraprofessional training needs for traumatic brain injury rehabilitation. *Journal of Head Trauma Rehabilitation, 8*(1), 88–101.

Beers, S. R. (1992). Cognitive effects of mild head injury in children and adolescents. *Neuropsychology Review, 3*(4), 281–320.

Bergland, M. (1996). Transition from school to adult life: Key to the future. In: A. Goldberg (Ed.), *Acquired Brain Injury in Childhood and Adolescence* (pp. 171–194). Springfield, IL: Charles C. Thomas.

Blosser, J. L., & DePompei, R. (2002). *Pediatric traumatic brain injury: Proactive intervention* (2nd ed.). New York: Delmar.

Brain Injury Association (1999). *Fact and figures on pediatric brain injury*. Alexandria, VA: Author.
Brown, G., Chadwick, O., Shaffer, D., Rutter, M., & Traub, M. (1981). A prospective study of children with head injuries: Psychiatric sequelae. *Psychological Medicine, 11*, 63–78.
Cooley, E. A., Glang, A., & Voss, J. (1997). Making connections: Helping children with ABI build friendships. In: A. Glang, G. H. S. Singer & B. Todis (Eds), *Children with Acquired Brain Injury: The School's Response* (pp. 255–275). Baltimore, MD: Paul H. Brookes.
Deaton, A. V. (1997). Understanding and overcoming the challenging behaviors of students with ABI. In: A. Glang, G. Singer & B. Todis (Eds), *Children with Acquired Brain Injury: The School's Response* (pp. 203–227). Baltimore, MD: Paul H. Brookes.
DePompei, R., Blosser, J., Savage, R., & Lash, M. (1999). *Back to school after a moderate to severe brain injury*. Wake Forrest, NC: L&A Publishing/Training.
Deshler, D. D., Ellis, E. S., & Lenz, B. K. (1996). *Teaching adolescents with learning disabilities: Strategies and methods* (2nd ed.). Denver, CO: Love.
DiScala, C., Osberg, J. S., & Savage, R. C. (1997). Children hospitalized for traumatic brain injury: Transition to postacute care. *Journal of Head Trauma Rehabilitation, 12*(2), 1–10.
Duhaime, A. C., Christian, C. W., Rorke, L. B., & Zimmerman, R. A. (1998). Non-accidental head injury in infants – the "shaken baby syndrome." *New England Journal of Medicine, 338*, 1822–1829.
Eslinger, P. J., Grattan, L. M., Damasio, H., & Damasio, A. R. (1992). Developmental consequences of childhood frontal lobe damage. *Archives of Neurology, 49*, 764–769.
Ewing-Cobbs, L., & Fletcher, J. M. (1987). Neuropsychological assessment of head injury in children. *Journal of Learning Disabilities, 20*, 526–535.
Ewing-Cobbs, L., Fletcher, J. M., Levin, H. S., Francis, D. J., Davidson, K., & Miner, M. E. (1997). Longitudinal neuropsychological outcome in infants and preschoolers with traumatic brain injury. *Journal of the International Neuropsychological Society, 3*, 581–591.
Ewing-Cobbs, L., Iovino, I., Fletcher, J. M., Miner, M. E., & Levin, H., S. (1991). Academic achievement following traumatic brain injury in children and adolescents. Paper presented at the 19th Annual Meeting of the International Neuropsychological Society (February), San Antonio, TX.
Faye, G., Jaffe, K., Polissar, N., Liao, S. Rivara, J., & Martin, K. (1994). Outcome of pediatric traumatic brain injury at three years: A cohort study. *Archives of Physical and Medical Rehabilitation, 73*, 540–547.
Feeney, T. J., & Ylvisaker, M. (1995). Choice and routine: Antecedent behavioral interventions for adolescents with severe traumatic brain injury. *Journal of Head Trauma Rehabilitation, 10*(3), 67–86.
Feeney, T. J., & Ylvisaker, M. (1997). A positive, communication-based approach to challenging behavior after ABI. In: A. Glang, G. H. S. Singer & B. Todis (Eds), *Children with Acquired Brain Injury: The School's Response* (pp. 229–254). Baltimore, MD: Paul H. Brookes.
Fletcher, J. M., Ewing-Cobbs, L., Francis, D. J., & Levin, H. S. (1995). Variability in outcomes after traumatic brain injury in children: A developmental perspective. In: S. H. Broman & M. E. Michel (Eds), *Traumatic Head Injury in Children* (pp. 3–21). New York: Oxford University Press.
Garth, J., Anderson, V., & Wrennal, J. (1997). Executive functions following moderate to severe frontal lobe injury: Impact of injury and age at injury. *Pediatric Rehabilitation, 1*(2), 99–108.
Glang, A., Singer, G., Cooley, E., & Tish, N. (1992). Tailoring Direct Instruction techniques for use with elementary students with brain injury. *Journal of Head Trauma Rehabilitation, 7*(4), 93–108.

Goodwin, J. E. B., & Larson, L. E. (1999). *Going to college when a student has a brain injury.* Wake Forrest, NC: L&A Publishing/Training.

Greenspan, A. I., & MacKenzie, E. J. (1994). Functional outcome after pediatric head injury. *Pediatrics, 94*(4), 425–432.

Hahn, Y. S., Fuchs, A. M., Flannery, A. M., Barthel, M. J., & McLone, D. G. (1988). Factors influencing post-traumatic seizures in children. *Neurosurgery, 22,* 864–867.

Halpern, A. S. (1985). Transition: A look at the foundations. *Exceptional Children, 51,* 479–486.

Janus, P. L. (1996). Educational issues in providing appropriate services for students with acquired brain injury. In: A. Goldberg (Ed.), *Acquired Brain Injury in Childhood and Adolescence* (pp. 195–202). Springfield, IL: Charles C. Thomas.

Kaufmann, P. M., Fletcher, J. M., Levin, H. S., & Miner, M. E. (1993). Attentional disturbance after pediatric closed head injury. *Journal of Child Neurology, 8,* 348–353.

Kaufman, J., & Blanchon, D. (1996). Managed care for children with special needs: A care coordination model. *Journal of Care Management, 2*(2), 46–59.

Kehle, T. J., Clark, E., & Jenson, W. R. (1996). Interventions for students with traumatic brain injury: Managing behavioral disturbances. *Journal of Learning Disabilities, 29*(6), 632–642.

Klonoff, H., Clark, C., & Klonoff, P. S. (1993). Long-term outcome of head injuries: A 23-year follow up study of children with head injuries. *Journal of Neurology, Neurosurgery & Psychiatry, 56,* 410–415.

Kinsella, G. J., Prior, M., Sawyer, M., Ong, B., Murtagh, D., Eisenmajer, R., Bryan, D., Anderson, V., & Klug, G. (1997). Predictors and indicators of academic outcome in children two years following traumatic brain injury. *Journal of the International Neuropsychological Society, 3,* 608–616.

Kraemer, B. R., & Blacher, J. (1997). An overview of educationally relevant effects, assessment, and school reentry. In: A. Glang, G. H. S. Singer & B. Todis (Eds), *Students with Acquired Brain Injury* (pp. 3–31). Baltimore, MD: Paul H. Brookes.

Lazar, M. F., & Mendalino, S. (1995). Cognitive outcome and behavioral adjustment following traumatic brain injury. *Journal of Head Trauma Rehabilitation, 10*(5), 55–63.

Levin, H. S., Culhane, K. A., Mendelsohn, E., Lilly, M. A., Bruce, D., Fletcher, J. M., Chapman, S. B., Harward, H., & Eisenberg, H. M. (1993). Cognition in relation to magnetic resonance imaging in head-injured children and adolescents. *Neurosurgery, 11,* 668–673.

Levin, H. S., & Eisenberg, H. M. (1979). Neuropsychological impairment after closed head injury in children and adolescents. *Journal of Pediatric Psychology, 4,* 389–402.

Markowitz, J., & Linehan, P. (2001, January). QTA: Traumatic brain injury. *Project Forum.* (Available from the National Association of State Directors of Special Education Inc., 1800 Diagonal Rd., Suite 320, Alexandria, VA 22314; http://www.nasdse.org).

Michaud, L. J., Duhaime, A. C., & Jaffee, K. M. (1999). Specific problems associated with pediatric brain injury. In: M. Rosenthal, J. Kreutzer, E. Griffith & B. Pentland (Eds), *Rehabilitation of the Adult and Child with Traumatic Brain Injury* (3rd ed., pp. 345–355). Philadelphia, PA: F. A. Davis Company.

Michaud, L. J., Duhaime, A. C., & Lazar, M. F. (1997). Traumatic brain injury. In: M. L. Batshaw (Ed.), *Children with Disabilities* (4th ed., pp. 595–617). Baltimore: Paul H. Brookes.

Mira, M. P., & Tyler, J. S. (1991). Students with traumatic brain injury: Making the transition from hospital to school. *Focus on Exceptional Children, 23*(5), 1–12.

Parker, R. S. (1994). Neurobehavioral outcome of children's mild traumatic brain injury. *Seminars in Neurology, 14*(1), 67–73.

Patton, J. R., & Blalock, G. (Eds) (1996). *Transition and students with learning disabilities: Facilitating the movement from school to adult life.* Austin, TX: Pro-Ed.

Price, B. H., Doffner, K. R., Stowe, R. M., & Mesulam, M. M. (1990). The comportmental learning disabilities of early frontal lobe damage. *Brain, 113*, 1383–1394.

Savage, R. C. (1991). Identification, classification, and placement issues for students with traumatic brain injuries. *Journal of Head Trauma Rehabilitation, 6*(1), 1–9.

Savage, R. C. (1997). Integrating rehabilitation and education services for school-age children with brain injuries. *Journal of Head Trauma Rehabilitation, 12*(2), 11–20.

Savage, R. C. (1998). Comparing students with autism and students with brain injuries. Unpublished manuscript, The May Center for Education and NeuroRehabilitation, Boston, MA.

Savage, R C. (2000). An analysis of 15,024 children with TBI. Paper presented at the Brain Injury Association 20th Symposium (August), Chicago, IL.

Savage, R., & Wolcott, G. (Eds) (1995). *An educator's manual: What educators need to know about students with traumatic brain injury.* Washington, D.C.: Brain Injury Association.

Singer, W., & Savage, R. C. (2000). *Medications for children with brain injuries.* Wake Forrest, NC: L&A Publishing/Training.

Taylor, H. G., & Alden, J. (1997). Age-related differences in outcomes following childhood brain insults: An introduction and overview. *Journal of the International Neuropsychological Society, 3*, 555–567.

Teasdale, G., & Jennett, B. (1974). Assessment of coma and impaired consciousness: A practical scale. *Lancet, 2*, 81–84.

Torner, J. C., Choi, S., & Barnes, T. Y. (1999). Epidemiology of head injuries. In: D. W. Marion (Ed.), *Traumatic Brain Injury* (pp. 9–29). New York: Thieme.

Tyler, J. S. (1997). Preparing educators to serve children with traumatic brain injury. In: A. Glang, G. H. S. Singer & B. Todis (Eds) *Children with Acquired Brain Injury: The School's Response* (pp. 323–341). Baltimore, MD: Paul H. Brookes.

Tyler, J., Blosser, J., & DePompei, R. (1999). *Teaching strategies for students with brain injuries.* Wake Forrest, NC: L&A Publishing/Training.

Tyler, J. S., & Mira, M. P. (1999). *Traumatic brain injury in children and adolescents: A sourcebook for teachers and other school personnel* (2nd ed.). Austin, TX: Pro-Ed.

Tyler, J. S., & Wilkerson, L. R. (1999). Planning school transition for students with TBI. *Brain Injury Source, 3*, 14–16, 54.

Tyler, J. S., Wilkerson, L. R., & DePompei, R. (2002). *Managing in-school transitions.* Wake Forrest, NC: L&A Publishing/Training.

U.S. Department of Education, Office of Special Education Programs (1999). *Implementation of the individuals with disabilities education act: Twenty-first annual report to congress.* Washington, D.C.: Author.

Valko, A. S. (1999). Rehabilitation and disabilities. In: D. W. Marion (Ed.), *Traumatic Brain Injury* (pp. 269–282). New York: Thieme.

Wehman, P. (1996). *Life beyond the classroom: Transition strategies for young people with disabilities* (2nd ed.). Baltimore, MD: Paul H. Brookes.

Weiner, H L., & Weinberg, J. S. (2000). Head injury in the pediatric age group. In: P. R. Cooper & J. G. Golfinos (Eds), *Head Injury* (4th ed., pp. 419–456). New York: McGraw-Hill.

Yeates, K. O., Luria, J., Bartkowski, H., Rusin, J., Martin, L., & Bigler, E. D. (1999). Postconcussive symptoms in children with mild closed-head injuries. *Journal of Head Trauma Rehabilitation, 14*, 337–350.

Ylvisaker, M., Chorazy, A. J. L., Feeney, R. J., & Russell, M. L. (1999). Traumatic brain injury in children and adolescents: Assessment and rehabilitation. In: M. Rosenthal, J. Kreutzer, E. Griffith & B. Pentland (Eds), *Rehabilitation of the Adult and Child with Traumatic Brain Injury* (3rd ed., pp. 356–392). Philadelphia, PA: F. A. Davis Company.

Ylvisaker, M., & Feeney, T. J. (1998). School reentry after traumatic brain injury. In: M. Ylvisaker (Ed.), *Traumatic Brain Injury Rehabilitation: Children and Adolescents* (2nd ed., pp. 369–387). Boston, MA: Butterworth-Heinemann.

Ylvisaker, M., Feeney, T. J., & Mullins, K. (1995). School reentry following mild traumatic brain injury: A proposed hospital-to-school protocol. *Journal of Head Trauma Rehabilitation, 10,* 42–49.

Ylvisaker, M., Feeney, T. J., & Szekers, S. F. (1998). Social-environmental approach to communication and behavior. In: M. Ylvisaker (Ed.), *Traumatic Brain Injury Rehabilitation: Children and Adolescents* (2nd ed., pp. 271–298). Boston, MA: Butterworth-Heinemann.

Ylvisaker, M., Hartwick, P., & Stevens, M. B. (1991). School reentry following head injury: Managing the transition from hospital to school. *Journal of Head Trauma Rehabilitation, 6,* 10–22.

Ylvisaker, M., Todis, B., Glang, A., Urbanczyk, B., Franklin, C., DePompei, R., Feeney, T., Maxwell, N. M., Pearson, S., & Tyler, J. S. (2001). Educating students with TBI: Themes and recommendations. *Journal of Head Trauma Rehabilitation, 16,* 76–93.

STUDENTS WITH GIFTS AND TALENTS

Vera I. Daniels

INTRODUCTION

For many years, giftedness has been closely linked with the concept of intelligence. This association began during the early part of the nineteenth century when two French psychologists Alfred Binet and Theodore Simon (1905) were commissioned by government officials in Paris to devise a test to provide a means for schools to determine the educability of students based on intellectual ability. The result was an individual test of intelligence known as the Binet-Simon Scales. The Binet-Simon Scales were revised and standardized by Lewis Terman, an American psychologist, and published in 1916 as the Stanford-Binet Intelligence Scale. Based on what the test measured, Terman (1925) considered as gifted only those children having an intelligence quotient (IQ score) of 140 or higher on the Stanford-Binet Intelligence Scale or a comparable test of intelligence. His views on giftedness were narrowly defined. He postulated that intelligence is fixed and determined by heredity. His unidimensional perspective of intelligence generated a great deal of controversy among psychologists in studying both the nature and assessment of intelligence.

Researchers challenging Terman's views on intelligence soon came to realize that the intellect was multidimensional, composed of a variety of distinct intellectual abilities and functions that could be identified, assessed, and measured. They also came to recognize that a single test of intelligence could only measure a portion of an individual's true intellectual capacity, and that a high aptitude or IQ score was only one of the many factors to be considered as being characteristic of giftedness. J. P. Guildford (1950, 1959), a key contributor to the multidimensional theory of intelligence, formulated a model theory of intelligence known as the "Structure of the Intellect" that changed the conceptions of giftedness. Guildford's model portrayed intelligence as having three distinct dimensions – operations, products, and contents – within which 120 independent factors are related to intellectual and creative activity. Guildford's work influenced other researchers to consider intelligence as a broader concept. Cattell (1971), for example, distinguished between two kinds of intelligence – fluid and crystallized intelligence. Gardner (1983) postulated a theory of "multiple intelligences" in which he hypothesized intelligence to constitute seven types of intelligence – linguistic, logical-mathematical, spatial, musical, kinesthetic, interpersonal, and intrapersonal intelligence. Sternberg (1985) introduced a triarchic theory of human intelligence in which intellectual performance is conceived as comprising three parts – analytic, synthetic, and practical intelligence. Today, the term giftedness is used to refer not only to individuals who have high IQ scores on an individual test of intelligence, but also to individuals with demonstrated high aptitudes on creativity measures. While some authorities (e.g. Getzels & Jackson, 1962; Renzulli, 1978; Torrance, 1962) put forth the notion that creativity is an important component of giftedness that is composed of abilities that are different from those measured by traditional intelligence tests, others (e.g. Treffinger, 1986) regard creativity as a distinctly separate entity having no correlation with superior intelligence or high academic achievement. Still, there are others (e.g. Clark, 1988) who view creativity as the highest form of giftedness because of the complex human functions that are involved. Another term which is also associated with giftedness is "talented". As used today, talented denotes individuals who demonstrate superior skills or abilities, usually in the visual or performing arts, that are a natural part of their repertoire. However, being identified as talented does not necessarily imply a high or superior degree of intelligence as measured or defined by tradition.

DEFINITIONS OF GIFTEDNESS

Concepts such as gifted and talented have been used extensively throughout the literature to refer to individuals who have superior abilities, or show the potential for performing remarkable high levels of accomplishment (when compared to their age-mates) in one or more domains or areas of performance. While the terms "giftedness" and "talentedness" are sometimes used synonymously, "giftedness often refers to exceptional intelligence or academic ability, while talent is often used to indicate exceptional artistic or athletic ability" (Hunt & Marshall, 2002, p. 456).

Because giftedness can manifest itself in a number of different ways, it is hard to agree on a single universally accepted definition of giftedness. Problems associated with defining giftedness has perplexed educators, psychologists, and researchers for decades. They have emerged in part because of the different theoretical views on giftedness. For example, Renzulli (1978) put forth a three-ring theory of giftedness – above average intelligence, high creativity, substantial task commitment – and considered as gifted only those individuals who possessed these three clusters or traits. Other issues in defining giftedness have emerged from the research on this topic, the wide range of characteristics associated with children having superior or extraordinary skills and abilities, and the various terminologies used. Although definitions of giftedness still remain a complex and controversial subject, the most widely used definitions of giftedness are those proposed by the federal government. While these definitions have been criticized (e.g. Renzulli, 1978) for their lack of consistency and specificity in providing school districts with the direction needed to more accurately identify students with gifts and talents, many states have adopted definitions of giftedness that are similar to federal definitions (Council of State Directors of Programs for the Gifted, 1985, cited in Pendarvis, Howley & Howley, 1990).

In an investigation of state and federal definitions of gifted, Cassidy and Hossler (1992) found that most states have adopted either the 1978 federal definition of giftedness as written or definitions of giftedness similar to federal definitions, with no states adopting more contemporary definitions such as that advanced by Gardner (1983) or Sternberg (1985). Table 1 shows federal definitions of giftedness that have been adopted over the years. While these definitions tend to reflect educational, societal, economic, political, and cultural attitudes of the times, myriad problems have been associated with their use. For example, the 1970 federal definition is somewhat vague. It offers little direction to states and school districts for identifying giftedness; and it recognizes only intellectual and creative giftedness, thereby creating biases that may cause school districts to ignore other traits or areas of giftedness that may be demonstrated by children.

The Marland definition (1972) somewhat rectified the problems inherent in the 1970 definition. This definition enumerated six types of giftedness – general intellectual ability, specific academic aptitude, creative or productive thinking, leadership ability, visual and performing arts, and psychomotor ability – and it recognizes children with *potential* ability for giftedness in one or more of the

Table 1. Federal Definitions of Gifted and Talented Children.

Source	Definition
U.S. Department of Education, 1970	The term gifted and talented children means, in accordance with objective criteria presented by the Commissioner, children who have outstanding ability or creative talent, the development of which requires special activities or services not ordinarily provided by local education agencies.
Education of the Gifted and Talented: Report to the Congress of the United States by the U.S. Commissioner of Education (Marland, 1972)	Gifted and talented children are those identified by professionally qualified persons who, by virtue of outstanding abilities, are capable of high performance. These children who require differentiated educational programs in order to realize their contribution to self and society. Children capable of high performance include those with demonstrated achievement and/or potential ability in any of the following areas, singly or in combination: (1) General intellectual ability; (2) Specific academic aptitude; (3) Creative or productive thinking; (4) Leadership ability; (5) Visual and performing arts; (6) Psyhcomotor ability.
The Gifted and Talented Children's Education Act of 1978	The term "gifted and talented children" means children and, whenever applicable, youth who are identified at the preschool, elementary, or secondary level as possessing demonstrated or potential abilities that are evidence of high performance capabilities in areas such as intellectual, creative, specific academic, or leadership ability, or in the performing and visual arts, and who by reason thereof, require services or activities not ordinarily provided by the school.
Education Consolidation and Improvement Act of 1981	Gifted children are those who give evidence of high performance capability in areas such as intellectual, creative, artistic, leadership capacity, or specific academic fields, and who require services or activities not provided by the school in order to fully develop such capabilities.
U.S. Department of Education, 1988	The term "gifted and talented" students means children and youth who give evidence of high performance capability in areas such as intellectual,

Table 1. Continued.

Source	Definition
	creative, artistic, or leadership capacity, or in specific academic fields, and who require services or activities not provided by the school in order to fully develop such capabilities.
Jacob K. Javtis Gifted and Talented Students Act (1993)	Children and youth with outstanding talent perform or show the potential for performing at remarkably high levels of accomplishment when compared with others of their age, experience or environment. These children and youth exhibit high performance capability in intellectual, creative, and/or artistic areas, possess an unusual leadership capacity, or excel in specific academic fields. They require services or activities not ordinarily provided by the schools. Outstanding talents are present in children and youth form all cultural groups, across all economic strata, and in all areas of human endeavor.

six areas. Children who fall under the auspices of "potentially gifted" are underachieving students, ethnic minority students, economically disadvantaged and at-risk students, students with disabilities (e.g. gifted students with learning disabilities, visual impairments, hearing impairments, physical disabilities), and other academic or physically challenged persons who may not be demonstrating giftedness in school. The 1972 definition also acknowledges that students with gifts and talents require "differentiated educational programs" (and services) that extend beyond those typically provided by regular school programs. The 1978 definition is undergirded by Marland's 1972 definition. This definition highlights giftedness as occurring at the preschool, elementary, and secondary levels and it continues to recognize potentially gifted students. The 1978 definition also continues to emphasize the need for "services or activities" not ordinarily provided by regular school programs. The most notable difference between the 1972 and 1978 definitions of giftedness is the elimination of psychomotor ability among the areas of giftedness.

The 1981 definition of giftedness, while somewhat similar to the 1978 definition, is less inclusive in its descriptors of distinguishing features of giftedness. While this definition does not specifically highlight giftedness as occurring at the different grade levels, it does reference high performance in specific academic fields thus linking the need for school districts to provide specialized programs for children identified as gifted. In addition, this definition excludes reference to children with potential ability for giftedness. Apparently, the 1988 definition resembles the 1981 definition. Like the 1981 definition, this definition acknowledges the need for specialized programs for children who are gifted and it excludes reference to potentially gifted children. A noticeable feature of this definition not evident in the 1981 definition is its reference to both "gifted" and "talented" youth.

The most current definition (1993) of giftedness represents significant advantages over previous definitions. Besides recognizing a broad range of giftedness, this definition also recognizes children and youth from all cultural groups, economic strata, and areas of human endeavor. The 1993 definition is noteworthy because it is the first time that a federal definition of giftedness has recognized "giftedness" as occurring in underserved and neglected populations. This definition offers much promise for unmasking the hidden potential of minority, disadvantaged, and at-risk youth, including children with disabilities who demonstrate extraordinary abilities in the presence of their disability. As Richert (1985) explained, one advantage to using a federal definition of giftedness is the legitimacy of national law behind it. Another is its comprehensiveness and applicability to diverse settings.

In general, definitions of giftedness tend to reflect a number of purposes. They may be used to: (a) identify and count children with gifts and talents; (b) diagnose, label, and place students in specially designed accelerated programs to meet their unique educational needs; (c) enable professionals to communicate more effectively about students and their needs; (d) help determine priorities for funding for educational programs; and (e) facilitate legislative efforts on behalf of children with gifts and talents. Regardless of how giftedness is defined, the fact remains that these individuals possess above-average intelligence and extraordinary skills and abilities in specific areas of performance.

PREVALENCE OF GIFTEDNESS

Determining the prevalence estimates for children receiving services in gifted education programs is complicated. First, there is no current federal mandate that requires educational services for students identified as gifted as there are for students with disabilities. Consequently, the number of children receiving services in specialized programs for students with gifts and talents are not reported by the states to the federal government. It also means that there is no national reporting system for obtaining statistical data on the number of children served in gifted education programs by the different states. Second, not all states or local school districts provide services to children with gifts and talents. As Jost (1997) noted in his examination of the 1996 *State of the States Gifted and Talented Education Report* by the Council of State Directors of Programs for the Gifted, approximately half of the states require gifted education programs. According to Jost, "Programs to identify gifted students and provide educational services for them are required in 24 states, while 18 states and the District of Columbia have no such mandates. Eight states only require the identification of gifted students . . ." (p. 268).

Typical estimates for the number of school-age children receiving services in gifted programs range from 3% to 5% of the total school population (Marland, 1972). The U.S. Department of Education estimates about 5% of the school population, or 3 million youngsters nationwide (see Jost, 1997). Higher percentages are estimated when an IQ cutoff score of 115 is used. These estimates could range from 3% to 15% or even 20% of the school-age population. While prevalence estimates for students with gifts and talents tend to fluctuate from one source to the next, the actual number of children identified as being gifted and talented can depend on several factors – federal reports, legislation, definitions of giftedness, the evaluative criteria used to identify giftedness, IQ cutoff scores, regulations of various states for giftedness, the appropriateness of instruments for the population of students being tested, qualifications of individuals who conduct evaluations, funding sources, and the amount of funding appropriated for gifted education programs.

IDENTIFICATION AND ASSESSMENT

Procedures for identifying children for gifted education programs is a persistent concern of educators in both general and special education. Although many gifted young children show indices of high potential before they begin school, usually they are not formerly identified until third or fourth grade (Hunt & Marshall, 2002). Richert (1985) listed six principles that should underline identification. They are:

(1) *Advocacy*. Identification should be designed in the best interest of all students.
(2) *Defensibility*. Procedures should be based on the best available research and recommendations.
(3) *Equity*. Procedures should guarantee that no one is overlooked. The civil rights of students should be protected. Strategies should be outlined for identifying the disadvantaged gifted.

(4) *Pluralism*. The broadest defensible definition of giftedness should be used.
(5) *Comprehensiveness*. As many possible gifted learners should be identified and served.
(6) *Pragmatism*. Whenever possible, procedures should allow for the modification and use of tools and resources on hand (pp. 68–69).

Although the current trend is to recognize giftedness as an intellectual trait that reflect multiple characteristics, there still remains an absence of sufficient standardized measures to adequately identify the academic, intellectual, and creative potentials of some children. Many children with gifts and talents (and potentially gifted youngsters) are not identified by school systems, especially those who come from cultural, linguistic, and economically disadvantaged backgrounds (e.g. Chinn & Hughes, 1987) or from subcultures with values that differ from mainstream society. Problems with the identification of children with gifts and talents from underserved populations may be attributed to a number of factors. As Karnes and Collins (1984) noted, these factors may include:

(1) Not having the same opportunities to develop and express their intelligence at an early age as children with gifts and talents from more advantaged backgrounds.
(2) Parents who place little or no emphasis upon intellectual development or the development of particular abilities and talents.
(3) The economic pressures of parents that causes them not to have time to spend with their children.
(4) A lack of exposure to books and other educational experiences that are provided to advantaged children.
(5) A lack of the dominate society's value of the gifts and talents valued by members of non-mainstreamed society.

Concerns about the identification of students with gifts and talents led to a study being commissioned by the U.S. Department of Education. This study, the *National Report on Identification, Assessment, and Recommendations for Comprehensive Identification of Gifted and Talented Youth*, revealed some interesting, yet disturbing information about existing practices that might undermine support for gifted programs. They include:

(1) Several categories of giftedness are simply not being addressed.
(2) Education equity is being violated in the identification of significant subpopulations.

(3) Identification instruments are being used to identify categories of giftedness for which they were not designed.
(4) Instruments and procedures are being used at inappropriate stages for identification.
(5) Multiple criteria are being combined inappropriately (Richert, 1985, p. 69).

Thus, identifying children who are gifted is a complex and complicated matter. While intelligence quotient (IQ) tests and achievement tests are a central part of the identification process, they should not be used as the sole index or determinant for identifying gifted and talented children. Current best practices for identifying gifted and talented learners calls for a multidemensional assessment approach in which assessment data are gathered from a wide variety of sources (e.g. formal and informal tests; nominations by teachers, peers, parents, or others knowledgeable of the student's special abilities; and direct observations) to make identification and placement decisions.

Intelligence Tests

Individual tests of intelligence provide a major source of information for determining the general cognitive ability or intellectual giftedness of children and adolescents. The two most commonly used standardized tests of intelligence are the Stanford Binet and the Weschler Intelligence Scale for Children (WISC-III). Other frequently used tests for cognitive abilities include the Differential Aptitude Tests, Cognitive Abilities Test, and the Kaufman Assessment Battery for Children. A number of criticisms have been associated with the use of conventional tests of intelligence. Perhaps most notable are those which relate to the restrictiveness of what these tests measure, and the limitations of these tests when used to measure the abilities of children from cultural, linguistic, and economically disadvantaged backgrounds.

Achievement Tests

Achievement tests provide a major source of information for identifying giftedness. These tests assess knowledge of specific academic content across a range of subject areas. Achievement tests may be group or individually administered. Group achievement tests are valuable as a screening instrument. However, individual tests of achievement are preferred when making identification and placement decisions. Among the frequently used group tests of academic achievement are the California Achievement Tests, the Metropolitan Achievement Tests, the Stanford Achievement Tests, and the Iowa Tests of

Basic Skills. Individualized tests of academic achievement which are commonly used include the Peabody Individual Achievement Test-Revised, the Wide Range Achievement Test-Third Edition, the Wechsler Individual Achievement Test-Revised, and the Woodcock-Johnson III (formerly, the Woodcock-Johnson Psychoeducational Battery).

While both intelligence and achievement tests have the potential to provide invaluable information about students' abilities, strengths, weaknesses, and programmatic and instructional needs, caution must be taken to reduce the overreliance on such measures for identifying gifted learners. Reliance on such measures as a primary means for identification has come under much criticism. This criticism has focused primarily on: (a) educational equity for minority groups such as African Americans, Hispanics, and Native Americans; (b) the use of identification instruments for purposes for which they have not been designed; (c) stages at which instruments and procedures are being used to identify potential gifts and talents; (d) the inappropriate ways in which data are being combined when multiple criteria is being used to identify giftedness; and (e) the screening procedures used in present practices (i.e. achievement tests, IQ tests, grades, and teacher nominations) which eliminate some children from gifted programs (Richert, 1987). Today, educators use multiple identification criteria for giftedness that draw from both formal and informal assessment procedures. In addition to intelligence and achievement tests, assessments for giftedness may include creativity measures, visual and performing arts measures, portfolio assessments, nominations, observations, interviews, and other assessment techniques.

Creativity Tests

Tests of creativity are useful measures for identifying creative abilities of students. Such measures may include Torrance Test of Creative Thinking (TTCT), Group Inventory for Finding Interests (GIFFI), Group Inventory for Finding Creative Talent (GIFT), Khatena Torrance Creative Perception Inventory, and the Preschool and Kindergarten Interest Descriptor (PRIDE).

Visual and Performing Arts Measures

Screening for giftedness in visual and performing arts may constitute observations, recommendations from professional artists, or nominations from teachers, peers, or significant others knowledgeable of the child's special abilities and talents. Other measures may include, for example, the Seashore Measures of Musical Talents, the Bentley Measures of Musical Abilities,

Standardized Tests of Musical Talent, Horn Art Aptitude Inventory, the Maier Art Tests, and ASSETS – A Survey of Students' Educational Talents and Skills.

Portfolio Assessments

Portfolios are made up of student work samples, collected over time, from a variety of sources and content areas. They are especially useful for substantiating the special abilities and creative talents of children with disabilities, and children who are members of underserved and neglected populations. Portfolio assessments document a student's affective and cognitive growth. They can also merge both quantitative and qualitative assessment data together to produce a broader reflection of a student's skills and abilities that may not be obtainable through conventional assessment measures.

Nominations

Nominations of giftedness can take on various forms. They can be made by a teacher, parent, peer, the student, or a significant other who has knowledge of the extraordinary abilities or creative talents of the student. Teacher nominations are one of the most frequently used screening devices for identifying students with gifts and talents. They are based on the teacher's professional judgements of a student's performance in relation to other students. Interestingly, teacher nominations are considered to be the least effective and reliable (Gallagher, 1966). Researchers (e.g. Jacobs, 1971) have found that parent nominations are much more reliable in identifying gifted and talented students. The reliability of parental judgments have been attributed to the amount of contact that parents have with their child and their conservativeness in assessing their child's abilities.

Observations

An observation is an informal technique that can be used to study any type of student behavior. This procedure is useful in collecting data on school related student types of behavior (e.g. appropriate or inappropriate behavior, academic or social behavior) and describing various patterns of behavior in the learning environment (McLoughlin & Lewis, 1994). Observations are also useful for anecdotal material to substantiate information reported by others (e.g. teachers, peers, administrators, and parents) about the gifts and talents demonstrated by students.

Interviews

Interviews, another informal information gathering strategy, are the oral equivalent of questionnaires (McLoughlin & Lewis, 1994). An interview can be used to gather descriptive data not otherwise available or accessible through conventional measures. The informant of an interview may be the student, his peers, teachers, parents, or other individuals or professionals knowledgeable of the student's extraordinary skills, abilities, and talents.

FACTORS THAT CONTRIBUTE TO GIFTEDNESS

Hereditary Factors

Historically, it was generally believed that heredity (our individual genetic makeup) and other biological factors were the primary determinants of giftedness. Researchers now recognize genetic inheritances as only one of many complex factors that can be used to explain the development of the human intellect and giftedness. While genetic factors determine in part, the range within which a person will function, environmental factors (e.g. family, culture, and school) determine the extent to which the individual functions in that range (Hallahan & Kauffman, 2000).

Environmental Factors

Environmental factors include family, cultural, and school factors. The following subsections discuss these factors.

Family factors. Family factors are perhaps the most powerful influence in defining giftedness. Such factors may include the socioeconomic level of the family, parenting practices, or the number of children in the family. Family expectations, the child's interactions with siblings, nutrition, access of the child to medical care and treatment, and the roles of parents in nurturing, encouraging, and channeling the extraordinary abilities demonstrated by their child may also influence giftedness.

Cultural factors. Cultural factors (e.g. attitudes, values, beliefs, and customs) can contribute to the development of gifts and talents. Cultural factors are influenced by the social context (environment) of the child and may differ substantially from one socioeconomic level to the next.

School factors. Schools foster the development of students' gifts, talents, and creative abilities. Schools can provide enrichment programs and curricular activities to help students with superior intellectual and creative abilities to achieve to their potential.

Despite the numerous theories and hypothesis about which factors contribute to the development of giftedness, it is obvious that the debate has far exceeded the nature vs. nurture controversy of the past. As Clark (1992) pointed out:

> High intelligence, whether expressed in cognitive abilities such as the capacity to generalize, to conceptualize, or to reason abstractly, or in specific academic ability, leadership, creative behavior expressed through visual and performing arts, results from the interaction between inherited and acquired characteristics. This interaction encompasses all of the physical, mental, and emotional characteristics of the person and all of the people, events, and objects entering the person's awareness. As no two people have identical physical, mental, and emotional properties, neither do they have the same environment (p. 10).

FACTORS THAT ENHANCE AND INHIBIT GIFTEDNESS

The degree to which heredity and the environment contribute to giftedness is well documented throughout the literature. Researchers have come to realize that the aggregate interactions between genetic endowment and environmental contributions are directly linked to giftedness. They have also come to recognize that the genetic patterns and anatomical structure of the individual, and the individuals' environment, encompasses "all of the physical, mental, and emotional characteristics of the person and all of the people, events, and objects entering the person's awareness" (Clark, 1992, p. 10).

Regarding factors that enhance and inhibit giftedness, one can surmise that children who have limited interactions and exposure to environmental stimuli will have limited opportunities to develop or enhance their gifts and talents; children who have boundless exposure to such influences will have increased opportunities to enhance their gifts and talents (Clark, 1992). Examples of indices of environmental influences that can enhance and inhibit giftedness, or the potential for giftedness, is presented in Table 2.

CHARACTERISTICS OF STUDENTS WITH GIFTS AND TALENTS

Students who are gifted manifest a wide array of abilities and degrees of difference from their agemates. Some may demonstrate outstanding cognitive ability and aptitude. Others may demonstrate extraordinary leadership characteristics or psychomotor skills. Still, there are others who may demonstrate

Table 2. Some Factors that Enhance and Inhibit Giftedness.

Factors that Enhance Giftedness
- meaningful, challenging, and conceptually rich differentiated curricular;
- innovative teaching techniques and the use of technologies;
- student involvement in class projects that have purpose, direction, meaning, and specific outcomes;
- recognition of student accomplishments;
- stimulating and nurturing environment;
- field experiences for community-based learning opportunities;
- encouragement and attention;
- economic (environmental) conditions.

Factors that Inhibit Giftedness
- boredom;
- poor teaching, poor educational experiences, limited opportunities to learn, inappropriate curriculum;
- poverty, unfavorable environmental conditions;
- insufficient infant stimulation;
- inadequate health care;
- family disorganization, single parent families;
- abuse, neglect, drugs.

extraordinary ability in the visual and performing arts (e.g. painting, sculpting, drawing, dancing, singing, playing musical instruments, and performing dramatically). Depending on the individual, the nature and magnitude of these differences may affect their social, emotional, educational, and psychological well being (Hallahan & Kauffman, 2000). The sections that follow describe some of the cognitive, academic, social-emotional, and physical characteristics of gifted and talented individuals commonly cited in the literature.

Cognitive

Gifted and talented learners have unusual cognitive (information processing) abilities. They have the remarkable ability to use and manipulate large amounts of information, and the ability to rapidly acquire, retain, and learn new information. These learners also have exceptional generalization and comprehension skills. They can generalize information quickly, and easily comprehend abstract concepts and complex relationships. In addition, these youngsters have excellent memories. They perform well on memory tasks; and they have the capacity to learn more rapidly and easier than their peers. Cartwright, Cartwright and Ward (1989) listed the following characteristics of highly able students that fall within the cognitive domain to include:

- Ability to ask many questions and be often not satisfied with "simple" answers.
- Ability to have good memories and be often exceptionally facile at retaining numbers and other symbols.
- Ability to begin to read at an early age and be often several grade levels above age-mates.
- Ability to like to experiment, hypothesize, and test out new ideas.
- Ability to have good reasoning abilities and understand quickly.
- Ability to have strong vocabularies.

Because gifted students' cognitive development is accelerated, it sometimes causes problems in the classroom. Many gifted students are often ahead of the class, as reflected by their performance on academic tasks. As such, they become easily bored (or impatient) with the pace of instruction; and they find conventional approaches that teachers use to instruction less motivating, less challenging, and less rewarding. Additionally, because of their advanced attributes, gifted children are not content to leave facts alone. This causes some teachers to perceive them as negative rather than positive. Others may view them as nonconformists. Still, there are others who feel threatened by their advanced abilities. Gifted students, as Karnes and Collins (1984) explained, are more likely to "display behaviors displeasing to teachers if the educational setting emphasizes drill and repetitious activities geared to grade-level expectations. The lack of challenge and subsequent boredom may produce disruptive behavior, inattention, disinterest, demands of relevancy, questions, arguments, or challenge to authority" (p. 6).

Academic

Gifted children are often described as intellectually curious. These children show a strong desire to learn, have an intense need for mental stimulation, and have difficulty conforming to the thinking of others (Silverman, 1995). Gifted students are also highly motivated learners and are quite persistent in the pursuit of interests and questions (Tuttle & Becker, 1980). Additionally, gifted students are generally recognized by their teachers for their superior achievement. They often excel in academic content areas (especially, math and science) well above average when compared to their age-mates.

While it is widely known that gifted youngsters perform well in school, not all gifted students perform at high levels in all school subjects. Contrary to popular belief, not all gifted students are straight "A" students or high achievers, and not all straight "A" students and high achievers are gifted students (Karnes

& Collins, 1984). Like students with disabilities, high ability students also show both inter- and intra-individual differences in their performance.

Social-Emotional

One of the most common misconceptions about children who are gifted is that they are socially inept and emotionally unstable (Cartwright, Cartwright & Ward, 1989; Hallahan & Kauffman, 2000). While it is true that some students with gifts and talents may feel different, misunderstood, and socially isolated (Hunt & Marshall, 2002), the fact is most gifted persons are healthy, well-adjusted, emotionally independent, and stable individuals who are sensitive to the needs of others (Cartwright, Cartwright & Ward, 1989; Hallahan & Kauffman, 2000). These children also have an advanced level of moral behavior and sense of justice; and they are quick to point out incongruities in situations (Cartwright, Cartwright & Ward, 1989).

Gifted students tend to maintain a positive self-image and a high level of self-awareness (Cartwright, Cartwright & Ward, 1989). Even though their classmates may perceive them as a "show-off," it does not always lead to peer alienation. In most cases, gifted students are not social outcasts (Karnes & Collins, 1984). The majority of these youngsters are popular among their peers, and are often leaders in many social situations (Karnes & Collins, 1984). They enjoy decision making, and like to assume responsibility for the group (Cartwright, Cartwright & Ward, 1989). In addition, gifted youngsters are cooperative and they adjust to change easily. Negative behaviors typically are not demonstrated by gifted students, and are mainly triggered by undue stressors imposed on them by peers, parents, or teachers (Karnes & Collins, 1984).

Physical

Although early research by Terman depicted gifted youngsters as stronger, bigger, and healthier than their age-mates, we now know that gifted children do not differ substantially from other children. The most noticeable difference in the physical appearance of gifted children typically occur when these youngsters are accelerated by several grades to provide for a more appropriate curriculum.

There are many profiles of high ability children presented in the literature. Clark (1988, 1992, 1997) presented what may be considered the most comprehensive list of characteristics of gifted children under five major headings – cognitive (thinking), affective (feeling), physical, intuitive, and societal.

Table 3. Common Characteristics of Gifted Learners.

- has high level of intellectual ability;
- has above average vocabulary, and enjoys communicating and socializing with older children, adolescents and adults;
- has excellent memory and recall capabilities;
- learns quickly, rapidly, easily, and retains what is learned;
- can comprehend easily;
- has exceptional cognition and information processing abilities;
- has high levels of skills in reasoning and problem solving;
- has ability to think abstractly, analytically, and critically;
- is intellectually curious, enjoys new and challenging experiences;
- has wide range of interests, and is an avid reader;
- is cooperative;
- is easily bored;
- is sensitive to the feelings of others;
- has unusual ability to lead, inspire, and influence others;
- has ability to make sound judgments;
- is a keen observer;
- gets pleasure from intellectual challenge;
- shows originality in intellectual work;
- shows creative ability in such things as music, art, dance, drama;
- sets high standards for self and is self-critical in evaluating and correcting own efforts.

Regardless of the characteristics cited, it is important to remember that these traits represent only a birds-eye view of the many characteristics of gifted and talented individuals. Table 3 presents some of the frequently reported characteristics of gifted children (e.g. Clark, 1992; ERIC Clearinghouse on Handicapped and Gifted Children, 1990; Karnes & Collins, 1984; Tuttle & Becker, 1980; Silverman, 1995).

NEGLECTED GROUPS OF GIFTED AND TALENTED STUDENTS

The unmasking of hidden potential of students from culturally diverse and economically disadvantaged backgrounds is problematic. It becomes more difficult when it involves students who demonstrate intellectual giftedness or extraordinary abilities in the presence of a disability. It is a well known fact that students from culturally diverse, economically disadvantaged, migrant, rural or inner-city areas, and disabled populations are grossly underrepresented in gifted education programs. Educators (e.g. Chinn & Hughes, 1987; Harris & Ford, 1991; Maker, 1996; Patton, 1992; Richert, 1997) have been grappling with this issue for decades. As Passow and Frasier (1996) stated, "Even with the significant and constant increases in both numbers and proportions of racial/ethnic minority and economically disadvantaged students in the public school population that have occurred in recent decades, underrepresentation of these students in programs for the gifted seems not to have changed substantially" (p. 198).

Perhaps one of the major reasons for the widespread failure to identify gifted students from under-identified and under-served populations is the procedures that are currently used to evaluate and identify giftedness. Another reason why a substantial proportion of children from traditionally underrepresented populations are not identified is because most teachers are not able or skilled in the ability to recognize gifts and talents in minority populations. A third reason for the disproportionate representation of youngsters from under-served populations in gifted education programs may be attributed to the instructional methods that teachers use in the classroom. In general, most teachers tend not to engage children regularly in learning tasks and activities that allow them to demonstrate their intellectual giftedness or potential for giftedness. Oftentimes, these children are confined to the traditional curricular that is not suited to their learning needs.

Other factors that contribute to the underrepresentation of gifted learners from neglected groups in gifted education programs include biases in the content of IQ tests; the definition, procedures, and criteria used to identify giftedness; the differences between the learning (cognitive) styles of minority and majority (white, middle-class) students; and the differences between the teaching styles of minority and majority teachers. Similarly, children of migrant families are grossly underrepresented in gifted education programs. Their lack of representation is primarily due to the frequent mobility of the family which interrupts the continuity of their schooling, learning, and general academic progress. Underserved populations are neglected because "the conditions and opportunities they are exposed to are insufficient to nurture, stimulate, and guide the full potential of their individual abilities" (Cline & Schwartz, 1999, p. 3). Despite the emphasis on discriminatory practices and the lack of educational equity for minority, at-risk, economically disadvantaged, and disabled youths, standardized assessment measures that are currently employed still are inadequate for identifying giftedness among these sub-groups of students.

Recognizing the fact that there are no perfect instruments for identifying giftedness among children from underserved populations (i.e. cultural and linguistically diverse students, economically disadvantaged students, at-risk students, students with disabilities, and migrant students), the most promising methods for identification are those which take into account multiple sources.

Such sources may include formal measures (e.g. intelligence tests, achievement tests, and creativity measures) and informal measures (e.g. portfolio artifacts, teacher nominations, peer nominations, nominations by other individuals who have knowledge of the student's special gifts and talents, direct observations, and interviews).

EDUCATIONAL CONSIDERATIONS

Efforts to provide enhanced educational opportunities for students who are gifted and talented has been inundated with problems. This may be due in part to the lack of a federal law requiring the implementation of an individualized education program that is designed to meet the unique needs of students with gifts and talents such as that required of students with disabilities under the 1997 Individuals with Disabilities Education Act (IDEA). It may also be due to problems associated with not having a single universally acceptable definition of giftedness, the differing philosophical viewpoints and beliefs about giftedness, and the educational needs of highly able learners.

It is without question that school systems have a major responsibility in the education of students with disabilities. This responsibility is mandated under IDEA. However, school systems also have an obligation and responsibility for the rights of students with gifts and talents to a free and appropriate public education. Currently, only one major federal law, the Jacob K. Javits Gifted and Talented Students Act, acknowledges the need for special programs for gifted and talented youths. Unfortunately, this Act falls short of mandating these services. School systems are responsible for determining the definition of giftedness, the procedures for identifying gifted students, the types of gifted children it is capable of serving, the structure through which these children will be provided educational services, and the personnel who will provide these services. Although school systems have gone to great lengths to improve the quality of educational services that are provided to students who are gifted and talented, advocates of the gifted and talented feel that schools are still negligent in helping these students achieve their full potential (Jost, 1997). In fact, it has been reported that as many as 20% of the students who drop out of school are gifted students (Ford, 1996).

Because of their unique abilities and diverse education needs, gifted students need to be exposed to a variety of innovative instructional approaches and service delivery systems. These youngsters also need to have curricula and instruction designed to accommodate their abilities and advance their cognitive learning styles. Unfortunately, many gifted students spend most of their day in regular classroom settings and are involved in traditional general education programs which focus on activities and curricula that are not suited to meet their unique capabilities or interests (Westberg, Archambault, Dobyns & Salvin, 1993).

Thus, without an advanced or enriched curricula, students with gifts and talents will fall short of their potential, or worst, lose interest in school (Jost, 1997) and become candidates for a variety of school-related behavior problems. According to Karnes and Collins (1984), "For gifted students, grade-level assignments may not only impede their achievement, but may also produce negative connotations of formal education. [Moreover] drill and repetition of activities already understood can only produce boredom, dislike of school, and underdeveloped potential abilities" (p. 7).

The lack of an appropriate curricula may also lead to higher dropout rates for gifted students. Educational programs for students with gifts and talents should have three prevailing characteristics: a curriculum designed to accommodate the students' advanced cognitive skills; instructional strategies consistent with learning styles of gifted students in the particular content areas of the curriculum; and administrative arrangements facilitating appropriate grouping of students for instruction (Van Tassel-Baska, 1998, cited in Hallahan & Kauffman, 2000). Although many programs fall short of these characteristics, Ford, Russo and Harris (1995), and Russo, Harris and Ford (1996) provided an intriguing discussion on the need for developing an appropriate educational program for gifted children, and the legal imperatives for meeting the education needs of gifted children. The following section provides a brief discussion on selected curricular adaptions and service delivery options commonly used to provide instruction to gifted students.

Curricular Differentiation

Curricular differentiation can vary from enrichment of the regular education curricula (e.g. individualized instruction, independent study, computer-assisted instruction, and contracting), to various program options and service delivery models (e.g. internships, mentoring programs, special courses, and specialized programs in various subject areas). There are a number of reasons why a differential educational curricula should be used. A differentiated curricula can stimulate higher-order thinking skills, prevent the loss of creative thinking skills, and create a learning environment that encourages students to achieve their full potential (Cartwright, Cartwright & Ward, 1989). Such curricula can also reduce underachievement, lower dropout rates, aid in the prevention of delinquency, and promote interactions with peers (see Cartwright, Cartwright & Ward).

Enrichment

Like students with disabilities, gifted students have educational needs which must be met on a daily basis. Meeting the needs of high ability students often will far exceed challenges that teachers face when integrating students with disabilities in their classroom. Because gifted and talented children manifest a remarkable ability to handle, comprehend, and understand complex ideas beyond their classmates, enrichment of the core content of the regular education curriculum is needed to facilitate learning. Enrichment activities can provide students with experiences that extend and broaden their knowledge and skills of the existing curriculum in breadth or depth, tempo or pace, and kind (Passow, 1979). Clark (1997) explained that "Enrichment can refer to adding disciplines or areas of learning not normally found in the regular curriculum, using more difficult or in-depth material to enhance the core curriculum, or enhancing the teaching strategies used to present instruction" (p. 204).

While the enrichment approach is recognized as the most common means by which we serve students with gifts and talents, it is also characterized as the most "abused" approach. As Hardman, Drew, and Egan (1999) noted, the enrichment approach ". . . is often applied in name only and in a sporadic fashion, without well-delineated objectives or rationale" (p. 529). It is also "often used by school systems in a superficial fashion as a token economy response to the demands of parents of children who are gifted" (Hardman et al., p. 529). Despite the drawbacks to this approach, it is used at varying levels to respond to instructional needs of gifted and talented youths.

Acceleration

Acceleration is one of the most common forms of specialized programming for children who are gifted. Acceleration could mean skipping a grade, taking advanced placement in selected courses for high school or college credit, individualized instruction, ability grouping, curriculum compacting, or some other form of curricular adjustment. In the past, grade skipping was a common administrative practice in providing instructional programming to students with superior abilities. However, today, educators are less enthusiastic about this approach. The decline in enthusiasm for this practice resulted from beliefs that grade skipping could lead to gifted students becoming socially maladjusted and could cause students to experience significant gaps in learning (Hardman et al., 1999).

Although acceleration provides gifted students with an opportunity to learn at rates that are congruent with their capabilities, it does not provide them with the differentiated curriculum that is needed to address their specific learning needs (Schiever & Maker, 1997). According to Hardman et al. (1999) "the major benefits of acceleration, as established by research and effective practice, include improved motivation and confidence and early completion of advanced or professional training" (p. 528).

Service Delivery Systems

The use of service delivery systems is another means by which services are provided to gifted students. Interestingly, the structure of these service delivery alternatives resemble those for students with disabilities. Clark's (1997) model for ability grouping is one example of a comprehensive service delivery continuum model for students who are gifted. This model postulates 11 learning environments for students who are gifted – the general education classroom, the general education class with cluster, the general education class with pullout, the general education class with cluster and pullout, the individualized classroom, the individualized classroom with cluster, the individualized classroom with pullout, the individualized classroom with cluster and pullout, special class with some integrated classes, special class, and special school.

SUMMARY

Students who are gifted and talented have many outstanding attributes in a variety of areas. Some may demonstrate superior intellectual, academic, and creative abilities while others may demonstrate remarkable skills in visual and performing arts. The problem inherent in defining giftedness is the many attributes that are identified with giftedness, and the problematic nature by which evaluations are conducted. Although an individual test of intelligence can identify high achievers, a multidimensional approach to identification is needed if we are to identify all children with gifts and talents, especially those from underserved and neglected populations. While efforts to provide enhanced educational opportunities for gifted and talented students are inundated with problems, most school districts do attempt to provide a differentiated curricular to meet the needs of high ability students. What is needed is a federal law that mandates a free and appropriate individualized education program for all students with gifts and talents similar to that provided for children with disabilities.

REFERENCES

Binet, A., & Simon, T. (1905). Méthodes nouvelles pour le diagnostic du niveau intellectuel des anormaux [New methods for determining the intellectual capacity of people with mental retardation]. *L'Année Psychologique, 11,* 191–244.
Cartwright, G. P., Cartwright, C. A., & Ward, M. E. (1989). *Educating special learners.* Belmonth, CA: Wadsworth.
Cassidy, J., & Hossler, A. (1992). State and federal definitions of the gifted: An update. *Gifted Child Quarterly, 15*(1), 46–53.
Cattell, R. B. (1971). *Abilities: Their structure, growth, and action.* Boston: Houghton Mifflin.
Chinn, P. C., & Hughes, S. (1987). Representation of minority students in special education classes. *Remedial and Special Education, 8*(4), 41–46.
Clark, B. (1988). *Growing up gifted: Developing the potential of children at home and at school* (3rd ed.). Columbus, OH: Charles E. Merrill.
Clark, B. (1992). *Growing up gifted: Developing the potential of children at home and at school* (4th ed.). New York: Macmillan.
Clark, B. (1997). *Growing up gifted: Developing the potential of children at home and at school* (5th ed.). New York: Macmillan.
Cline, S., & Schwartz, D. (1999). *Diverse populations of gifted children: Meeting the needs in the regular classroom and beyond.* Upper Saddle River, NJ: Prentice-Hall.
ERIC Clearinghouse on Handicapped and Gifted Children (1990). *Giftedness and the gifted: What's it all about* (ERIC EC Digest No. E476). Reston, VA: Author.
Ford, D. Y. (1996). *Reversing underachievement among gifted black students: Promising practices and programs.* New York: Teachers College Press.
Ford, D. Y., Russo, C. J., & Harris J. J. (1995). Meeting the educational needs of the gifted: A legal imperative. *Roeper Review, 17*(4), 224–228.
Gallagher, J. J. (1985). *The gifted child* (3rd ed.). Newton, MA: Allyn and Bacon.
Gallagher, J. J. (1966). *Research summary on Gifted Child Education.* Springfield, IL: State Department of Public Education.
Gardner, J. (1983). *Frames of mind: The theory of multiple intelligences.* New York: Basic Books.
Getzels, J. W., & Jackson, P. W. (1962). *Creativity and intelligence: Explorations with gifted students.* New York: John Wiley and Sons.
Guildford, J. P. (1950). Creativity. *American Psychologist, 5,* 444–454.
Guildford, J. P. (1959). Three faces of intellect. *American Psychologist, 14,* 469–479.
Hallahan, D. P., & Kauffman, J. M. (2000). *Exceptional learners: Introduction to special education* (8th ed.). Needham Heights, MA: Allyn and Bacon.
Hardman, M. L., Drew, C. J., & Egan, M. W. (1999). *Human Exceptionality: Society, School, and Family* (6th ed.). Needham Heights, MA: Allyn and Bacon.
Harris, J. J., & Ford, D. Y. (1991). Identifying and nurturing the promise of gifted Black American children. *Journal of Negro Education, 60*(1), 3–18.
Hunt, N., & Marshall, K. (2002). *Exceptional children and youth: An introduction to special education* (3rd ed.). Boston: Houghton Mifflin.
Jacobs, J. C. (1971). Effectiveness of teachers and parent identification of gifted children as a function of school level. *Psychology in the Schools, 8,* 140–142.
Jost, K. (1997). Educating gifted students. *The CQ Researcher, 7*(12), 265–288.
Karnes, F. A., & Collins, E. C. (1984). *Handbook of instructional resources and references for teaching the gifted* (2nd ed.). Boston: Allyn and Bacon.

Maker, C. J. (1996). Identification of gifted minority students: A national problem, needed changes and a promising solution. *Gifted Child Quarterly, 40*(1), 41–50.

Marland, S., Jr. (1972). *Education of the gifted and talented: Report to the Congress of the United States by the U.S. Commissioner of Education*. Washington, D.C.: U.S. Government Printing Office.

McLoughlin, J. A., & Lewis, R. B. (1994). *Assessing special students* (4th ed.). Upper addle River, NJ: Prentice-Hall.

Passow, A. H. (Ed.) (1979). *The gifted and the talented: Their education and development. The 78th yearbook of the National Society for the Study of Education*. Chicago: University of Chicago Press.

Passow, A. H., & Frasier, M. M. (1996). Towards improving identification of talent potential among minority and disadvantaged students. *Roeper Review, 18*(3), 198–202.

Patton, J. M. (1992). Assessment and identification of African-American learners with gifts and talents. *Exceptional Children, 59*(2), 150–159.

Pendarvis, E. D., Howley, A. A., & Howley, C. B. (1990). *The abilities of gifted children*. Englewood Cliffs, NJ: Prentice Hall.

Renzulli, J. S. (1978). What makes giftedness? Reexamining a definition. *Phi Delta Kappan, 60*(3), 180–184, 261.

Richert, E. S. (1985). Identification of gifted children in the United States: The need for pluralistic assessment. *Roeper Review, 8*(2), 68–72.

Richert, E. S. (1987). Rampant problems and promising practices in the identification of disadvantaged gifted students. *Gifted Child Quarterly, 31*(4), 149–154.

Richert, E. S. (1997). Excellence with equity in identification and programming. In: N. Colangelo & G. A. Davis (Eds), *Handbook of Gifted Education* (2nd ed., pp. 75–88). Needham Heights, MA: Allyn and Bacon.

Russo, C. J., Harris, J. J., & Ford, D. Y. (1996). Gifted education and the law: A right, privilege, or superfluous? *Roeper Review, 18*(3), 179–182.

Schiever, S. W., & Maker, C. J. (1997). Enrichment and acceleration: An overview and new directions. In: N. Colangelo & A. D. Davis (Eds), *Handbook of Gifted Education* (2nd ed., pp. 113–125). Needham Heights, MA: Allyn and Bacon.

Silverman, L. K. (1995). Highly gifted children. In: J. L. Genshaft, M. Bireley & C. L. Hollinger (Eds), *Serving Gifted and Talented Students: A Resource for School Personnel* (pp. 124–160). Austin, TX: PRO-ED.

Sternberg, R. J. (1985). *Beyond IQ: A triarchic theory of human intelligence*. Cambridge, England: Cambridge University Press.

Terman, L. M. (1925). *Mental and physical traits of a thousand gifted children (Genetic studies of genius: Vol. 1)*. Stanford, CA: Stanford University Press.

Torrance, E. P. (1962). *Guiding creative talent*. Englewood Cliffs, NJ: Prentice Hall.

Treffinger, D. J. (1986). Research on creativity. *Gifted Child Quarterly, 30*(1), 15–19.

Tuttle F. B., Jr., & Becker, L. A. (1980). *Characteristics and identification of gifted and talented students*. Washington, D.C.: National Education Association.

Westberg, K. L., Archambault, F., Dobyns, S., & Salvin, T. (1993). The classroom practices observation study. *Journal of the Education of the Gifted, 16*(2), 120–146.

PART 3.
LIFE SPAN ISSUES AND SPECIAL POPULATIONS

EARLY CHILDHOOD SPECIAL EDUCATION

Vivian I. Correa and Hazel Jones

INTRODUCTION

Over the past 15 years, the field of early childhood special education has experienced some of the most exciting and significant reforms in special education. The amendment of the Education of All Handicapped Children's Act (PL 99-457) in 1986 provided the impetus for states to offer services to children with disabilities from birth through two years of age under Part C, and mandated free and appropriate public education for children ages three through five under Part B. Prior to 1986, most efforts to provide services to young children with disabilities and their families were supported by research and demonstration projects funded by the federal government or by a handful of local community agencies (e.g. ARC, United Cerebral Palsy) committed to early intervention in spite of the scarcity of resources for such programs (Smith, 2000).

Enormous gains have been made since 1986 in assuring that *all* young children with disabilities, birth to age FIVE, have *access* to early childhood special education services. However, as a field, it is imperative to move beyond the provision of access to the provision of the highest *quality* services. Today, multiple challenges are encountered in providing quality services to young children and their families. Early childhood special educators report having increased caseloads and greater demands placed on them for consultation and collaboration with general early childhood educators. Furthermore, an increasing proportion of the children served in early intervention settings come from

---
Effective Education for Learners with Exceptionalities, Volume 15, pages 351–372.
Copyright © 2003 by Elsevier Science Ltd.
All rights of reproduction in any form reserved.
ISBN: 0-7623-0975-X

culturally and/or linguistically diverse backgrounds while some children experience devastating poverty and unsafe living conditions. Some states can barely fund the minimal requirements for early intervention services and report severe shortages of qualified early childhood special educators. In this chapter, we provide an overview of the recommended practices in early childhood special education and describe the challenges we face in providing services that address the diverse needs of young children and their families today. We start by describing the philosophical underpinnings of early childhood special education. Next, we outline some current trends in service delivery models, assessment practices, and instructional approaches for meeting the needs of young children with disabilities in diverse settings. Lastly, we address issues of personnel preparation in early childhood special education.

PHILOSOPHICAL UNDERPINNINGS OF EARLY CHILDHOOD SPECIAL EDUCATION

The philosophical underpinnings of modern practices in early childhood special education (ECSE) can be traced back to the collaborative work of two national organizations, the National Association for the Education of Young Children (NAEYC), and the Division of Early Childhood (DEC) of the Council for Exceptional Children. Each organization has developed documents stating their philosophy and recommended practices (Bredekamp & Copple, 1997; DEC Task Force, 1993; Odom & McLean, 1996; Sandall, McLean & Smith, 2000). Not surprisingly, the two groups have much in common in their philosophical approaches to serving young children with and without disabilities. The three primary values and beliefs that drive the practice of early childhood special education are the following:

(1) all young children are valued and full participants in their families, communities, and schools;
(2) high quality early intervention can help ensure that all young children reach their full developmental potential and attain functional skills in areas of communication, mobility, social competence, cognition, and self-care; and
(3) families benefit from consistent and supportive partnerships and collaborations with service providers (Sandall et al., 2000, p. 151).

In assuring that all children are valued and respected, ECSE embraces the concepts of cultural responsiveness and respect for children and families from diverse cultural, linguistic, social, and economic backgrounds. Interventionists must develop cultural competence and implement intervention strategies that are respectful of and appropriate to the beliefs, values, and traditions of families from varying cultural and linguistic groups (Barrera, 2000; Kalyanpur & Harry, 1999; Lynch & Hanson, 1997; Miller & Stayton, 2000). Furthermore, early childhood special educators should adopt a resource-based approach to intervention that stresses "supports and resources that develop and strengthen families' sense of parenting competence and confidence" (Trivette & Dunst, 2000, p. 42). The importance of the families' informal supports (kinship, friends, community, church), should be understood while also acknowledging that some families rely primarily on formal supports (professionals). It is the responsibility of early childhood educators to enhance the informal supports for families and empower them to use their own social networks.

To ensure that all young children reach their full developmental potential and attain functional skills in all areas of development, early childhood special educators are required to have comprehensive knowledge and skills in assessment, curriculum, and instructional strategies in order to promote positive outcomes for young children. Intervention in the child's natural environment also requires coordination of services with a variety of personnel including early childhood educators, related service personnel, and program administrators. "Collaboration requires shared goals, open and effective communication, and a willingness to solve problems as a team" (Sandall, McLean, Santos & Smith, 2000, p. 9). Transdisciplinary models of teaming, collaboration, and consultation have been effective in ECSE (McWilliam, 2000; Thomas, Correa & Morsink, 2001). This approach to teaming involves professionals from different disciplines working together, with one member of the team working directly with the family. Transdisciplinary teaming makes intervention more holistic and integrates the expertise of individual team members from various disciplines.

It is apparent that the goal of early intervention is to provide learning opportunities for children in natural settings. The right of all children to participate actively and meaningfully with their families and communities has been referred to as the principle of normalization. Effective methods for including young children with disabilities in family childcare homes, childcare centers, and public schools have been studied extensively over the years (Gurlanick, 2001; Thurman, Cornwell & Ridener-Gottwald, 1997). If a child with disabilities is identified at birth, services often begin in the hospital and move to the home, community, and eventually to the school. Early childhood special educators are charged with creating a seamless system of services including smooth transitions for children and families from one program to the next. A seamless system has no delays or gaps between services for children from birth to age two, under Part C of IDEA, and children age three to five, under Part B of IDEA (Bowe, 2000). The next section of this chapter will address several service delivery options available for meeting the needs of children with disabilities from birth through age five.

SERVICE DELIVERY OPTIONS IN EARLY CHILDHOOD SPECIAL EDUCATION

A goal of early childhood special education is individualization of services for children with disabilities and their families. In collaboration with families, ECSE personnel are asked to provide services in natural environments that meet the needs of the child and family. Several options have been used in early intervention and preschool programs. According to Graham and Bryant (1993), the most frequent model of service delivery for infants and toddlers is home-based, while for preschool children it is public school based. However, multiple models of service delivery have emerged as families and ECSE personnel have worked toward a greater continuum of service activities in natural environments. A seamless system of service delivery starting with hospital care and moving to community based settings is presented in Fig. 1.

Neonatal Intensive Care

Services for many newborns with disabilities begin in the hospital and in neonatal intensive care units (NICU). This environment is often intimidating and distressing for families of newborns who have or are at risk for disabilities. Many advances have been made in the way that services are provided in the

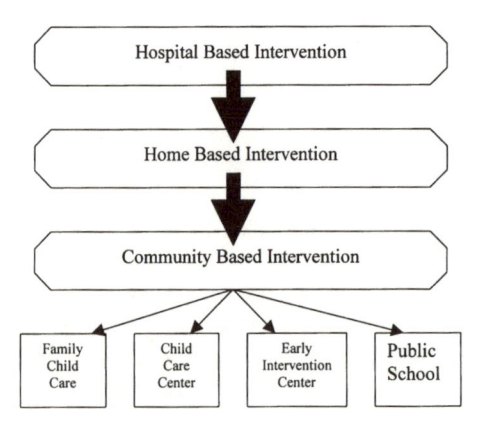

Fig. 1. A Seamless Model of Early Intervention.

NICU. Thurman et al. (1997) reported on the trend towards creating family focused intervention in the NICU. Personnel in the NICU frequently acknowledge the importance that families play in the health and development of newborns. In many NICU settings, a family-friendly environment is created to encourage parents and family members to spend time with the newborn. Technological advances in neonatal intensive care allow families to more easily hold, feed, and interact with their newborns. The strict medical approach to intervention has given way to a more family oriented approach. NICU staff, including social workers, nurses, and peer counselors, provide ongoing support to families as they cope with their newborns' medical conditions. Early interventionists are often hired to serve on the NICU team and to provide support and information to families about early childhood special education. Often, infants leave the NICU with an established Individualized Family Service Plan (IFSP) and support services to follow once the infant goes home. This is a critical period in a families' life and often sets the stage for future family-professional relationships and interactions.

Home-Based Intervention

Home visitation models have been used extensively over the years. One of the most recognized models of home-based intervention was the Portage Project funded in 1969 to provide educational services to preschool children and their families in rural areas. The model continues to be used today although states vary significantly in how they provide Part C services. In a study of 20 states' Part C programs, Spiker et al. (2000) found that service coordination took on various forms including: (a) use of "preliminary-to-ongoing" vs. "single" service coordinator model; (b) personnel from independent agency vs. program providing direct services; (c) service coordinators with single vs. multiple roles with families; and (d) service coordinators who serve only infant/toddlers vs. other ages of clients. Furthermore, the authors found that most Part C programs provided services first by public agency agencies and then by private program or providers under contract with the local agency.

Not surprising, early interventionists serving infants under 18 months of age typically provide in-home services one day per week, working closely with the primary caregiver on early stimulation activities. The advantage of this model of service delivery is that learning takes place in the child's natural environment, encouraging generalization of skills directly to the home setting. Early interventionists are able to observe the child in the home setting and understand the role that family culture plays in the care of the child. Additionally, families are not burdened by transportation requirements. To solve the problem of families being isolated from other families of children with disabilities and children being isolated from peer social interactions, some programs have incorporated a center-based component to their model. In those cases, families are encouraged to attend meetings at a central location in order to foster social interactions and family support groups. The home plus center model appears to be an effective approach to serving infants and toddlers with disabilities.

Community-Based Intervention

At some point in the early intervention system, children and families transition from home to community based services. Often, the transition is necessary because family members are required to work and can no longer stay at home with the infant. In some cases, families choose to place their children in family child care settings (usually a mother who is caring for her own preschoolers and serves six to eight children in her home). This model of service delivery for children with disabilities is becoming more common as states provide more support and training to family child care providers (Thurman et al., 1997; Buell, Gamel-McCormick & Hallman, 1999). In other cases, families seek out high quality child care centers that support the inclusion of children with disabilities. Unfortunately, inclusive community child care programs are not widely available to families, and when available they require extensive collaboration and consultation between early childhood educators, early childhood special educators, and related service personnel.

School-Based Intervention

The transition from Part C services to Part B services can also involve a transition from home to the community and public school. When the child turns three years of age, services are typically transferred to community child care programs, Head Start programs, or public school classroom settings. A transition plan is required at least 90 days before the child turns three years of age, and involves the family and personnel from both the exiting and receiving programs. McWilliam (2000) described a continuum of service models ranging from most segregated to most integrated which included one-on-one pull-out; small group pull-out; one-on-one in classrooms, group activities, individualized within routines, and pure consultation. Overall, a variety of classroom models from self-contained to inclusive settings are used for educating preschool children with disabilities. However, the DEC of the Council for Exceptional Children support "the continued development, implementation, evaluation, and dissemination of *full inclusion* supports, services, and systems that are of high quality for all children" (cited in Sandall et al., 2000, p. 150). Early childhood educators, early childhood special educators, and related service personnel must be trained and prepared to implement inclusive practices for each individual child and family.

Much is known about creating quality inclusive programs for young children with disabilities (Guralnick, 2001). In recent years, the research focus has moved from "how to include" children with disabilities to "what makes a quality inclusive program." Inclusion in early childhood special education is implemented in very different ways across state and local education agencies. It is estimated that 50% of all children with disabilities who are receiving services are being served in inclusive settings (U.S. Department of Education, 1998). Those settings, however, are varied. In a recent report on defining inclusive practices, Odom et al. (1999) found that programs varied on two levels: (a) the structure or organization of the program; and (b) the range of service delivery models. Table 1 outlines the different types of inclusive programs and ranges of service delivery.

Experience has shown that inclusion for preschool children with disabilities has been very effective. However, there are many complex variables that affect the success of inclusive programs. In a recent article reviewing the literature on inclusion, Odom (2000) concluded that:

- Children with and without disabilities make positive gains in inclusive settings.
- School systems are more likely to include children with mild disabilities than children with severe disabilities.
- There is less social interaction between children with disabilities and their peers in inclusive settings than between typically developing peers.
- Individualized instructional strategies and techniques must be implemented in order to produce positive outcomes for preschoolers with disabilities.
- Teachers and family members generally have positive attitudes toward inclusion.
- School administrators influence the success of inclusion by implementing policies that promote inclusive programs (e.g. funding, staffing, and standards).
- Cultural and linguistic diversity of families and communities have an impact on inclusion for preschoolers with disabilities from those backgrounds.

Including preschoolers with disabilities in general education settings can be complicated, time consuming, and require extraordinary skills in collaboration and family involvement. General classroom modifications should be designed to be straightforward. The accommodations most often used by teachers in

Table 1. Different Types of Inclusive Programs and Range of Services.

TYPES OF INCLUSIVE PROGRAMS

Community-Based Child Care	Children attend non-profit and for-profit preschools and child care centers located outside of public school buildings. Both the community-based child care and the public school agencies participate in the funding and organization of these programs.
Head Start Programs	Chldren attend programs which Head Start agencies fund and organize.
Public School Early Childhood Education	Children attend early childhood and early childhood special education classes in public schools. These programs are operated through public schools.
Public School Head Start Combination	Children attend Head Start classrooms away from or within public school buildings. In these settings, the public school system administers the contract for Head Start services.
Public School Child Care	Children attend tuition-based child care programs organized by the public school system.
Dual Enrollment	Children divide their days between early childhood education programs and inclusive or nonintegrated special education programs.

RANGE OF INCLUSIVE SERVICES

Itinerant Teaching Model – Direct Service	Services are provided regularly by visiting special education teachers and other service providers in early chldhood education settings.
Itinerant Teaching Model – Collaborative/Consultative	Special education teachers and service providers consult with early childhood teachers to incorporate individualized goals into the classroom curriculum.
Team Teaching Model	Early childhood and special education teachers share teaching roles in the same classroom, collaborating on planning and leading activities.
Early Childhood Teacher Model	Early childhood teachers plan, implement, and supervise classroom activities for children with and without disabilities.
Early Childhood Special Education	Early childhood special education teachers plan, implement, and supervise classroom activities. Children without disabilities are brought into the classroom.
Integrative/Inclusive Activities	Children with and without disabilities attend separate classrooms, but participate in joint activities for a portion of the day.

Excerpted from Odom, S., Horn, E., Marquart, J., Hanson, M., Wolfbert, R., Beckman, P., Lieber, J., Li, S., Schwartz, I., Janko, S., & Sandall, S. (1999). On the forms of inclusion: Organizational context and individualized service delivery models. *Journal of Early Intervention, 22,* 185–199.

inclusive settings include: (a) adapting curriculum for children with sensory, physical, or cognitive disabilities; (b) learning to pace instruction and adjust the amount of time needed for each activity; (c) providing a hierarchy of prompts and physical assistance for completing an activity; (d) determining effective behavioral management programs; (e) obtaining appropriate adaptive equipment and materials; and (f) making physical adaptations to the school environment (Lieber, Schwartz, Sandall, Horn & Wolery, 1999). Although much is known about inclusion in ECSE, it is not surprising that more research is needed in this area. Odom (2000) acknowledged that future research on inclusion ought to focus on the quality of the programs, such as evaluating: (a) actual child engagement in classroom routines; (b) effective instructional strategies and intensity within naturalistic learning models; (c) social interactions and relationships between teachers, peers, and preschoolers with disabilities; and (d) the models of funding that best promote inclusive practices. Additionally, the costs of inclusion and the barriers related to funding policies in states and local education agencies should be researched. Until state and local policies are developed to better support inclusion, families will continue to face enormous amounts of resistance to receiving quality services for their children in inclusive settings. Clearly, inclusion remains a "serious socio-political issue that has strong proponents and opponents" (Bricker, 2000, p. 17).

IDENTIFICATION AND ASSESSMENT OF YOUNG CHILDREN WITH DISABILITIES

Identification and assessment of young children with disabilities is multifaceted and requires a multidisciplinary approach. Families also play an important role in the process. For infants and toddlers, the evaluation begins with the family identifying the developmental needs of their child. The multidisciplinary evaluation team then gathers information on the resources, priorities, and concerns of the family and supports and services necessary to enhance the family's capacity to meet the developmental needs of their infant or toddler with disabilities (IDEA, 1997). This process is known as family assessment. Any assessment that is conducted must be voluntary on the part of the family. Early intervention personnel must assess the family using appropriate methods and procedures, including a personal interview with the family. For preschoolers aged three through five, families are involved in the assessment process by providing information on the child's development. Parents should provide the assessment team with relevant functional and developmental information about their child. In doing its work, the assessment team gathers information on how the child can be involved in the general curriculum.

Child find programs are the earliest forms of screening and assessment for identifying children who have disabilities or who are at risk for disabilities. Under both Part B and C of IDEA, states are required to develop programs that identify, at an early age, children who are at risk for disabilities. Kenny and Culbertson (1997) report that physicians and other primary-care providers are natural and excellent choices to perform screening, because families regularly take children to doctors, well-baby pediatric clinics, and hospitals. For children from significantly low socioeconomic backgrounds or who have no medical insurance, the emergency room may be the first place medical-care providers have access to infants or preschoolers for developmental screening. Some of the most common screening instruments used for young children include the Denver II (Frankenburg et al., 1990), the Battelle Developmental Inventory (Newborg, Stock, Wnek, Guidubaldi & Svinicki, 1984), and the Minnesota Child Development Inventory (Ireton & Thwing, 1974).

Naturalistic Approaches to Assessment

Standardized and norm-referenced assessments of young children suspected of having disabilities have been used for many years (see Culbertson & Willis, 1993 for full discussion). However, the appropriateness and validity of using these methods of assessment with young children has come under serious criticism (Bagnato, Neisworth & Munson, 1996; Bagnato & Neisworth, 2000; McConnell, 2000; NAEYC, 1991; Neisworth & Bagnato, 2000). In more recent years, professionals have recommended the use of more developmentally appropriate, authentic, and naturalistic approaches to assessment (Bowe, 2000; Linder, 1993; Sandall et al., 2000). Some of their recommended practices include the following:

- Using transdisciplinary team approaches that emphasize play based arena assessments.
- Including multiple sources and measures collected across various environments.
- Collaborating with families on gathering information and making decisions about their child's assessment.
- Understanding how culture, language, and socioeconomic status influences the assessment process and outcomes for children and families.
- Promoting the idea that assessment is ongoing, flexible, and built on team consensus.

Several curriculum-based assessment instruments have been developed such as the Assessment, Evaluation, and Programming Systems for Infants and Children

(AEPS) (Bricker, 1993), the Assessment, Evaluation, and Programming Systems for Preschoolers (Briker & Pretti-Frontczak, 1996), and the Work Sampling Systems (WSS) (Meisels, Liaw, Dorfman & Nelson, 1995). These evaluation tools are designed to link a performance-based assessment of a child with developmentally appropriate curricula, individualized planning, and instructional procedures. Although they are very useful in monitoring developmental gains and children's progress in early intervention, McConnell (2000) recommended that a combination of assessment approaches be used to better evaluate both progress and the rate of change children make in a program.

Performance-based instruments expose the skills and competencies children acquire, while general outcome measures expose how quickly the child acquires the skills to meet the academic demand of a later classroom environment (McConnell, 2000). When using general outcome measures, particular domains or areas are indexed against a common long-term goal. For example, with a general outcomes based approach, the early interventionists would not only measure a child's progress on specific semantic and syntax skills, but would also monitor the outcomes related to a more global goal of the child's use of gestures, sounds, and words to express his/her needs to others (Priest et al., 2001). This approach would typically incorporate measurements across an extended period of time and development (e.g. every three months). "General outcome measures more directly measure child progress in a broader developmental context, allowing interventionists and others to determine whether current situations are leading to desired rates of development toward long term goals" (see McConnell, p. 46).

Lastly, an ecobehavioral approach to evaluation and assessment is being used more widely in early intervention programs (McConnell, 2000). This approach can improve the ability to identify conditions associated with a child's desired or undesired developmental outcomes and identify potentially effective treatment conditions or components of the treatment setting. Most of the work documenting the effectiveness of this approach in assessment examined the impact of environmental variables in one or multiple settings on the child's behaviors (Malmskog & McDonnell, 1999). The use of functional behavioral assessments and behavioral intervention plans are of widespread interest since the requirements for discipline and behavioral intervention have been outlined more specifically in the reauthorized IDEA 1997.

Integrating the wealth of information gathered from a high quality assessment can be time-consuming and challenging for ECSE professionals. One method for collecting the multiple sources of information is the use of portfolios. According to Bowe (2000), a portfolio can include records of direct observations, video or tape recordings, photographs, checklists and rating scales, passports [notebook of parent-teacher communication], and more traditional criterion-referenced and norm-referenced tests. Furthermore, researchers with the Early Childhood Research Institute on Measuring Growth and Development (1998) developed a comprehensive assessment decision making model that includes "frequent monitoring of child program and growth, formal decision rules for identifying desirable and undesirable rates of progress and growth, explicit procedures for producing data to help evaluate the likely merit of different intervention options, and a formal and explicit role for parents and families in evaluating all data and informing all decisions" (McConnell, 2000, p. 47). Improved methods for assessing child development and early intervention programs are clearly on the horizon.

CURRICULUM, INSTRUCTION, AND INTERVENTION IN EARLY CHILDHOOD SPECIAL EDUCATION

Although many definitions of curriculum exist, the definition used in this section will be that of Wolery and Sainato (1996). Using their definition, curriculum has three elements: (1) the content to be taught; (2) the methods used to determine the content for each child; and (3) the methods used to ensure that the content identified for each child is acquired and used. Curriculum content includes those behaviors, skills, and abilities that may be targets of intervention for young children with disabilities as well as those skills that would be appropriate for most young children. The methods for ensuring acquisition and use of content are the environmental arrangements determined appropriate for each child including choice of materials, furniture, and equipment, as well as specific intervention strategies deemed appropriate by the team through the IEP process.

Curriculum content often draws from a number of theoretical approaches. Garguilo and Kilgo (2000) described five theoretical models typically used in ECSE. The *developmental curriculum model* is based on theories of typical child development and includes sequenced milestone skills that children are expected to achieve. Children's acquisition of more advanced skills is supported through their interactions with the physical and social aspects of the environment. The *developmental-cognitive curriculum model* is based on the work of Piaget. The content is similar to the developmental curriculum model with an emphasis placed on the development of cognitive skills. The *academic (or preacademic) skills model* is closely related to the first two models in that it assumes development is based on a group of core skills typically taught to young children. Preacademic skills are often those thought necessary for school readiness, for example., an underlying behavior needed to learn or perform a specific task. Preacademic skills come from every area of development and as such, could all be labeled as readiness skills (Allen & Schwartz, 1996). The *behavioral curriculum model* is based on the learning principals of behavioral psychology. These theorists (e.g. Skinner & Bijou) propose that children are motivated to learn by their environment and therefore highlights the importance of the activities in which the child engages and the skills necessary to do so. This model places emphasis on the use of direct instruction procedures (e.g. prompting, shaping, and reinforcement). In the *functional curriculum model,* functional skills having immediate relevance to a child are emphasized. These skills tend to be based on the demands of the environment and those required to perform tasks of daily living (e.g. dressing and eating). The child's proficiency in acquiring age appropriate skills holds more importance than his or her developmental age.

There are advantages and disadvantages to each of the aforementioned curriculum models, however, early childhood programs rarely adhere strictly to any one model. Rather, a combination of approaches is most often the case. Decisions about the use of a particular curriculum model are based on a number of factors including: (a) goals of the program; (b) philosophical beliefs as well as attitudes and education of the teachers; (c) values, beliefs and traditions of the families involved; and (d) age and developmental levels of the children enrolled.

Child-Focused Intervention

Regardless of the curriculum model implemented, children with disabilities need specialized instruction based on their unique needs as determined by the team and specified as their individual goals and objectives on the IEP or IFSP. The recommended practice for implementing this instruction is the use of child-focused intervention. Doing so involves making decisions about how children are taught, where they are taught, and how to monitor progress to make adjustments in instruction and goals (Wolery, 2000). Child-focused intervention are based on the premise that promoting children's learning and development is a primary concern of early intervention, that learning and development are significantly influenced by children's interactions with their social and physical environment, and that intervention methods selected are based on research. Wolery points out that implementing the recommended practices in child-focused intervention is a complex process. It requires adults to "do specific things (design environments, individualize and adapt practices and use systematic procedures) in very purposeful ways to produce specific outcomes" (see Wolery, p. 31). These DEC recommended practices have been designed to be a guide for planning and implementing effective interventions that promote learning and development.

Naturalistic Instructional Approaches

Naturalistic instruction is a generic term for specific, specialized interventions known as milieu teaching (Kaiser, Yoder & Keetz, 1992), incidental teaching (Hart & Risley, 1968; Warren & Kaiser, 1986), and activity-based instruction (Bricker, Pretti-Frontczak & McComas, 1998). The value of these approaches is that they allow individual instruction to occur without disruption of the classroom or home routines. They may prove to be particularly useful in inclusive early childhood classrooms where teachers feel that they cannot and do not want to provide *different* interventions (i.e. those that would point out his or her disability) for children with disabilities. Naturalistic instructional approaches have the following characteristics in common. *One feature common to all approaches is the importance of following the child's lead and interests.* By following the child's lead, the adult engages in an activity of interest to the child and increases the likelihood of continued interaction. *The second common feature is embedding learning opportunities in ongoing routines and activities that occur across the day.* When instruction on individual goals and objectives occurs in these activities, multiple opportunities and contexts for practice and generalization are provided. *Another common feature is the use of naturally occurring consequences (or reinforcement) as part of the activity.* Since objects and events are those of interest and desired by the child, consequences are more meaningful and are more likely to increase the desired behavior.

The research literature on the effectiveness of these approaches is growing. Naturalistic approaches have been effectively used with children with diverse abilities to teach communication skills (Hart & Risley, 1968, 1975; Kaiser et al., 1992; Warren & Kaiser, 1986), imitation (Venn, Wolery, Werts, Morris, DeCesare & Cuffs, 1993), and fine motor skills (Fox & Hanline, 1993). Initial studies on the effectiveness of these approaches in inclusive classroom settings are encouraging (Grisham-Brown & Hemmeter, 1997; Horn, Lieber, Li, Sandall & Schwartz, 2000) but limited. Although these approaches require complex planning for implementation, their value for use in inclusive settings is likely to prompt continued development of methods to support their use in the classroom (Horn et al., 2000; Odom, 2000).

Technology Applications

The 1997 reauthorization emphasizes the use of technology applications with *all* children with disabilities as necessary to increase, maintain, or improve their functional capabilities. This includes children with disabilities in early intervention and preschool programs. The appropriate use of technology applications can be a valuable tool in enhancing the lives of young children with disabilities as well as improve teaching and learning for children, families, and professionals. As a result, the use of technology applications has become commonplace in schools and early childhood settings (Brett, 1997). This popularity has also led to the development of a number of innovative programs and services providing information and technical assistance in the use of technology applications with young children. The PennTECH Assistive Technology Early Intervention Program of the Pennsylvania Department of Education, Activating Children Through Technology (ACTT) (Hutinger & Johanson, 2000), and the National Center to Improve Practice (NCIP) are just a few programs and projects that provide training, equipment loan programs, assistance with policy development, as well as software and hardware adaptations.

Technology applications for young children fall into several categories and range on a continuum from low-tech (e.g. velcro) to high-tech (e.g. computers). The recommended categories of technology used to provide access to natural learning environments and early childhood curriculum are motor, cognitive/perceptual, communication, medical, social interactions, adaptive, daily living, play, and academic (Stremel, 2000). Parette and Murdick (1998) mentioned visual, listening, and leisure as assistive technology areas that may facilitate the inclusion of a child with disabilities. If technology is used appropriately, the benefits to children, their families, and the professionals who serve them can be astounding. Examples of these effects were seen in a recent report of the Early Childhood Comprehensive Technology System (ECCTS). Based on this report, there were documented positive outcomes for children (e.g. there was progress in all areas of development including social-emotional growth as measured by the Brigance, the Behavior Interaction Tool), increased technology skills among teachers, and maintenance of the system in the school partners (Hutinger & Johanson, 2000).

Although the evidence strongly points to the potential of technology applications to improve the lives of children with disabilities and their families, there are obstacles that may hinder its use. Parette and Murdick (1998) described three such obstacles: (1) lack of training; (2) technology abandonment (i.e. unused assistive technologies); and (3) expense. Given the potential for technology applications to improve access to and increased independence in the natural environment, continued efforts should be made to ensure adequate training in assessment and use of technology as well as knowledge of funding sources. Research to provide a framework for inservice, preservice, and policy development is also needed if technology is to develop fully the promise it holds for children with disabilities, families, and professionals (Lesar, 1998).

PERSONNEL PREPARATION TRENDS IN EARLY CHILDHOOD SPECIAL EDUCATION

The job of the early childhood special education professional has become more challenging as advances have been made in the field. Today, the roles and responsibilities associated with the job of educating young children with disabilities birth to age five go beyond the traditional work of child intervention. Early childhood special educators are also required to develop knowledge and skills in collaboration, teaming, consultation, service coordination, supervision, advocacy, and administration. A career in ECSE entails extraordinary efforts in systems change and leadership. Furthermore, the models of service delivery in early childhood special education require that personnel work in a variety of settings including hospitals, private homes, family child care homes, private and public child care facilities, and private and public school settings.

It is not surprising, then, that institutions that prepare early childhood special educators are rethinking and reinventing the essential components of ECSE programs. One of most significant advances in reforming the preparation of early childhood special educators came with the call for unification of the fields of early childhood and early childhood special education. In the early 1990s, the Association of Teacher Education (ATE), the Division of Early Childhood (DEC), and the National Association for the Education of Young Children (NAEYC) began a dialogue on the need for preparing all individuals who work with children in early childhood settings to posses knowledge and skills for working with young children with disabilities. The dialogue eventually led to a position paper endorsed by all three organizations that supported a framework for personnel standards in early childhood, early childhood special education, and related services professionals (DEC, NAEYC & ATE, 1995). These three organizations further recommended that "personnel standards be derived from empirically defensible knowledge and clearly articulated philosophical assumptions about what constitutes effective early education and early intervention for young children with special needs and their families" (Miller & Stayton, 2000, p. 91). Lastly, it was recommended that early childhood licenses should be freestanding and separate from existing general education elementary or secondary special education licenses.

The guidelines developed for ECSE are based on performance standards in the categories of: (a) child development and learning; (b) curriculum development and implementation; (c) family and community relationships; (d) assessment and evaluation; (e) field experiences; and (f) professionalism (DEC, NAEYC & ATE, 1995). Integral to the content preservice and inservice teachers must learn in ECSE is the process or delivery model involved in preparing teachers. Several researchers have suggested what quality professional development programs in early childhood special education should contain (Bailey, 1996; Buysse, Wesley & Able-Boone, 2001; Fenichel & Eggbeer, 1991). Table 2 outlines the key components of inservice and preservice preparation programs.

The impetus created by the unification and collaboration of the fields of early childhood and early childhood special education has led to reform in EC and ECSE teacher preparation programs. Several models for unifying or blending early childhood and early childhood special education have been implemented (Correa, Hartle, Jones, Kemple, Rapport & Smith-Bonhue, 1997; Kemple, Hartle, Correa & Fox, 1994; Miller & Stayton, 1998, 1999; Winton, McCollum & Catlett, 1997). Furthermore, the move toward more inclusive education and integrated transdisciplinary therapy has spurred new techniques for personnel preparation for paraprofessionals, related service personnel, and early childhood educators. As the field of early intervention expands and the roles of early interventionists become more complex there ought to be added training at both the inservice and preservice levels. Great gains have been made in the preparation of early childhood professionals, however, new ideas and knowledge

Table 2. Key components of inservice and preservice preparation programs.

(1) Create a preparation program built on a framework of concepts that are common to all disciplines working with young children and their families (Fenichel & Eggbeer, 1991).
(2) Establish a core of knowledge on inclusion and family-centered practices that can be integrated throughout the curricula of personnel preparation programs in various disciplines (Bailey, 1996).
(3) Provide individualized supervision and support during formal preparation and throughout the stages of a professional's career including mentoring programs (Fenichel & Eggbeer, 1991).
(4) Arrange opportunities throughout personnel preparation programs to respond to conflicting values held by families and other professionals (Bailey, 1996).
(5) Incorporate knowledge and skills in problem solving for professionals who face ethical challenges by using case method instruction to resolve thorny issues in early intervention (Bailey, 1996).
(6) Build "communities of practice" by including families, university faculty, researchers, policy makers, administrators, and service providers to inform and translate the necessary knowledge base for preparation programs (Buysse, Wesley & Able-Boone, 2001).
(7) Emphasize the knowledge and skills necessary for professionals to feel comfortable with collaboration and consultation through self-reflection and practice in teaming with professionals and families (Dinnebeil, Hale & Rule, 1999; Wesely, Buysse & Keyes, 2000; Thomas, Correa & Morsink, 2001).
(8) Create opportunities for direct involvement with young children and families from culturally and linguistically diverse backgrounds as well as teenage parents, parents with disabilities, and homeless families (Fenichel & Eggbeer, 1991; Kalyanpur & Harry, 1999; Lynch & Hanson, 1997).

from our research to practice and from our practice back to research must continue to be disseminated. Furthermore, more early childhood special education personnel from culturally and linguistically diverse backgrounds must be recruited and retained. The needs of diverse children would be better met by professionals who understand the culture and linguistic demands of this population. No doubt, the quality of services for children with disabilities and families depends on the recruitment of quality professionals into ECSE and their continued professional development.

FUTURE DIRECTIONS

Despite the significant progress that has been made over the past two decades, much work is still needed to insure that all young children with disabilities receive the most appropriate and effective services. We have constructed a foundation for a comprehensive system of services for young children with disabilities and their families. We have advanced our knowledge base in multiple areas including inclusion (Guralnick, 2000; Odom, 2000), assessment and instructional strategies (Hemmeter, 2000; McConnell, 2000), ECSE curriculum (Bruder, 1997), and personnel preparation (Miller & Stayton, 2000). The new DEC recommended practices provide the road map for the future of ECSE.

We must continue to "push the envelope" on the philosophical goals of improving early childhood special education services for children and families. We have become significantly a more diverse population and that diversity will challenge us to providing services that are culturally responsive to young children and their families. The numbers of children living in "high-risk" environments continue to trouble us as a profession. Today, early interventionists are being challenged to meet the needs of these vulnerable children and families exposed to conditions such poverty, HIV, drug abuse, violence, and homelessness. Since the passage of the landmark early intervention legislation in 1986 (PL 99-457), we have made tremendous advances in understanding the perplexing issues that face early childhood special educators today. In collaboration with families, professionals from various disciplines, and policy makers, we will continue to make great headway!

REFERENCES

Allen, K. E., & Schwartz, I. S. (1996). *The exceptional child: Inclusion in early childhood education* (3rd ed.). Albany, NY: Delmar Publishers.
Bagnato, S. J., Neisworth, J. T., & Munson, J. (1997). *LINKing: Assessment and early intervention.* Baltimore: Paul H. Brookes.

Bagnato, S. J., & Neisworth, J. T. (2000, Spring). Assessment is adjusted to each child's developmental needs. *Birth through Five Newsletter, 1*(2), 1.
Bailey, D. B. (1996). An overview of interdisciplinary training. In: D. Bricker & A. Widerstrom (Eds), *Preparing Personnel to Work with Infants and Young Children and Their Families: A Team Approach* (pp. 3–22). Baltimore: Paul H. Brookes.
Barrera, L. (2000). Honoring differences: Essential features of appropriate ECSE services for young children from diverse sociocultural environments. *Young Exceptional Children, 3*(4), 17–24.
Bowe, F. G. (2000). *Birth to five early childhood special education* (2nd ed.). Albany, NY: Delmar Publishers.
Bredekamp, S., & Copple, C. (1997). *Developmentally appropriate practice in early childhood programs* (Rev. ed.). Washington, D.C.: National Association for the Education of Young Children.
Brett, A. (1997). Assistive and adaptive technology: Supporting competence and independence in young children with disabilities. *Dimensions of Early Childhood, 25*(3), 14–15, 18–20.
Bricker, D. D. (1993). *The assessment, evaluation, and programming system for infants and young children: Vol. 1. AEPS measurement for birth to three years.* Baltimore: Paul H. Brookes.
Bricker, D. D. (2000). Inclusion: How the scene has changed. *Topics in Early Childhood Special Education, 20,* 14–19.
Bricker, D. D., & Pretti-Frontczak, K. L. (Eds) (1996). *The assessment, evaluation, and programming system for infants and young children: Vol. 3 AEPS measurement for three to six years.* Baltimore: Paul H. Brookes.
Bricker, D., Pretti-Frontczak, K., & McComas, N. R. (1998). *An activity-based approach to early intervention* (2nd ed.). Baltimore: Brookes.
Bruder, M. B. (1997). The effectiveness of specific educational/developmental curricula for children with established disabilities. In: M. Guralnick (Ed.), *The Effectiveness of Early Intervention* (pp. 523–548). Baltimore: Paul H. Brookes.
Bryant, D., & Graham, M. (1993). *Implementing early intervention: from research to effective practice.* New York: The Guilford Press.
Buell, M. J., Gamel-McCormick, M., & Hallam, R. (1999). Inclusion in childcare context: Experiences and attitudes of family childcare providers. *Topic in Early Childhood Special Education, 19,* 217–224.
Buysse, V., Wesley, P., & Able-Boone, H. (2001). Innovations in professional development: creating communities of practice to support inclusion, In: M. Guralnick (Ed.), *Early Childhood Inclusion Focus on Change* (pp. 179–200). Baltimore: Paul H. Brookes.
Correa, V., Hartle, L., Jones, H., Kemple, K., Rapport, M. J., & Smith-Bonhue, T. (1997). The Unified PROTEACH early childhood program at the University of Florida. In: L. Blanton, C. Griffin, J. Winn & M. Pugach (Eds), *Teacher Education in Transition: Collaborative Practices in General and Special Education* (pp. 84–105). Denver, CO: Love Publishing.
Culbertson, J., & Willis, D. J. (Eds) (1993). *Testing young children: A reference guide for developmental, psychoeducational, and psychosocial assessments.* Austin, TX: Pro-Ed.
Bricker, D., Pretti-Frontczak, K., & McComas, N. (1998). *Activity-based approach to early intervention.* Baltimore: Paul H. Brookes.
Dinnebeil, L., Hale, L., & Rule, S. (1999). Early intervention program practices that support collaboration. *Topics in Early Childhood Special Education, 19,* 225–235.
Division for Early Childhood (DEC), National Association for the Education of Young Children (NAEYC), & Association of Teacher Educators (ATE) (1995). *Personnel standards for early education and early intervention: Guidelines for licensure in early childhood special education.* Denver, CO: Division of Early Childhood.

Division for Early Childhood Task Force on Recommended Practices (1993). *DEC recommended practices: Indicators of quality in programs for infants and young children with special needs and their families*. Reston, VA: Council for Exceptional Children.

Early Childhood Institute on Measuring Growth and Development (1998). *Research and development of individual growth and development indicators for children between birth and age eight* (Vol. 4). Minneapolis: University of Minnesota.

Fenichel, E. S., & Eggbeer, L. (1991). Preparing practitioners to work with infants, toddlers, and their families: Four essential elements of training. *Infants and Young Children*, 4(2), 56–62.

Fox, L., & Hanline, M. F. (1993). A preliminary evaluation of learning within developmentally appropriate early childhood settings. *Topics in Early Childhood Special Education*, 13, 308–327.

Frankenburg, W. K., Dodds, J. B., Archer, P., Bresnick, B., Maschka, P., Edelman, N., & Shapiro, H. (1990). *Denver II screening manual*. Denver, CO: Denver Developmental Materials.

Garguilo, R. M., & Kilgo, J. (2000). *Young children with special needs*. Albany, NY: Delmar Publishers.

Grisham-Brown, J., & Hemmeter, M. L. (1997). Effectiveness of embedded skill instruction on skill acquisition, maintenance and generalization. Paper presented at the Division of Early Childhood Conference, Pheonix.

Guralnick, M. J. (2001). *Early childhood inclusion: Focus on change*. Baltimore: Paul H. Brookes.

Hart, B., & Risley, T. R. (1968). Establishing the use of descriptive adjectives in the spontaneous speech of disadvantaged children. *Journal of Applied Behavior Analysis*, 1, 109–120.

Hart, B., & Risley, T. R. (1975). Incidental teaching of language in preschool. *Journal of Applied Behavior Analysis*, 8, 411–420.

Hemmeter, M. J. (2000). Classroom-based interventions: Evaluating the past and looking toward the future. *Topics in Early Childhood and Special Education*, 20, 56–61.

Horn, E., Lieber, J., Li, S., Sandall, S., & Schwartz, I. (2000). Supporting young children's IEP goals in inclusive settings through embedded learning opportunities. *Topics in Early Childhood Special Education*, 20, 208–223.

Hutinger, P. L., & Johanson, J. (2000). Implemeting and maintaining an effective early childhood comprehensive technology system. *Topics in Early Childhood Special Education*, 20, 159–173.

Individuals with Disabilities Education Act Amendment of 1997, PL 105-17, 20 U.S.C. & 1400 *et seq.*

Ireton, H., & Thwing, E. (1974). *Manual for the Minnesota child development inventory*. Minneapolis, MN: Behavior Science Systems.

Kaiser, A., Yoder, P., & Keetz, A. (1992). Evaluating milieu teaching. In: S. F. Warren & J. Reichle (Eds), *Causes and Effects in Communication and Language Intervention* (Vol. 1, pp. 9–47).

Kalyanpur, M., & Harry, B. (1999). *Culture in special education*. Baltimore: Paul H. Brookes.

Kemple, K. M., Hartle, L. C., Correa, V. I., & Fox, L. (1994). Preparing teachers for inclusive education: The development of a unified teacher program in early childhood and early childhood special education. *Teacher Education and Special Education*, 17, 38–51.

Kenny, T. J., & Culbertson, J. L. (1997) Developmental screening for preschoolers. In: J. L. Culbertson & D. J. Willis (Eds), *Testing Young Children: A Reference Guide for Developmental, Psychoeducational, and Psychosocial Assessment* (pp. 42–64). Austin, TX: Pro-Ed.

Lasar, S. (1998) Use of assistive technology with young children with disabilities: Current status and training. *Journal of Early Intervention*, 21, 146–159.

Lieber, J., Schwartz, I., Sandall, S., Horn, E., & Wolery, R. A. (1999). Curricular considerations for young children in inclusive settings. In: C. Seefeldt (Ed.), *The Early Childhood Curriculum: Current Findings in Theory and Practice* (pp. 93–118). New York: Teachers College Press.

Linder, T. W. (1993). *Transdisciplinary play-based intervention: Guidelines for developing a meaningful curriculum for young children.* Baltimore: Paul H. Brookes.

Lynch, E. W., & Hanson, M. J. (1997). *Developing cross-cultural competence: A guide for working with young children and their families* (2nd ed.). Baltimore: Paul H. Brookes.

Malmskog, S., & McDonnell, A. P. (1999). Teacher-mediated facilitation of engagement by children with developmental delays in inclusive preschools. *Topics of Early Childhood Special Education, 19,* 203–216.

McConnell, S. R. (2000). Assessment in early intervention and early childhood special education: Building on the past to present into our future. *Topics in Early Childhood Special Education, 20,* 43–48.

McWilliam, R. A. (2000). Recommended practices in interdisciplinary models. In: S. Sandall, M. E. McLean & B. J. Smith (Eds), *DEC Recommended Practices in Early Intervention/Early Childhood Special Education* (pp. 47–54). Longmont, CO: Sopris West.

Meisels, S. J., Liaw, F. R., Dorfman, A., & Nelson, R. N. (1995). The Work Sampling System: Reliability and validity of a performance assessment for young children. *Early Childhood Research Quarterly, 10,* 277–296.

Miller, P. S., & Stayton, V. D. (1998). Blended interdisciplinary teacher preparation in early education and intervention: A national study. *Topics in Early Childhood Special Education, 18*(1), 49–58.

Miller, P. S., & Stayton, V. D. (1999). Higher education culture – A fit or misfit with reform in teacher education? *Journal of Teacher Education, 50,* 290–302.

Miller, P. S., & Stayton, V. D. (2000). Recommended practices in personnel preparation. In: S. Sandall, M. E. McLean & B. J. Smith (Eds), *DEC Recommended Practices in Early Intervention/Early Childhood Special Education* (pp. 77–106). Longmont, CO: Sopris West.

National Association for the Education of Young Children and National Association of Early Childhood Specialists in State Departments of Education (1991). *Position statement: Guidelines for appropriate curriculum content and assessment in programs serving children ages three through eight* (NAEYC No. 725). Washington, D.C.: Author.

Neisworth, J. T., & Bagnato, S. J. (2000). Recommended practices in assessment. In: S. Sandall, M. E. McLean & B. J. Smith (Eds), *DEC Recommended Practices in Early Intervention/Early Childhood Special Education* (pp. 17–27). Longmont, CO: Sopris West.

Newborg, J., Stock, J. R., Wnek, L., Guidubaldi, J., & Svinicki, J. (1984). *Battelle developmental inventory.* Allent, TX: DLM Teaching Resources.

Odom, S. L. (2000). Preschool inclusion: What we know and where we go from here. *Topics in Early Childhood Special Education, 20*(1), 20–27.

Odom, S. L., & McLean, M. E. (1996). *Early intervention/early childhood special education: Recommended practices.* Austin, TX: Pro-Ed.

Odom, S., Horn, E., Marquart, J., Hanson, M., Wolfbert, R., Beckman, P., Lieber, J., Li, S., Schwartz, I., Janko, S., & Sandall, S. (1999). On the forms of inclusion: Organizational context and individualized service delivery models. *Journal of Early Intervention, 22,* 185–199.

Parett, H. P., & Murdick, N. L. (1998). Assistive technology and IEPs for young children with disabilities. *Early Childhood Education Journal, 25,* 193–198.

Priest, J., McConnell, S., Walker, D., Carta, J., Kaminski, R., McEvoy, M., Good, R., Greenwood, C., & Shinn, M. (2001). General growth outcomes for young children: Developing a foundation for continuous progress measurement. *Journal of Early Intervention, 24,* 163–180

Sandall, S., McLean, M. E., & Smith, B. J. (2000). *DEC Recommended Practices in Early Intervention/Early Childhood Special Education.* Longmont, CO: Sopris West.

Sandall, S., McLean, M. E., Santos, R. M., & Smith, B. J. (2000). DEC's new recommended practices: The context for change. In: S. Sandall, M. E. McLean & B. J. Smith (Eds), *DEC Recommended Practices in Early Intervention/Early Childhood Special Education* (pp. 5–16). Longmont, CO: Sopris West.

Smith, B. (2000). The federal role in early childhood special education policy in the next century: The responsibility of the individual. *Topics in Early Childhood Special Education, 20,* 7–13.

Spiker, D., Hebbeler, K., Wagner, M., Cameto, R., & McKenna, P. (2000). A framework for describing variations in state early intervention systems. *Topics in Early Childhood Special Education, 20,* 195–207.

Stremel, K. (2000). DEC recommended practices in technology applications. In: S. Sandall, M. E. McLean & B. J. Smith (Eds), *DEC Recommended Practices in Early Intervention/Early Childhood Special Education* (pp. 17–27). Longmont, CO: Sopris West.

Thomas, C., Correa, V., & Morsink, C. (2001). *Interactive teaming: Enhancing programs for students with special needs.* Upper Saddle River, NJ: Prentice-Hall.

Thurman, S. K., Cornewell, J. R., & Ridener-Gottwald, S. (1997). *Contexts of early intervention: Systems and settings.* Baltimore: Paul H. Brookes.

Trivette, C. M., & Dunst, C. J. (2000). Recommended practices in family-based practices. In: S. Sandall, M. E. McLean & B. J. Smith (Eds), *DEC Recommended Practices in Early Intervention/Early Childhood Special Education* (pp. 39–46). Longmont, CO: Sopris West.

U.S. Department of Education (1998). *To assure the free appropriate public education of all children with disabilities: Twentieth annual report to Congress on the implementation of the Individuals with Disability Act.* Washington, D.C.: Author.

Venn, M. L., Wolery, M., Werts, M. G., Morris, A., DeCesare, L. D., & Cuffs, M. S. (1993). Embedding instruction in art activities to teach preschoolers with disabilities to imitate their peers. *Early Childhood Research Quarterly, 8,* 277–294.

Warren, S. F., & Kaiser, A. P. (1986). Incidental language teaching: A critical review. *Journal of Speech and Hearing Disorders, 51,* 291–299.

Wesley, P. W., Buysse, V., & Keyes, L. (2000). Comfort zone revisited: Effects of child characteristics on professional comfort in providing consultation. *Journal of Early Intervention, 23,* 106–115.

Winton, P. J., McCollum, J. A., & Catlett, C. (1997). *Reforming personnel preparation in early intervention.* Baltimore: Paul H. Brookes.

Wolery, M. (2000). Recommended practices in child-focused interventions. In: S. Sandall, M. E. McLean & B. J. Smith (Eds), *DEC Recommended Practices in Early Intervention/Early Childhood Special Education* (pp. 17–27). Longmont, CO: Sopris West.

Wolery, M., & Sainato, D. M. (1996). General curriculum and intervention strategies. In: S. L. Odom & M. E. McLean (Eds), *Early Intervention/Early Childhood Special Education: Recommended Practices.* Austin, TX: Pro-Ed.

TRANSITIONS TO ADULTHOOD FOR YOUTH WITH DISABILITIES

Mary E. Morningstar and Kagendo Mutua

INTRODUCTION

Central to the goals of public education in the U.S. in the twenty-first century, is the focus on interventions and educational practices that lead to the achievement of valued educational outcomes for all students. Recent federal statutes and educational reform movements point to a renewed commitment to improving educational outcomes and to equipping all high school graduates with skills necessary for achieving success in the global marketplace. Those valued educational outcomes are at the core of recent federal legislation including, Goals 2000: Educate America Act, and PL 103-239, the 1994 School-to-Work Opportunities Act, as well as recent educational reform initiatives, including the Secretary's Commission on Achieving Necessary Skills (SCANS). While these initiatives are ostensibly geared to *all* students, some researchers (e.g. Phelps & Hanley-Maxwell, 1997) are concerned as to which of those initiatives were intended to include students with disabilities. Whether the clause, "all students" tacitly omits students with disabilities or not, the relevance of the outcomes espoused by these reform initiatives to students with disabilities is undeniable. The critical question is, How can reform initiatives such as transition help all learners to maximize their fullest potential? In this chapter, we will frame transition as a process by which youth with disabilities are systematically equipped with skills necessary for realizing valued post-secondary outcomes promised to all secondary school students. In addition, we will discuss transition within its historical, philosophical, and legal contexts that form the background for model development and best practices.

HISTORICAL FOUNDATIONS OF TRANSITION PROGRAMS

The techniques that are today regarded as essential elements of transition programming did not originate at the enactment of Individuals with Disabilities Education Act (IDEA). Rather, what we now refer to as "transition services" for youth with disabilities was evident in programs developed during the 1930s for deaf students, and the 1940s for students with mental retardation (Rusch, Szymanski & Chadsey-Rusch, 1992). It was not until the 1960s, however, that educational and vocational models were developed in a comprehensive manner. Indeed, transition experts (e.g. Halpern, 1992) have suggested that comprehensive transition techniques have their origins in the work study programs of the 1960s. According to Halpern, work study and transition programs share a focus on several similar elements, including establishing formal linkages with rehabilitation services (adult agencies), providing vocational instruction, and providing community experiences. However, work study programs were a collaboration between local state offices of rehabilitation services and local public schools in providing students with mild disabilities an integrated academic, social, and vocational curriculum along with community work experiences aimed at promoting community adjustment and productivity.

Despite the proliferation of the work study model in the 1960s, it essentially died in the 1970s primarily because of flawed funding mechanisms and the "similar benefits" requirement of the 1973 amendments to the Vocational Rehabilitation (VR) Act. This requirement stipulated that federal VR funds could not be used to pay for services that were a primary responsibility of another agency. With the passage the Education for All Handicapped Children Act (PL 94-142) in 1975, providing an appropriate education to all students with disabilities became the primary responsibility of public schools. Within PL 94-142, community work experiences were considered a part of the student's educational program, therefore, rehabilitation agencies could no longer pay for this service. Without the VR funding, schools could not always support work programs for students with disabilities, thus, these programs were often discontinued. In 1977, the Career Education Implementation Incentive Act (PL 95-207) became the second federal precursor to transition programming. In 1971, concerns with the high drop-out rates led to the introduction of career education programs (Brolin, 1993; Marland, 1971). The establishment of the Office of Career Education in 1974 and the passage in 1977 of the Career

Education Implementation Incentive Act helped to establish career education at the forefront of public education agenda. While career education programs did not specifically include students with disabilities, increased federal attention and funding during the 1970s broadened the focus, thus ensuring that students with disabilities were included (Isaacson & Brown, 1993). When it was repealed as planned in 1982, career education programs lost significant ground. Federal involvement was only intended as "seed money" to encourage the development and expansion of models that would be integrated within the regular educational program. In reality, without the infusion of federal funds, career education programs, as a separate educational priority, fell by the wayside.

Early Models of Transition Planning and Services

Follow-up studies in the early 1980s pointed to a need to systematically plan and develop models of serving students with disabilities at the secondary level in order to provide educational experiences necessary for student achievement of positive post-school outcomes Research showed that particular subpopulations of students with disabilities were experiencing particularly dismal post-school outcomes, particularly with regard to gender, ethnicity and severity of the disability (Blackorby & Wagner, 1996). Indeed, follow-up studies conducted prior to IDEA's 1990 mandate for transition services (e.g. Hasazi, Gordon & Roe, 1985) and studies conducted after legislation mandated transition planning (e.g. the National Transition Longitudinal Study [NLTS]) reported by Blackorby and Wagner (1996), and subsequent analyses of these and similar efforts (Furney, Hasazi & DeStefano, 1997; National Council on Disability, 2000; Szymanski, 1994) have all consistently indicated that adult outcomes for many youth with disabilities continues to remain problematic. As a consequence, several models have been proposed with the intent of providing the critical educational experiences to facilitate the transition from school to post-school settings.

Over the past two decades, models of transition planning and services have been promulgated, first through federal incentives, and more recently because of new federal regulations. Yet, as discussed earlier, training youth with disabilities for life after high school is not a new phenomenon. Early vocational programs such as cooperative workstudy programs, career education, along with the postschool follow-up research foreshadowed the development of subsequent models of transition, including the Office of Special Education and Rehabilitation Services (OSERS) "Bridge" Model and Halpern's Community Adjustment Model, to mention a few. Just two years after the repeal of the Career Education Implementation Incentive Act, and "one school generation after guaranteeing the right to a free and appropriate education for all children with disabilities" (Will, 1984, p. 1), a new federal transition initiative emerged. This model focused exclusively on the transition of students with disabilities from school to employment. According to the Office of Special Education and Rehabilitation Services (OSERS), transition was defined as the "bridge between the security and structure offered by the school and the opportunities and risks of adult life" (Will, p. 2). This Bridge Model delineated three types of services that could be offered to students with disabilities upon exit from public school programs:

(1) Transition *without special services* for students with disabilities who make the transition by relying on their own resources or those generic services available to all students.
(2) Transition with *time-limited services* for students with disabilities seeking specialized short-term services in order to secure employment (e.g. vocational rehabilitation services).
(3) Transition with *ongoing services* for students with severe disabilities who need ongoing support to sustain employment.

As it appears, this federal support for the Bridge Model resulted in the infusion of discretionary funding into transition programs for students with disabilities. This funding allowed for the development of new and innovative models of transition planning and services. In reaction to the OSERS narrow focus on transition to employment, Halpern (1985) proposed that *community adjustment* (i.e. living successfully in the community) should be the goal of transition programs. In his model he emphasized community adjustment and advocated that transition programs should include a focus on community living and social and interpersonal networks as well as employment. All three of the elements of community adjustment are necessary for success. The expanded focus on community adjustment considerably enhanced the one-dimensional aspect of the OSERS transition model.

Over the last decade, due to the ongoing federal support for transition research and program development, an extensive literature base has developed (Halpern, Lindstrom, Benz & Nelson, 1991; Kohler, DeStefano, Wermuth, Grayson & McGinty, 1994; Patton & Dunn, 1999; Rusch & DeStefano, 1989). Much of the information regarding models and best practices, however, has not been well-substantiated with empirical evidence of improved outcomes (Greene & Albright, 1995; Johnson & Rusch, 1993; Kohler, 1993). In more recent studies seeking to apply a more rigorous criteria of best practices, Kohler and colleagues have developed a taxonomy of transition practices for students with disabilities

(Kohler, 1996, 1998). There appears to be, at minimum, face validity for indicators of effective transition programs (Clark & Kolestoe, 1995). Identified best practices of transition programs have been summarized by Morningstar, Kleinhammer-Tramill and Lattin (1999) to include:

(1) A focus on *community outcomes* when developing curriculum and instruction.
(2) The importance of *interagency collaboration* both during planning and in the formal sharing of resources.
(3) The necessity of an individualized *method of planning* for transition.
(4) The importance of *family and support network involvement* in planning and decision making.

While not consistently identified as a best practice early on, the critical role that *student self-determination* and *student involvement* play in transition planning is now considered to be a priority outcome for special education (Ward & Halloran, 1993). Thus, self-determination should be considered a cornerstone of quality school programs in the 21st Century.

The Decade of Transition-related Legislation

The decade of the nineties has seen the emergence of several educational initiatives that have been projected to have a profound effect on educational outcomes of all students, and particularly of students with disabilities. Among the key policy initiatives are School-to-Work Opportunities Act of 1994, Goals 2000: Educate America Act, Improving America's Schools Act of 1994, and IDEA of 1990 and subsequent IDEA 1997 Amendments. The following subsections present a brief overview of these laws and their impact on transition programming for youth with disabilities.

Goals 2000: Educate America Act and the Improving America's Schools Act of 1994. The passage of Goals 2000 in 1994 was a culmination of the standards-based reform movement that began in the 1980s and became more focused with passage of Goals 2000 and the Improving America's Schools Act (the reauthorized Elementary and Secondary Education Act) in 1994. For the field of special education, the standards-based reform movement was one of the more challenging initiatives of the 1990s – it involves an alignment of standards, assessments, and accountability systems to provide a coherent framework for curriculum, instruction, personnel development, technology, school finance, integrated services, and virtually every educational activity in order to improve student outcomes. Accountability systems linked with standards-based reform tend to link school accreditation (high-stakes for schools) and/or graduation (high-stakes for students) with student progress on state and local assessments (Morningstar et al., 1999). The standards-based reform movement appears to have taken root with support from the political leaders ranging from governors to chief state school officers, and models of school reform are being used as public agenda-building tools to raise awareness of the need to improve schools and raise expectations for and performance of all students.

School-to-Work Opportunities Act of 1994. In 1994, the School-to-Work Opportunities Act (STW) was authorized. The law provided start-up funds to stimulate development of state and local partnerships between business, labor, education, and community-based organizations which would prepare and support youth to enter high-skill careers. The major efforts of STW include: (a) coordinating school-based learning, work-based learning; and (b) connecting activities between school and business settings. Unlike previous career and vocational education legislation, the STW Act was explicitly inclusive of students with disabilities and was compatible with IDEA transition requirements because it supported individualized career planning and coordinated education/work experiences by age 16 or earlier to prepare students for positive post-school and career outcomes.

When initially authorized, the STW Act was viewed by the administration of the U.S. Department of Education as an essential component of standards-based reform as promoted by Goals 2000 (Riley, 1995). Goals 2000 promoted improvement of state and local education systems so that students leave high school with the necessary skills to succeed in a competitive and rapidly changing global economy. The STW Act complemented Goals 2000 by ensuring that students learned essential workplace skills and had relevant career experiences (Smith & Scoll, 1995). However, the challenge remains to integrate STW career and work experiences within the increasingly narrow academic focus of current standards-based reforms efforts.

IDEA 1990 amendments. From approximately 1980–1990, the U.S. Department of Education used discretionary funding to promote transition planning and services. During this decade, a number of model demonstration and research grants focusing on transition were funded. However, wide discrepancies existed among states in their provision of transition services (DeStefano & Wermuth, 1992). The 1990 reauthorization of the Education for All Handicapped Children's Act, renamed The Individuals with Disabilities Education Act (IDEA), alleviated inconsistencies by mandating that transition planning for students in special education must begin at age 16 or younger when appropriate. IDEA required that transition planning focus on students' postschool outcomes and that these outcomes be achieved through services and supports provided by a variety of agencies, not just the schools.

The 1990 IDEA expanded previous federal special education law regarding how an individualized educational program (IEP) was to be developed for a young adult with disabilities. IEPs for students with disabilities who were at least 16 years old were now required to include a statement of needed transition services focusing on postschool outcomes (e.g. postsecondary education, vocational training, integrated employment, supported employment, continuing and adult education, adult services, independent living, and community participation) and including interagency linkages, if needed. Schools were responsible for ensuring that a range of experiences, services, and supports were available to the student so that he or she could work toward achieving the desired outcomes. Transition services included instruction, community experiences, the development of employment experiences and other postschool adult outcomes, and if appropriate, daily living skills and functional vocational assessment. Additionally, 1990 IDEA required that the transition plan reflect the needs, preferences, and interests of the young adult with disabilities and that it be developed with input and active participation from the student and family, school staff, relevant adult service agencies, and other community members. Finally, IDEA stated that other community agencies that may be involved with the student must be included in the transition planning process. This meant that schools needed to develop relationships with community agencies to ensure that certain services were provided to students before they exited high school. While schools were not required to provide all of the needed transition services, they were responsible for ensuring that identified transition services were provided. Therefore, interagency linkages and coordination were considered to be critical aspects of providing comprehensive transition planning for students with disabilities.

IDEA 1997 amendments. The 1997 amendments to IDEA reflect the influence of standards-based reform and, like other education legislation from the mid-1990s, the reauthorized IDEA continues to focus on student outcomes. IDEA's transition planning requirements lowered the age of identification of students' transition needs to age 14 and the development and implementation of a transition plan for all students with disabilities starting at the age of 16 (or younger, when deemed appropriate). In addition, IDEA now requires that IEPs show how students with disabilities will address state and local standards and how they will participate in state assessments, in keeping with standards-based reform. Clearly, the overall intent of these changes in IDEA is to ensure that students with disabilities progress toward the same high standards to which other students must achieve and that states' and schools' accountability systems include students with disabilities. IDEA clearly specifies that schools must focus attention on outcomes and be responsible for ensuring that a planning process is in place to identify, work toward, and plan for these post-school outcomes. In turn, the effectiveness of these secondary programs may be judged by the success of their students in meeting state and local standards and by their success in postschool life (DeStefano & Wermuth, 1992; Turnbull, Bateman & Turnbull, 1993).

The 1997 reauthorization of IDEA appears to provide the needed leverage to create secondary school reforms that will ensure successful adult outcomes for students with disabilities. The unique aspects of the law that are the impetus for change in schools include: (a) the development of interagency linkages; (b) broadening the scope of curricula and programs to include instruction, related services, community experiences, and employment; (c) increasing performance expectations for students with disabilities in conjunction with standards-based curriculum and holding states and schools accountable for the post-school outcomes students achieve; (d) involving students, parents and community agencies in the planning process; and (e) changing the role of many school professionals to one of service coordination (Morningstar et al., 1999). In sum, many of the federal initiatives and subsequent mandates are a systematic attempt to resolve the poor economic, social, and educational outcomes for young adults with disabilities. Legislation such as IDEA sets in place the minimal compliance requirements for school districts to provide transition planning and services. It is clear, however, that without attention to significant exemplary practices in education and secondary school and adult service reform, the impact of transition services on the lives of young adults with disabilities will be minimal. With this in mind, the next section reviews models and best practices of exemplary transition programs for students with disabilities.

ENSURING EFFECTIVE TRANSITION PLANNING FOR YOUTH WITH DISABILITIES

IDEA 1990 and it's subsequent reauthorization in 1997 provided the federal definition of transition and mandated the provision of services for students with disabilities by age 14. IDEA defines "transition services" as:

A coordinated set of activities for a student with a disability that:

(a) are designed within an outcome-oriented process, which promotes movement from school to post-school activities, including post-secondary education, vocation training, integrated employment (including supported

employment), continuing and adult education, adult services, independent living, or community participation;
(b) are based upon the individual student's needs, taking into account the student's preferences and interests; and
(c) include instruction, related services, community experiences, the development of employment and other post-school adult living objectives, and, when appropriate, acquisition of daily living skills and functional vocational evaluation (Section 602[30]).

Three important elements of this definition are: (a) focusing on an outcome-oriented process; (b) taking student preferences and interests into consideration; and (c) requiring a coordinated effort among schools and other community services.

Implementing the Requirements of IDEA

Since 1990, IDEA makes it clear that students, family members, schools, and community agencies must focus on what will happen to a student once that student leaves high school. It requires that the focus of planning be on similar outcomes as for any adult, including independent living, employment, and full participation in the community. Planning for adult outcomes requires that schools be held more accountable for providing an educational program that will more likely lead to success in adult life. This means that all goals and objectives in the IEP must reflect what the student is expected to know or be able to do to meet his or her desired postschool outcomes. The outcome-oriented approach to transition planning allows key stakeholders to think about and plan for the student's adult life. According to IDEA, transition services must be based upon *student needs, taking into account student preferences and interests.* IDEA requires educators to focus on more than just student needs or deficits. The transition plan becomes one in which the student and family's dreams for the future are at the center. A critical aspect of this student-centered planning is to ensure that the student is actively involved in his or her own educational and transition planning. Today, there are several self-determination curricula that have been developed to enable students with disabilities become actively involved in their transition process.

There is an explicit expectation within IDEA that all of the services and supports needed for transition are coordinated; thereby ensuring that the services not only meet the student's needs, but are not duplicated by several agencies. Schools are required to coordinate the transition planning process by linking it with all of the various agencies and support service providers that are involved in the provision of transition services. The coordinated set of activities relies heavily on services and people within and outside of the school setting. This requirement is very different from what was typically in place for IEPs. In the past, schools have been solely responsible. Now schools are required to work with outside agencies and invite them to IEP meetings. The coordinated set of activities also includes interagency linkages and responsibilities of others that are documented in the IEP. Clearly, those who are involved in transition planning must carefully consider a variety of ways that transition services could be provided. Certainly, this would require that the methods of providing transition services are coordinated so that they are effective for the student.

Connecting Transition with the IEP

During a student's secondary school years, the Individualized Education Program (IEP) can be thought of as the road map for reaching a student's final destination: the student's and family's vision of the future. Therefore, it is critical that a sufficient amount of time and energy be given to this process. In it's broadest definition, transition planning is an ongoing process that begins with informal and person-centered planning and culminates in the development of the transition plan during an IEP meeting. The process then continues with ongoing review of transition goals, objectives, and strategies. Transition planning guides the development of the IEP so that the focus remains on the dreams, preferences, and strengths of the student. The regulations for IDEA specify that the following must be included in the IEP:

(1) For each student with a disability beginning at age 14 (or younger if deemed appropriate by the IEP team), and updated annually, a statement of the transition service needs of the student under the applicable components of the student's IEP that focuses on the student's courses of study (such as participation in advanced-placement courses or a vocational educational program); and
(2) For each student beginning at age 16 (or younger, if determined appropriate by the IEP team), a statement of needed transition services for the child, including, when appropriate, a statement of the interagency responsibilities or any needed linkages.
(3) Transfer of rights. In a State that transfers rights at the age of majority, beginning at least one year before a student reaches the age of majority under State law, the student's IEP must include a statement that the student

has been informed of his or her rights under Part B of the Act, that will transfer upon reaching the age of majority, consistent with Section 300.517. (34 CFR Section 300.347).

When transition first became mandated, the federal requirement was to develop a *statement of needed transition services* beginning at age 16. Further, IDEA 1990 required that the statement of needed transition services be based upon the needs, preferences and interests of the student, and include interagency responsibilities or linkages or both, if appropriate. The focus of transition planning is the desired postschool outcomes for the student. Finally, the statement of needed transition services must also identify the specific transition services to be provided by the school and/or outside agencies. Transition services included instruction, community experiences, related services, the development of employment and other postschool adult living objectives, and if necessary, daily living skills or functional vocational evaluations. With the reauthorization of IDEA in 1997, transition planning was required to begin at an earlier age for students with disabilities. For a lot of students and their families, age 16 was too late to begin the process of planning for the transition to adult life. Therefore, the new requirements of IDEA require a modified form of transition planning to begin at age 14. As it stands, IDEA 1997 mandates schools to identify a student's transition needs (the *statement of transition service needs*) at age 14 and to address these needs in the applicable components of the student's IEP as well as through the student's courses of study. The postschool outcomes specified by IDEA is the basis for identifying transition needs for younger students (i.e. employment, independent living, and community participation). This requirement is not intended to supplant, but rather to augment the more specific statement of needed transition services that are required to be included in an IEP beginning at age 16. It does not however, provide for more comprehensive transition planning such as involving outside agencies.

IDEA and its corresponding regulations are not specific when it comes to defining what constitutes *courses of study*. However, the interpretation of the regulations specifies courses of study as a "multi-year description of coursework to achieve a student's desired postschool goals" (Storms, O'Leary & Williams, 2000). Therefore, courses of study reflects the student's transition service needs in such a way as to "be meaningful to the student's future and motivate the student to complete his or her education" (34 CFR Section 300.347, Appendix A). Focusing on long-range courses of study for a student is required of IEP teams beginning at age 14 and continuing annually until the student graduates with a high school diploma or is no longer eligible for IDEA services.

Table 1. Suggestions for Preparing Students for Understanding Rights

Preparing Students for Understanding Their Rights
- Students should understand their disability and be able to advocate for themselves.
- Students should understand why they receive special education services.
- Students should receive written and oral notification of meetings.
- Students should be notified of changes in placement with explanations on why those changes occurred. This notification should be in the communication mode best suited to each individual student.
- Students should participate and assist in the direction of the IEP meetings.
- Students should receive explanations on the type and purpose of evaluations.
- Students should be involved in the interpretation of test results.
- Students should be given the opportunity to review their educational records.
- Students should know their rights under the Rehabilitation Act and the Americans with Disabilities Act.
- Students should participate in self-advocacy and self-determination training.
- Students, their parents and teachers should meet prior to the student's 18th birthday to discuss specific rights and the implications of those rights in the educational process.

Source: Student rights: What you need to know. (1998, Winter). What's Working in Transition: Transition News, Information, and Resources from Minnesota. Minneapolis, MN: University of Minnesota.

Apparently, this language in IDEA emphasizes the importance of including students with disabilities in general education. Therefore, when identifying transition needs beginning at age 14, IEP teams should first examine what courses and programs are currently available from general education. This might include taking a consumer math class, or attending the vocational education program at the high school. Effectively meeting the identified transition service needs of students beginning at age 14 would require: (a) identifying the desired postschool outcomes; and (b) identifying courses the student should take to work toward these long-range adult goals.

The new IDEA requirement mandates that at the IEP meeting one year prior to the students 18th birthday (the usual age of majority for most states), students and parents are to be notified of the specific rights which will transfer to the student once the student turns 18. Documentation of this notification must then be included in the IEP. The rights that will transfer from the parent to the student include: (a) notification of meetings; (b) notification and consent for evaluation; (c) selection of participants of IEP meetings; (d) approval of the contents of the IEP; and (e) approval regarding change of placement. For students who may be deemed legally incompetent to make important life decisions, schools should provide parents with necessary information to begin guardianship proceedings with local district courts. Assisting students and their parents in the transfer of rights once the student reaches the age of majority is an important task. Today, a variety of self-determination and transition curricula have been developed to assist schools in this effort (Field & Hoffman, 1996; Martin & Marshall, 1996; Powers, Sowers, Turner, Nesbitt, Knowles & Ellison, 1996; Wehmeyer & Kelchner, 1995; Van Reusen, Bos, Schumaker & Deshler, 1994). Table 1 provides suggestions for helping students in assuming their rights at age of majority.

Summarizing the Transition Planning Process

Educators involved in the transition planning process must: (a) identify preferences, interests and needs of the student; (b) develop a vision for the future; (c) develop a transition IEP; (d) implement the transition IEP; and (e) evaluate the results. Following, is further discussion of these imperatives.

Identifying preferences, interests and needs. The best way to identify appropriate preferences, interests, and needs for a student is to develop a process so the student, his or her family, and professionals can gather necessary information and create a vision for the future. This requires focusing on the student's strengths, contributions, interests, and dreams. This is the first step in identifying the preferences and interests of students and families. In addition, families and advocates must be aware of the possibilities for their child – this can be done by: (a) exposing children and youth with disabilities to successful role models (i.e. adults with similar disabilities leading interesting lives); and (b) talking with other parents. If students with disabilities are to fully participate in the transition planning process, then they must possess the skills and confidence necessary to make decisions about their future. Students must be allowed to directly participate in different work and community activities in order to make informed choices about their future. In addition, it is critical that students have the opportunities to make relevant and important choices about their life and to learn from their mistakes when these happen. Direct instruction and training in choice-making and self-advocacy are important and there are many different curricula available that do this.

Developing a vision for the future. Developing a vision of a quality adult life for a student with disabilities directly relates to the post-school outcomes identified in the IEP. Everyone involved should provide their perspectives and priorities, discuss them as a group, and then the student and family should have the ultimate decision. Transition planning teams need to gather information from all stakeholders involved with the transition process (e.g. the student, his or her family, teachers, adult service providers involved with the student and family, friends and neighbors) and develop the vision for the future based upon this input. Having a vision of the future developed by critical stakeholders is often what excites and motivates the team to plan and act. Using person-centered planning methods is an excellent way to develop a meaningful vision for the future (c.f. Clark, 1998; Menchetti & Piland, 1998; and Morningstar, Kleinhammer-Tramill & Lattin, 1998 for more specific information on using person-centered planning techniques during transition planning).

Developing a transition IEP. Goals, objectives, and milestones developed for the IEP should directly link to the identified postschool outcomes and should be developed and agreed upon by all members of the planning team, especially the student and his or her family. Goals and objectives should be flexible enough to meet the unique needs of the student's vision for the future. Goals and objectives that do not specifically relate to one or more of the postschool outcomes should not be included in the IEP.

Implementing the transition IEP. The IEP will be implemented using instruction, related services, community experiences, and, in some cases, functional vocational evaluation. In addition, each IEP for students aged 16 years old may have some interagency linkages and responsibilities. It is important to document outside agency activities and to follow-up to ensure the provision of these services as well as to reconvene the IEP team as needed.

Evaluating results. As the school year progresses, the IEP team reviews and evaluates the effectiveness of the goals and objectives, and determines whether goals are being met in the time frame that was established, and if the goals and instructional techniques are meeting the student's needs. If transition services are not being provided by the agency that agreed to provide them, then it is necessary to reconvene the transition IEP team to determine how such services will be provided. IEP teams may not delete goals and objectives, but may change the timelines or the person(s) responsible for it. It is not always necessary to reconvene the entire IEP team, but the key individuals involved must meet again. Information from evaluating the IEP is used to both expand the IEP and to think about the next year's IEP.

CHALLENGES FACING TRANSITION IN THE 21st CENTURY

The past several decades have brought tremendous attention to strategies for implementing effective transition planning and services. The emergence of current research and best practices, however, have not sufficiently addressed some of the most critical pressures facing educators, families, youth and our society, including cultural and ethnic diversity issues, students with disabilities living in poverty, and youth from rural communities.

Cultural and Ethnic Diversity

The mainstream U.S. beliefs about success, which are mirrored in the IDEA transition outcomes for students with disabilities, are often in direct conflict with the values and beliefs of other cultural groups. While a focus among professionals regarding the transition experiences of culturally diverse students appears to be increasing (Navarrete & White, 1994), it is disappointing to note that research on culturally diverse populations of students and families in transition is still relatively small. The voices of family members and students from cultures different from the dominant one in the U.S. are not being heard regarding their hopes, dreams, and concerns about transition. Results of studies focusing on postschool outcomes for specific groups of culturally diverse students with disabilities are discouraging. For instance, the National Longitudinal Transition Survey (NLTS) indicated that the transition outcomes for Hispanic youth were found to have significantly lower rates of employment and independent living than their white peers (Blackorby & Wagner, 1996). Additionally, some have argued that the concepts inherent in self-determination (i.e. self-advocacy, individual autonomy, and self-control) are antithetical to the values of Hispanic families, and therefore, could lead to conflict (Kalyanpur & Harry,1999; Turnbull & Turnbull, 2001). Also, students with and without disabilities from an Apache reservation in Arizona equally experienced poverty, unemployment, disenfranchisement, and lack of opportunity (Shafer & Rangasamy, 1995). These researchers concluded that the explicit IDEA transition goals of employment and independent living are both elusive and, in many instances, culturally inappropriate. The values inherent in transition, based upon values such as independence, individualization, and competition, directly conflict with Native American values of cooperation, interdependence and communal responsibility (Clay, 1992). In addition, African American youth with disabilities (particularly males) are much less likely than their white peers to be employed three to five years after high school, and when employed, are earning substantially less (see Blackorby & Wagner, 1996). Discouragingly, African American youth continue to be over-represented within the category of mental retardation (Harry, Grenot-Scheyer, Smith-Lewis, Park, Xin & Schwartz, 1995), yet are often less likely to be served by community adult agencies upon graduation (Sailor, 1994). The implications of these results are that large numbers of African American youth with disabilities are cut off from formal services and supports necessary for successful adult life.

Equally disturbing is the disproportionate representation of students from culturally and linguistically diverse backgrounds in programs for students with disabilities (Artiles & Trent, 1994; Oswald, Coutinho, Best & Singh, 1999). The greatest overrepresentation in special education is among African American, non-Hispanic students, with Native American students slightly overrepresented. African American students are twice as likely to be enrolled in programs for students with mental retardation (USDOE, 1999). Additionally, most recent federal data indicate that children from racial minority groups were more likely to have two or more co-occurring disabilities (USDOE, 2000). While it was not clear from this analysis that this disproportionality is due to racial bias in the special education eligibility process, poverty among racial minority groups, or other factors, there are additional emotional and financial costs associated with supporting children and youth with multiple disabilities, particularly as these youth transition to adult services. Apparently, issues surrounding cultural diversity and transition are multifaceted and complex. Addressing the needs of culturally diverse students and their families in transition requires a reexamination of assumptions about ideal postschool goals for students in that they may not meet the needs of cultural and ethnic minorities.

Despite increasing ethnicity among families and students in the U.S., many school professionals still have limited direct experiences with cultural traditions other than their own (Harry et al., 1995). Those most closely associated with the problems and barriers to parent-professional interactions have emphasized the importance of going beyond multicultural education to developing "cultural reciprocity" as a cornerstone of educational services (Harry, Kalyanpur & Day, 1999; Kalyanpur & Harry, 1999). Moving toward cultural reciprocity will require professionals to reconsider values and assumptions inherent to their belief systems. The good news is that researchers, families, and others concerned with issues related to cultural diversity have begun the process of addressing the best way to do this. Table 2 provides examples of ways to increase professionals' cultural competence and increase reciprocal relationships between parents and professionals.

Youth in Poverty

Research has suggested that of a wide array of variables (i.e. race, ethnicity, education, and skill levels), a family's socioeconomic status is one of the most powerful predictor of adult success for children (Kerchhoff, Campbell, Trott & Kraus, 1989). Therefore, it is evident that poverty is a critical issue that pervasively impacts the likelihood of success in secondary education and transition. Nearly one in six American children and youth live in poverty and

Table 2. Steps to Achieving Cultural Competence and Reciprocity.

General Strategies	Source
(1) Professionals should ask rather than make assumptions about what language is spoken at home and by which members.	Harry et al., (1995)
(2) Goal setting should take into account the cultural and family norms for personal and social development, this is particularly true regarding employment and independent living goals.	
(3) Develop a clear understanding of the cultural interpretations of the disability. Many cultures differ in the meanings attributed to the disability. These views may affect how the family copes.	
(4) Professionals should respect the child-rearing practices of the culture and not place blame on the family for differences with those in the US.	
(5) Professionals have an important responsibility to ensure that parents have access to all sources of information including advocacy groups and that materials explaining rights and responsibilities are made available in the native language or through personalized explanations by speakers of the family's language.	
(6) Enhance self-awareness by understanding who you are from a variety of perspectives including your family origins and your beliefs, biases, and behaviors. Be aware that your beliefs and values may be very different from the families you work with.	Turnbull & Turnbull (1997)
(7) Enhance cultural-specific awareness by learning about different cultural groups in terms of child-rearing practices and family patterns. Be careful not to stereotype but become familiar with the general traditions, customs and values of the families in your community.	
(8) Enhance culture-generic awareness by identifying values and practices that are found in all cultures. This is a way to develop come common ground when working with families from different cultures.	
(9) Enhance cultural issues related to the disability by understanding how cultural views influence the definition and meaning of the disability and therefore, the family-professional roles, communication patterns, and expectations and anticipated outcomes.	
(10) Establish alliances with culturally diverse families by taking a personalized approach to working with the family.	
(11) Outcomes and strategies for facilitating transition to adulthood that promote self-esteem, community interdependence, and inclusion need to be developed.	Shafer & Rangasmy (1995)

Table 2. Continued.

General Strategies	Source
(12) Improve the multicultural competence of team members by: — Providing opportunities for team members to learn about differing world views and be aware of their own views, values and cultures. — Providing opportunities for team members to learn about intercultural communication, including nonverbal communication. — Subscribing to resources that focus on multicultural issues including journals and internet discussion groups. — Gathering feedback from families regarding their satisfaction with special education services	Navarette & White (1994)
(13) Expose Culturally diverse students and families to a variety of role models and resources: — Subscribe to magazines which highlight culturally diverse role models and use these in various content areas. — Develop mentor programs with role models of color in the community with students.	

Source: Wehmeyer, M., Morningstar, M., & Husted, D. (1999). *Family Involvement in Transition Planning and Implementation.* Austin, TX: Pro-Ed (reproduced with permission of the Publisher).

are more likely to be poor today than 30 years ago (Children's Defense Fund, 2001), and it has been noted that "the major cause of child abuse, crime, drug and alcohol addiction, interpersonal problems and general antisocial behavior is poverty" (Edgar, 1990, p. 4). Unfortunately, poverty is even more prevalent in families that have a child with disabilities. Recent research indicates that disability risk is higher among children living in poverty and in single-parent households (Fujiura & Yamaki, 2000). While these findings are not yet conclusive, Fujiura and Yamaki concluded that they were "highly suggestive and should be a source of concern" (p. 194). This is especially of concern when confronted with recent federal data indicating that students with two or more co-occurring disabilities were more likely to live with a single parent (36%) or no parent (50%) than students with a single disability (32%); and it's been suggested that students with co-occurring disabilities were more likely than students with one disability to live below the poverty level (USDOE, 2000).

The greatest number of special education students come from low-income families who live in urban (47%); and in rural areas (34%) (USDOE, 1996). To call the interaction of geographic location, poverty, and disability distressing is to grossly understate the problem. For example, researchers have reported that in 165 urban schools serving 140,000 students, more than 80% of the entire population lives in poverty (Gottlieb, Alter, Gottlieb & Wishner, 1994). As Gottlieb et al. concluded:

> The vast majority of children who are classified as learning disabled and placed in special education in many urban school districts are not disabled in the sense demanded by legislation and regulation. Instead, they are children who suffer the many ravages of poverty, not the least of which is its effect on academic performance (p. 456).

Sadly, the recent passage of the Personal Responsibility and Work Opportunity Reconciliation Act of 1996 (the Welfare Reform act) could make post-school outcomes even less attainable for youths with disabilities. Welfare Reform's five-year limit on public assistance creates greater competition among workers for even those low-skill employment opportunities that have been considered "underemployment" for many young adults with disabilities (Gerry, 1997). Based on figures from the Urban Institute (1996), the National Technical Assistance Center on Welfare Reform (NTACWF) estimated that at least 50% of the remaining welfare recipients – those who constitute the population who are "difficult to employ" – have mild to moderate disabilities. Moreover, Gerry estimated that approximately 55% of young adults who have dropped out of school and who now must complete adult education to remain eligible for welfare benefits have mild to moderate disabilities and need transition services as well as continued education.

Youth from Rural Communities

A large body of research focusing on special education in rural communities in the U.S. has pointed to the complexity of challenges involved in the delivery of special education services and more specifically, transition services to students with disabilities within those areas. Some of those challenges include: (a) sheer isolation of many rural communities; (b) inability to hire and retain qualified personnel; (c) lack of appropriate transition services options; and (d) diminished funding pools (Clark & White, 1985; Coombe, 1993; Greenwood, 1992; Helge, 1981). In addition, the very problems facing youth with disabilities in non-rural areas exist in rural communities as well, including a large number of students living in poverty, and acute problems in providing services to students with low incidence and severe disabilities (Snell & Brown, 2000). Jointly, all these factors conspire to make the provision of transition services to adolescents with disabilities within rural communities almost an impossible task. Researchers (e.g. Mallory, 1995) have found that rurality in and of itself presents challenges and opportunities to professionals engaged in providing transition services specifically, and special education services in general. Those researchers have found what they have termed as a rural ethic that is not found in non-rural communities. For instance, there is a greater sense of "community" and communal responsibility to childrearing, a stronger division of labor, and a stronger ethic of caring and taking care of the others. This rural ethic does auger well for the implementation of transition services given that the success to transition programming is predicated upon collaboration. However, the success of such programs rest on the value that professionals place on harnessing and utilizing community strengths and redefining transition outcomes with the view of preparing youth with disabilities for success as adults living in a rural community.

CONCLUSIONS

We believe that transition is best viewed as a process by which youth with disabilities learn the skills necessary for achieving the valued post-school outcomes anticipated by all youth exiting high school. This definition has room for the complexity of issues facing youth with disabilities and their families. As history has shown, the transformation to what we today call "transition" is the result of years of research, policy development, and an accumulation of best practices. By all accounts, those who are most closely involved in the challenges facing America's schools today do not consider the preparation of youth with disabilities for the transition to adulthood as static. Each decade has brought renewed importance to certain components of transition as well as additional pressures for special educators, families and youth with disabilities in considering how best to prepare youth for adult life. Given the current environment in which schools are operating, especially with the new pressures of academic standards and state and district assessment, it may be time for special educators to closely examine and perhaps realign how we think about and provide transition services.

One common denominator of youth with disabilities making the transition to adult life is that they can all be considered to have complex support needs, especially when it comes to finding and sustaining employment, living independently, and attaining postsecondary education and training. Transition planning and services is moving away from traditional categorical approaches to providing special education, to one that instead focuses on the student's desired postschool outcomes, takes into account the student's strengths and interests, and develops transition plans that meet these unique support needs.

This approach would work well for *all* youth preparing to make the transition to adulthood. Perhaps it is time to seriously consider how to blend the best of special education and transition services within the current context of general education, and particularly the factors driving secondary school reform.

Distilling what we know to be effective practices for transition has never been an easy task. Currently, there does appear to be agreement as to what are essential elements that ensure successful transitions (Johnson & Rusch, 1993; Kohler, 1993, 1998). Dimensions of a quality transition program have been described in this chapter with *student self-determination* as the cornerstone. An underlying belief in student self-determination is considered to be a foundation of school programs tied directly to quality of life outcomes (Morningstar et al., 1999). The other four components of transition discussed previously (i.e. individualized planning, family and support network involvement, community outcomes, and interagency collaboration) cannot be considered outside of this self-determination perspective. For example, *individualized planning* is central to self-determination in that it offers a perspective on the unique needs and aspirations of the student. However, individualized planning can only facilitate self-determination to the extent that the individual and those closest to him or her are actively involved in this process. Therefore, educators involved in transition must ensure that students and family members do not become disenfranchised from the process.

The *involvement of family and support networks* is at the heart of transition because, ultimately, a student's quality of life depends upon his or her ability to realize personal goals *with the support of* those who are closest to them. In fact, family involvement is understood to be one of the few consistent factors leading to successful school and adult outcomes (Kohler, 1993; Pleet, 2000). Certainly, transition to adulthood is a time of tremendous change for adolescents and their families, particularly as it influences emergent adult roles of the student and a shift from parent-directed decisions to one in which the student takes the lead. It is clear, however, that students with disabilities continue to seek out the support and guidance from family members and friends during transition, probably more so than they do professionals (Morningstar, Turnbull & Turnbull, 1996). Establishing a network of support may in fact be one of the most important features of transition planning that will ensure success long after the student leaves school.

The last two, *focusing on community outcomes* and *interagency collaboration*, are critical to transition and strongly influenced by efforts to promote self-determination. We must take into account the range of environments in which students are involved as well as encourage all of the possibilities for participating in continued learning, living arrangements and life style, recreation, work and career development, and other aspects of citizenship. Collaborating with agencies outside of school offers the opportunity to develop a network of formal supports so that students can achieve their desired adult outcomes. The quality of interagency collaboration is, however, largely linked to how well this network supports the individual in accomplishing his or her goals.

The field of transition has grown up considerably over the course of the past 20 years since it was first identified as a major priority of the Department of Education. Much of the expansion of how we think about transition is due to the emergence of research and the identification of model programs and services for youth and families. Transition, like all major educational efforts, however, does not exist in a vacuum. Societal pressures and priorities have significantly impacted how we provide such services. The regulatory language found in the reauthorization of IDEA reflects a major influence affecting all educational systems, that is standards-based educational reform. Like other educational legislation from the mid-1990s, IDEA has a renewed focus on student outcomes, particularly for evidence of postschool success for youth with disabilities. Additionally, IDEA regulations now are aligned with the central tenets of standards-based reform that is, focusing on high expectations and holding schools accountable for student outcomes. It is now being argued that high expectations and standards for all students *and* the individualization of goals and instruction is achievable. IDEA offers the necessary balance between excellence and equity and access to the general curriculum for students with disabilities.

However, some parents and special educators are fearful that students with disabilities will lose the special rights and safeguards to which they are entitled under IDEA. This becomes even more apparent during the secondary school years when the nature and focus of high schools is predominantly academic. Special education, and in particular transition, has been described as at a crossroads in which the old mode of doing business, namely, following procedural guidelines, must now make way for a focus on student outcomes. Parents and teachers alike may not fully understand the importance of this shift from IEP compliance to accountability. They may need information and support in order to make the conversion from thinking solely about the individualized needs of their child to understanding the big picture, namely access to the general curriculum, how this impacts students needs pertaining to progress in the general curriculum, and inclusion in state and district accountability systems.

Perhaps it's time the field of transition listened more closely to the current message of "catching the wave" of school reform (Halpern, 1999). The current focus within school reform efforts appears to be almost exclusively on academic performance rather than developing the skills needed for a successful adult life. As it currently stands, however, special education in general and stakeholders concerned with the transition to adulthood for youth with disabilities in particular, have been essentially left out of the reform discussion, while changes are happening that significantly impact youth with disabilities, their families, and special educators. Perhaps it's time to address the reality that special education can no longer remain separate from the rest of the school and society. While proponents of standards-based reform may be primarily concerned with traditional academics, paying minimal attention to standards of learning leading to the adult roles and outcomes so important to those involved in the field of transition, it may be necessary to join this effort (Halpern, 1999). Stakeholders concerned with transition for youth with disabilities may not agree with all of the aspects of general education reform, but the direction now being pursued by educational policymakers is unavoidable. Therefore, given all we know to be right about how to prepare youth with disabilities and their families for the transition to adulthood, we must work with our general education colleagues to achieve common goals for all students, including how best to prepare youth for adult life.

What is the future of transition? The answer isn't always clear. A growing body of evidence seems to support the transition programs and practices addressed in this chapter. However, the field of transition is faced with sometimes new and always challenging pressures. Three such complex challenges facing transition addressed in this chapter (i.e. youth and families living in poverty, the emerging ethnic and linguistic diversity of our society, and youth from rural communities) must be seriously addressed so as to avoid robbing society of an important portion of the next generation of young adults. Without direct and concerted attention to the challenges facing poor, rural, and ethnically diverse students with disabilities and their families, the results may be headed for a crisis. The future for transition services for youth with disabilities must be open to the current tide of school reform, take into consideration the challenges facing secondary schools and society, and retain the best elements that the field has found to be most effective.

REFERENCES

Artiles, A. J., & Trent, S. C. (1994). Overrepresentation of minority students in special education: A continuing debate. *Journal of Special Education, 27*(4), 410–437.

Blackorby, J., & Wagner, M. (1996). Longitudinal postschool outcomes of youth with disabilities: Findings from the national longitudinal transition study. *Exceptional Children, 62*(5), 399–413.

Brolin, D. E. (1993). *Life-centered career education: A competency-based approach* (4th ed.). Reston, VA: Council for Exceptional Children.

Bullis, M., & Cheney, D. (1999). Vocational and transition interventions for adolescents and young adults with emotional or behavioral disorders. *Focus on Exceptional Children, 31*(7), 1–24.

Chadsey-Rusch, J., Rusch, F., & O'Reilly, M. (1991). Transition from school to integrated communities. *Remedial and Special Education, 12*(6), 23–33.

Children's Defense Fund (2001, April 17). *The Children's Defense Fund reviews the state of America's children and says it's time to do whatever it takes to "leave no child behind"* [on-line press release]. Available: http://www.childrensdefense.org/release010417.htm

Clark, G. M. (1998). *Assessment for transitions planning.* Austin, TX: Pro-Ed.

Clark, G. M., & Kolstoe, O. P. (1995). *Career development and transition education for adolescents with disabilities* (3rd ed.). Boston: Allyn and Bacon.

Clark, G. M., & White, W. J. (1985). Issues in providing career and vocational education to secondary-level mildly handicapped students in rural settings. *Career Development for Exceptional Individuals, 8,* 42–49.

Clay, J. A. (1992). Native American independent living. *Rural Special Education Quarterly, 11*(1), 41–50.

Coombe, E. (1993). Planning transition to employment in rural areas for students with disabilities: start with a good local fit. *Rural Special Education Quarterly, 12*(3), 3–7.

DeStefano, L., & Wermuth, T. (1992). IDEA (PL 101-476): Defining a second generation of transition services. In: F. Rusch, L. DeStefano, J. Chadsey-Rusch, L. A. Phelps & E. Szymanski (Eds), *Transition from School to Adult Life: Models, Linkages, and Policy* (pp. 537–550). Sycamore, IL: Sycamore Press.

deFur, S. H., & Taymans, J. M. (1995). Competencies needed for transition specialist in vocational rehabilitation, vocational education, and special education. *Exceptional Children, 62,* 38–51.

Edgar, E. (1990). Education's role in improving our quality of life: Is it time to change our world view? *Beyond Behavior,* (Winter), 9–13.

Field, S., & Hoffman, A. (1996). *Steps to self-determination: A curriculum to help adolescents learn to achieve their goals.* Arlington, VA: Council for Exceptional Children.

Fujiura, G. T., & Yamaki, K. (2000). Trends in demography of childhood poverty and disability. *Exceptional Children, 66,* 187–199.

Furney, K. S., Hasazi, S. B., & DeStefano, L. (1997). Transition policies, practices, and promises: Lessons from three states. *Exceptional Children, 63,* 343–355.

Gerry, M. (1997). *Report to the management team of the National Technical Assistance Center on Welfare Reform.* Kansas City, MO: Author.

Greene, G., & Albright, L. (1995). "Best practices" in transition services: Do they exist? *Career Development for Exceptional Individuals, 18*(1), 1–2.

Greenwood, R. (1992). Transition to the work setting in rural areas. *Human Services in the Rural Environment, 15*(3), 21–25.

Halpern, A. (1985). Transition: A look at the foundations. *Exceptional Children, 51,* 479–486.

Halpern, A. (1992). Transition: New wine in old bottles. *Exceptional Children, 58*(3), 202–211.

Halpern, A. (1999). *Transition: Is it time for another rebottling?* [on-line]. Paper presented at the 1999 Annual OSEP Project Directors' Meeting (June), Washington, D. C. Avaliable: http://www.ed.uiuc.edu/sped/tri/hapern99.htm

Halpern, A., Lindstrom, L. E., Benz, M. R., & Nelson, D. J. (1991). *Community transition team model: Team leader's manual.* Eugene, OR: University of Oregon Press.

Harry, B., Grenot-Scheyer, M., Smith-Lewis, M., Park, H., Xin, F., & Schwartz, I. (1995). Developing culturally inclusive services for individuals with severe disabilities. *Journal of the Association for Persons with Severe Disabilities, 20*(2), 99–109.

Harry, B., & Kalyanpur, M. (1994). Cultural underpinnings of special education: implications for professional interactions with culturally diverse families. *Disability and Society, 9*(2).

Harry, B., Kalyanpur, M., & Day, M. (1999). *Building cultural reciprocity with families: Case studies in education.* Baltimore, MD: Paul H. Brookes.

Hasazi, S., Gordon, L., & Roe, C. (1985). Factors associated with the employment status of handicapped youth exiting high school from 1975 to 1983. *Exceptional Children, 51,* 455–469.

Helge D. I. (1981). Problems in implementing comprehensive special education programming in rural areas. *Exceptional Children, 47*(7), 514–520.

Isaacson, L. E., & Brown, D. (1993). *Career information, career counseling, and career development* (5th ed.). Boston: Allyn and Bacon.

Johnson, J. R., & Rusch, F. R. (1993). Secondary special education and transition services: identification and recommendations for future research and demonstration. *Career Development for Exceptional Individuals, 16*(1), 1–18.

Kalyanpur, M., & Harry, B. (1999). *Culture in special education: Building reciprocal family-professional relationships.* Baltimore, MD: Paul H. Brookes.

Kohler, P. (1993). Best practices in transition: Substantiated or implied? *Career Development for Exceptional Individuals, 16*(2), 107–121.

Kohler, P. (1996). Preparing youth with disabilities for future challenges: A taxonomy for transition programming. In: P. D. Kohler (Ed.), *Taxonomy for Transition Programming: Linking Research and Practice* (pp. 1–62). Champaign, IL: Transition Research Institute. University of Illinoins at Urbana-Champaign.

Kohler, P. (1998). Implementing a transition perspective of education: A comprehensive approach to planning and delivering secondary education and transition services. In: F. Rusch & J. Chadsey (Eds), *Beyond High School: Transition from School to Work* (pp. 179–205). Belmont, CA: Wadsworth.

Kohler, P. A., DeStefano, L., Wermuth, T. R., Grayson, T. E., & McGinty, S. (1994). An analysis of exemplary transition programs: How and why are they selected? *Career Development for Exceptional Children, 17*(2), 187–202.

Marland, S. P., Jr. (1971). *Career education now.* Speech presented before the annual convention of the National Association of Secondary School Principals, Houston.

Martin, J. E., & Marshall, L. H. (1996). ChoiceMaker: Infusing self-determination instruction into the IEP and transition process. In: D. J. Sands & M. L. Wehmeyer (Eds), *Self-determination Across the Life Span: Independence and Choice for People with Disabilities* (pp. 211–232). Baltimore, MD: Paul H. Brookes.

Menchetti, B. M., & Piland, V. C. (1998). The personal career plan: A person-centered approach to vocational evaluation and career planning. In: F. R. Rusch & J. C. Chadsey (Eds), *Beyond High School: Transition from School to Work* (pp. 319–337). Belmont, CA: Wadsworth Publishing Co.

McDonnell, J., Mathot-Buckner, C., & Ferguson, B. (1996). *Transition programs for students with moderate/severe disabilities.* Pacific Grove, CA: Brooks/Cole.

Morningstar, M. E., Turnbull A. P., & Turnbull, H. R. (1995). What do students with disabilities tell us about the importance of family involvement in transition from school to adult life? *Exceptional Children, 62,* 249–260.

Morningstar, M. E., Kleinhammer-Tramill, P. J., & Lattin D. L. (1999). Using successful models of student-centered transition planning and services for adolescents with disabilities. *Focus on Exceptional Children, 31*(9).

Navarette, L. A., & White, W. J. (1994). School to community transition planning: Factors to consider when working with culturally diverse students and families in rural settings. *Rural and Special Education Quarterly, 13*(1).

Oswald, D. P., Coutinho, M. J., Best, A. M., & Singh N. N. (1999). Ethnic representation in special education. *The Journal of Special Education, 32*(4), 194–206.

Patton, J. R., & Dunn, C. (1999). *Transition from school to young adulthood: Basic concepts and recommended practices.* Austin, TX: Pro-Ed.

Phelps, L. A., & Hanley-Maxwell, C. (1997). School-to-work transition for youth with disabilities: A review of outcomes and practices. *Review of Educational Research, 67*(2), 197–226.

Pleet, A. (2000, November 15). *Parent participation and students' post school outcomes* [on-line]. National Transition Alliance, University of Illinois, Champaign, IL. Retrieved from http://ici.umn.edu/ncset/events/transcripts/2000/00_11_15.pdf

Powers, L. E., Sowers, J., Turner, A., Nesbitt, M., Knowles, E., & Ellison, R. (1996). TAKE CHARGE: A model for promoting self-determination among adolescents with disabilities. In: L. E. Powers, G. H. S. Singer & J. Sowers (Eds), *On the Road to Autonomy: Promoting Self-Competence for Children and Youth with Disabilities* (pp. 291–322). Baltimore, MD: Paul H. Brookes.

Riley, R. W. (1995). Reflections on Goals 2000. *Teachers College Record, 96*(3), 380–388.

Rusch, F. R., & DeStefano, L. (1989). Transition from school to work: Strategies for young adults with disabilities. *Interchange, 9*(3) 1–2.

Rusch, F. R., Szymanski, E., & Chadsey-Rusch, J. (1992). The emerging field of transition services. In: F. Rusch, L. DeStefano, J. Chadsey-Rusch, L. A. Phelps & E. Szymanski (Eds), *Transition from School to Adult Life: Models, Linkages, and Policy* (pp. 5–17). Sycamore, IL: Sycamore Press.

Sailor, W. (1994). Inclusive practices in community services for culturally diverse young adults with disabilities. Unpublished manuscript, University of Kansas, Lawrence.

Shafer, M. S., & Rangasamy, R. (1995). Transition and Native American youth: A follow-up study of school leavers on the Fort Apache Indian Reservation. *Journal of Rehabilitation, 61*(1).

Smith, M. S., & Scoll, B. W. (1995). The Clinton human capital agenda. *Teachers College Record, 96*(3), 389–404.

Snell, M. E., & Brown, F. (2000). *Instruction of students with severe disabilities* (5th ed.). Columbus, OH: Merrill.

Storms, J., O'Leary, E., & Williams, J. (2000). *Transition requirements: A guide for states, districts, schools, universities and families.*

Szymanski, E. (1994). Transition: life-span and life-space considerations for empowerment. *Exceptional Children, 60*(5), 402–410.

Turnbull A. P., & Turnbull, H. R. (2001). *Families, professionals and exceptionality: Collaborating for empowerment* (4th ed.). Columbus, OH: Merrill Prentice Hall.

Turnbull, H. R., Bateman, D. F., & Turnbull, A. P. (1993). Family empowerment. In: P. Wehman (Ed.), *The ADA Mandate for Social Change.* Baltimore, MD: Paul H. Brookes.

U.S. Department of Education, Office of the Under Secretary, Planning and Evaluation Service (1999, April 8). *Federal education legislation enacted in 1994: An evaluation of implementation and impact (executive summary)* [On-line]. Available: www.ed.gov/offices/OUS/eval/1994legislation.html

U.S. Department of Education (1996). *Eighteenth Annual Report to Congress on Implementation of the Individual with Disabilities Education Act.* Washington, D.C.: Author.

Van Reusen, A. K., Bos, C. S., Schumaker, J. B., & Deshler, D. D. (1994). *The self-advocacy strategy for education and transition planning.* Lawrence, KS: Edge Enterprises.

Ward, M. J., & Halloran, W. D. (1993). Transition issues for the 1990s. *OSERS News in Print: Transitions, 6*(1), 4–5.

Wehmeyer, M. L., & Kelchner, K. (1995). *Whose life is it anyway? A student-directed transition planning process.* Arlington, TX: The Arc National Headquarters.

Wehmeyer, M. L., Morningstar, M., & Husted, D. (1999). *Family involvement in transition planning and implementation.* Austin, TX: Pro-Ed.

Will, M. (1984). *OSERS programming for the transition of youth with disabilities: Bridges from school to working life.* Washington, D.C: Author.

THE MYTH OF SOCIOECONOMIC DISSONANCE: WORKING WITH HOMELESS STUDENTS IN SPECIAL EDUCATION CONTEXTS

Lynn K. Wilder and Festus E. Obiakor

INTRODUCTION

The Masai people, great warriors from the grasslands of Eastern Africa, greet each other by asking, "How are the children?" The intended response is, "*All the children are well*" (Morrison, 2000). In the U.S., a more accurate response to that same question might be, "Most of the children are well." Children who are homeless or children who have disabilities do not fair as well as most. Those who are homeless *and* have disabilities fair the poorest of all (Hausman & Hammen, 1993; Heflin & Rudy, 1991; Reed & Sautter, 1990; Russell & Williams, 1988; Shea & Bauer, 1997). A good measure of the success of a society is how it treats its weakest members. In the same vein, a good measure of the success of a school community is how it educates its most vulnerable students. Truly good teachers increase their own abilities by teaching students who are weaker than themselves. These students then become truly good students who teach others; all benefit. As educators in the United States, we have much to learn about how to effectively educate our most vulnerable, at-risk students. This chapter focuses on the myth of socioeconomic dissonance and on how to work with homeless students in special education contexts.

SOCIOECONOMIC DISSONANCE

Socioeconomic dissonance can be described as the discord between groups with differing socioeconomic status. No one would dispute that the middle socioeconomic status of teachers differs from the lower socioeconomic status of their students who live in poverty. But, the critical question remains, does socioeconomic difference necessarily indicate dissonance or conflict between teachers and their students with disabilities from low socioeconomic groups? The following are case studies that help explain this phenomenon:

Case 1

In a special education college course, a guest speaker was invited to discuss the importance of obtaining parental permission before evaluating a child for special education classification and placement. One student, a general educator, raised her hand to comment that securing that permission in her school would be nearly impossible, and then she noted, "I have worked in a school in a poor neighborhood for many years and I can tell you none of those parents care at all about their children."

Case 2

In one college class, there was a discussion on the influx of Hispanic students of working class and migrant parents into the local school district. One Anglo American paraeducator, who had worked for several years in an elementary school resource room with many Hispanic students from transient families, made this revealing comment privately, "Until I had this class, I thought all Hispanics were poor, lazy, and dumb."

As indicated in Cases 1 and 2, socioeconomic differences sometimes do engender opposition between teachers and students with disabilities who live in poverty, especially when those teachers and students have preconceived ideas about the behavior of individuals from other groups. Cultural behavior can sometimes be defined by socioeconomic status (Goldstein, Glick & Gibbs, 1998); therefore, some teachers expect the behavior of students with disabilities who are of low socioeconomic status to be different from the behavior of students with disabilities who are of higher socioeconomic status. Their expectations of their low socioeconomic students with disabilities are lower. It is easy to imagine how school personnel without experience with students with disabilities who live in extreme poverty might espouse negative attitudes toward these students; their attitudes would be expressed in ignorance (Obiakor, 1994, 1999a, b, 2001).

It appears that educators see in their poor students and their poor parents what they expect to see in them (Obiakor, 1999b). Researchers have demonstrated that teacher expectations are a powerful influence on the academic and behavioral success of students (Brophy, 1986; Duncan, 1993; Ford, 1992; Grossman, 1995; Spring, 1994); for instance, Grossman emphasized that teachers expect less from students with low socioeconomic status. As he stated, "Many teachers, psychologists, and administrators are prejudiced against non-European American and poor students" (p. 63). Therefore, teachers may lower their expectations even further for students with disabilities who are poor. Earlier, Grossman (1991) noted that "the elimination of teacher prejudice is the first and most important step educators can take to ensure that only students who require special education services are referred to and accepted into special education programs, and that once accepted, they receive culturally appropriate special education services" (p. 23). Culturally appropriate services tend to be truly individualized when programs respond to differences and styles that students bring to school (see Obiakor, 2001). Surely, homeless individuals with disabilities will have needs unlike the needs of any other students. As consequence, general and special educators are professionally obligated to address them.

SOCIOECONOMIC STATUS: EFFECTS ON BEHAVIORAL RATING SCORES

Wilder (1999) conducted a study using Braaten's (1998) *Behavioral Objective Sequence* (BOS) to determine whether there was a difference between how students with identified emotional/behavioral disorders (EBD) perceived their social/behavioral competencies and how their teachers perceived them. The study investigated whether selected student or teacher demographic variables predicted teacher and student discrepancies in behavioral ratings for youth with EBD.

The BOS is a comprehensive, developmentally sequenced, observation-based assessment that examines competencies, not deficits like many behavioral rating scales, to determine a student's level of prosocial functioning in school. It consists of prosocial skills identified by teachers as skills students need to master in order to succeed socially and behaviorally in the school. Since homeless students may have serious social/ behavioral needs (Bassuk & Rubin, 1987; Lively & Kleine, 1996; Wells, 1990), a behavioral rating scale like the BOS appears valuable in assessing social/behavioral function and in selecting appropriate social and behavioral instruction for students with disabilities who are homeless. According to this study, one of the student demographic variables that emerged as a predictor of discrepancies between student and teacher ratings was student socioeconomic status. Although Wilder's study used a small research sample (N = 56 students), its findings corroborated the finding that student socioeconomic status affects teacher perceptions and subsequently teacher expectations and interactions (Friedman, 1976; Grossman, 1995; Smith, 1988).

The complex social phenomenon demonstrated by Wilder's 1999 study has many possible implications. Some might suggest that the differences in perception of student social competencies point to an imbalance of power and a difference in cultural norms between students with disabilities who are from low socioeconomic groups and their teachers (Campbell-Whatley, Algozzine & Obiakor, 1997) or that the differences reflect prejudicial attitudes of teachers (Grossman, 1991; Obiakor, 1999a; Winzer & Mazurek, 1998). Quite possibly, low socioeconomic students' social behaviors are not those that are valued and espoused by the school culture (Obiakor, 2001; Wilder, Jackson & Smith, 2001). Many general and special educators see differences as deficits. As a consequence, they stigmatize all students with low socioeconomic status and those who are racially and culturally different by expecting them to be less emotionally, socially, and academically adept. Low socioeconomic students are frequently referred for special education services (Kauffman, 2000). Of course, not all teachers exhibit prejudice toward students with low socioeconomic status. However, enough teachers do reveal prejudice that the answer to the question of whether socioeconomic difference necessarily predicts dissonance or conflict between teachers and their students from low socioeconomic groups appears to be that sometimes it does.

HOMELESS STUDENTS IN SPECIAL EDUCATION CONTEXTS

If teachers frequently refer low socioeconomic students for special education because of their biases, then most likely they will refer homeless students as well. Given their circumstances, homeless students have high rates of developmental delay, language disabilities, poor physical health, anxiety, depression, mental illness, and behavioral problems (Bassuk & Rosenberg, 1988; Bassuk & Rubin,1987; Institute of Medicine, 1988; Leshner, 1992). However, the assumption that all homeless students will have academic and social/behavioral difficulties is dangerous. Many homeless students with disabilities succeed in school despite extremely difficult personal challenges associated with not having a permanent home, such as not knowing where to sleep, how to get food, where to wash and get clean clothes, where to put their few possessions so they are not stolen, and where to go for emotional support since homeless parents may be preoccupied with their own problems. Parental problems sometimes include physical or sexual abuse and neglect of their children (Heflin & Rudy, 1991; Newman, 1999). In addition, homeless students with disabilities and their parents frequently worry about how to find a school and whether they can enroll without immunization records, how to get to school, whether someone will send for their special education records and where they will be placed, where to get school supplies and monies for fees, how to befriend peers and teachers, and how to adjust to constantly changing expectations in new schools. After school hours, they must figure out how to complete their homework without proper supplies, a computer or adaptive technology, a library card, or transportation (Wilder, 2002).

As a result of the aforementioned difficulties, most homeless students experience emotional turmoil (Leshner, 1992); school phobia is not an unusual phenomenon for homeless students (Tower & White, 1989). Since families of homeless students with disabilities have inadequate resources and personal difficulties, the students themselves have disabilities, and their teachers may expect less of them, it is not difficult to understand why these students might be at serious risk of educational failure (Hausman & Hammen, 1993; Linehan, 1992). However, resources can be allocated, and teacher expectations can be changed. Surprisingly, it is these very circumstances that sometimes cause students to demonstrate strength, independence, an uncanny ability to adjust to new situations, stamina, and academic engagement – in short, school success (Finn & Rock, 1997). Personnel in the schools must help these students cope successfully with their challenges.

Young Homeless Students

Young homeless students with disabilities have little if any control over their living circumstances. They probably move frequently, own few possessions, wear dirty and unfashionable clothes, experience hunger and cold, have health and dental needs, experience social and emotional needs, and possibly endure physical and/or sexual abuse and neglect, along with peer chastisement (Heflin & Rudy, 1991; Newman, 1999). They tend to miss school often, change schools frequently, and experience academic and behavioral difficulties (Linehan, 1992; Rountree, 1996). School personnel should acknowledge that there is little that younger homeless children can do to improve their living circumstances or school circumstances, but responsive adults in schools can and must act in the following manner:

(1) School district personnel are required by the McKinney Act to locate young homeless students within their boundaries and enroll them in school (Douvanis & Douvanis, 1995).
(2) Administrators can provide school enrollment on-site in shelters (Wilder, in press).

(3) If homeless parents come to school to enroll their children, school office personnel should inform them that their children have the right to attend their old school for a year with the school arranging transportation, or they have the option to attend the school where they are presently residing (Rountree, 1996).

(4) School office personnel should immediately enroll the children in free meal programs; arrange for needed transportation; send for academic, special education, and immunization records (if they exist); and alert only the appropriate school personnel of the students' homelessness (Douvanis & Douvanis, 1995; Tower & White, 1989). A student's inability to produce records should not preclude school attendance.

(5) Informed school health nurses can ensure that homeless students have vision, hearing, medical, and dental screenings and can connect the students and their families with health-related services (Johnson, 1992).

(6) Administrators can initiate an expedited referral and evaluation procedure for students' special education placement if former records cannot be located, and they may arrange counseling services if needed.

(7) Administrators can spend Chapter One funds to provide clothing for homeless students who are inappropriately clothed (Johnson, 1992).

(8) Administrators can allow homeless students to shower in school facilities and can provide space for their personal belongings (Wilder, in press).

(9) Administrators can seek donations from businesses for school fees and school supplies (Wilder, in press).

(10) Administrators should provide inservice training for teachers to inform them of the needs of homeless children and teach them their responsibilities (Linehan, 1992; Quint, 1994).

(11) Teachers should teach social/behavioral skills of the dominant culture and provide numerous opportunities for practice and generalization in order to improve the resiliency of homeless students and to improve their treatment by their peers in the school context (Gordon, 1995).

(12) Teachers are also responsible for instructing the other students to accept the homeless students as important members of the school community and to refrain from harassing them (Guetzloe, 1997; Sagor, 1996).

(13) Administrators should provide academic support services, for example, the provision of mentors (Ogbu, 1992) and after-school tutoring programs in shelters to reduce the risk of academic failure (Finn & Rock, 1997).

The characteristics, needs, and effective education of homeless students with disabilities differ according to age. Students who experience academic failure in late elementary school are at an increased risk of drug abuse, delinquency, violence, pregnancy, and dropping out of school (Hawkins, Catalano & Miller, 1992). The transition from elementary school to middle school is extremely difficult for most students. Sadly, when students need ever increasing adult support, they enter a school environment that fosters less personal student-teacher interactions, has more students per classroom, places more emphasis on competition, demands academic performance based on test scores, and offers less support from school personnel. As a result, students often begin to display negative attitudes toward school (U.S. Department of Health and Human Services, 1997).

Homeless Adolescent Students

Like younger homeless students, homeless adolescents may experience physical or sexual abuse, but unlike them, they have probably left their parents and live without families in shelters, in cars, on the street, or with various friends (Ysseldyke, Algozzine & Thurlow, 2000). Parental divorce, addictions, incarceration, insufficient finances, or other parental crises may precipitate a transient lifestyle for adolescents with disabilities. In addition, they may leave home because they have conflicts with their parents that cause them to feel unloved; they may be running from the law. Their parents may expel them from their homes because they have addictions, or have become teen parents. Homeless teens sometimes work as prostitutes, steal to support themselves, or work full time jobs that preclude consistent school attendance (Rothman, 1991; U.S. Department of Health and Human Services, 1997). Homeless youth are often difficult for school and social service agency personnel to locate (Powers & Jaklitsch, 1992). Unaccompanied youth account for about 7% of the homeless population (Mayors' Sixteenth Annual Report, *Hunger and Homelessness in America's Cities*, 2000). The more these adolescents move, the greater the risk that they will engage in criminal behavior and drug-related problems (Hawkins et al., 1992), but many resilient youth survive and succeed in school.

Although the school attendance of young homeless children is sometimes sporadic, the enrollment, attendance, and academic achievement of homeless youth are worse (Powers & Jaklitsch, 1992). One in four homeless adolescents qualifies for special education services; half produce below average or failing school work (Bassuk & Rubin, 1987; Hausman & Hammen, 1993). Most display negative relationships with peers and teachers. Early patterns of stressors in their lives tend to result in poor social/behavioral adjustment (Wells, 1990; Werner & Smith, 1992), and they are likely to have pervasive needs for psychological care (Rothman, 1991). Since peers with homes tend to ridicule them, adolescent homeless students resist trusting peers as friends and most isolate themselves from the social context of the school community. Their emotional turmoil may be expressed in acts of aggression or withdrawal (Grossman, 1991; Tower & White, 1989). As a consequence, teachers should be taught during inservice sessions to understand the source and function of these emotionally charged behaviors and to avoid overreactions with impatience and anger that will further isolate the homeless student (Beck & Malley, 1998; Linehan, 1992). Teachers can improve their effectiveness with homeless students with disabilities by teaching them about risk and resiliency factors.

REDUCING REDUCING RISKS AND BUILDING RESILIENCY: HELPING HOMELESS STUDENTS TO MAXIMIZE THEIR FULLEST POTENTIAL

In recent years, there has been a plethora of research on risk and resiliency (protective) factors. Risk factors add to the probability that at-risk youth will fail in school, and protective factors make school success more likely for students who are at greatest risk of educational failure (Hawkins et al., 1992). Teachers must help homeless youth with disabilities to recognize risk factors that lead to school failure: aggression, violence, other persistent anti-social behavior, substance abuse, sexual activity, teen pregnancy, gang membership, at-risk peer associations, negative attitudes toward education and toward acculturation. When these students recognize the risk factors, they can be taught how to stay away from destructive behaviors and why they should do so (Hawkins et al., 1992). The great difficulty is that some homeless youth with disabilities do not desire to adjust to the school culture because they feel alienated and stigmatized, and they do not trust those who attempt to teach them (Long, 1997; Powers & Jaklitsch, 1992). Unfortunately, those who attempt to teach them may not have the knowledge, skills, patience, persistence, or desire to serve these youth in an on-going relationship. Homeless youth with disabilities must have trusted mentors who encourage them to avoid risk factors, adopt protective strategies, and demonstrate unconditional regard for their personal welfare. Teachers can and should assume this role or try to acquaint the adolescent with someone who will.

School personnel should teach homeless youth with disabilities to recognize behavior and activities that build resiliency and protect them from school failure. Some productive activities that students participate in when they are successful within the school culture are cross-age tutoring, club membership, athletics, music, drama, art, and service learning (Tower & White, 1989). These activities channel students' energies in a positive manner, serving as protective factors in their lives (Finn & Rock, 1997; Pisapia & Westfall, 1994; Westfall & Pisapia,

1994). Other protective factors teachers must teach to homeless adolescents with disabilities are how educational engagement will increase their chances for school success; how consistent attendance at counseling sessions may improve their emotional stability; how productive extra curricular and service activities may increase their sense of well-being; how vocational training will help prepare them for successful adult employment; how prosocial skills training will increase their social/behavioral skills and their level of social comfort in the dominant culture; and how life skills training will help prepare them for adult life (Wilder, 2001).

It is most critical that homeless adolescents reflect, by verbalizing or writing, on how their experiences have caused them to develop positive personal traits and exactly what positive traits they possess (Finn & Rock, 1997; Westfall & Pisapia, 1994). They can then be taught through understanding and appreciating those traits viewed as helping them to gain resiliency and learn social/behavioral, academic, vocational, and problem solving skills that homelessness might improve their chances of success in school and subsequently in adult life. The power of the positive approach should not be understated (Epstein, 1999; Saleeby, 1992; Seligman & Csikszentmihalyi, 2000). Confident homeless adolescents with disabilities can even learn to share their experiences with others. The more protective factors they can nurture, the more resilient they can become. Homeless youth need step-by-step support in this journey, given by responsive, caring, and kind adults (Long, 1997). Thus, it is important that homeless adolescents stay in the same school with the same support system for at least a year.

One additional protective factor that may improve outcomes for some homeless students with disabilities is their involvement in organized religion. Although the research is sometimes contradictory, some evidence supports the tenet that some religious engagement improves students' social/behavioral skills. Religious membership may provide the family-like socialization structure (much like gang membership) through which students who are at-risk desire to be accepted by other members of their particular faith and will thus acculturate (Johnson, Jang, Larson & Li, 2001). Religiosity has been positively correlated with student well-being and self-esteem; it has also demonstrated positive correlations with the inhibition of premarital sexual behavior, alcohol and drug abuse, and suicide (Payne, Bergin, Bielema & Jenkins, 1991). Private religious organizations are another type of social service agency that school personnel may encounter when working with homeless youth with disabilities since they frequently fund and operate homeless shelters.

General and special education teachers and other school personnel should provide the adult understanding and emotional support that homeless adolescents with disabilities need if they are to remain in school (Wilder, in press). "Emotional support means the ability to take a stand with the student and not against him or her" (Long, 1997, p. 245). Earlier, Brophy (1986) stated that low socioeconomic students "are more likely to require warmth and support in addition to good instruction and to need more encouragement for their efforts and praise for their successes" (p. 1073). Providing this support changes both the teacher and the student. Learning to change is not only advantageous for homeless students with disabilities; it enhances educators also. With this emotional support, some homeless adolescents demonstrate remarkable resiliency and thrive despite their circumstances. Consider Case 4 for further descriptions.

Case 4

Don was adopted as an infant into a very wealthy family. As the only child, he was not allowed to perform household chores or make decisions on his own. As a teen, he was given a cell phone, a sports car, and a furnished and paid for apartment. He became irresponsible and began partying frequently. As a result, his adopted parents cut off his living expenses, and he had no place to live but on the street. Then he moved to a men's homeless shelter for addicts funded by a private religious organization and lived there for about two years. He attended classes on-site at the shelter to improve his educational level, attended group counseling sessions to overcome his substance addictions, was employed at the shelter industries and, eventually, maintained a steady job on the "outside" at a copy shop. The last hurdle he had yet to conquer was re-establishing a relationship with his adoptive parents. Success for Don came because several responsive adults supported him at critical junctures in his struggle to survive life's stressors.

It is important that general and special educators act on behalf of homeless youth with disabilities to help them maximize their fullest potential. Not only are they required by the McKinney Act to locate homeless adolescents within their boundaries and enroll them in school (Douvanis & Douvanis, 1995), they are also required by the Individuals with Disabilities Act (IDEA) to educate students with exceptionalities. The mentality that we are trying to be nice should be avoided. We must do what we do because it is professionally responsible. To buttress professionally responsible behavior, general and special educators must:

(1) Enroll even unaccompanied homeless adolescents and try immediately to contact parent(s) or guardian(s); document all attempts to do so.

(2) Inform the appropriate local social service agency personnel that an unaccompanied minor needs a guardian and work with judges as they appoint school social workers to serve as guardians.
(3) Provide school enrollment, tutorial services, or even instructional services onsite in large shelters for homeless youth.
(4) Establish a safe and secure school environment with clear academic and behavioral expectations, regular routines, and responsive adults.
(5) Provide homeless youth with disabilities with vocational counseling and job exploration opportunities.
(6) Refer homeless youth to any appropriate, available educational support services to decrease their chances of being academically/behaviorally at risk of school failure.
(7) Develop mentoring programs as effective tools for students at risk of school failure.
(8) Teach housed and homeless, rich and poor, students with and without disabilities to treat each other with respect.

CONCLUSIONS

An American public official once stated, "The stability of every society . . . has depended on the resignation of the poor to their poverty" (Wood, McDonnell, Pfordresher, Fite & Lankford, 1989, p. 594). We have frequently encountered this attitude expressed by individuals working for social service agencies and special education programs. This attitude reflects a prejudice unacceptable among those who work with homeless students with disabilities: the attitude that change is impossible for the homeless. General and special educators working with homeless students with disabilities must comprehend that they can help their students to:

(1) Emotionally cope with their present conditions by using all available resources (e.g. mentors, counselors, interpreters if needed, and supportive, not critical peers and other school personnel who can teach them to recognize and use resiliency factors to achieve success in the school culture).
(2) Work to solve their problems, whether financial, health-related, or of other sorts by teaching them problem solving, critical thinking, functional academic, self-care, vocational, and social/behavioral skills and by affording them the opportunity to practice and generalize these skills.

(3) Increase the students' knowledge by teaching them academic skills according to their intellectual level in order to increase their chances of completing the greatest education possible for them (i.e. increase their ability to earn their living, use their leisure time productively, and subsequently increase their social status).

It is the task of general and special educators to hold out whatever hope of improved life circumstances they can and to work to ensure that homeless students with disabilities have access to the basic living resources and special educational services they deserve. Often the school is the only stable social entity in the homeless student's life (Reed & Sautter, 1990). It is imperative that educators believe homeless students with disabilities want to succeed and they help them in any way necessary to do so. And, most importantly, educators must work to retain homeless students with disabilities in the same school for at least a year so at least some of these goals can be realized.

Our premise in this chapter is that socioeconomic dissonance should be a myth. Significant negative differences between school personnel and families who are in extreme poverty exist only in the minds and hearts of those who embrace this myth; the reality is that, fundamentally, beneath the ragged exterior the poor are no different than the middle class educators who teach them. General and special education teachers who are brave enough to visit students with disabilities and their parents in their places of residence (i.e. street, shelter, or other) learn that poor parents, even parents with serious addictions or mental illness, love their children. Each time educators have the opportunity to sit opposite a family in extreme poverty, their thoughts should be "under different conditions, that could be my child and me." This possible attitude will help teachers appreciate, not negate, blame, or denigrate the circumstances of homeless students with disabilities and their parents. We believe educators must learn to look beyond the outward appearance and unusual behavior of individuals and into the hopes, desires, and dreams of the heart. A critical consideration for teachers is what part they will play in their students' growth and learning. Although there is a tendency for those in power to minimize and blame minority groups, including the poor and those with certain disabilities, for their own circumstances, labeling and fault-finding have not been shown to be effective methods for improving educational outcomes. (Wilder et al., 2001). For this reason, socioeconomic dissonance between educators and students with disabilities and their parents who live in extreme poverty should remain the great myth, not the reality, of the new millennium.

REFERENCES

Bassuk, E. L., & Rosenberg, L. (1988). Why does family homelessness occur? A case-control study. *American Journal of Public Health, 78,* 783–788.

Bassuk, E., & Rubin, L. (1987). Homeless children: A neglected population. *American Journal of Orthopsychiatry, 57*(2), 279–286.

Beck, M., & Malley, J. (1998). A pedagogy of belonging. *Reclaiming Children and Youth, 7,* 133–141.

Braaten, S. (1998). *Behavioral Objective Sequence.* Champaign, IL: Research Press.

Brophy J. (1986). Teacher influences on student achievement. *American Psychologist, 41,* 1069–1077.

Campbell-Whatley, G. D., Algozzine, B., & Obiakor, F. E. (1997). Using mentoring to improve academic programming for African American male youths with mild disabilities. *The School Counselor, 44,* 362–366.

Douvanis, G., & Douvanis, C. (1995). When the student has no mailbox. *Journal for a Just and Caring Education, 1*(2), 142–150.

Duncan, G. (1993). Racism as a developmental mediator. *Educational Forum, 57,* 360–369.

Epstein, M. (1999). Using strength-based assessment in programs for children with emotional and behavioral disorders. *Beyond Behavior, 9*(2), 25–27.

Finn, J. D., & Rock, D. A. (1997). Academic success among students at risk for school failure. *Journal of Applied Psychology, 82,* 221–234.

Ford, B. A. (1992). Multicultural education training for special educators working with African-American youth. *Exceptional Children, 59,* 107–114.

Friedman, P. (1976). Comparison of teacher reinforcement schedules for students with different social class backgrounds. *Journal of Educational Psychology, 68,* 286–293.

Goldstein, A., Glick, B., & Gibbs, J. C. (1998). *Aggression replacement training: A comprehensive intervention for aggressive youth* (2nd ed.). Champaign, IL: Research Press.

Gordon, K. A. (1995). Self-concept and motivational patterns of resilient African American high school students. *Journal of Black Psychology, 21,* 239–256.

Grossman, H. (1991). Special education in a diverse society: Improving services for minority and working class students. *Preventing School Failure, 36*(1), 19–27.

Grossman, H. (1995). *Special education in a diverse society.* Needham Heights, MA: Allyn-Bacon.

Guetzloe, E. (1997). The power of positive relationships: Mentoring programs in the school and community. *Preventing School Failure, 41*(3), 100–105.

Hausman, B., & Hammen, C. (1993). Parenting in homeless families: The double crisis. *American Journal of Orthopsychiatry, 63,* 358–368.

Hawkins, J. D., Catalano, R. F., & Miller, J. Y. (1992). Risk and protective factors for alcohol and other drug problems in adolescence and early adulthood: Implications for substance abuse prevention. *Psychological Bulletin, 112*(1), 64–105.

Heflin, L. J., & Rudy, K. (1991). *Homeless in need of special education: Exceptional children at risk.* Reston, VA: ERIC Clearinghouse on Handicapped and Gifted Children. (ERIC Document Reproduction Service No. ED 399 167)

Institute of Medicine (1988). *Homelessness, health, and human needs.* Washington, D.C.: National Academy Press.

Johnson, J. F. (1992). Educational support services for homeless children and youth. In: J. H. Stronge (Ed.), *Educating Homeless Children and Adolescents: Evaluating Policy and Practice* (pp. 153–178). Newbury Park, CA: Sage.

Johnson, B. R., Jang, S. J., Larsen, D. B., & Li, S. D. (2001). Does adolescent religious commitment matter? A reexamination of the effects religiosity in delinquency. *The Journal of Research in Crime and Delinquency, 38*(1), 22–44.

Kauffman, J. M. (2000). *Characteristics of emotional and behavioral disorders of children and youth* (7th ed.). Upper Saddle River, NJ: Merrill.

Leshner, A. I. (1992). *Outcasts on main street: Report of the Federal Task Force on Homelessness and Severe Mental Illness*. Washington, D.C.: National Institute of Mental Health.

Linehan, M. F. (1992). Children who are homeless: Educational strategies for school personnel. *Phi Delta Kappan*, (September). Bloomington, IN: Phi Delta Kappan.

Lively, K. L., & Kleine, P. F. (1996). *The school as a tool for survival for homeless children*. New York: Garland.

Long, N. J. (1997). The therapeutic power of kindness. *Reclaiming Children and Youth, 5*(4), 242–246.

Mayors' 16th Annual Status Report (2000). *Hunger and homelessness in America's cities* [On-line]. Available: www.usmayors.org/uscm/news/press_release/documents/hunger_release.html

Morrison, A. B. (2000). No more strangers. *Ensign, 30*(September), 16–20.

Newman, R. (1999). *Educating homeless children: Witness to a cataclysm*. New York: Garland.

Obiakor, F. E. (1994). *The eight step multicultural approach: Learning and teaching with a smile*. Dubuque, IA: Kendall/Hunt.

Obiakor, F. E. (1999a). Multicultural education: Powerful tool for educating learners with exceptionalities. In: F. E. Obiakor, J. O. Schwenn & A. F. Rotatori (Eds), *Advances in Special Education: Multicultural Education for Learners with Exceptionalities* (pp. 1–14). Stamford, CT: JAI Press.

Obiakor, F. E. (1999b). Teacher expectations of minority exceptional learners: Impact on "accuracy" of self-concepts. *Exceptional Children, 66*(Fall), 39–53.

Obiakor, F. E. (2001). *It even happens in "good" schools: Responding to cultural diversity in today's classrooms*. Thousand Oaks, CA: Corwin Press.

Ogbu, J. U. (1992). Understanding cultural diversity and learning. *Educational Researcher, 21*(8), 5–14.

Payne, I. R., Bergin, A. E., Bielema, K. A., & Jenkins, P. H. (1991). Review of religion and mental health: Prevention and the enhancement of psychosocial functioning. *Prevention in Human Services, 9*, 11–40.

Pisapia, J., & Westfall, A. (1994). *Developing resilient schools and resilient students. Research brief No. 19*. Richmond, VA: Metropolitan Educational Research Consortium.

Powers, J. L., & Jaklitsch, B. (1992). Adolescence and homelessness: The unique challenge for secondary educators. In: J. H. Stronge (Ed.), *Educating Homeless Children and Adolescents: Evaluating Policy and Practice* (pp. 115–132). Newbury Park, CA: Sage.

Quint, S. (1994). *Schooling homeless children: A working model for America's public schools*. New York: Teachers College Press.

Reed, S., & Sautter, R. C. (1990). Children of poverty: The status of 12 million young Americans. Phi Delta Kappan Special Report (June). Bloomington, IN: Phi Delta Kappan.

Rothman, J. (1991). *Runaway and homeless youth: Strengthening services to families and youth*. White Plains, NY: Longman.

Rountree, M. (1996). Opening school doors to the homeless. *Thrust for Educational Leadership, 26*(1), 10–13.

Russell, S. C., & Williams, E. U. (1988). Homeless handicapped children: A special education perspective. *Children's Environments Quarterly, 5*, 3–7.

Sagor, R. (1996). Building resiliency in students. *Educational Leadership*, (September), 38–43.

Saleebey, D. (1992). *The strengths perspective in social work practice*. New York: Longman.
Seligman, M. E. P., & Csikszentmihalyi, M. (Eds) (2000). Happiness, excellence, and optimal functioning [special issue]. *American Psychologist, 55*.
Shea, T. M., & Bauer, A. M. (1997). *An introduction to special education: A social skills perspective* (2nd ed.). Madison, WI: Brown & Bench.
Smith, M. K. (1988). Effects of children's social class, race, and gender on teacher expectations for children's academic performance. In: C. Heid (Ed.), *Multicultural Education: Knowledge and Perceptions* (pp. 101–117). Bloomington, IN: Indiana University Center for Multicultural Education.
Spring, J. (1994). *American education* (6th ed.). White Plains, NY: Longman.
Tower, C. C., & White, D. J. (1989). *Homeless students*. Washington, D.C.: National Education Association of the United States.
U.S. Department of Health and Human Services (1997). *Understanding youth development: Promoting positive pathways of growth*. (CSR Publication No. 105-95-1735). Washington, D.C.: Author.
Wells, A. (1990). Educating homeless children. *The Education Digest* (April), 30–33.
Werner, E. E., & Smith, R. S. (1992). *Overcoming the odds: High risk children from birth to adulthood*. Ithaca, NY: Cornell University Press.
Westfall, A., & Pisapia, J. (1994). *At risk students: Who are they and what helps them succeed?* Richmond, VA: Metropolitan Research Consortium.
Wilder, L. K. (1999). Student vs. teacher perception of student behavior for youth with emotional/behavioral disorders: Accurate assessment (Doctoral Dissertation). Ann Arbor, MI: UMI.
Wilder, L. K. (2002). The homeless are people too: Including homeless students in educational programming. In: F. E. Obiakor, P. A. Grant & E. A. Dooley (Eds), *Educating all: Refocusing the Comprehensive Support Model* (pp. 64–84). Springfield, IL: Charles C. Thomas.
Wilder, L. K. (2001). Success in college for students with disabilities. *Theories and Practices in Supervision and Curriculum, 12*, 31–34.
Wilder, L. K., & Gunsalus, C. (2001). Managing problem behaviors of students with disabilities in inclusive settings. *OASCD Journal, 11*(1), 40–43. Oklahoma City, OK: OASCD.
Wilder, L. K., Jackson, A. P., & Smith, T. B. (2001). Secondary transition of multicultural learners: Lessons from the Navajo Native American experience. *Preventing School Failure, 45*(3), 119–124.
Winzer, M. A., & Mazurek, K. (1998). *Special education in multicultural contexts*. Upper Saddle River, NJ: Prentice-Hall.
Wood, K. M., McDonnell, H., Pfordresher, J., Fite, M. A., & Lankford, P. (1989). *Classics in world literature*. Glenview, IL: Scott, Foresman.
Ysseldyke, J. E., Algozzine, B., & Thurlow, M. L. (2000). *Critical issues in special education* (3rd ed.). Boston: Houghton Mifflin.

FAMILY AND SCHOOL PARTNERSHIPS: BUILDING BRIDGES IN GENERAL AND SPECIAL EDUCATION

Jean Ann Summers, Karen Gavin,
Tonya Purnell-Hall and Jason Nelson

INTRODUCTION

The concept of inclusion in special education leads to extensive discussions, as exemplified throughout this book, about how to bring together what has become two parallel systems – "general" and "special" – into a unified system of education. Each field has developed practices that could profitably contribute to improvements in practices in the other. We have learned over the last few decades that inclusion practices, when done well, have mutual benefits for all concerned: for children both with and without exceptionalities, for professionals in general and special education, and for overall reform of the system as a whole. This chapter focuses on one of the critical components of effective education in both general and special education: the relationships between families and schools. We hope to make the same case about the value of "inclusion" for family partnerships that others make about the value of inclusion in the classroom. We argue that the development of a comprehensive plan for inclusion and school reform should incorporate a synthesis of thinking and practice with respect to family-school relationships – the result would be a system in which families in all their range of diversity are linked in partnership with schools and other resources in the community, to meet the educational needs of all children, regardless of their special needs and strengths.

Certainly, the goal of developing strong partnerships between families and schools is the same in both the general and special education fields: to enhance children's developmental and educational outcomes. The same issues and challenges have faced both fields and have caused educators often to fall short of their goals in both fields. As in all other aspects of special education, however, the concepts, research, and practice principles of family-school relationships for families of students with disabilities, have evolved separately from the thinking in the general education field. This parallel development has meant that the solutions to challenges and ideas for enhancing positive partnerships have for the most part proceeded without opportunities for educators in either field to cross-pollinate, leading educators to "reinvent the wheel," so to speak. We believe solutions for healthy partnerships between home and school, that maximize the strengths of school and community for the benefit of all children, will not be achieved until general and special educators are able to synthesize the best ideas from both fields. In sections that follow, we seek answers to a series of questions: What are the current conceptualizations or ideal models of family-school partnerships in general and special education, and what are the strategies related to those concepts? What are some of the issues and opportunities facing family-school partnerships in both general and special education? And finally, what is needed to realize the ideal models?

CONCEPTUAL FRAMEWORKS OF FAMILY-SCHOOL PARTNERSHIPS

General Education Concepts

The primary focus in general education research related to family-school partnerships, was traditionally on the importance of parental influence on child development and student achievement. For example, Grolnick & Slowiaczek (1994) defined parent involvement as "the dedication of resources by the parent to the child within a given domain" (p. 238). Many researchers have focused on family demographic variables, such as socioeconomic status, maternal education, and number of children in the household, as a means for predicting students' success in school. More recent studies have focused on process variables (e.g. family communication patterns, family routines, parenting styles, parent-child attachment, parental expectations and aspirations) which influence children's development (Grolnick, Benjet, Kurowski & Apostoleris, 1997; Halle,

Kurtz-Costes & Mahoney, 1997; Hart & Risley, 1996; Zellman & Waterman, 1998). The assumption is that the home environment provides an enriched or deprived learning environment that makes the child more or less prepared for the formal classroom.

In an attempt to develop a conceptual framework to explain this process, early educational researchers (e.g. Bloom, 1964) postulated specific parent actions, such as modeling work habits or setting expectations for academic achievement as critical factors for predicting school success. In this same vein, Singh, Bickley, Trivette, Keith, and Anderson (1995) proposed that most definitions of parent involvement fall into four major categories: (1) parental academic aspirations and expectations for children; (2) participation in school activities and programs; (3) home structure that supports learning (e.g. monitoring homework and imposing rules about television watching); and (4) parent-child communication about school and achievement. Notably, these models of parent involvement are clearly not defining any sense of family-school *partnership*, in the usual understanding of partnership as a relationship with mutual expectations among all parties. There is an underlying assumption that it is the family's responsibility to comply with the judgments of professionals and help children meet the expectations of the school. There are no reciprocal expectations for schools to conform to any family expectations or definitions about children's development or achievement. A different viewpoint has emerged more recently, through the work of Epstein (1996) and her colleagues. Epstein (1996) used Bronfrenner's (1979) ecological model to propose a social theory of "overlapping spheres of influence" as a model for understanding family-school partnerships. Specifically, Epstein's theoretical perspective postulated that, "the most effective families and schools had overlapping, shared goals and missions concerning children, and conducted some work collaboratively" (p. 214). Epstein postulates that these overlapping "spheres of influence" come together through a mutual focus on the "child-as-student in interactions between families and schools, parents and teachers, or other influential participants" (Hidalgo, Siu, Bright, Swap & Epstein, 1995, p. 499). Within these overlapping spheres of influence are six major types of partnerships that help families, schools, and communities assist in children's education and development. Within each partnership are a multitude of activities and practices with varying levels of shared responsibility between teachers, parents, students and other significant members within the community or society. The six partnership types include (Epstein, 1992):

Type 1: Basic Obligations of Families: Assisting families in their responsibilities to promote children's health and safety, develop parenting strategies, establish positive home conditions that foster learning and appropriate behavior. Schools may conduct parent workshops, home visits, family support programs or promote information exchanges to help families understand their child taking into account their age and grade level.

Type 2: Basic Obligations of Schools: Communicating effectively with families about school events and children's progress. Communications include telephone calls, school newsletters, report card exchange, and informative materials about a variety of educationally related issues.

Type 3: Involvement at School: Parent volunteering to assist the students or the school. Volunteering includes classroom parent, school safety volunteer, or assisting a classroom teacher or other school official. This also includes family attendance to school related-events such as school performances, sporting events, or other activities.

Type 4: Involvement in Learning Activities at Home: Involving families in their child's learning through monitoring and assisting educational activities at home, such as homework and other school-related tasks. Schools provide families with the information to understand and effectively interact with their children during home learning activities.

Type 5: Involvement in Decision Making, Governance, and Advocacy: Parents serving in participatory roles in committees or other school groups. Training parents to be leaders in decision-making skills and true contributors to school decisions.

Type 6: Collaboration with Community Organizations: Collaborating with local and regional businesses, colleges and universities, and other agencies to share responsibility for children's learning and development.

Special Education Concepts

Turnbull and Turnbull (1997) provided a succinct review of the evolving views of parents' roles in special education. Some of these views may have changed over time, but most linger on, at least as undercurrents of assumptions about the nature of the family-school partnerships. As Turnbull and Turnbull noted, the first view of families, held throughout the first half of the twentieth century, was that parents are the cause of their child's disability, either through genetic transmission of the disability, or through poor parenting practices or harmful behaviors such as substance abuse. This viewpoint exists side by side to the view that parents need training to enhance their role as teachers of their children. In this view, parents are recruited as supplementary teachers or therapists and taught how to provide therapies, behavior management, or early stimulation, for their children in the home. Just as in general education, these earlier views of parental roles in special education convey the message that parents are expected to be passive recipients of professional judgments and faithful followers of their recommendations (see Turnbull & Turnbull, 1997). In other words, schools know best; therefore, the "best" families follow the lead of the school.

Another set of parental roles in special education, however, contradict these expectations of passivity, inadequacy, and compliance. These roles arise from the historic exclusion of children with disabilities from educational services, and the gradual recognition that schools need to be compelled by some outside force to provide appropriate services. Initially, parents responded to this exclusion by organizing associations, such as The ARC (originally called the National Association for Parents and Friends of Mentally Retarded Children), United Cerebral Palsy, and so on. At their early stages, these groups were sources of funding and development of local services for children and adults with disabilities (Turnbull & Turnbull, 1997). But increasingly, they were the organizational framework through which parents served as political advocates for change. Through these organizations, parents brought successful litigation establishing the rights of children with special needs to an education, and finally legislation, such as the Individuals with Disabilities Education Act, or IDEA, first passed in 1975 passed in 1975 as the Education of All Handicapped Children's Act (PL 94-142) and subsequently amended and expanded (1997, 34 CFR Part 300). Because of this earlier successful advocacy effort, it is hardly surprising that a study of Congressional intent during the debate over the original bill reveals that Congress viewed parents as a key mechanism for enforcement of IDEA (Turnbull, Turnbull & Wheat, 1982), and thus arose the role of parents as active decision makers for their children. There are a variety of "power tools" parents are given in the law to assure their child receives services, such as rights to see the child's records, rights to participate and approve of their child's Individualized Education Plan, rights to due process procedures, to mention a few. In short, in contrast to the "parental inadequacy" view of parents held by the traditional parent involvement conceptualizations (of parents as cause or parents in need of training), this set of roles is a kind of "school inadequacy" view that schools cannot or will not meet educational needs of children with disabilities without parental involvement as advocates and decision makers.

In the meantime, another view of the role of families of children and adults with disabilities was evolving outside the educational sphere, from the increasing push to include people with disabilities in the community. Again, Bronfrenbrenner's (1979) influence appears. His ecological framework led to the recognition of the importance of families in the overall ecology in which the child or adult resides. Thus the recognition grew that a broad array of family supports was necessary to maintain the child both in the school and the community at large. Advocates began to call for a reversal of the "agency centered/parent involvement" expectation that families should comply with the needs of the service system, to a "family centered/family support" expectation that the service system (defined as an array of health, educational, and social services) should come together to meet the needs of the whole child and family (Turnbull & Summers, 1985). This family-centered orientation is most evident in early intervention and early childhood special education services. It was codified in the 1986 amendments (PL 99-457) to PL 94-142, creating early intervention services for infants and toddlers with disabilities, and explicitly stating that the purpose of early intervention was "to *support families* to meet the special and developmental needs of their child" (IDEA, 1997, 34 CFR Part 303, Section 631(a)(4), emphasis added). It also mandated the development of an Individualized Family Support Plan, or IFSP, rather than the IEP specified for children with disabilities from age 3–21.

The changes in the law both reflected current thinking and fueled continuing development of conceptualizations of family-centered practice. Dunst and Trivette (1989) reviewed a number of early intervention models and classified them as professional-centered, family-focused, family-allied, and family-centered. The professional-centered model is more like the traditional parent involvement model, in which parents are the passive recipients of professional decisions, and services are provided by professionals. Associated with this is the family-allied model (see Dunst & Trivette) in which parents are expected to work under the direction of early interventionists to work with their child on specific goals, which are generally identified by the professional. The family-focused model (Bailey, McWilliam, Darkes, Hebbeler, Simeonsson, Spiker & Wagner, 1998) views parents and early interventionists as collaborators in decision making about the goals and services for the child. Finally, the family-centered model (see Dunst & Trivette) views the family as the primary decision maker as well as the primary vehicle for delivering the interventions. The role of professionals is to empower families to identify their strengths, to supplement those strengths to meet needs, and to otherwise serve as a resource to the family.

Beyond the field of early intervention and early childhood special education services, the family-centered or family-focused, strengths-based point of view is similar to person-centered planning approaches such as Group Action Planning (Turnbull, Turnbull & Blue-Banning, 1994), the Making Action Plans or MAPs process (Falvey, Forest, Pearpoint & Rosenberg, 1994), and Personal Futures Planning (Mount & Zwernick, 1988). All these processes utilize family, friends, and peers to consider the student's strengths, mobilize resources to meet needs, and develop goals for both the student and his or her support network.

The role of professionals in all these processes is primary facilitative, to serve as a resource for the student, family, and friends in selecting goals and developing strategies.

Regardless of the exact terminology used, there is general agreement in the field about the basic components or characteristics that distinguish family-centered orientations to educational or other services. These components have been identified through surveys of family preferences (e.g. Mahoney, O'Sullivan & Dinnebaum, 1990; Summers, Dell'Oliver, Turnbull, Benson, Santelli, Campbell & Siegel-Causey, 1990), through development and evaluation of professional training and service models, or through synthesis of the literature (e.g. Bailey et al., 1998; Dunst, Trivette & Deal, 1994). They include:

(1) *Empowering the family as the primary decision maker*. Families are recognized for their expertise in understanding their child's needs and strengths, as well as their understanding of their own family's values, preferences, and resources. Therefore schools are expected to give primary recognition of parents' preferences and consideration of their assessments of their child, in developing educational plans.
(2) *Recognition of whole-family, whole-child needs*. Educational needs of the child are part of a larger profile of needs and strengths of that child, and further, the needs and strengths of all members of the child are equally important. Therefore, schools are expected to collaborate with other agencies throughout the community, to meet a broad range of support needs.
(3) *Strengths-perspective*. Goals, educational outcomes and strategies are built on the strengths and resources of the child and family, rather than based on a deficit-correction orientation.
(4) *Flexibility*. Families and students are culturally diverse and require different approaches to honor those differences. Further, families and students are constantly changing. Schools are therefore expected to respond flexibility to changing needs or circumstances of the family and student.
(5) *Sensitivity and respect*. Coping with a child's special needs or serving as an advocate for one's child is stressful and highly emotional; parents should not be expected to be dispassionate participants in the educational process. Professionals need to respect and be sensitive to family's emotional well-being.

Are family-centered practices superior to other orientations toward serving students, especially very young students, with disabilities? The answer is unclear. Some researchers argue that family-centered practice is incompatible with the need to be directive with parents in such aspects as enhancing the quality of the parent-child interaction (Baird & Peterson, 1997). Others note that empirical evidence of the effectiveness of family-centered practice, in terms of developmental outcomes for the child, has not been demonstrated (Eiserman, Weber & McCoun, 1995). These arguments are countered by responses that the critique of family-centered practice is inaccurate (e.g. Mahoney & Wheeden, 1997). It may well be that the arguments about the efficacy of family-centered practice are moot. That is, family-centered practice is in essence a philosophy or value, similar to the idea of treating people with dignity, and therefore not open to empirical investigation; it shapes practice because it is "the right thing to do," not necessarily because it has been objectively demonstrated to lead to better child outcomes. Professional associations concerned with early intervention services have embraced the family-centered approach in developing principles and recommended practice indicators (NAEYC, 1996). Therefore, practitioners can assume that these principles reflect current thinking about "best practice" in family-school partnerships in special education. The question is, where does that lead them? What are the applications of these frameworks in the day-to-day interactions between families and professionals in education?

COMMON THREADS IN FAMILY PROFESSIONAL PARTNERSHIPS

There are clearly a number of commonalities in the general and special education fields, related to family-professional partnerships. The concepts of family-centered practice articulated by special education are more "practice guidelines" for positive relationships, while the framework for family relationships in general education provide more concrete roles, activities, and expectations. The two are not incompatible. Special educators have noted these similarities and have described the ways that ideas about family-professional relationships in special education can fit into a conceptual framework for family relationships in general education (e.g. Turnbull & Turnbull, 1997). Using Epstein's six types of partnership roles as a framework for discussion, we describe some current service models and practices in general and special education.

Type One: Building Parenting Skills

General education. In both general and special education, the primary focus for building parenting skills has been in the early childhood arena. The content of parent education and its intended outcomes are as varied as the designers of parent education models. Parenting education is defined as "the process of providing parents and other primary caregivers with specific knowledge and childrearing skills with the goal of promoting the development and competence of their children" (Mahoney, Kaiser, Girolmetto, MacDonald, Robinson, Safford & Spiker, 1999). As in any topical area of child development, this definition is not universally accepted, with other researchers in the early childhood field suggesting that the focus on childrearing skills and developmental outcomes for children is too narrow. For example, some practitioners and researchers call for relationship-focused parenting education, fostering reciprocal and satisfying interactions between parents and their children, leading to secure and emotionally healthy development (Bromwich, 1997; Weston, Ivins, Heffron & Sweet, 1997). In general, however, parenting education usually consists of providing parents with: (a) information about child development; (b) general parenting strategies; (c) activities to enhance positive parent-child interaction; (d) strategies for teaching children specific skills; and (e) management of problem behavior (see Mahoney et al., 1999).

In the general education field, parent education is usually, though not always, focused on so-called "at risk" families, such as low-income parents, teen parents, or families at risk for child abuse. An exception is the Parents as Teachers (PAT) program, which in many states serves families of young children from all income levels. PAT provides support and child development information for first-time parents with children from newborns to five years old. Families receive parenting information during home visits with a PAT educator and parent group meetings with other program families. PAT educators help parents develop age appropriate expectations for and engage in educationally relevant interactions with their child (Parents as Teachers, 2000). Head Start (and now Early Head Start, serving infants and toddlers) is the most comprehensive national early childhood intervention program to date, and has a heavy emphasis on parent involvement and parent training. The basic Head Start principles include health education, parent involvement, parent advocacy/leadership, parent education and home education. Parent education includes teaching/helping parents learn about the social, emotional, physical, and cognitive development of children in addition to promoting parenting activities that facilitate the child's progress. Specifically, parents are encouraged to engage in activities, which stimulate learning or skills acquisition. For example, parents are taught to interact with their child during play activities or to foster language skills using scaffolding during conversation. For even more challenged families, more intensive parent education is provided through such models as family preservation programs, focused on working with families whose children are one step from being removed from the home due to abuse or neglect (Summers et al., 1990). These programs typically include short-term and intensive, in-home participation by a parent educator who provides parents with a "crash course" on appropriate parenting along with other family support services intended to move the family out of crisis and onto a more healthy path.

While early childhood programs support the basic premise of Epstein's Type One involvement, families with older children are less likely to seek parenting information and attend parenting workshops (Epstein & Dauber, 1991). Parents of elementary and middle school students contact the school for help building "positive home conditions that support school learning and behavior all across the school years" (see Epstein & Dauber, p. 290). School officials and families are inclined to collaborate about ways to increase student achievement and promote appropriate school conduct. For example, for a middle school student experiencing difficulties in language arts, the school may meet with the family, provide information about age-appropriate expectations, and develop plans to assist the student through the use of resources in the home and in the school. Parents of adolescents also seek information regarding events in their child's future (e.g. graduation, college, employment). While academics and school conduct are still important, in the absence of any significant problems, parents turn to the school for information about graduation requirements, career planning and development, vocational training, college placement exams, and financial assistance for college.

Special education. Providing parents with skills and knowledge to help them support their child's development is one of eight expected family support outcomes for family-centered early intervention services (Bailey et al., 1998). In general, parent education in special education provides similar content (e.g. behavior management, understanding of developmental milestones) as parenting education for families with typically developing children. But in early intervention, the concept of parent education also includes equipping parents with specialized skills to meet their child's special needs. Current "best practice" in early intervention suggests the efforts of therapists should be focused not on working directly with the child once or twice a week, but rather on teaching parents how to incorporate therapeutic activities into the daily family routine, so that the child receives much more "intervention" than possibly could be provided by the therapists with their limited time to work with the child (Shearer & Shearer, 1977).

Is parent education effective? That depends on the parent education model, the quality of its implementation, and the types of outcomes being measured. Some studies suggest that the quality of parent-child interactions is strongly related to child development (see Mahoney, Boyce, Fewell, Spiker & Wheeden, 1998), and that parent-implemented interventions can be even more effective than therapist implemented interventions (see Kaiser, Hancock & Hester, 1998).

Other studies have found little or no improvement in children's development when parents have been the target of change (see Eiserman et al., 1995). These studies, however, did not account for the quality or the degree to which the parent education was successfully implemented, or have been critiqued on the basis of other research design flaws (see Mahoney et al.).

Type Two: Communication between Home and School

General education practice. Communication practices between home and school are a common issue. Typical common communication strategies that most schools employ include school newsletters or memos, telephone calls, and parent-teacher conferences. In addition to these, some schools have adopted more innovative strategies for communicating with families: e-mail, teacher home visits, teacher telephone hotlines, daily or weekly home-school notes, or bilingual parent liaisons. Communication between the home and school focuses around disseminating information about school events (e.g. school picture day, standardized testing, and school carnival) or informing parents about individual student progress (e.g. academic weaknesses, school conduct, social skills, and peer relations).

However, increasingly schools are encouraging a dialogue between home and school as compared to a monologue with the school telling the parent about his/her own child. Studies have found that even the most satisfied parents report a desire for more contact between home and school. Although many parents desire more information *from* the school, they also seek more opportunities to interact *with* school officials (Gettinger & Guetschow, 1998).

Communication in special education. In special education, there are both legally required forms of communication, and there are "recommended practices" to enhance positive communication between home and school. In the case of legal requirements, IDEA requires that parents must be notified in writing from the beginning, when their child is being referred for evaluation for special education services. Further, the law specifies that notification must be in the family's "preferred language." The law also requires that parents be given detailed information about their rights (again, in their own language). Finally, parents are to be included in their child's Individualized Education Plan meetings on an annual basis, and are to have copies of all the assessment materials and IEP documents. Ideally, these legal communications should not be delivered in a "legalistic" way; that is, they should be written in ways that are easy to understand and nonthreatening. Unfortunately, this is not always the case.

Just as in general education, however, the most effective communication between home and school in special education is informal, regular, and positive.

Some special education teachers use journals or diaries, in which both the parent and teacher can keep a running dialogue about the day's happenings at school or events at home (Turnbull & Turnbull, 1997). Other schools use regular phone calls to stay in touch with parents. Regardless of the form of the communication, parents emphasize the importance of communicating *positive* events along with the problems encountered. A note or phone call home about a child's achievement or a positive event at school, goes a long way toward creating a positive atmosphere between home and school (see Turnbull & Turnbull).

Type Three: Volunteering

General education. The concept of parent volunteering in education conjures up stereotypical images of parents (mostly mothers) participating in school bake sales or carnivals, going along on field trips, or participating in the Parent Teacher Association. Fathers (again, stereotypically) have been recruited as volunteers to help build playground equipment or otherwise improve the school environment. With a broader conceptualization of family partnerships, however, there has been increasing use of volunteers, such as retirees ("foster grandparents"), to provide one-on-one tutoring for students in schools. Also, the growing tendency to develop enriched and more highly relevant curricula for students has led schools to recruit parents and other community members, to help develop the linkage between what students are learning in school, and the "real world" applications of that learning. Examples include parents visiting the school to talk about their careers, or students visiting parents' work sites to learn how math, literacy, science, or other concepts are applied on the job.

Special education. In special education, the roles of volunteers have until recently followed a similar line of thought as in general education (i.e. using parents as fund raisers and as auxiliary tutors in classrooms). A more recent development for using family resources to support individual students, expands the concept of volunteerism and capitalizes on family strengths. There are a set of similar strategies, variously labeled MAPs (Falvey et al., 1994), Group Action Planning (GAP) (Turnbull, Turnbull & Blue-Banning, 1994), Personal Futures Planning (Mount & Zwernick, 1988) and Essential Lifestyles Planning (Smull & Harrison, 1992). All these processes were intended initially for use with students who have severe disabilities, but they have also been used with students with milder needs. The student, parents, other family members, friends, and any others who have a substantial interest in the student and family come together in an informal setting, most often the family home. The group considers the students' dreams and strengths, along with "nightmares" and needs. Each person in the group takes some responsibility to implement an agreed-upon action plan. The focus is on the creation of a supportive setting in school, home, and community which capitalizes on the student's strengths and talents and which also provides the supports required to meet his or her needs. In the MAPs or GAP, school professionals are not the focal point – instead, family and friends take responsibility, both for deciding on the plan and for providing the needed supports. Since its focus is on a broader, whole-community and whole-family plan for the student, the process is not intended to be a substitute for the IEP process. It can, however, *inform* the IEP process, as instructional outcomes may be selected that support the goals of the MAPs action plan, and some of the identified instructional strategies specified on the IEP may take advantage of the family members or other volunteers who are participating in the MAPs, to reinforce or participate in these strategies.

Type Four: Extending Learning in Home

General education. The influence of home learning activities has been documented extensively in child development and education research. As indicated in the discussion of parenting education, many early childhood programs, including Early/Head Start and Parents as Teachers provide parents with information and training about engaging young children in developmentally appropriate activities. In addition to young children, families with elementary school-aged children are commonly the recipients of information about home learning programs and strategies. Once children reach school age, programs cater to parents' desires to assist their child on homework lessons or to teach new skills. Pre-literacy and literacy skills are the most common skills that parents want to strengthen and that schools tend to encourage (Christensen, Rounds & Gorney, 1992). Literacy programs offered to parents usually include a structured program format to increase letter recognition, word or reading fluency, reading comprehension, phonics or other literacy-related skills.

Schools frequently encourage home learning activities for families with children in junior and senior high school. This can be either formal programs or informal activities in the home. For example, Epstein and associates developed Teachers Involve Parents in Schoolwork (TIPS), an interactive homework program for teachers, parents, and students (National Network of Partnership Schools, 2001). TIPS provides structured activities that allow parents to be more involved with their child's daily educational responsibilities, and helps parents to feel more competent to "teach" the homework lesson. TIPS provides parents with explicit direction to facilitate learning by making the student responsible for their homework.

Special education. Programs emphasizing home learning activities in early childhood special education and early intervention, have been initially described as parent education activities. Other types of home learning activities for special education students usually involve efforts to coordinate interventions and to maximize generalization for students learning new skills and behaviors. Home and school coordination of learning activities is especially important for students with challenging behaviors. This is true not only because a consistent environment is a critical component for meeting those students' needs, but also because families are often equally stressed by the student's challenging behaviors and may need help to cope at home and in the community.

An example of using home-school partnerships for student learning is the Positive Behavior Support (PBS) technology, which seeks alternatives to coercive or aversive interventions (Sailor & Carr, 1994). PBS assumes that problem behavior occurs for reasons that can be detected through systematic investigation (Sailor & Carr, 1994); when those reasons are identified, teachers and parents can then work together to teach more socially acceptable alternatives to difficult behavior that accomplish the same functions for the student. The school-wide PBS system also includes support at the family and community level (Sugai, Horner, Dunlap, Hieneman, Lewis, Nelson, Scott, Liaupson, Sailor, Trnbull, Turnbull, Wickham, Wilcox & Ruef, 2000). In the PBS model, families are seen as critical members of the team, because their intimate knowledge of their child's history, idiosyncrasies, preferences, and special abilities is essential to helping professionals analyze the functional purpose of the student's behavior in the first place (Turnbull & Turnbull, in press). In the second place, families are seen as critical to carrying out and supporting positive change in the home and community, that complement the school's positive behavioral support team (Turnbull & Turnbull, in press).

Type Five: Decision Making

General education. The cultivation of parents as leaders and decision-makers in general education is often focused on organizing parents as advocates for schools. Examples are the nationally organized Parent Teacher Association, or more local, single-school organizations commonly referred to as Parent Teacher Organizations (Sullivan, 2000). While the national PTA participates in national-level advocacy on educational issues, local PTOs tend to focus more on an individual school or school district. Representatives from the PTO, for example, may participate on school site-based councils or other governance bodies in a school or district. Parent involvement in educational decision making includes training for parent leadership, or training to recruit and empower other parents to participate in their child's education. An example is the National Coalition for Parent Involvement in Education (NCPIE, 2000), which provides information and education about ways to improve family and school partnerships. A more focused example of parent leadership development is the Parent Academy, begun in Baltimore and subsequently disseminated in a number of other states, which offers training and information to parent leaders to recruit and train other parents as school volunteers (Parent Academy Newsletter, 1996).

Developing parents as decision-makers and advocates is often a component of broader models for school reform. For example, the Comer School Model considers development of positive partnerships with families as a critical component of school reform (Comer, 2000; Comer & Haynes, 1991). The parent program in the Comer system includes three levels: A School Planning and Management Team which includes parents elected by other parents, a systematic effort to encourage parents to attend and volunteer in school activities, and a series of general activities (e.g. open house, carnival night, a Holiday program) which parents are encouraged to attend on a regular basis (see Comer & Haynes). Evaluations of these programs suggest that parent leadership development can be very effective. An example is the evaluation of the Commonwealth Institute for Parent Leadership (CIPL) (Corbett & Wilson, 2000). CIPL is a statewide program in Kentucky, consisting of a series of workshops intended to train parent leaders to enhance their working relationships with teachers and to increase their ability to evaluate the quality of instruction they observe in schools. The evaluation found that the training effectively increased participants' confidence, willingness, and skills in involvement; the primary barriers were resistance from principals and teachers who did not welcome greater parent participation in their schools (see Corbett & Wilson).

Special education. The legal mandates for parent involvement in developing IEPs have been accompanied by federally appropriated resources to accomplish that goal, in the form of the Parent Training and Information Centers network, funded by the U.S. Office of Special Education. These Centers, located in every state, provide information to parents on their legal rights with respect to special education, and education on effective strategies for working with professionals. In addition, national associations exist for parents and family members for just about any type of disability, including, to mention a few: Down Syndrome Congress, Federation of Families for Children's Mental Health, National Association for Parents of the Visually Impaired, United Cerebral Palsy, Autism Society of America, and Children and Adults with Attention-Deficit/ Hyperactivity Disorder. Added to these are associations such as the National Parent to Parent Network – an organization devoted to helping establish and maintain local parent support groups (more specifically, programs matching a "veteran" parent of a child with a disability, with a parent who has recently discovered his or her child has that disability). The list of organizations, advocacy groups, and service programs to support and nurture parents of special education students as decision makers, is nearly endless.

In contrast to general education, decision-making for parents in special education focuses less on whole-school involvement and more on parents participating in assessments of their child's strengths and needs, developing his or her IEP, and monitoring the implementation of the plan. Some authors (e.g. Crais & Belardi, 1999; Nagle, 2000) argue that a critical step in developing meaningful partnerships with parents occurs at the time of their introduction to the "world" of special education (i.e. their referral for evaluation and assessment). Nagle (2000) noted that the evaluation process may be the first contact families have had with school professionals. These first encounters set the stage for future expectations and interactions between families and professionals (Crais & Belardi, 1999). Encouraging parents' active involvement in assessing the child, identifying instructional outcomes and strategies, and determining placement, is not only the law; it has practical benefits. Parents are seen as the experts on their child and the information they can provide about what their child can and cannot do in different settings and situations, is invaluable (Crais, 1993; Nagle, 2000; Wolfendale, 1998). Not only can parents contribute necessary information regarding their child's developmental, social, and medical history, they can also provide logistical information such as the "best time" for testing in order to get the child's optimum performance (Davis & Hathaway, 1987). Information gathered from parents increases the reliability and validity of the assessment (see Crais & Belardi, 1999). Establishing a collaborative relationship with parents during the assessment process is also important in determining the effectiveness of program planning and interventions (Miller & Hanft, 1998; Shriver, Kramer & Garnett, 1993). Suggestions for ways to give parents meaningful opportunities to participate in decision-making include simply having an attitude of respect (e.g. Christenson, 1995); asking parents to observe, inform, and describe their child's behavior (Crais); giving parents an opportunity to look at and respond to test results before meetings (Wise, 1995); and writing and sharing jargon-free reports that include explicit descriptions of what the results mean (Sandy, 1986; Weddig, 1984; Wiener & Kohler, 1986).

Type Six: Collaborating with the Community

General education. Educational reform efforts often involve restructuring schools to meet the demands of a corporate America that needs a workforce ready to participate in an information-based, high tech economy involving a partnership with the community at large (Buttery & Anderson, 1999; Darling-Hammond & Sclan, 1996). This means including the local business community as active participants in teaching students. Second, policy makers and educators have increasingly recognized that broader social issues like poverty, high crime and violence, teen parenting, and substance abuse, have a strong influence on a school's ability to successfully educate students. The current fragmented approach to solving problems through a variety of health, social service, and law enforcement programs, has been seen as an ineffective way of addressing these complex issues. Service integration and interagency collaboration, including schools as a part of this effort, has long been advocated as a critical strategy to attack some of our most difficult social problems (see Schorr, 1989). The highly visible presence of schools in the community have led many to focus on school-linked approaches to achieving service integration (Center for the Future of Children Staff, 1992). Some authorities believe that establishing school-linked services is an essential component of educational reform. According to Jihl and Kirst (1992): "A sick child cannot learn, and a challenging curriculum cannot be mastered by a child confronting chaos at home. The schools cannot solve all these problems alone or be the only organization enabling parents to be more responsible and effective with their children" (p. 98).

Programs that are considered "school-linked services," may encompass a range of models, from informal collaborative contacts between schools and other services, to formally integrated agencies (Volpe, Batra, Bomio & Costin, 1999). They also include both "bottom up" initiatives begun by community members, and "top-down" policy initiatives at the state level (Volpe et al., 1999). A school-linked services program should be shaped to the unique needs and resources of the community it serves (Gomby & Larson, 1992); therefore, programs tend to be flexible, offer a variety of services based on expressed community needs, and have a high degree of variability in administrative structures (Volpe et al., 1999). In a typical program, services – administered by other health and social service agencies as well as by the school district – may be located in a neighborhood school, where they are accessible to the community. Types of services offered may include adult education and job training, school-based health clinics, preschool and/or before- and after-school child care, youth mentoring, and other youth activities and services.

Evaluation of these programs is difficult since each is unique; however, there is evidence that school-linked services can make dramatic differences for students and for their communities (Gomby & Larson, 1992). For example, one evaluation of 16 schools involved in a school linked "Caring Communities" program in Missouri, found that school attendance increased and suspensions decreased dramatically, while academic performance scores also improved (Local Investment Commission, 1998). Successful school-linked services also means improved partnerships with parents; for example, the Caring Communities evaluation found not only that parents gained tangible services such as job placements and new job skills, but also that the number of parents participating as volunteer mentors or tutors increased dramatically. Further, in these schools attendance at parent/teacher conferences increased from below 70% to between 90 and 100% (see Local Investment Commission). In short, school-linked service programs offering a variety of services that are clearly relevant to families, have the effect of bringing parents into the schools. And when they come, they appear to stay.

Special education. In special education, collaboration is not only a recommended practice but also is mandated by IDEA (1997, 34 CFR Part 300). However, collaboration is mandated only at the transition points, from early intervention for infants and toddlers to the special education system, and from secondary special education to the adult vocational education and disabilities services system. At the early childhood stage, the law requires coordination among health, education, and social service programs to assure comprehensive supports are provided. At the transition from age 36 months to preschool, more collaboration is required to assure appropriate services are in place. At the other end of the age spectrum, collaboration between special education and Vocational Rehabilitation is mandated to assure transition from school to adult services.

Attention to collaboration at these transition points has become a major policy issue because stress for families and students is high during these times of uncertainty. Families may, for example, face concern about losing early intervention staff to whom they have become very attached, or have concerns about moving to a program with less emphasis on these close relationships with families (Hadden & Fowler, 1997). In early intervention programs emphasizing family-centered approaches to planning for transitions, parents receive information and education about their program options, their educational rights, how to communicate effectively with staff about their children, how to prepare for meetings, and how to prepare their children for new settings (Noonan & Ratokalau, 1991; Spiegel-McGill, Reed, Konig & McGowan, 1990). At the other end of the age spectrum in special education, there is less thought about involving families in transitions to adult services, but there are program examples suggesting that the same principles apply (i.e. parents need to be provided with information about options, an orientation to the world of adult services, and strategies for preparing their son or daughter for their new life). In short, family involvement in the overall collaborative process is accepted as recommended practice for transition planning both in early childhood and in adult transition services.

CREATING OPPORTUNITIES FOR FAMILY-SCHOOL PARTNERSHIPS

Thus far, we have explored the meanings and expected roles in both special and general education for families and school professionals, at each of Epstein's six levels of family-school partnerships. While on the surface there may be a number of differences in approaches to families between the two systems, a closer look suggests that these differences are more in the degree of emphasis of the various roles of partnerships, than any substantive disagreements about the importance and the nature of family and school partnerships. For example, in special education there is more emphasis on families as decision-makers; in general education there is more emphasis on families as volunteers. This does not mean that general educators believe in discouraging parents as decision makers or that special educators do not welcome or want parents as volunteers. It means, rather, that the ways of thinking about family involvement have led to variations in emphasis and strategies for accomplishing healthy family-school partnerships. There are indeed a number of similarities in the kinds of practices and attitudes toward families that are suggested as "recommended practice" at each of the six levels, to encourage optimal partnerships.

Another – perhaps more unfortunate – similarity between the fields of family-school partnerships in general and special education, is that the recommended practices described here are more often found in textbooks and journal articles, than in the schools and neighborhoods of the society. In the "real world," relationships between school professionals and families in both general and special education tend to be a source of stress and concern. Many professionals blame parents for problems seen in students; and many parents blame schools for a number of problems besetting society in general and their children in particular. In short, while there are no shortages of creative suggestions and recommended practices that appear to be highly effective in bridging the gap between schools and families, the divide stubbornly remains. The reasons why these "ideal" models of family-school partnerships have failed, in many places, to touch the "real world" experiences of parents and professionals, lie, first, in the changing nature of families, and second, in the more-or-less unchanging nature of professional development and support. Following are subsections that discuss how family-school partnerships can be enhanced.

The Changing Nature of Families

Many of the expected roles of parents in education are based on an assumption that families fit a traditional structure: both parents living in the same household with their children, with father working and mother remaining at home. However, that traditional structure is no longer the typical profile of families in the United States. In the first place, increasing numbers of women have joined the labor force. In 1999, 69.8% of married mothers were employed, as were 78.5% of unmarried mothers (Bureau of Labor Statistics, 2000). Although the growth of one-parent households appears to be slowing, they still comprise 27% of family households with children (Dept. of Commerce News, 1998). The significance for educators is clear: one cannot count on parents to be available for conferencing, receiving phone calls, volunteering, or otherwise participating in school activities during the school day. Nor can one assume that even the most conscientious parents will have unlimited emotional and physical reserves to enable them to help children with homework, engage in numerous learning activities with their children, or participate in after-school events.

Further changes in family structure relate to the high rate of divorce in the society today. The fact that single parents head "only" 27% of households is testimony to the rate of remarriage and blended family structures. Foster parent families are also on the rise, as are the numbers of grandparents assuming primary parenting roles (Hanson & Lynch, 1992). Finally, there is an increasing acceptance for families with same-sex couples raising children (Copeland & White, 1991). All these demographic indicators raise the question of just *who* we mean when we refer to parents. The implications of these demographic shifts for family-school relationships are not academic. Educators encounter numerous legal and practical headaches when, for example, a stepfather and a biological father both show up at a teacher conference or an IEP meeting, or when there is a court order restricting access of one parent to his or her child.

Another issue related to changing families in America is the increasing diversity in the society. For example, the fact that populations of Asian and Hispanic Americans are increasing at a much faster rate than numbers of African-Americans or Euro-Americans is a continuing trend (Hanson & Lynch, 1992; U.S. Census Bureau, 1996). America is fast approaching a time when Euro-Americans will no longer be considered the "majority" ethnic group in the society. The implications of cultural diversity for schools include language differences, which create a vast number of issues for educators and for educational assessment. In special education, the law mandates that communication with parents must be in the language in which the parent is most comfortable. Similarly, evaluations of children for special services must be conducted in the child's language and utilize a "culture-free" measure of the child's cognitive and functional abilities. The selection of evaluation measures must take into account language and cultural differences. But these differences may also lead families to quite different conclusions about their child's abilities than the school's assessment.

Cultural differences affect family and school relationships in many different ways beyond language and assessment issues. For example, values and beliefs about parenting and child rearing vary widely across cultures (Kalyanypur & Harry, 1992). The strong orientation toward Euro-American parenting beliefs has led to criticism of many parent education programs (see Mahoney et al., 1999). One of the more volatile examples lies in the tendency of many Asian, African-American, and Hispanic families to have a more authoritarian approach to childrearing, including the use of corporal punishment and more directive interactions (see Kalyanpur & Rao, 1991). While the more explicit expression of authority often used in African American families may be viewed as harsh or even abusive in many Euro-American families, this parenting style may in fact be quite functional, as long as the child recognizes parental authority as exercised in the context of a loving relationship (Delpit, 1988). Misinterpretation by educators of parental "harshness," coupled with legal requirements that schools must report suspected abuse, has created numerous controversies between schools and the ethnic communities they serve. Other cultures also have different views of child development. Euro-American cultural values emphasize developing independence and achievement in children. Cultures like Hispanic or Asian groups, with less emphasis on these values, may have later-age expectations for their child's development, or may not see the importance of encouraging a child to take independent action; these groups may be seen by Euro-Americans as "over-protective" (Harry, 1992b). Similarly, Native Americans view children as unique and complete at birth, resulting in a noninterfering style of parenting which Euro-American professionals may view as neglectful (Everett, 1983). Not only are there misinterpretations of motives between families and schools with different cultural emphases, the school may be pursuing goals with children that are counter to the family's.

Still other facets of cultural diversity are the family's beliefs about relationships with professionals and their communication style. Obvious examples of communication issues are the direct approach (i.e. "getting to the point") of many Euro-American professionals vs. the more indirect style preferred by parents of some cultures, which may lead them to conclude the professional is rude or disrespectful; or the habit of deference toward professionals which may lead to a conclusion that the parent is in agreement with the educator when that is not the case at all (Harry, 1992a). Beyond communication issues, a more fundamental difference may be the concept of professionalism itself. This is the belief inculcated through professional training, that competence is based in the rationality and science of the discipline, and that the educator's "professional self" rather than one's "personal self" is to be presented in interactions with parents. In contrast, families from other cultures may place a far greater emphasis on personal relationships, expecting the teacher to display both personal and "public" facets of his or her life (Harry, 1992a). Based on the above, it is important that general and special educators understand cultural variables that affect their interactions with families.

Closing the Gaps in Personnel Development for Teachers

In recent years, a number of school districts across the nation have developed programs to foster more interaction between families and schools. Unfortunately, many educators are not adequately prepared to work with families, not interested in or comfortable working with families, or not supported in their partnerships with families (Brand, 1996; Katz & Bauch, 1999; Tichenor, 1997). This problem can be compounded by families who do not feel comfortable or welcome in the educational setting, possess limited opportunities to interact with school officials, differ in their cultures, linguistic backgrounds, or lifestyles (Morris, Taylor, Knight & Wasson, 1996). Coupled with teacher characteristics and idiosyncrasies, it is a wonder that parents and teachers ever interact.

When families and educators engage in stable and supportive partnership, it is often the result of the classroom teacher's invitation and encouragement (Epstein & Dauber, 1991; Gavin & Greenfield, 1998; Katz & Bauch, 1999). Prepared with multiple "tools of the trade," teachers who successfully partner with and engage parents often possess specific ideas and activities for working with parents (Katz & Bauch, 1999). Also, teachers with a strong sense of efficacy in their teaching are more likely to engage families in a partnership (Greenwood & Hickman, 1991). Teaching pre-service and in-service teachers about family-school relationship development in addition to quality training in a teacher education programs could increase the likelihood that collaborative relationships occur between both general and special educators and the families they serve.

PERSPECTIVES

Given the nature of changing families with multiple needs and minimal time, and the current (poor) state of teacher preparation to interact with families, it is no wonder that successful family-school partnerships tend to remain more in the ideal realm than in the world of everyday practice. To paraphrase the maxim often quoted about real estate, the three most important factors in effective family-school partnerships are relationships, relationships, and relationships. In fact, effective partnerships between anyone – interagency collaboration, intra-agency teamwork, and parent-professional interactions – depend strongly on the degree to which the participants on both sides share a sense of comfort, trust, and communication with one another Time and again, parent satisfaction surveys and studies of family preferences suggest that the quality of the collaborative partnership depends most critically on the one-to-one, interpersonal relationships established between the parents and the professionals (Dinnebeil, Hale & Rule, 1996; Summers, Steeples, Peterson, Naig, McBride, Wall, Liebow, Swanson & Stowitschek, 2001).

We have already noted the critical need for teacher preparation and other professional curricula to include relationships with families as part of their curricula. In addition, schools need to provide a supportive atmosphere to encourage positive family relationships. This includes appropriate resources for reduced case loads and available staff (such as school social workers and parent liaisons) to allow for time and expertise to interact with families. It also includes flexible policies (e.g. flextime for early childhood workers to make evening or weekend home visits), as well as clear expectations and rewards for staff to cultivate positive relationships with parents. In addition, it includes continuing in-service education, especially including families as equal partners in the training, in order to develop opportunities to dialogue and create open lines of communication and understanding.

In the end, parents cannot be expected to complete their side of the partnership without preparation and continuing support. Schools need to adopt and actively market programs that are available in both general and special education, to provide parents with the skills to participate as active decision makers. Inclusion of parents and other family members in professional in-service activities – especially those involving team development, communication, and relationship building – will go a long way toward getting everyone "on the same page." But it is important to remember that not every parent is available or inclined to participate in such leadership activities. The cliché about "starting where the student is" is equally applicable to parents. This means that an array of options for participation will help to maximize parent relationships with the schools. Families who come into the school for concrete help, such as employment or GED training in school-linked services programs, may stay for other activities involving their child's academic program. Parents of children with behavior or academic challenges, who are asked their opinion, and who are also contacted when there are positive achievements to report, may learn that interacting with the school is not a painful experience after all. The point is that creating a welcoming atmosphere for parents to come into the school is both the most difficult challenge, yet the easiest of all – doing away with our stereotypes and treating parents as human beings with whom professionals have something in common.

REFERENCES

Baird, S., & Peterson, J. (1997). Seeking a comfortable fit between a family-centered philosophy and infant-parent interaction in early intervention: Time for a paradigm shift? *Topics in Early Childhood Special Education, 17*(2), 139–164.

Bailey, D. B., McWilliam, R. A., Darkes, L. A., Hebbeler, K., Simeonsson, R. J., Spiker, D., & Wagner, M. (1998). Family outcomes in early intervention: A framework for program evaluation and efficacy research. *Exceptional Children, 64*(3), 313–328.

Bloom (1964). *Stability and change in human characteristics.* Chicago, IL: University of Chicago Press.

Brand, S. (1996). Making parent involvement a reality: Helping teachers develop partnerships with parents. *Young Children, 51,* 76–81.

Bromwich, R. (1997). *Working with families and their infants at risk: A perspective after 20 years of experience.* Austin, TX: Pro-Ed.

Bronfrenbrenner, U. (1979). *The ecology of human development: Experiments by nature and design.* Cambridge, MA: Harvard University.

Bureau of Labor Statistics (2000). Employment characteristics of families summary. http://stats.bls.gov/newsrels.htm

Buttery, T., & Anderson, P. J. (1999). Community, school, and parent dynamics: A synthesis of literature and activities. *Teacher Education Quarterly, 26*(4), 111–122.

Center for the Future of Children staff (1992). Analysis. *The Future of Children, 2*(1), School Linked Services, 6–18.

Christensen, S., Rounds, T., & Gorney, D. (1992). Family factors and student achievement: An avenue to increase students' success. *School Psychology Quarterly, 7*(3), 178–206.

Christenson, S. L. (1995). Families and schools: What is the role of the school psychologist? *School Psychology Quarterly, 10,* 118–132.

Comer, J. (2000). *Building successful partnerships: A guide for developing parent and family involvement programs.* New York: Origin Book Sales, Inc.

Comer, J. P., & Haynes, N. M. (1991). Parent involvement in schools: An ecological approach. *Elementary School Journal, 91*(3), 271–277.

Copeland, A. P., & White, K. M. (1991). *Studying families.* Newbury Park, CA: Sage.

Corbett, D., & Wilson, B. (2000). "I didn't know I could do that": Parents learning to be leaders through the Commonwealth Institute for Parent Leadership. Malvern, PA: Unpublished report to the Pew Charitable Trusts.

Crais, E. R. (1993). Families and professionals as collaborators in assessment. *Topics in Language Disorders, 14,* 29–40.

Crais, E. R., & Belardi, C. (1999). Family participation in child assessment: Perceptions of families and professionals. *Infant-Toddler Intervention, 9,* 209–238.

Darling-Hammond, L., & Sclan, E. M. (1996). Who teaches and why: Dilemmas of building a profession for twenty-first century schools. In: J. Sikula, T. J. Buttery & E. Guyton (Eds), *Handbook of Research on Teacher Education* (pp. 67–101). New York: Macmillan.

Davis, S. T., & Hathaway, D. J. (1987). Preparing for your child's assessment: A guide for the pre-school parent. *The Exceptional Parent, 17,* 36–40.

Delpit, L. (1988). The silenced dialogue: Power and pedagogy in educating other people's children. *Harvard Educational Review, 58*(3), 280–298.

Dinnebeil, L. A., Hale, L. M., & Rule, S. (1996). A qualitative analysis of parents' and service coordinators' descriptions of variables that influence collaborative relationships. *Topics in Early Childhood Special Education, 16,* 322–347.

Dinnebeil, L. A., Hale, L. M., & Rule, S. (2000). Early intervention program practices that support collaboration. *Topics in Early Childhood special Education, 19,* 225–235.

Dunst, C. J., & Trivette, C. M. (1989). An enablement and empowerment perspective of case management. *Topics in Early Childhood Special Education, 8,* 87–102.

Dunst, C. J., Trivette, C. M., & Deal, A. G. (Eds) (1994). *Supporting and strengthening families, Volume 1: Methods, strategies and practices.* Cambridge, MA: Brookline Books.

Eiserman, W. D., Weber, C., & McCoun, M. (1995). Parent and professional roles in early intervention: A longitudinal comparison of the effects of two intervention configurations. *Journal of Special Education, 29,* 20–44.

Epstein, J. (1992). School and family partnerships. In: M. Alkin (Ed.), *Encyclopedia of Educational Research* (6th ed., pp. 1139–1161). New York: Macmillan.

Epstein, J. (1996). Perspectives and previews on research and policy for school, family, and community partnerships. In: A. Booth & J. Dunn (Eds), *Family-School Links: How Do They Affect Educational Outcomes?* (pp. 209–246). Mahway, NJ: Lawrence Erlbaum.

Gettinger, M., & Guetschow, K. W. (1998). Parental involvement in schools: Parent and teacher perceptions. *Journal of Research and Development in Education, 32,* 38–52.

Epstein, J., & Dauber, S. (1991). School programs and teacher practices of parent involvement in inner-city elementary and middle schools. *The Elementary School Journal, 91,* 289–305.

Everett, F., Proctor, N., & Cartmell, B. (1983). Providing psychological services to American Indian children and families. *Professional Psychology: Research and Practice, 14*(5), 588–603.

Falvey, M. A., Forest, M., Pearpoint, J., & Rosenberg, R. (1994). Building connections. In: J. S. Thousand, R. A. Villa & A. I. Nevin (Eds), *Creativity and Collaborative Learning: A Practical Guide to Empowering Students and Teachers* (pp. 347–368). Baltimore: Brookes.

Gavin, K., & Greenfield, D. (1998). A comparison of levels of involvement for parents with at-risk African American kindergarten children in classrooms with high vs. low teacher envouragement. *Journal of Black Psychology, 24,* 404–417.

Gomby, D. S., & Larson, C. S. (1992). Evaluation of school-linked services. *The Future of Children, 2*(1), School Linked Services, 68–84.

Greenwood G., & Hickman, C. (1991). Research and practice in parent involvement: Implications for teacher education. *The Elementary School Journal, 91,* 279–288.

Grolnick, W., Benjet, C., Kurowski, C., & Apostoleris, N. (1997). Predictors of parental involvement in children's schooling. *Journal of Educational Psychology, 89,* 538–548.

Grolnick, W., & Slowiaczek, M. (1994). Parents' involvement in children's schooling: A multidimensional conceptualization and motivational model. *Child Development, 65,* 237–252.

Hadden, S., & Fowler, S. A. (1997). Preschool: A new beginning for children and parents. *Teaching Exceptional Children, 30,* 36–39.

Halle, T., Kurtz-Costes, B., & Mahoney, J. (1997). Family influences on school achievement in low-income, African American children. *Journal of Educational Psychology, 89*(3), 527–537.

Hanson, M. J., & Lynch, E. W. (1992). Family diversity: Implications for policy and practice. *Topics in Early Childhood Special Education, 12*(3), 283–306.

Harry, B. (1992a). An ethnographic study of cross-cultural communication with Puerto Rican-American families in the special education system. *American Educational Research Journal, 29,* 417–494.

Harry, B. (1992b). Developing cultural self-awareness: The first step in values clarification for early interventionists. *Topics in Early Childhood Special Education, 12*(3), 333–350.

Hart, B., & Risley, T. (1994). *Meaningful differences in the everyday experience of young American children.* Lawrence, KS: Brookfield.

Hidalgo, N., Siu, S., Bright, J., Swap, S., & Epstein, J. (1995). Research on families, schools, and communities: A multicultural perspective. In: J. A. Banks (Ed.), *Handboook of Research on Multicultural Education* (pp. 498–524). New York: Macmillan.

IDEA, Individuals with Disabilities Education Act Amendments of 1997. Final Regulations. 34 CFR Part 300. Assistance to states for the education of children with disabilities.

IDEA, Individuals with Disabilities Education Act Amendments of 1997. Final Regulations. 34 CFR Part 303. Early intervention program for infants and toddlers with disabilities.

Jihl, J., & Kirst, M. (1992). Getting ready to provide school-linked services: What schools must do. *The Future of Children*, 2(1), School Linked Services, 95–106.

Kaiser, A. P., Hancock, T. B., & Hester, P. P. (1998). Parents as co-interventionists: Research on applications of naturalistic language teaching procedures. *Infants and Young Children*, 10(4), 1–11.

Kalyanpur, M., & Harry, B. (1999). *Culture in special education: Building reciprocal family-professional relationships.* Baltimore, MD: Paul H. Brookes Publishing Co.

Kalyanpur, M., & Rao, S. S. (1991). Empowering low-income, black families of handicapped children. *American Journal of Orthopsychiatry*, 61, 523–532.

Katz, L., & Bauch, J. (1999). The Peabody family involvement initiative: Preparing preservice teachers for family/school collaboration. *The School Community Journal*, 9, 49–69.

Local Investment Commission (1998). Measuring the impact of caring communities in Jackson County. St. Louis, MO: The Family Investment Trust. Website: www.mofit.org/evallinc.htm

Mahoney, G., Kaiser, A., Girolametto, L., MacDonald, J., Robinson, C., Safford, P., & Spiker, D. (1999). Parent education in early intervention: A call for a renewed focus. *Topics in Early Childhood Special Education*, 19(3), 131–140.

Mahoney, G., Boyce, G., Fewell, R., Spiker, D., & Wheeden, C. A. (1998). The relationship of parent-child interaction to the effectiveness of early intervention services for at-risk children and children with disabilities. *Topics in Early Childhood Special Education*, 18, 5–17.

Mahoney, G., O'Sullivan, P., & Dinnebaum, J. (1990). A national study of mothers' perceptions of family-focused intervention. *Journal of Early Intervention*, 14, 133–146.

Mahoney, G., & Wheeden, C. A. (1997). Parent-child interaction – The foundation for family-centered early intervention practice: A response to Baird and Peterson. *Topics in Early Childhood Special Education*, 17(2), 165–184.

Miller, L. J., & Hanft, B. E. (1998). Building positive alliances: Partnerships with families as the cornerstone of developmental assessment. *Infants and Young Children*, 11, 49–60.

Morris, V., Taylor, S., Knight, J., & Wasson, R. (1996). Preparing teachers to reach out to families and communities. *Action in Teacher Education*, 18, 10–22.

Mount, B., & Zwernick, K. (1988). *It's never too early, it's never too late: A booklet about personal planning for persons with developmental disabilities, their families and friends, case managers, service providers, and advocates.* St. Paul, MN: Metropolitan Council.

Nagle, R. J. (2000). Issues in preschool assessment. In: B. A. Bracken (Ed.), *The Psychoeducational Assessment of Preschool Children* (3rd ed., pp. 19–32). Boston: Allyn and Bacon.

National Coalition for Parent Involvement in Education (2001, March). Developing family/school partnerships: Guidelines for schools and school districts. www.ncpie.org/ncpieguidelines.html

National Association for the Education of Young Children, Division of Early Childhood/Council for Exceptional Children, & National Board of Professional Teaching Standards (1996). *Guidelines for preparation of early childhood professionals.* Washington, D.C.: National Association for the Education of Young Children.

National Network of Partnership Schools (2001, January) [On-line]. http://www.csos.jhu.edu/p2000/tips/TIPSmain.htm

Noonan, M. J., & Ratokalau, N. B. (1991). PPT: The Preschool Preparation and Transition Project. *Journal of Early Intervention, 15,* 390–398.

Parent Academy School Volunteer Program (2001, March). First Quarter 1996 Online Newsletter. http://www.charm.net/wizards/parent/news1q1996.htm

Parents as Teachers (2000, December) [On-line]. Available: http//www.patnc.org/abouruswhatispat.asp

Sandy, L. R. (1986). The descriptive-collaborative approach in psychological report writing. *Psychology in the Schools, 23,* 395–400.

Sailor, W., & Carr, E. G. (1994). Should only positive methods be used by professionals who work with children and youth? (Reply to Mulick). In: E. Gambril & M. Mason (Eds), *Children: Controversial Issues.* Los Angeles: Sage Publications.

Schorr, L. B. (1989). *Within our reach: Breaking the cycle of disadvantage.* New York: Doubleday.

Shearer, M. S., & Shearer, D. E. (1977). Parent involvement. In: J. Jordan, A. Hayden, M. Karnes & M. Ward (Eds), *Early Childhood Education for Exceptional Children* (pp. 85–106). Reston, VA: Council for Exceptional Children.

Shriver, M. D., Kramer, J. J., & Garnett, M. (1993). Parent involvement in early childhood special education: Opportunities for school psychologists. *Psychology in the Schools, 30,* 264–273.

Singh, K., Bickley, P., Trivette, P., Keith, T., Keith, P., & Anderson, E. (1995). The effects of four components of parental involvement on eighth grade student achievement: Structural analysis of NELS-88 data. *School Psychology Review, 24*(2), 299–317.

Smull, M., & Harrison, S. B. (1992). *Supporting people with severe reputations in the community.* Alexandria, VA: National Association of State Mental Retardation Program Directors.

Spiegel-McGill, P., Reed, D. J., Konig, C. S., & McGowan (1990). Parent education: Easing the transition to preschool. *Topics in Early Childhood Special Education, 9,* 66–77.

Sugai, G., Horner, R., Dunlap, G., Hieneman, M., Lewis, T., Nelson, C. M., Scott, S., Liaupson, C., Sailor, W., Turnbull, A., Turnbull, R., Wickham, D., Wilcox, B., & Ruef, M. (2000). Applying positive behavior support and functional behavioral assessment in schools. *Journal of Positive Behavior Interventions, 2,* 131–143.

Sullivan, T. (2000, August). [On-line]. *PTO Today, 2*(1). Available: http://www.ptotoday.com/0800ptopta2.html

Summers, J. A., Dell'Oliver, C., Turnbull, A. P., Benson, H. A., Santelli, E., Campbell, M., & Siegel-Causey, E. (1990). Examining the Individualized Family Service Plan process: What are family and practitioner preferences? *Topics in Early Childhood Special Education, 10,* 78–99.

Summers, J. A., Steeples, T., Peterson, C., Naig, L., McBride, S., Wall, S., Liebow, H., Swanson, M., & Stowitschek, J. (2001). Policy and management supports for effective service integration in Early Head Start and Part C programs. *Topics in Early Childhood Special Education, 21,* 16–30.

Tichenor, M. (1997). Teacher education and parent involvement: Reflections from preservice teachers. *Journal of Instructional Psychology, 24,* 233–240.

Turnbull, A. P., & Summers, J. A. (1987). From parent involvement to family support: Evolution to revolution. In: S. M. Pueschel, C. Tingey, J. W. Rynders, A. C. Crocker & D. M. Crutcher (Eds), *New Perspectives on Down Syndrome* (pp. 289–306). Baltimore: Brookes.

Turnbull, A. P., & Turnbull, H. R. (1997). *Families, professionals, and exceptionality: A special partnership.* Columbus, OH: Merrill.

Turnbull, A. P., Turnbull, H. R., & Blue-Banning, M. J. (1994). Enhancing inclusion of infants and toddlers with disabilities and their families: A theoretical and programmatic analysis. *Infants and Young Children, 7*(2), 1–14.

Turnbull, A. P., & Turnbull, H. R. (in press). Extending a school-wide approach of positive behavior interventions and support to families and the community. In: A. P. Turnbull & H. R. Turnbull (Eds), *Families, Professionals, and Exceptionality: Collaborating for Empowerment* (4th ed.). Upper Saddle River, NJ: Merrill Prentice Hall.

Turnbull, H. R., Turnbull, A. P., & Wheat, M. (1982). Assumptions about parental participation: A legislative history. *Exceptional Education Quarterly, 3*(2), 1–8.

U.S. Bureau of the Census (1996). [On-line]. Percent distribution of projected households by type: 1995–2010. Available: http://www.census.gov/population/projections/nation/hh-fam.html

U.S. Department of Commerce News (2001). [On-line]. Growth in single fathers outpaces growth in single mothers, Census Bureau reports. *United States Department of Commerce News.* U.S. Census Bureau, Public Information Office. Available: http://www.census.gov/Press-Release/cb98-228.html

Volpe, R., Batra, A., Bomio, S., & Costin, D. (1999). *Third generation school-linked services for at risk children.* Toronto, Ontario: Dr. R. G. N. Laidlaw Research Centre, Institute of Child Study, Department of Human Development and Applied Psychology, University of Toronto.

Weddig, R. R. (1984). Parental interpretation of psychoeducational reports. *Psychology in the Schools, 21,* 477–481.

Weston, D., Ivins, B., Heffron, M. C., & Sweet, N. (1997). Formulating the centrality of relationships in early intervention: An organizational perspective. *Infants and Young Children, 9*(3), 1–12.

Wiener, J., & Kohler, S. (1986). Parents' comprehension of psychological reports. *Psychology in the Schools, 23,* 265–270.

Wise, P. S. (1995). Best practices in communicating with parents. In: A. Thomas & J. Grimes (Eds), *Best Practices in School Psychology – III* (pp. 279–287). Washington, D.C.: National Association of School Psychologists.

Wolfendale, S. (1998). Involving parents in child assessments in the United Kingdom. *Childhood Education, 74,* 355–358.

Zellman, G., & Waterman, J. (1998). Understanding the impact of parent school involvement on children's educational outcomes. *The Journal of Educational Research, 91*(6), 370–380.

MULTICULTURAL LEARNERS WITH EXCEPTIONALITIES IN GENERAL AND SPECIAL EDUCATION SETTINGS

Herbert Grossman, Cheryl A. Utley and Festus E. Obiakor

INTRODUCTION

Despite the requirements of federal laws such as the Individuals with Disabilities Education (IDEA) of 1997, a disproportionate number of minority students continue to be placed in special education (e.g. Oswald & Coutinho, 2001; National Research Council, 2002). IDEA 1997 is a comprehensive piece of legislation intended to provide a more equitable program for multicultural learners with exceptionalities against discrimination. Major concepts of service delivery for this law include services and rights that respect the dominant language of the student and family. By logical extension, multicultural learners must be referred for special education services based upon need – not culturally, ethnic, or linguistic differences. Apparently, these learners fall through the cracks of the general education system and, in many cases, are referred for special education services.

Currently, assessment and instructional procedures for teaching multicultural learners with exceptionalities are designed for English proficient, middle-class, suburban, European American students, with well educated parents who have the time and resources to help them gain the most that they can from the regular education systems. This chapter describes demographic profiles of multicultural groups in the United States and the intrinsic and extrinsic causes of ethnic and socioeconomic disparities. Given major demographic changes, we identify challenges facing general and special educators. These challenges involve addressing issues of teacher bias, teacher expectations, assessment, and learning and teaching style incompatibilities. To transform these challenges in general and special education, a paradigm shift in multicultural teaching and learning is proposed.

DEMOGRAPHIC PROFILES OF MULTICULTURAL CHILDREN IN THE UNITED STATES

The U.S. is a more heterogeneous society than it has ever been and the trends toward increasing heterogeneity will continue and perhaps quicken its pace. The U.S. Bureau of the Census (1990) has revealed data showing significant changes in the number and distribution of multicultural populations, changes in immigration and migration patterns and changes in ethnic group population characteristics. According to Aponte and Wohl (2000), the year 2000 census ushered in new changes in the type of multiracial ethnic data collected. The racial/ethnic categories identified in the demographic profile included the following labels: Black/African American, Non-Hispanic White/White, Spanish/Hispanic/Latino, Asian/Pacific Islander, American Indian, Eskimo or Aleutian backgrounds.

Of the total U.S. population of 267,636,061, there are 12.6% Black/African American, 10.2% Spanish/Hispanic/Latino, 3.6% Asian/Pacific Islanders, and 0.0% Indians/Eskimos/Aleuts (U.S. Bureau of the Census, 1990). Researchers have noted that the number and percentage of multicultural persons over the last decade have rapidly increased and it is projected that these numbers and percentages will dramatically change by the years 2030 and 2050. For example, the non-Hispanic/White population will steadily decline from 72% to 60% in 2030, then to 53% in 2050. By the year 2030, it is projected that 14.4% of the population will be Black/African American, 18.9% Spanish/Hispanic/Latino, 7.0% Asian/Pacific Islanders, and 1.0% American Indians/Eskimos/Aleuts (U.S. Bureau of the Census, 1996). By the year 2050, it is projected that 15.4% of the population will be Black/African American, 24.5% Spanish/Hispanics/ Latinos, 8.7% Asian/Pacific Islanders, and 1.1% American Indians/Eskimos/Aleuts.

Trends in Poverty Statistics

Educators are challenged to provide equitable educational outcomes for children living in poverty or adverse environmental circumstances. During much of the last two decades, children in the U.S. have experienced higher rates of poverty in urban, suburban, and rural areas. In addition, the child poverty rate "continues to exceed older children, ages six through 17, and is more than double the rate for adults, ages 18 through 64, and the elderly, ages 65 and above" (National Center for Children in Poverty, 1999, p. 1). In the document, *Changing America: Indicators of Social and Economic Well-Being by Race and Hispanic Origin* (Council of Economic Advisors for the President's Initiative on Race, 1998), poverty increased to 22.5% to 25.0%. For African American young children, the child poverty rate is 40% and for Hispanic children, the rate increased to 38% and more rapidly than for other groups (Spickard, Fong & Ewalt, 1996). Many immigrant and refugee families and children live in poverty because they are unable to find permanent employment or jobs that pay high wages. As a consequence, their financial resources tend to be limited making it difficult for them to provide adequate diet, health care, housing arrangements, and living conditions for their children (Drachman, 1996).

Intrinsic and Extrinsic Causes of Cultural and Socioeconomic Disparities

Many educators fail to understand the intrinsic and extrinsic causes of ethnic and socioeconomic disparities and believe that poor, multicultural learners with exceptionalities are predisposed to have problems in school. According to Grossman (1995), intrinsic causes refer to a host of factors including biomedical problems (e.g. health care and nutrition, substance abuse, acquired immune deficiency syndrome), genetic differences as related to cognitive ability, theories of cultural deprivation and educational disadvantage (e.g. self-concept, cognitive and linguistic abilities, educational aspirations). He noted that:

> Educators who locate the causes of these disparities within students themselves tend to favor solutions that change students or accommodate educational approaches to their assumed differences or made inadequacies. Educators who believe that some students are brought up in disadvantaged cultures that do not prepare them to succeed in school usually favor modifying the students' culturally influenced, attitudes and behavior . . . Educators believe there are genetic differences among students from different ethnic and socioeconomic backgrounds that make it difficult for them to use higher-level cognitive processes typically suggest that teachers should reduce the goals they hope to achieve with these students and should adapt their methods for achieving them to these students' assumed limitations (p. 15).

Extrinsic causes of ethnic and socioeconomic disparities refer to explanations of school failure that may be attributed outside the students. In many cases, educational approaches implemented in the schools are ill-suited to the context (or living conditions) of multicultural learners with and without exceptionalities. For example, immigrant and refugee students, upon, entering the U.S. may experience culture shock and engage in aggressive behaviors because they have not received the educational assistance they need to adjust to a new school and community environment. These students may encounter contextually inappropriate educational practices such as prejudice and discrimination in the educational system (e.g. biased expectations, poor evaluation, and poor treatment of students).

A second example is illustrated by the difficulties encountered by multicultural learners attending rural schools. In rural school districts, implementing comprehensive special education services is very difficult (Helge, 1991). For example, travel to remote locations with vast distances between population groups, impassable roads during inclement weather, and low population density makes it difficult to provide special education services to multicultural learners with exceptionalities. Remote and impoverished school districts suffer from a lack of social, psychological, and family counseling services. These obstacles prevent many families from being involved in the special education process, and make it extremely difficult to offer services at reasonable costs. In addition, special educational services are provided by uncertified and poorly prepared personnel.

CHALLENGES IN EDUCATING MULTICULTURAL LEARNERS

This section presents challenges faced by general and special educators in providing appropriate special education services to multicultural learners. These challenges include: (a) shortages in personnel staff; (b) biased teacher expectations; (c) tracking and low ability grouping; (d) prejudicial assessment; and (e) learning and teaching style incompatibles with multicultural learners.

Shortages in General and Special Education Personnel

Despite the language and multicultural diversity of the schools, the majority of general and special educators are Anglo-American, monolingual speakers of English and the composition of the teaching or professional force fail to reflect the changing ethnic and language composition of children to be served (Cook & Hoe, 1995; Wald, 1996; Zeichner, 1993). Data compiled by professional organizations have revealed several trends in the shortage of multicultural personnel in special education (American Association of Colleges for Teacher Education ([AACTE], 1994; National Center for Education Statistics [NCES], 1997; Choy, Henke, Alt, Medrich & Bobbitt, 1993). For example, data by the NCES revealed that 13.5% of the U.S. teaching force was composed of CLD personnel, whereas 31.4% of all students represented diverse populations. In supply-and-demand research in special education, Cook and Boe (1995) compared the ethnic and racial composition of special education teachers and students in public schools. The supply of special education teaching professionals representing diverse populations was approximately 14%, whereas the percentage of students in special education programs representing multicultural populations was about 32%.

Currently, there is a nationwide shortage of educational professionals who are culturally and linguistically competent to assess and instruct linguistically different students in their native languages. Because of this shortage, school districts do not have qualified bilingual general and special educators who are competent in conducting non-biased assessments and providing bilingual special education services. When bilingual special education services are not available, linguistically different learners with exceptionalities remain in bilingual education classrooms, without a formal individualized education plan (IEP), without being formally identified, and the Bilingual Education Department remains responsible for their education (Baca & Cervantes, 1998; Grossman, 1995). Basically, the underlying issues associated with the supply and demand of culturally and linguistically diverse teachers and professionals include:

(1) Individuals representing multicultural population do not consider teaching as a career because of the lure of alternative careers.
(2) Variables such as poverty, standardized tests, and certification exams continue to have a disparate effect on the number of multicultural students who are enrolling in postsecondary educational programs.
(3) Barriers such as alienation in the higher education setting, discrimination, and additional educational requirements necessary for certification, increased attrition/retention rates of teachers of color in urban, inner city areas are greater.

Collectively, these statistics have continued to have a tremendous impact on the successes and failures of general and special educators who are qualified to teach multicultural learners with exceptionalities. These disparities create a number of conditions that detract from excellence in education for all students and from building a successful multicultural society.

Issues of Teacher Bias, Behavior, and Expectations

The current educational system has a mainstream cultural bias which adversely affects the education of multicultural learners. This bias is manifested in preconceived limiting and inaccurate expectations about multicultural learners from diverse cultures (Obiakor, 1991a, b). In addition, a lack of awareness, sensitivity and understanding of diverse cultures by school personnel interferes with the delivery of appropriate educational programs, reinforces negative stereotypes, and interferes with the development of productive relationships with teachers, peers, parents, and adults. This next section presents a number of issues related to teacher bias, behavior, and expectation. To understand issues surrounding minority status, general and special educators must understand their social context on poverty and affluence, social class stratification, educational inequality, and race (Janesick, 1995; Ogbu, 1974, 2002). Earlier studies on education and race by Rist (1971, 1978), Schofield (1982), and Cusick (1983) documented the effects of teacher behaviors and beliefs on the dynamics of racial interaction in desegregated elementary, middle, and high schools. For example, Schofield's findings revealed that academics were emphasized to such a great extent that social goals to nurture positive interracial relationships among African American and White students were virtually nonexistent. Teachers' beliefs were based upon one of three perspectives: the "natural progression assumption," the "colorblind view of interracial schooling," and "assimilation." The natural progression theory postulated that African American and White relationships developed naturally without planned extracurricular activities. A second belief, "colorblind view of interracial schooling" was based on the notion that it was inappropriate to discuss the topic of race, prejudice, or discrimination. A discussion on these topics implied that one must be racist or prejudiced, thus, any reference to race related issues were discouraged, unapproachable, and masqueraded as part of general problems such as discipline or attendance. With regard to teachers' beliefs about assimilation, they believed that integration of African Americans into mainstream society will be achieved in terms of behavior, economic status, education, and access to educational opportunities. The findings from Cusick's study supported the egalitarian ideal of providing opportunities for social, political, and economic equality for urban minority high school students. Standards and discipline policies were established to maintain order, prevent conflicts between African American and White students, and keep troublemakers out of school. As in the Schofield study, there were no discussions about race and the social interactions between African American and White students.

In a different study, Rist (1971) documented how teachers acted out their prejudices against poor students. He remarked that:

> When a teacher bases her expectations of performance on the social status of the student and assumes that the higher the social status, the higher the potential of the child, those children of low and social status suffer a stigmatization outside of their own choice or

will. Yet there is a greater tragedy than being labeled as a slow learner, and that is being treated as one. The differential amounts of control-oriented behavior, the lack of interaction with the teacher, and ridicule from one's peers, and the caste aspects of being placed in lower reading groups all have implications for the future lifestyle and value of education for the child ... Given the treatment of poor children from the beginning of their kindergarten experience, for what class strata are they being prepared other than that of the lower class? It appears that the public school system not only mirrors the configurations of the larger society, but also significantly contributes to maintaining them. Thus the system of public education in reality perpetuates what it is ideologically committed to eradicate – class barriers which result in inequality in the social and economic life of the citizenry (pp. 107–108).

With demographic changes in society, general and special educators must confront the issue of teacher expectation as they explore innovative ways to teach multicultural learners with and without exceptionalities. Obiakor (1999a) observed that, "when teachers fail to respond to intra-individual and inter-individual differences, processes of identification, assessment, classification, placement, and instruction become loaded with inappropriate assumptions, negative stereotypes, and illusionary conclusions" (p. 207). He further noted that "students respond positively or negatively to their environmental stimuli (e.g. parents, peers, teachers, and paraprofessionals). In general and special education, the ways students are identified or the expectations placed on them can have positive or negative influence" (p. 208).

Although a few studies failed to find significant ethnic and class differences in teacher expectations of their students (Flynn, 1983; Heller, 1985, Huebner & Cummings, 1986; Jaeger & Freijo, 1975), a good number of studies have found such bias (Beady & Hansell, 1980; Bennett, 1979; Campos, 1983; Dao, 1991; Dusek & Joseph, 1983; Figueroa & Gallegos, 1978; Grant, 1984; Ogbu, 1978; Sue & Kitano, 1973). To illustrate the impact of teacher expectations on multicultural learners, Obiakor (1999b) presents the following cases for analyses:

Case No. 1: Roberta was a 14-year-old immigrant from Mexico. She had only been in the U.S. for three months. She was experiencing some difficulties with the English language while trying to adjust to the American culture. She was new and had not made friends in the school. She did not want to sound different, therefore, she did not participate in class. She was shy and isolated herself from her peers. She rarely participated in class and seemed to have trouble getting started with her class work. Her teacher acknowledged that she was very respectful and polite and tried several times to engage her in conversation but she said very little each time. It was six weeks into the school year and her teacher was not able to get much information from her. She was very concerned that she failed to adjust well in school activities. Her teacher recommended that she be tested for attention deficit disorder and/or emotional disturbance.

Case No. 2: Don was a 12-year-old Native American boy of average intelligence and performed at his grade level. He was very mechanical and enjoyed taking things apart and putting the pieces together. He wanted to be an automobile mechanic when he finished high school. His family was financially poor. He wore very dirty clothes. He appeared sick and tired most of the time and often slept in class. He did not get along well with his peers because they ridiculed and called him derogatory names. His teacher was worried that he snapped easily and lost control. For this reason, he wanted him to be tested for emotional disturbance.

Case No. 3: William was a 10-year-old African American male. He was very big for his age and was always aware of his physical appearance and size. He had difficulty focusing on his tasks and rarely completed his assignments but always wanted to help others. Although he tried to be nice and friendly to his peers, they did not always accept him, and this made him very upset. His teacher wrote a note to the counselor requesting for a conference with him and the counselor. According to the teacher, "William appears not be understand simple directions. He wanders in and out of the classroom and constantly does annoying things. Whatever is happening to him is beyond his control and he might need professional help."

Case No. 4: Hoshino was a 10-year-old Asian American male. His attendance had been very regular and he made good grades in his classes. He was very sociable and got along well with his peers. His demeanor began to change, and he became frequently angry and resentful. He lost his temper easily and often argued with his teacher. He got frustrated with the teacher when she tried to talk to him and sometimes he was rebellious. She came to the counselor and reported, "I am worried about Hoshino. He argues over anything I say to him, even things that will help him. We are constantly fighting over issues. I believe he is emotionally disturbed." The counselor tried to contact Hoshino's parents and discovered that they were going through a divorce. They were engaged in an ugly court battle over the children and their properties. There was no peace at home and Hoshino was considering running away (pp. 208–209).

Each of the above cases presented by Obiakor (1999b) exposed a multicultural learner in a unique and challenging classroom scenario. Teachers evaluated the behavior of students in a biased manner. Case No. 1 reveals an immigrant minority who was trying to adjust to the educational system of the United States. The student was shy and maybe withdrawn. The critical question is: Does shyness indicate emotional disturbance? It appears that the teacher's expectation was not fulfilled, and the unlikely solution was to get rid of the student. In Case No. 2, the teacher was not concerned that the student's peers ridiculed him for his poverty, however, he was quick to recommend him for testing for emotional disturbance. Case No. 3 deals with a student who was said to be "nice and friendly," but unaccepted by his peers because of his physical maturity. In a class where students did not get along with a fellow student, it was the teacher's responsibility to foster peer relationships. Rather than attempt to refer the student for counseling, the teacher should have fostered positive relationships through positive actions (e.g. letting students know that they are all valuable elements of the class; picking a "Person of the Day," a "Teacher of the Week," or a "Leader of the Month;" allowing students to say positive things orally and in writing about their classmates). In Case No. 4, the teacher needed to know other variables that impinged upon the student's learning – such a knowledge should not have been used to label or categorize the student; it should have been used to reduce the stressor or crisis confronting the student. It is very important that teachers try to know their students to avoid unrealistic expectations, stereotypic tendencies, inaccurate generalizations, and illusory conclusions. Clearly, disruptive behavior, inadequate motivation, lack of participation in school, and poor achievement that multicultural learners are caused, at least in part, by biased expectations, evaluation, and treatment they receive in school. Therefore, problems will not be solved until teachers correct their biased attitudes and beliefs and behave more democratically as they serve the needs of students as a whole. To some educators (e.g. Obiakor, 2001; Obiakor et al., 2002), the elimination of teacher prejudice and discrimination is the first and most important step to ensure the delivery of culturally appropriate education services.

Tracking and Low-Ability Grouping

Research confirms that poor and multicultural learners are much more likely to be placed in low-track and low-ability groups than European American middle-class students. Chun (1988) observed that tracking and ability grouping have been justified on the grounds that:

> ... Students learn better when they are grouped with other students who are similar to them academically; that the placement process used to sort students into groups is accurate and fair and, in addition, reflects past achievements and innate abilities; that slower students develop more positive attitudes in relation to themselves and their schools if they are not sorted into groups with students who are more capable; that it is easier for teachers to accommodate individual differences in homogeneous groups; that similar students are easier to manage (p. 94).

However, research on these approaches have indicated that they typically do more harm than good. Hall (1997) reported that:

> The reasons for the differential performance as a result of tracking or ability grouping are found in the very different experiences children in lower groups have compared to higher ones. There is less instructional time, less material covered, lower difficulty or material presented, lower teacher quality and, even when the same teachers have both high and low tracks, the latter receive lower quality instruction. There are also lower teacher expectations and encouragement, more teacher interruptions of student responses and different advice about educational and occupational options. These results have been found to occur as early as first grade... and this placement can have persistent effects over several years and perhaps longer, partly because of teacher and parent expectations... all have observed the assignment to groups has numerous problems and inaccuracies: many children are miscategorized (students with identical abilities placed in widely varying groups or students' abilities miscalculated) or assignments vary by class size, school organizational processes and constraints. It is no wonder then that grouping and tracking rather than narrowing differences exacerbates them with major consequences over the length of students' academic careers (pp. 21–22).

As noted earlier, multicultural learners are not placed in ability groups in an accurate and fair manner. Biased teacher expectations and behaviors are reflected in the assignment of multicultural learners to low-ability groups when objective evaluation of their performance would not justify their placement. In some cases, ability grouping is used to resegregate students and not to enhance their learning. Despite the progress in providing equal educational opportunities to all students, the educational system has consistently perpetuated inequality in school, thus causing many students to misbehave, tune out, and drop out.

Prejudicial Assessment

Federal laws in special education (e.g. IDEA 1997) have consistently recognized nondiscriminatory assessment as a fundamental ingredient in special education. The primary objective of nondiscriminatory assessment is to provide an unbiased, multifaceted, multi-disciplinary, and professionally sound evaluation. To a large extent, this ensures that an evaluation process adheres to assessment standards and procedures. The evaluation team must follow specific IDEA standards related to cultural bias and the validation of tests. Turnbull and Turnbull (2000) outlined IDEA standards and procedures relating to the student, cultural bias, test validity, and administration, as follows:

(1) Tests and other materials are provided and administered in the student's native language or other mode of communication unless it is not feasible to do so [20 U.S.C. Section 1414 (b)(3)(A)ii].

(2) Tests and other materials that are selected and administered to children with limited English proficiency measure the extent to which the child has a disability and needs special education, rather than measuring the child's English language skills [34 C.F.R. 300.532(a)(2)].
(3) The team must ensure that all standardized tests [20 U.S.C. Section 1414 (b)(3)(B)] have been validated for the specific purpose for which they are used.
(4) Tests and other materials are administered by trained and knowledgeable personnel; and are administered in accordance with any instruction from the test's producers (p. 140).

Not long ago, Turnbull, Turnbull, Shank and Leal (1999) noted that nondiscriminatory assessment helps to: (a) determine whether or not a student has a disability; (b) determine the nature of the disability and the special education and related services that he/she should receive; and (c) identify specific special education and related services in order to develop an appropriate, individualized educational plan (IEP) for a student with a disability. Within nondiscriminatory assessment standards and procedures are: (a) breadth of the assessment; (b) administration of the assessment procedures; (c) timing of the assessment, parental notice, and consent; and (d) interpretation of the assessment information. Although the provisions of IDEA 1997 are to guarantee an appropriate education for students with disabilities, problems of misclassification, misidentification, and misassessment continue to exist when African American learners are evaluated using conventional, traditional psychometric testing procedures (Obiakor, 1994, 1999b).

The issue of test bias is currently a hotly debated topic in the psychological literature today as in the 1970s, 1980s, 1990s and 2000s (Grossman, 1995; Karr & Schwenn, 1999; Midgette, 1995; Obiakor, 1994, 1999b, 2001; Obiakor, Algozzine, Thurlow, Ogisi, Enwefa, Enwefa & McIntosh, 2002; Ogbu, 2002; Samuda, Feuerstein, Kaufman, Lewis & Sternberg, 1998; Sandoval, Frisby, Gelsinger, Scheuneman & Grenier, 1998). One important underlying principle of the assessment process is that tests should not be racially or culturally discriminatory in the psychological examination of multicultural learners. From a historical perspective, questions about test bias, issues on psychological testing, factors associated with test construction, and the educational use of tests for African American learners have stimulated debates among psychologists, social scientists, and educators. For example, a major consideration in the evaluation of special education programs for multicultural learners with exceptionalities is the possibility that the psychological testing process was conceptualized as a means of determining eligibility for placement rather than as a link to the provision of individualized educational programs.

A major criticism regarding the use of standardized intelligence tests is that they may be culturally biased against poor, minority children as compared to majority children. Because of differences in cultures, languages, values, and experiential backgrounds, assessment tools are used inappropriately to assess the intelligence of minority children (Utley, Haywood & Masters, 1992; Valencia & Suzuki, 2001). If one examines the technical adequacy of the intelligence test for predicting school-related performance, then the assumption that this test is valid for all segments of the population is valid. However, if one examines the quality of educational programming as the conceptual basis for testing, then the psychometric assessment of children is questionable. Given the relatively poor academic achievement and serious behavior problems of some multicultural learners in different classroom settings, diagnostic information to guide the teaching-learning process is essential (Padilla & Lindholm, 1995). One very important issue that must be resolved in the psychoeducational assessment of African American children is the utility of standardized assessment in the development of effective educational programs (Utley, Haywood & Masters, 1990). Although standardized intelligence test scores are used for purposes of classification and diagnosis, they are not prescriptive. Instructional issues raise questions as to the prescriptive contribution of the diagnostic process. Standardized intelligence tests are not used to identify a child's *functional* needs (e.g. cognitive processing and adaptive behavior), they are supposed to be used to develop instructional practices designed to minimize discrepancies between learning performance and learning potential. Sewell (1987) eloquently argued that "given the relatively poorer academic performance of minority children, assessment dictated by academic problems and geared to provide diagnostic information to guide the teaching-learning process is vitally necessary" (p. 431). He further remarked that "the conceptual model guiding the assessment process should satisfy the fundamental requirement of identifying cognitive processes so that the instructional needs of the individual can be served in a nondiscriminatory context" (p. 433). In this context, psychometric theory is of no particular value if standardized intelligence tests cannot demonstrate a beneficial link to instructional outcomes for African American learners. Therefore, it is imperative that teachers and school psychologists demonstrate that the use of standardized intelligence tests leads to effective instructional practices for multicultural learners with exceptionalities.

LEARNING AND TEACHING STYLE INCOMPATIBILITIES

According to Winzer and Mazurek (1994), cultural diversity means "that there are significant differences in students' performance and interactions in broad areas such as verbal and nonverbal communication, orientation modes such as conceptions of time, social values, and cognitive tempo. Cultural differences in learning may be especially apparent in three areas: learning styles, communication styles, and language differences" (p. 153). Multicultural learners are very heterogeneous in their learning and behavioral styles, however, research has shown that multicultural learners may have the following characteristics: (a) participatory vs. passive learning; (b) involved personal relationships vs. distant relationships; (c) dependent vs. independent learning; (d) peer vs. adult oriented learning; (e) individualistic vs. group-oriented learning; (e) reflective/analytical vs. impulsive/spontaneous cognitive styles; (f) global perception vs. analysis of details; and (g) motivational style.

Many general and special educators know very little about the cultural traits, behaviors, values, and attitudes different multicultural learners bring to the classroom and how they affect the ways students act out and interact with peers and adults in instructional and social situations. Unfortunately, multicultural learners often are unprepared for the instructional techniques they are exposed to in school because their learning and behavior styles do not match their teachers' instructional styles. Teaching styles that are incompatible with multicultural learners'styles of learning tend to be rigid, uncreative, characterized by low expectations and ignore the impact of culture and language, learning, and thinking. Mismatches between students' and teachers' behavioral, communication, learning, and perceptual styles can impair students ability to express themselves, use problem-solving skills, and develop positive student-teacher relationships (Daniels, 2001; Grossman, 1995; Shade & New, 1993). To address this teaching challenge, there are multidimensional ways in which educators can handle the incompatibilities and discontinuities between students' cultural characteristics and the norms, expectations, and methods that prevail in most schools. They can accommodate their methods to students' characteristics, help students assimilate to the approaches that are typically found in American schools, assist students to become bicultural, and empower themselves to resolve their cultural conflicts.

FOSTERING MULTICULTURAL TRANSFORMATION IN GENERAL AND SPECIAL EDUCATION PROGRAMS

Conceptually, multicultural education is defined using several different ways, frameworks, typologies, or approaches. Collectively, these approaches emphasize one of many aspects of multicultural education such as (a) educational equity; (b) cultural pluralism; (c) human relations; (d) social reconstruction; (e) school reform and restructuring; (f) teachers' educational practices;

(g) cross-cultural competence. Consequently, definitions have led to misinterpretations, misconceptions, and myths about basic assumptions, beliefs, and structures within schools. To advance the field and reduce the multiple meanings of multicultural education, Banks (1992, cited in Lockwood) suggested that "scholars need to develop a higher level of consensus about what the term means. Such agreement is beginning to form among academics. The consensus centers around a primary goal for multicultural education, which is to increase educational equality for both gender groups, for students from diverse ethnic and cultural groups, and for exceptional students" (p. 24). In the same vein, Grant and Ladson-Billings (1997) stated that "as scholars continue to study multicultural education and try to define it to meet the context of the ever-changing society, the meanings that characterize the different approaches will change, and/or some of the approaches will give way to make room for new ideas and meanings. This is as it should be, because if multicultural education is to be accepted and affirmed, scholars and practitioners must understand its meanings and continue to refine its definition so the multicultural education is appropriate for the time and social context" (p. 176). Recently, Nieto (2001) defined multicultural education as:

... A process of comprehensive school reform and basic education for all students. It challenges and rejects racism and other forms of discrimination in schools and society and accepts and affirms the pluralism (ethnic, racial, linguistic, religious, economic, and gender, among others) that students, their communities, and teachers reflect. Multicul-tural education permeates the schools' curriculum and instructional strategies, as well as the interactions among teachers, students, and families, and the very way that schools conceptualize the nature of teaching and learning. Because it uses critical pedagogy as its underlying philosophy and focuses on knowledge, reflection, and action (praxis) as the basis for social change, multicultural education promotes democratic principles of social justice (p. 305).

Banks (1992, cited in Lockwood) summarized the underlying assumptions of multicultural education, as follows:

(1) Multicultural education is a reform movement designed to bring about educational equity for all students, including those from different races, ethnic groups, social classes, exceptionality, and sexual orientation.
(2) Multicultural education should help students to develop the knowledge, attitudes, and skills to participate in a democratic and free society ... Multicultural education promotes the freedom, abilities and skills to cross ethnic and cultural boundaries to participation in other cultures and groups.
(3) Multicultural education is for all children, not just for African Americans or Hispanics or Native Americans, but for all students.
(4) The multicultural classroom, students hear multiple voices and multiple perspectives. They hear the voice of different ethnic and cultural groups.

(5) The aims of multicultural education should always be the same, regardless of the setting. However, the strategy points and methods may have to be contextualized.
(6) A multicultural curriculum can be taught with almost any materials if the teachers have the knowledge, skills, and attitudes needed to transform their thinking and consequently the school curriculum.
(7) Multicultural education is an inclusive and cementing movement... It attempts to bring various groups that have been on the margins of society to the center of society (pp. 23–27).

The implications of multicultural perspectives for general and special educators are that: (a) behaviors are influenced by culture: (b) learning and social interactions are inextricably connected and inseparable from cognition; and (c) both teachers and students are engaged in the process of constructing knowledge through shared social activities and dialogue. Therefore, general and special educators are challenged to: (a) interpret the social behaviors of learners from culturally diverse backgrounds; (b) distinguish academic and social behaviors from deficits; and (c) employ instructional strategies effective to help these learners maximize their schooling experiences and acquire the most productive interpersonal skills (Cartledge, Lee & Feng, 1995).

Providing a culturally appropriate education for multicultural learners has been accepted as a goal and policy statements have been issued by the federal government and educational organizations emphasizing the importance of multicultural education. A few years ago, Grossman (1995) noted that "because there is no legal definition of culturally appropriate education, there are many different approaches aimed at increasing respect for diversity, reducing prejudice, improving interethnic group relations, and resolving cultural incompatibilities between students' styles of learning and behavior and educators' styles of instruction" (p. 87). Additionally, he recommended various approaches to address the educational difficulties of multicultural learners in schools, some of which include:

(1) Increasing respect for diversity, reducing prejudice, and improving interethnic group relations.
(2) Discussions of differences and similarities among different multicultural groups.
(3) The inclusion of students' cultures in the curriculum and classroom.
(4) Implementing a proactive antibias curriculum program.
(5) Eliminating teacher bias.
(6) Eliminating curriculum bias.

(7) Teaching about prejudice.
(8) Teaching an emancipatory and transformative curriculum to change biased discriminatory aspects of society (pp. 87–98).

CONCLUSION

In this chapter, we addressed critical issues related to the education of multicultural learners in general and special education settings. We explained that traditional methods of identification, assessment, categorization, placement, and instruction have failed to yield fruitful dividends. Demographic shifts in our society call for innovative ways to challenges caused by: (a) shortages in general and special education personnel; (b) biased teacher expectations; (c) tracking and low-ability grouping; (d) prejudicial assessment; (e) learning and teaching style incompatibilities with multicultural learners. We conclude that addressing these challenges will help in fostering multicultural transformation in general and special education problems.

REFERENCES

American Association of Colleges for Teacher Education (1994). *Teacher education pipeline III: Schools, colleges, departments of education enrollments by race, ethnicity, and gender.* Washington, D.C.: Author.

Aponte, J. F., & Wohl, J. (2000). *Psychological intervention and cultural diversity* (2nd ed.). Needham Heights, MA: Allyn & Bacon.

Baca, L. M., & Cervantes, H. T. (1998). *The bilingual special education interface* (3rd ed.). Upper Saddle River, NJ: Merrill.

Beady, C. H., & Hansell, S. (1980). *Teacher race and expectations for student achievement.* ERIC Document Reproduction Service No. ED 200-695.

Bennett, C. I. (1979). The effects of student characteristics and task performance on teacher expectations and attributions. *Dissertation Abstracts International, 40,* 979–980-B.

Campos, F. (1983). *The attitudes and expectations of student teachers and cooperating teachers toward students in predominantly Mexican American schools: A qualitative data perspective.* ERIC Document Reproduction No. ED 234-026.

Cartledge, G., Lee, J., & Feng, H. (1995). Cultural diversity: Multicultural factors in teaching social skills. In: G. Cartledge & J. F. Milburn (Eds), *Teaching Social Skills to Children and Youth* (pp. 328–355). Needham Heights, MA: Allyn & Bacon.

Chun, E. W. (1988). Sorting black students for success and failure: The inequality of ability grouping and tracking. *Urban League Review, 11*(1–2), 93–106.

Cook, L. H., & Hoe, E. E. (1995). Who is teaching students with disabilities? *Teaching Exceptional Children, 28,* 70–72.

Council of Economic Advisors for the President's Initiative on Race (1998). *Changing America: Indicators of social and economic well-being by race and Hispanic Origin.* Online at http://www.whitehouse.gov/WH/EOP/CEA/html/publications.html

Cusick, P. A. (1983). *The egalitarian ideal and the American high school.* New York: Longman.

Daniels, V. I. (2001). Responding to the learning needs of multicultural learners with gifts and talents. In: C. A. Utley & F. E. Obiakor (Eds), *Special Education, Multicultural Education, School Reform: Components of Quality Education for Learners with Mild Disabilities* (pp. 140–154). Springfield, IL. Charles C. Thomas.

Dao, M. (1991). Designing assessment procedures for educationally at-risk Southeast Asian-American students. *Journal of Learning Disabilities, 24*(10), 594–601.

Drachman, D. (1996). Immigration statuses and their influence on service provision, access, and use. In: P. L. Ewalt, E. M. Freeman, S. A. Kirk & D. L. Poole (Eds), *Multicultural Issues in Social Work* (pp. 117–133). Washington, D.C.: National Association of Social Workers.

Dusek, J. B., & Joseph, G. (1983). The bases of teacher expectancies: A meta-analysis. *Journal of Educational Psychology, 75*(3), 327–346.

Figueroa, R. A., & Gallegos, E. A. (1978). Ethnic differences in school behavior. *Sociology of Education, 51*, 289–298.

Flynn, T. M. (1983). IQ tests and placement. *Integrated Education, 21*, 124–126.

Grant, L. (1984). Black females' "place" in desegregated classrooms. *Sociology of Education, 57*, 98–110.

Grant, C. A., & Ladson-Billings, G. (1997). *Dictionary of multicultural education*. Phoenix, AZ: Oryx Press.

Grossman, H. (1995). *Teaching in a diverse society*. Needham Heights, MA: Allyn & Bacon.

Hall, P. M. (1997). *Race, ethnicity, and multiculturalism: Policy and practice*. New York: Garland.

Helge, D. (1991). *Rural, exceptional, at risk*. Reston, VA: Council for Exceptional Children.

Heller, K., A., Holtzman, W. H., & Messick, S. (1982). *Placing children in special education: A strategy for equity*. Washington, D.C.: National Academy Press.

Huebner, E. S., & Cummings, J. A. (1986). Influence of race and test data ambiguity upon school psychologists' decisions. *School Psychology Review, 15*(3), 410–417.

Jaeger, R., & Freijo, T. (1975). Race and sex as concomitants of composite halo in teachers' evaluative ratings of pupils. *Journal of Educational Psychology, 67*(2), 226–237.

Janesick, J. (1995). Our multicultural society. In: E. L. Meyen & T. M. Skrtic (Eds), *Special Education, Student Disability: Traditional, Emerging, and Alternative Perspectives* (4th ed., pp. 713–728). Denver, CO: Love.

Karr, S., & Schwenn, J. O. (1999). Multimethod of assessment of multicultural learners. In: F. E. Obiakor, J. O. Schwenn & A. F. Rotatori (Eds), *Multicultural Education for Learners with Exceptionalities* (Vol. 12, pp. 105–120). Stamford, CT: JAI Press.

Lockwood, A. T. (1992). Education for freedom. *Focus in Change, 7*(Summer), 23–29.

Midgette, T. E. (1995). Assessment of African American exceptional learners: New strategies and perspectives. In: B. A. Ford, F. E. Obiakor & J. M. Patton (Eds), *Effective Education of African American Exceptional Learners: New Perspectives* (pp. 3–26). Austin, TX: Pro-Ed.

National Center for Education Statistics, U.S. Department of Education (1997). *Statistical analyses report: Profiles of students with disabilities as identified in NELS: 88* (Technical Report No 97–254). Washington, D.C.: U.S. Department of Education.

National Center for Children in Poverty (1999). *Young children in poverty: A statistical update*. New York: The Joseph L. Mailman School of Public Health of Columbia University.

Nieto, S. (2001). *Affirming diversity: The sociopolitical context of multicultural education* (3rd ed.). New York: Longman.

Obiakor, F. E. (1994). *The eight-step multicultural approach: Learning and teaching with a smile*. Dubuque, IA: Kendall/Hunt.

Obiakor, F. E. (1999a). Teacher expectations of minority exceptional learners: Impact on "accuracy" of self-concepts. *Exceptional Children, 66*, 39–53.

Obiakor, F. E. (1999b). Teacher expectations: Impact on accuracy of self-concepts of multicultural exceptional learners. In: F. E. Obiakor, J. O. Schwenn & A. F. Rotatori (Eds), *Advances in Special Education: Multicultural Education for Learners with Exceptionalities* (Vol. 12, pp. 205–216). Stamford, CT: JAI Press.

Obiakor, F. E. (2001). *It even happens in "good" schools: Responding to cultural diversity in today's classrooms.* Thousand Oaks, CA: Corwin Press.

Obiakor, F. E., Algozzine, B., Thurlow, M., Gwalla-Ogisi, N., Enwefa, S., Enwefa, R., & McIntosh, A. (2002). *Addressing the issue of disproportionate representation: Identification and assessment of culturally diverse students with emotional or behavioral disorders.* Arlington, VA: The Council for Children with Behavioral Disorders, the Council for Exceptional Children.

Ogbu, J. U. (1974). *The next generation: An ethnography of education in an urban neighborhood.* New York: Academic Press.

Ogbu, J. U. (1978). *Minority education and caste: The American in cross-cultural perspective.* New York: Academic Press.

Ogbu, J. U. (2002). Cultural amplifiers of intelligence: IQ and minority status in cross-cultural perspective. In: J. M. Fish (Ed.), *Race and Intelligence: Separating Science from Myth* (pp. 241–278). Mahwah, NJ: Lawrence Erlbuam.

Oswald, D. P., & Coutinho, M. J. (2001). Trends in disproportionate representation in special education: Implications for multicultural education. In: C. A. Utley & F. E. Obiakor (Eds), *Special Education, Multicultural Education, and School Reform: Components of Quality Education for Learners with Mild Disabilities* (pp. 53–73). Springfield, IL: Charles C. Thomas.

Padilla, A. M., & Lindholm, K. J. (1995). Quantitative educational research with ethnic minorities. In: J. A. Banks & C. A. McGee-Banks (Eds), *Handbook of Research on Multicultural Education* (pp. 201–225). New York: MacMillan.

Rist, R. C. (1971). Student social class and teacher expectations: The self-fulfilling prophecy in ghetto education. In: *Challenging the myths: The schools the Blacks and the poor.* Cambridge, MA: Harvard University Press.

Rist, R. C. (1978). *The invisible children.* Cambridge, MA: Harvard University Press.

Samuda, R., Feuerstein, R., Kaufman, A. S., Lewis, J. E., & Sternberg, R. J. (1998). *Advances in cross-cultural assessment.* Thousand Oaks, CA: Sage.

Sandoval, J., Frisby, C. L., Gelsinger, K. F., Scheuneman, J. D., & Grenier, J. R. (1998). *Test interpretation and diversity: Achieving equity in assessment.* Washington, D.C.: American Psychological Association.

Schofield, J. W. (1982). *Black and white in school: Trust, tension, or tolerance.* New York: Praeger.

Sewell, T. E. (1987). Dynamic assessment as a non-discriminatory procedure. In: C. S. Lidz (Ed.), *Dynamic Assessment: An Interactional Approach to Evaluating Learning Potential* (pp. 426–445). New York: The Guilford Press.

Shade, B. J., & New, C. A. (1993). Cultural influences on learning: Teaching implications. In: J. A. Banks & C. A. McGee Banks (Eds), *Multicultural Education: Issues and Perspectives* (2nd ed., pp. 317–331). Needham Heights, MA: Allyn & Bacon.

Spickard, P. R., Fong, R., & Ewalt, P. L. (1996). Undermining the very basis of racism – its categories. In: P. L. Ewalt, E. M. Freeman, S. A. Kirk & D. L. Poole (Eds), *Multicultural Issues in Social Work* (pp. 14–20). Washington, D.C.: National Institute of Social Workers.

Sue, S., & Kitano, H. H. L. (1973). Stereotypes as a measure of success. *Journal of Social Issues*, 29(3), 83–98.

SUMMARY COMMENTS
ACHIEVING EFFECTIVE EDUCATION FOR LEARNERS WITH EXCEPTIONALITIES THROUGH RESEARCH AND PRACTICE

Charles R. Greenwood

INTRODUCTION

Delays in bringing research findings and discoveries into practice are a constant issue in all professions where research is intended to inform practice. A hundred years ago, a physician would offer a patient a list of possible treatments, all thought equally effective (no systematic research existed one way or the other supporting any of these options), and the patient was asked to choose (Carnine, 1995). Today, medical practice is informed by research and professional practice standards are based on research findings. Moreover, it is the stated policy of many professional organizations that their practices and standards of practice are subject to change in the face of new research findings. Even so, many patients suffer needlessly because their doctor is unaware of the latest information. For example, convincing evidence demonstrating that bacteria (i.e. Helicobacter pylori) caused ulcers and that antibiotic medication is an effective cure has been reported in the medical literature since 1982 (Centers for Disease Control, 2000). The public, however, even many doctors still believe ulcers are caused by stress (The Kansas City Star, 1996). Consequently, many ulcer patients who could be cured if checked for the bacteria and treated correctly, are not. Instead, they suffer needlessly because of the gap between research and practice.

Effective Education for Learners with Exceptionalities, Volume 15, pages 465–473.
© 2003 Published by Elsevier Science Ltd.
ISBN: 0-7623-0975-X

Equivalent advances and discoveries in special education research exist today (e.g. Carnine, 1997). Consider just a few. Today, persons with moderate to severe disabilities live lives in the broader community when previously they were cared for in institutions. Children with Downs syndrome engage and succeed in school when previously thought retarded and not educated. Students with learning disabilities make significant academic progress because learning strategies help them master basic skills when previously these practices did not exist. Ninety-five percent of children with severe reading problems can learn to read at average levels given early intervention when previously early identification of reading problems and early intervention were not possible. Persons with physical disabilities learn, communicate, and locomote because of computer technology and assistive devices that help them hold jobs and care for themselves when previously they were unable to do so. Like so many significant discoveries that we take for granted (e.g. air travel and space flight), these were not thought possible a 100 or even 50 years ago. It has taken this long, for this knowledge of physics, aerodynamics, and special education among others, to advance from concept, invention, and discovery to everyday practice. Every day, thousands bet their lives on the fact that airplanes will fly and that pilots know how to fly them safely! Every day, parents send their children to school believing that their teachers are well trained and know how to teach their children!

It continues to be surprising that it takes time for new knowledge to reach practice. In general education, for example, research findings emerged in the 1970s reporting that the ability to manipulate spoken language, for example as in rhyming, segmenting, and blending sounds, a class of skills known collectively today as "phonemic awareness," was an important skill on the path to learning to read (Liberman, Shankweiler, Fischer & Carter, 1974). However, some 20 years later in the mid-1990s this growing body of knowledge was relatively unknown to general education teachers and no teacher friendly tools existed to support classroom instruction of these skills. Today, five or six years later, there are several of these tools for teachers (e.g. O'Connor, Notari-Syverson & Vadasy, 1996, 1998), this knowledge is included in the training of new teachers, methods exist for monitoring students progress learning these skills (Kaminsky & Good, 1996), and this knowledge is increasingly in the hands and practice of teachers in local schools. How research makes its way from discovery to practice, and the mechanisms a profession uses to bridge between the two, are fundamentally important because they directly impact the effectiveness of the profession and the social costs and benefits at stake of not using new expertise (e.g. Levine, 1995). Unfortunately in education, as compared to more highly effective disciplines, there is a sense that research findings are even slower coming into practice (Levine, 1995; Malouf & Schiller, 1995; Viadero, 1994).

STRENGTHENING THE VALUE OF RESEARCH IN TEACHER EDUCATION

My vision for general and special education in the 21st century is that we tackle educational problems and reap the benefits of doing so. Our first step must be to strengthen the value of research on learning and teaching in preservice teacher training programs (Fuchs & Fuchs, 1990). We must make sure that research knowledge and research-validated practices are at the heart for what we choose to teach teachers in training. This can be accomplished if we make measurable change in student learning our criterion for selecting which practices we will and will not teach teachers in training (Greenwood & Maheady, 1997). By focusing strongly on evidence of student learning resulting from the use of instructional practices, regardless of the paradigm that underpins the practice, we can improve student learning and also avoid the paradigm wars that cause us to lose sight of our purpose as educators – *to improve student learning* (Kromrey, Hines, Paul & Rosselli, 1996).

CREATING A STRONG MARKET FOR RESEARCH-VALIDATED PRACTICES IN LOCAL SCHOOLS

Beyond strengthening the link between research and preservice teacher preparation, our approach must focus on improving the market among teachers and parents for research-validated instructional intervention practices. If teachers and parents believe that better student outcomes can be achieved through improved practices or by improving existing practices, research and the profession will move to a higher level of effectiveness much to the joy of the public and policy makers. *Absolutely no progress can be made bridging the gap between research and practice without the active, voluntary participation of teachers, regardless of the participation of school administrators and parents.* Because teachers are the professionals ultimately delivering instruction, nothing really important can be accomplished without their grass roots support and participation. Teachers must "buy in" to the belief that research informs instructional practice. As faculty members and, as members of educational professional associations, teachers who know the value of research and of translating research into practice are fundamental to a market for research-validated practice. Unfortunately, many teachers currently hold less than favorable beliefs about the value of educational research and too many see it as unrelated to what they do in the classroom (e.g. Kaestle, 1993). My vision is that teacher educators who are able to demonstrate the value of research on learning and teaching, who teach research-validated practices, and who require their trainees to document their own instructional effectiveness in terms of measures of student learning, will challenge this belief. Similarly so, teachers' professional organizations and educational policy organizations will promote the expectation that not all instructional practices are made equal and that those with the "best evidence in student learning outcomes" will be selected and used by classroom teachers. Supporting this goal, these organizations, like similar organizations in other highly effective professionals will inform and alert their members about advances in research and practice.

Teachers must play a role in targeting research questions, potential solutions, and the criteria used for determing success. If teachers are to value research, it must be relevant to classroom instruction. Among classroom teachers, my colleagues and I have used the term "street validity" to characterize this kind of relevance to classroom instruction. Too often, researchers have asked and answered questions with little practical value. Too often, solutions developed by researchers have been unwieldy and unsustainable (Kaestle, 1993). To change this situation, researchers must involve teachers in the process of targeting, testing, and evaluating practices considered to be potential solutions (Abbott, Walton, Tapia & Greenwood, 1999; Fuchs & Fuchs, 1998). My vision is that local school classrooms will increasing become the laboratories for research on teaching and learning. And, that within these settings, teachers and researchers together in partnership will conceptualize, plan, carry out, and measure the effects of new instructional interventions. Journals reporting this kind of work with high relevance to teachers are listed in Table 1. Supporting the motivation necessary for this to occur, local schools, city and state educational units, and colleges of education will need to actively support in their policies, and particularly in their criteria for promotion and professional advancement, that research activities in local schools be required, and thus, highly valued.

We know that brief workshops do not change teachers' classroom practices. However, a mix of training, classroom consultation with modeling, demonstration, and feedback over a year or more is effective changing practice. This form of ongoing continuing professional development requires a systematic *collaboration/consultation* component in local schools that allows teachers and researchers to work together to identify and implement effective instructional approaches (e.g. Baker & Smith, 2001; Boudah & Knight, 1999; Logan & Stein, 2001; Vaughn, Hughes, Schumm & Klingner, 1998). In these examples, collaborations were established between researchers and teachers (e.g. Baker & Smith,

Table 1. Journals Publishing Research Focused on Classroom and Teacher Practices.

Journal	Publisher
• TEACHING Exceptional Children	Council for Exceptional Children
• Learning Disabilities Research and Practice	Lawrence Erlbaum
• Proven Practice	Sopris West
• Intervention in School and Clinic	Pro-Ed, Inc.
• Journal of Behavioral Education	Kluwer Academic/Human Sciences Press
• Education and Treatment of Children	Pressley Ridge Schools

2001) or between a school-based, research-lead teacher and classroom teachers (Logan & Stein, 2001), so that research knowledge could be brought into ongoing, sustained professional activities in local schools (Blue prints for bridging the gap. Online at http//: www.lsi.ukans.edu/jg/blueprnt.htm). My vision is that this form of professional development will become standard at least until new research suggests a better way.

Between research and practice lies a step requiring "translating research into practice." Unfortunately, translation of research to practice is too often "an uneven, unsystematic process" but necessary for actually reaping benefits contained in new knowledge. Translation is required if improved practices are to be brought to scale. Simply publishing research findings in professional journals is not enough to change practice even in professions other than education. Unfortunately, this step is not recognized or at least it is underestimated in importance and time to achieve. In the physical/biomedical sciences, this step is known as "technology transfer" and it means developing the tools and processes necessary to bring new products that are based on new research knowledge to market. For instance, to make a new cancer-fighting drug available to consumers may require developing a new company with the new means of producing quantities of the drug for sale. It may also entail more research to further understand the utilization of the new product. The parallel process in education is when research-validated practices are newly developed as training, curricula, software, media, and/or text, tools that enable learning by teachers and delivery to students. While sounding a lot like technology transfer, this process in education has often failed because the practices developed for dissemination lacked relevance (value to teachers) and trustworthy evidence of their success promoting student learning outcomes. Therefore, they were not used and if so, did not work. Schools and universities need professionals whose role is to translate what has been shown to be effective so that it may be accessed by teachers and usable by them.

In a number of research programs recently supported by the U.S. Department of Education and National Institute for Mental Health, for example, this translation step is increasing described as "implementation research" where the purpose is not to invent or establish effectiveness – these steps being prerequisites, but rather to learn how effective a practice is when implemented in a range of typical educational settings and conditions. Translation of the practice for utilization and dissemination follows from this kind of research. In support of translating research to practice, any number of professional roles in schools or teachers' professional organizations should be responsible for identifying relevant research findings and translating them for use by local teachers. My vision is that translation will become systematic at multiple levels in the schools, in the professional organizations, in policy, in research, and in teacher training. *I believe that teacher utilization is a test of success, and so too are improved student learning outcomes.* Two criteria must be used to test success, utilization and resulting student learning. First, teachers must use the practice(s) given its availability in a usable form and the opportunity to learn it. If they do not, we have the problem of relevance mentioned previously. Second, its use will lead to improved learning outcomes for students who experience it. Using both criteria is important, because utilization is an indicator of program implementation and because acceleration in student learning should result given the use of the practice. In the case of either success or failure, we need to understand that failure to achieve student learning is not due to failure to implement the practice, rather a problem in the practice itself. Baker and Smith (2001) provide a nice description of how local elementary school faculty included new phonemic awareness procedures in their curriculum and used formative evaluation measures of reading to evaluate successful implementation. My vision is that both success criteria will be used in local schools and school systems as standards.

Teachers must monitor the frequency and quality of their use of the practice in collaboration with their colleagues, collaborators, coaches, and partners. Observational measures will be particularly useful for this purpose. For example, Implementation Checklists can be developed for measuring the fidelity of implementation and is one very good example, particularly when the assessment items are mapped to the steps, procedures, and sequences of the actual practice so that they may be used as feedback for teachers first learning the practice and as a check for sustained use. Formative measures of students progress in the curriculum, like Curriculum-based Measurement (CBM – Shinn, 1989; 1998) or Dynamic Indicators of Early Basic Literacy Skills (DIBELS – Kaminsky & Good, 1996), are particularly good methods for monitoring students progress because they can be administered frequently, and their results can be used for instructional decision making. Standardized achievement tests and high stakes tests are not particularly helpful in this way because they are not administered frequently enough such that they can be used by classroom teachers in adapting ongoing teaching. Teachers need to know which students are making progress and which are not so that instruction may be changed accordingly. Achievement tests are, however, helpful indicators of the percentage of students reaching a standard of performance at a particular point (grade level) in their schooling.

CONCLUSION

My vision is that teaching will be more effective in this new century because of a systematic effort made to bridge the gap between research and practice. Our students will learn better and faster, and enjoy the experience more, when how they are taught is based on the most current and advanced knowledge of effective practice. This goal is achievable, I believe, when we require that effectiveness be expressed in terms of measured growth in student learning linked to utilization of specific instructional interventions. This goal can be achieved when evidence of this kind is used by the profession to select its practices for teacher preparation and its standards of practice. Like other "highly effective" professions (e.g. medicine and engineering), my vision is that our stated policies will include the fact that our current practices are based on accumulated research evidence but that they are subject to change given new research findings. Hopefully, all teachers will understand that there is a strong and important science of learning and teaching, and that what they do as teachers must be guided by what is known to work in local classrooms. As a result, teachers and researchers will be eager to work with one another on problems relevant to classroom instruction. My vision is that the work of educational researchers who are not interested in classroom practice and who do not intend to conduct research relevant to practice will not be made part of the teacher-training curriculum because they are not studying phenomena that will be in the control of classroom teachers or the effort to teach.

Just as parents expect improved outcomes from the services they receive from the practitioners of other professions, they should expect improved outcomes in student performance and learning at school, regardless of their child's status (e.g. disability, English language learner, race, socioeconomic status, etc.). My vision is that the public perception of teachers and education will change from that of a professional group with limited ability to advance its effectiveness, one that is endlessly caught up in paradigm wars of relatively little importance to its consumers, to one of clarity of goals, standards of practice based on evidence in student learning, and accomplishment accelerating the performance and satisfaction of students, parents, and policy makers. I know that many will see comparing education to medicine or engineering to be comparing apples with oranges. However, this is only true if one assumes a weak science of learning and, that in education, we do not expect research to contribute to improved student outcomes and practices leading to these outcomes. If this is the case (and I reject that it is), we should immediately stop fooling the public and policy makers who commit resources to educational research and expect value added to student learning as a result.

In sum, like the stunning advances in the quality of life produced through accumulated research over the last 100, 50, and recent years in all fields including education and special education, those of the next 100 years will seem slow to those of us engaged in the work at the moment, but progress will be apparent one decade to the next. If we want progress faster, launching a systematic effort like the one I have suggested, or the ones suggested throughout this book, may just speed things up to the benefit of all.

REFERENCES

Abbott, M., Walton, C., Tapia, Y., & Greenwood, C. R. (1999). Research to practice: A 'blueprint' for closing the gap in local schools. *Exceptional Children, 65*(3), 339–352.

Baker, S., & Smith, S. (2001). Linking school assessments to research-based practices in beginning reading: Improving programs and outcomes for students with and without disabilities. *Teacher Education and Special Education, 24*(4), 315–332.

Blue prints for bridging the gap. Online at http://www.lsi.ukans.edu/jg/blueprnt.htm

Boudah, D. J., & Knight, S. L. (1999). Creating learning communities of research and practice: Participatory research and development. In: D. M. Byrd & D. J. McIntyre (Eds), *Research on Professional Development Schools: Teacher Education Yearbook VII* (pp. 97–114). Thousand Oaks, CA: Corwin Press.

Carnine, D. (1995). The professional context for collaboration and collaborative research. *Remedial and Special Education, 16*(6), 368–371.

Carnine, D. (1997). Bridging the research-to-practice gap. *Exceptional Children, 63*(4), 513–521.

Centers for Disease Control (2000). *Ulcers.* (on line http://www.cdc.gov/ncidod/dbmd/hpylori.htm).

Fuchs, D., & Fuchs, L. S. (1990). Making educational research more important. *Exceptional Children, 57*(2), 102–107.

Fuchs, D., & Fuchs, L. (1998). Researchers and teachers working together to adapt instruction for diverse learners. *Learning Disabilities Research and Practice, 13*(3), 162–170.

Greenwood, C. R., & Maheady, L. (1997). Measurable change in student performance: Forgotten standard in teacher preparation? *Teacher Education and Special Education, 20*, 265–275.

Kaminski, R. A., & Good, R. H. (1996). Toward a technology for assessing basic early literacy skills. *School Psychology Review, 25*, 215–227.

Kansas City Star (1996). *Bacteria causes ulcers* (February 4). Kansas City, MO.

Kaestle, C. F. (1993). Research news and comment: The awful reputation of education research. *Educational Researcher, 22*(1), 23–31.

Kromrey, J. D., Hines, C. V., Paul, J., & Rosselli, J. (1996). Creating and using a multiparadigmatic knowledge base for restructuring teacher education in special education: Technical and philosophical issues. *Teacher Education and Special Education, 19*(2), 87–101.

Levine, M. (1995). 21st century professional education: How education could learn from medicine, business, and engineering. *Education Week, 14*(19), 33–36.

Liberman, I. Y., Shankweiler, D., Fischer, F. W., & Carter, B. (1974). Explicit syllable and phoneme segmentation in the young child. *Journal of Experimental Child Psychology, 18,* 201–212.

Logan, K. R., & Stein, S. S. (2001). The research lead teacher model. *Teaching Exceptional Children, 33*(3), 38–45.

Malouf, D. B., & Schiller, E. P. (1995). Practice and research in special education. *Exceptional Children, 61,* 414–424.

O'Connor, R. E., Notari-Syverson, A., & Vadasy, P. F. (1996). Ladders to literacy: The effects of teacher-led phonological activities for kindergarten children with and without disabilities. *Exceptional Children, 63,* 117–130.

O'Connor, R. E., Notari-Syverson, A., & Vadasy, P. (1998). First grade effects of teacher-led phonological activities in kindergarten for children with mild disabilities: A follow-up study. *Learning Disabilities Research and Practice, 13,* 43–52.

Shinn, M. R. (1989). *Curriculum-based measurement: Assessing special children.* New York: Guilford.

Shinn, M. R. (Ed.) (1998). *Advanced applications of curriculum-based measurement.* New York: The Guilford Press.

Vaughn, S., Hughes, M. T., Schumm, J. S., & Klingner, J. (1998). A collaborative effort to enhance reading and writing instruction in inclusion classrooms. *Learning Disability Quarterly, 21*(1), 57–74.

Viadero, D. (1994). The great divide: The gap between research and practice is wider in education than in other fields, such as medicine and business. *Teacher Magazine, 5*(October), 22–24.

SUBJECT INDEX

achieving cultural competence 389–390
attention deficit hyperactivity disorder
   139–154
   assessment and identification 144–148
   classroom management 150–151
   concerns for education 140–141
   diagnosing 143
   definitions/classification 141–144
   parent involvement 152–153
   treatment and intervention 148–153
      best practices 149
      medication 148–152
      self monitoring strategies 151–152
autism spectrum disorder 195–232
   characteristics 198–199
   diagnosis 212–216
   definitions 195–196
   etiology 199–200
   medication 220
   prevalence 199
   treatment 216
   social impairment 207–209

behavioral objective sequence 403
bridge model for transition 375

central coherence theory of autism
   205–207
child-focused intervention 363
cognitive disability 77-99
   causes 87
   classification levels 81
   definitions 80–83
      federal 83
      AAMR revised 83–87
   learning characteristics 90–93
   learning potential 93–94

minority children 89
models 78–79
new concept 77–78
collaborative consultation 186
collaborative language 189–191
comprehensive support model 6–7
control theory of autism 209–212
craft of teaching 8–10
critical race theory 46–47

deaf education 238–243
   best practices 243–250
   bilingual bicultural 242
   oral approach 238–243
   total communication 241–242
dynamic assessment 183–184

early childhood special education
   351–372
   identification and assessment 359–362
   instruction 359–366
   personnel preparation 366–368
   philosophy 352–354
   service delivery options 354–359
educational equity 19–21
effective special education 465–473
emotional and behavioral disorders
   119–138
   funding 122–126
   model training programs 131–133
   number served 119
   Professional Development Schools
      (PDS) 129–131
   restructuring teacher education
      126–129
executive function deficits in autism
   203–205

family-school partnerships 418–424
family professional partnerships 424–435
  building parenting skills 424–427
  changing nature of families 435–438
  communication 427–428
  community collaboration 432–434
  decision making 430–432
  home learning 429–430
  volunteering 428–429
federal initiatives 26–37
  goals 2000 29–30
  New Freedom Initiative Act 28
  No Child Left Behind Act of 2001 28
  school to work opportunities 33–35
  special education law 31–33
  title 1, 30–31
  Workforce Investment Act of 1998 36–37
federal government's roles in education 22–24

gifted and talented atudents 325–348
  assessment 333–336
  characteristics 337–341
  contributing factors 336–337
  definitions 326–330
  educational programming 343–346
  identification 331–333
  neglected groups 341–343
  prevalence 330–331

health impairment 283–298
  definition 283
  needs 287–290
  parental roles 291–292
  protective laws 285
  school concerns 292
  teacher roles 290–291
hearing impairment 233–257
  causes 237–238
  definitions 234–236
  professional's training 250–252
  technological advances 252–253
home-based intervention 355–356
homeless students 401–415
  intervention 408–411
  special education context 404–408

IDEA 381–384
  IDEA 1990 amendments 378–379
  IDEA 1997 amendments 379–380
inclusive education 44–45

learning community 7–8
learning disabilities 99 117
  assessment 102–104
  classification 100–102
  discrepancy formula 100
  educational services delivery alternatives 108–110
  instruction 107–108
  placement concerns 104–107
litigation 24
  case law 24
  Brown vs Board of Education 25

multicultural education 458–459
  assumptions 458–459
  defined 458
multicultural learners 445–463
  demographic profile 446–448
  educational challenges 448–456
  intervention concerns 456–457
  transformation issues 457–460
multidimensional teaching learning process 10–14

naturalistic approaches to assessment 360–362

parents as teachers program 425
performance assessment 184
positive behavior aupport 430
prejudicial assessment 454–456
professional development schools 129–131
pullout programs 185

research in teacher education 467
research validated practices in education 467

school based intervention 356–359
school based health centers 293
severe and multiple disabilities 155–180

Subject Index

abilities not deficits 156
advocacy 160–161
educational programming 163–172
  early childhood 164–166
  elementary 166–169
  middle school 169–171
  high school 171–172
extended classroom concept 159
inclusiveness 157–158
parents, families, and friends 158–159
support vs readiness 156–157
teacher collaboration 159
socioeconomic discrepancy 402–403
speech and language disorders 181–193
  assessment 182–184
  service delivery models 184–189
systemic school change effort 51–69
  district 62–69
  local school 56–62
  professionals 53–56
  students 51–53

teacher bias 449–453
teacher shortages 448–449

theory of mind-autism 201–203
transformed schools 49–50
transitional programming to adulthood 373–399
  challenges 386–392
  effective planning 380–386
  historical foundations 374–380
traumatic brain injury 299–323
  classification 301–304
  educational programs 308–310
  effects of injury 306–308
  incidence and prevalence 300–301
  instructional interventions 312–315
  teacher training 318
  transitional planning 315–318

visual impairment 259–282
  characteristics 264–266
  definitions 259–262
  educational implications 269–278
  professionals 266–269
  service planning 278–280
visual systems 267